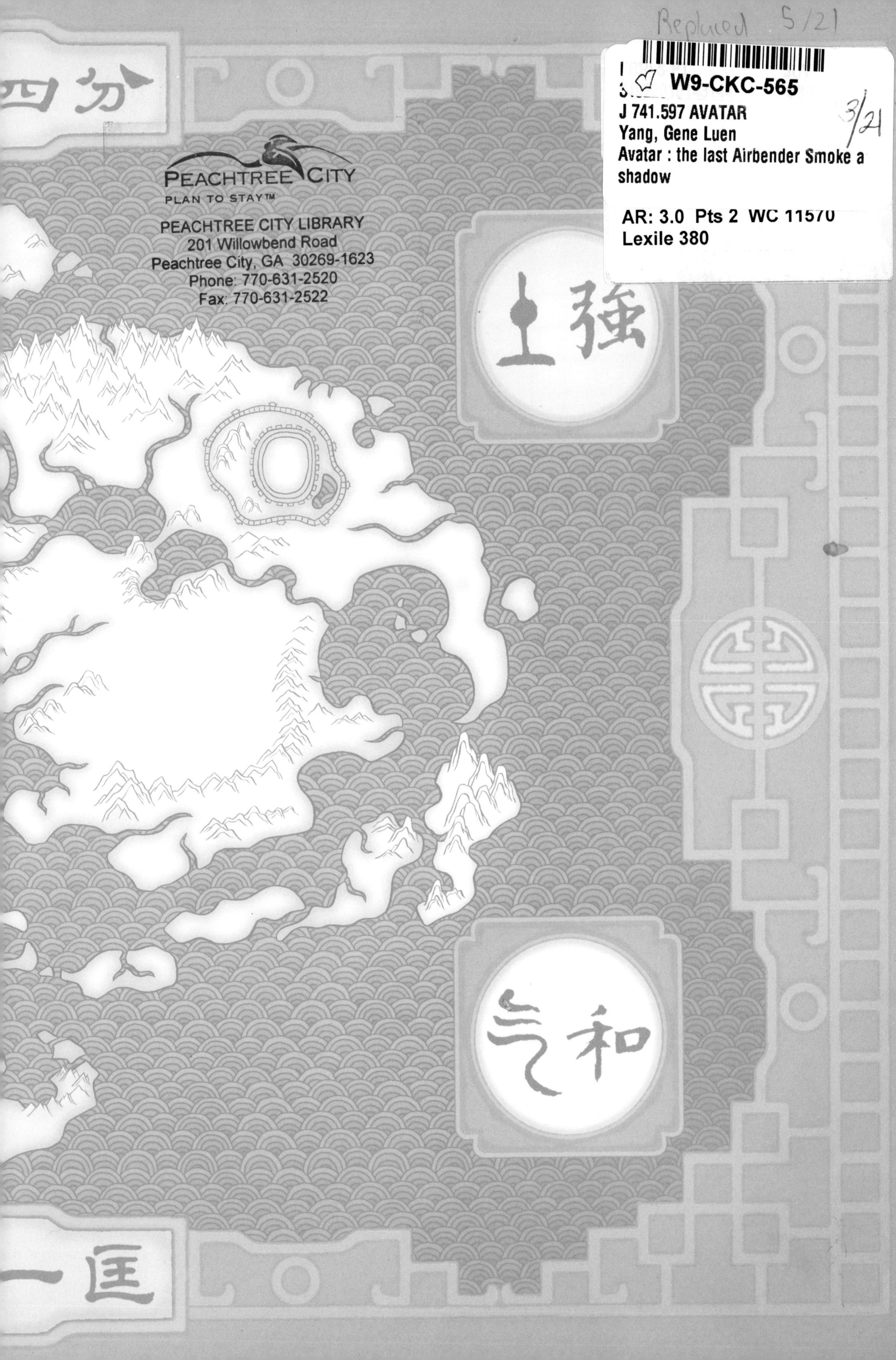
強
和

AVATAR
THE LAST AIRBENDER

Created by

BRYAN KONIETZKO

**MICHAEL DANTE
DiMARTINO**

nickelodeon

降世神通

AVATAR

THE LAST AIRBENDER

SMOKE AND SHADOW

GENE
LUEN YANG
Script

GURIHIRU
Art & Cover

MICHAEL
HEISLER
Lettering

DARK HORSE BOOKS

MIKE RICHARDSON
Publisher

DAVE MARSHALL
Editor

AARON WALKER
Associate Editor

RACHEL ROBERTS
Assistant Editor

SANDY TANAKA
Collection Designer

CHRISTIANNE GOUDREAU
Digital Art Technician

Translation by AKI YANAGI

Special thanks to LINDA LEE,
KAT VAN DAM, JAMES SALERNO, *and* JOAN HILTY
at Nickelodeon, and to BRYAN KONIETZKO *and*
MICHAEL DANTE DIMARTINO.

9 10 8

ISBN 978-1-50670-013-7 Nick.com DarkHorse.com First edition: September 2016

Published by **DARK HORSE BOOKS**, a division of Dark Horse Comics LLC, 10956 SE Main Street, Milwaukie, OR 97222

To find a comics shop in your area, visit comicshoplocator.com.

This book collects *Avatar: The Last Airbender—Smoke and Shadow* Parts 1 through 3.

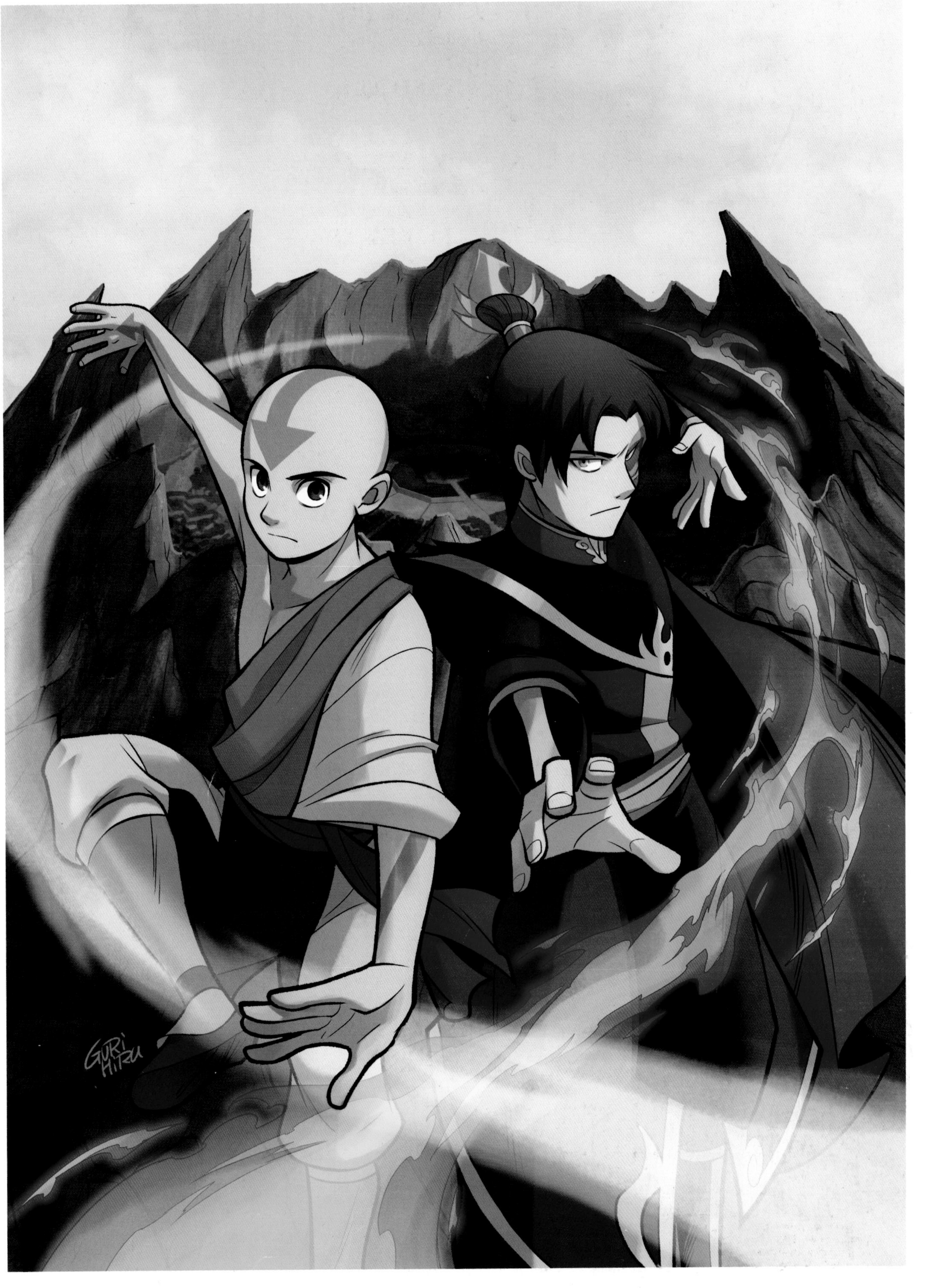
GURI
HIRU

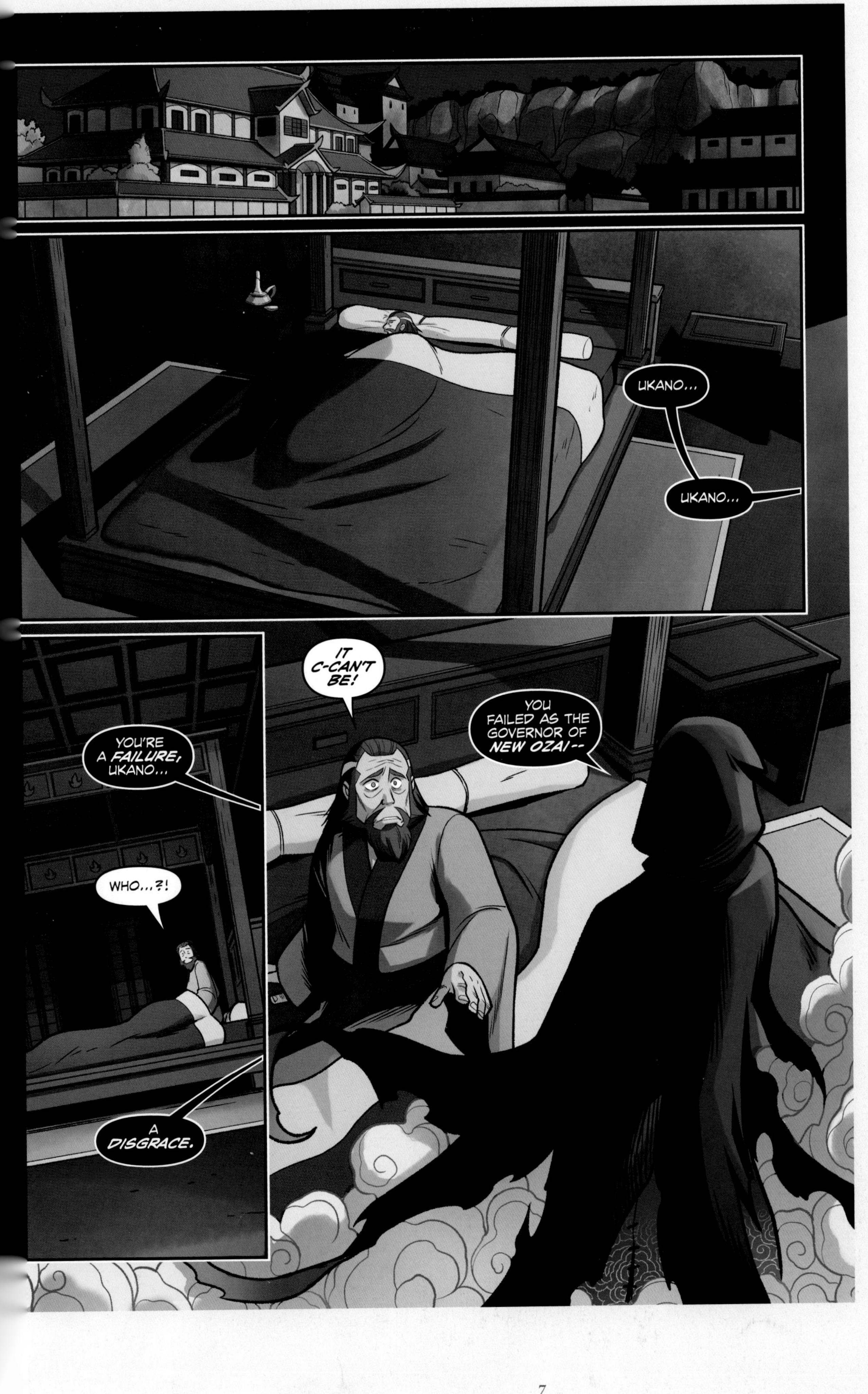

UKANO...
UKANO...
IT C-CAN'T BE!
YOU FAILED AS THE GOVERNOR OF NEW OZAI--
YOU'RE A FAILURE, UKANO...
WHO...?!
A DISGRACE.

GENE LUEN YANG: *Mai's father first appeared in the episode "Return to Omashu." Omashu had fallen to the Fire Nation, and he was appointed governor. One of the first things he does onscreen is beg Azula's forgiveness. For* Smoke and Shadow*, we decided to fill out his character a bit. We gave him a name—Ukano—and expanded on his cowardliness.*

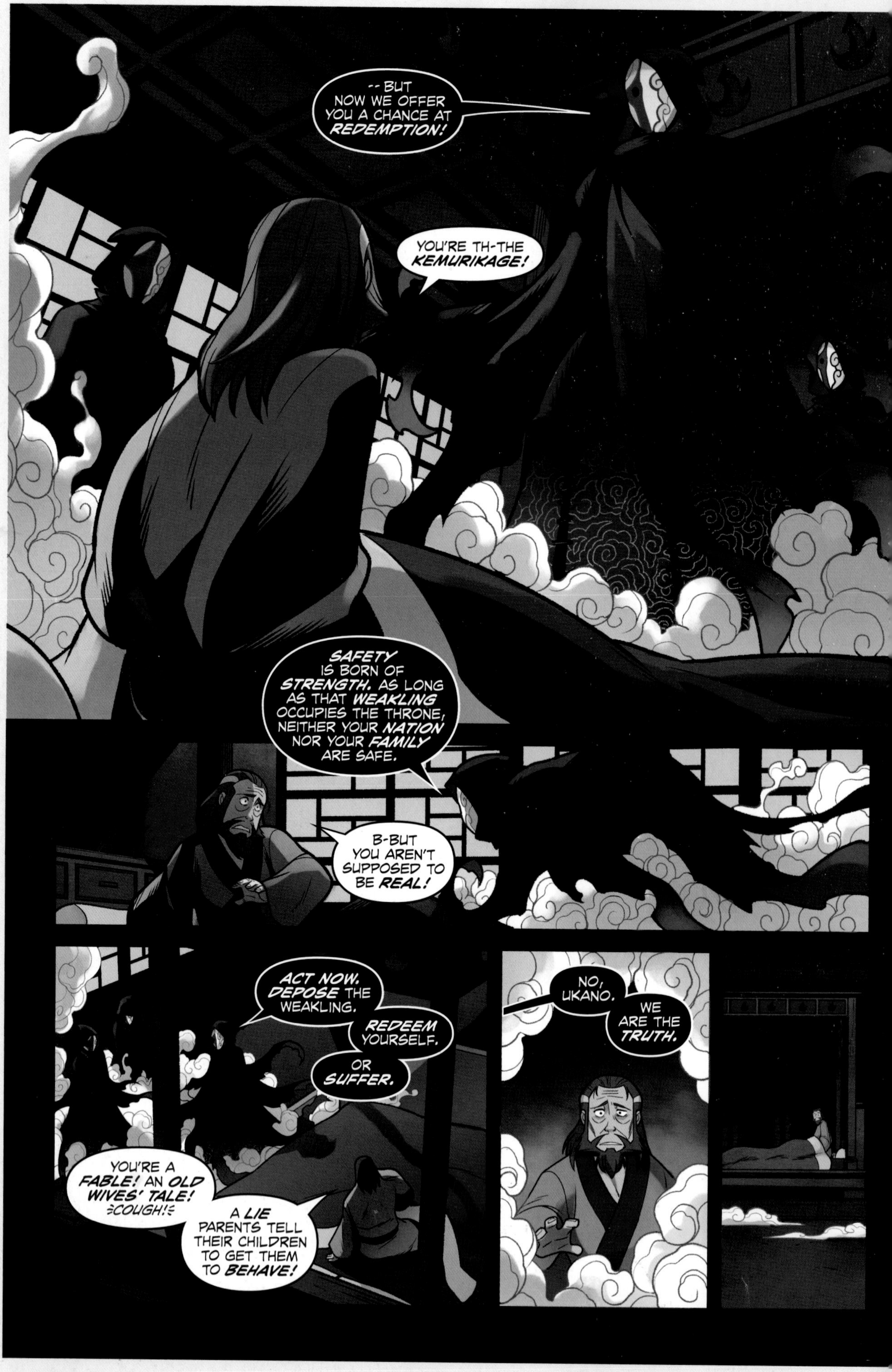
-- BUT NOW WE OFFER YOU A CHANCE AT REDEMPTION!
YOU'RE TH-THE KEMURIKAGE!
SAFETY IS BORN OF STRENGTH. AS LONG AS THAT WEAKLING OCCUPIES THE THRONE, NEITHER YOUR NATION NOR YOUR FAMILY ARE SAFE.
B-BUT YOU AREN'T SUPPOSED TO BE REAL!
YOU'RE A FABLE! AN OLD WIVES' TALE! ≥COUGH!≤
ACT NOW. DEPOSE THE WEAKLING.
REDEEM YOURSELF.
OR SUFFER.
A LIE PARENTS TELL THEIR CHILDREN TO GET THEM TO BEHAVE!
NO, UKANO.
WE ARE THE TRUTH.

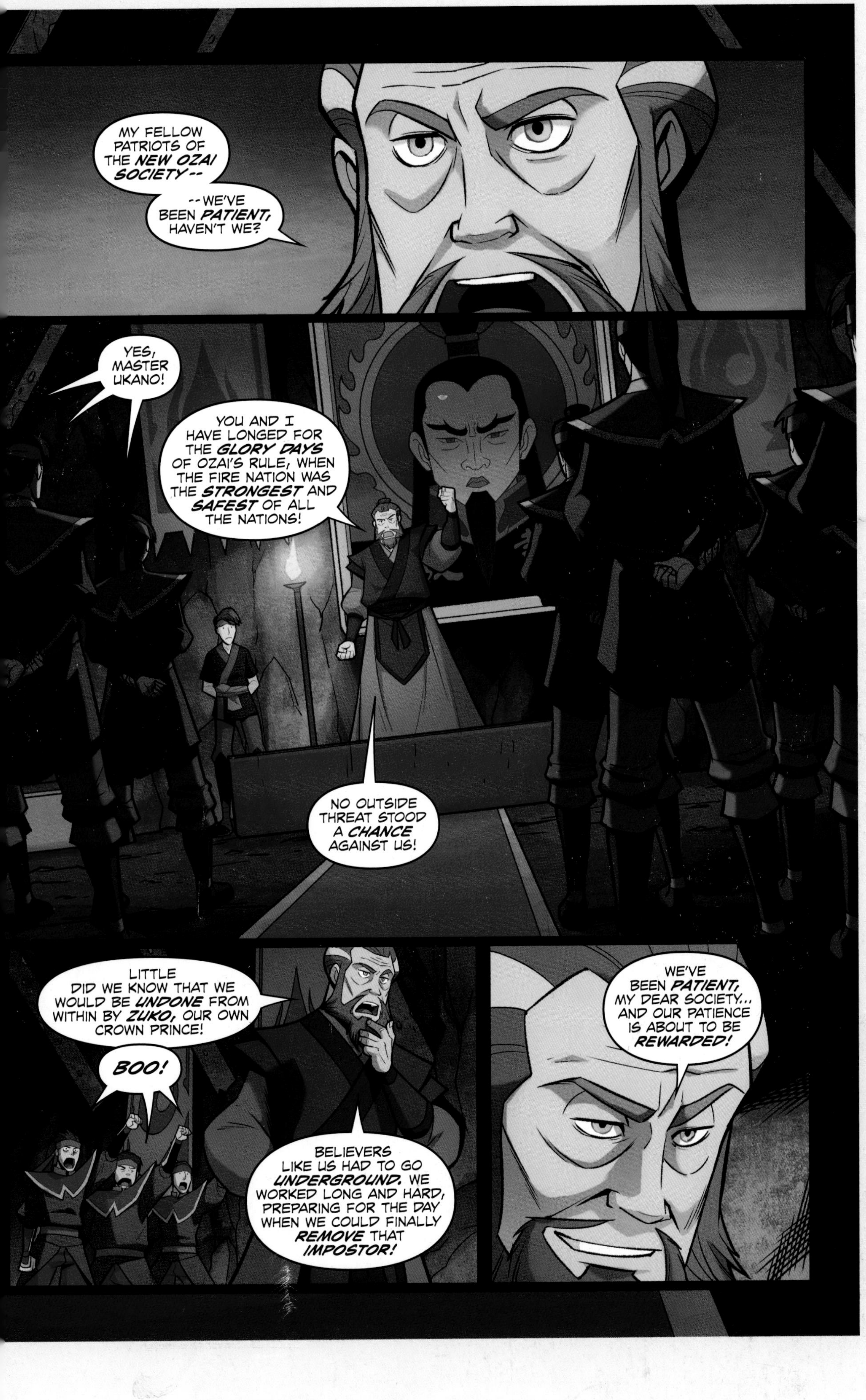
MY FELLOW PATRIOTS OF THE NEW OZAI SOCIETY--
--WE'VE BEEN PATIENT, HAVEN'T WE?
YES, MASTER UKANO!
YOU AND I HAVE LONGED FOR THE GLORY DAYS OF OZAI'S RULE, WHEN THE FIRE NATION WAS THE STRONGEST AND SAFEST OF ALL THE NATIONS!
NO OUTSIDE THREAT STOOD A CHANCE AGAINST US!
LITTLE DID WE KNOW THAT WE WOULD BE UNDONE FROM WITHIN BY ZUKO, OUR OWN CROWN PRINCE!
BOO!
BELIEVERS LIKE US HAD TO GO UNDERGROUND. WE WORKED LONG AND HARD, PREPARING FOR THE DAY WHEN WE COULD FINALLY REMOVE THAT IMPOSTOR!
WE'VE BEEN PATIENT, MY DEAR SOCIETY... AND OUR PATIENCE IS ABOUT TO BE REWARDED!

GLY: *The New Ozai Society first appeared in "Rebound," a short story we did for* Free Comic Book Day 2013. *The whole story was focused on Mai, one of my favorite characters from the original series. She and Zuko broke up (again) in* The Promise. *"Rebound" showed that there still might be something there. In many ways, "Rebound" laid the groundwork for* Smoke and Shadow.

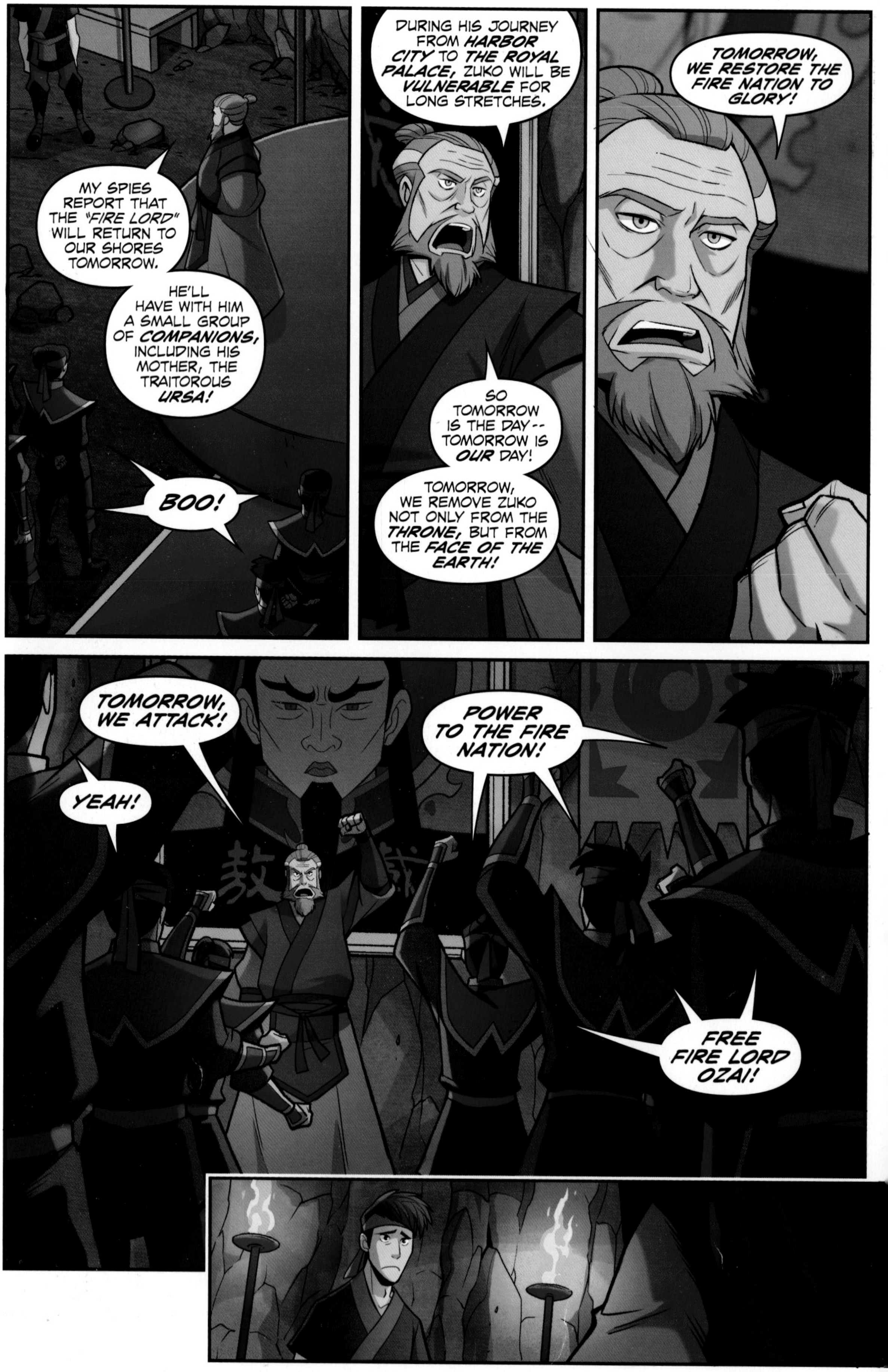
MY SPIES REPORT THAT THE "FIRE LORD" WILL RETURN TO OUR SHORES TOMORROW.
HE'LL HAVE WITH HIM A SMALL GROUP OF COMPANIONS, INCLUDING HIS MOTHER, THE TRAITOROUS URSA!
BOO!
DURING HIS JOURNEY FROM HARBOR CITY TO THE ROYAL PALACE, ZUKO WILL BE VULNERABLE FOR LONG STRETCHES.
SO TOMORROW IS THE DAY-- TOMORROW IS OUR DAY!
TOMORROW, WE REMOVE ZUKO NOT ONLY FROM THE THRONE, BUT FROM THE FACE OF THE EARTH!
TOMORROW, WE RESTORE THE FIRE NATION TO GLORY!
TOMORROW, WE ATTACK!
YEAH!
POWER TO THE FIRE NATION!
FREE FIRE LORD OZAI!

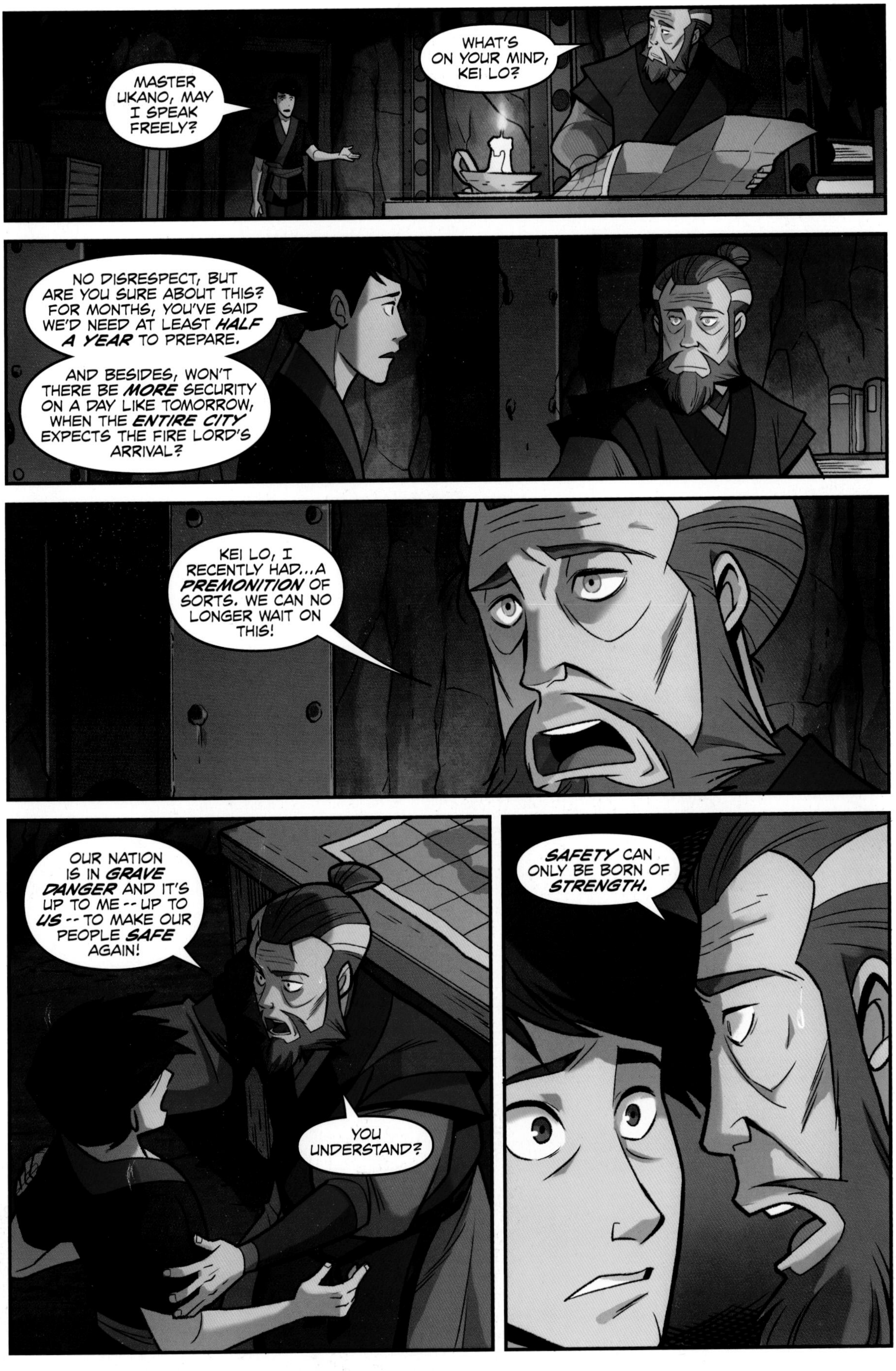
MASTER UKANO, MAY I SPEAK FREELY?
WHAT'S ON YOUR MIND, KEI LO?
NO DISRESPECT, BUT ARE YOU SURE ABOUT THIS? FOR MONTHS, YOU'VE SAID WE'D NEED AT LEAST HALF A YEAR TO PREPARE.
AND BESIDES, WON'T THERE BE MORE SECURITY ON A DAY LIKE TOMORROW, WHEN THE ENTIRE CITY EXPECTS THE FIRE LORD'S ARRIVAL?
KEI LO, I RECENTLY HAD...A PREMONITION OF SORTS. WE CAN NO LONGER WAIT ON THIS!
OUR NATION IS IN GRAVE DANGER AND IT'S UP TO ME -- UP TO US -- TO MAKE OUR PEOPLE SAFE AGAIN!
YOU UNDERSTAND?
SAFETY CAN ONLY BE BORN OF STRENGTH.

GLY: *Kei Lo also made his debut in "Rebound." He confessed his sincere feelings for Mai right before he betrayed her. Here, we're establishing him as a decent fellow, someone worthy of being a real love interest for Mai.*

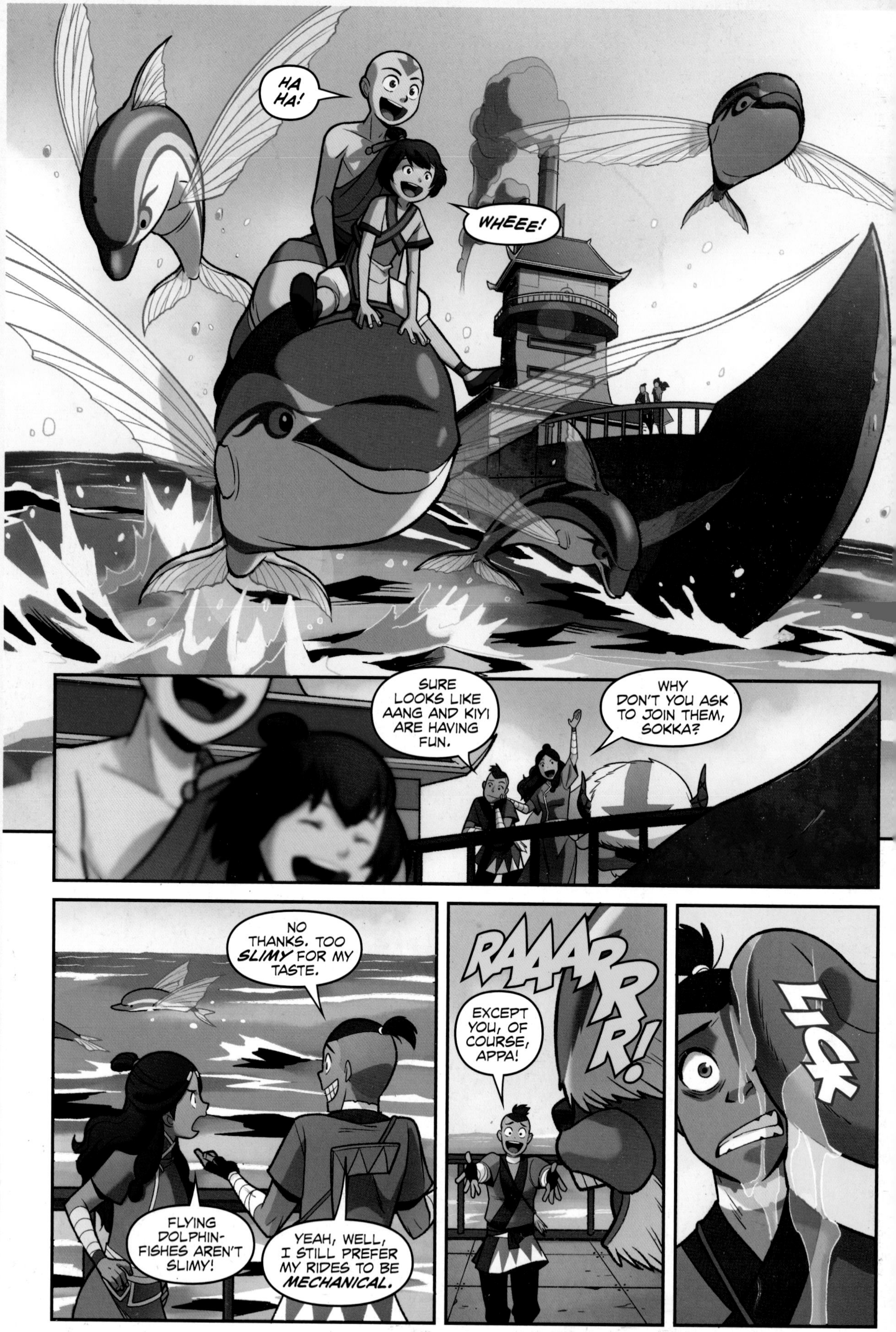
HA HA!
WHEEE!
SURE LOOKS LIKE AANG AND KIYI ARE HAVING FUN.
WHY DON'T YOU ASK TO JOIN THEM, SOKKA?
NO THANKS. TOO SLIMY FOR MY TASTE.
FLYING DOLPHIN-FISHES AREN'T SLIMY!
YEAH, WELL, I STILL PREFER MY RIDES TO BE MECHANICAL.
RAAARRR!
EXCEPT YOU, OF COURSE, APPA!
LICK

GLY: *Originally, I had a different hybrid animal for this scene. After Mike read my script, he suggested dolphin-fish, which he'd just used in "Korra Alone," the second episode of* The Legend of Korra *Book Four. They turned out to be a perfect fit here.*

GLY: *Ah. Appa's slobber. Always good for a laugh.*

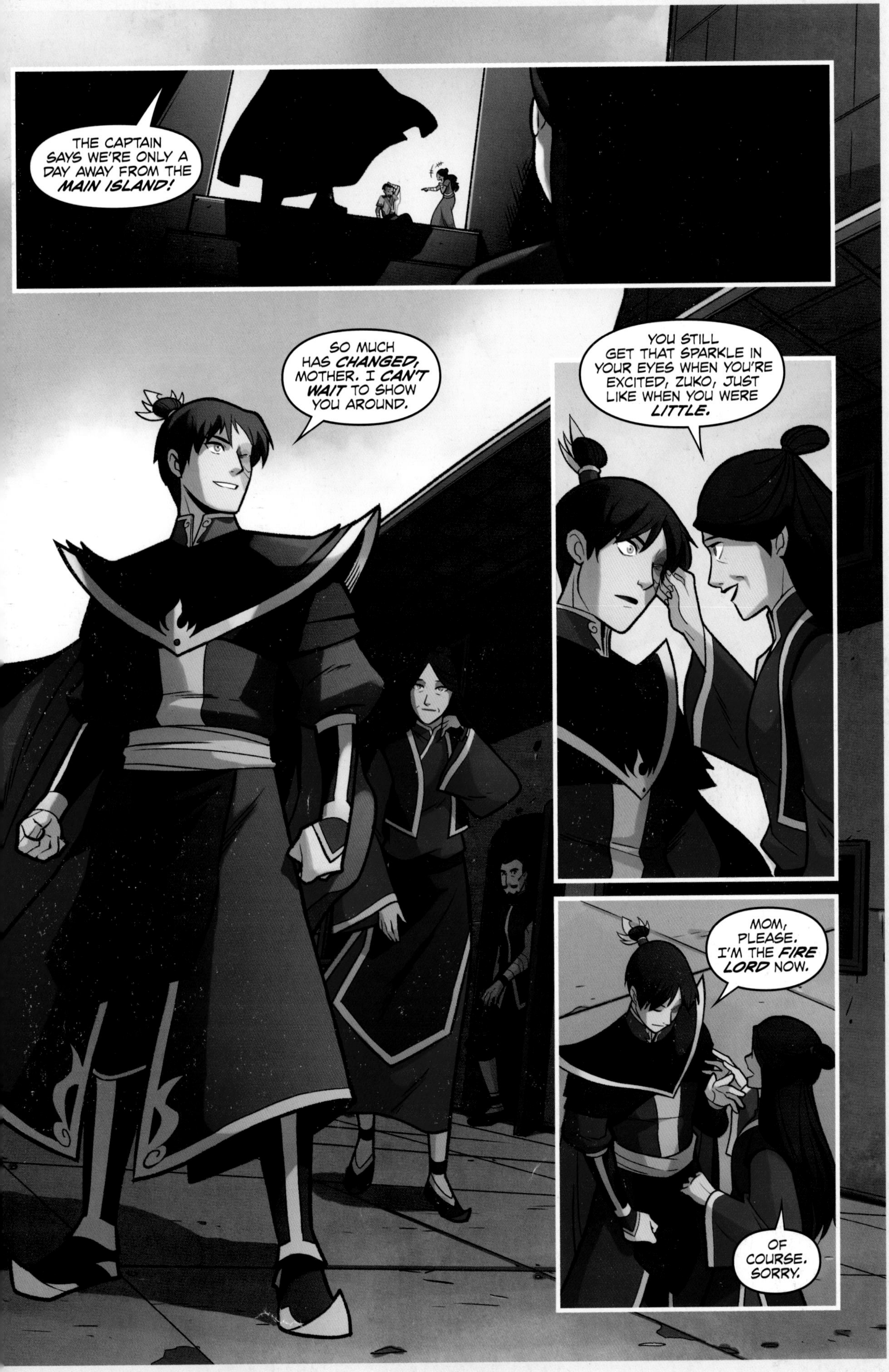
THE CAPTAIN SAYS WE'RE ONLY A DAY AWAY FROM THE MAIN ISLAND!
SO MUCH HAS CHANGED, MOTHER. I CAN'T WAIT TO SHOW YOU AROUND.
YOU STILL GET THAT SPARKLE IN YOUR EYES WHEN YOU'RE EXCITED, ZUKO, JUST LIKE WHEN YOU WERE LITTLE.
MOM, PLEASE. I'M THE FIRE LORD NOW.
OF COURSE. SORRY.

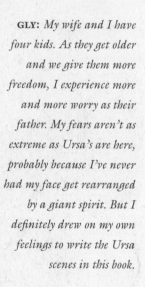

GLY: *My wife and I have four kids. As they get older and we give them more freedom, I experience more and more worry as their father. My fears aren't as extreme as Ursa's are here, probably because I've never had my face get rearranged by a giant spirit. But I definitely drew on my own feelings to write the Ursa scenes in this book.*

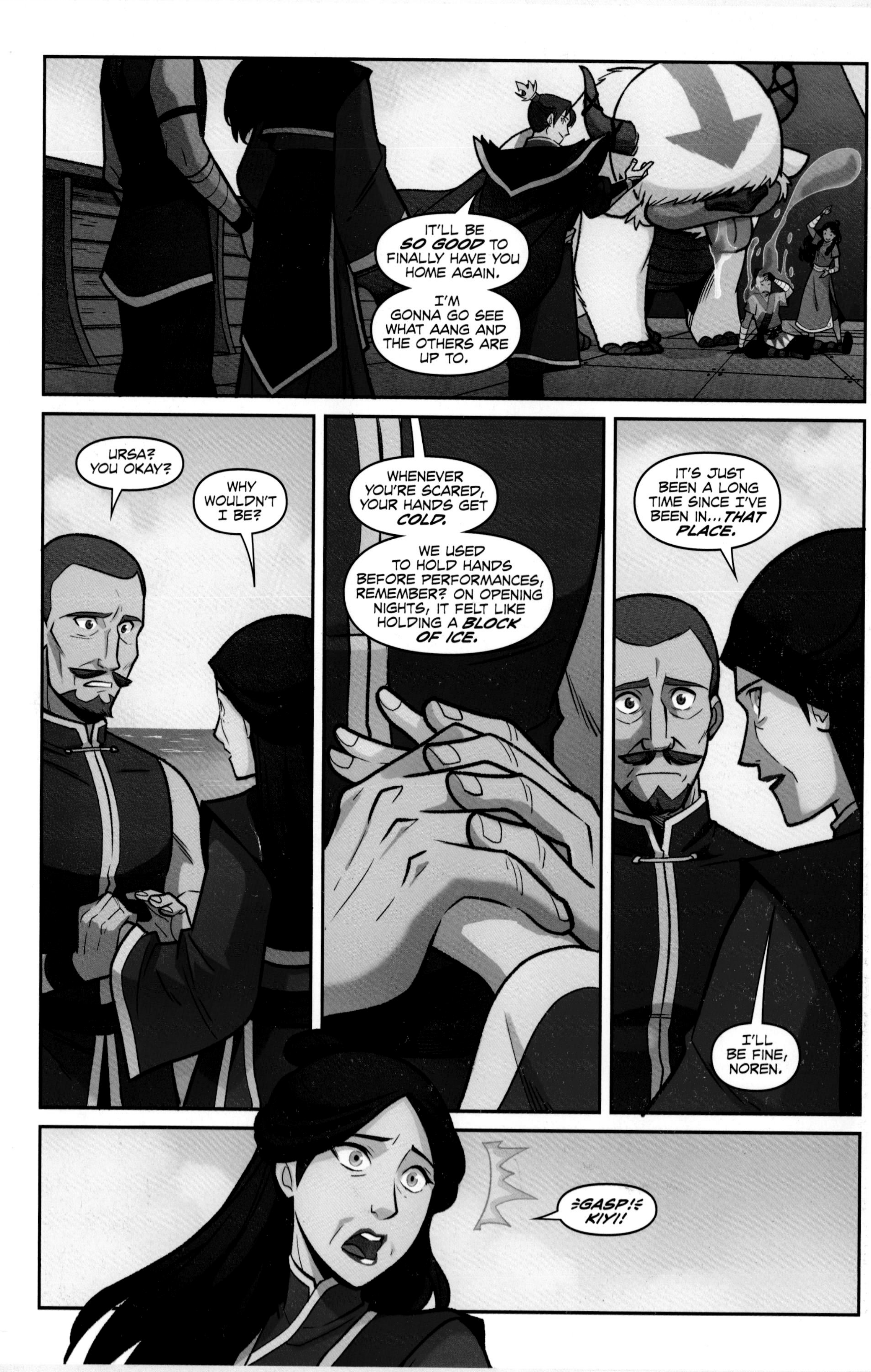
IT'LL BE SO GOOD TO FINALLY HAVE YOU HOME AGAIN.
I'M GONNA GO SEE WHAT AANG AND THE OTHERS ARE UP TO.
URSA? YOU OKAY?
WHY WOULDN'T I BE?
WHENEVER YOU'RE SCARED, YOUR HANDS GET COLD.
WE USED TO HOLD HANDS BEFORE PERFORMANCES, REMEMBER? ON OPENING NIGHTS, IT FELT LIKE HOLDING A BLOCK OF ICE.
IT'S JUST BEEN A LONG TIME SINCE I'VE BEEN IN... THAT PLACE.
I'LL BE FINE, NOREN.
GASP! KIYI!

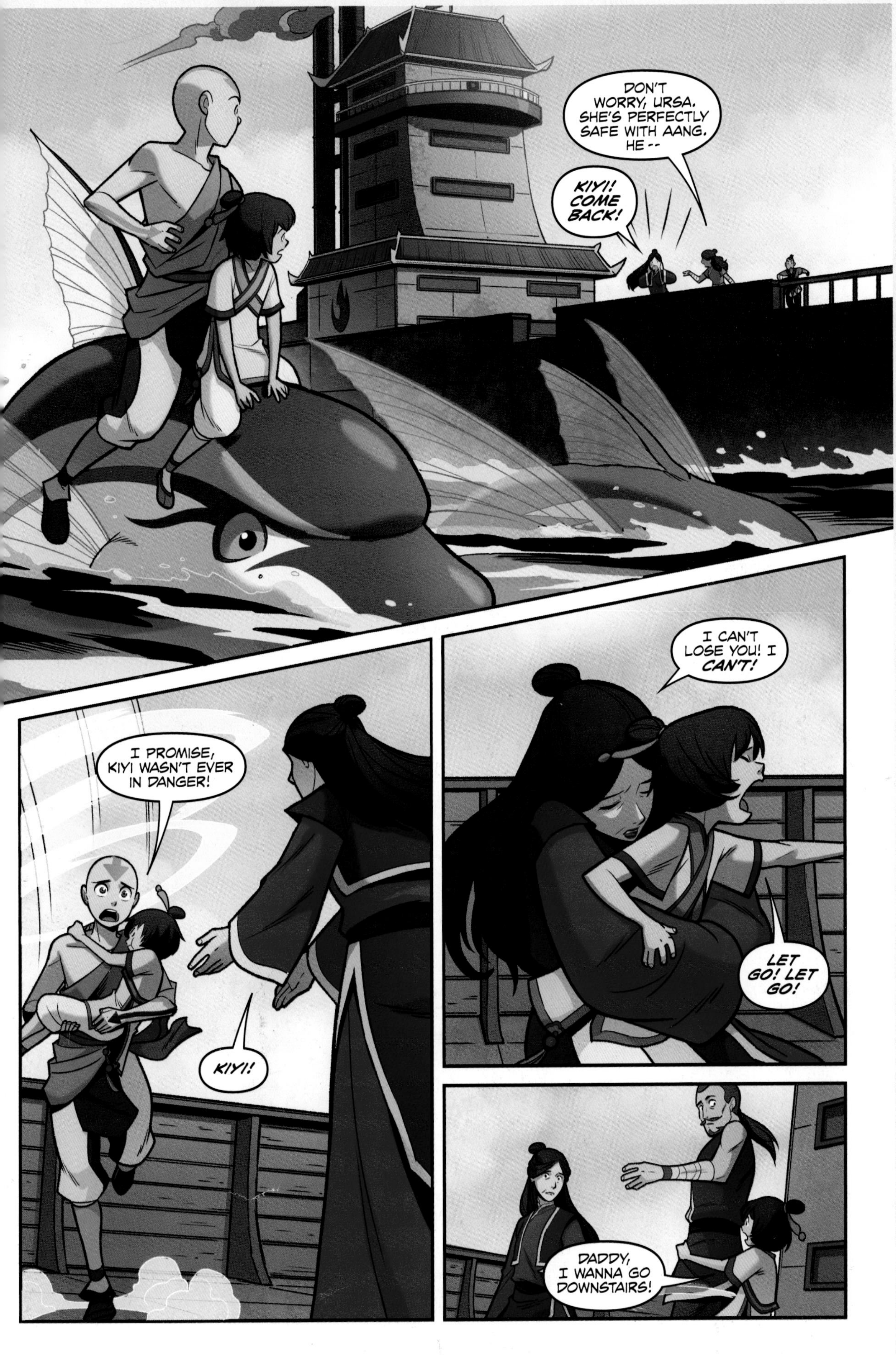
DON'T WORRY, URSA. SHE'S PERFECTLY SAFE WITH AANG. HE --
KIYI! COME BACK!
I PROMISE, KIYI WASN'T EVER IN DANGER!
KIYI!
I CAN'T LOSE YOU! I CAN'T!
LET GO! LET GO!
DADDY, I WANNA GO DOWNSTAIRS!

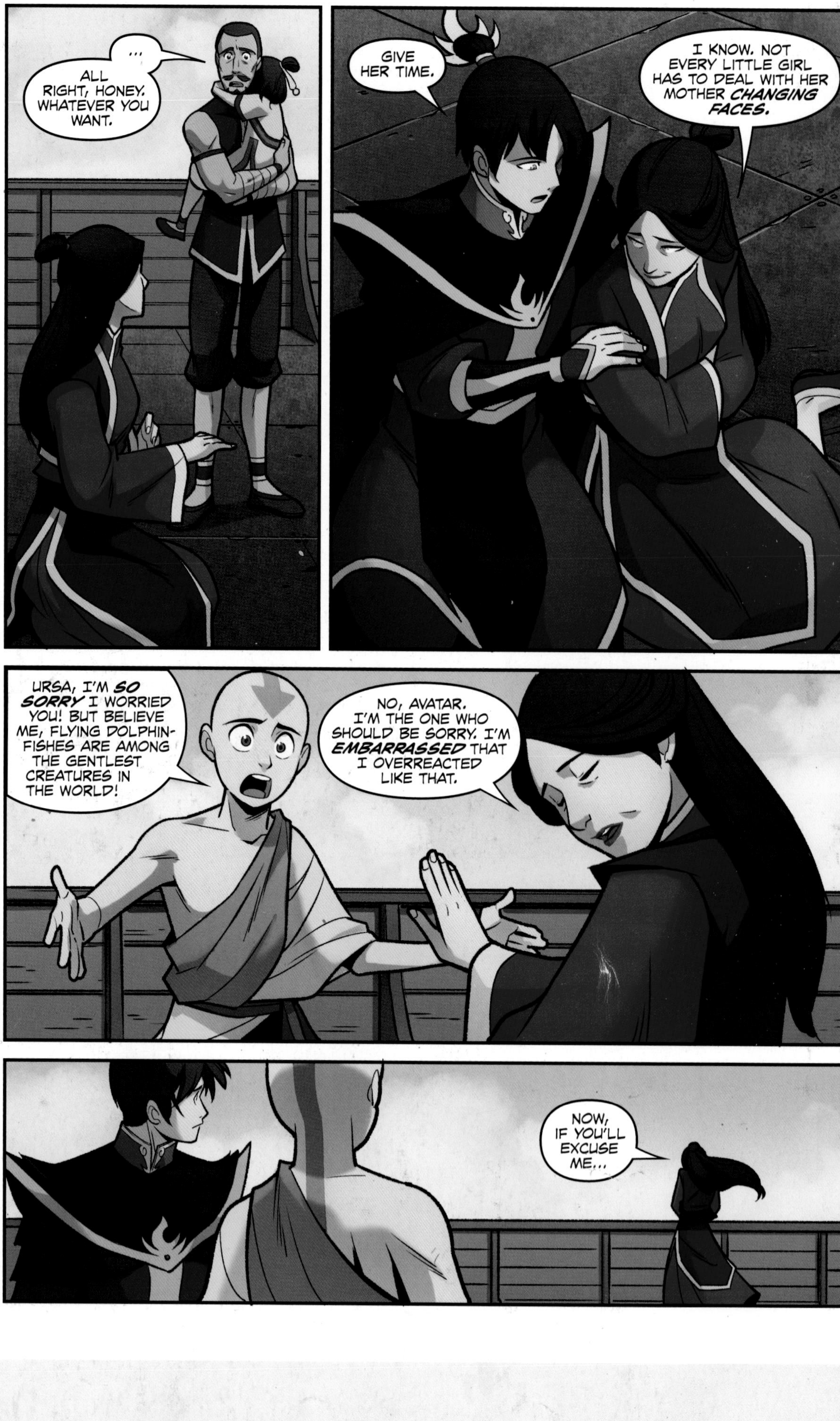
...
ALL RIGHT, HONEY. WHATEVER YOU WANT.
GIVE HER TIME.
I KNOW. NOT EVERY LITTLE GIRL HAS TO DEAL WITH HER MOTHER CHANGING FACES.
URSA, I'M SO SORRY I WORRIED YOU! BUT BELIEVE ME, FLYING DOLPHIN-FISHES ARE AMONG THE GENTLEST CREATURES IN THE WORLD!
NO, AVATAR. I'M THE ONE WHO SHOULD BE SORRY. I'M EMBARRASSED THAT I OVERREACTED LIKE THAT.
NOW, IF YOU'LL EXCUSE ME...

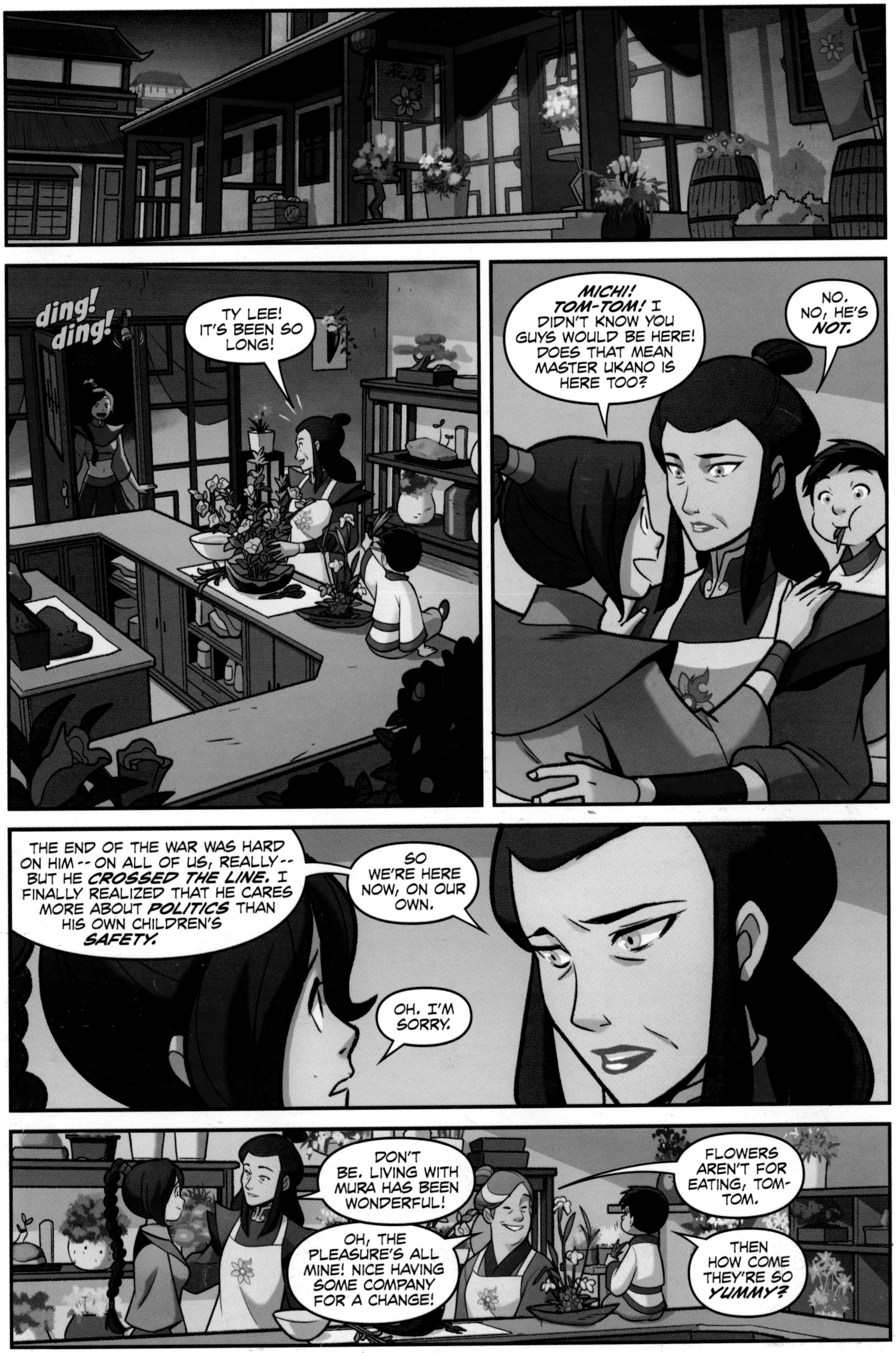
ding! ding!
TY LEE! IT'S BEEN SO LONG!
MICHI! TOM-TOM! I DIDN'T KNOW YOU GUYS WOULD BE HERE! DOES THAT MEAN MASTER UKANO IS HERE TOO?
NO. NO, HE'S NOT.
THE END OF THE WAR WAS HARD ON HIM--ON ALL OF US, REALLY--BUT HE CROSSED THE LINE. I FINALLY REALIZED THAT HE CARES MORE ABOUT POLITICS THAN HIS OWN CHILDREN'S SAFETY.
SO WE'RE HERE NOW, ON OUR OWN.
OH. I'M SORRY.
DON'T BE. LIVING WITH MURA HAS BEEN WONDERFUL!
OH, THE PLEASURE'S ALL MINE! NICE HAVING SOME COMPANY FOR A CHANGE!
FLOWERS AREN'T FOR EATING, TOM-TOM.
THEN HOW COME THEY'RE SO YUMMY?

GLY: *Auntie Mura's flower shop was designed by cartoonist Ryan Hill. I think he did a great job, especially with the shop's logo.*

GURIHIRU: *To make the flower shop fit in with the world of* Avatar, *we made it Eastern style with many bonsai plants. Mai's mother is performing ikebana-style flower arrangement.*

GLY: *Here, Gurihiru perfectly captured the personalities of both Ty Lee and Mai.*

G: *Mai appears here for the first time since* The Promise. *She is one of our favorite characters, so we were happy that we could finally draw her again.*

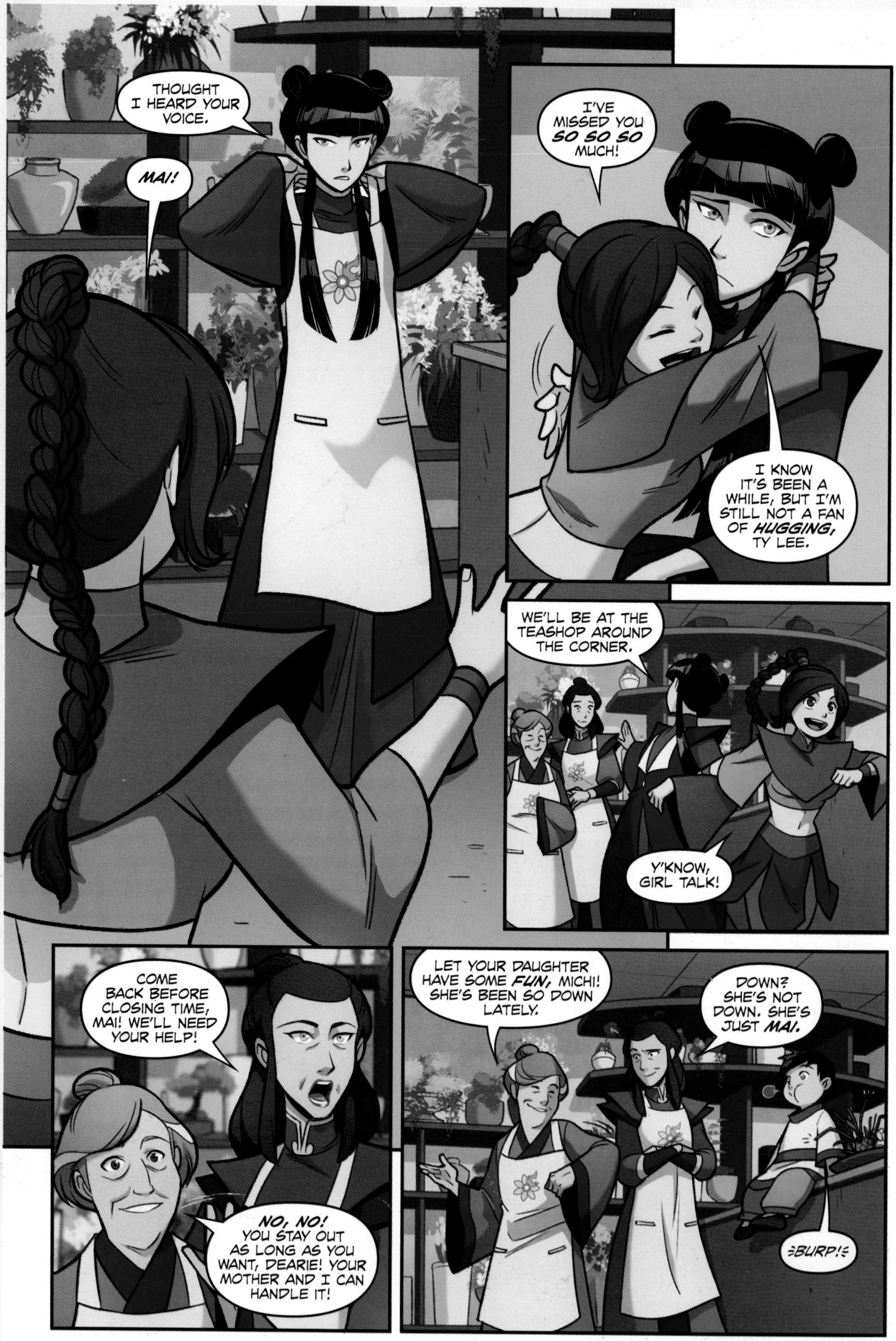
THOUGHT I HEARD YOUR VOICE.
MAI!
I'VE MISSED YOU SO SO SO MUCH!
I KNOW IT'S BEEN A WHILE, BUT I'M STILL NOT A FAN OF HUGGING, TY LEE.
WE'LL BE AT THE TEASHOP AROUND THE CORNER.
Y'KNOW, GIRL TALK!
COME BACK BEFORE CLOSING TIME, MAI! WE'LL NEED YOUR HELP!
NO, NO! YOU STAY OUT AS LONG AS YOU WANT, DEARIE! YOUR MOTHER AND I CAN HANDLE IT!
LET YOUR DAUGHTER HAVE SOME FUN, MICHI! SHE'S BEEN SO DOWN LATELY.
DOWN? SHE'S NOT DOWN. SHE'S JUST MAI.
BURP!

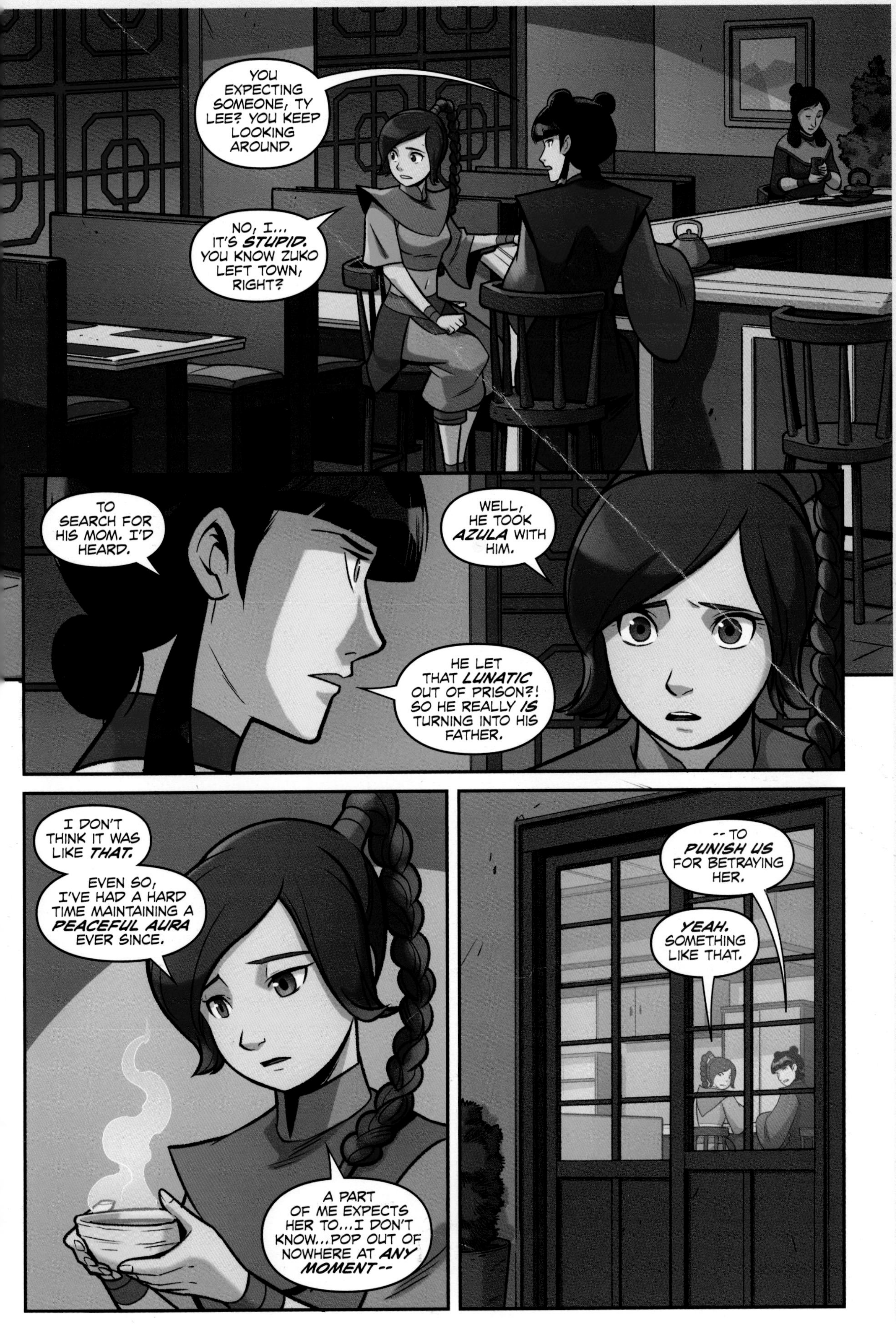
YOU EXPECTING SOMEONE, TY LEE? YOU KEEP LOOKING AROUND.
NO, I... IT'S STUPID. YOU KNOW ZUKO LEFT TOWN, RIGHT?
TO SEARCH FOR HIS MOM. I'D HEARD.
WELL, HE TOOK AZULA WITH HIM.
HE LET THAT LUNATIC OUT OF PRISON?! SO HE REALLY IS TURNING INTO HIS FATHER.
I DON'T THINK IT WAS LIKE THAT.
EVEN SO, I'VE HAD A HARD TIME MAINTAINING A PEACEFUL AURA EVER SINCE.
A PART OF ME EXPECTS HER TO...I DON'T KNOW...POP OUT OF NOWHERE AT ANY MOMENT--
--TO PUNISH US FOR BETRAYING HER.
YEAH. SOMETHING LIKE THAT.

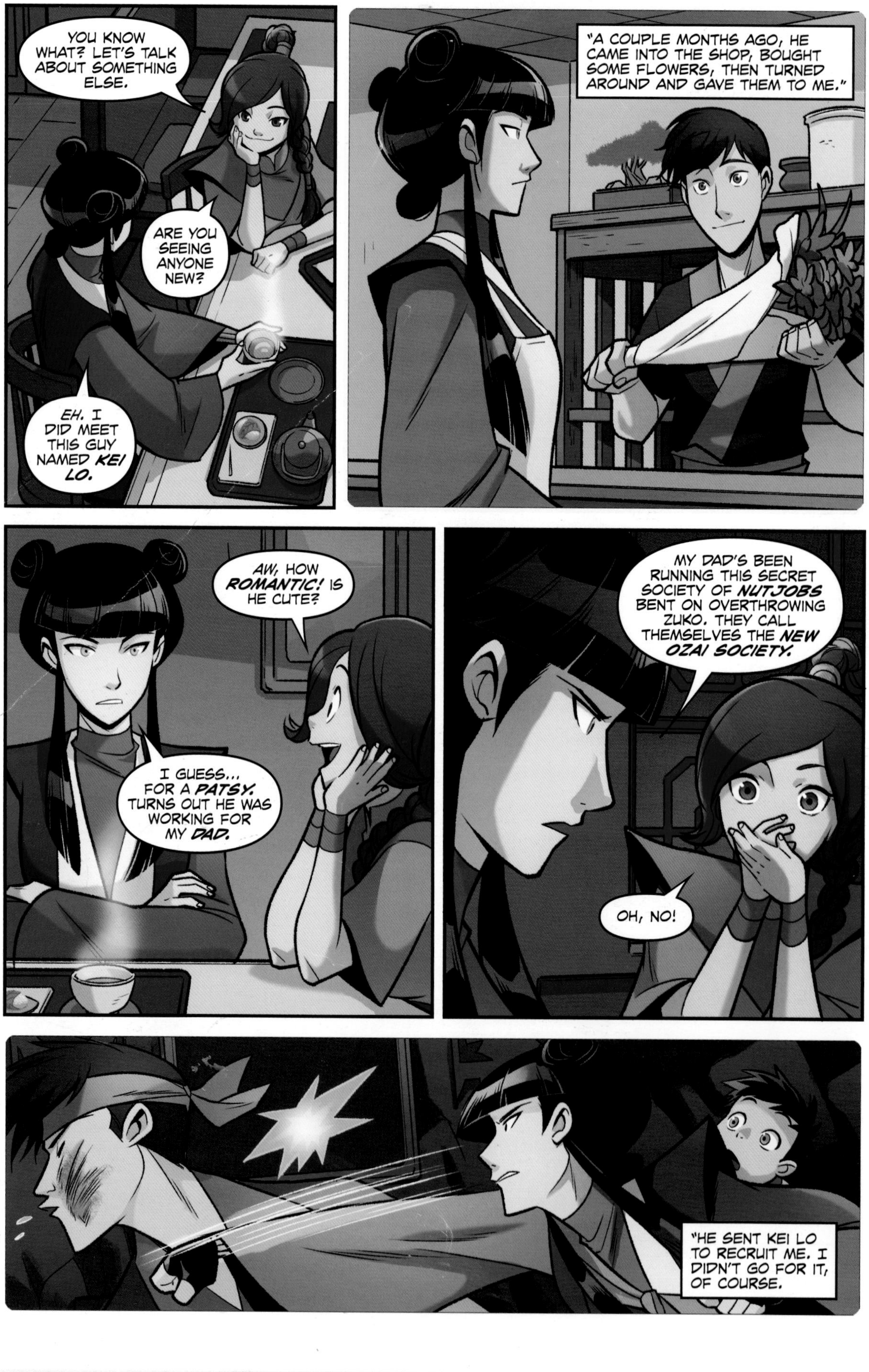
YOU KNOW WHAT? LET'S TALK ABOUT SOMETHING ELSE.
ARE YOU SEEING ANYONE NEW?
EH. I DID MEET THIS GUY NAMED KEI LO.
"A COUPLE MONTHS AGO, HE CAME INTO THE SHOP, BOUGHT SOME FLOWERS, THEN TURNED AROUND AND GAVE THEM TO ME."
AW, HOW ROMANTIC! IS HE CUTE?
I GUESS... FOR A PATSY. TURNS OUT HE WAS WORKING FOR MY DAD.
MY DAD'S BEEN RUNNING THIS SECRET SOCIETY OF NUTJOBS BENT ON OVERTHROWING ZUKO. THEY CALL THEMSELVES THE NEW OZAI SOCIETY.
OH, NO!
"HE SENT KEI LO TO RECRUIT ME. I DIDN'T GO FOR IT, OF COURSE.

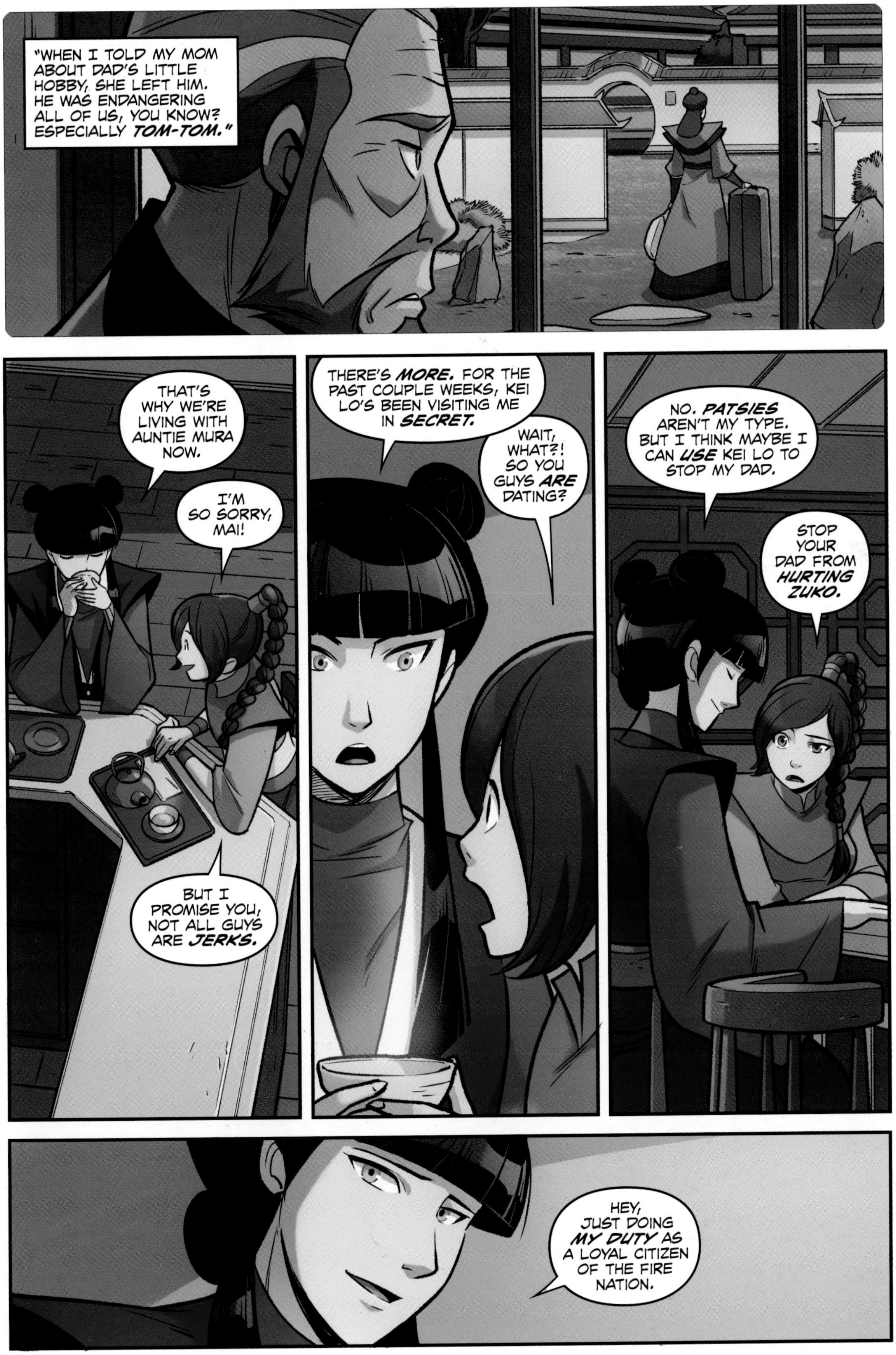
"WHEN I TOLD MY MOM ABOUT DAD'S LITTLE HOBBY, SHE LEFT HIM. HE WAS ENDANGERING ALL OF US, YOU KNOW? ESPECIALLY TOM-TOM."
THAT'S WHY WE'RE LIVING WITH AUNTIE MURA NOW.
I'M SO SORRY, MAI!
BUT I PROMISE YOU, NOT ALL GUYS ARE JERKS.
THERE'S MORE. FOR THE PAST COUPLE WEEKS, KEI LO'S BEEN VISITING ME IN SECRET.
WAIT, WHAT?! SO YOU GUYS ARE DATING?
NO. PATSIES AREN'T MY TYPE. BUT I THINK MAYBE I CAN USE KEI LO TO STOP MY DAD.
STOP YOUR DAD FROM HURTING ZUKO.
HEY, JUST DOING MY DUTY AS A LOYAL CITIZEN OF THE FIRE NATION.

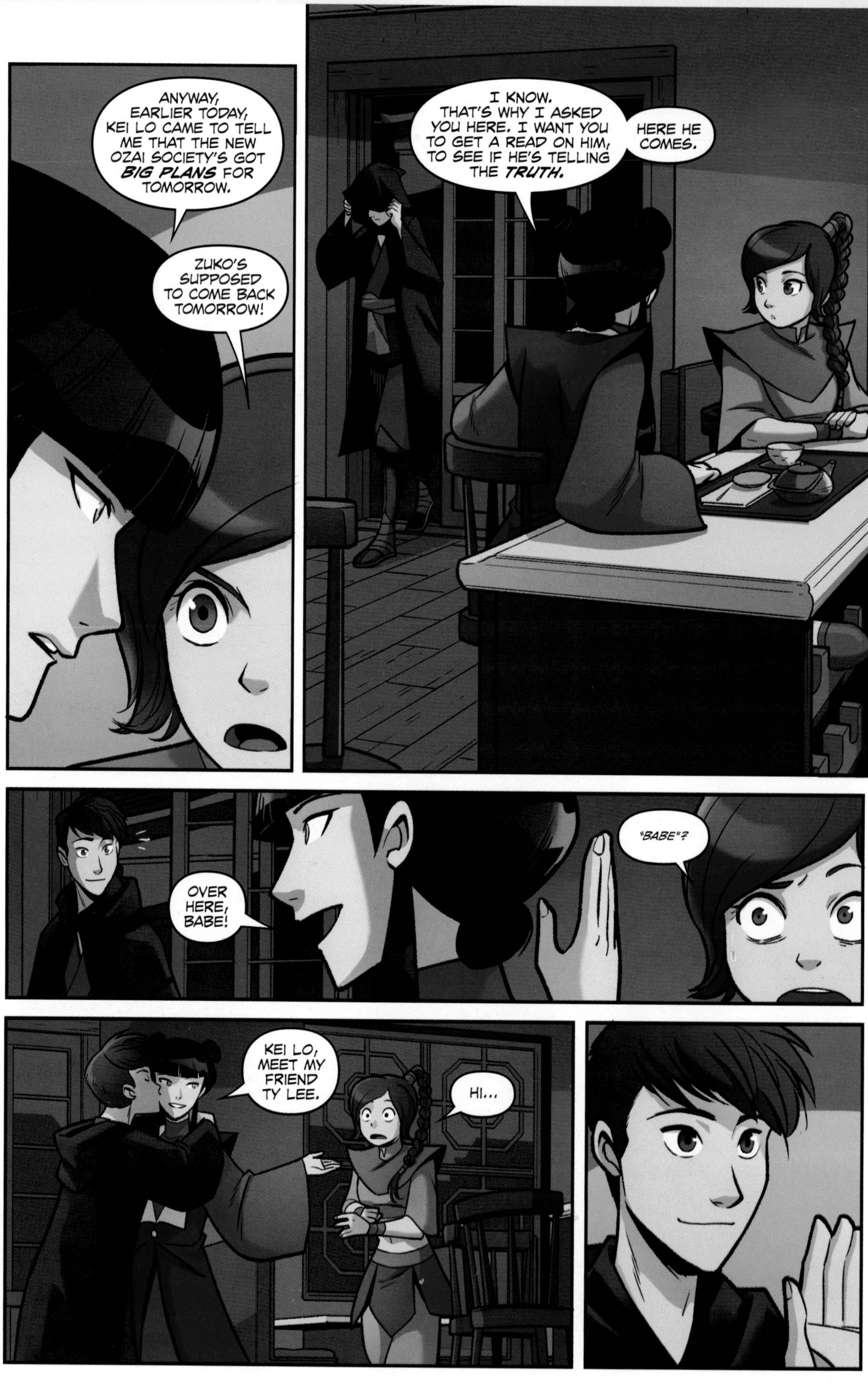
ANYWAY, EARLIER TODAY, KEI LO CAME TO TELL ME THAT THE NEW OZAI SOCIETY'S GOT BIG PLANS FOR TOMORROW.
ZUKO'S SUPPOSED TO COME BACK TOMORROW!
I KNOW. THAT'S WHY I ASKED YOU HERE. I WANT YOU TO GET A READ ON HIM, TO SEE IF HE'S TELLING THE TRUTH.
HERE HE COMES.
OVER HERE, BABE!
"BABE"?
KEI LO, MEET MY FRIEND TY LEE.
HI...

GLY: *I'm always looking for cute, saccharine names that couples can call each other. "Sweetie," Aang and Katara's go-to, is used in both* Avatar: The Last Airbender *and* The Legend of Korra. *"Babe" I got from two friends of mine. I love them but cringe a little inside every time I hear them use it. I chose it for Mai specifically because it is so not Mai.*

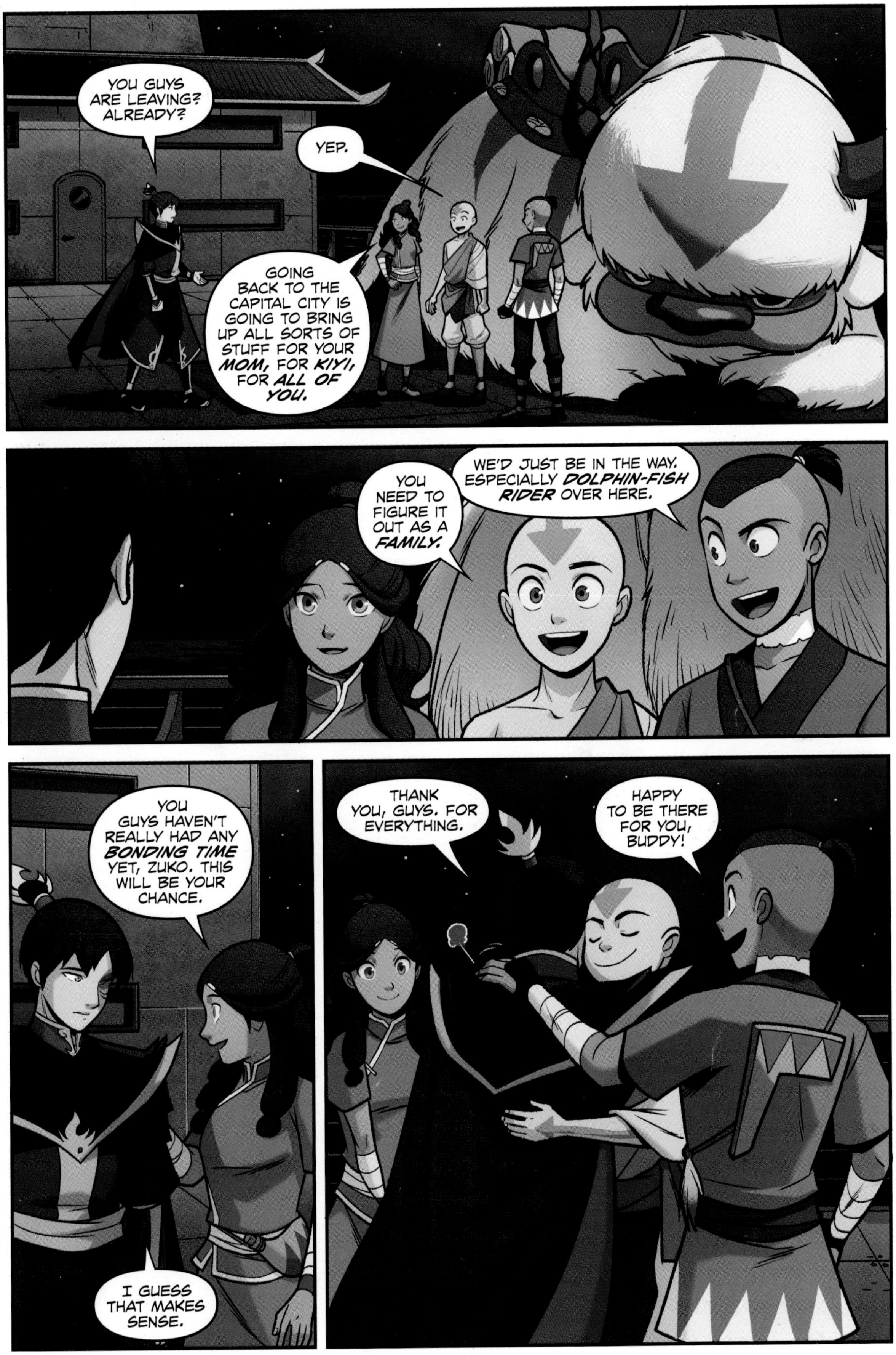
YOU GUYS ARE LEAVING? ALREADY?
YEP.
GOING BACK TO THE CAPITAL CITY IS GOING TO BRING UP ALL SORTS OF STUFF FOR YOUR MOM, FOR KIYI, FOR ALL OF YOU.
YOU NEED TO FIGURE IT OUT AS A FAMILY.
WE'D JUST BE IN THE WAY. ESPECIALLY DOLPHIN-FISH RIDER OVER HERE.
YOU GUYS HAVEN'T REALLY HAD ANY BONDING TIME YET, ZUKO. THIS WILL BE YOUR CHANCE.
I GUESS THAT MAKES SENSE.
THANK YOU, GUYS. FOR EVERYTHING.
HAPPY TO BE THERE FOR YOU, BUDDY!

GLY: *We debated whether to keep Katara and Sokka in this story longer. In the end, we decided to keep the focus on the Fire Nation family dynamic.*

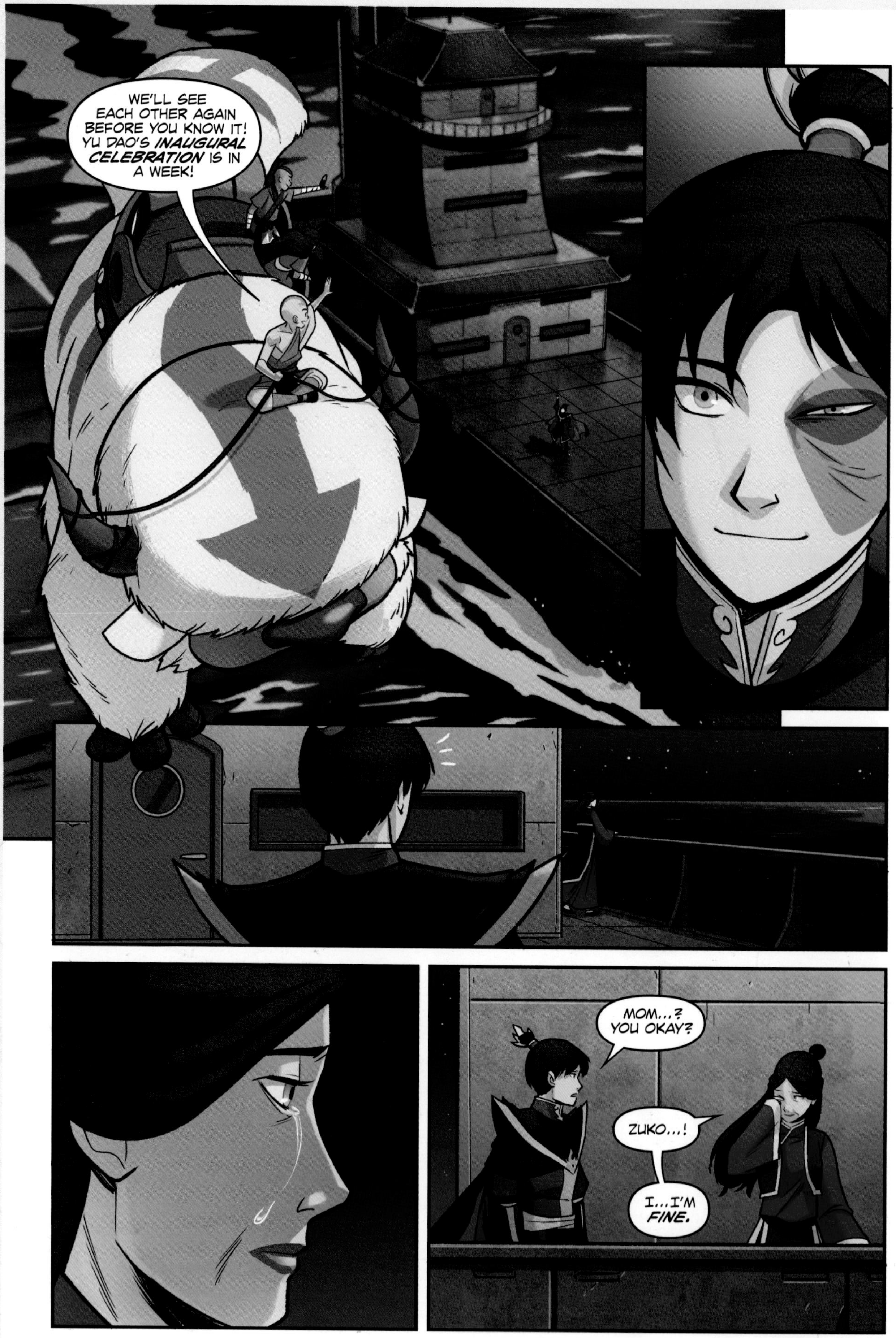
WE'LL SEE EACH OTHER AGAIN BEFORE YOU KNOW IT! YU DAO'S INAUGURAL CELEBRATION IS IN A WEEK!
MOM...? YOU OKAY?
ZUKO...!
I...I'M FINE.

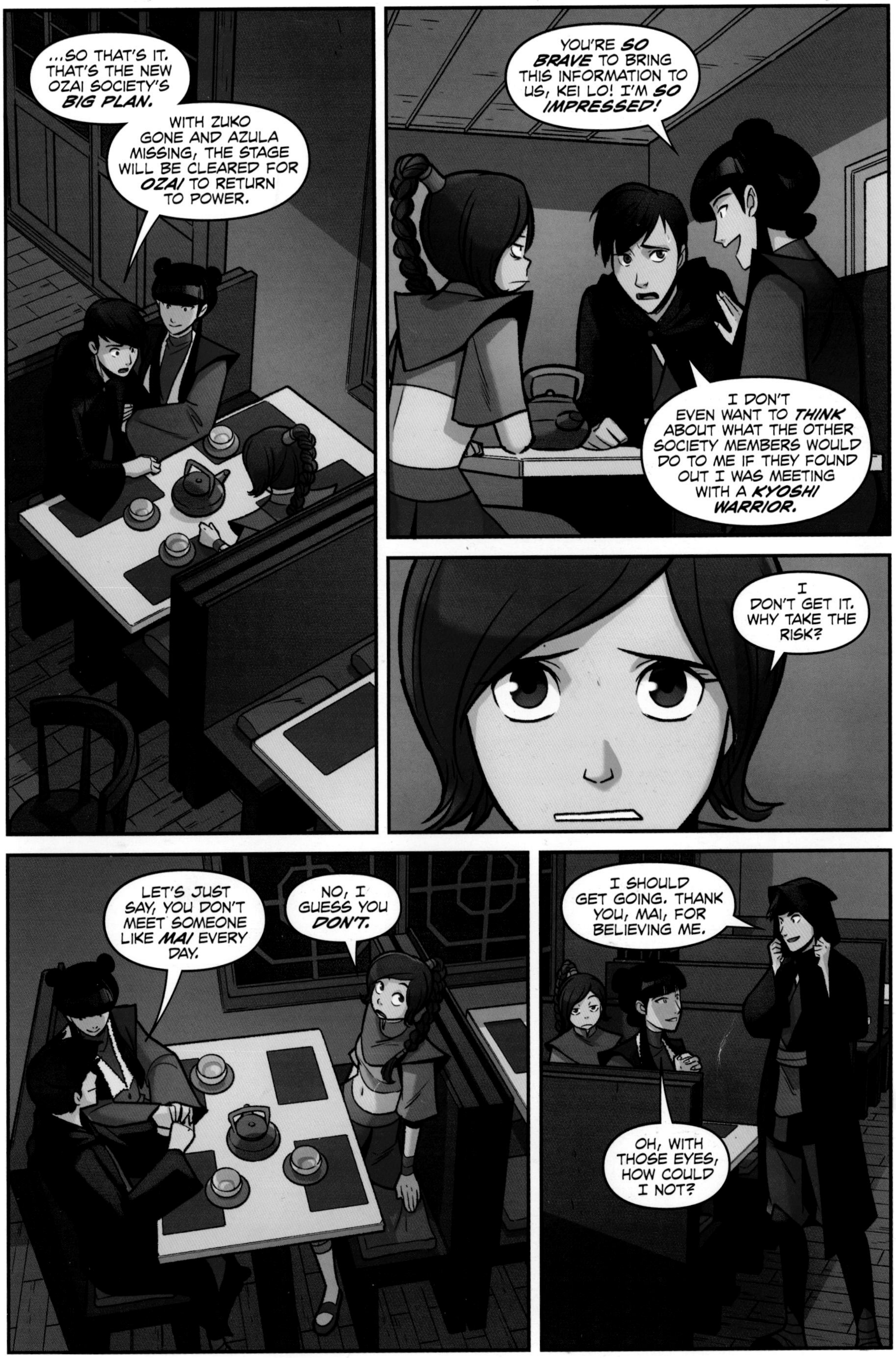
...SO THAT'S IT. THAT'S THE NEW OZAI SOCIETY'S BIG PLAN.
WITH ZUKO GONE AND AZULA MISSING, THE STAGE WILL BE CLEARED FOR OZAI TO RETURN TO POWER.
YOU'RE SO BRAVE TO BRING THIS INFORMATION TO US, KEI LO! I'M SO IMPRESSED!
I DON'T EVEN WANT TO THINK ABOUT WHAT THE OTHER SOCIETY MEMBERS WOULD DO TO ME IF THEY FOUND OUT I WAS MEETING WITH A KYOSHI WARRIOR.
I DON'T GET IT. WHY TAKE THE RISK?
LET'S JUST SAY, YOU DON'T MEET SOMEONE LIKE MAI EVERY DAY.
NO, I GUESS YOU DON'T.
I SHOULD GET GOING. THANK YOU, MAI, FOR BELIEVING ME.
OH, WITH THOSE EYES, HOW COULD I NOT?

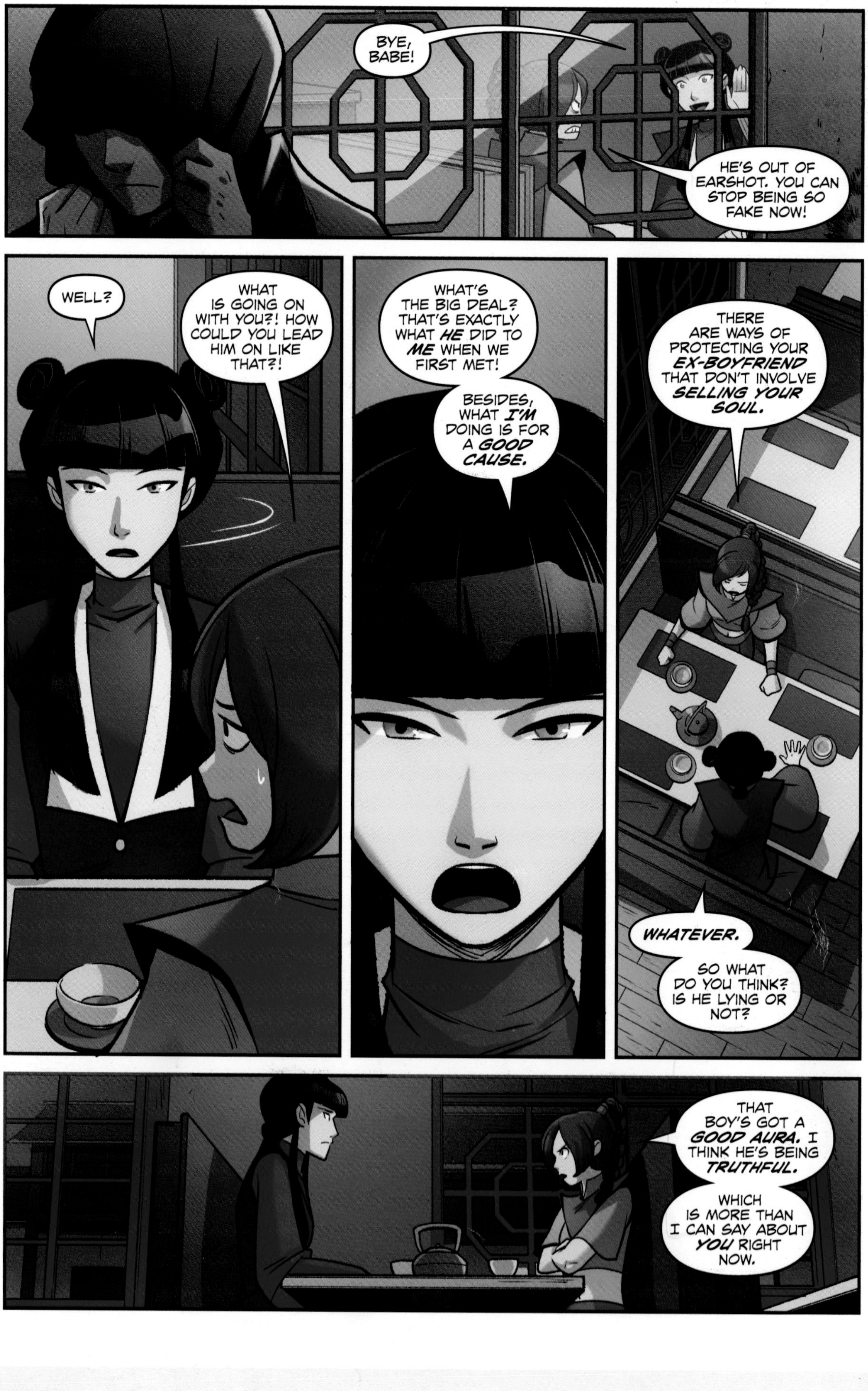
BYE, BABE!
HE'S OUT OF EARSHOT. YOU CAN STOP BEING SO FAKE NOW!
WELL?
WHAT IS GOING ON WITH YOU?! HOW COULD YOU LEAD HIM ON LIKE THAT?!
WHAT'S THE BIG DEAL? THAT'S EXACTLY WHAT HE DID TO ME WHEN WE FIRST MET!
BESIDES, WHAT I'M DOING IS FOR A GOOD CAUSE.
THERE ARE WAYS OF PROTECTING YOUR EX-BOYFRIEND THAT DON'T INVOLVE SELLING YOUR SOUL.
WHATEVER.
SO WHAT DO YOU THINK? IS HE LYING OR NOT?
THAT BOY'S GOT A GOOD AURA. I THINK HE'S BEING TRUTHFUL.
WHICH IS MORE THAN I CAN SAY ABOUT YOU RIGHT NOW.

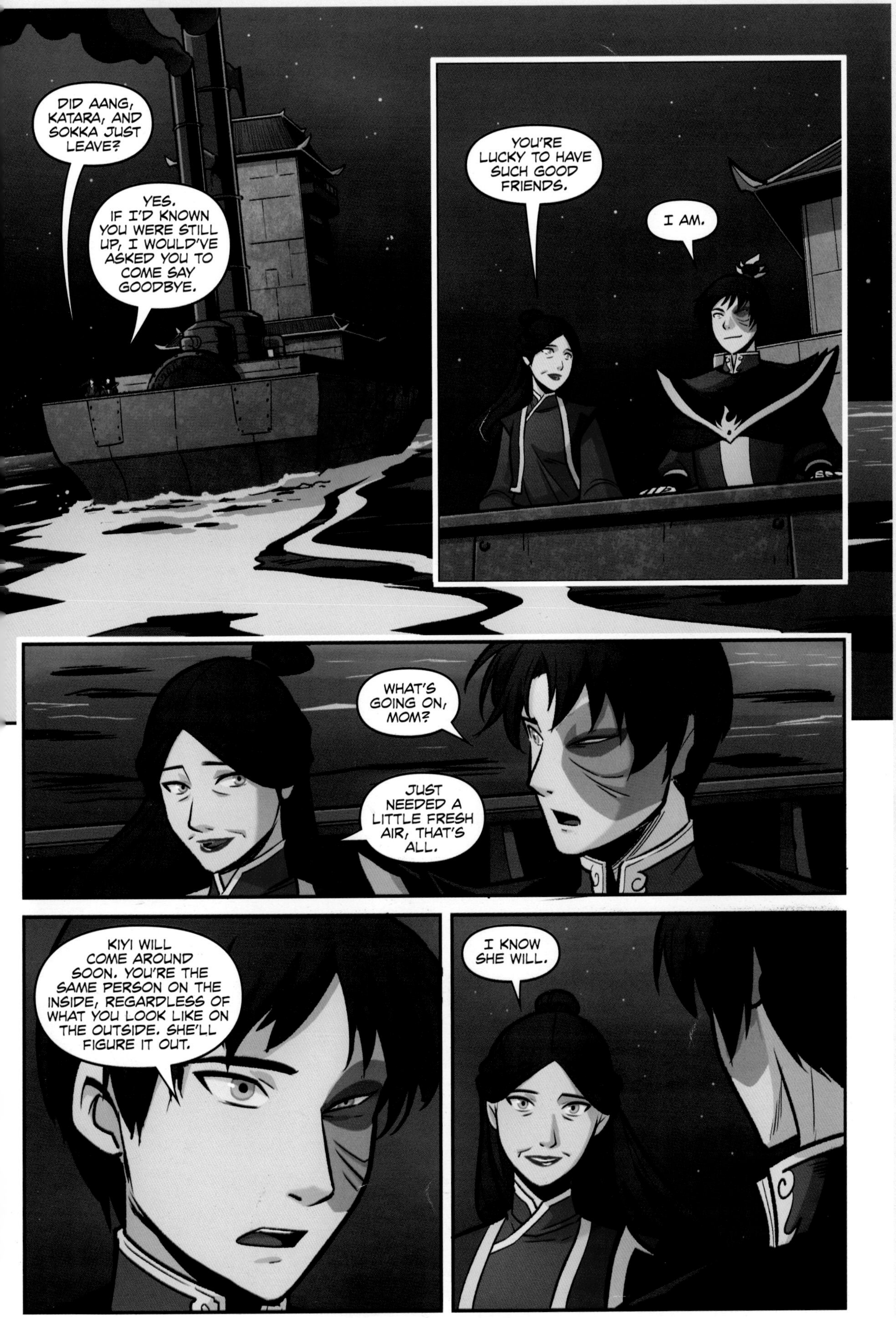
DID AANG, KATARA, AND SOKKA JUST LEAVE?
YES. IF I'D KNOWN YOU WERE STILL UP, I WOULD'VE ASKED YOU TO COME SAY GOODBYE.
YOU'RE LUCKY TO HAVE SUCH GOOD FRIENDS.
I AM.
WHAT'S GOING ON, MOM?
JUST NEEDED A LITTLE FRESH AIR, THAT'S ALL.
KIYI WILL COME AROUND SOON. YOU'RE THE SAME PERSON ON THE INSIDE, REGARDLESS OF WHAT YOU LOOK LIKE ON THE OUTSIDE. SHE'LL FIGURE IT OUT.
I KNOW SHE WILL.

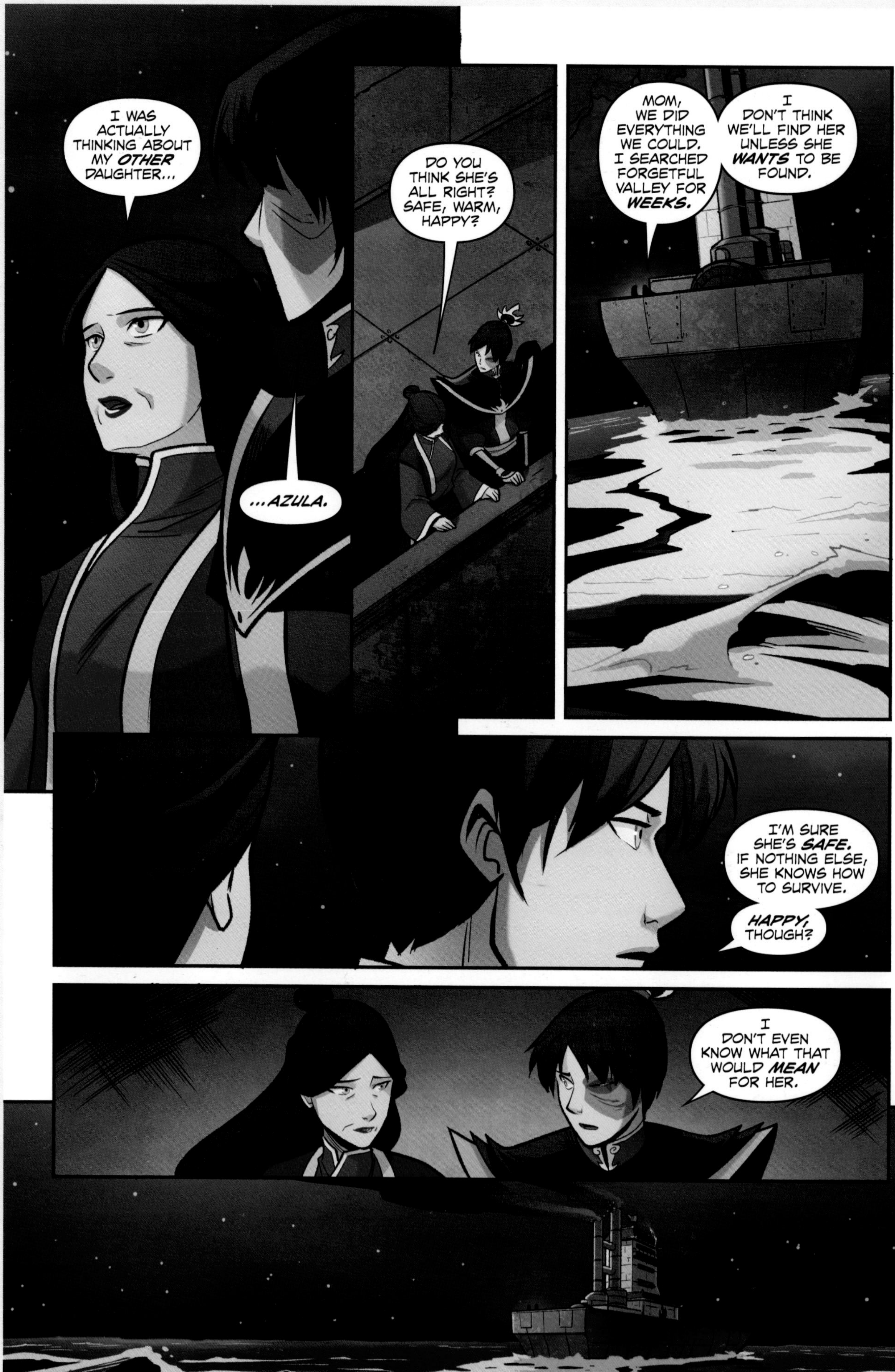
I WAS ACTUALLY THINKING ABOUT MY *OTHER* DAUGHTER...
...AZULA.
DO YOU THINK SHE'S ALL RIGHT? SAFE, WARM, HAPPY?
MOM, WE DID EVERYTHING WE COULD. I SEARCHED FORGETFUL VALLEY FOR *WEEKS.*
I DON'T THINK WE'LL FIND HER UNLESS SHE *WANTS* TO BE FOUND.
I'M SURE SHE'S *SAFE.* IF NOTHING ELSE, SHE KNOWS HOW TO SURVIVE.
HAPPY, THOUGH?
I DON'T EVEN KNOW WHAT THAT WOULD *MEAN* FOR HER.

GLY: *Zuko's referencing the final scenes of* The Search. *Ever since I was invited into the* Avatar: The Last Airbender *sandbox, I've been getting mail from* Avatar *fans. A good percentage of it is about Azula. Some folks want her to stay an antagonist. Others want her to switch sides.*

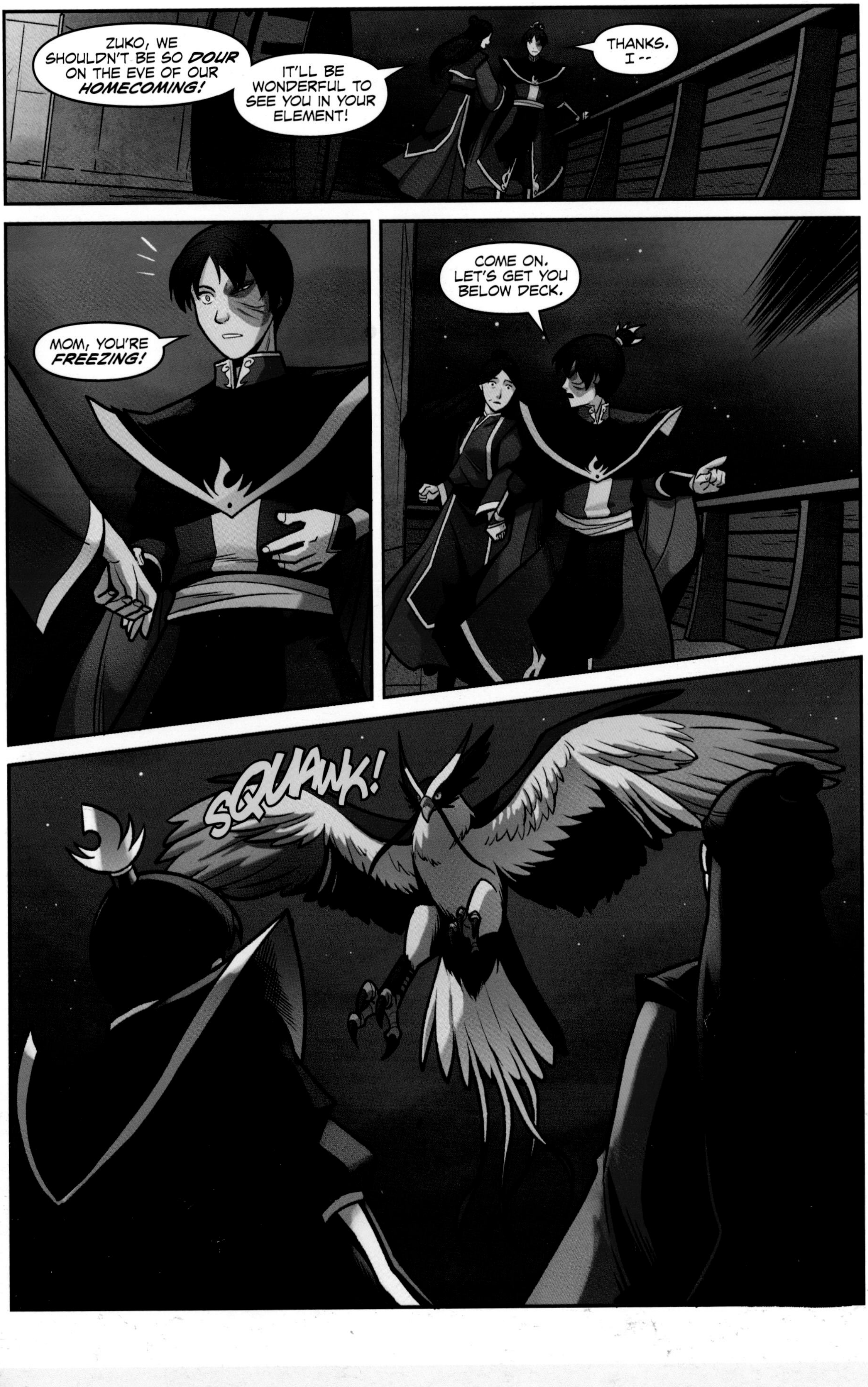
ZUKO, WE SHOULDN'T BE SO *DOUR* ON THE EVE OF OUR *HOMECOMING!*
IT'LL BE WONDERFUL TO SEE YOU IN YOUR ELEMENT!
THANKS. I --
MOM, YOU'RE *FREEZING!*
COME ON. LET'S GET YOU BELOW DECK.
SQUAWK!

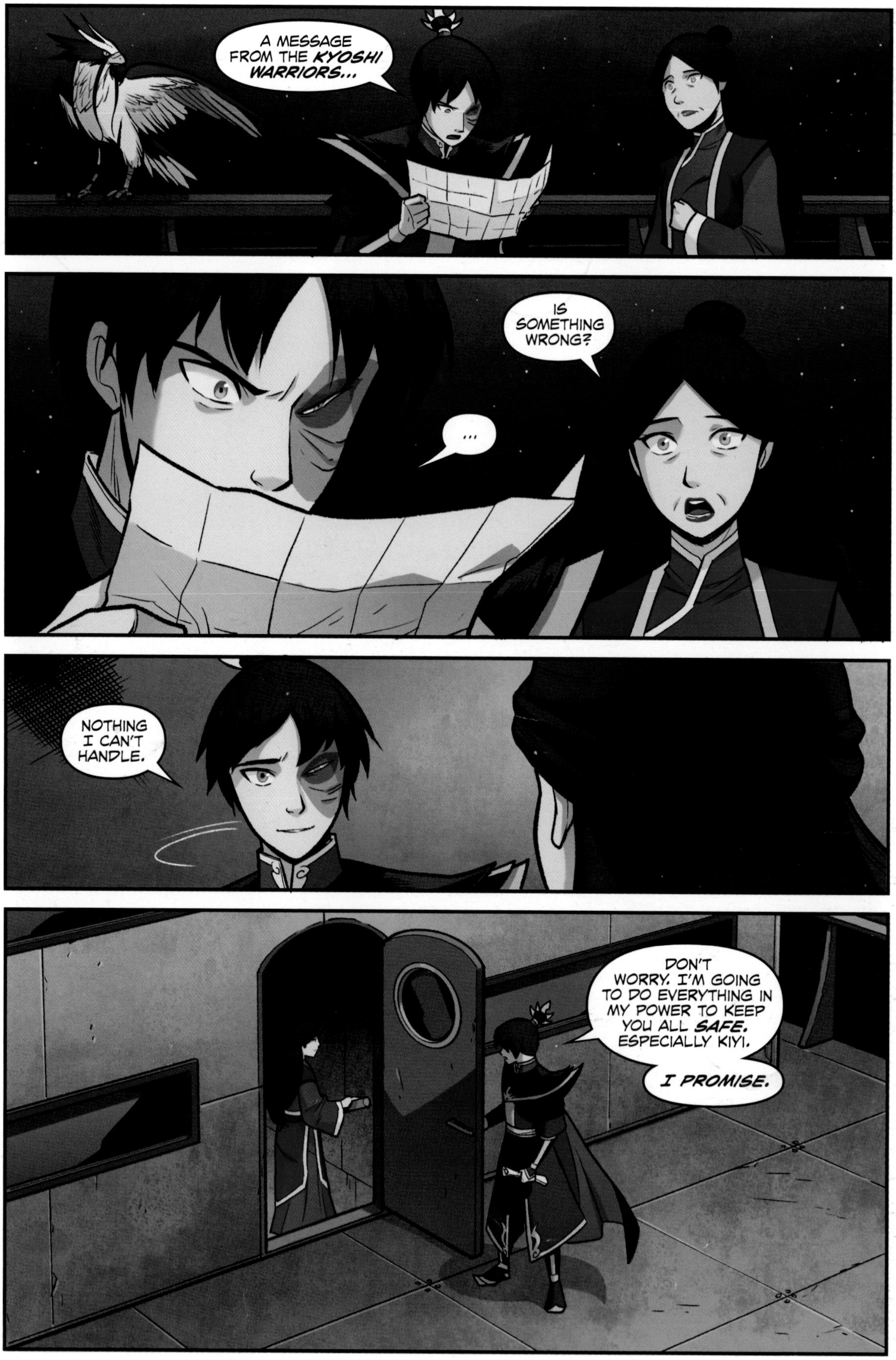
A MESSAGE FROM THE *KYOSHI WARRIORS...*
IS SOMETHING WRONG?
...
NOTHING I CAN'T HANDLE.
DON'T WORRY. I'M GOING TO DO EVERYTHING IN MY POWER TO KEEP YOU ALL *SAFE.* ESPECIALLY KIYI.
I PROMISE.

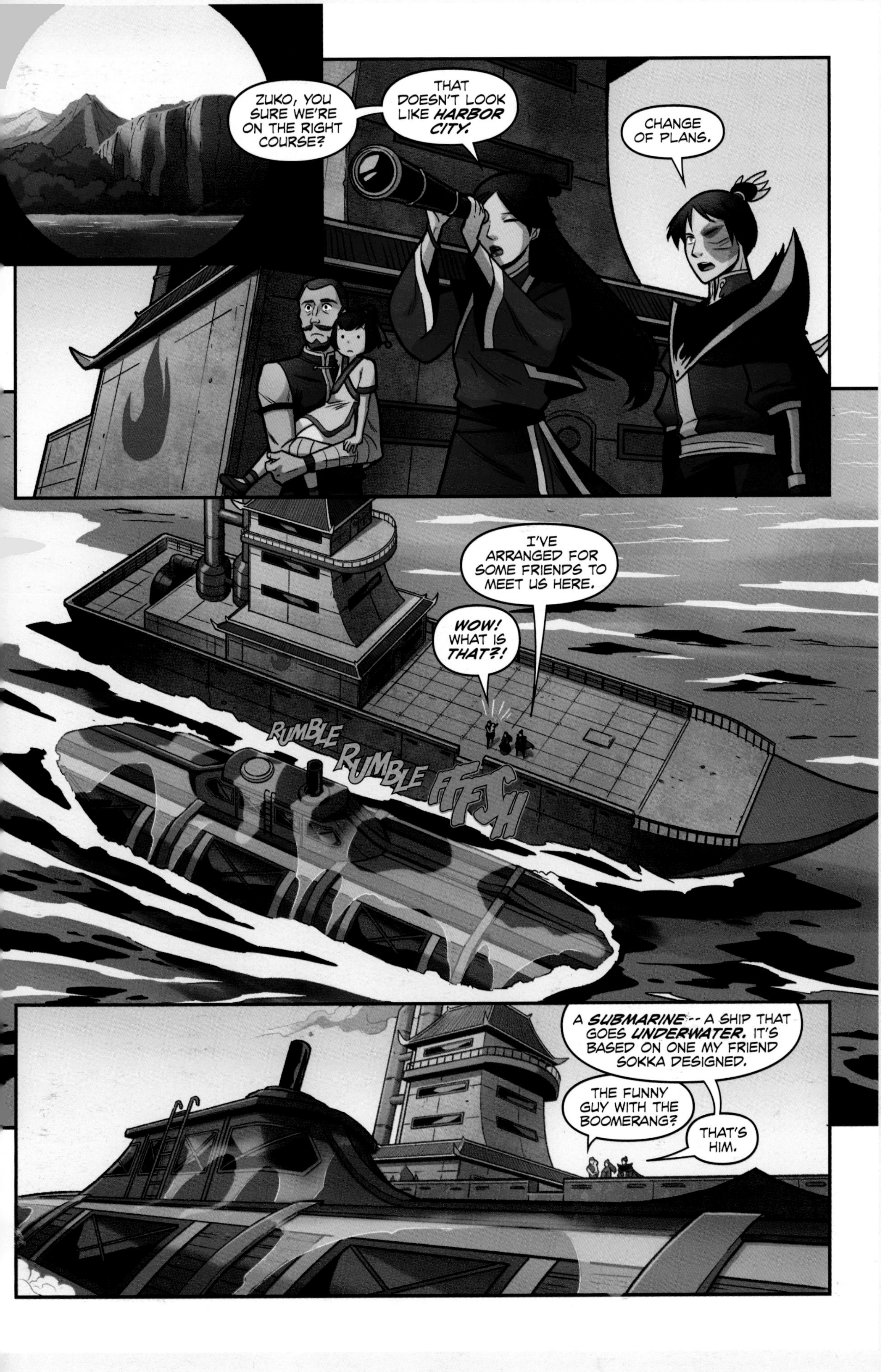
ZUKO, YOU SURE WE'RE ON THE RIGHT COURSE?
THAT DOESN'T LOOK LIKE HARBOR CITY.
CHANGE OF PLANS.
I'VE ARRANGED FOR SOME FRIENDS TO MEET US HERE.
WOW! WHAT IS THAT?!
RUMBLE RUMBLE FFFSH
A SUBMARINE-- A SHIP THAT GOES UNDERWATER. IT'S BASED ON ONE MY FRIEND SOKKA DESIGNED.
THE FUNNY GUY WITH THE BOOMERANG?
THAT'S HIM.

GLY: *I loved the waterbending-powered submarines that Sokka designed for the invasion of the Fire Nation in "The Day of Black Sun." Technology as awesome as that wouldn't just go away, of course. Here, we're showing that folks actually improved upon Sokka's original designs.*

G: *Since there weren't many references for the submarine, we had a hard time understanding the design.*

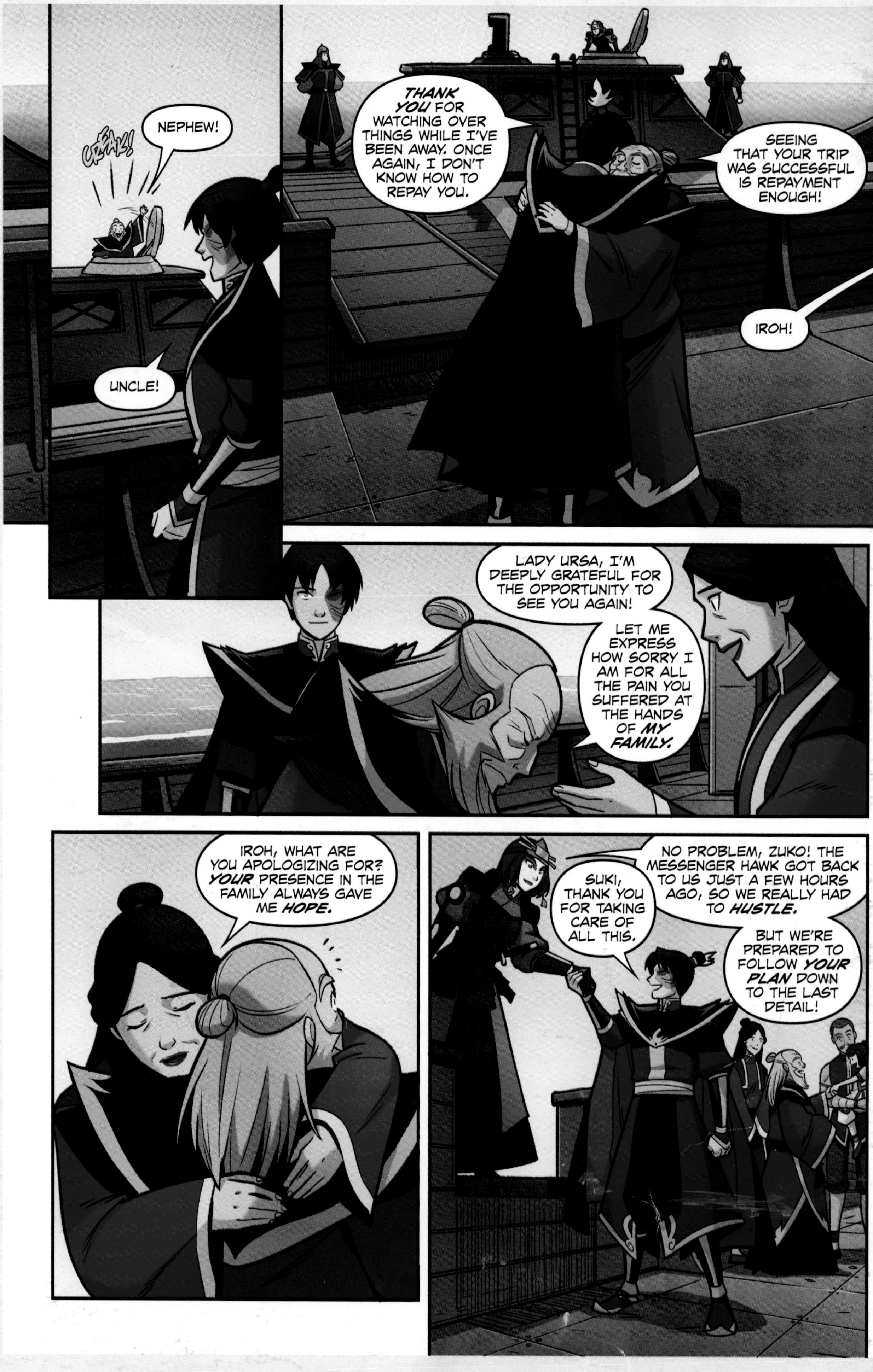
CREAK!
NEPHEW!
UNCLE!
THANK YOU FOR WATCHING OVER THINGS WHILE I'VE BEEN AWAY. ONCE AGAIN, I DON'T KNOW HOW TO REPAY YOU.
SEEING THAT YOUR TRIP WAS SUCCESSFUL IS REPAYMENT ENOUGH!
IROH!
LADY URSA, I'M DEEPLY GRATEFUL FOR THE OPPORTUNITY TO SEE YOU AGAIN!
LET ME EXPRESS HOW SORRY I AM FOR ALL THE PAIN YOU SUFFERED AT THE HANDS OF MY FAMILY.
IROH, WHAT ARE YOU APOLOGIZING FOR? YOUR PRESENCE IN THE FAMILY ALWAYS GAVE ME HOPE.
SUKI, THANK YOU FOR TAKING CARE OF ALL THIS.
NO PROBLEM, ZUKO! THE MESSENGER HAWK GOT BACK TO US JUST A FEW HOURS AGO, SO WE REALLY HAD TO HUSTLE.
BUT WE'RE PREPARED TO FOLLOW YOUR PLAN DOWN TO THE LAST DETAIL!

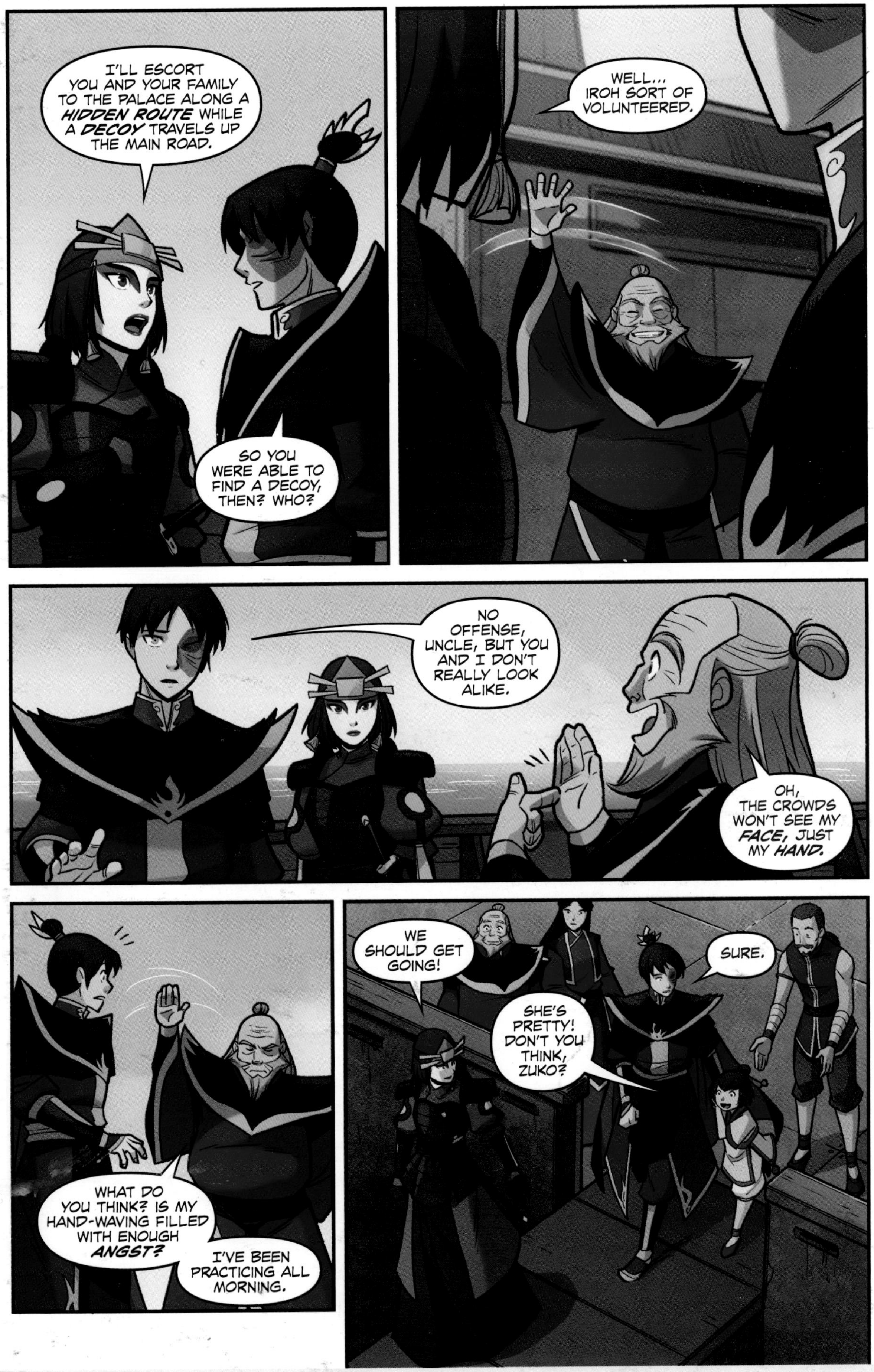
I'LL ESCORT YOU AND YOUR FAMILY TO THE PALACE ALONG A HIDDEN ROUTE WHILE A DECOY TRAVELS UP THE MAIN ROAD.
SO YOU WERE ABLE TO FIND A DECOY, THEN? WHO?
WELL... IROH SORT OF VOLUNTEERED.
NO OFFENSE, UNCLE, BUT YOU AND I DON'T REALLY LOOK ALIKE.
OH, THE CROWDS WON'T SEE MY FACE, JUST MY HAND.
WHAT DO YOU THINK? IS MY HAND-WAVING FILLED WITH ENOUGH ANGST?
I'VE BEEN PRACTICING ALL MORNING.
WE SHOULD GET GOING!
SURE.
SHE'S PRETTY! DON'T YOU THINK, ZUKO?

GLY: *In the script, I described this scene as "Iroh wears a grave expression as he waves his hand solemnly." Gurihiru nailed it.*

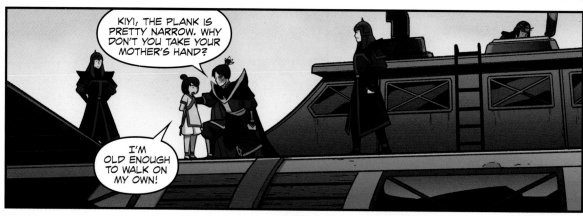

KIYI, THE PLANK IS PRETTY NARROW. WHY DON'T YOU TAKE YOUR MOTHER'S HAND?

I'M OLD ENOUGH TO WALK ON MY OWN!

I KNOW, BUT MAYBE *SHE'S* SCARED. SHE'S NEVER BEEN ON A SUBMARINE BEFORE.

THAT'S HER PROBLEM!

WILL YOU DO IT AS A FAVOR TO ME?

FINE.

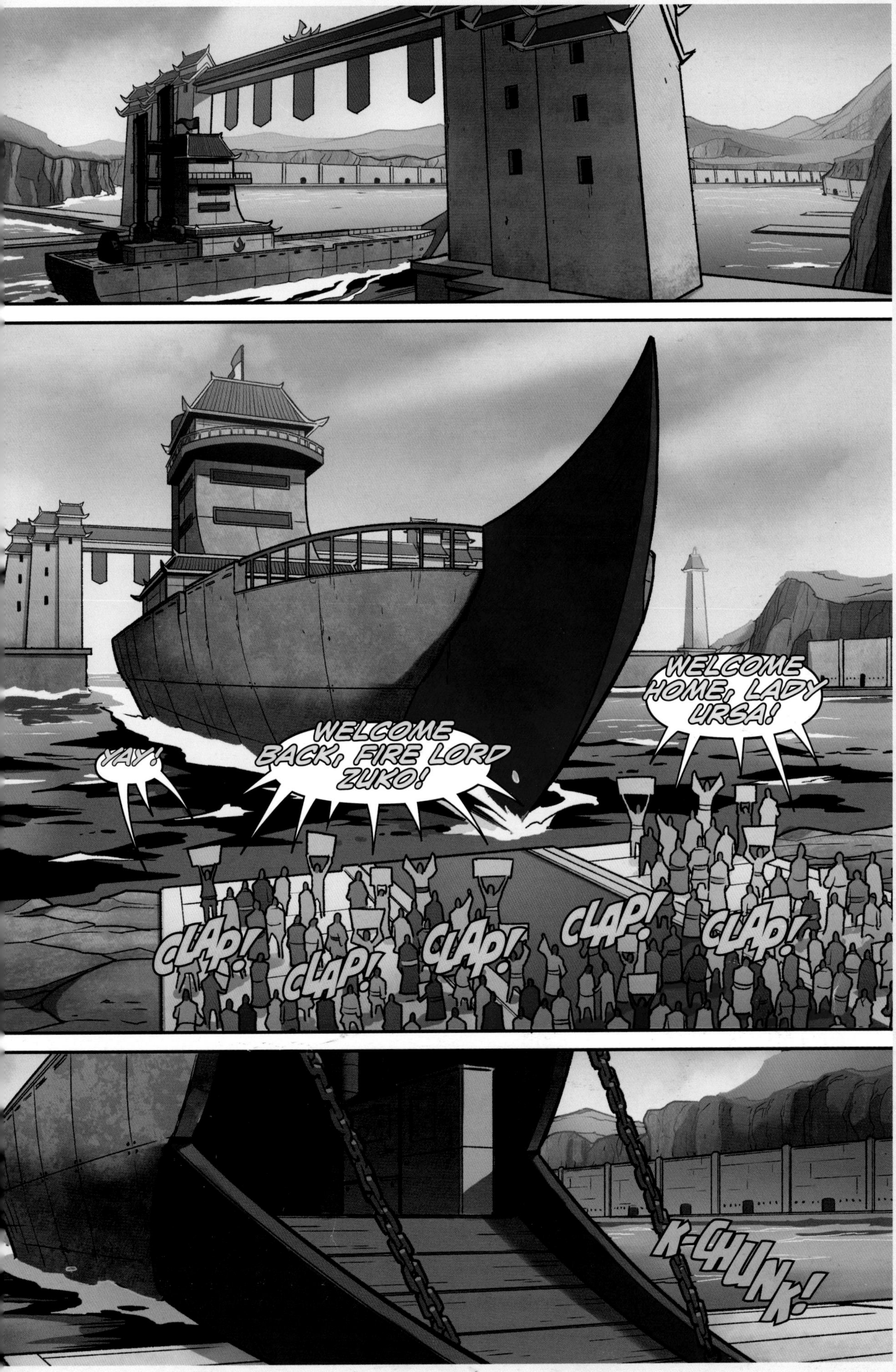
YAY!
WELCOME BACK, FIRE LORD ZUKO!
WELCOME HOME, LADY URSA!
CLAP! CLAP! CLAP! CLAP! CLAP!
K-CHUNK!

GLY: *The Fire Nation harbor, the Royal Plaza, the switchbacks leading up to and into the dormant volcano that holds the Capital City—all of it was created for the original show. And all of it serves as the perfect setting for the next few scenes. Mike and Bryan and their team put so much thought and care into their world building. Do that right, and you can support volume after volume of stories.*

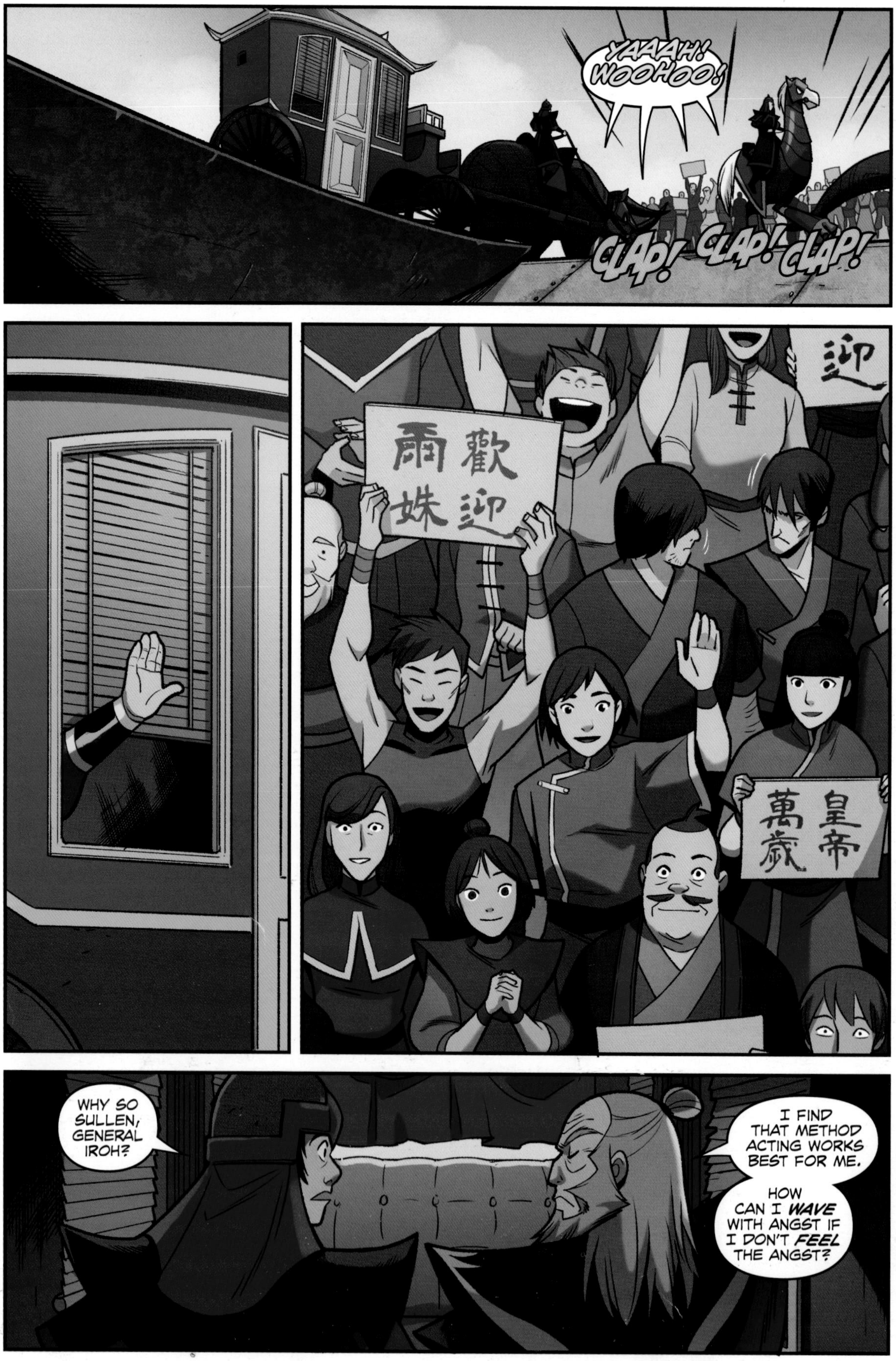
YAAAAH! WOOHOO!
CLAP! CLAP! CLAP!
歡迎雨姝
迎
皇帝萬歲
WHY SO SULLEN, GENERAL IROH?
I FIND THAT METHOD ACTING WORKS BEST FOR ME.
HOW CAN I *WAVE* WITH ANGST IF I DON'T *FEEL* THE ANGST?

GLY: *As in earlier stories, I needed my mom's help for the Chinese characters in this panel.*

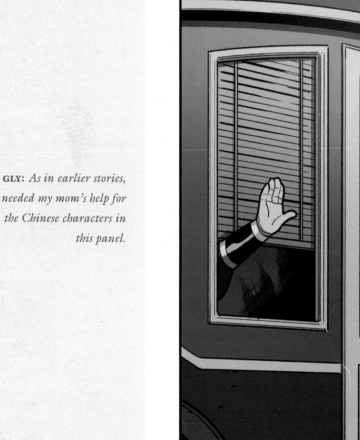

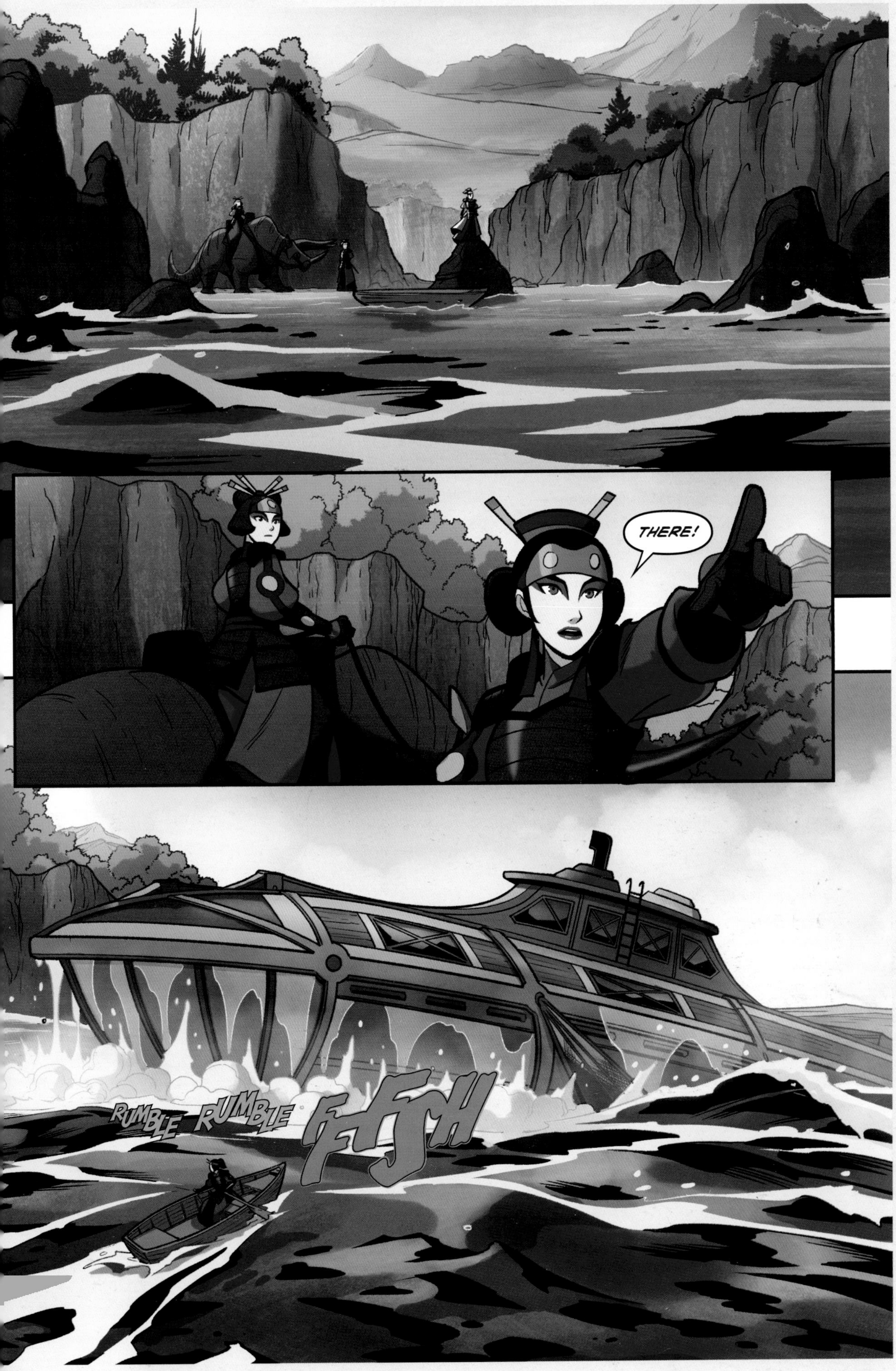
THERE!
RUMBLE RUMBLE
FFSH

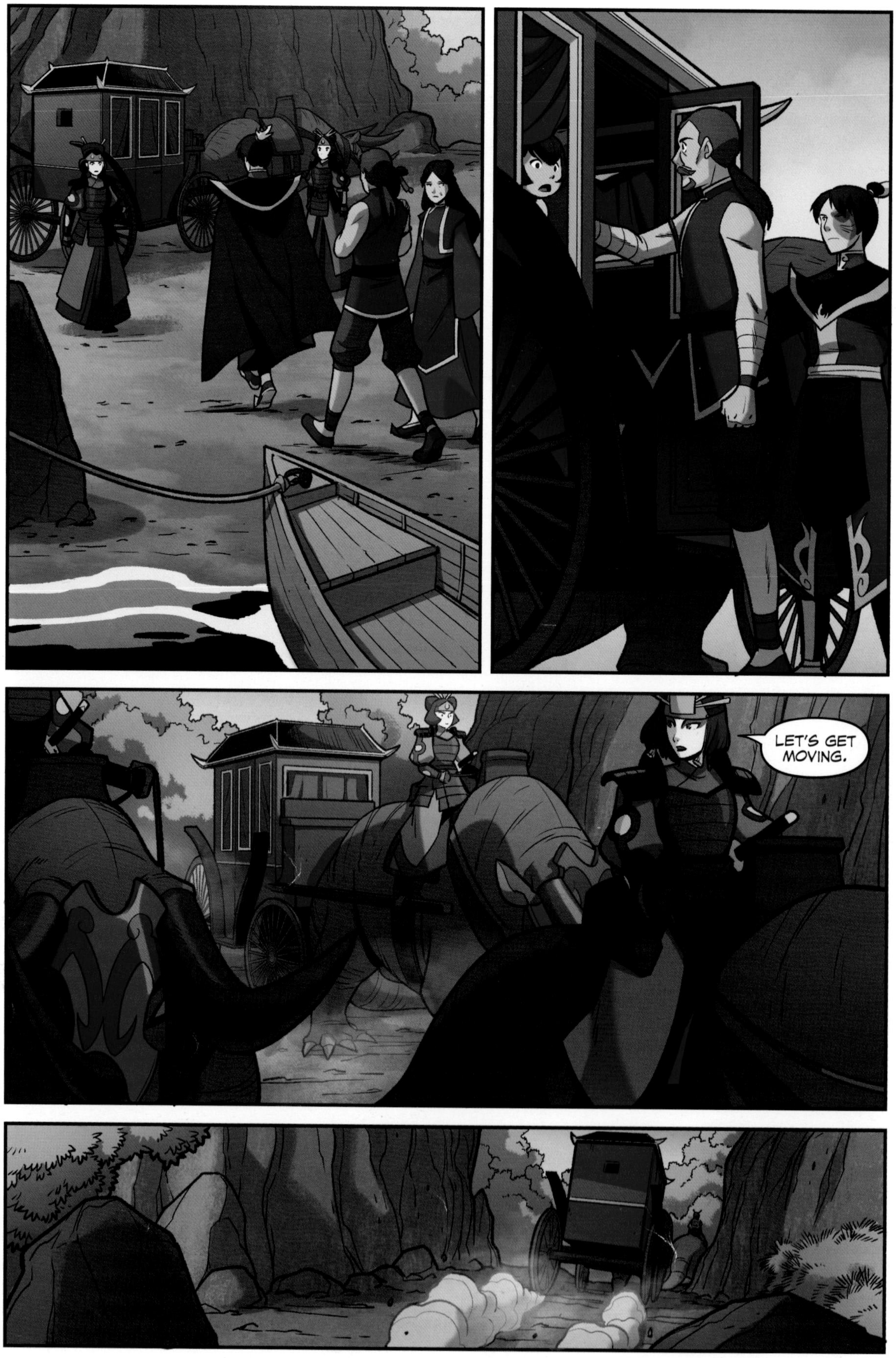
LET'S GET MOVING.

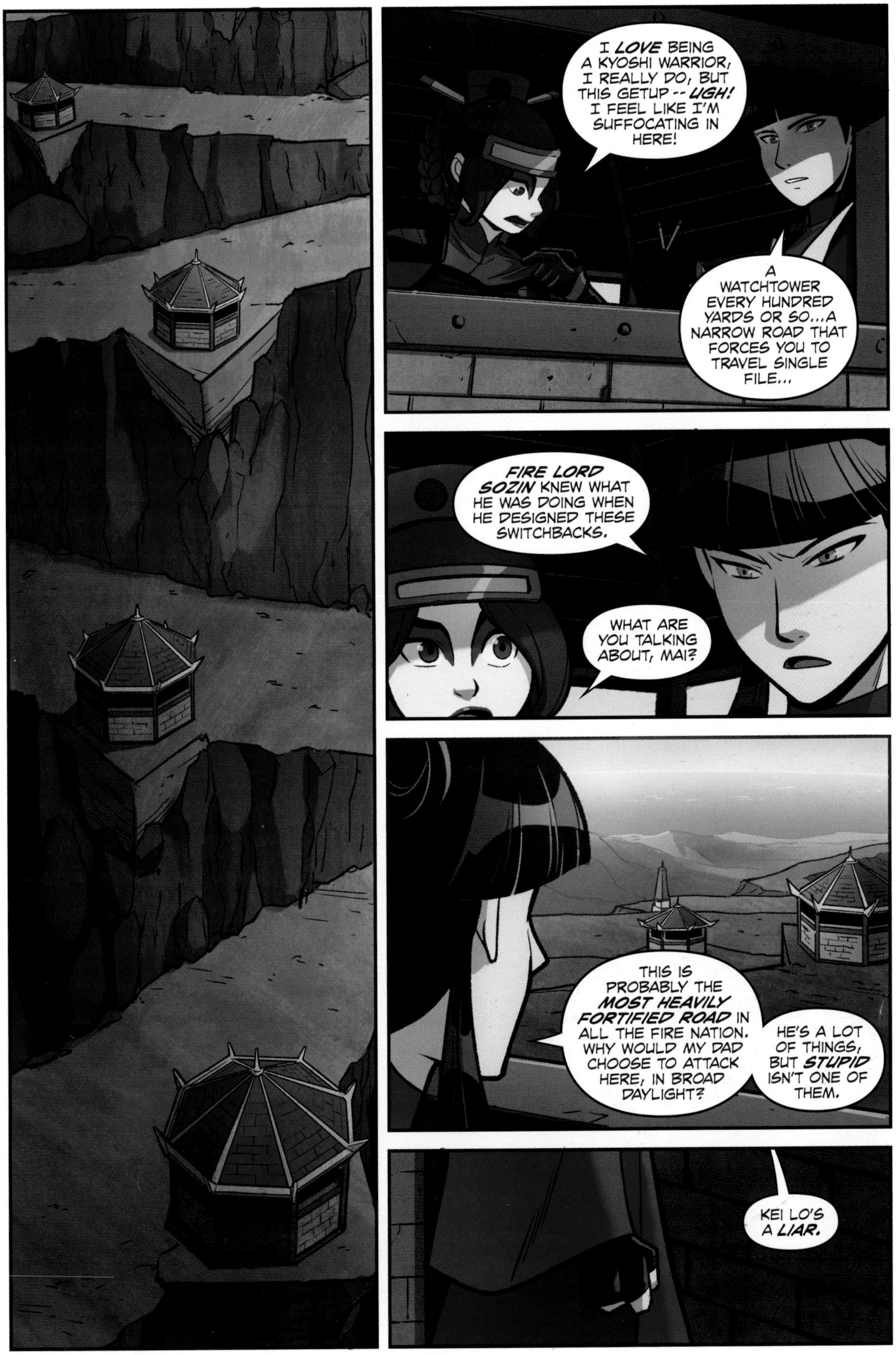
I LOVE BEING A KYOSHI WARRIOR, I REALLY DO, BUT THIS GETUP -- UGH! I FEEL LIKE I'M SUFFOCATING IN HERE!
A WATCHTOWER EVERY HUNDRED YARDS OR SO... A NARROW ROAD THAT FORCES YOU TO TRAVEL SINGLE FILE...
FIRE LORD SOZIN KNEW WHAT HE WAS DOING WHEN HE DESIGNED THESE SWITCHBACKS.
WHAT ARE YOU TALKING ABOUT, MAI?
THIS IS PROBABLY THE MOST HEAVILY FORTIFIED ROAD IN ALL THE FIRE NATION. WHY WOULD MY DAD CHOOSE TO ATTACK HERE, IN BROAD DAYLIGHT?
HE'S A LOT OF THINGS, BUT STUPID ISN'T ONE OF THEM.
KEI LO'S A LIAR.

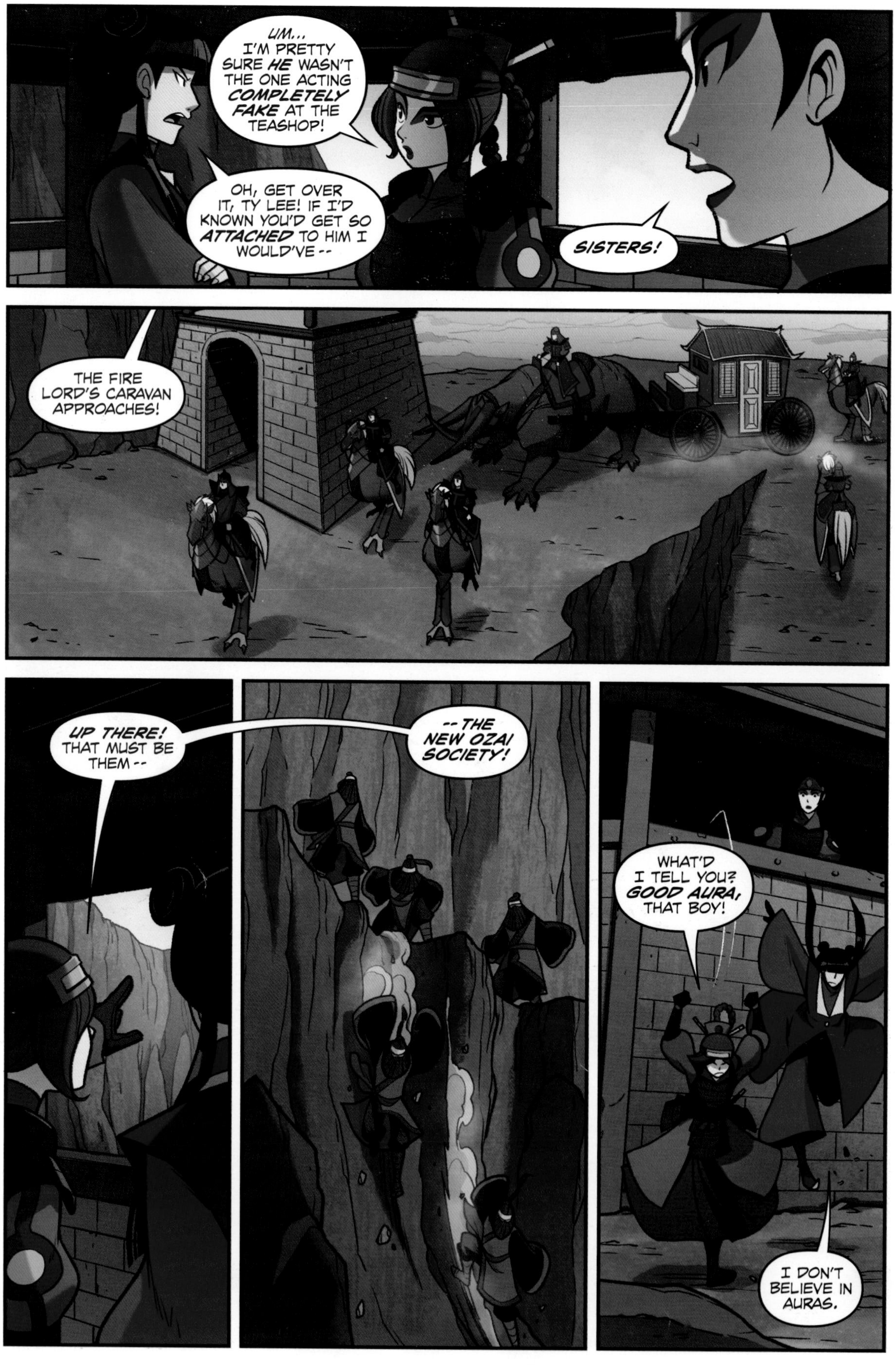
UM... I'M PRETTY SURE HE WASN'T THE ONE ACTING COMPLETELY FAKE AT THE TEASHOP!
OH, GET OVER IT, TY LEE! IF I'D KNOWN YOU'D GET SO ATTACHED TO HIM I WOULD'VE --
SISTERS!
THE FIRE LORD'S CARAVAN APPROACHES!
UP THERE! THAT MUST BE THEM --
-- THE NEW OZAI SOCIETY!
WHAT'D I TELL YOU? GOOD AURA, THAT BOY!
I DON'T BELIEVE IN AURAS.

GLY: *We asked Gurihiru to design uniforms for the New Ozai Society that were secretive and functional and cool. They knocked it out of the park.*

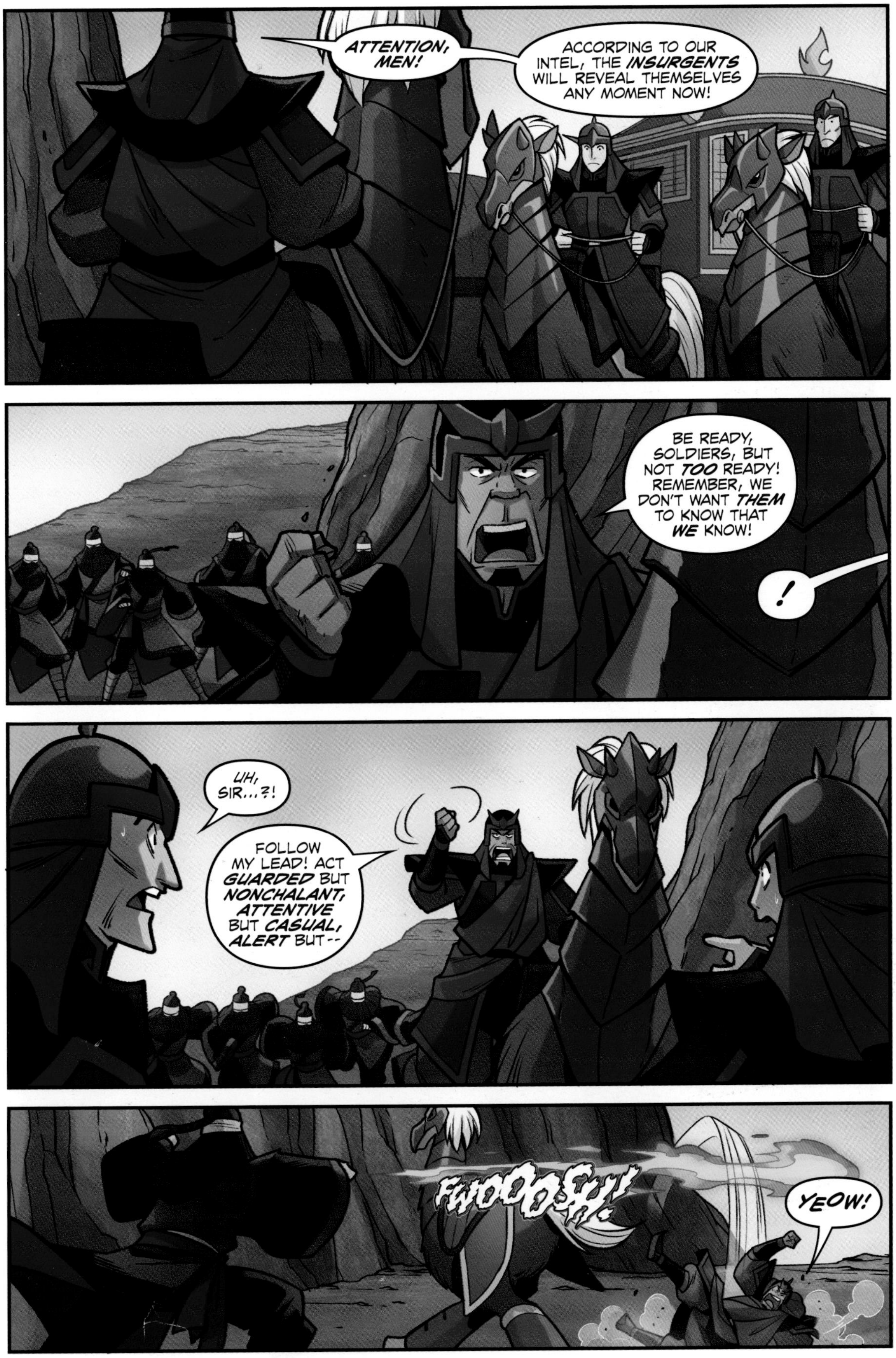
ATTENTION, MEN!
ACCORDING TO OUR INTEL, THE INSURGENTS WILL REVEAL THEMSELVES ANY MOMENT NOW!
BE READY, SOLDIERS, BUT NOT TOO READY! REMEMBER, WE DON'T WANT THEM TO KNOW THAT WE KNOW!
!
UH, SIR...?!
FOLLOW MY LEAD! ACT GUARDED BUT NONCHALANT, ATTENTIVE BUT CASUAL, ALERT BUT--
FWOOOSH!
YEOW!

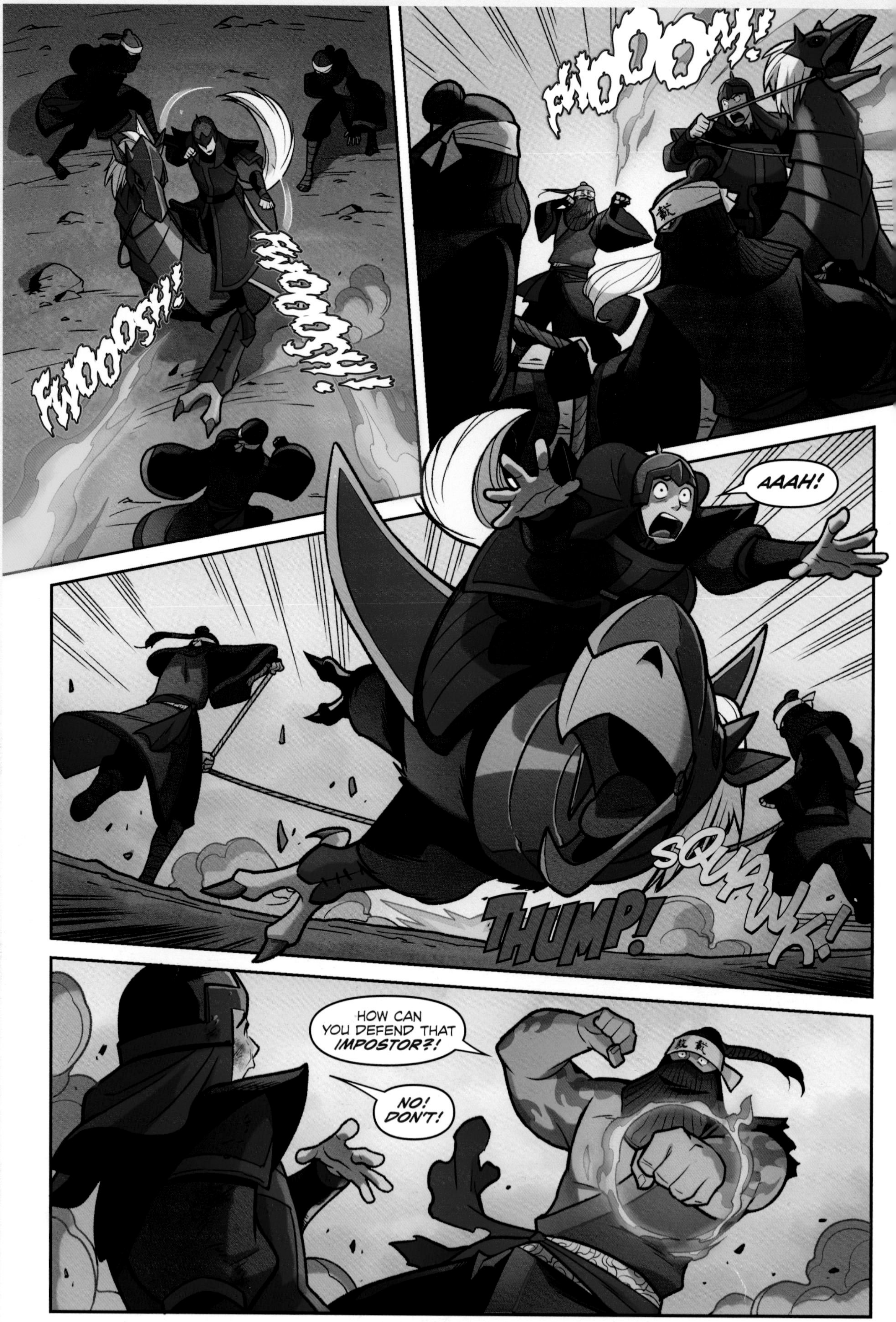
FWOOOSH!
FWOOOSH!
FWOOOM!
AAAH!
SQUAWK!
THUMP!
HOW CAN YOU DEFEND THAT *IMPOSTOR?!*
NO! DON'T!

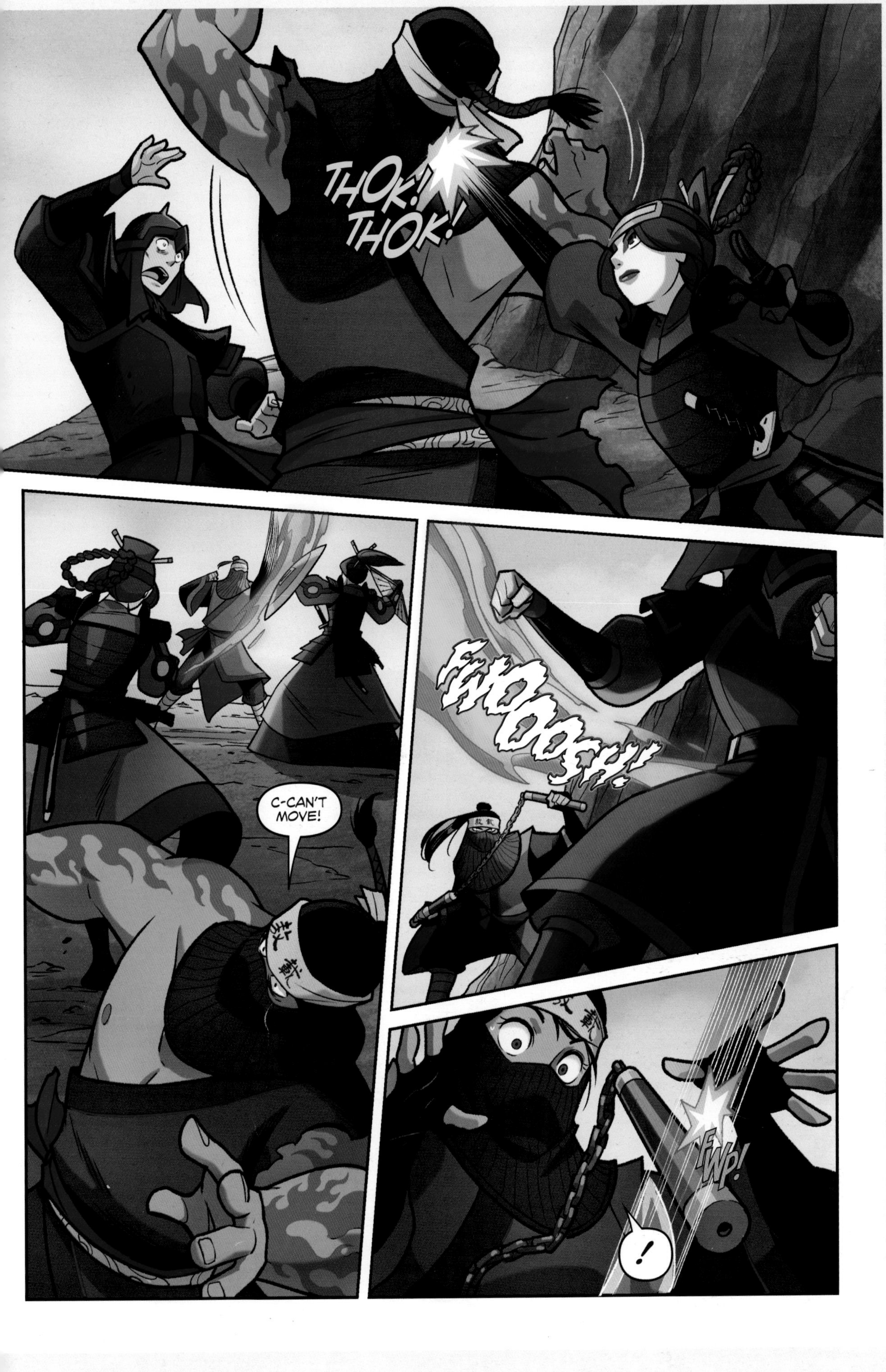
THOK! THOK!
C-CAN'T MOVE!
FWOOOSH!
FWP!
!

GLY: *I love how, even though New Ozai is a supposedly homogenous secret society, Gurihiru made every individual member look, well, individual.*

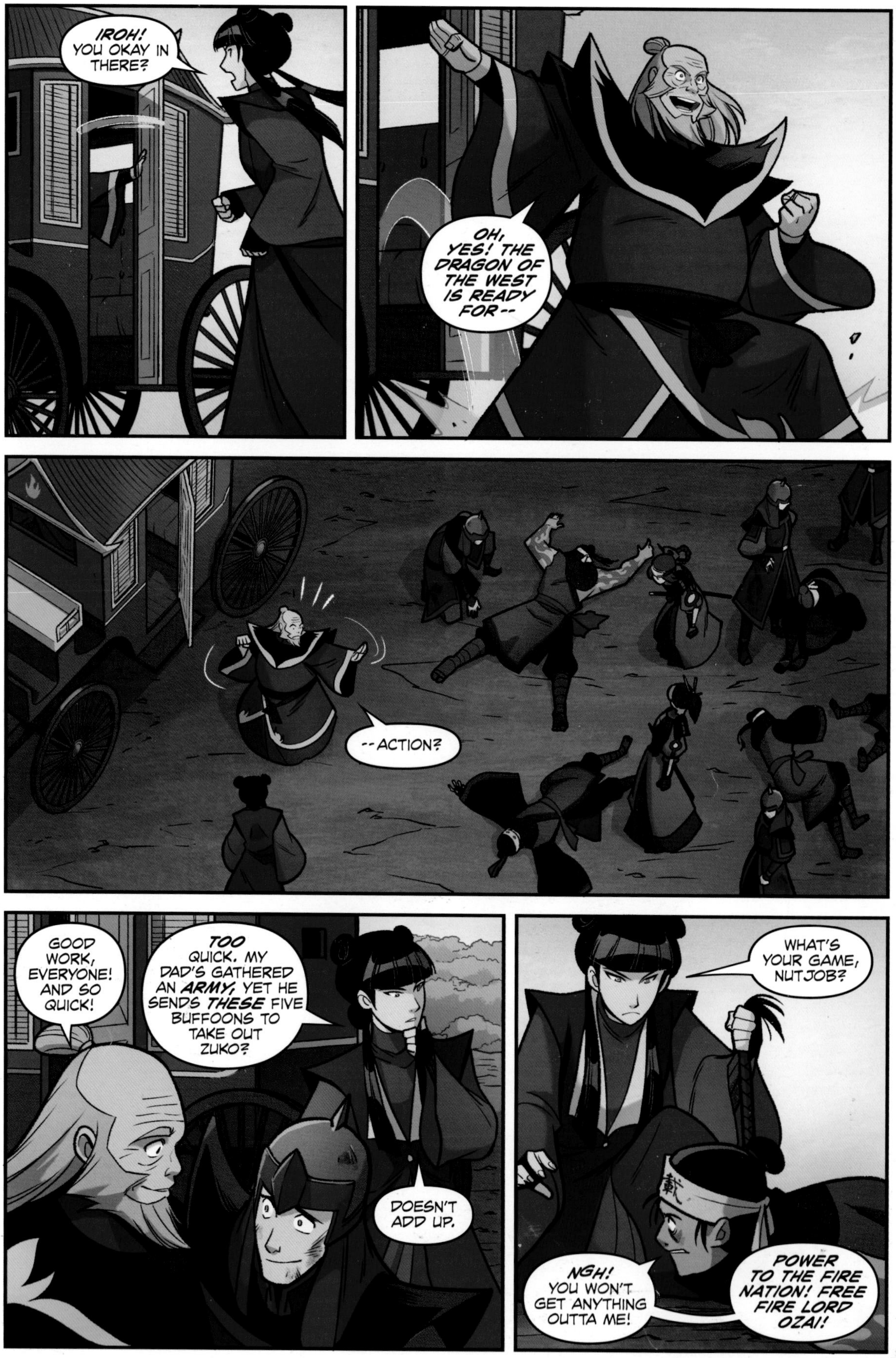
IROH! YOU OKAY IN THERE?
OH, YES! THE DRAGON OF THE WEST IS READY FOR--
--ACTION?
GOOD WORK, EVERYONE! AND SO QUICK!
TOO QUICK. MY DAD'S GATHERED AN ARMY, YET HE SENDS THESE FIVE BUFFOONS TO TAKE OUT ZUKO?
DOESN'T ADD UP.
WHAT'S YOUR GAME, NUTJOB?
NGH! YOU WON'T GET ANYTHING OUTTA ME!
POWER TO THE FIRE NATION! FREE FIRE LORD OZAI!

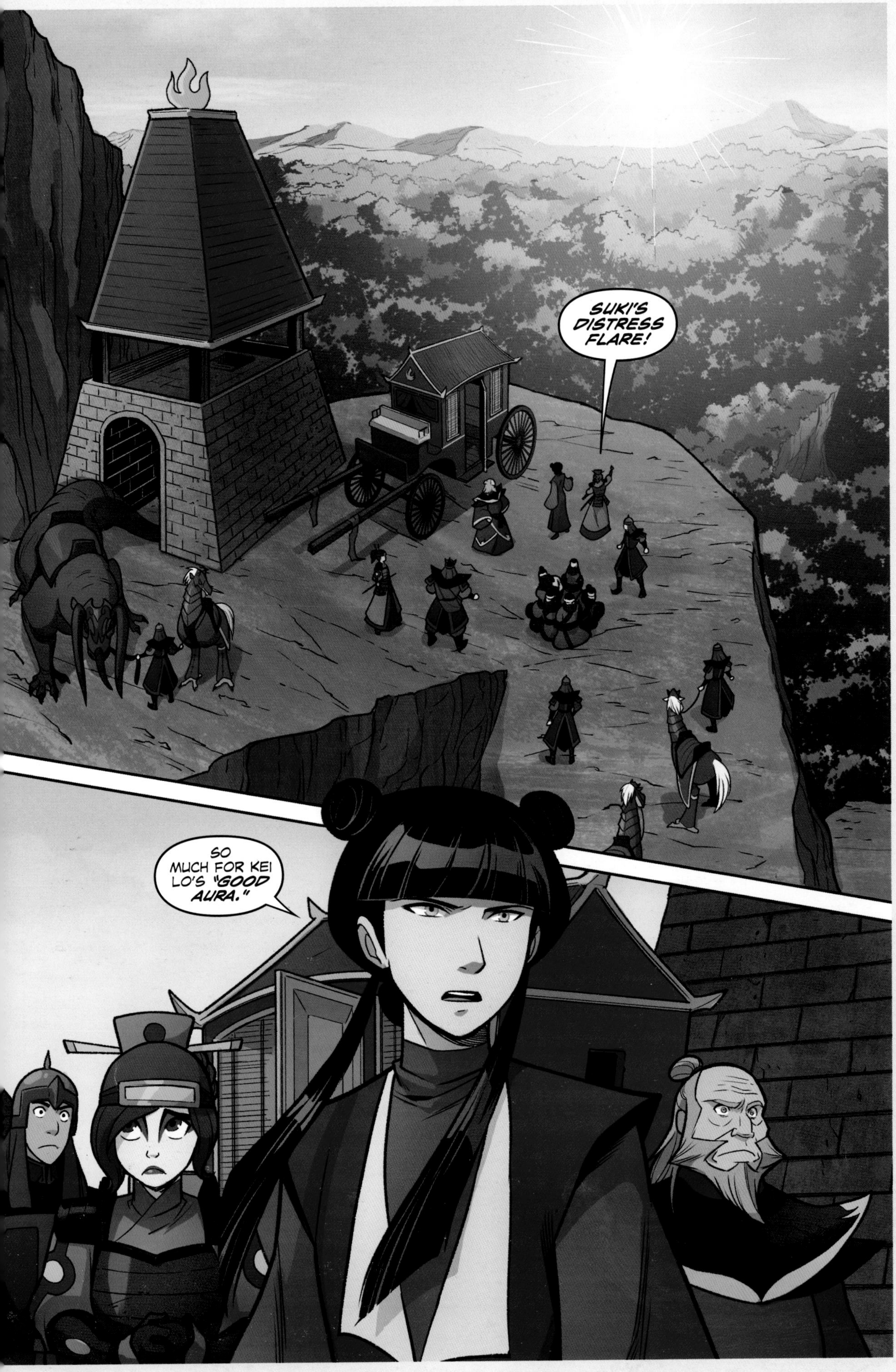
SUKI'S DISTRESS FLARE!
SO MUCH FOR KEI LO'S "GOOD AURA."

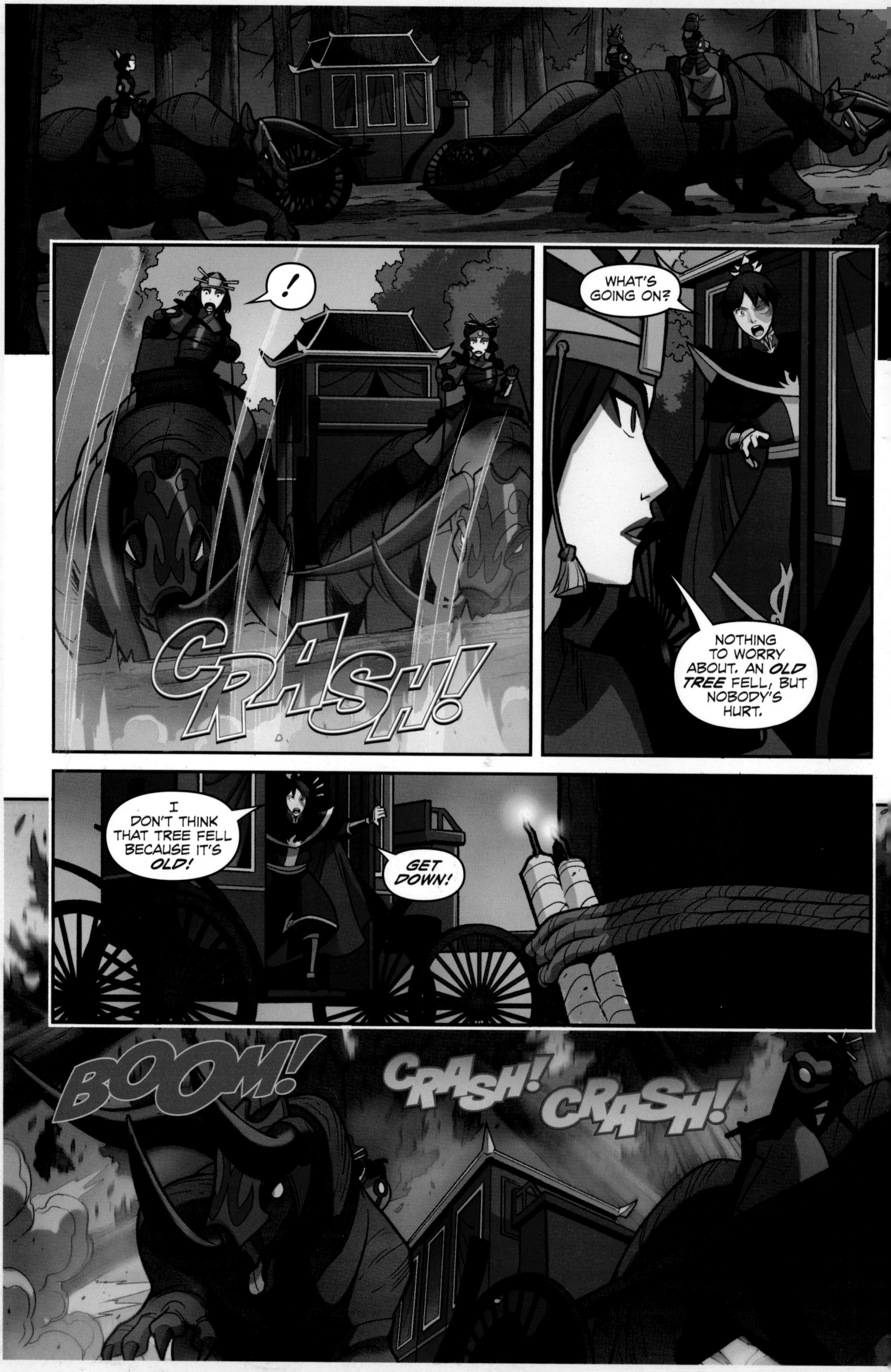
!
CRASH!
WHAT'S GOING ON?
NOTHING TO WORRY ABOUT. AN OLD TREE FELL, BUT NOBODY'S HURT.
I DON'T THINK THAT TREE FELL BECAUSE IT'S OLD!
GET DOWN!
BOOM!
CRASH! CRASH!

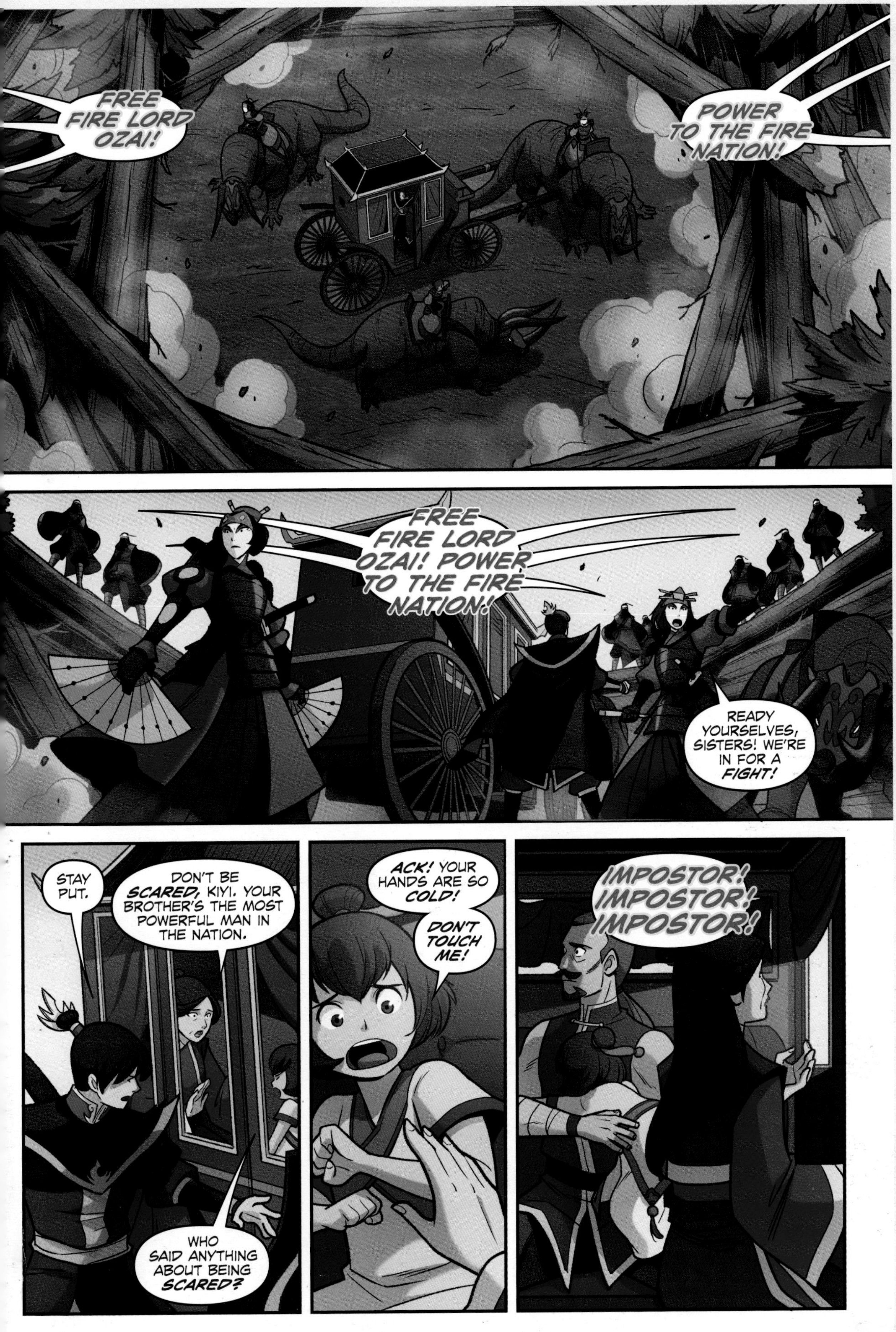
FREE FIRE LORD OZAI!
POWER TO THE FIRE NATION!
FREE FIRE LORD OZAI! POWER TO THE FIRE NATION!
READY YOURSELVES, SISTERS! WE'RE IN FOR A FIGHT!
STAY PUT.
DON'T BE SCARED, KIYI. YOUR BROTHER'S THE MOST POWERFUL MAN IN THE NATION.
WHO SAID ANYTHING ABOUT BEING SCARED?
ACK! YOUR HANDS ARE SO COLD!
DON'T TOUCH ME!
IMPOSTOR! IMPOSTOR! IMPOSTOR!

GLY: *This happens to me. When I get scared, my hands get cold.*

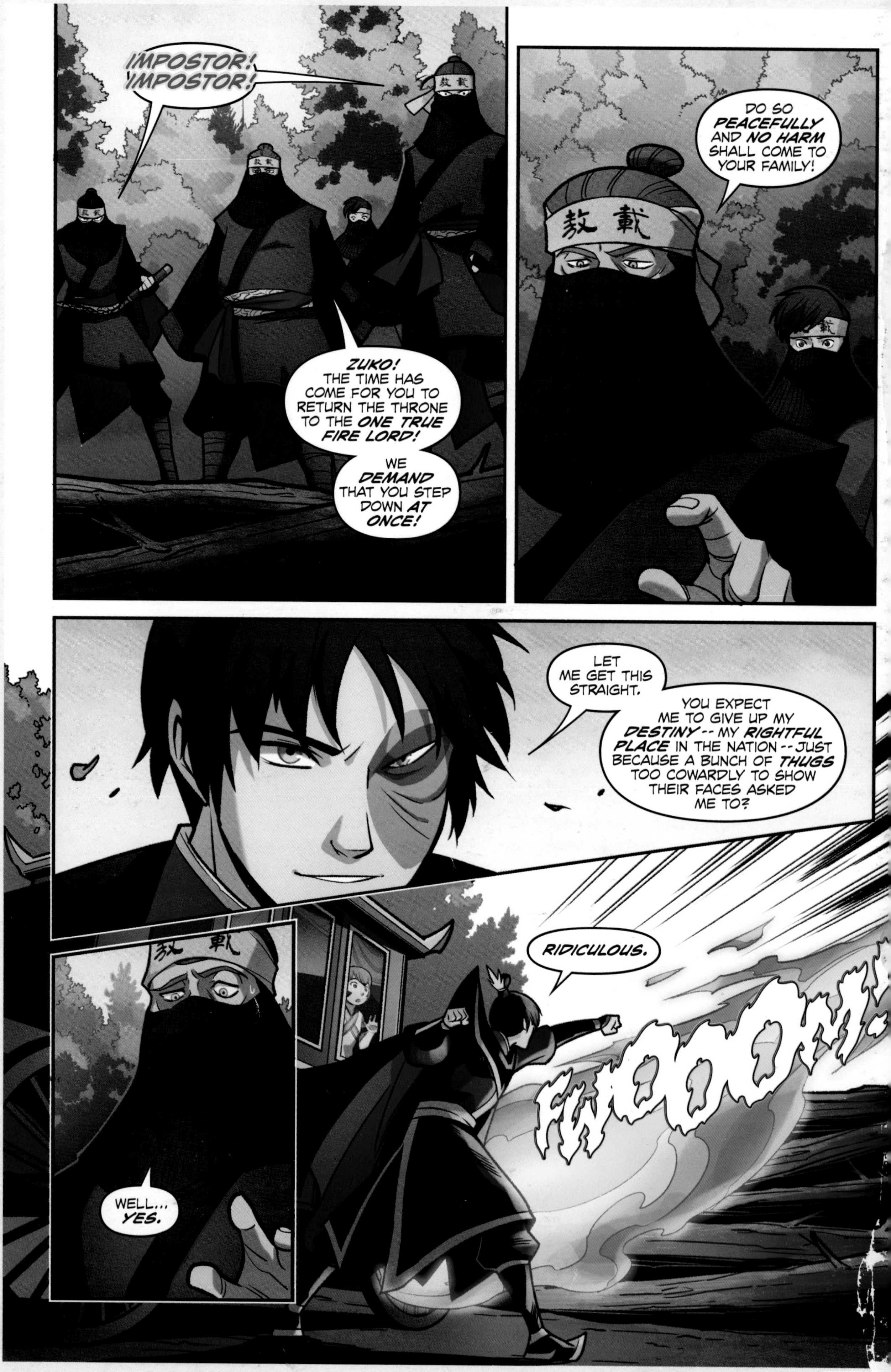
IMPOSTOR! IMPOSTOR!
ZUKO! THE TIME HAS COME FOR YOU TO RETURN THE THRONE TO THE ONE TRUE FIRE LORD!
WE DEMAND THAT YOU STEP DOWN AT ONCE!
DO SO PEACEFULLY AND NO HARM SHALL COME TO YOUR FAMILY!
LET ME GET THIS STRAIGHT.
YOU EXPECT ME TO GIVE UP MY DESTINY -- MY RIGHTFUL PLACE IN THE NATION -- JUST BECAUSE A BUNCH OF THUGS TOO COWARDLY TO SHOW THEIR FACES ASKED ME TO?
WELL... YES.
RIDICULOUS.
FWOOOM!

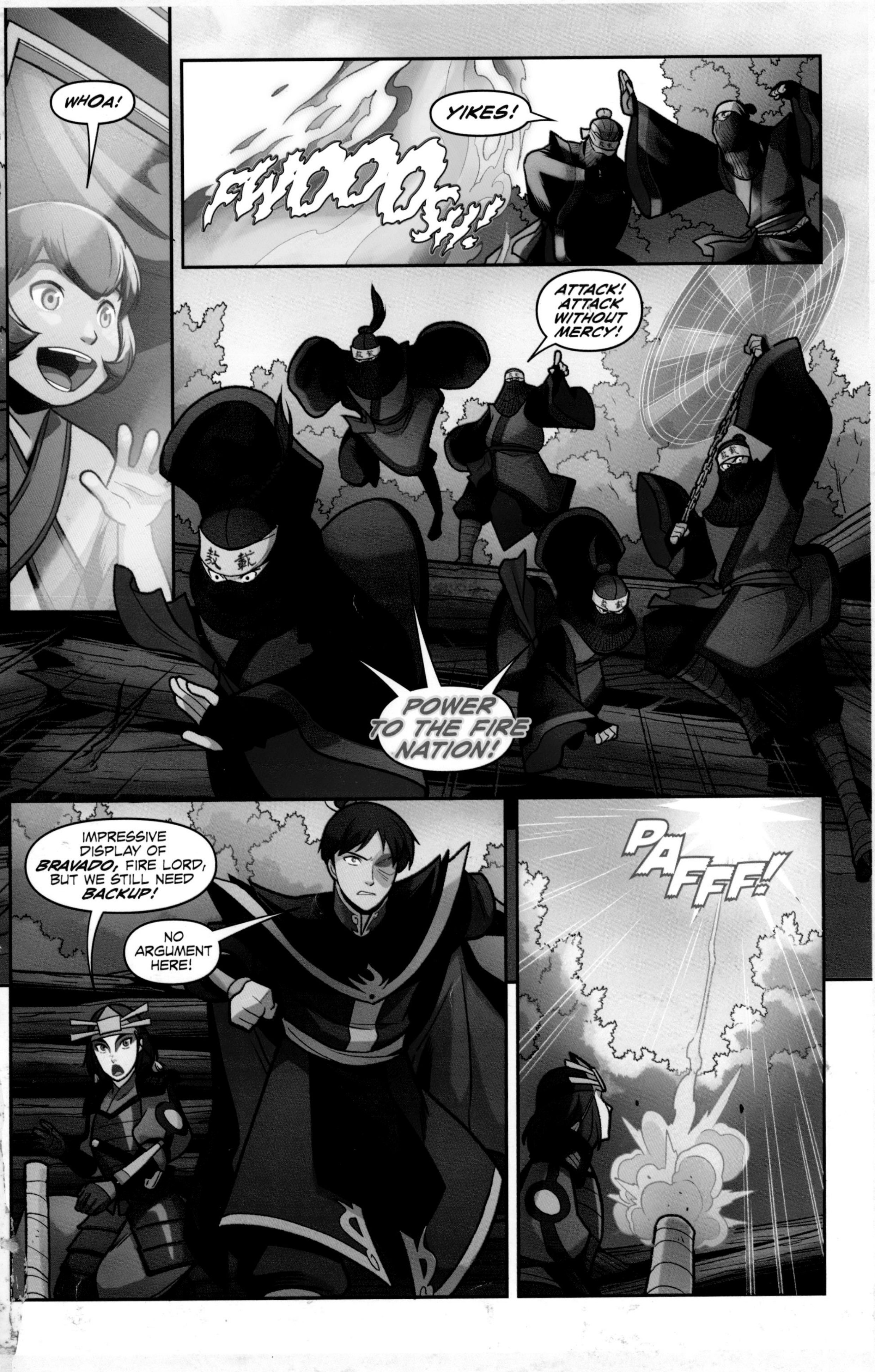
WHOA!
YIKES!
FWOOOSH!
ATTACK! ATTACK WITHOUT MERCY!
POWER TO THE FIRE NATION!
IMPRESSIVE DISPLAY OF BRAVADO, FIRE LORD, BUT WE STILL NEED BACKUP!
NO ARGUMENT HERE!
PAFFF!

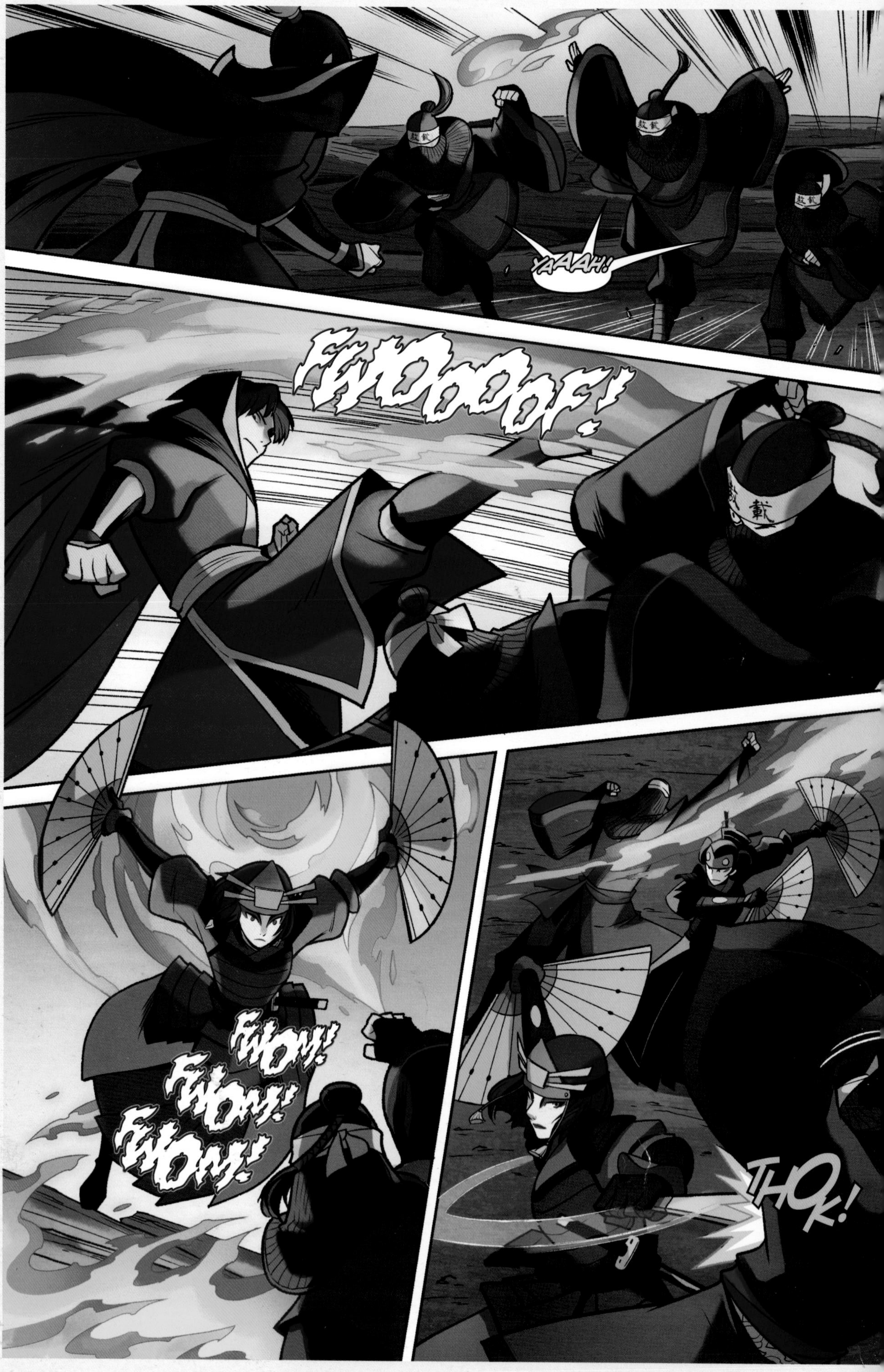
YAAAH!
FWOOOOF!
FWOM!
FWOM!
FWOM!
THOK!

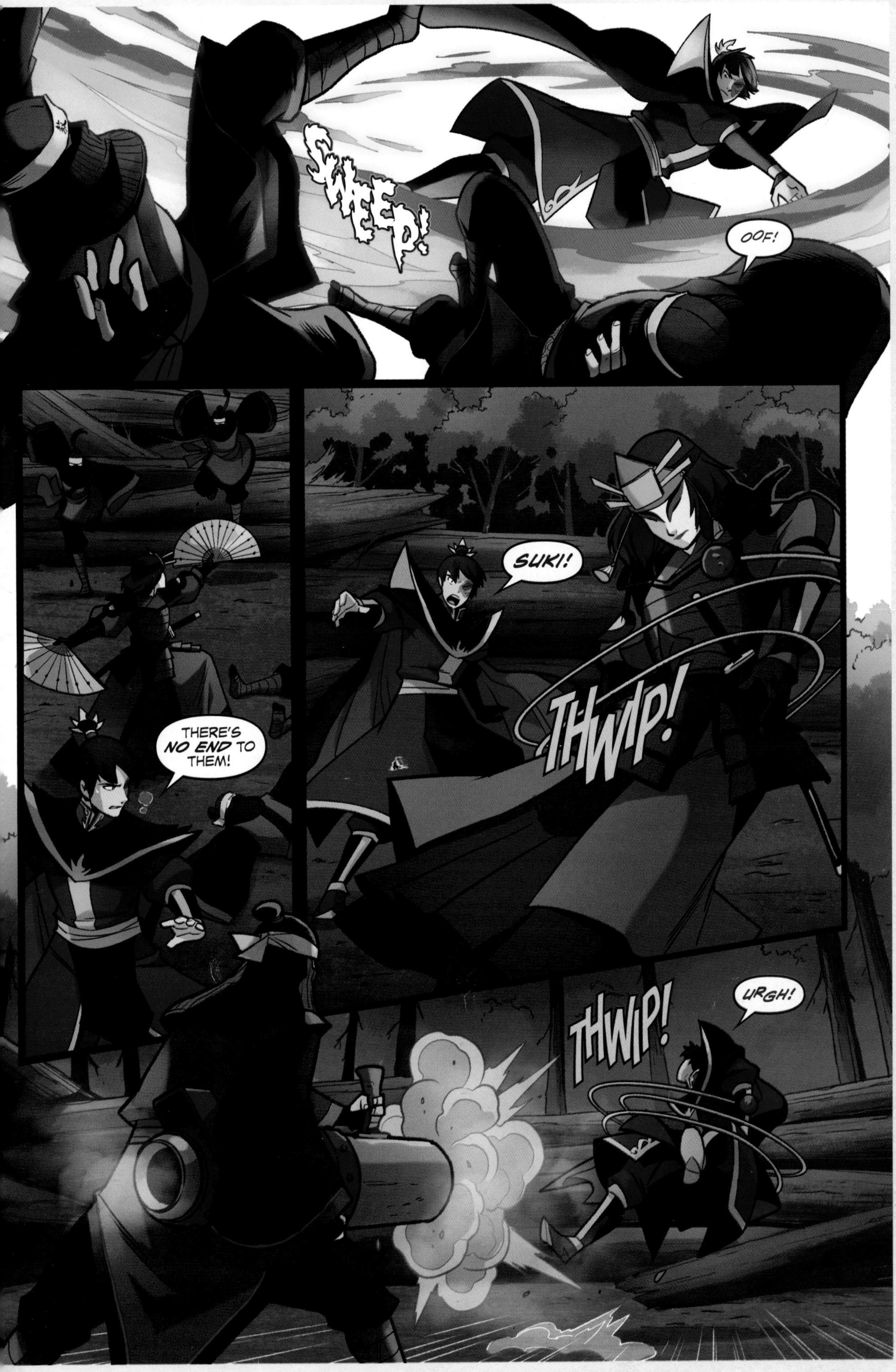
SWEEP!
OOF!
SUKI!
THERE'S NO END TO THEM!
THWIP!
THWIP!
URGH!

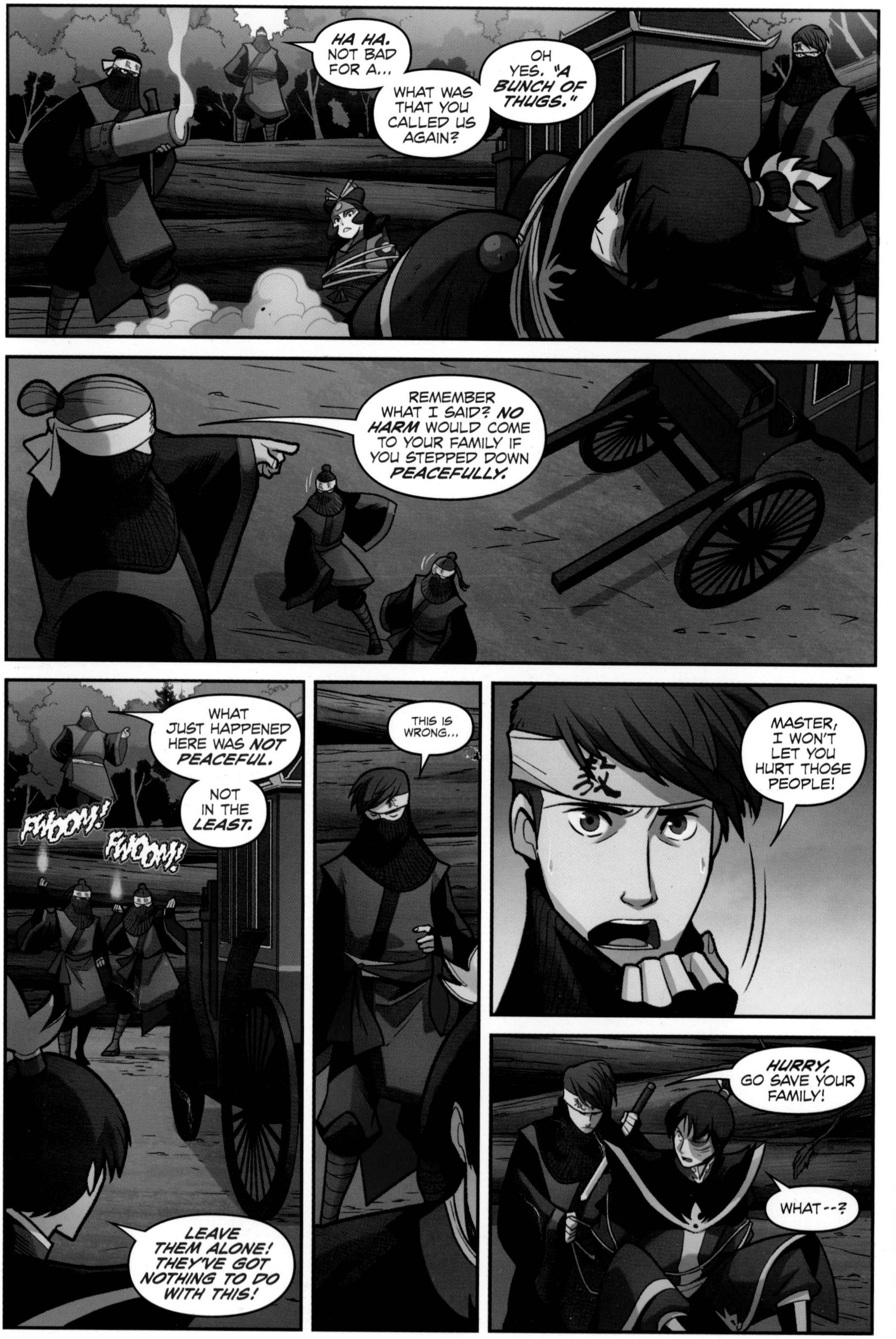
HA HA. NOT BAD FOR A...
WHAT WAS THAT YOU CALLED US AGAIN?
OH YES. "A BUNCH OF THUGS."
REMEMBER WHAT I SAID? NO HARM WOULD COME TO YOUR FAMILY IF YOU STEPPED DOWN PEACEFULLY.
WHAT JUST HAPPENED HERE WAS NOT PEACEFUL.
NOT IN THE LEAST.
FWOOM!
FWOOM!
LEAVE THEM ALONE! THEY'VE GOT NOTHING TO DO WITH THIS!
THIS IS WRONG...
MASTER, I WON'T LET YOU HURT THOSE PEOPLE!
HURRY, GO SAVE YOUR FAMILY!
WHAT--?

GLY: *We give Kei Lo his true heroic moment here. Without it, he's not really a romantic possibility for Mai.*

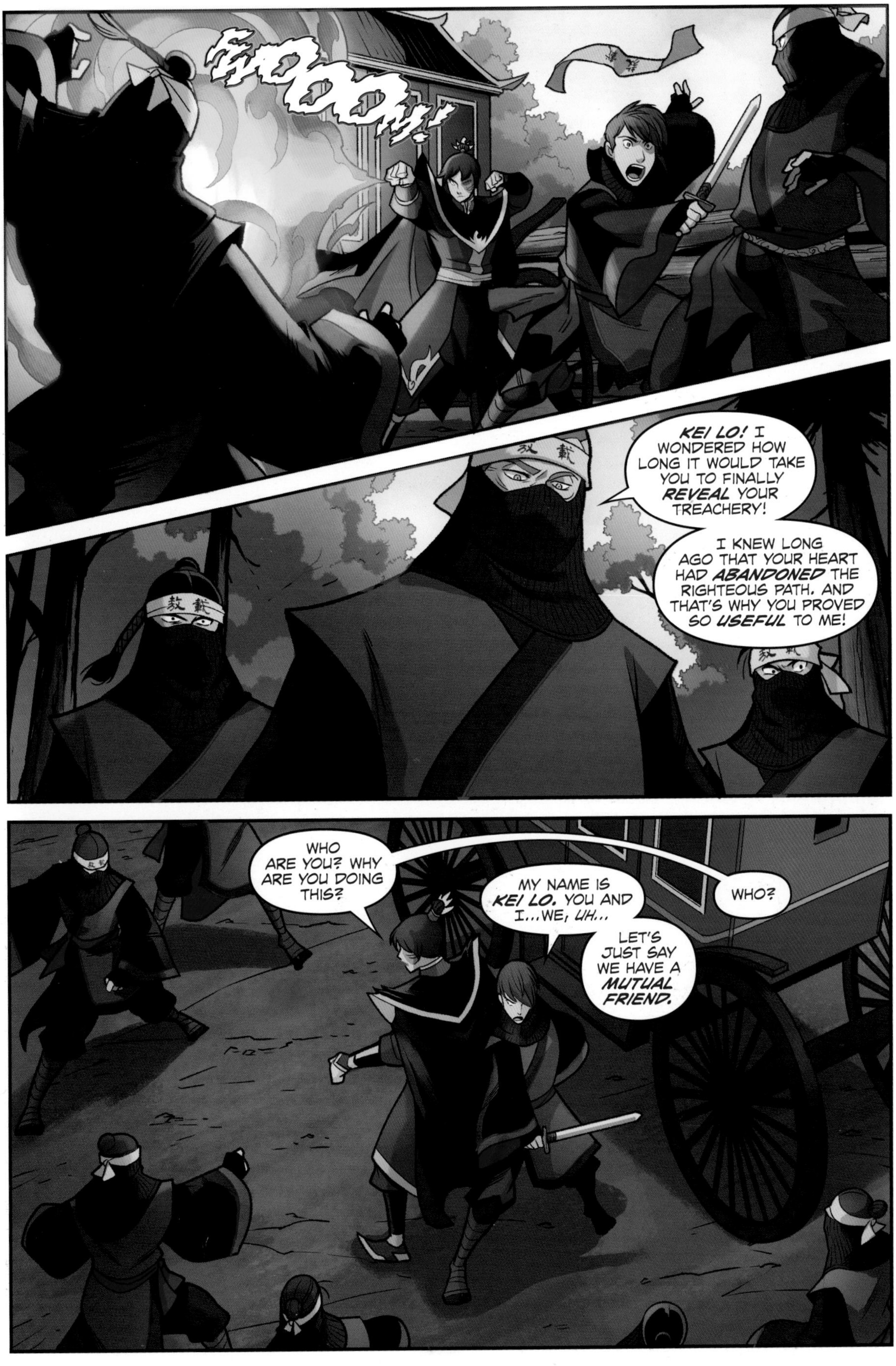
FWOOOM!
KEI LO! I WONDERED HOW LONG IT WOULD TAKE YOU TO FINALLY REVEAL YOUR TREACHERY!
I KNEW LONG AGO THAT YOUR HEART HAD ABANDONED THE RIGHTEOUS PATH. AND THAT'S WHY YOU PROVED SO USEFUL TO ME!
WHO ARE YOU? WHY ARE YOU DOING THIS?
MY NAME IS KEI LO. YOU AND I...WE, UH...
LET'S JUST SAY WE HAVE A MUTUAL FRIEND.
WHO?

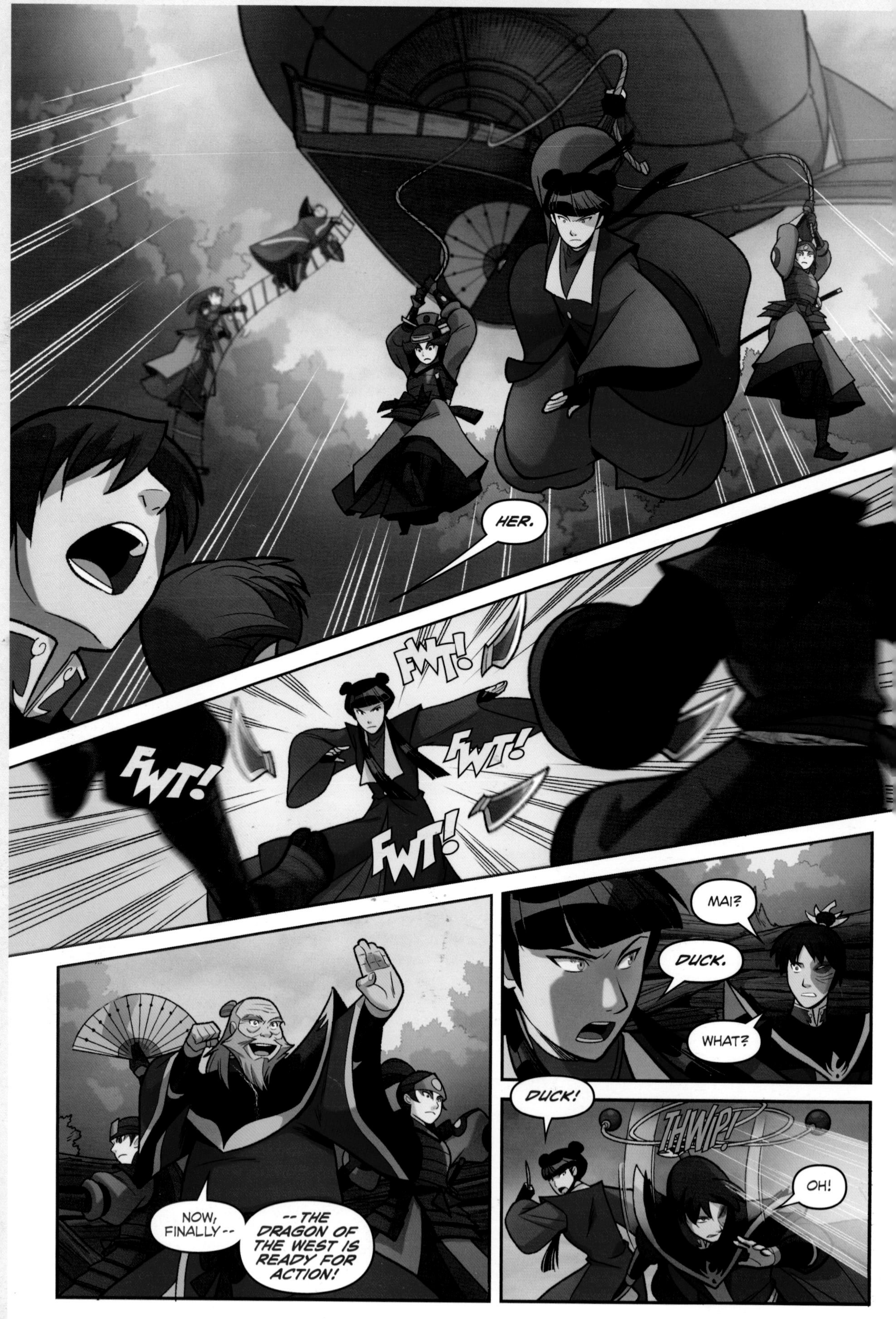
HER.
FWT!
FWT!
FWT!
FWT!
MAI?
DUCK.
WHAT?
NOW, FINALLY--
--THE DRAGON OF THE WEST IS READY FOR ACTION!
DUCK!
THWIP!
OH!

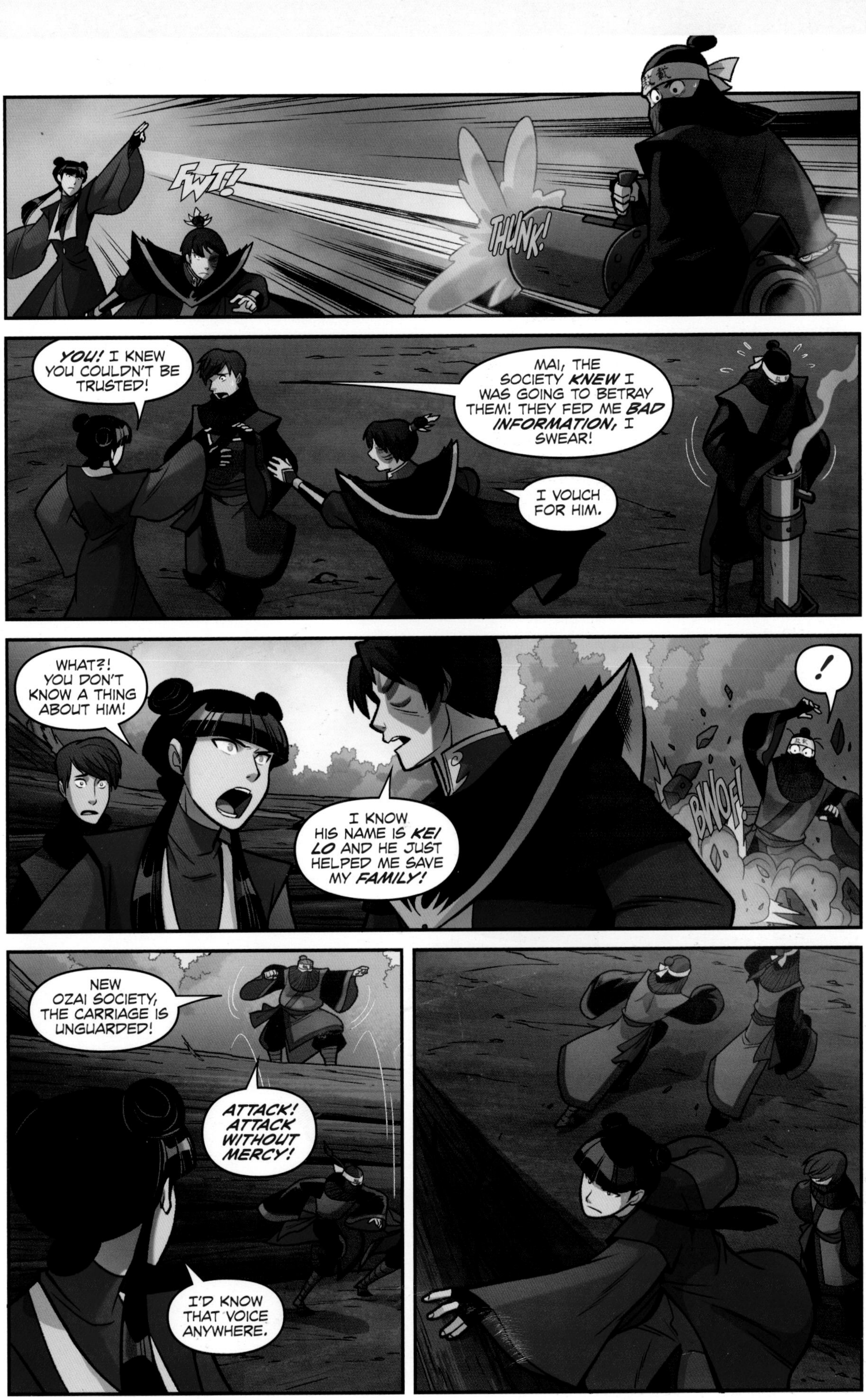
FWT!
THUNK!
YOU! I KNEW YOU COULDN'T BE TRUSTED!
MAI, THE SOCIETY KNEW I WAS GOING TO BETRAY THEM! THEY FED ME BAD INFORMATION, I SWEAR!
I VOUCH FOR HIM.
WHAT?! YOU DON'T KNOW A THING ABOUT HIM!
I KNOW HIS NAME IS KEI LO AND HE JUST HELPED ME SAVE MY FAMILY!
!
BWOF!
NEW OZAI SOCIETY, THE CARRIAGE IS UNGUARDED!
ATTACK! ATTACK WITHOUT MERCY!
I'D KNOW THAT VOICE ANYWHERE.

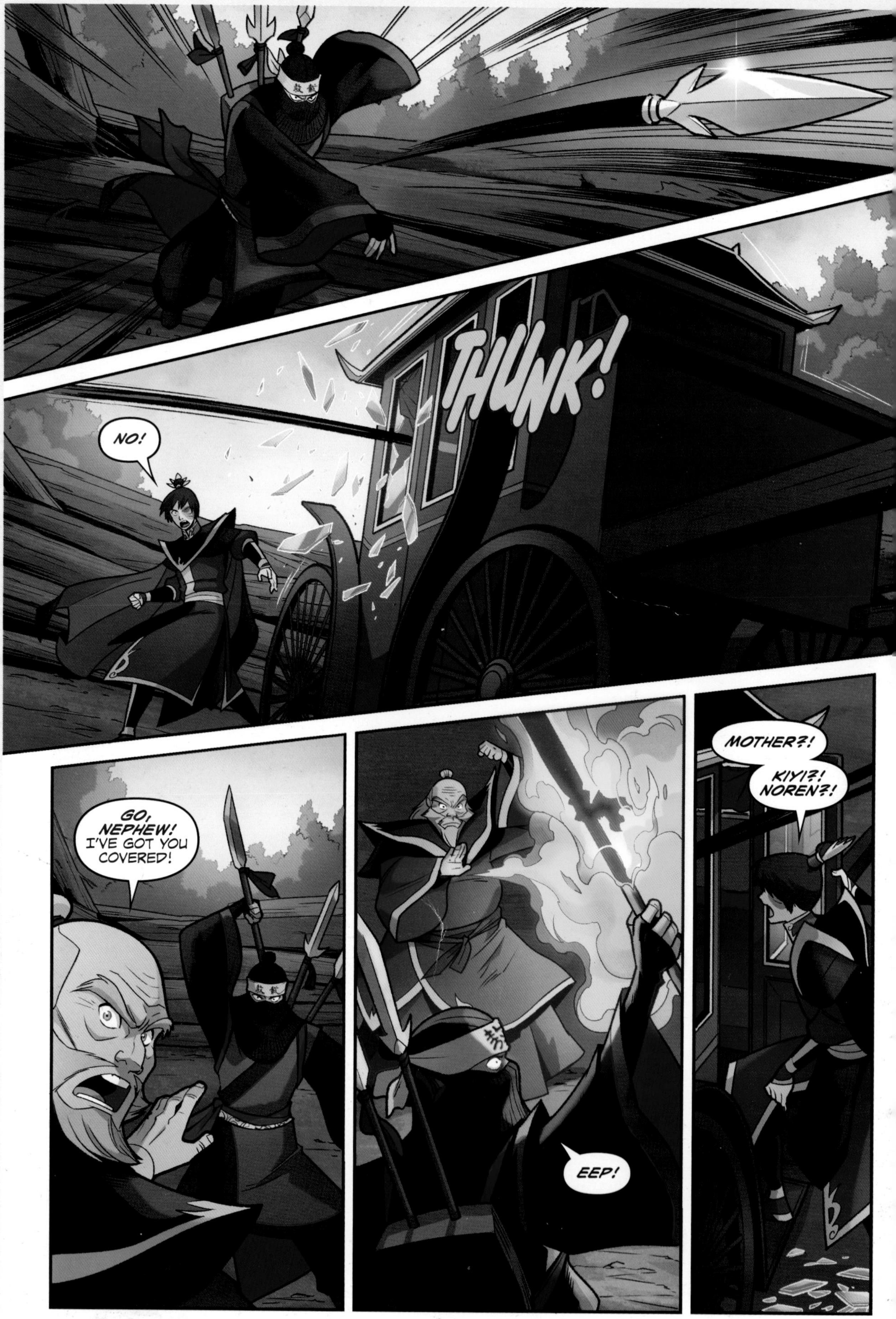
THUNK!
NO!
GO, NEPHEW! I'VE GOT YOU COVERED!
EEP!
MOTHER?!
KIYI?! NOREN?!

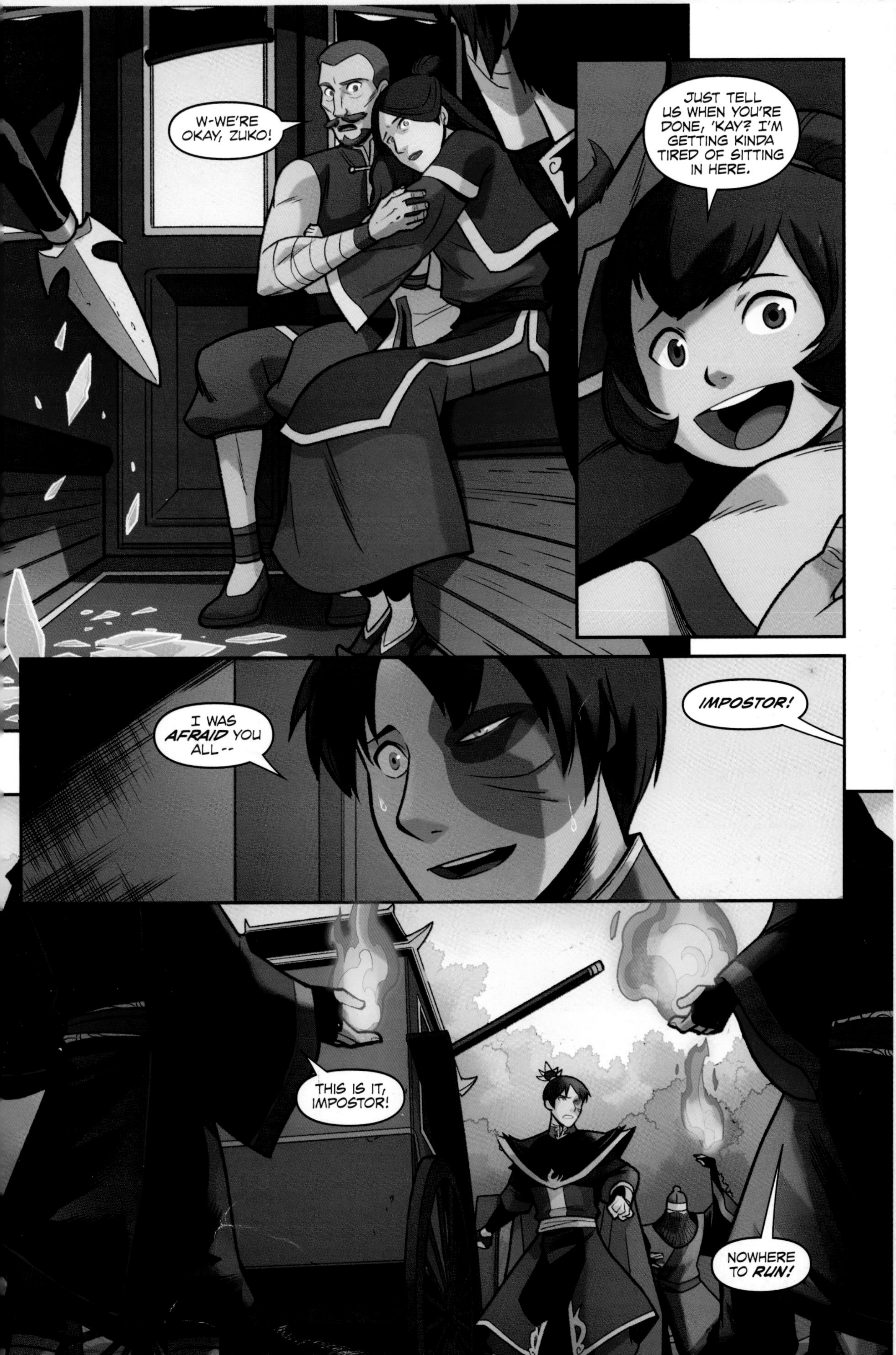
W-WE'RE OKAY, ZUKO!
JUST TELL US WHEN YOU'RE DONE, 'KAY? I'M GETTING KINDA TIRED OF SITTING IN HERE.
I WAS *AFRAID* YOU ALL--
IMPOSTOR!
THIS IS IT, IMPOSTOR!
NOWHERE TO *RUN!*

GLY: *As I was working and reworking the outline for* Smoke and Shadow, *fear emerged as the dominant theme for the book. It made sense. At the time, I was struggling with a lot of fear in my writing life. I had taken on multiple projects, a couple of which just seemed too big for me. In a lot of ways, writing* Smoke and Shadow *was therapy for me.*

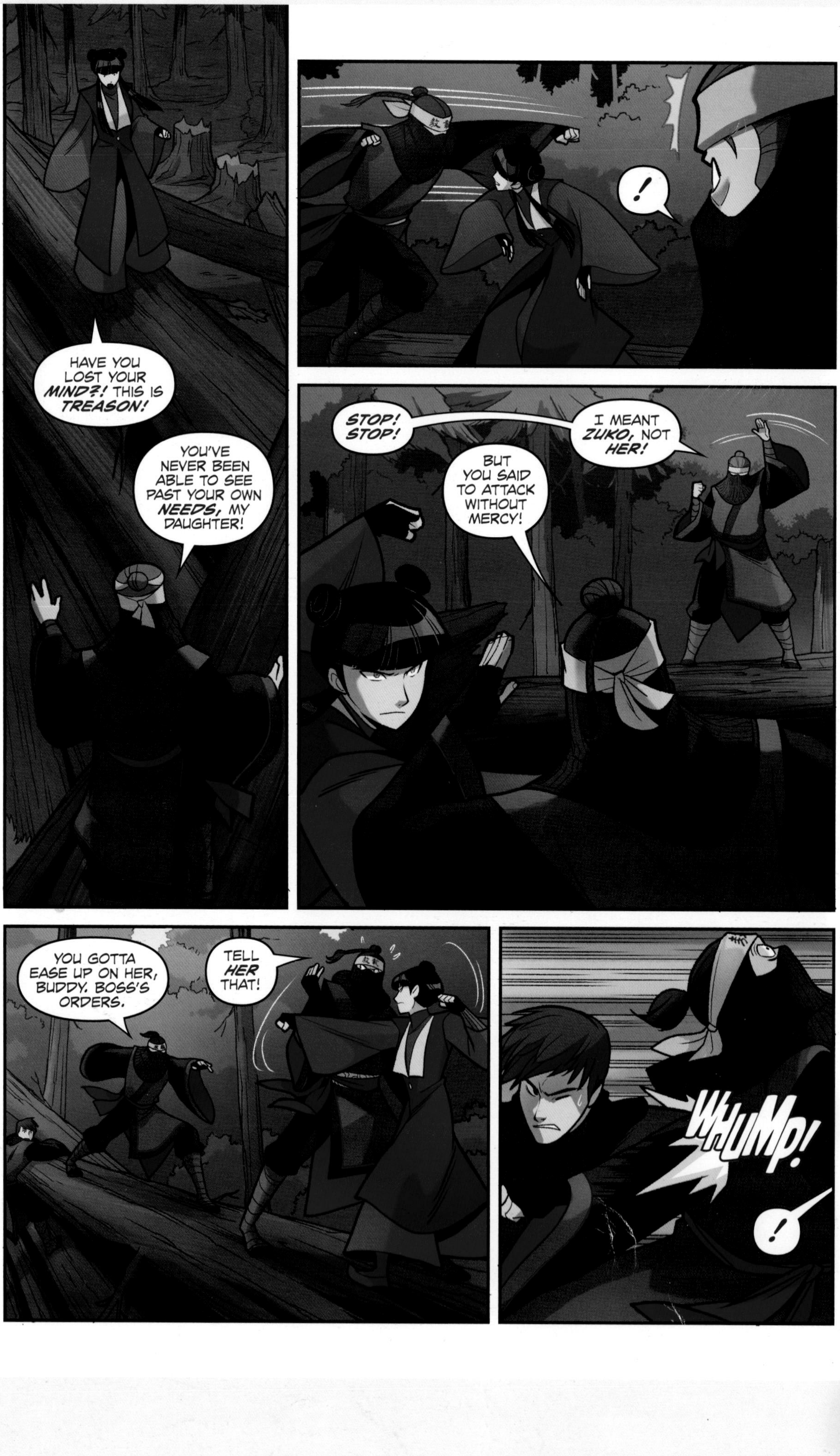
!
HAVE YOU LOST YOUR MIND?! THIS IS TREASON!
YOU'VE NEVER BEEN ABLE TO SEE PAST YOUR OWN NEEDS, MY DAUGHTER!
STOP! STOP!
I MEANT ZUKO, NOT HER!
BUT YOU SAID TO ATTACK WITHOUT MERCY!
YOU GOTTA EASE UP ON HER, BUDDY. BOSS'S ORDERS.
TELL HER THAT!
WHUMP!
!

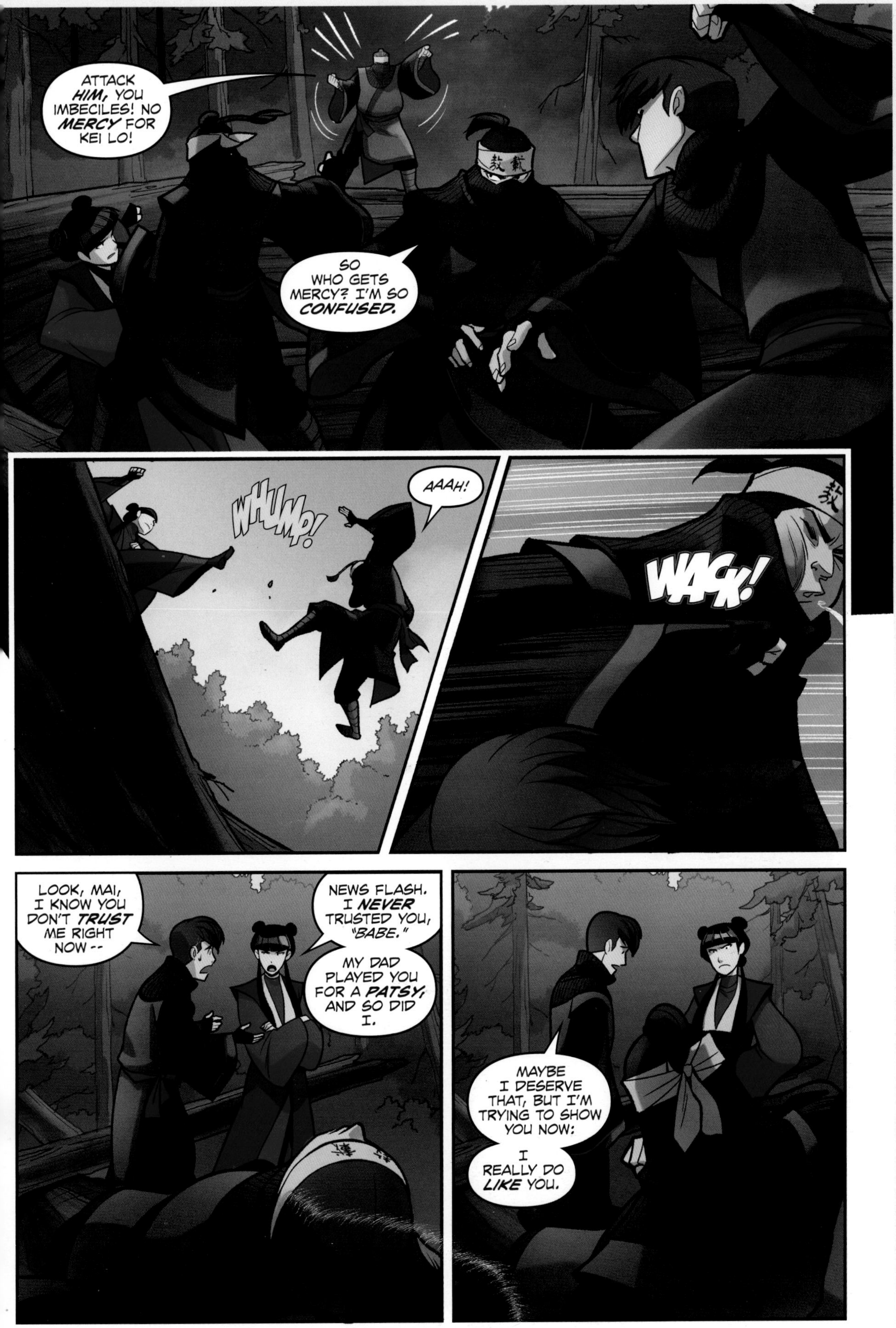
ATTACK HIM, YOU IMBECILES! NO MERCY FOR KEI LO!
SO WHO GETS MERCY? I'M SO CONFUSED.
WHUMP!
AAAH!
WACK!
LOOK, MAI, I KNOW YOU DON'T TRUST ME RIGHT NOW --
NEWS FLASH. I NEVER TRUSTED YOU, "BABE."
MY DAD PLAYED YOU FOR A PATSY, AND SO DID I.
MAYBE I DESERVE THAT, BUT I'M TRYING TO SHOW YOU NOW:
I REALLY DO LIKE YOU.

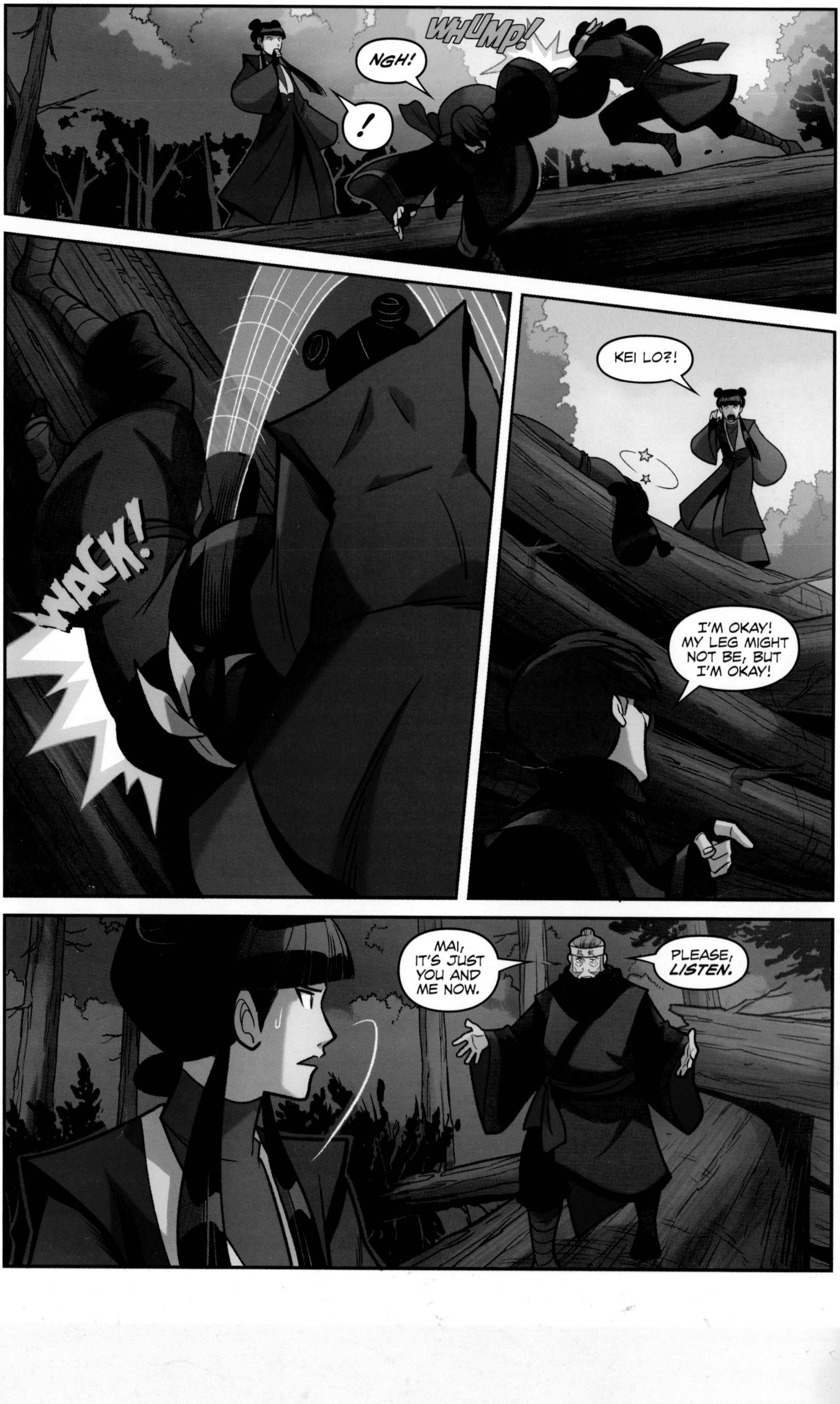
WHUMP!
NGH!
!
WACK!
KEI LO?!
I'M OKAY! MY LEG MIGHT NOT BE, BUT I'M OKAY!
MAI, IT'S JUST YOU AND ME NOW.
PLEASE, *LISTEN.*

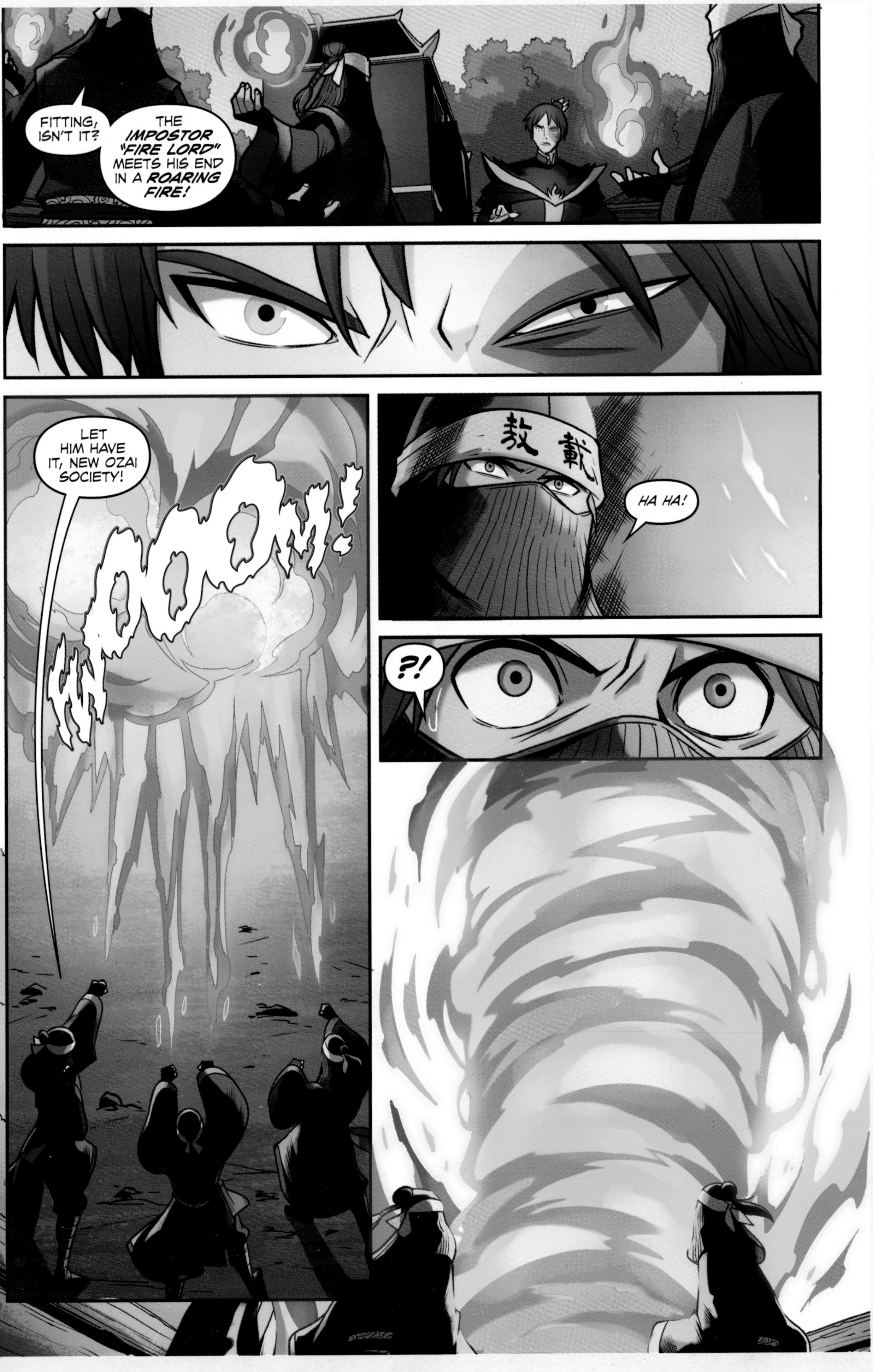
FITTING, ISN'T IT?
THE IMPOSTOR "FIRE LORD" MEETS HIS END IN A ROARING FIRE!
LET HIM HAVE IT, NEW OZAI SOCIETY!
WHOOOM!
HA HA!
?!

GLY: *The multicolored cone of fire is a nod to the episode "The Firebending Masters," one of the last episodes in the animated series.*

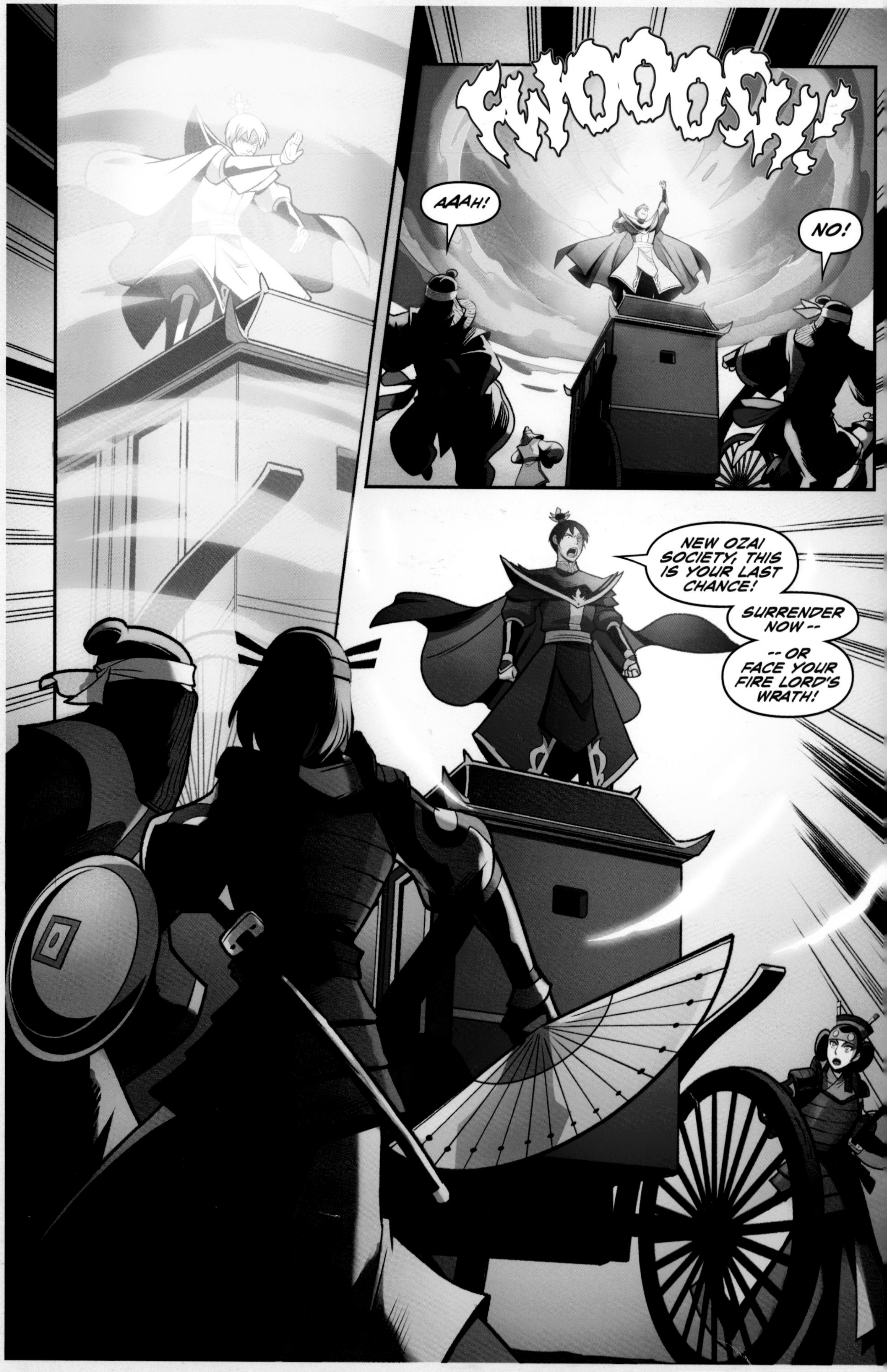
FWOOOSH!
AAAH!
NO!
NEW OZAI SOCIETY; THIS IS YOUR LAST CHANCE!
SURRENDER NOW --
-- OR FACE YOUR FIRE LORD'S WRATH!

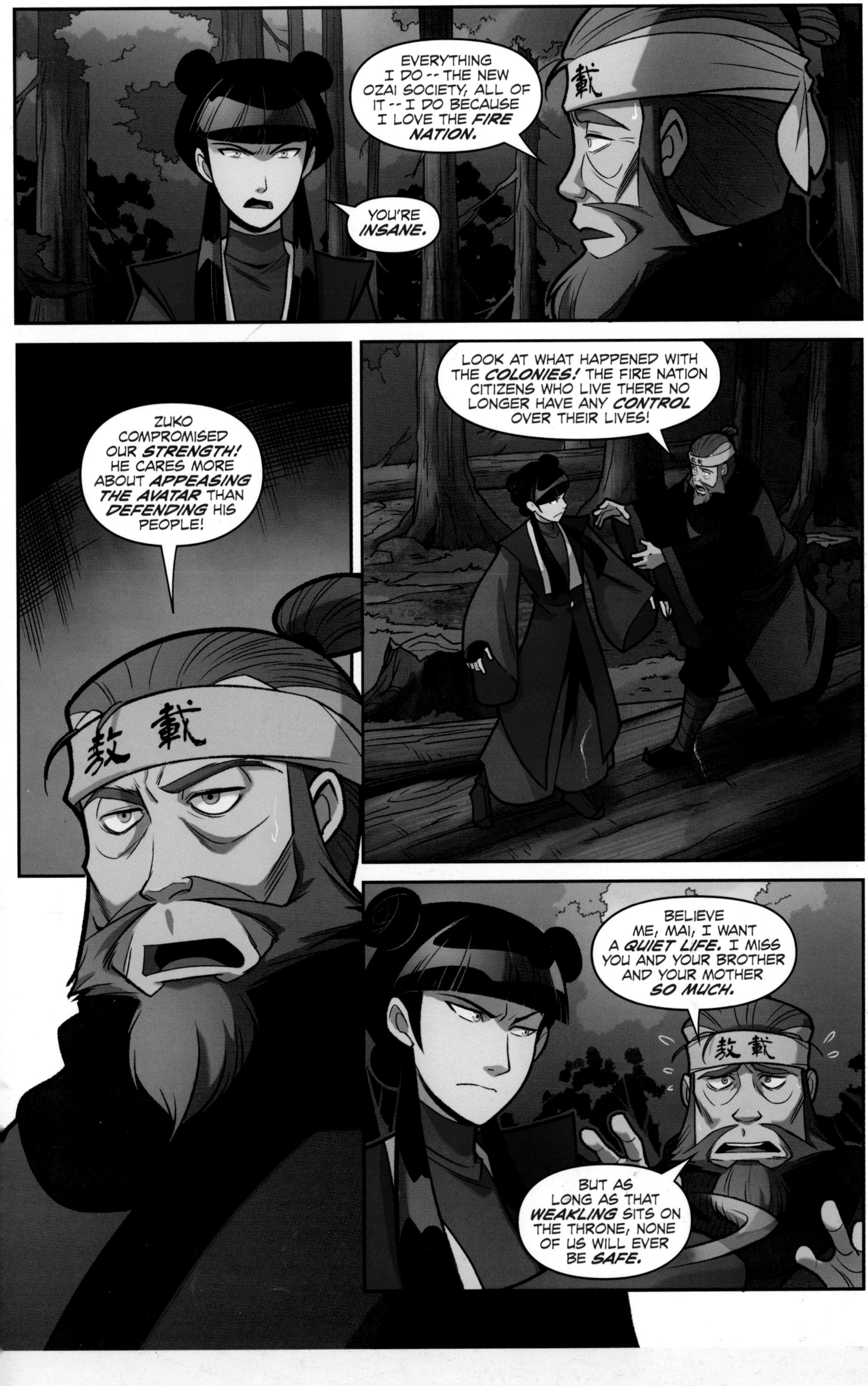
EVERYTHING I DO -- THE NEW OZAI SOCIETY, ALL OF IT -- I DO BECAUSE I LOVE THE FIRE NATION.
YOU'RE INSANE.
ZUKO COMPROMISED OUR STRENGTH! HE CARES MORE ABOUT APPEASING THE AVATAR THAN DEFENDING HIS PEOPLE!
LOOK AT WHAT HAPPENED WITH THE COLONIES! THE FIRE NATION CITIZENS WHO LIVE THERE NO LONGER HAVE ANY CONTROL OVER THEIR LIVES!
BELIEVE ME, MAI, I WANT A QUIET LIFE. I MISS YOU AND YOUR BROTHER AND YOUR MOTHER SO MUCH.
BUT AS LONG AS THAT WEAKLING SITS ON THE THRONE, NONE OF US WILL EVER BE SAFE.

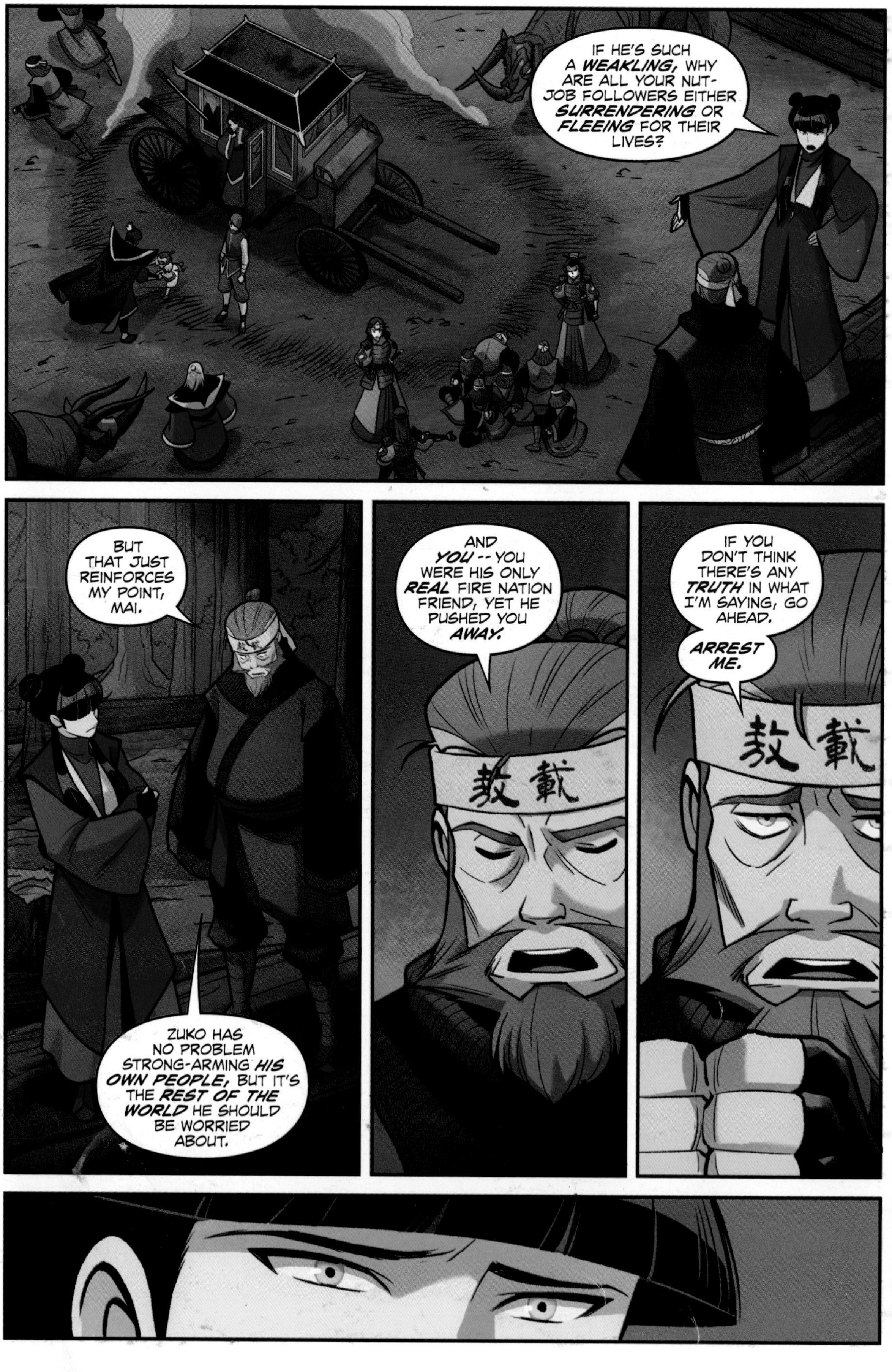
IF HE'S SUCH A WEAKLING, WHY ARE ALL YOUR NUT-JOB FOLLOWERS EITHER SURRENDERING OR FLEEING FOR THEIR LIVES?
BUT THAT JUST REINFORCES MY POINT, MAI.
ZUKO HAS NO PROBLEM STRONG-ARMING HIS OWN PEOPLE, BUT IT'S THE REST OF THE WORLD HE SHOULD BE WORRIED ABOUT.
AND YOU -- YOU WERE HIS ONLY REAL FIRE NATION FRIEND, YET HE PUSHED YOU AWAY.
IF YOU DON'T THINK THERE'S ANY TRUTH IN WHAT I'M SAYING, GO AHEAD.
ARREST ME.

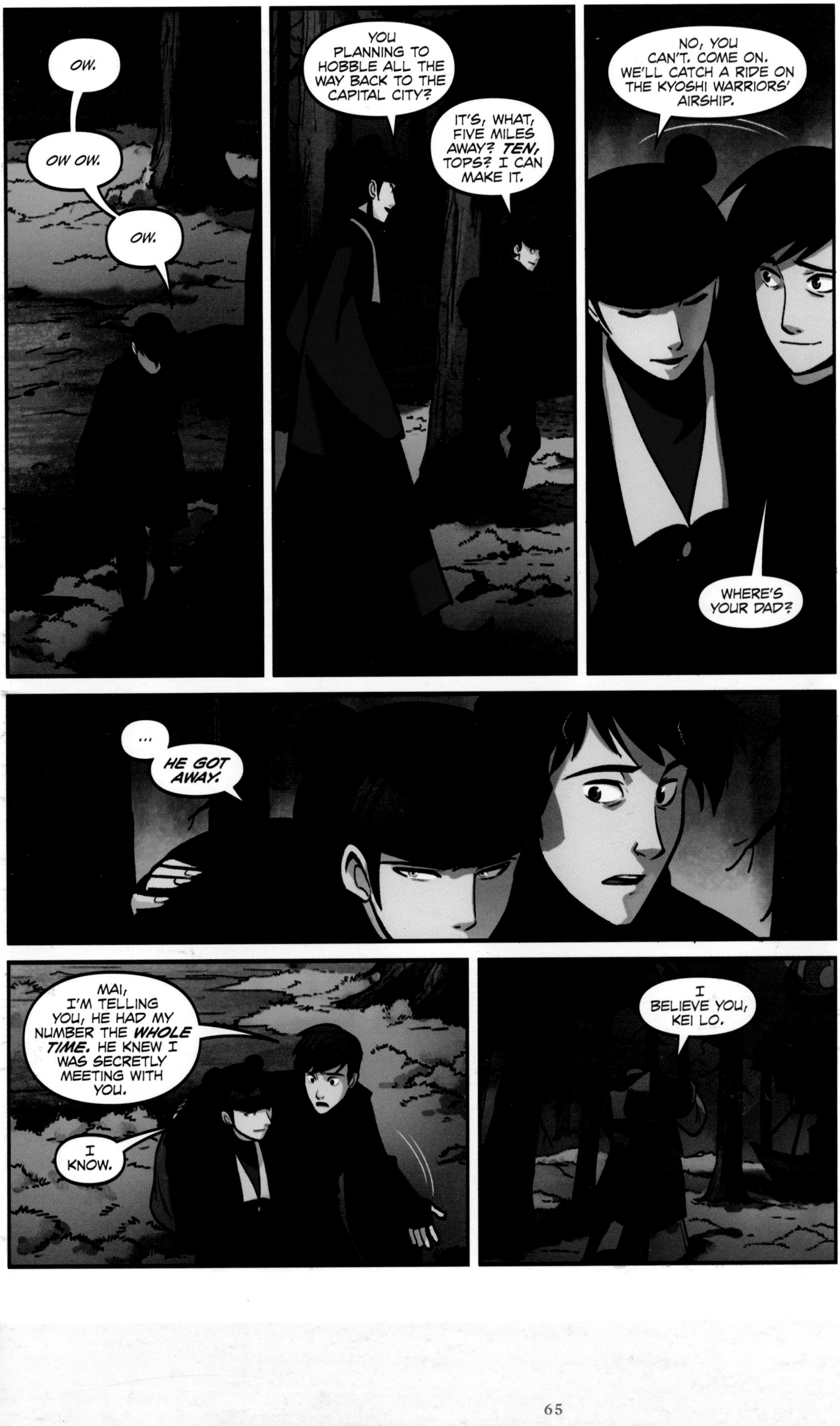
OW.
OW OW.
OW.
YOU PLANNING TO HOBBLE ALL THE WAY BACK TO THE CAPITAL CITY?
IT'S, WHAT, FIVE MILES AWAY? TEN, TOPS? I CAN MAKE IT.
NO, YOU CAN'T. COME ON. WE'LL CATCH A RIDE ON THE KYOSHI WARRIORS' AIRSHIP.
WHERE'S YOUR DAD?
...
HE GOT AWAY.
MAI, I'M TELLING YOU, HE HAD MY NUMBER THE WHOLE TIME. HE KNEW I WAS SECRETLY MEETING WITH YOU.
I KNOW.
I BELIEVE YOU, KEI LO.

GLY: *The physical pain that Kei Lo suffers throughout this story is foreshadowing.*

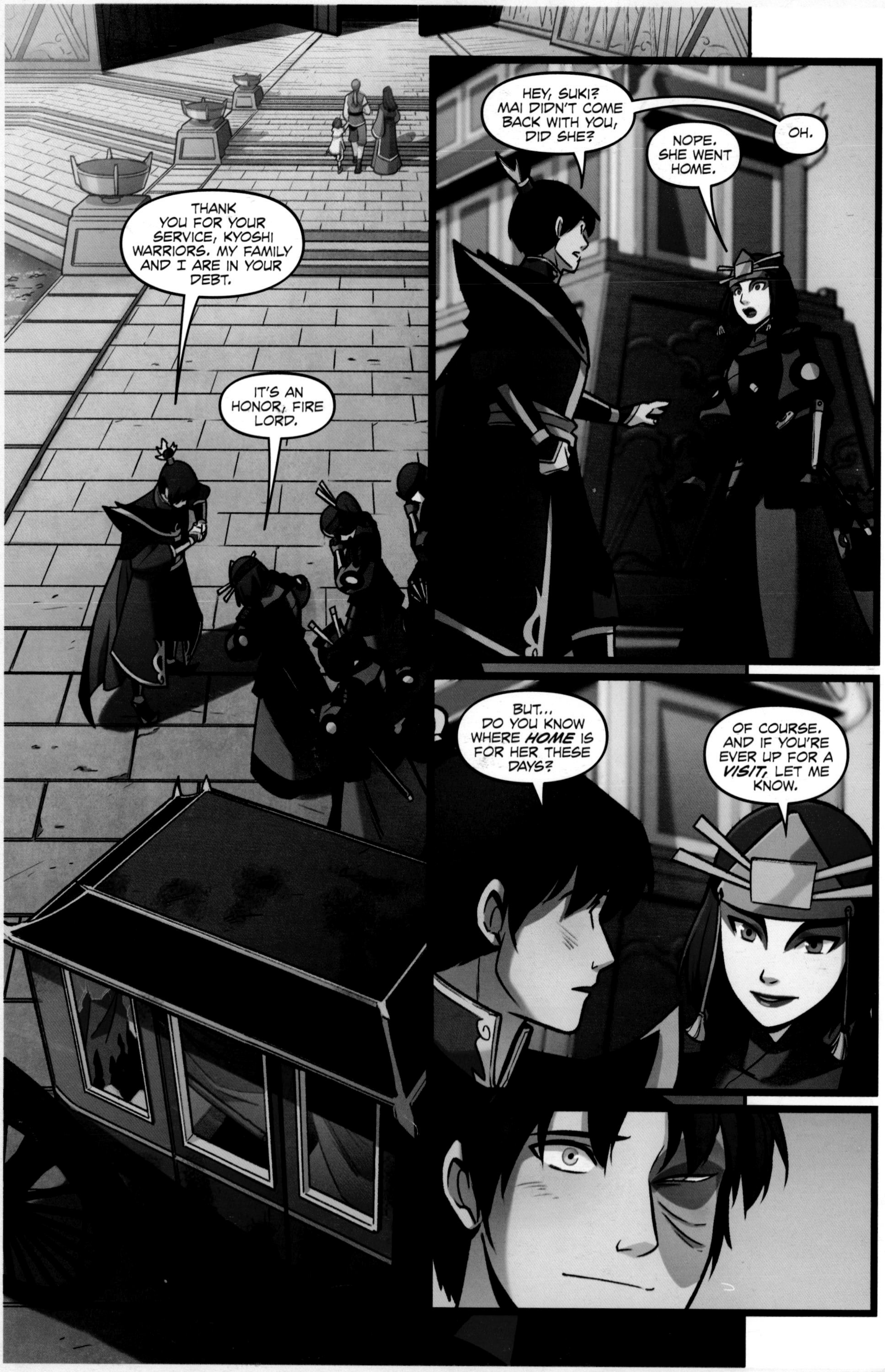
THANK YOU FOR YOUR SERVICE, KYOSHI WARRIORS. MY FAMILY AND I ARE IN YOUR DEBT.
IT'S AN HONOR, FIRE LORD.
HEY, SUKI? MAI DIDN'T COME BACK WITH YOU, DID SHE?
NOPE. SHE WENT HOME.
OH.
BUT... DO YOU KNOW WHERE *HOME* IS FOR HER THESE DAYS?
OF COURSE. AND IF YOU'RE EVER UP FOR A *VISIT,* LET ME KNOW.

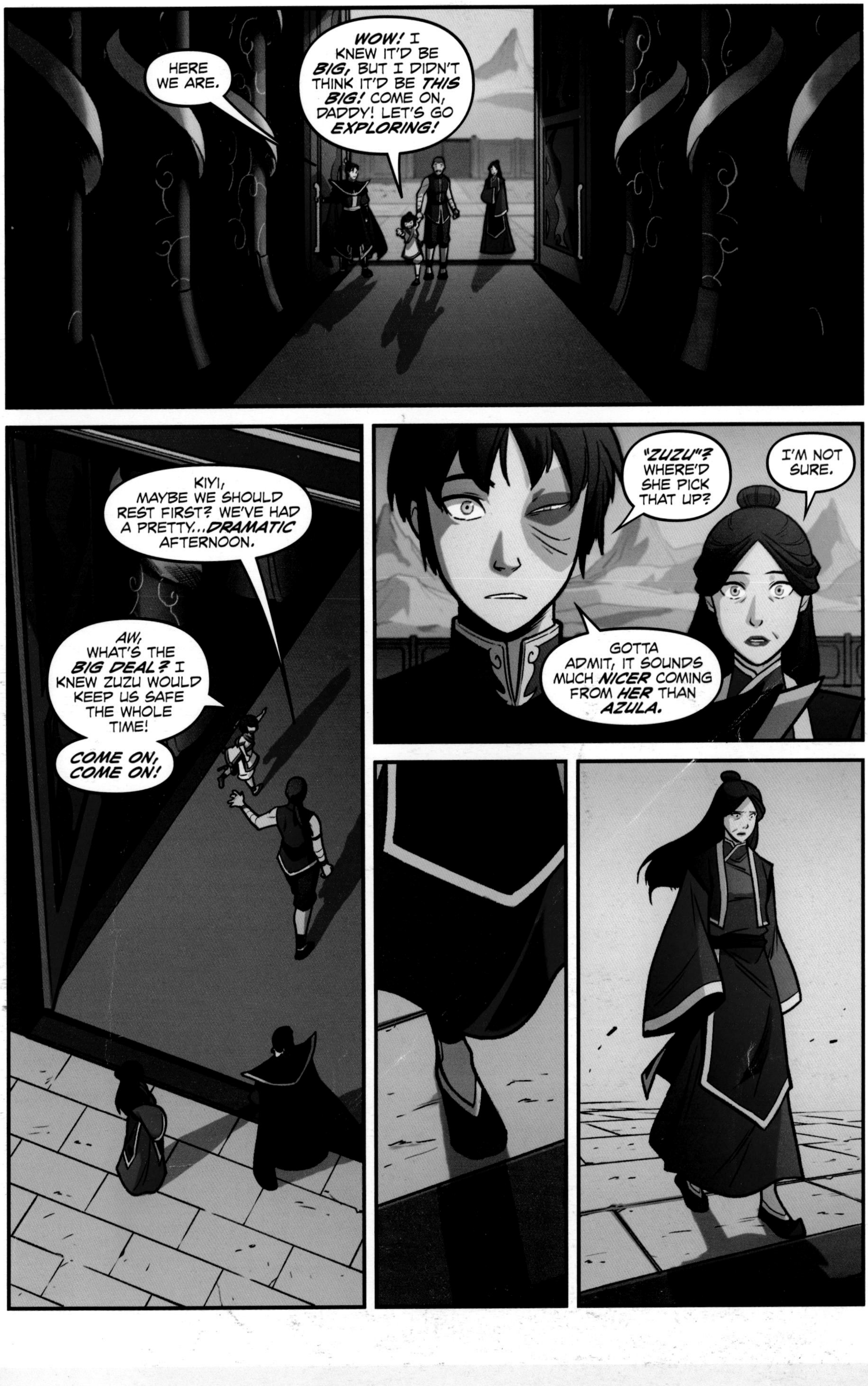
HERE WE ARE.
WOW! I KNEW IT'D BE BIG, BUT I DIDN'T THINK IT'D BE THIS BIG! COME ON, DADDY! LET'S GO EXPLORING!
KIYI, MAYBE WE SHOULD REST FIRST? WE'VE HAD A PRETTY...DRAMATIC AFTERNOON.
AW, WHAT'S THE BIG DEAL? I KNEW ZUZU WOULD KEEP US SAFE THE WHOLE TIME!
COME ON, COME ON!
"ZUZU"? WHERE'D SHE PICK THAT UP?
I'M NOT SURE.
GOTTA ADMIT, IT SOUNDS MUCH NICER COMING FROM HER THAN AZULA.

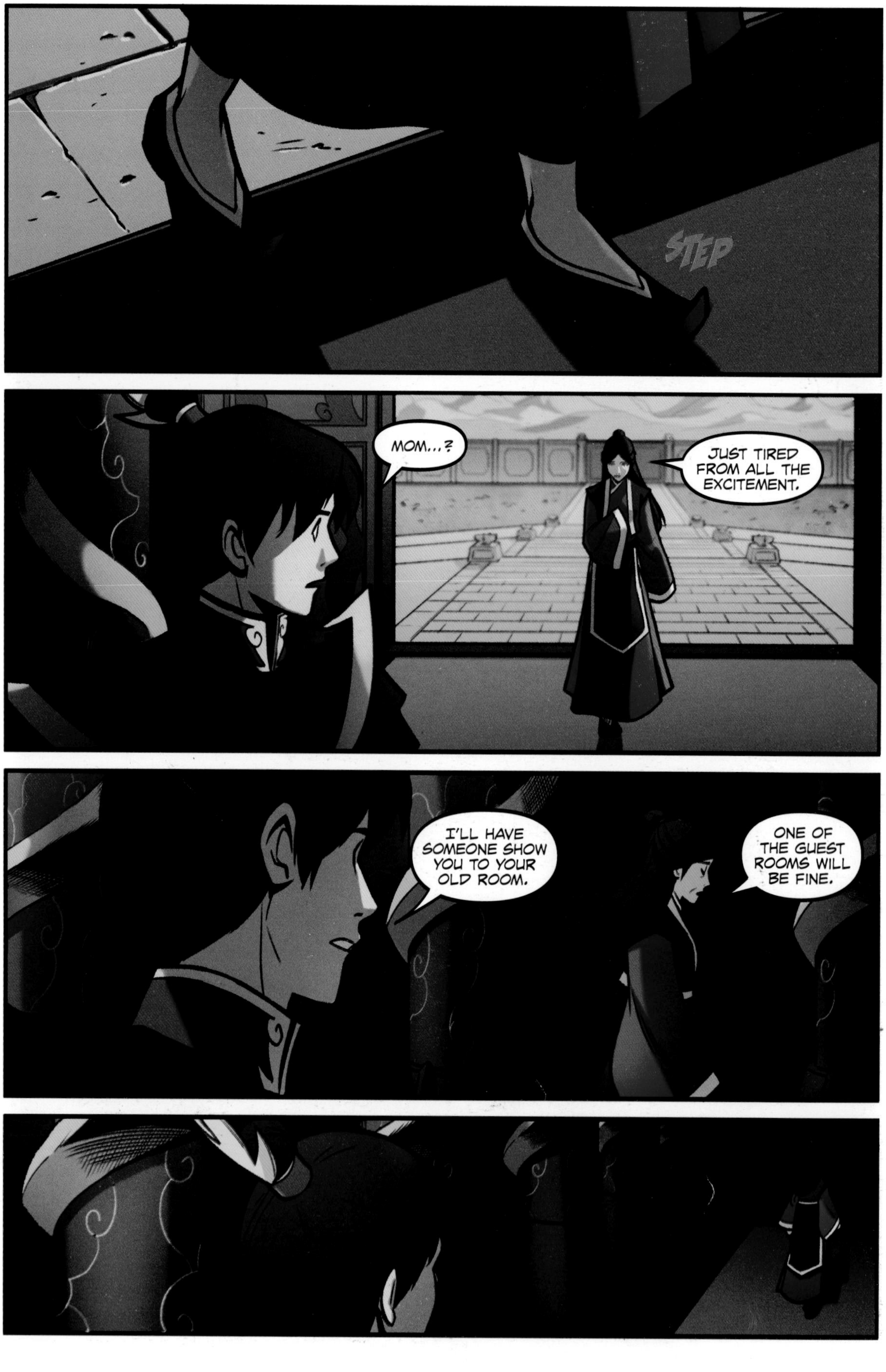
STEP
MOM...?
JUST TIRED FROM ALL THE EXCITEMENT.
I'LL HAVE SOMEONE SHOW YOU TO YOUR OLD ROOM.
ONE OF THE GUEST ROOMS WILL BE FINE.

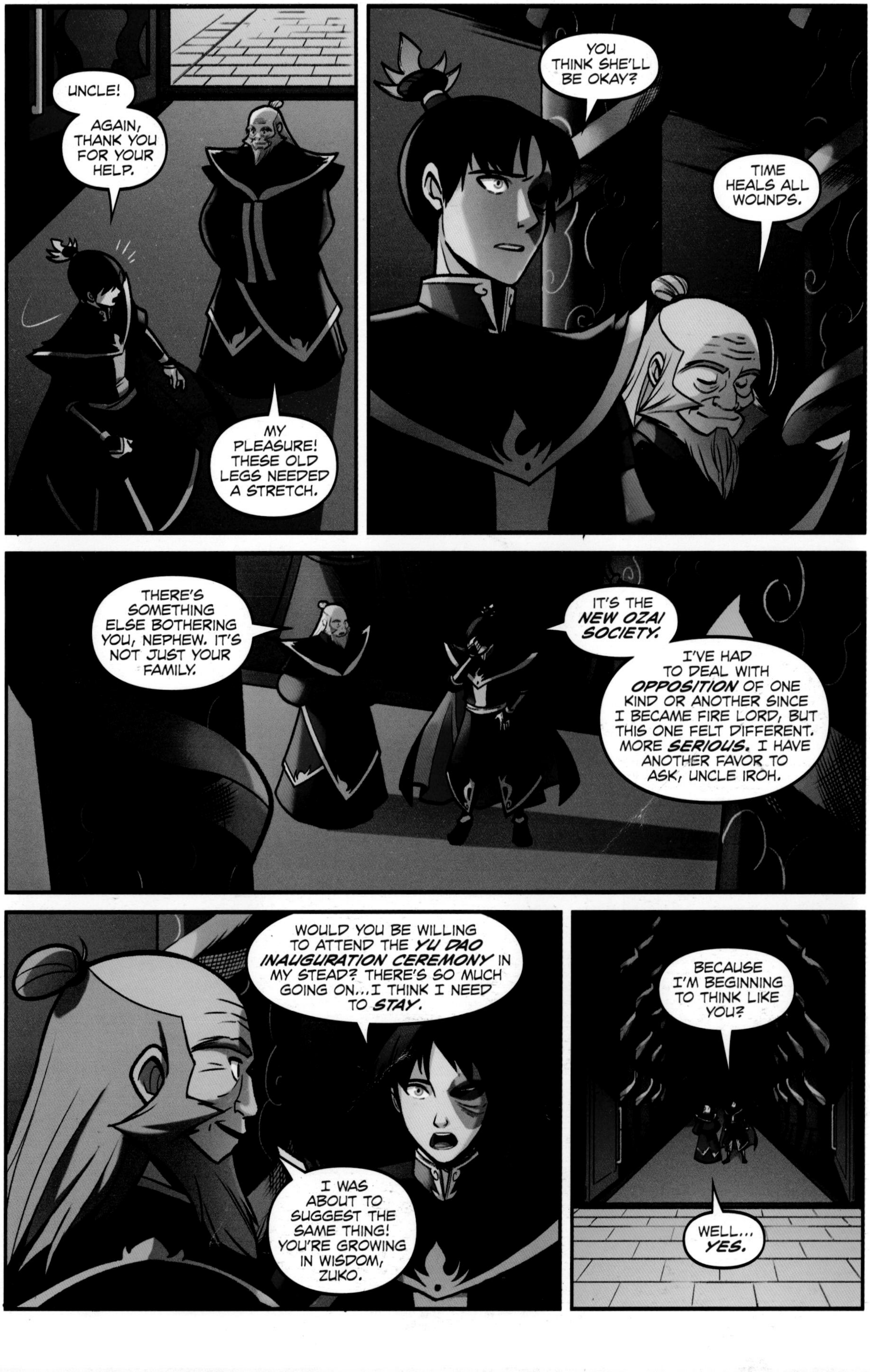
UNCLE!
AGAIN, THANK YOU FOR YOUR HELP.
MY PLEASURE! THESE OLD LEGS NEEDED A STRETCH.
YOU THINK SHE'LL BE OKAY?
TIME HEALS ALL WOUNDS.
THERE'S SOMETHING ELSE BOTHERING YOU, NEPHEW. IT'S NOT JUST YOUR FAMILY.
IT'S THE NEW OZAI SOCIETY.
I'VE HAD TO DEAL WITH OPPOSITION OF ONE KIND OR ANOTHER SINCE I BECAME FIRE LORD, BUT THIS ONE FELT DIFFERENT. MORE SERIOUS. I HAVE ANOTHER FAVOR TO ASK, UNCLE IROH.
WOULD YOU BE WILLING TO ATTEND THE YU DAO INAUGURATION CEREMONY IN MY STEAD? THERE'S SO MUCH GOING ON...I THINK I NEED TO STAY.
I WAS ABOUT TO SUGGEST THE SAME THING! YOU'RE GROWING IN WISDOM, ZUKO.
BECAUSE I'M BEGINNING TO THINK LIKE YOU?
WELL... YES.

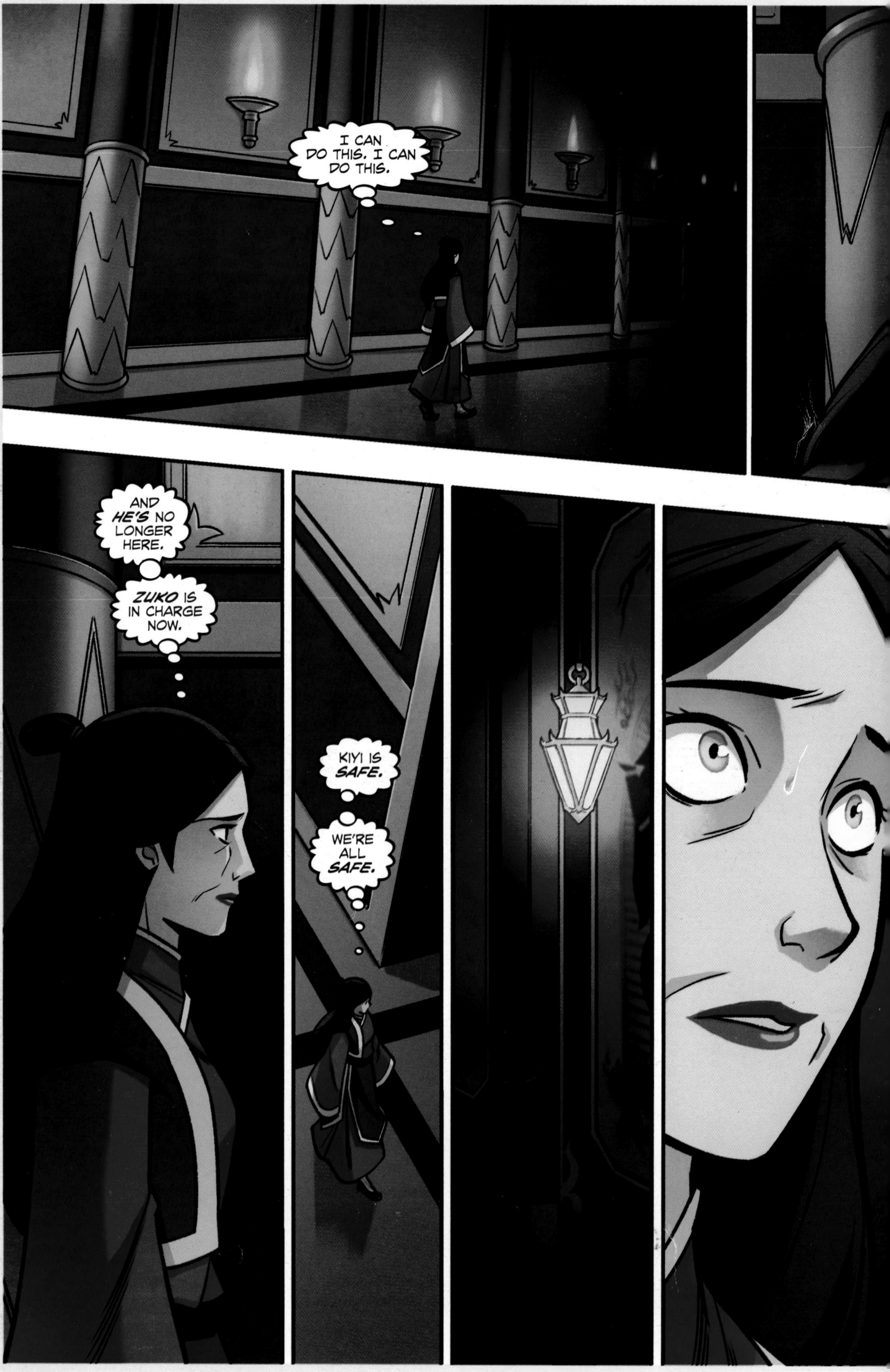
I CAN DO THIS. I CAN DO THIS.
AND HE'S NO LONGER HERE.
ZUKO IS IN CHARGE NOW.
KIYI IS SAFE.
WE'RE ALL SAFE.

GLY: *Gurihiru's use of color on this spread is just brilliant. That flash of bluish purple? Perfect.*

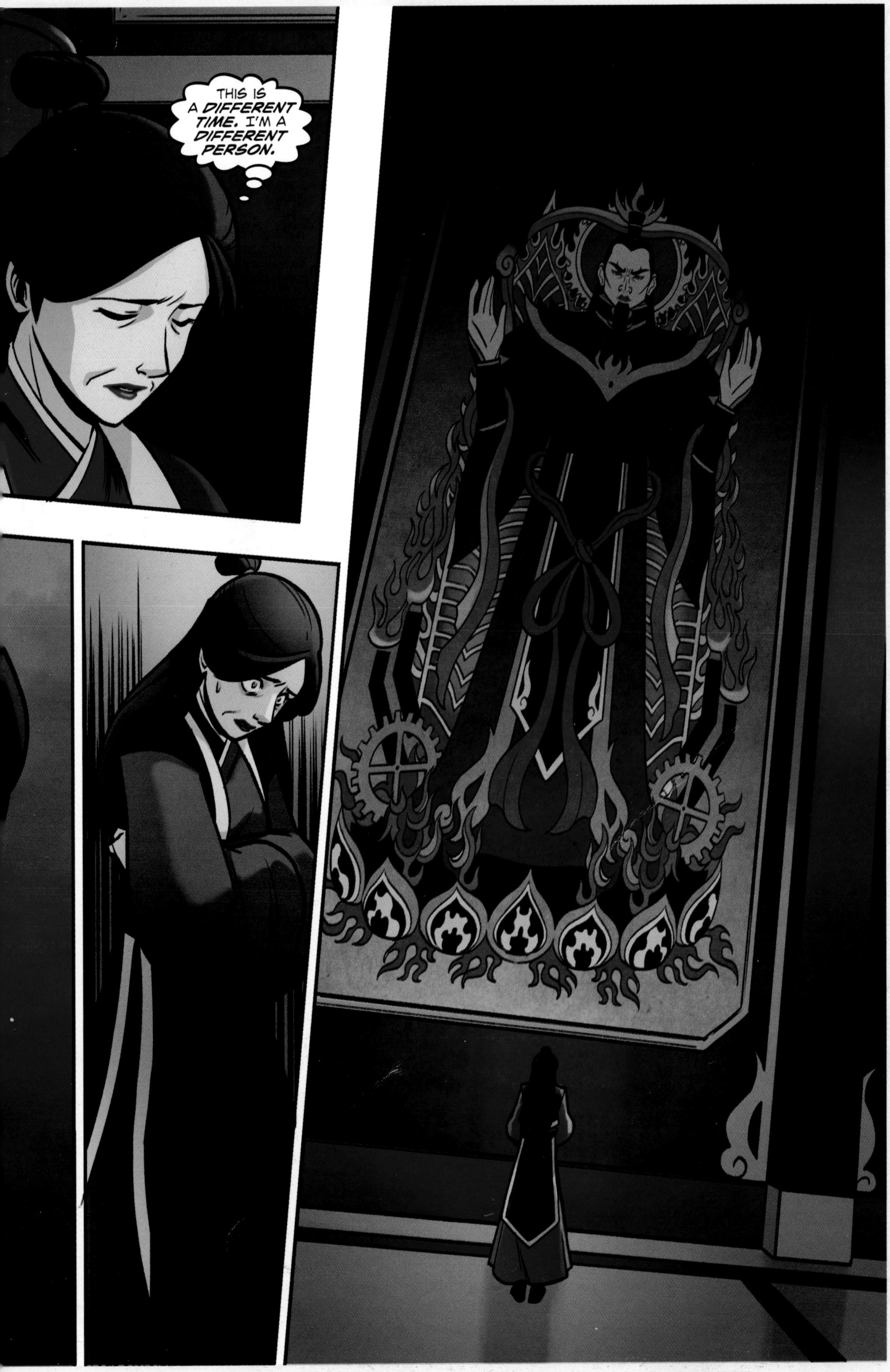
THIS IS A DIFFERENT TIME. I'M A DIFFERENT PERSON.

G: *We wanted to show how Ursa feared Ozai in this double-page spread. We thought it went well.*

GLY: *Every one of these books begins with a phone call between Mike, Bryan, a few of the editors, and me. During one of these phone calls, Mike and Bryan told me about an idea they'd had while they were working on the original series. They'd wanted to introduce an order of Fire Nation warrior women, sort of like the Fire Nation version of the Kyoshi Warriors. That idea ended up on the cutting-room floor, fortunately for Gurihiru and me. We were able to flesh them out by giving them a ghostly twist and a name: the Kemurikage.* Kemuri *is Japanese for "smoke,"* and kage *is Japanese for "shadow."*

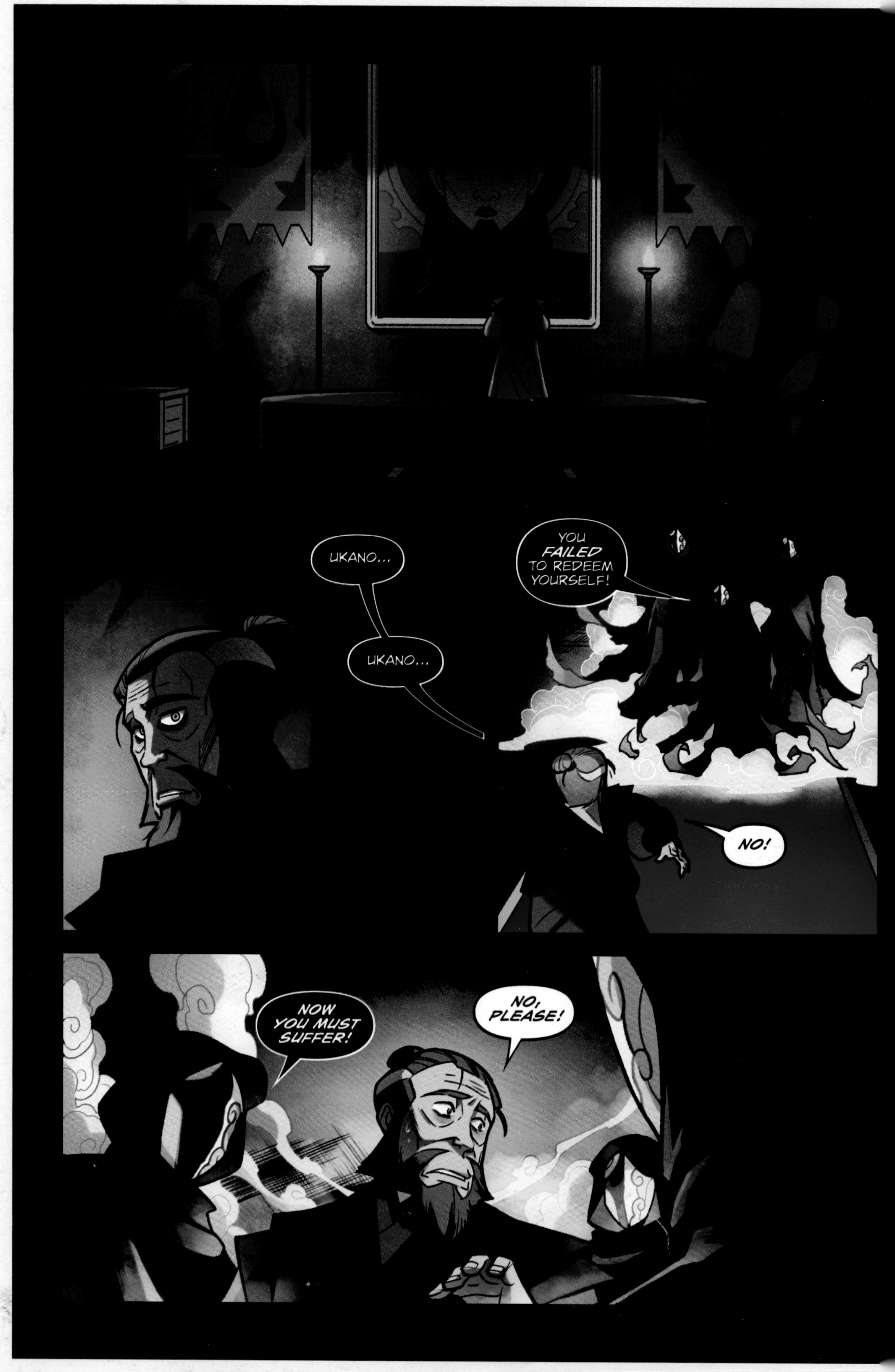
UKANO...
UKANO...
YOU FAILED TO REDEEM YOURSELF!
NO!
NOW YOU MUST SUFFER!
NO, PLEASE!

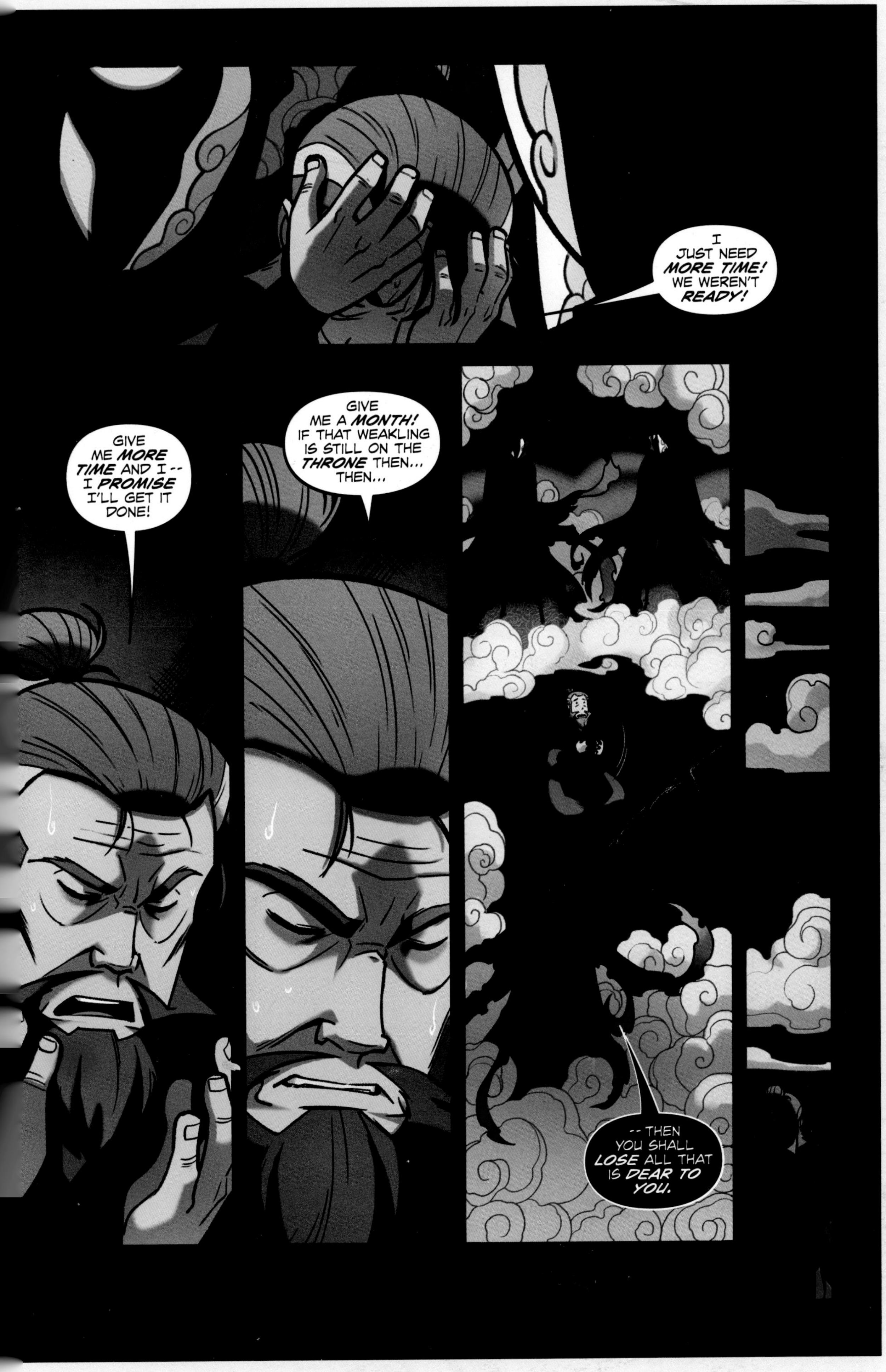
I JUST NEED MORE TIME! WE WEREN'T READY!
GIVE ME MORE TIME AND I -- I PROMISE I'LL GET IT DONE!
GIVE ME A MONTH! IF THAT WEAKLING IS STILL ON THE THRONE THEN... THEN...
-- THEN YOU SHALL LOSE ALL THAT IS DEAR TO YOU.

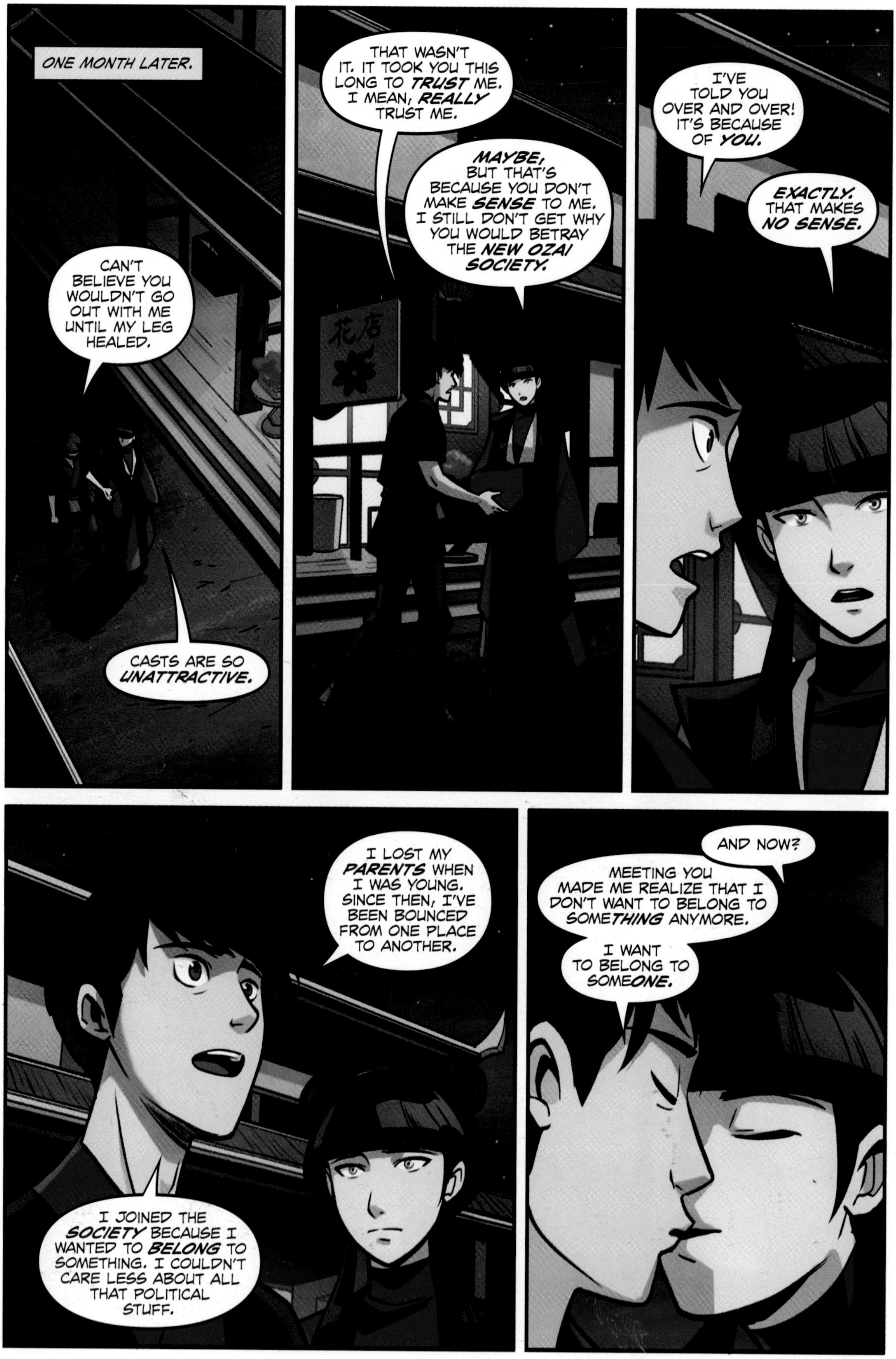
ONE MONTH LATER.
CAN'T BELIEVE YOU WOULDN'T GO OUT WITH ME UNTIL MY LEG HEALED.
CASTS ARE SO UNATTRACTIVE.
THAT WASN'T IT. IT TOOK YOU THIS LONG TO TRUST ME. I MEAN, REALLY TRUST ME.
MAYBE, BUT THAT'S BECAUSE YOU DON'T MAKE SENSE TO ME. I STILL DON'T GET WHY YOU WOULD BETRAY THE NEW OZAI SOCIETY.
花店
I'VE TOLD YOU OVER AND OVER! IT'S BECAUSE OF YOU.
EXACTLY. THAT MAKES NO SENSE.
I LOST MY PARENTS WHEN I WAS YOUNG. SINCE THEN, I'VE BEEN BOUNCED FROM ONE PLACE TO ANOTHER.
I JOINED THE SOCIETY BECAUSE I WANTED TO BELONG TO SOMETHING. I COULDN'T CARE LESS ABOUT ALL THAT POLITICAL STUFF.
AND NOW?
MEETING YOU MADE ME REALIZE THAT I DON'T WANT TO BELONG TO SOMETHING ANYMORE.
I WANT TO BELONG TO SOMEONE.

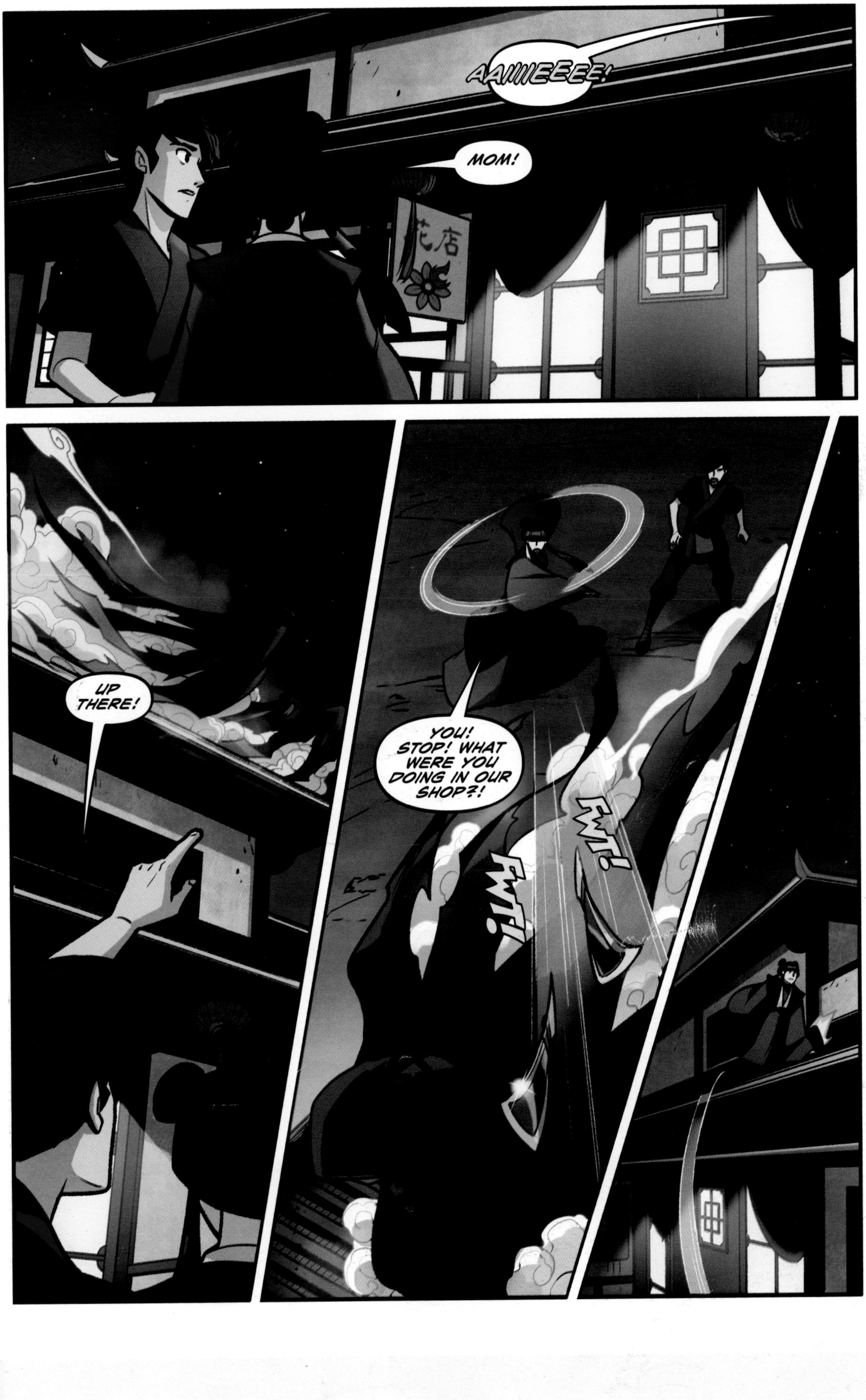
AAIIIIEEEEE!
MOM!
UP THERE!
YOU! STOP! WHAT WERE YOU DOING IN OUR SHOP?!
FWT!
FWT!

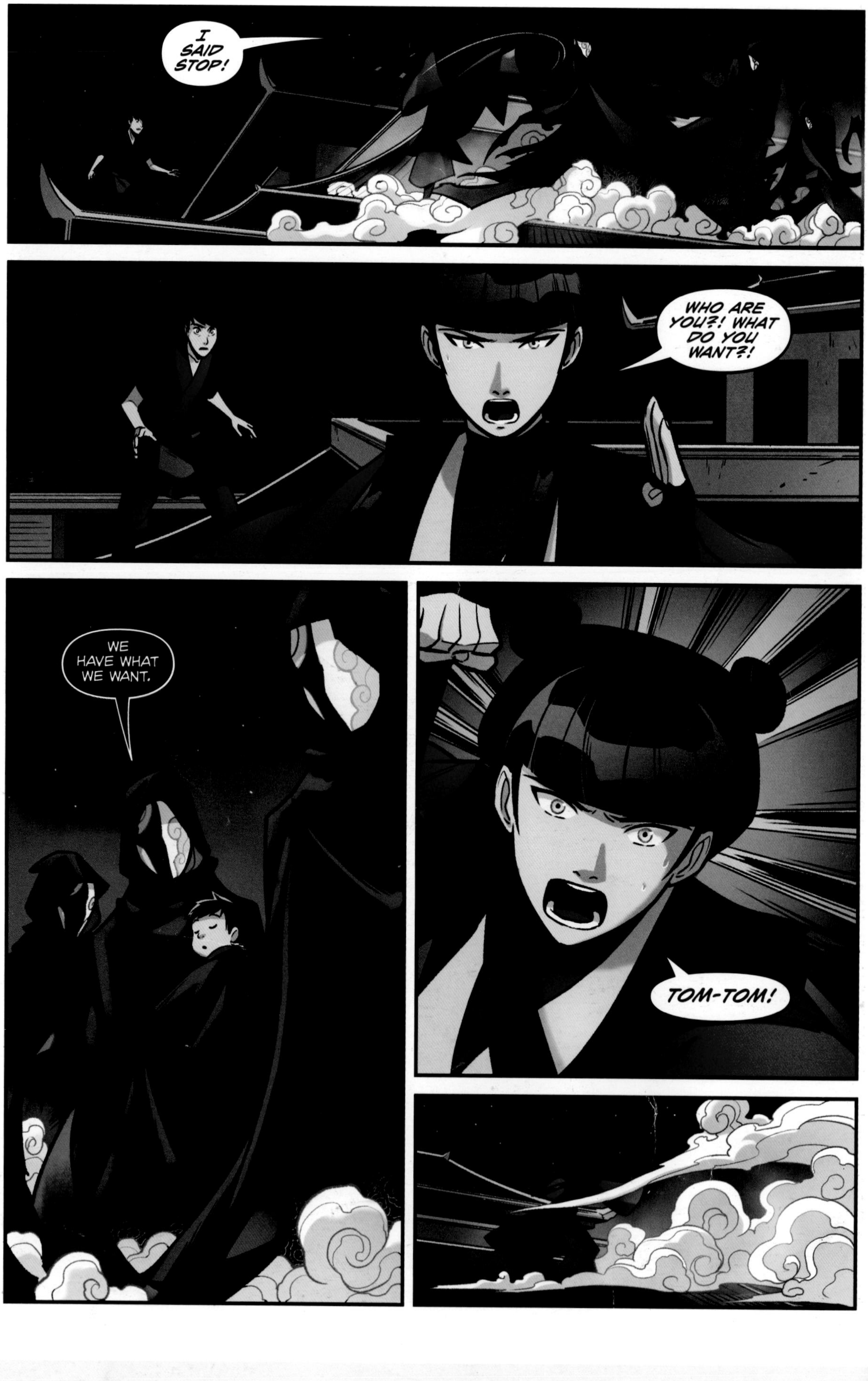
I SAID STOP!
WHO ARE YOU?! WHAT DO YOU WANT?!
WE HAVE WHAT WE WANT.
TOM-TOM!

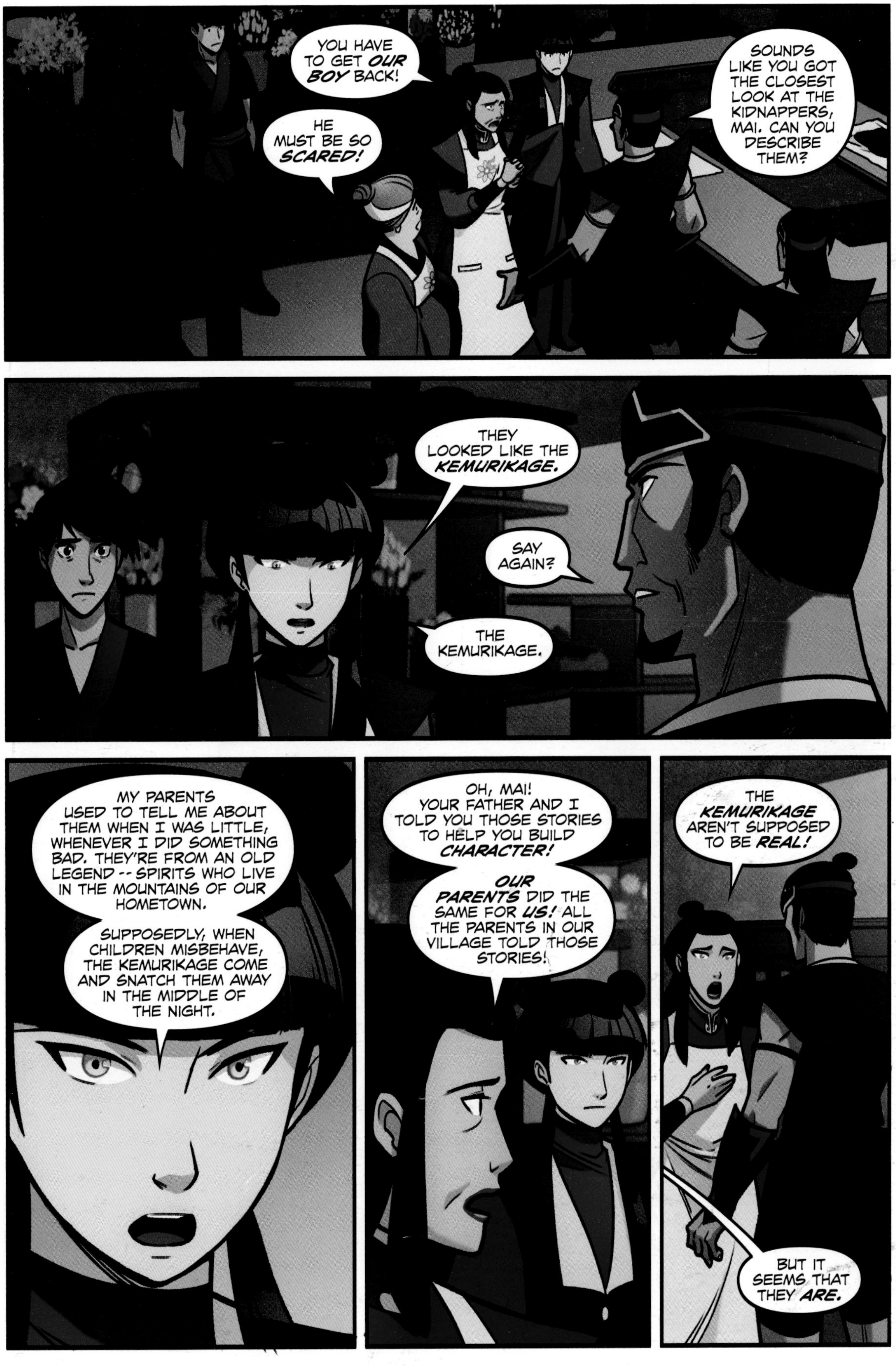
YOU HAVE TO GET OUR BOY BACK!
HE MUST BE SO SCARED!
SOUNDS LIKE YOU GOT THE CLOSEST LOOK AT THE KIDNAPPERS, MAI. CAN YOU DESCRIBE THEM?
THEY LOOKED LIKE THE KEMURIKAGE.
SAY AGAIN?
THE KEMURIKAGE.
MY PARENTS USED TO TELL ME ABOUT THEM WHEN I WAS LITTLE, WHENEVER I DID SOMETHING BAD. THEY'RE FROM AN OLD LEGEND -- SPIRITS WHO LIVE IN THE MOUNTAINS OF OUR HOMETOWN.
SUPPOSEDLY, WHEN CHILDREN MISBEHAVE, THE KEMURIKAGE COME AND SNATCH THEM AWAY IN THE MIDDLE OF THE NIGHT.
OH, MAI! YOUR FATHER AND I TOLD YOU THOSE STORIES TO HELP YOU BUILD CHARACTER!
OUR PARENTS DID THE SAME FOR US! ALL THE PARENTS IN OUR VILLAGE TOLD THOSE STORIES!
THE KEMURIKAGE AREN'T SUPPOSED TO BE REAL!
BUT IT SEEMS THAT THEY ARE.

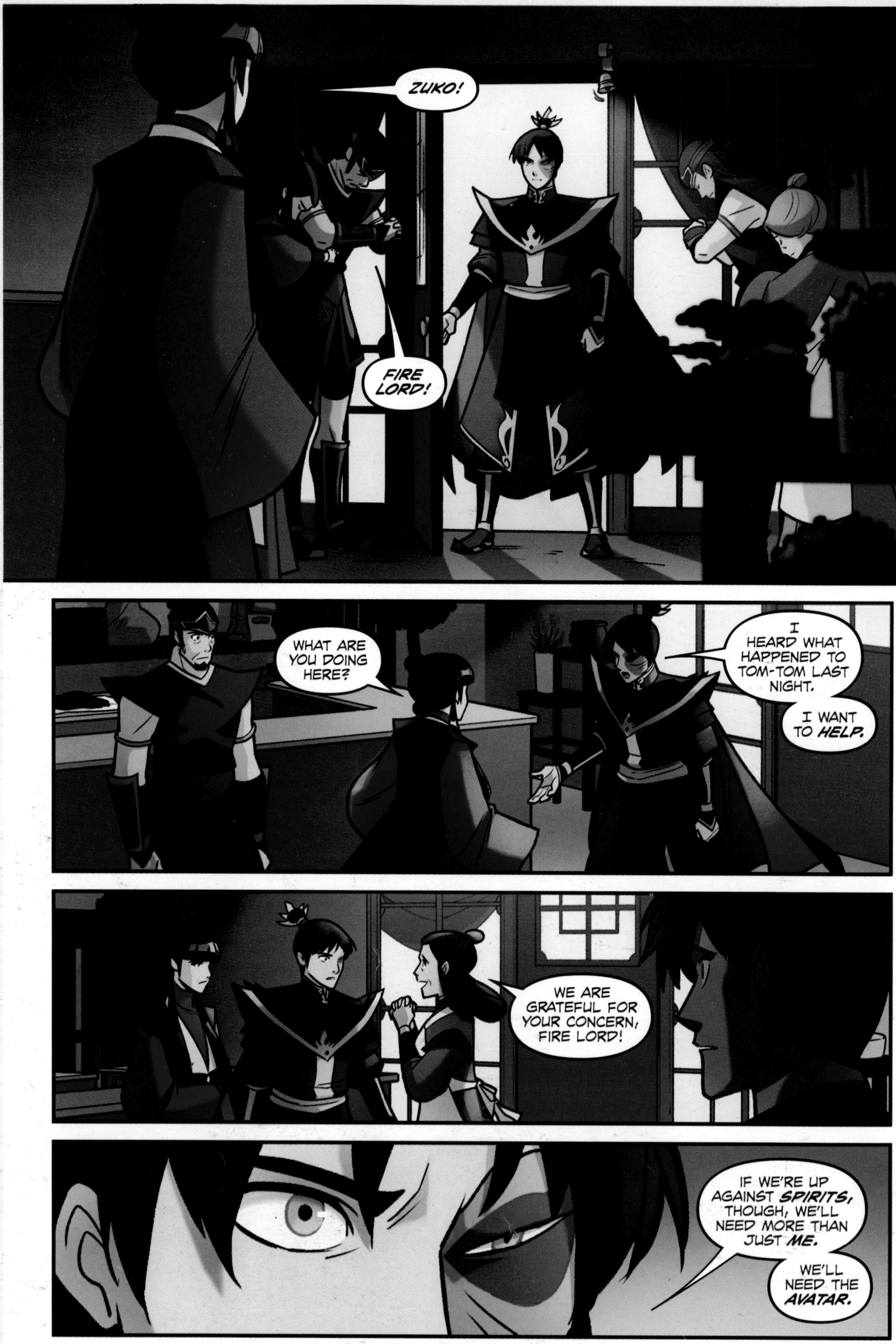
ZUKO!
FIRE LORD!
WHAT ARE YOU DOING HERE?
I HEARD WHAT HAPPENED TO TOM-TOM LAST NIGHT.
I WANT TO HELP.
WE ARE GRATEFUL FOR YOUR CONCERN, FIRE LORD!
IF WE'RE UP AGAINST SPIRITS, THOUGH, WE'LL NEED MORE THAN JUST ME.
WE'LL NEED THE AVATAR.

GLY: *Of course we're going to bring Avatar Aang back for the next chapter. The series is called* Avatar: The Last Airbender, *after all.*

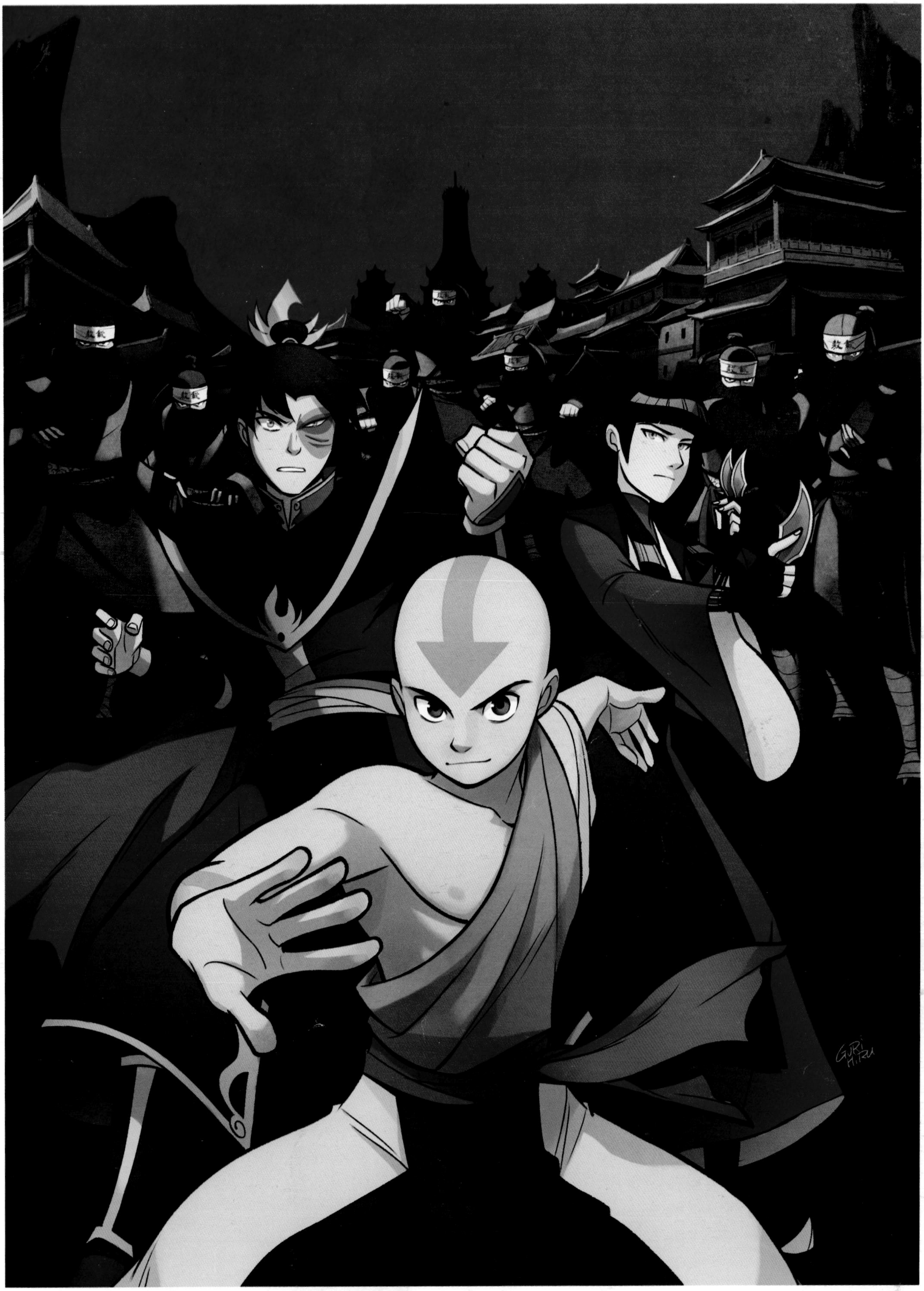
GURI HIRU

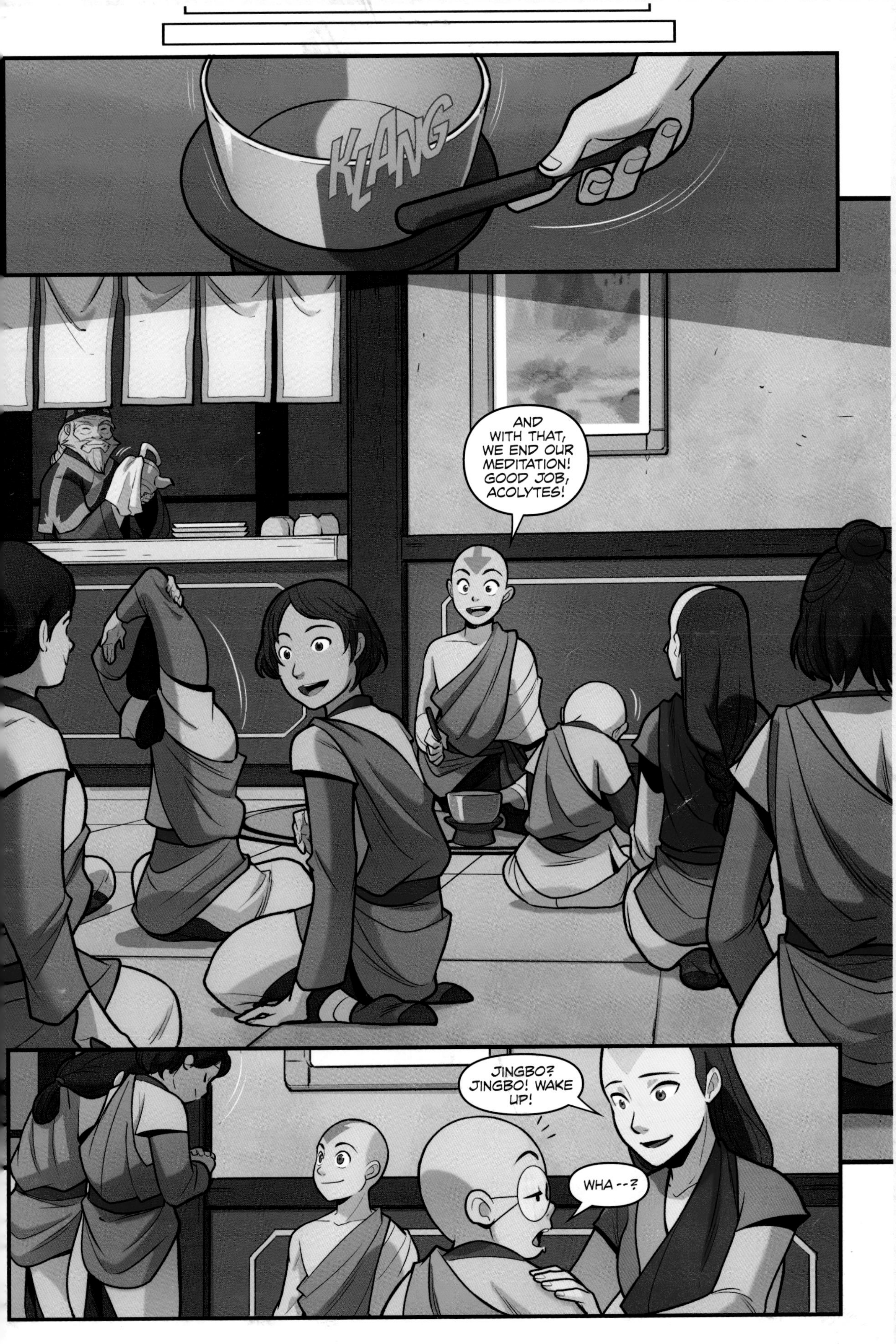
KLANG
AND WITH THAT, WE END OUR MEDITATION! GOOD JOB, ACOLYTES!
JINGBO? JINGBO! WAKE UP!
WHA--?

GLY: *That's the Avatarverse equivalent of a Tibetan singing bowl, often used to signal the beginning and end of meditation.*

G: *Before we started work on the second part of* Smoke and Shadow, *we had the chance to travel to China. We took many reference photos of the architecture, and they have been a big help in drawing the world of* Avatar.

GLY: *This scene takes place in Uncle Iroh's teashop, the Jasmine Dragon, which first appeared in the episode "The Guru." I love the green dragon pattern on the rug.*

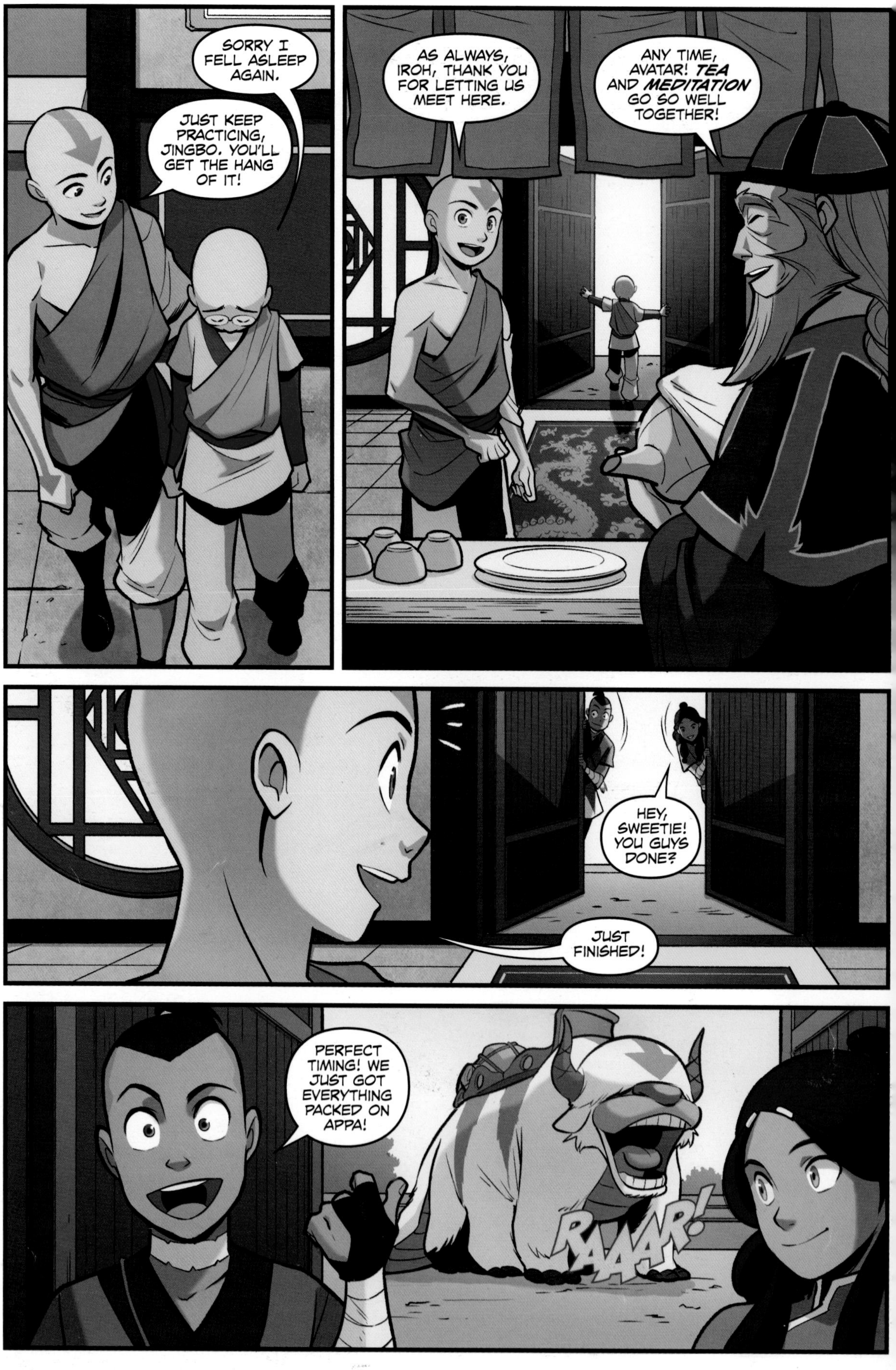
SORRY I FELL ASLEEP AGAIN.
JUST KEEP PRACTICING, JINGBO. YOU'LL GET THE HANG OF IT!
AS ALWAYS, IROH, THANK YOU FOR LETTING US MEET HERE.
ANY TIME, AVATAR! TEA AND MEDITATION GO SO WELL TOGETHER!
HEY, SWEETIE! YOU GUYS DONE?
JUST FINISHED!
PERFECT TIMING! WE JUST GOT EVERYTHING PACKED ON APPA!
RAAAR!

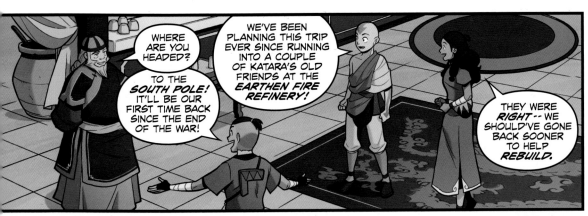

WHERE ARE YOU HEADED?

WE'VE BEEN PLANNING THIS TRIP EVER SINCE RUNNING INTO A COUPLE OF KATARA'S OLD FRIENDS AT THE *EARTHEN FIRE REFINERY!*

TO THE *SOUTH POLE!* IT'LL BE OUR FIRST TIME BACK SINCE THE END OF THE WAR!

THEY WERE *RIGHT* -- WE SHOULD'VE GONE BACK SOONER TO HELP *REBUILD.*

PLUS, WE'LL FINALLY GET TO SEE *DAD!*

AND GO *PENGUIN SLEDDING!*

AND EAT SOME OF AUNTIE ASHUNA'S *SEAL JERKY!*

WHAT? YOU HATE AUNTIE ASHUNA'S SEAL JERKY!

YOU MEAN I *HATED* AUNTIE ASHUNA'S SEAL JERKY!

ABSENCE MAKES THE HEART GROW *FONDER.*

LET'S GET MOVING! WEATHER'S PERFECT RIGHT NOW. IF WE HURRY, WE CAN PROBABLY GET TO --

SQUAWK!

!

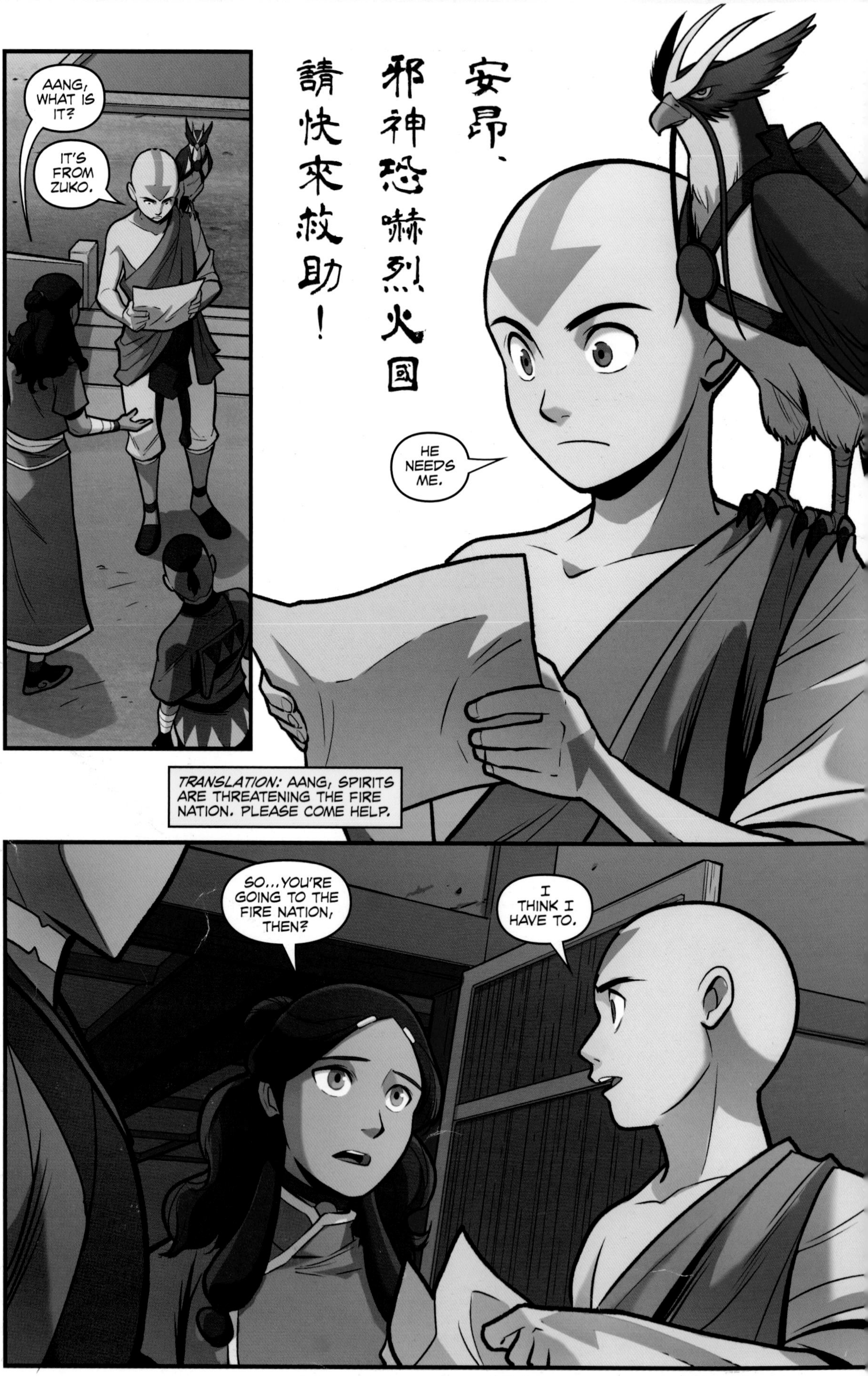
AANG, WHAT IS IT?
IT'S FROM ZUKO.
安昂、
邪神恐嚇烈火國
請快來救助！
HE NEEDS ME.
TRANSLATION: AANG, SPIRITS ARE THREATENING THE FIRE NATION. PLEASE COME HELP.
SO...YOU'RE GOING TO THE FIRE NATION, THEN?
I THINK I HAVE TO.

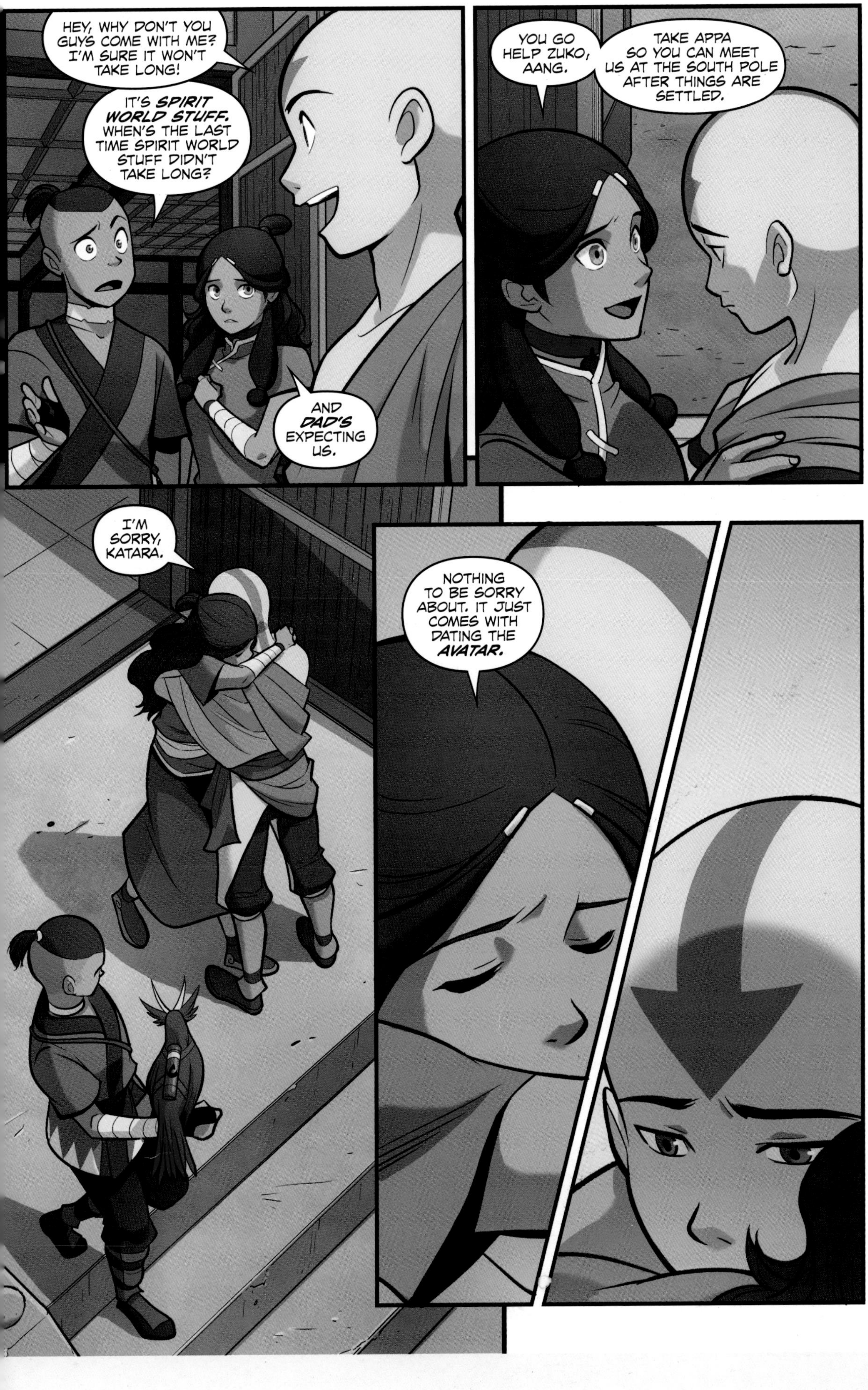
HEY, WHY DON'T YOU GUYS COME WITH ME? I'M SURE IT WON'T TAKE LONG!
IT'S SPIRIT WORLD STUFF. WHEN'S THE LAST TIME SPIRIT WORLD STUFF DIDN'T TAKE LONG?
AND DAD'S EXPECTING US.
YOU GO HELP ZUKO, AANG.
TAKE APPA SO YOU CAN MEET US AT THE SOUTH POLE AFTER THINGS ARE SETTLED.
I'M SORRY, KATARA.
NOTHING TO BE SORRY ABOUT. IT JUST COMES WITH DATING THE AVATAR.

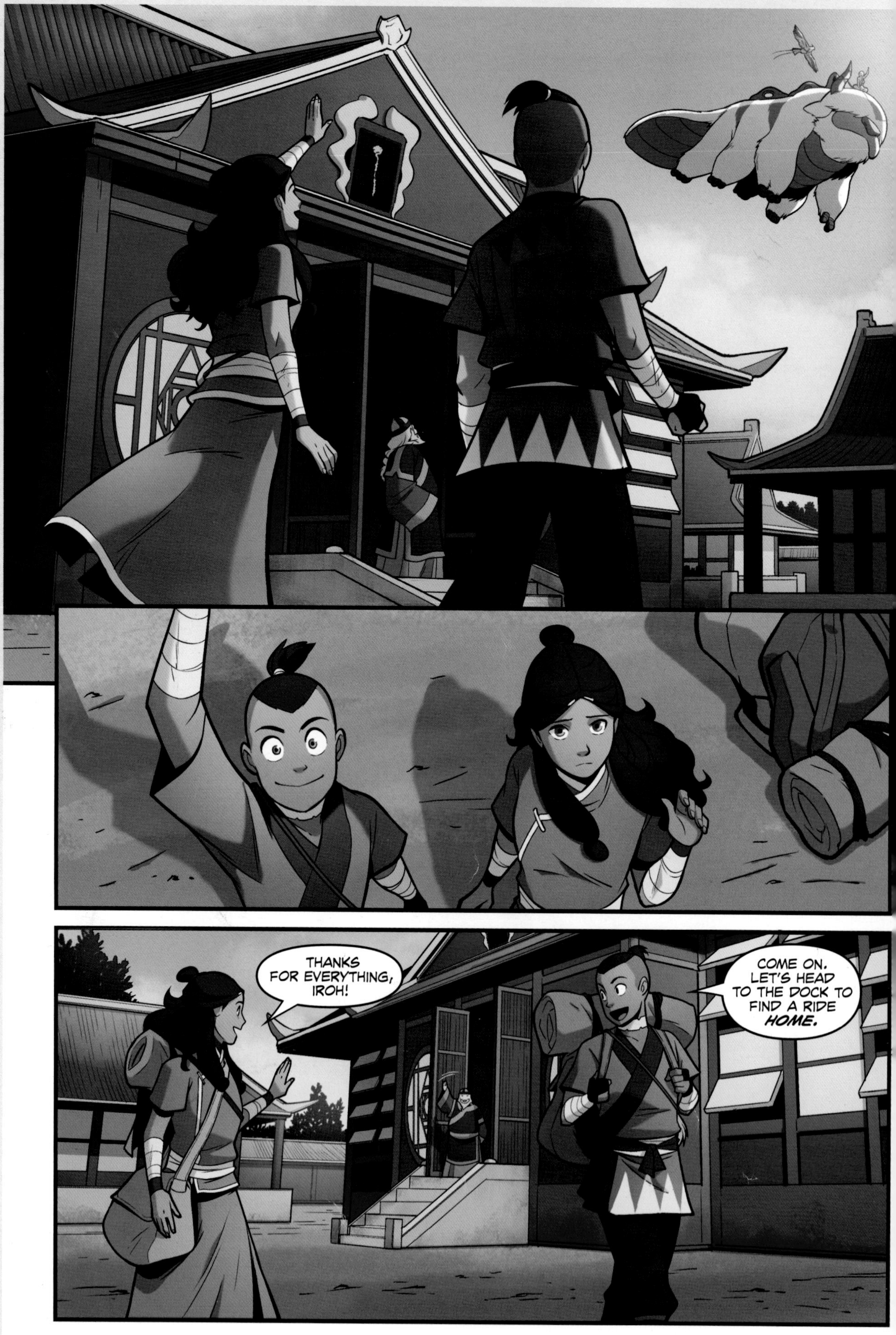
THANKS FOR EVERYTHING, IROH!
COME ON. LET'S HEAD TO THE DOCK TO FIND A RIDE ***HOME.***

G: *This is the last time we see Katara and Sokka in this series. It's a bit sad, since Sokka so often brightens the atmosphere. We will be seeing them more in the next series,* North and South*!*

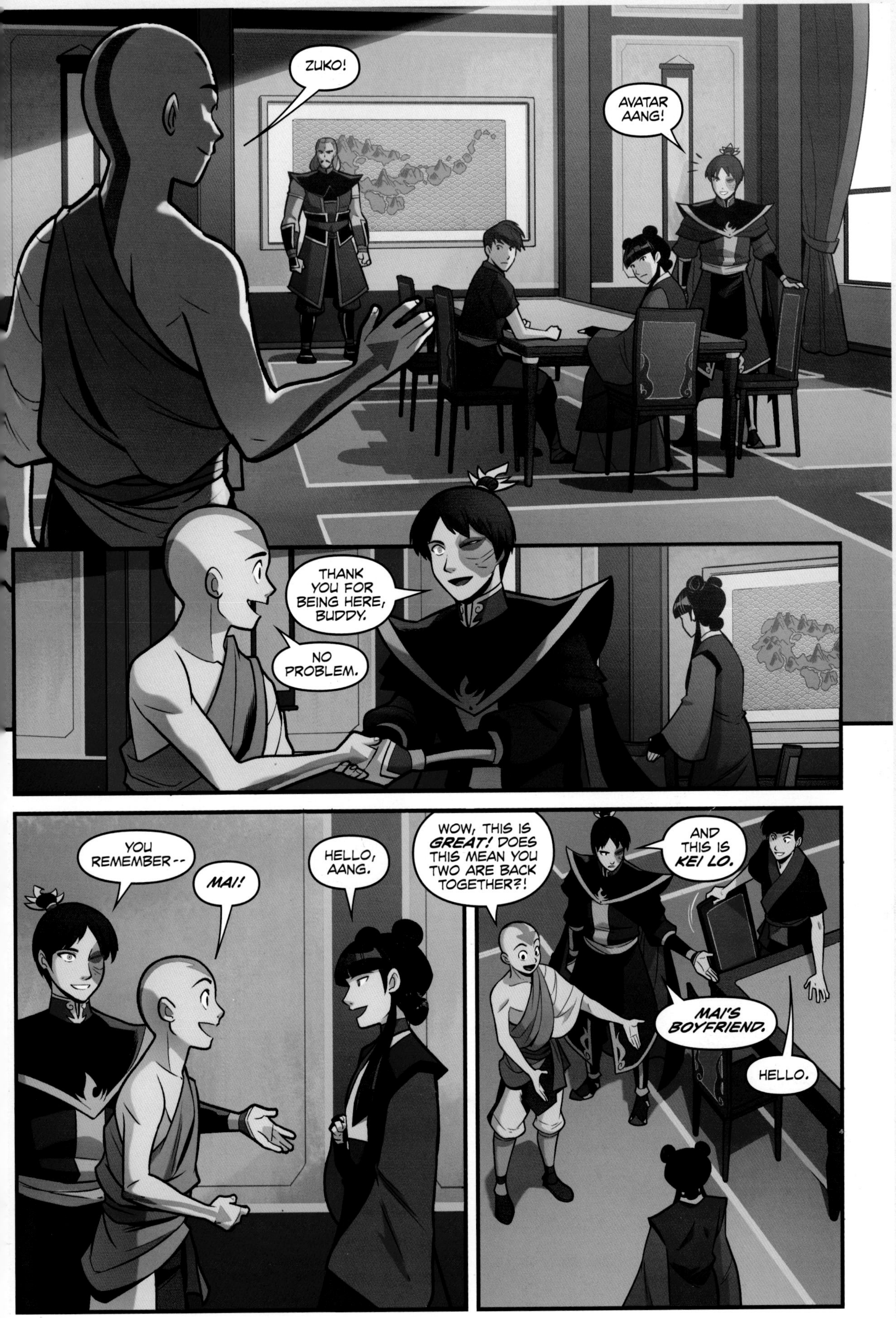
ZUKO!
AVATAR AANG!
THANK YOU FOR BEING HERE, BUDDY.
NO PROBLEM.
YOU REMEMBER--
MAI!
HELLO, AANG.
WOW, THIS IS *GREAT!* DOES THIS MEAN YOU TWO ARE BACK TOGETHER?!
AND THIS IS *KEI LO.*
MAI'S BOYFRIEND.
HELLO.

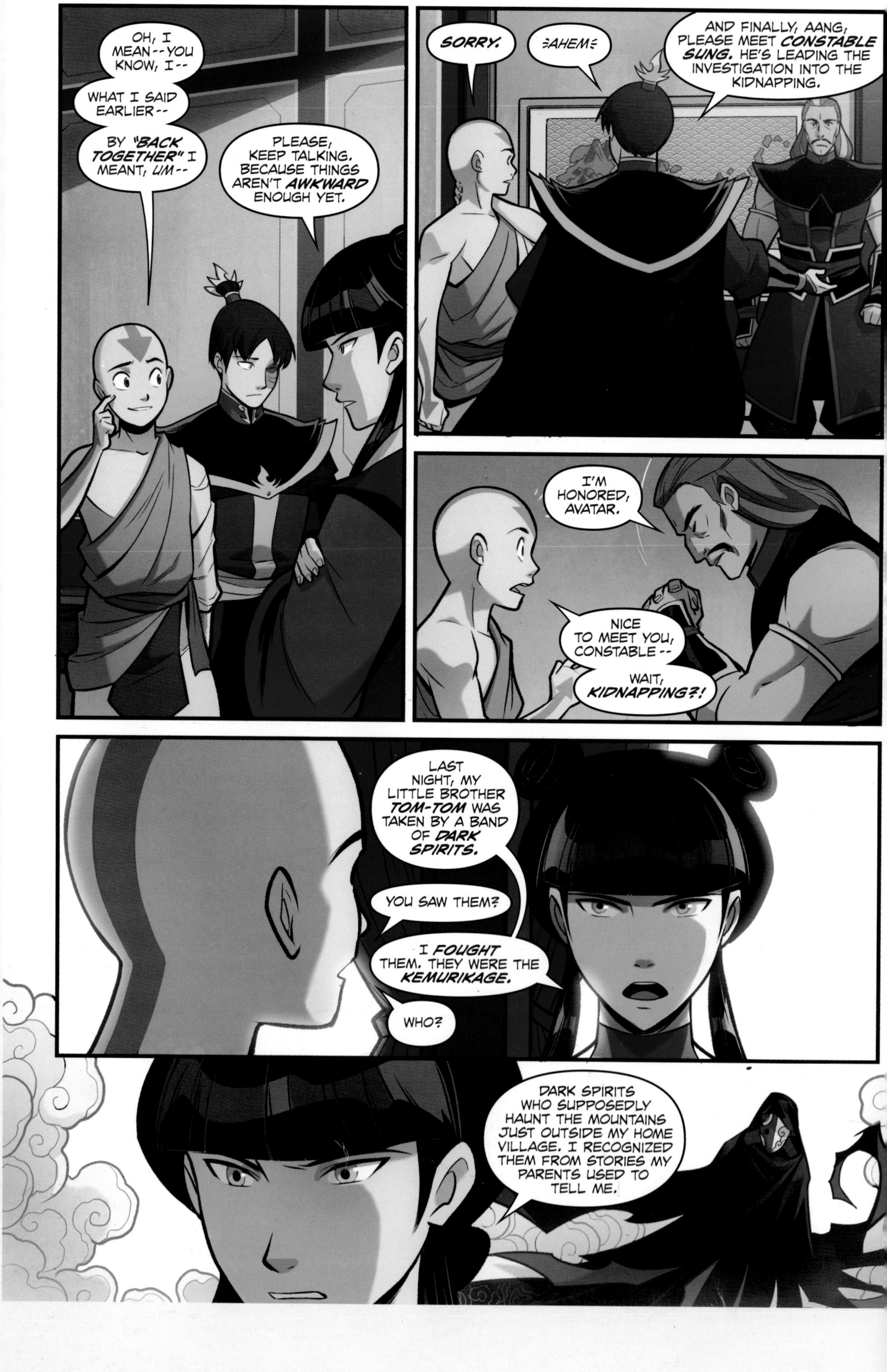
OH, I MEAN--YOU KNOW, I--
WHAT I SAID EARLIER--
BY "BACK TOGETHER" I MEANT, UM--
PLEASE, KEEP TALKING. BECAUSE THINGS AREN'T AWKWARD ENOUGH YET.
SORRY.
AHEM
AND FINALLY, AANG, PLEASE MEET CONSTABLE SUNG. HE'S LEADING THE INVESTIGATION INTO THE KIDNAPPING.
I'M HONORED, AVATAR.
NICE TO MEET YOU, CONSTABLE--
WAIT, KIDNAPPING?!
LAST NIGHT, MY LITTLE BROTHER TOM-TOM WAS TAKEN BY A BAND OF DARK SPIRITS.
YOU SAW THEM?
I FOUGHT THEM. THEY WERE THE KEMURIKAGE.
WHO?
DARK SPIRITS WHO SUPPOSEDLY HAUNT THE MOUNTAINS JUST OUTSIDE MY HOME VILLAGE. I RECOGNIZED THEM FROM STORIES MY PARENTS USED TO TELL ME.

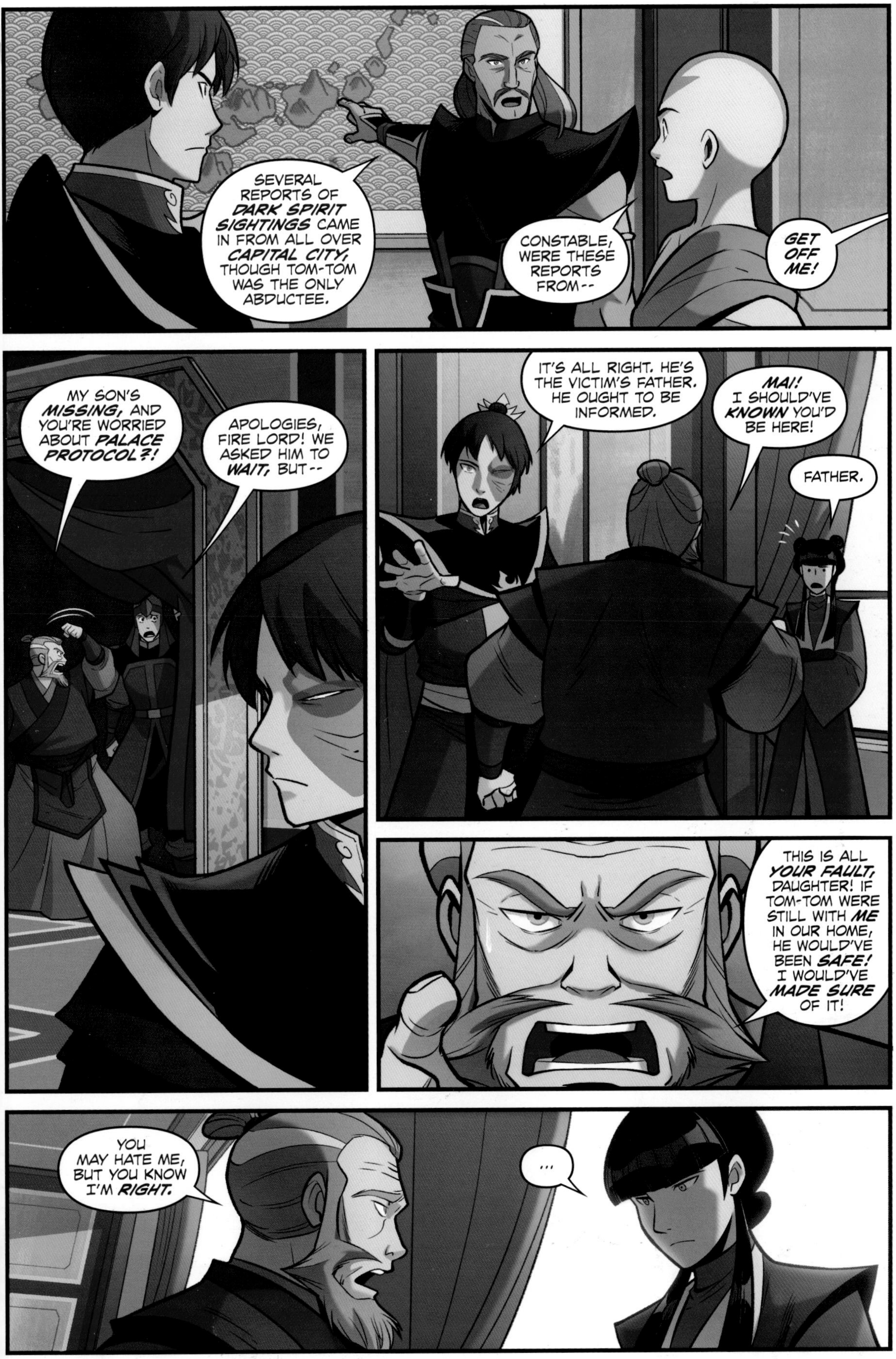
SEVERAL REPORTS OF DARK SPIRIT SIGHTINGS CAME IN FROM ALL OVER CAPITAL CITY, THOUGH TOM-TOM WAS THE ONLY ABDUCTEE.
CONSTABLE, WERE THESE REPORTS FROM--
GET OFF ME!
MY SON'S MISSING, AND YOU'RE WORRIED ABOUT PALACE PROTOCOL?!
APOLOGIES, FIRE LORD! WE ASKED HIM TO WAIT, BUT--
IT'S ALL RIGHT. HE'S THE VICTIM'S FATHER. HE OUGHT TO BE INFORMED.
MAI! I SHOULD'VE KNOWN YOU'D BE HERE!
FATHER.
THIS IS ALL YOUR FAULT, DAUGHTER! IF TOM-TOM WERE STILL WITH ME IN OUR HOME, HE WOULD'VE BEEN SAFE! I WOULD'VE MADE SURE OF IT!
YOU MAY HATE ME, BUT YOU KNOW I'M RIGHT.
...

G: *Fear can be a good thing—paying attention to our fears can keep us safe. But when does fear cross the line? When does fear become a hindrance rather than a help? That's the question Zuko's struggling with.*

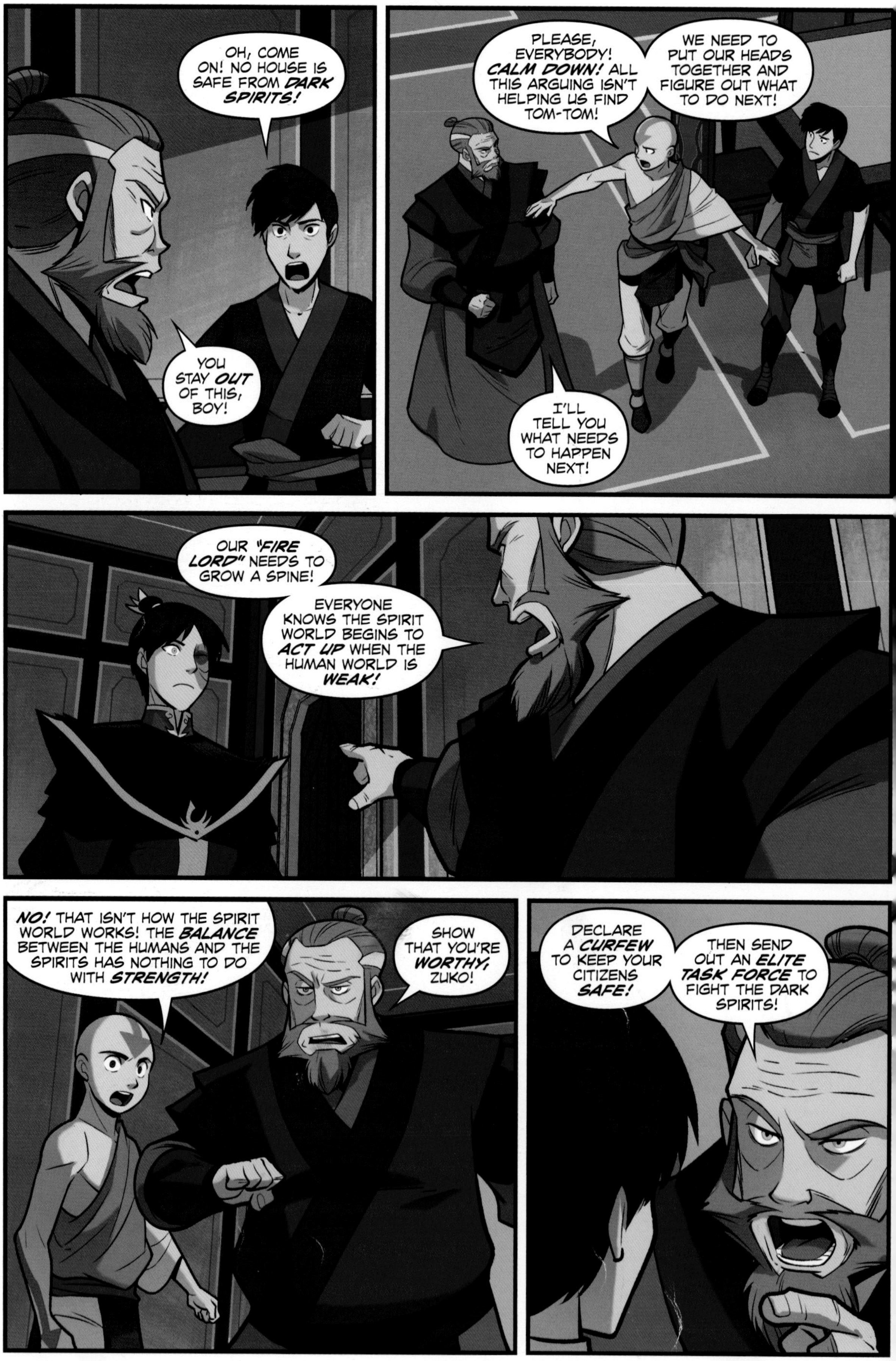
OH, COME ON! NO HOUSE IS SAFE FROM DARK SPIRITS!
YOU STAY OUT OF THIS, BOY!
PLEASE, EVERYBODY! CALM DOWN! ALL THIS ARGUING ISN'T HELPING US FIND TOM-TOM!
WE NEED TO PUT OUR HEADS TOGETHER AND FIGURE OUT WHAT TO DO NEXT!
I'LL TELL YOU WHAT NEEDS TO HAPPEN NEXT!
OUR "FIRE LORD" NEEDS TO GROW A SPINE!
EVERYONE KNOWS THE SPIRIT WORLD BEGINS TO ACT UP WHEN THE HUMAN WORLD IS WEAK!
NO! THAT ISN'T HOW THE SPIRIT WORLD WORKS! THE BALANCE BETWEEN THE HUMANS AND THE SPIRITS HAS NOTHING TO DO WITH STRENGTH!
SHOW THAT YOU'RE WORTHY, ZUKO!
DECLARE A CURFEW TO KEEP YOUR CITIZENS SAFE!
THEN SEND OUT AN ELITE TASK FORCE TO FIGHT THE DARK SPIRITS!

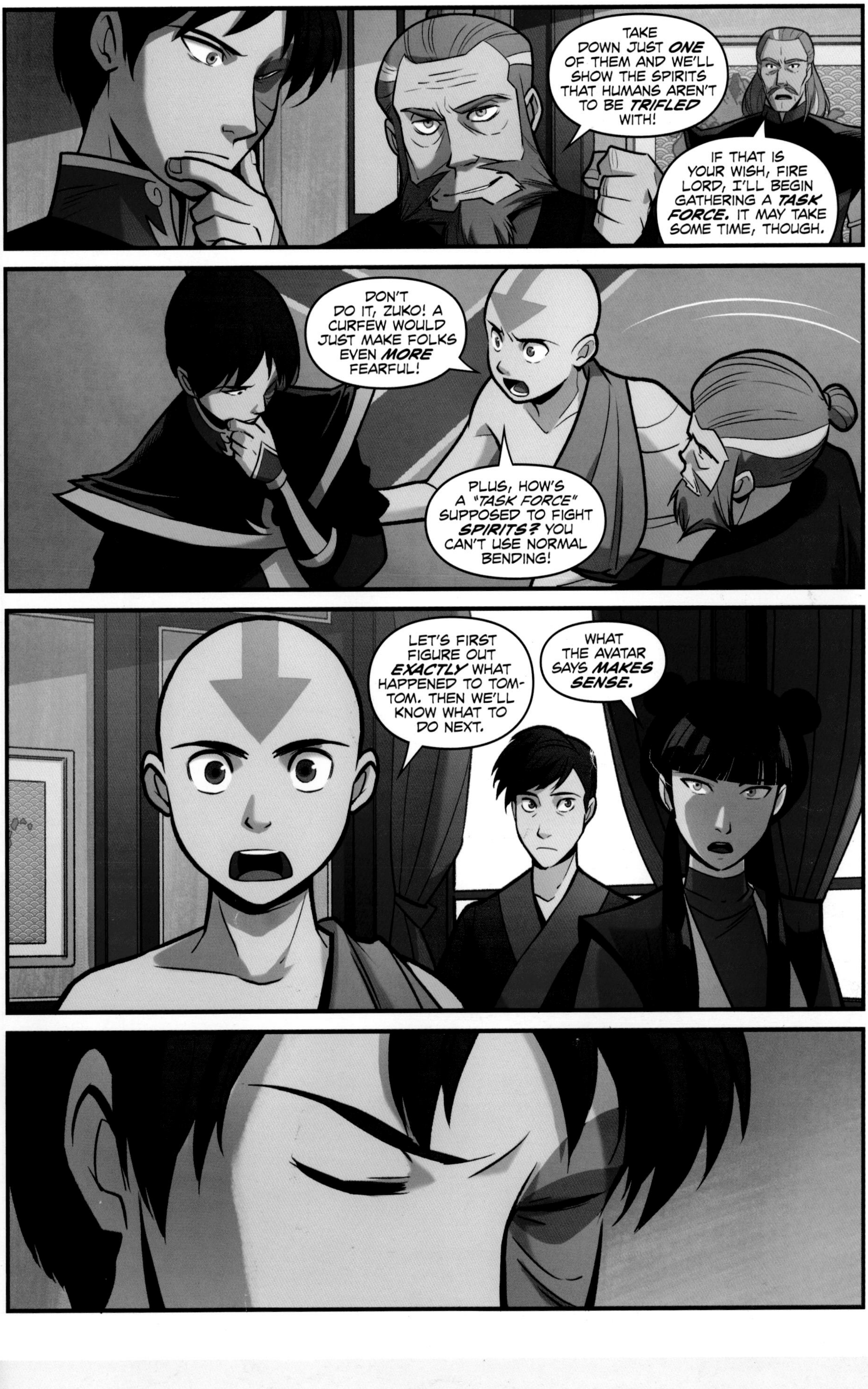
TAKE DOWN JUST ONE OF THEM AND WE'LL SHOW THE SPIRITS THAT HUMANS AREN'T TO BE TRIFLED WITH!
IF THAT IS YOUR WISH, FIRE LORD, I'LL BEGIN GATHERING A TASK FORCE. IT MAY TAKE SOME TIME, THOUGH.
DON'T DO IT, ZUKO! A CURFEW WOULD JUST MAKE FOLKS EVEN MORE FEARFUL!
PLUS, HOW'S A "TASK FORCE" SUPPOSED TO FIGHT SPIRITS? YOU CAN'T USE NORMAL BENDING!
LET'S FIRST FIGURE OUT EXACTLY WHAT HAPPENED TO TOM-TOM. THEN WE'LL KNOW WHAT TO DO NEXT.
WHAT THE AVATAR SAYS MAKES SENSE.

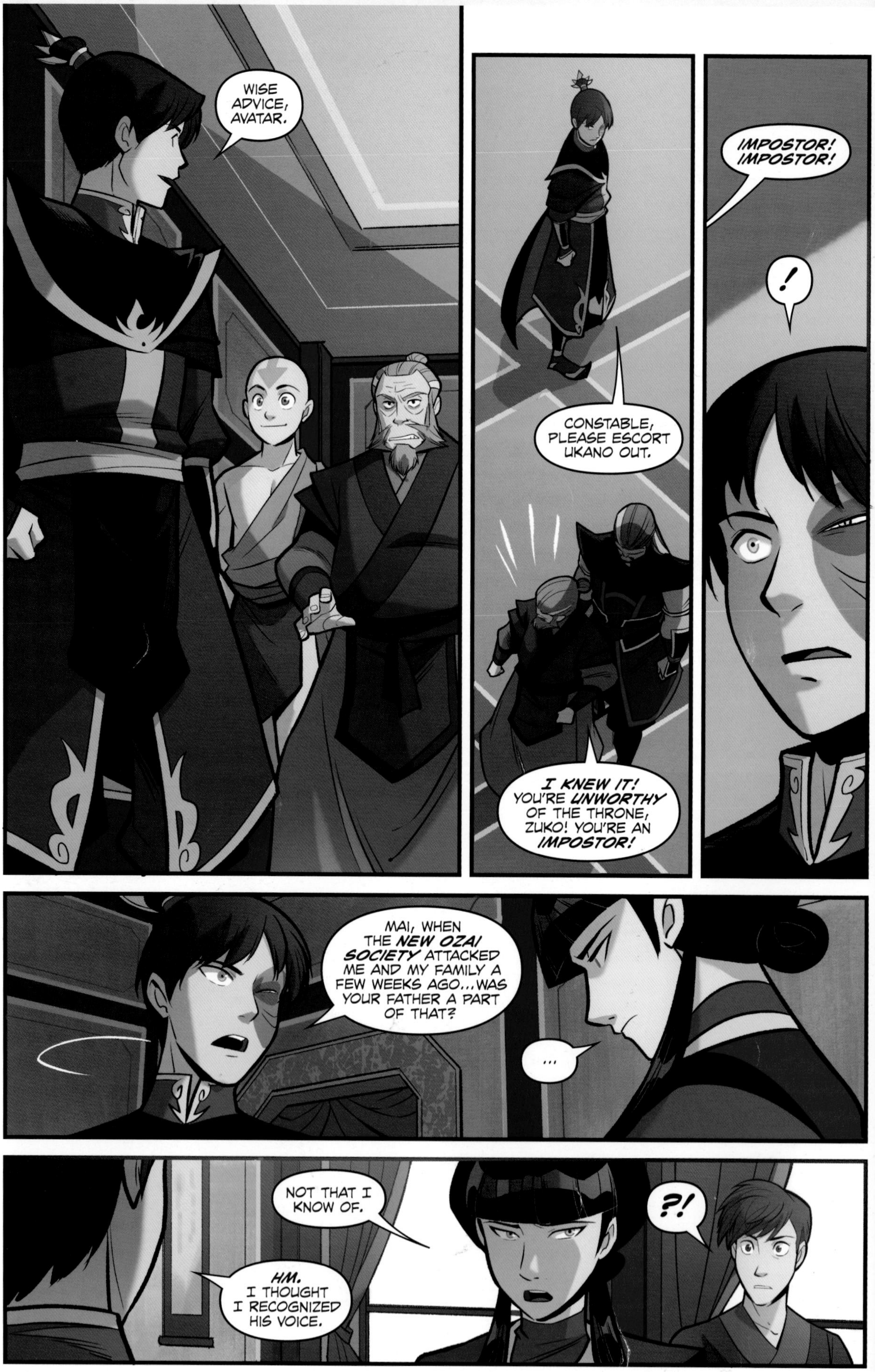
WISE ADVICE, AVATAR.
CONSTABLE, PLEASE ESCORT UKANO OUT.
I KNEW IT! YOU'RE UNWORTHY OF THE THRONE, ZUKO! YOU'RE AN IMPOSTOR!
IMPOSTOR! IMPOSTOR!
!
MAI, WHEN THE NEW OZAI SOCIETY ATTACKED ME AND MY FAMILY A FEW WEEKS AGO...WAS YOUR FATHER A PART OF THAT?
...
NOT THAT I KNOW OF.
HM. I THOUGHT I RECOGNIZED HIS VOICE.
?!

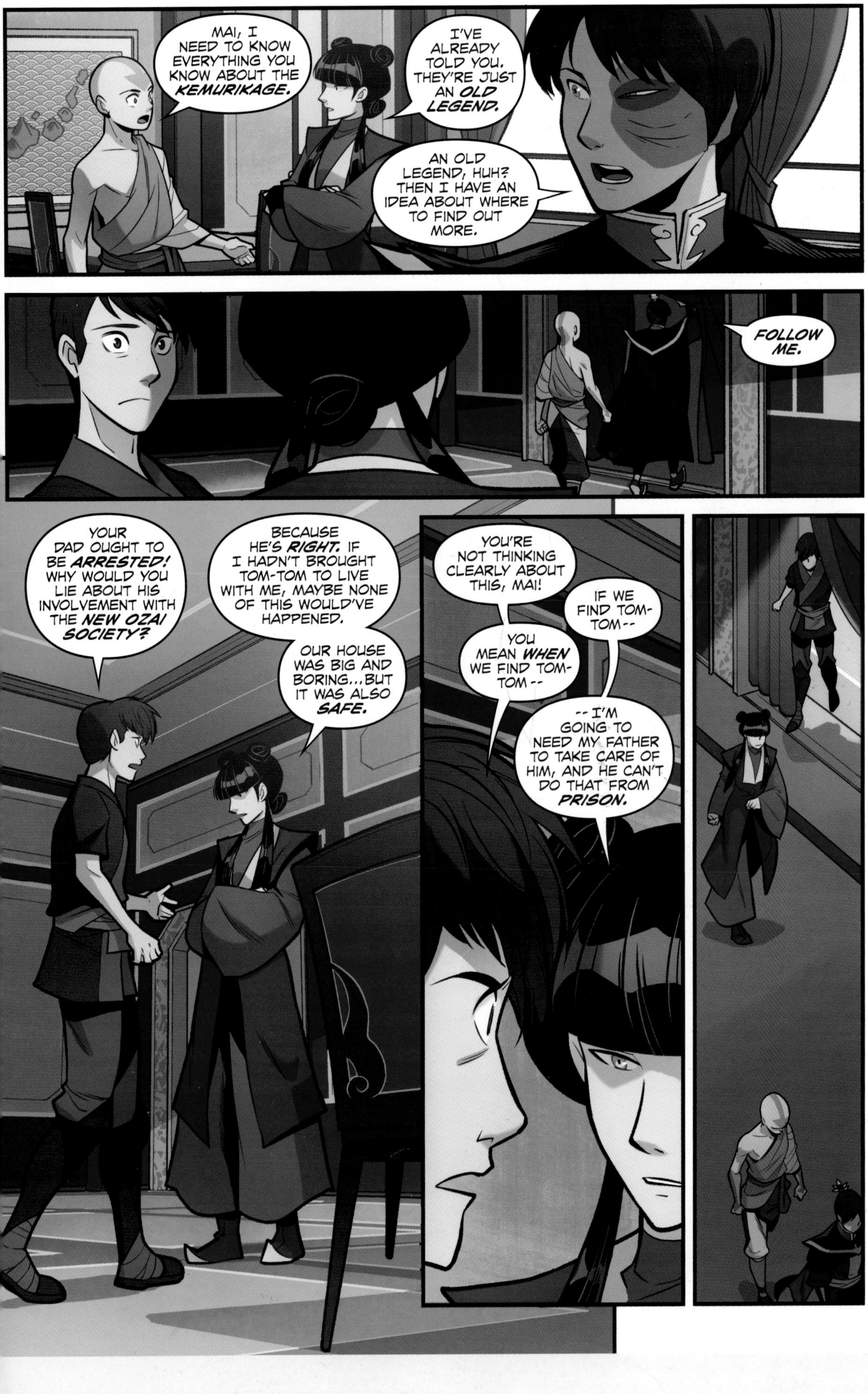
MAI, I NEED TO KNOW EVERYTHING YOU KNOW ABOUT THE KEMURIKAGE.
I'VE ALREADY TOLD YOU. THEY'RE JUST AN OLD LEGEND.
AN OLD LEGEND, HUH? THEN I HAVE AN IDEA ABOUT WHERE TO FIND OUT MORE.
FOLLOW ME.
YOUR DAD OUGHT TO BE ARRESTED! WHY WOULD YOU LIE ABOUT HIS INVOLVEMENT WITH THE NEW OZAI SOCIETY?
BECAUSE HE'S RIGHT. IF I HADN'T BROUGHT TOM-TOM TO LIVE WITH ME, MAYBE NONE OF THIS WOULD'VE HAPPENED.
OUR HOUSE WAS BIG AND BORING...BUT IT WAS ALSO SAFE.
YOU'RE NOT THINKING CLEARLY ABOUT THIS, MAI!
IF WE FIND TOM-TOM--
YOU MEAN WHEN WE FIND TOM-TOM--
--I'M GOING TO NEED MY FATHER TO TAKE CARE OF HIM, AND HE CAN'T DO THAT FROM PRISON.

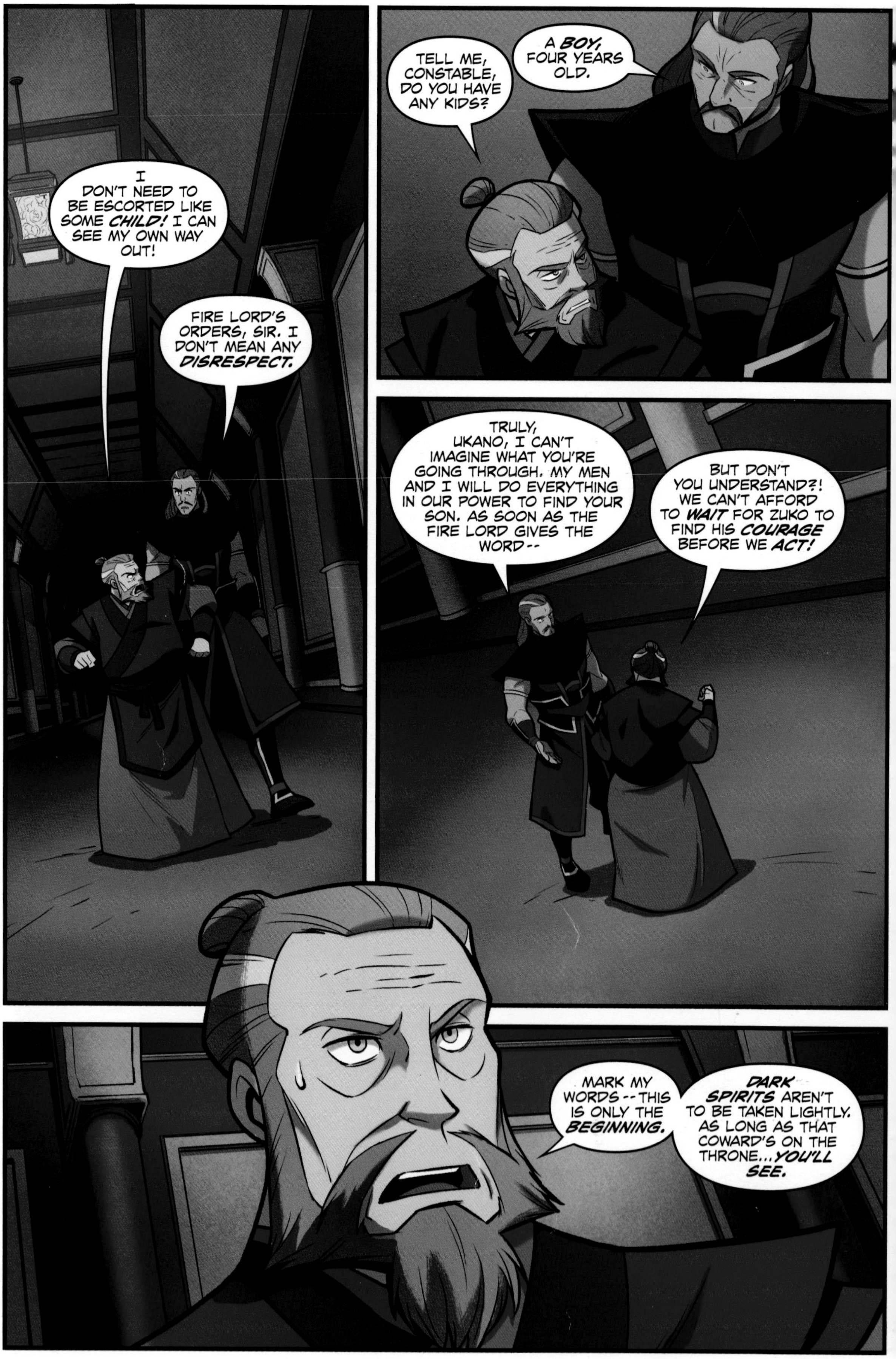
I DON'T NEED TO BE ESCORTED LIKE SOME CHILD! I CAN SEE MY OWN WAY OUT!
FIRE LORD'S ORDERS, SIR. I DON'T MEAN ANY DISRESPECT.
TELL ME, CONSTABLE, DO YOU HAVE ANY KIDS?
A BOY. FOUR YEARS OLD.
TRULY, UKANO, I CAN'T IMAGINE WHAT YOU'RE GOING THROUGH. MY MEN AND I WILL DO EVERYTHING IN OUR POWER TO FIND YOUR SON. AS SOON AS THE FIRE LORD GIVES THE WORD--
BUT DON'T YOU UNDERSTAND?! WE CAN'T AFFORD TO WAIT FOR ZUKO TO FIND HIS COURAGE BEFORE WE ACT!
MARK MY WORDS--THIS IS ONLY THE BEGINNING.
DARK SPIRITS AREN'T TO BE TAKEN LIGHTLY. AS LONG AS THAT COWARD'S ON THE THRONE...YOU'LL SEE.

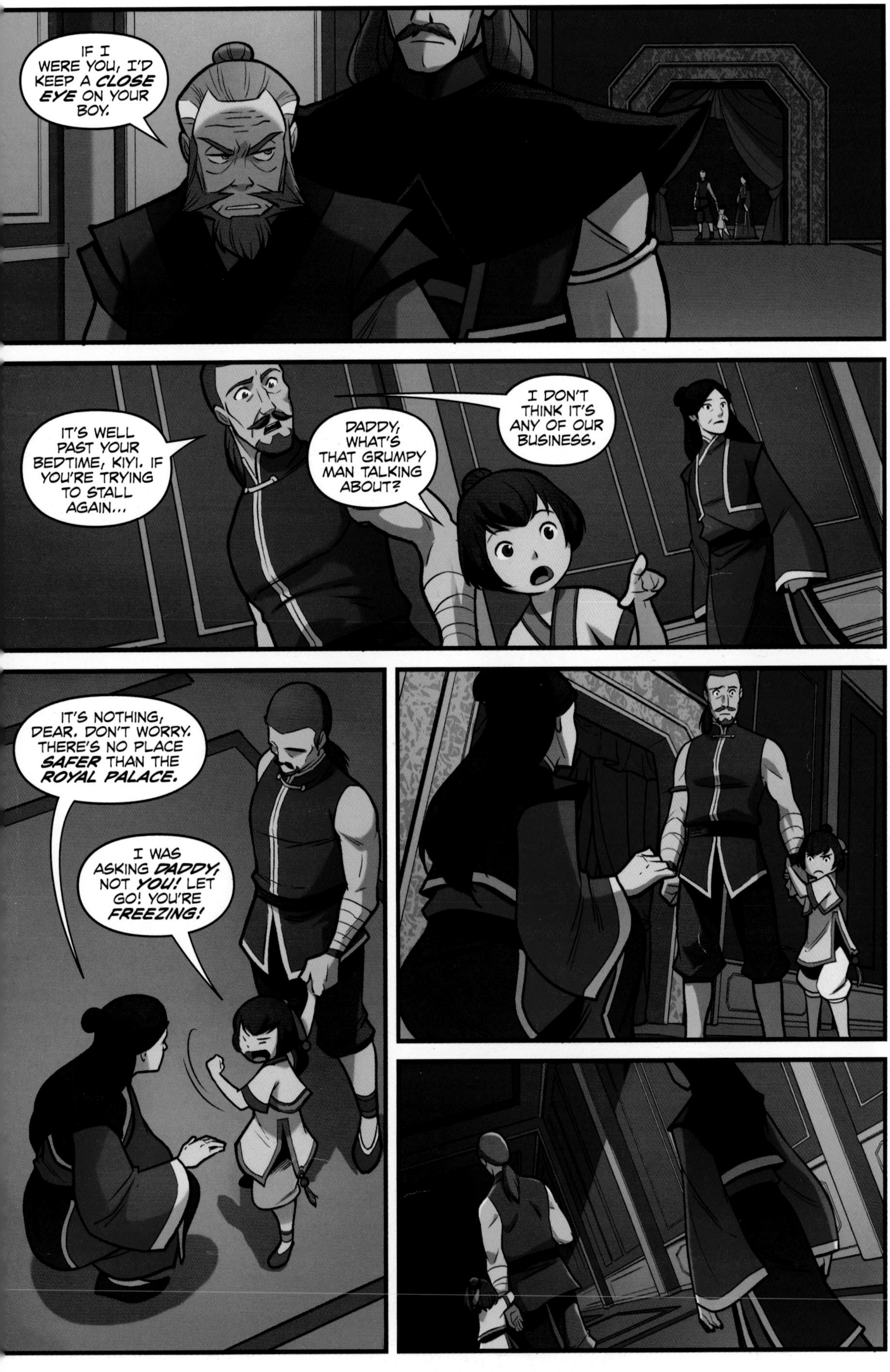
IF I WERE YOU, I'D KEEP A CLOSE EYE ON YOUR BOY.
IT'S WELL PAST YOUR BEDTIME, KIYI. IF YOU'RE TRYING TO STALL AGAIN...
DADDY, WHAT'S THAT GRUMPY MAN TALKING ABOUT?
I DON'T THINK IT'S ANY OF OUR BUSINESS.
IT'S NOTHING, DEAR. DON'T WORRY. THERE'S NO PLACE SAFER THAN THE ROYAL PALACE.
I WAS ASKING DADDY, NOT YOU! LET GO! YOU'RE FREEZING!

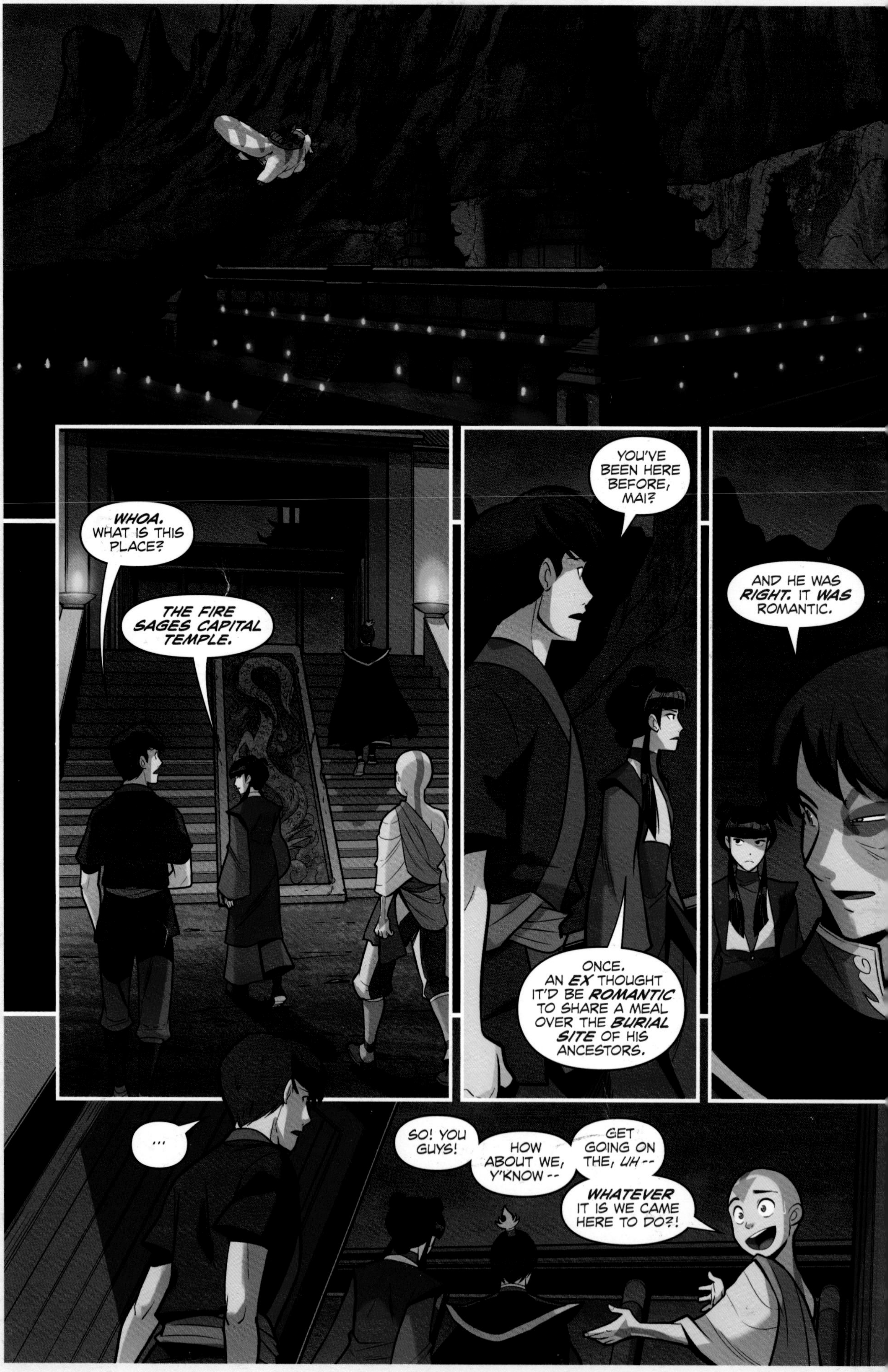
WHOA. WHAT IS THIS PLACE?
THE FIRE SAGES CAPITAL TEMPLE.
YOU'VE BEEN HERE BEFORE, MAI?
ONCE. AN EX THOUGHT IT'D BE ROMANTIC TO SHARE A MEAL OVER THE BURIAL SITE OF HIS ANCESTORS.
AND HE WAS RIGHT. IT WAS ROMANTIC.
...
SO! YOU GUYS!
HOW ABOUT WE, Y'KNOW --
GET GOING ON THE, UH --
WHATEVER IT IS WE CAME HERE TO DO?!

SO GOOD TO SEE YOU AGAIN, SHYU!

I'M SORRY IT'S BEEN SO LONG SINCE MY LAST VISIT. THINGS HAVE BEEN *BUSY.*

GREAT SAGE SHYU!

FIRE LORD! AVATAR! WHAT A PLEASANT SURPRISE!

YOU KNOW WHAT *FIRE SAGE KAJA* USED TO SAY -- THE *BUSIER* WE ARE, THE MORE ATTENTION WE MUST PAY TO OUR *INTERIOR LIFE.*

TRUE, BUT--

MY BROTHER SAGES AND I RECENTLY REVIVED A COUPLE OF *OLD PRACTICES* THAT MAY BE OF INTEREST TO YOU! IN FACT, I'M TEACHING A NEW *MEDITATION CLASS* THAT--

I'D LOVE TO HEAR MORE, SHYU -- I SWEAR -- BUT RIGHT NOW, MY FRIENDS AND I NEED TO GET INTO THE *DRAGONBONE CATACOMBS.*

≡SIGH≡ OF COURSE.

GLY: *The Fire Sages Capital Temple and the Dragonbone Catacombs beneath first showed up in the episode "The Avatar and the Fire Lord."*

Shyu, however, wasn't in that episode. He first appeared in "Avatar Roku." Shyu was the only Fire Sage still loyal to the old ways. On Crescent Island, he helped Aang get in touch with his past life.

Although we don't show it in the comics, Shyu was appointed Great Sage after the end of the war.

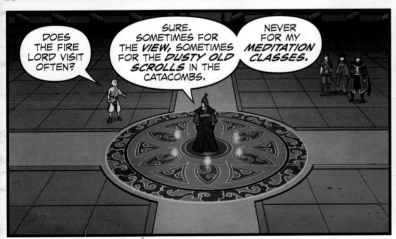

DOES THE FIRE LORD VISIT OFTEN?

SURE. SOMETIMES FOR THE *VIEW,* SOMETIMES FOR THE *DUSTY OLD SCROLLS* IN THE CATACOMBS.

NEVER FOR MY *MEDITATION CLASSES.*

GLY: *I just loved the way the Dragonbone Catacombs opened up in "The Avatar and the Fire Lord." That's why we gave it a full page here.*

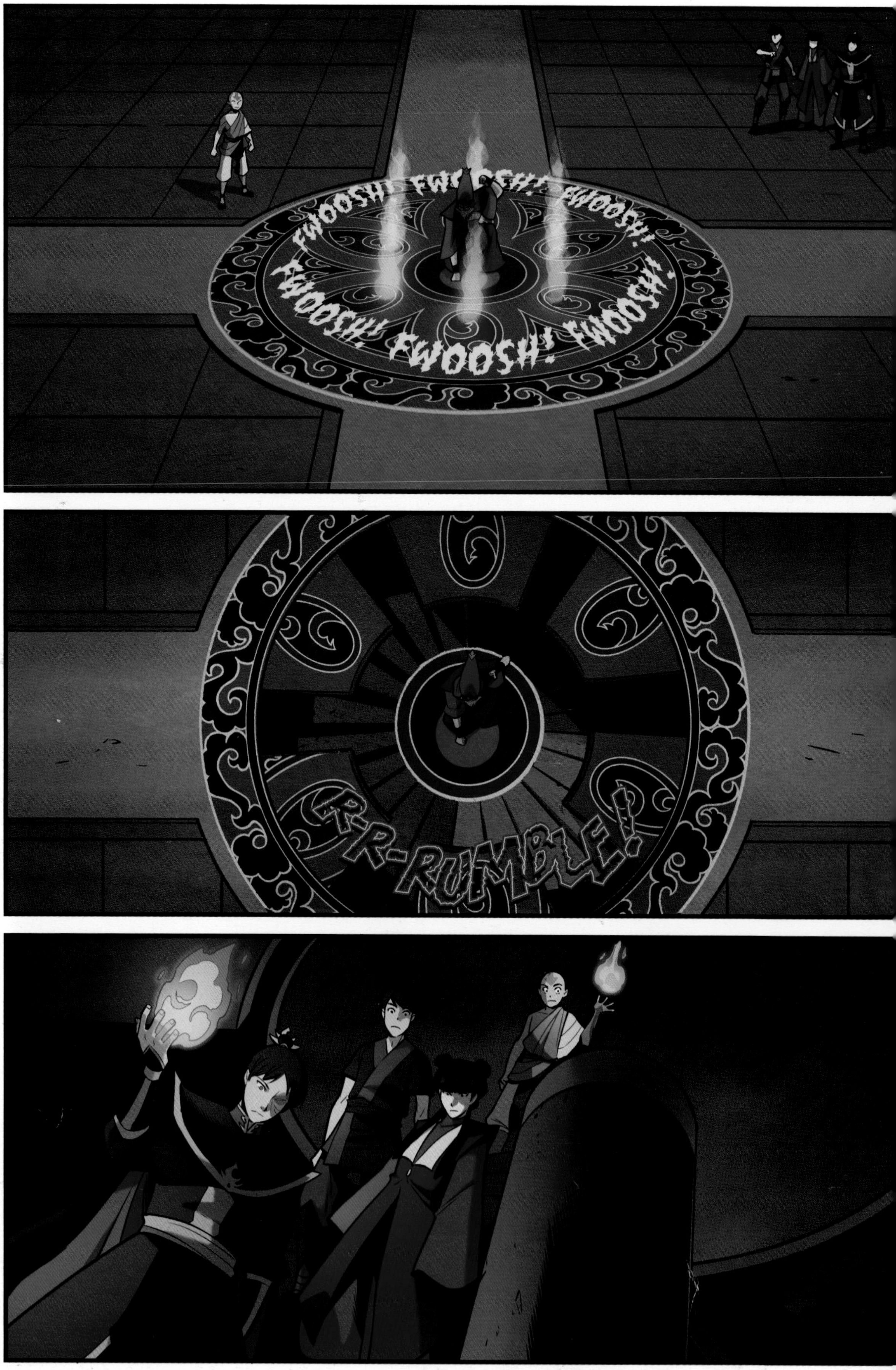
FWOOSH!
FWOOSH!
FWOOSH!
FWOOSH!
FWOOSH!
FWOOSH!
R-R-RUMBLE!

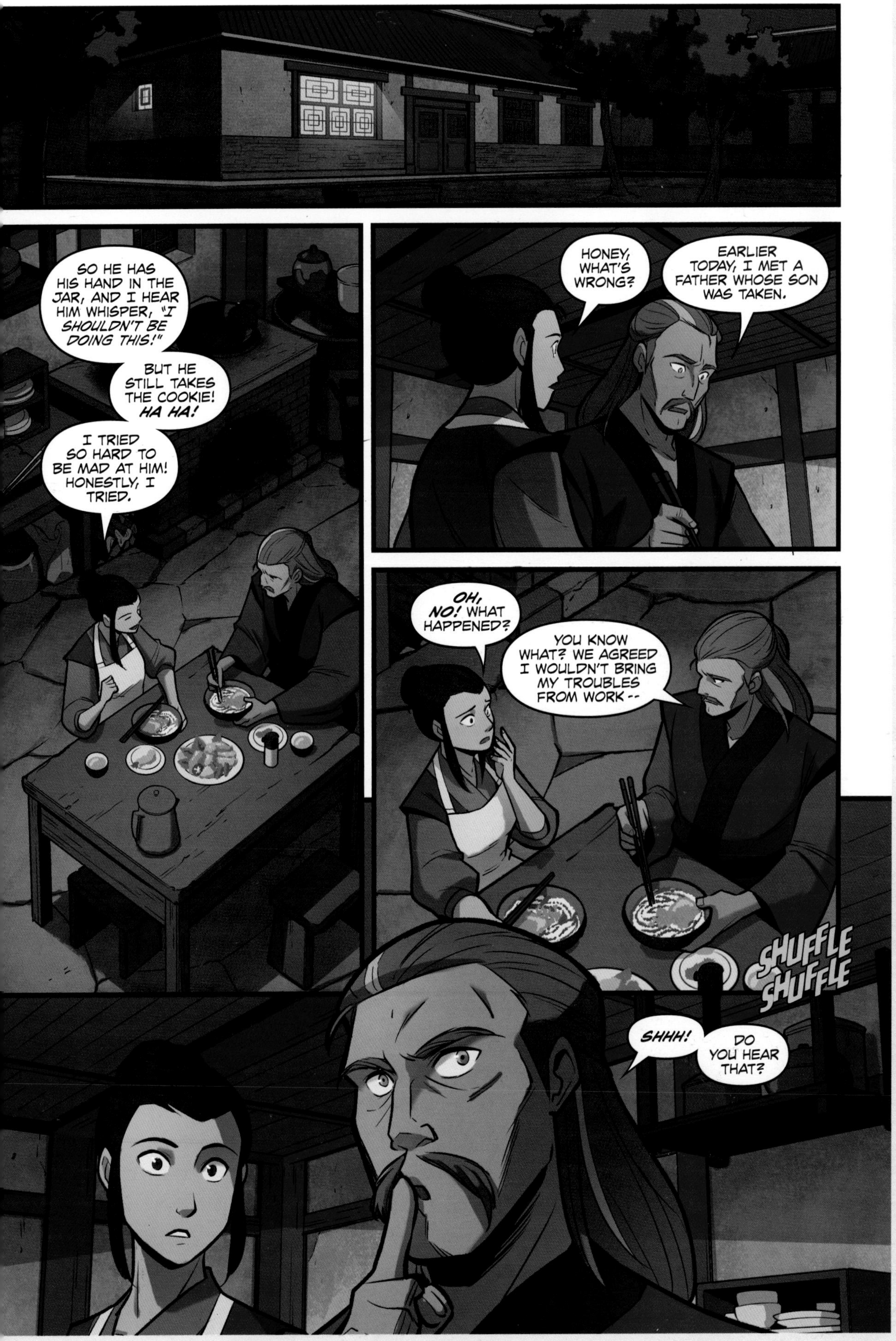
SO HE HAS HIS HAND IN THE JAR, AND I HEAR HIM WHISPER, "I SHOULDN'T BE DOING THIS!"
BUT HE STILL TAKES THE COOKIE! HA HA!
I TRIED SO HARD TO BE MAD AT HIM! HONESTLY, I TRIED.
HONEY, WHAT'S WRONG?
EARLIER TODAY, I MET A FATHER WHOSE SON WAS TAKEN.
OH, NO! WHAT HAPPENED?
YOU KNOW WHAT? WE AGREED I WOULDN'T BRING MY TROUBLES FROM WORK--
SHUFFLE SHUFFLE
SHHH!
DO YOU HEAR THAT?

GLY: *One of my kids actually did something like this.*

G: *Those two are eating udon. We always have fun thinking up meals and cooking scenes.*

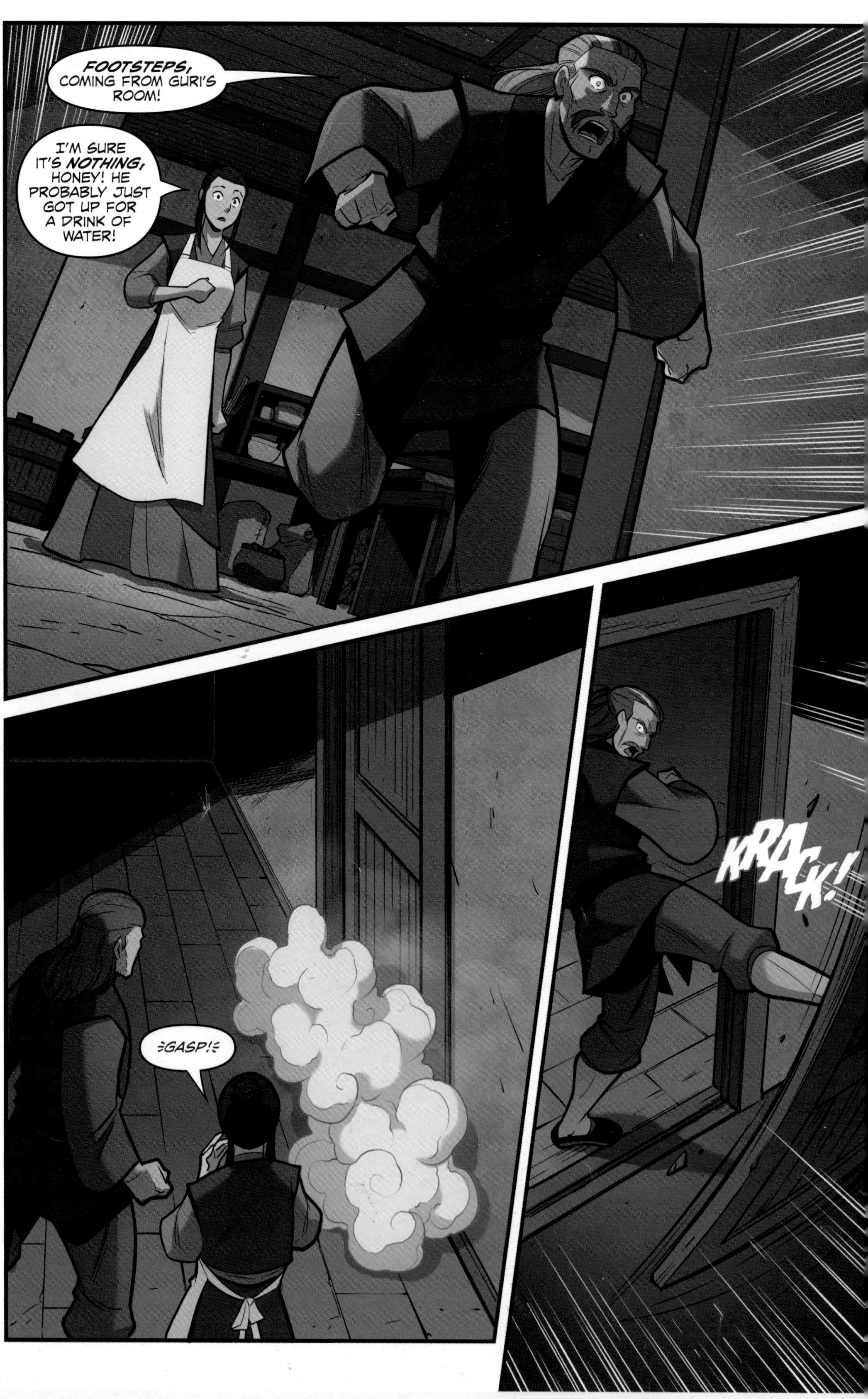
FOOTSTEPS, COMING FROM GURI'S ROOM!
I'M SURE IT'S NOTHING, HONEY! HE PROBABLY JUST GOT UP FOR A DRINK OF WATER!
KRACK!
GASP!

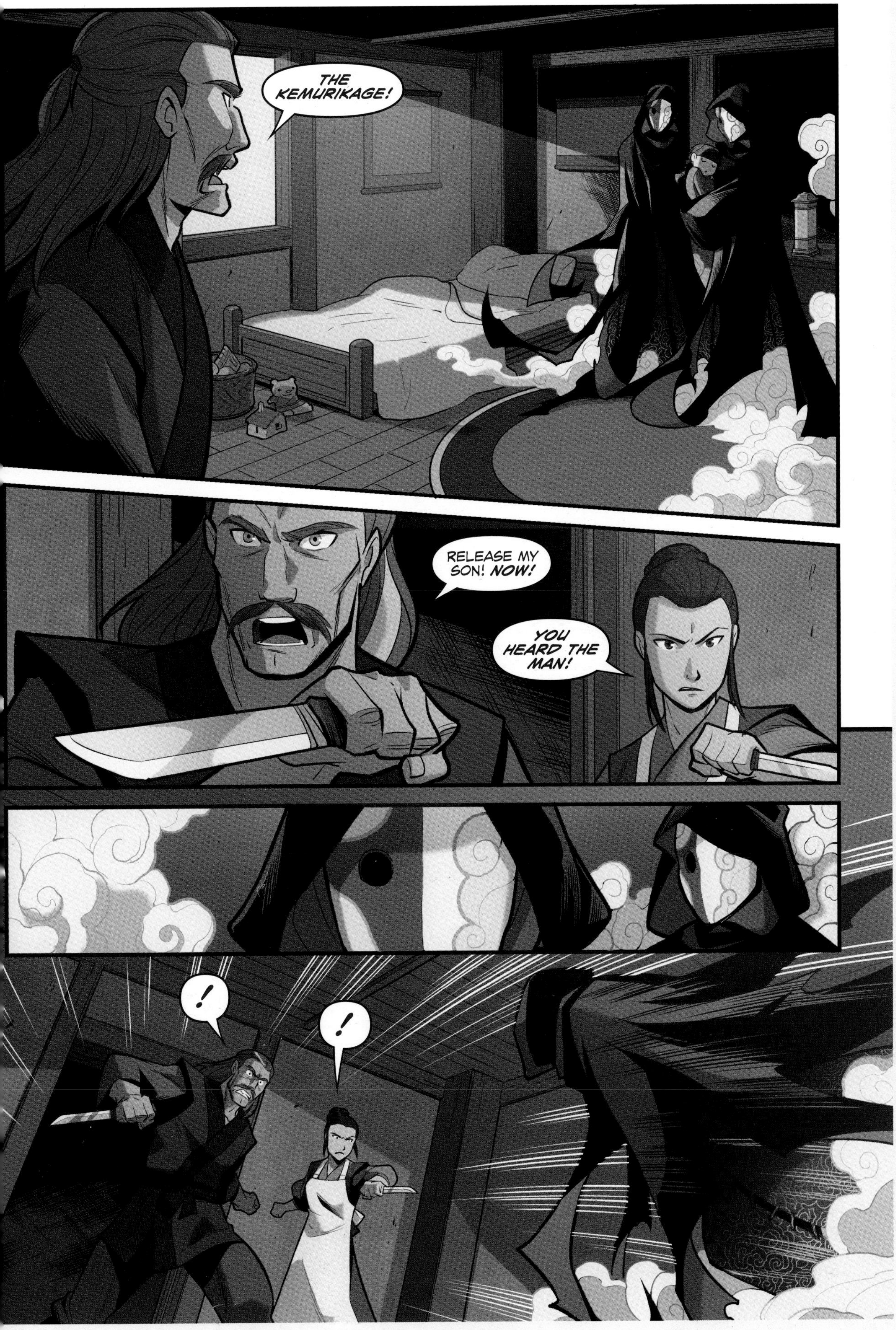
THE KEMURIKAGE!
RELEASE MY SON! NOW!
YOU HEARD THE MAN!
!
!

GLY: *In the first draft of the script, only the dad goes into the room to fight the Kemurikage. It didn't feel right . . . It didn't feel realistic. Moms fight for their kids. Always.*

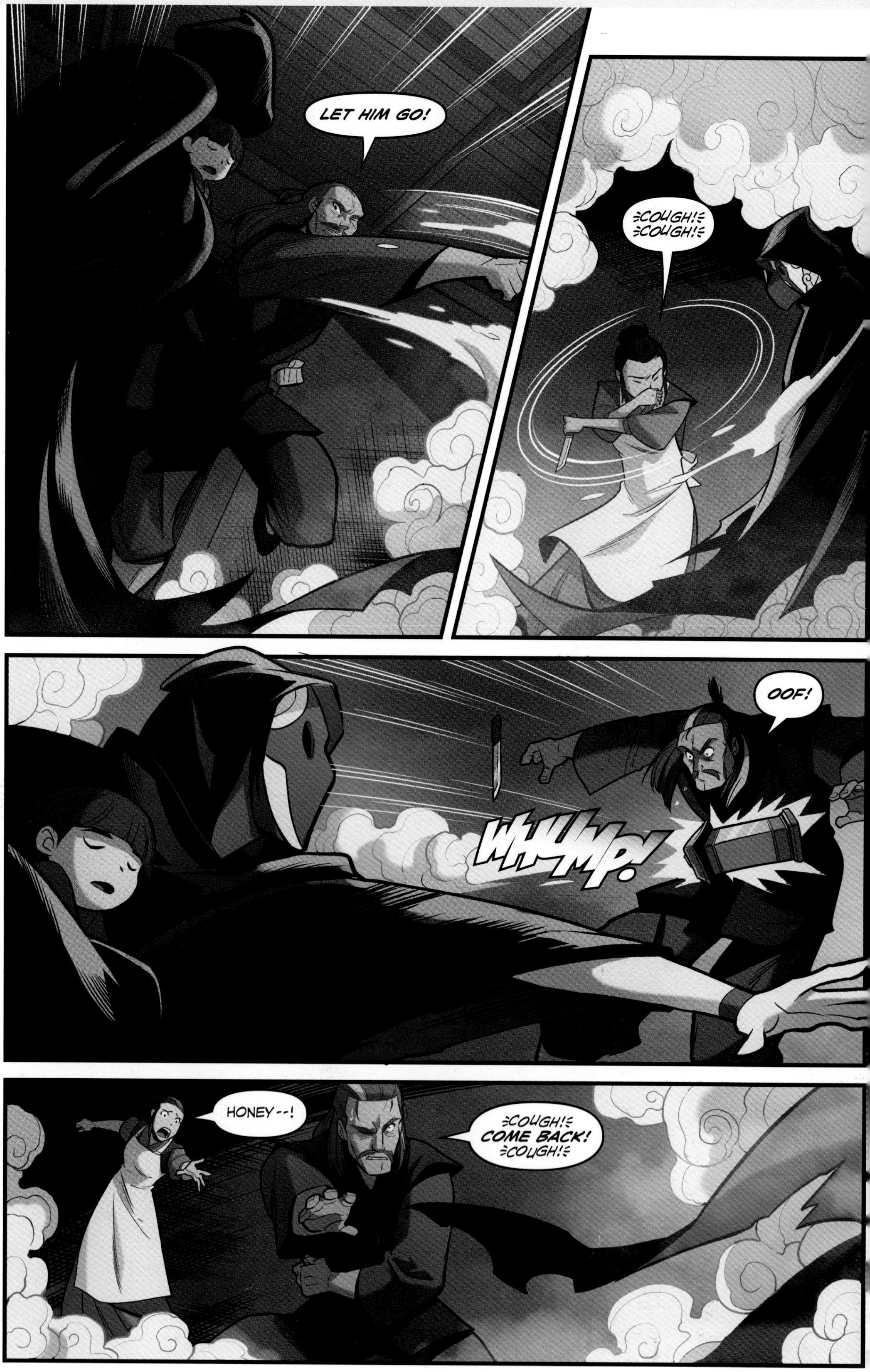
LET HIM GO!
COUGH! COUGH!
OOF!
WHUMP!
HONEY--!
COUGH! COME BACK! COUGH!

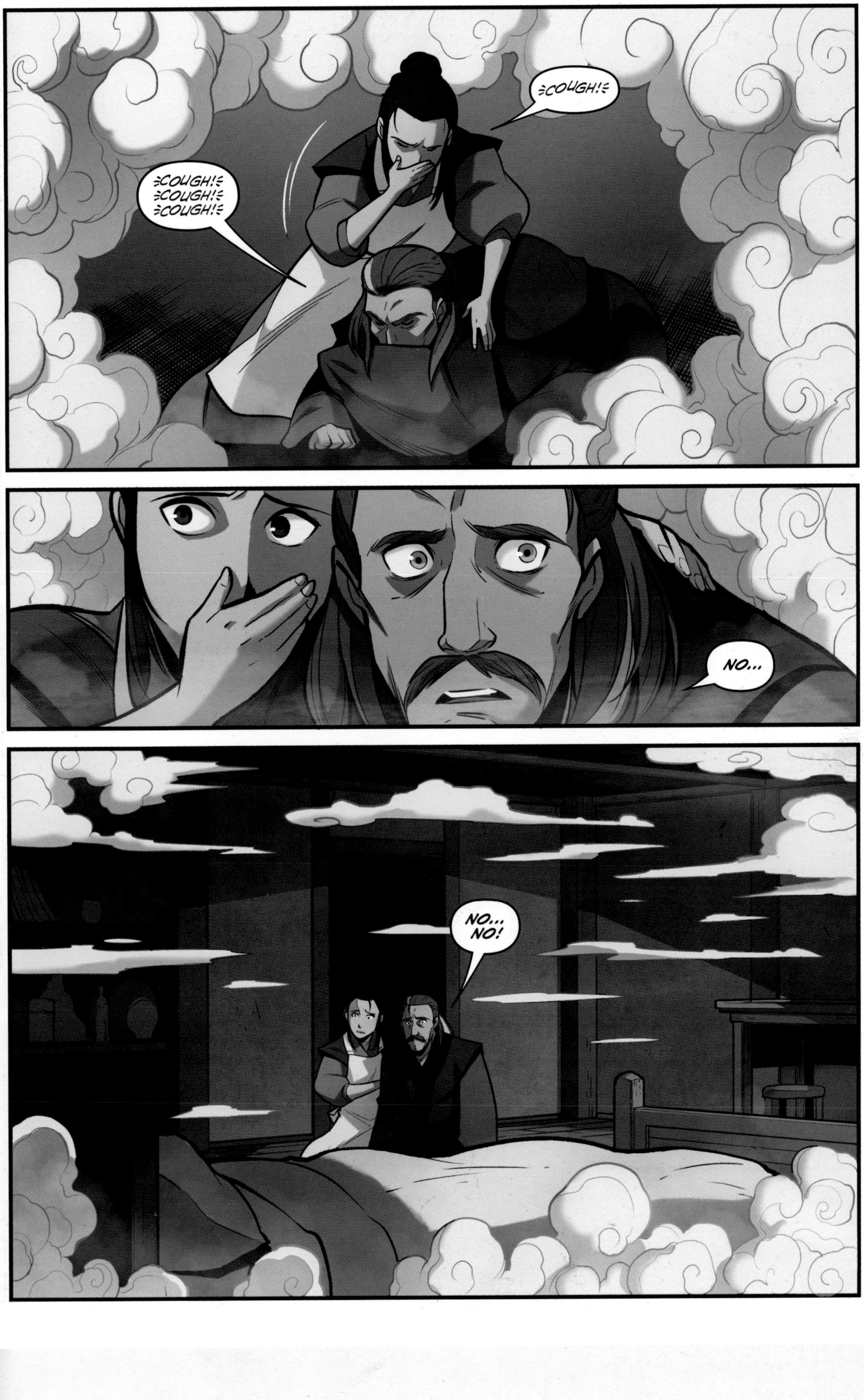
COUGH!
COUGH! COUGH! COUGH!
NO...
NO... NO!

G: This mural describes the history of the Fire Kingdom, but we had a hard time figuring out how these murals should look. We were inspired by the episode "The Firebending Masters."

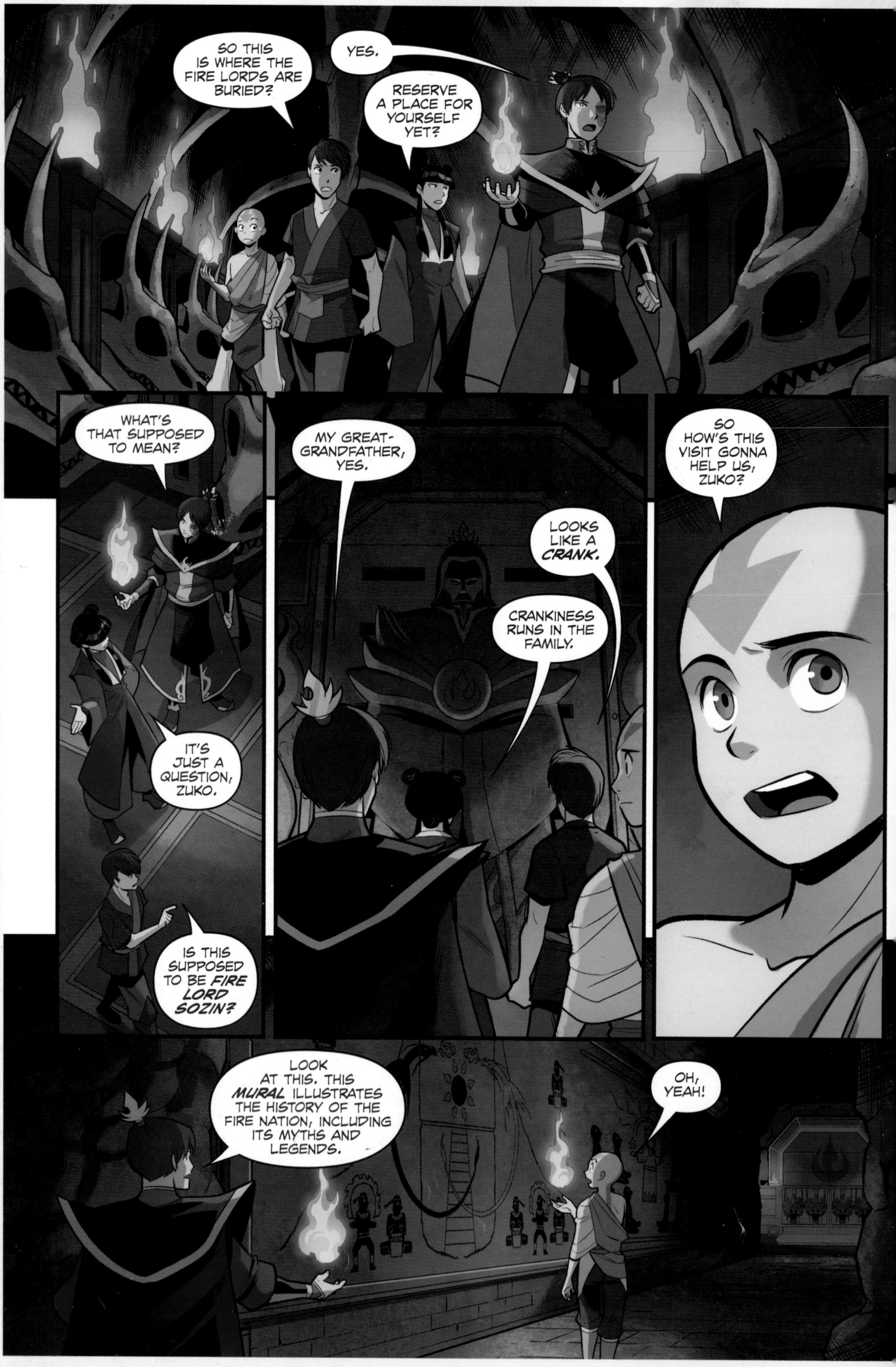
SO THIS IS WHERE THE FIRE LORDS ARE BURIED?
YES.
RESERVE A PLACE FOR YOURSELF YET?
WHAT'S THAT SUPPOSED TO MEAN?
IT'S JUST A QUESTION, ZUKO.
IS THIS SUPPOSED TO BE FIRE LORD SOZIN?
MY GREAT-GRANDFATHER, YES.
LOOKS LIKE A CRANK.
CRANKINESS RUNS IN THE FAMILY.
SO HOW'S THIS VISIT GONNA HELP US, ZUKO?
LOOK AT THIS. THIS MURAL ILLUSTRATES THE HISTORY OF THE FIRE NATION, INCLUDING ITS MYTHS AND LEGENDS.
OH, YEAH!

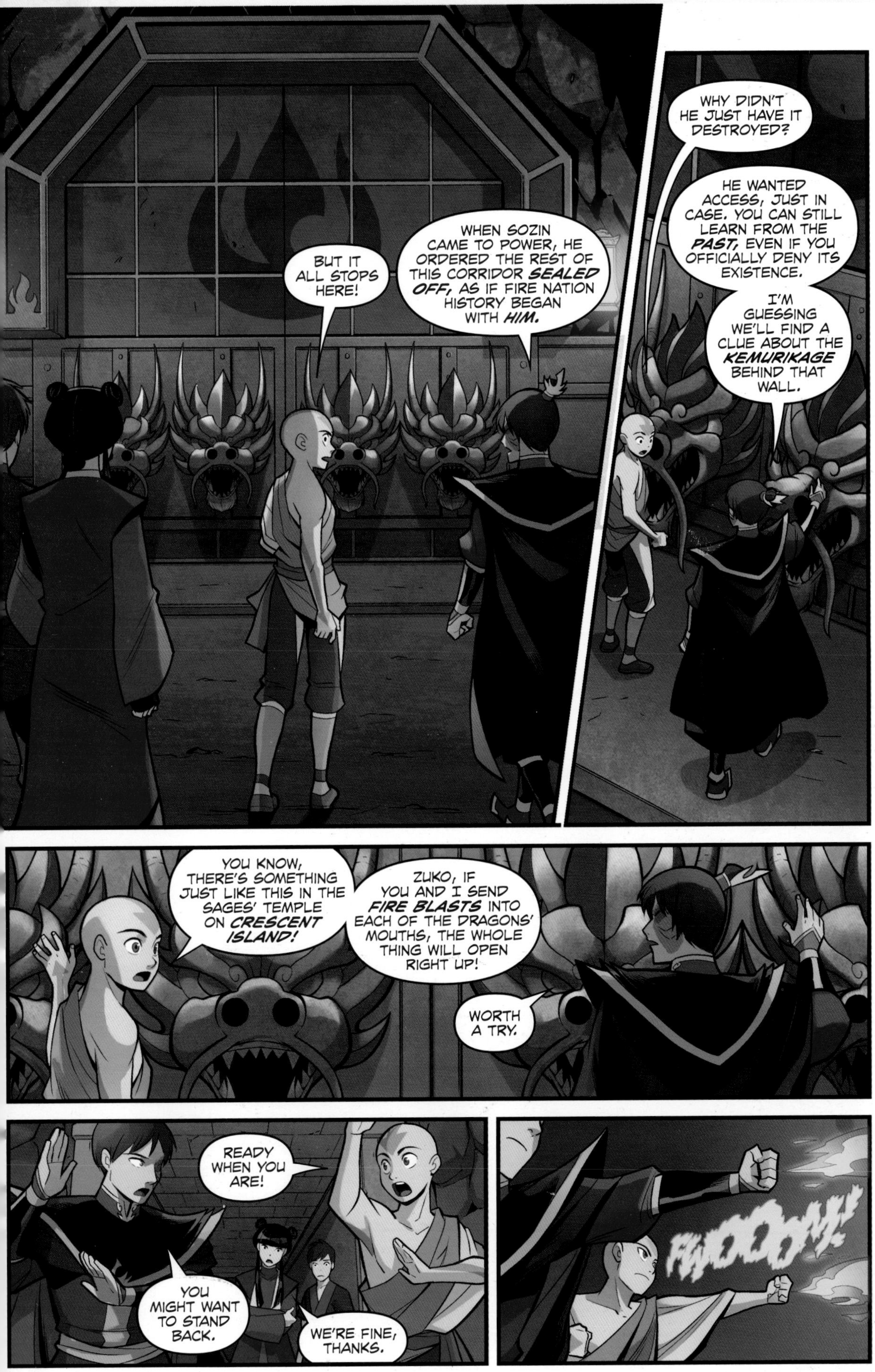
BUT IT ALL STOPS HERE!
WHEN SOZIN CAME TO POWER, HE ORDERED THE REST OF THIS CORRIDOR SEALED OFF, AS IF FIRE NATION HISTORY BEGAN WITH HIM.
WHY DIDN'T HE JUST HAVE IT DESTROYED?
HE WANTED ACCESS, JUST IN CASE. YOU CAN STILL LEARN FROM THE PAST, EVEN IF YOU OFFICIALLY DENY ITS EXISTENCE.
I'M GUESSING WE'LL FIND A CLUE ABOUT THE KEMURIKAGE BEHIND THAT WALL.
YOU KNOW, THERE'S SOMETHING JUST LIKE THIS IN THE SAGES' TEMPLE ON CRESCENT ISLAND!
ZUKO, IF YOU AND I SEND FIRE BLASTS INTO EACH OF THE DRAGONS' MOUTHS, THE WHOLE THING WILL OPEN RIGHT UP!
WORTH A TRY.
READY WHEN YOU ARE!
YOU MIGHT WANT TO STAND BACK.
WE'RE FINE, THANKS.
FWOOOOM!

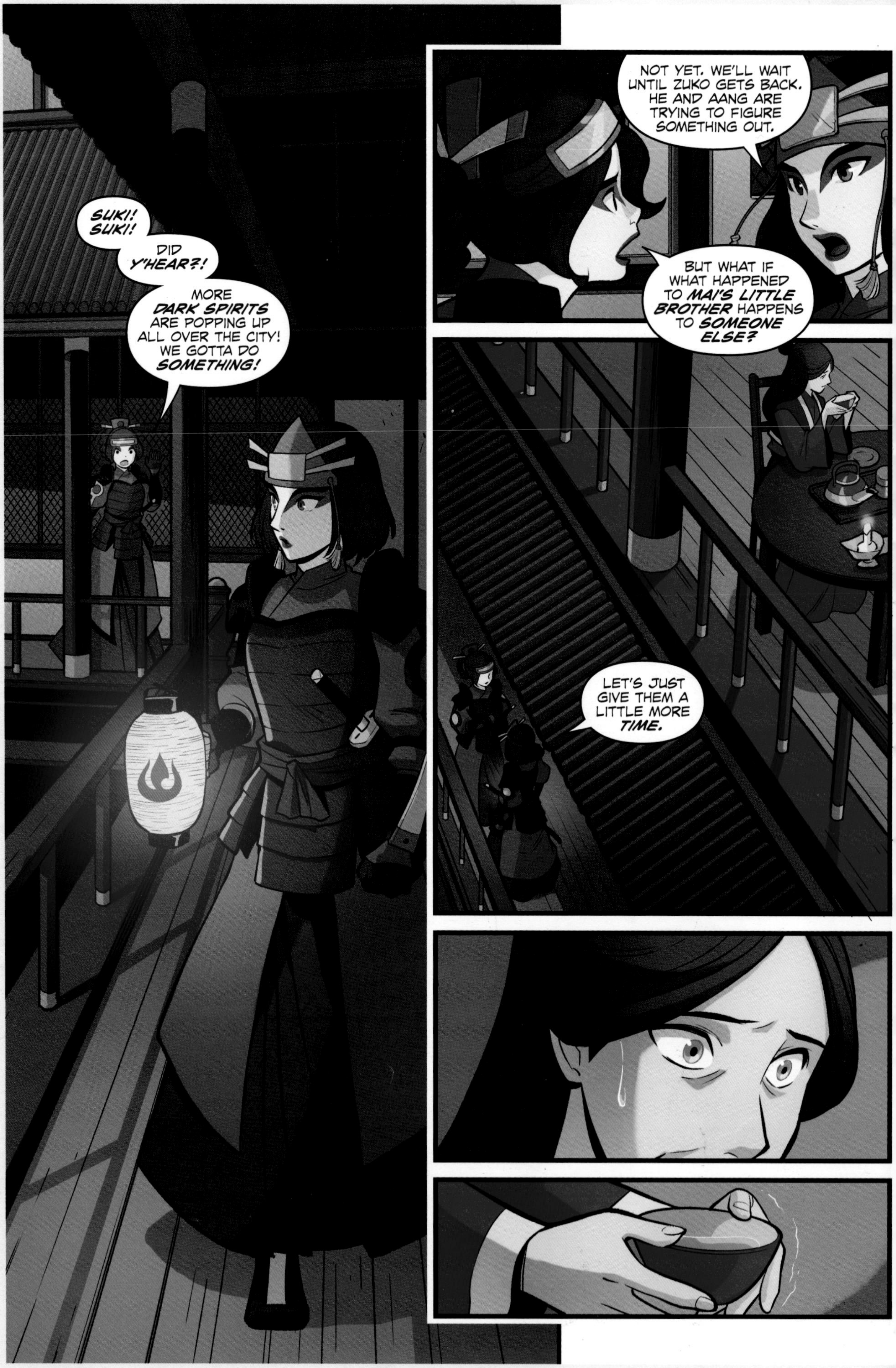
SUKI! SUKI!
DID Y'HEAR?!
MORE DARK SPIRITS ARE POPPING UP ALL OVER THE CITY! WE GOTTA DO SOMETHING!
NOT YET. WE'LL WAIT UNTIL ZUKO GETS BACK. HE AND AANG ARE TRYING TO FIGURE SOMETHING OUT.
BUT WHAT IF WHAT HAPPENED TO MAI'S LITTLE BROTHER HAPPENS TO SOMEONE ELSE?
LET'S JUST GIVE THEM A LITTLE MORE TIME.

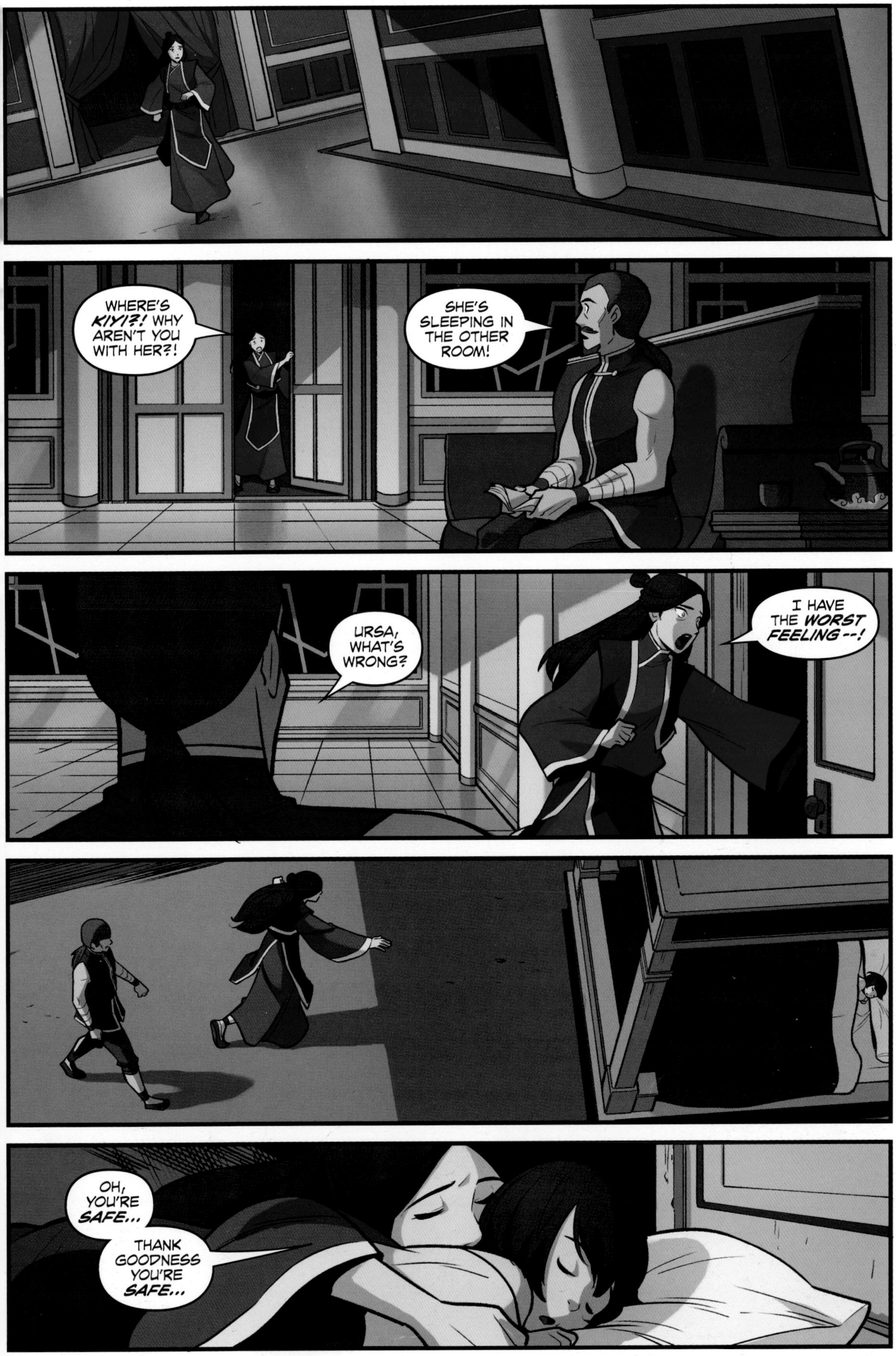
WHERE'S KIYI?! WHY AREN'T YOU WITH HER?!
SHE'S SLEEPING IN THE OTHER ROOM!
URSA, WHAT'S WRONG?
I HAVE THE WORST FEELING--!
OH, YOU'RE SAFE...
THANK GOODNESS YOU'RE SAFE...

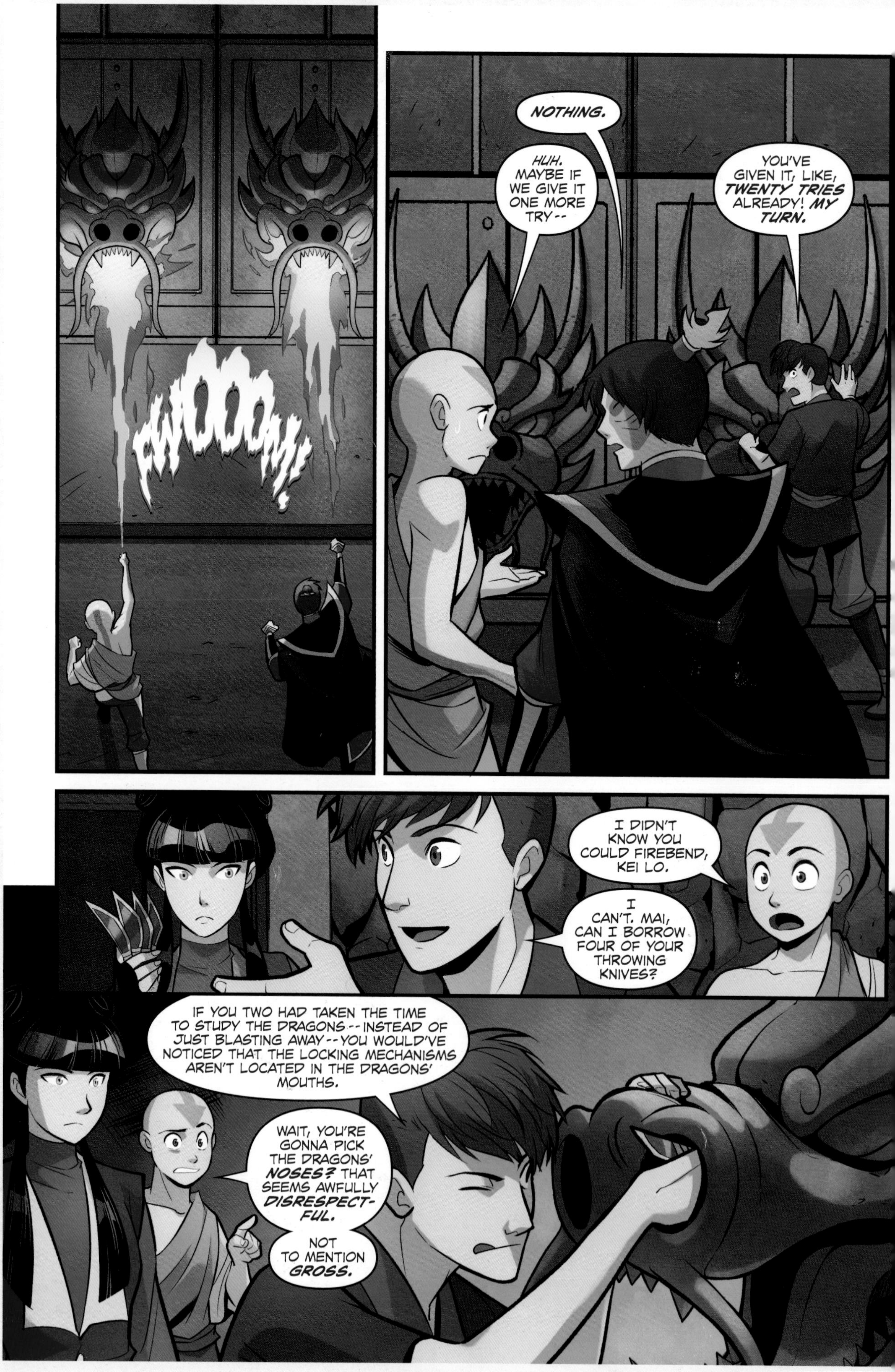
FWOOOM!
HUH. MAYBE IF WE GIVE IT ONE MORE TRY--
NOTHING.
YOU'VE GIVEN IT, LIKE, TWENTY TRIES ALREADY! MY TURN.
I DIDN'T KNOW YOU COULD FIREBEND, KEI LO.
I CAN'T. MAI, CAN I BORROW FOUR OF YOUR THROWING KNIVES?
IF YOU TWO HAD TAKEN THE TIME TO STUDY THE DRAGONS--INSTEAD OF JUST BLASTING AWAY--YOU WOULD'VE NOTICED THAT THE LOCKING MECHANISMS AREN'T LOCATED IN THE DRAGONS' MOUTHS.
WAIT, YOU'RE GONNA PICK THE DRAGONS' NOSES? THAT SEEMS AWFULLY DISRESPECT-FUL.
NOT TO MENTION GROSS.

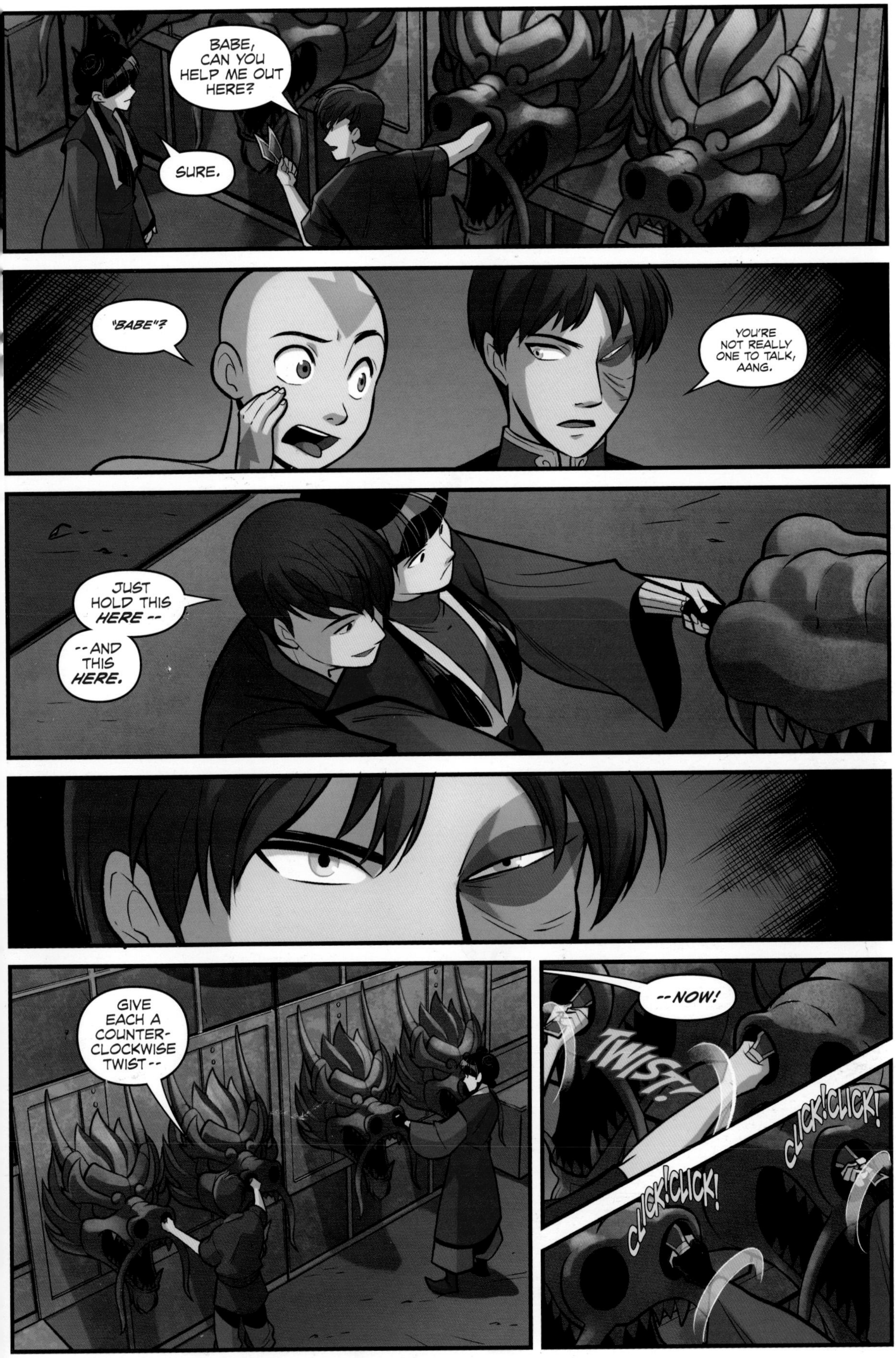
BABE, CAN YOU HELP ME OUT HERE?
SURE.
"BABE"?
YOU'RE NOT REALLY ONE TO TALK, AANG.
JUST HOLD THIS HERE --
--AND THIS HERE.
GIVE EACH A COUNTER-CLOCKWISE TWIST--
--NOW!
TWIST!
CLICK!CLICK!
CLICK!CLICK!

GLY: *I didn't want to repeat the sequence from "Avatar Roku," so I couldn't let these doors be opened with firebending. We had to come up with something different.*

I also wanted to give Kei Lo a chance to flirt with Mai. I figured it would give Zuko and Mai's conversation a few pages later some more oomph.

G: *Aang seems to be having a hard time being in the middle of the love triangle between Zuko, Mai, and Kei Lo, but we had fun drawing them.*

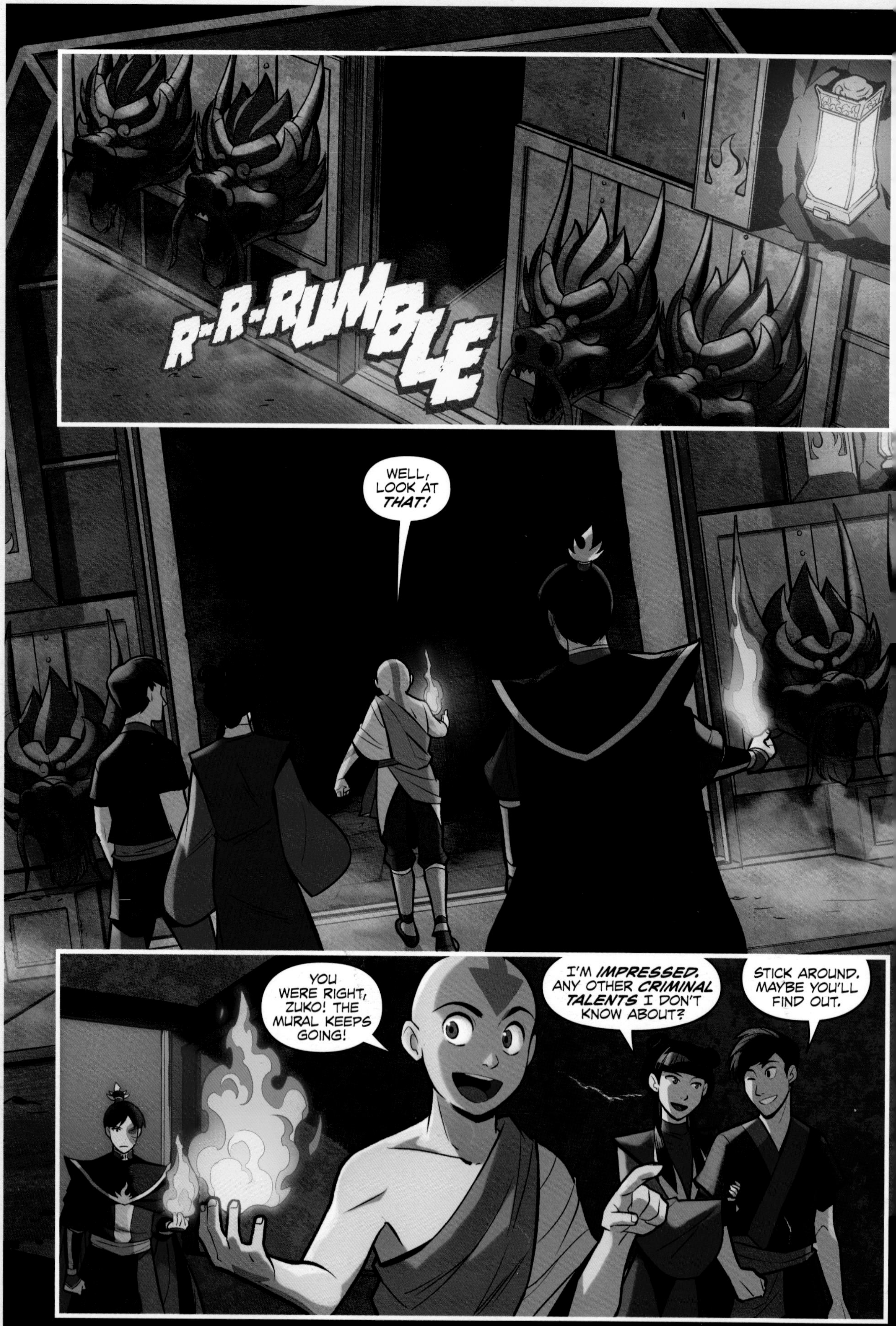
R-R-RUMBLE
WELL, LOOK AT *THAT!*
YOU WERE RIGHT, ZUKO! THE MURAL KEEPS GOING!
I'M *IMPRESSED.* ANY OTHER *CRIMINAL TALENTS* I DON'T KNOW ABOUT?
STICK AROUND. MAYBE YOU'LL FIND OUT.

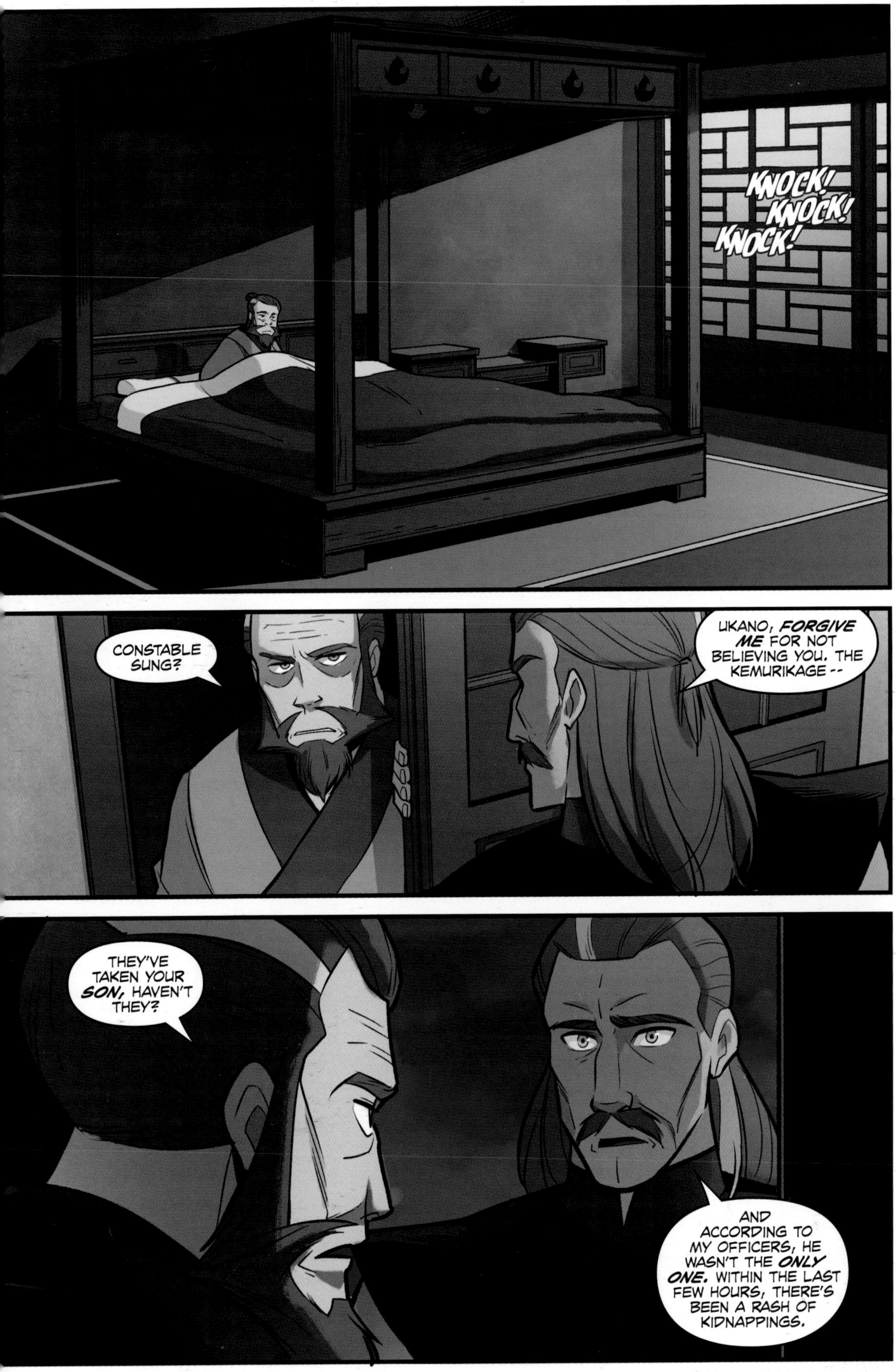
KNOCK! KNOCK! KNOCK!
CONSTABLE SUNG?
UKANO, FORGIVE ME FOR NOT BELIEVING YOU. THE KEMURIKAGE --
THEY'VE TAKEN YOUR SON, HAVEN'T THEY?
AND ACCORDING TO MY OFFICERS, HE WASN'T THE ONLY ONE. WITHIN THE LAST FEW HOURS, THERE'S BEEN A RASH OF KIDNAPPINGS.

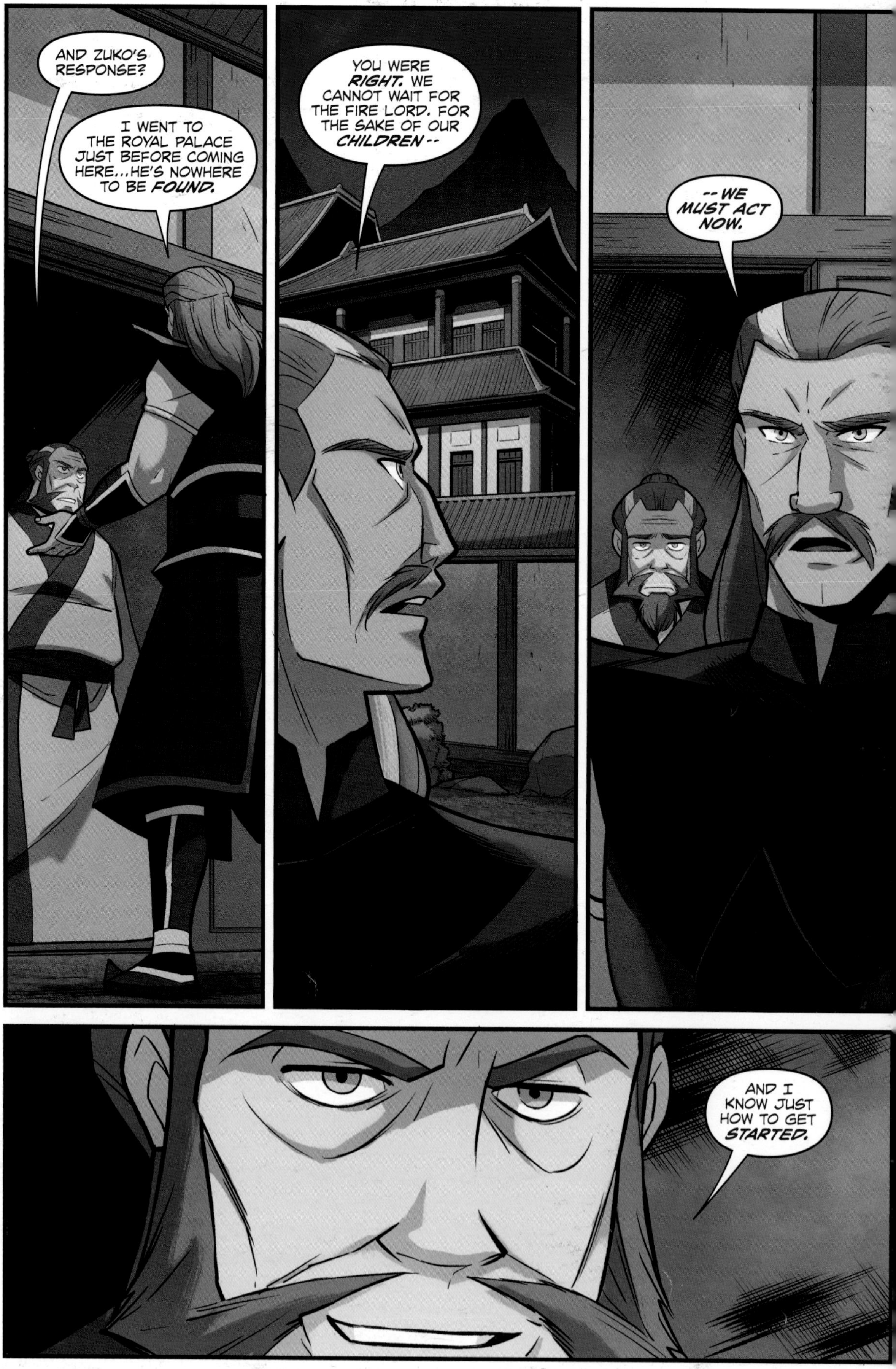
AND ZUKO'S RESPONSE?
I WENT TO THE ROYAL PALACE JUST BEFORE COMING HERE...HE'S NOWHERE TO BE FOUND.
YOU WERE RIGHT. WE CANNOT WAIT FOR THE FIRE LORD. FOR THE SAKE OF OUR CHILDREN--
--WE MUST ACT NOW.
AND I KNOW JUST HOW TO GET STARTED.

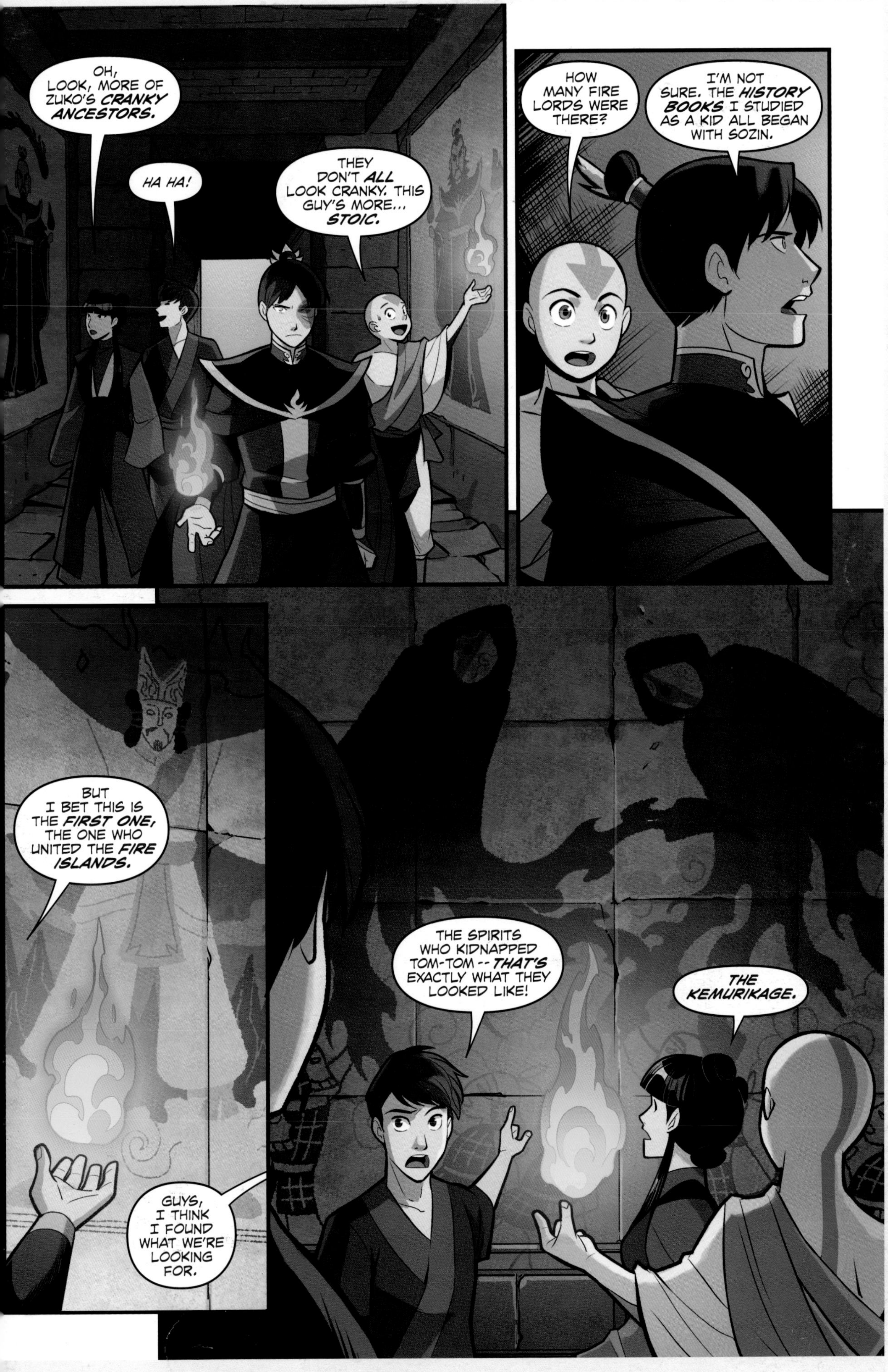
OH, LOOK, MORE OF ZUKO'S CRANKY ANCESTORS.
HA HA!
THEY DON'T ALL LOOK CRANKY. THIS GUY'S MORE... STOIC.
HOW MANY FIRE LORDS WERE THERE?
I'M NOT SURE. THE HISTORY BOOKS I STUDIED AS A KID ALL BEGAN WITH SOZIN.
BUT I BET THIS IS THE FIRST ONE, THE ONE WHO UNITED THE FIRE ISLANDS.
GUYS, I THINK I FOUND WHAT WE'RE LOOKING FOR.
THE SPIRITS WHO KIDNAPPED TOM-TOM--THAT'S EXACTLY WHAT THEY LOOKED LIKE!
THE KEMURIKAGE.

GLY: *As an* Avatar *fan, I hope we someday learn more about the first Fire Lord.*

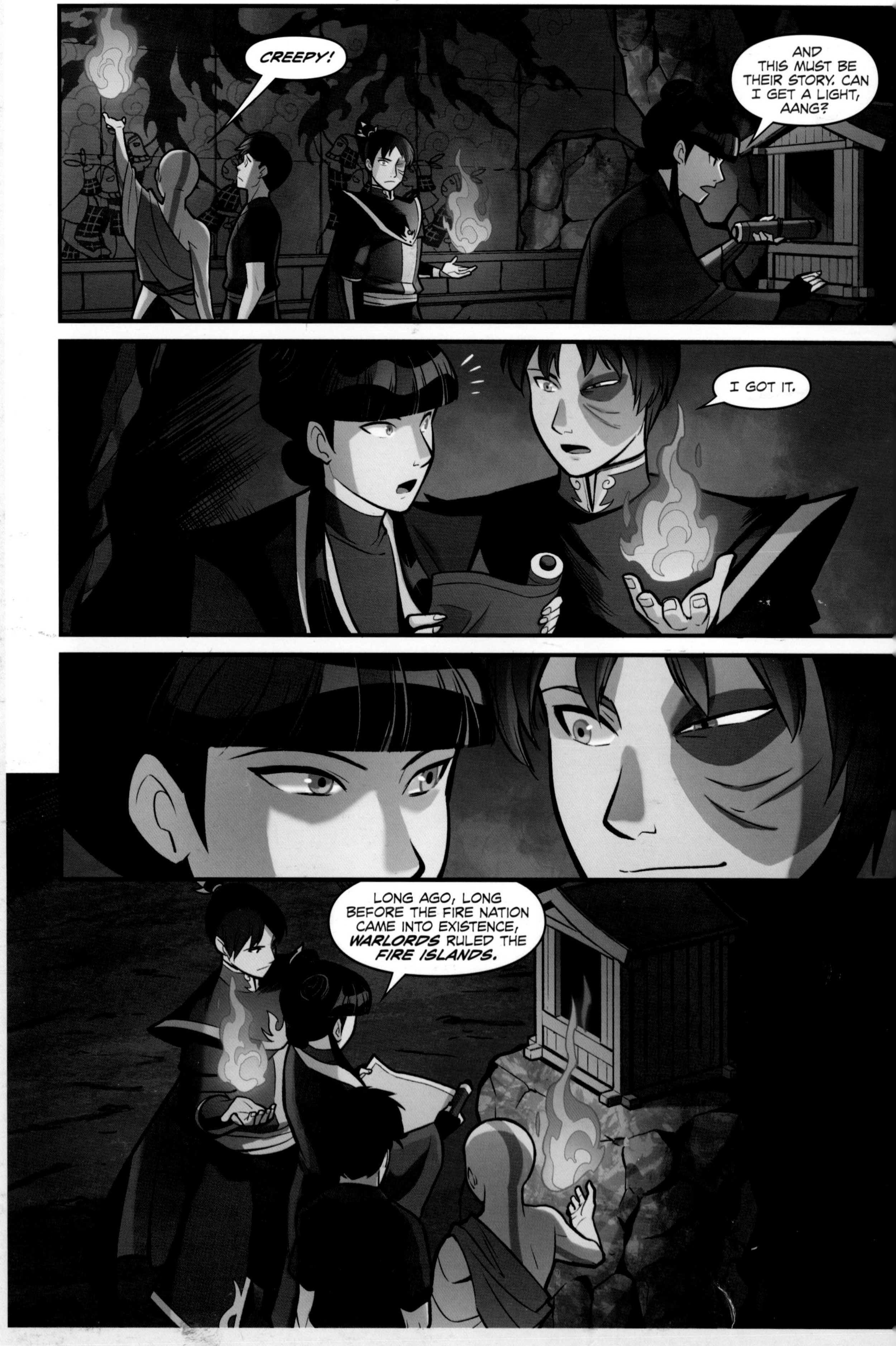
CREEPY!
AND THIS MUST BE THEIR STORY. CAN I GET A LIGHT, AANG?
I GOT IT.
LONG AGO, LONG BEFORE THE FIRE NATION CAME INTO EXISTENCE, **WARLORDS** RULED THE **FIRE ISLANDS.**

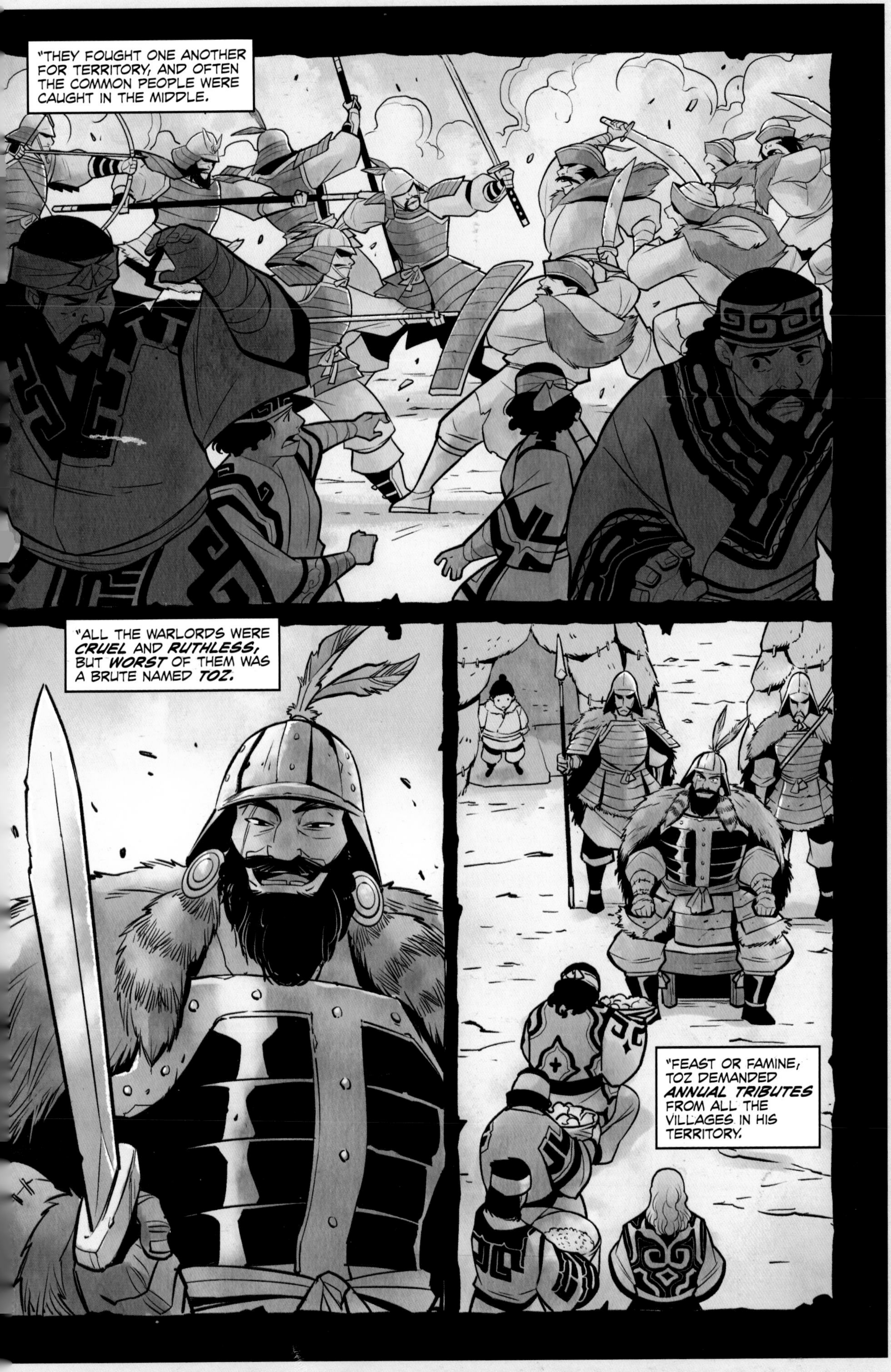
"THEY FOUGHT ONE ANOTHER FOR TERRITORY, AND OFTEN THE COMMON PEOPLE WERE CAUGHT IN THE MIDDLE.
"ALL THE WARLORDS WERE CRUEL AND RUTHLESS, BUT WORST OF THEM WAS A BRUTE NAMED TOZ.
"FEAST OR FAMINE, TOZ DEMANDED ANNUAL TRIBUTES FROM ALL THE VILLAGES IN HIS TERRITORY.

GLY: *Mike, Bryan, the editors, and I debated whether the legend of the Kemurikage was too bleak. In the end, we decided to run with it.*

G: *For the costumes in this sequence, we referenced the Ainu, an indigenous people who lived on the Kuril Islands.*

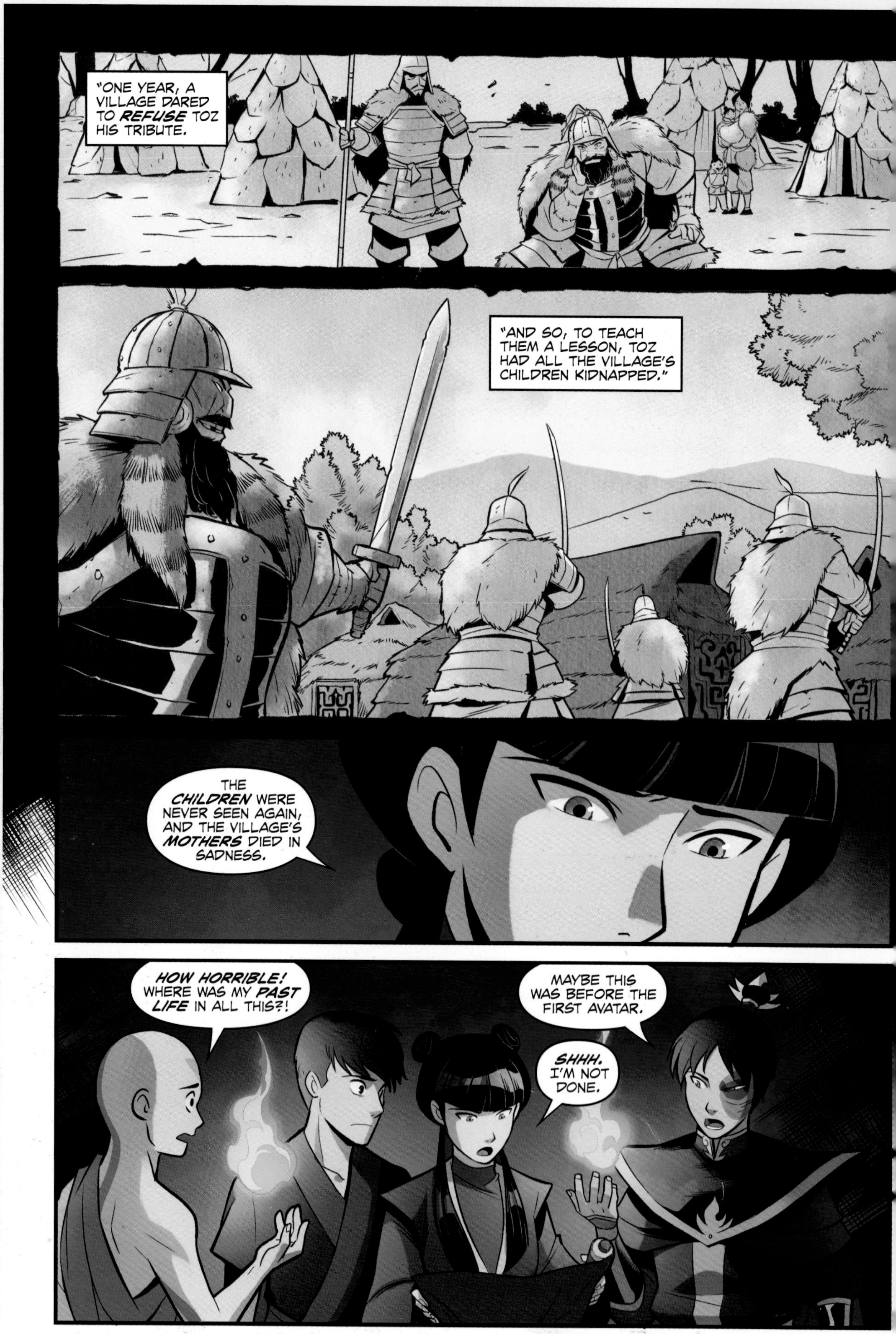
"ONE YEAR, A VILLAGE DARED TO *REFUSE* TOZ HIS TRIBUTE.
"AND SO, TO TEACH THEM A LESSON, TOZ HAD ALL THE VILLAGE'S CHILDREN KIDNAPPED."
THE *CHILDREN* WERE NEVER SEEN AGAIN, AND THE VILLAGE'S *MOTHERS* DIED IN SADNESS.
HOW HORRIBLE! WHERE WAS MY *PAST LIFE* IN ALL THIS?!
MAYBE THIS WAS BEFORE THE FIRST AVATAR.
SHHH. I'M NOT DONE.

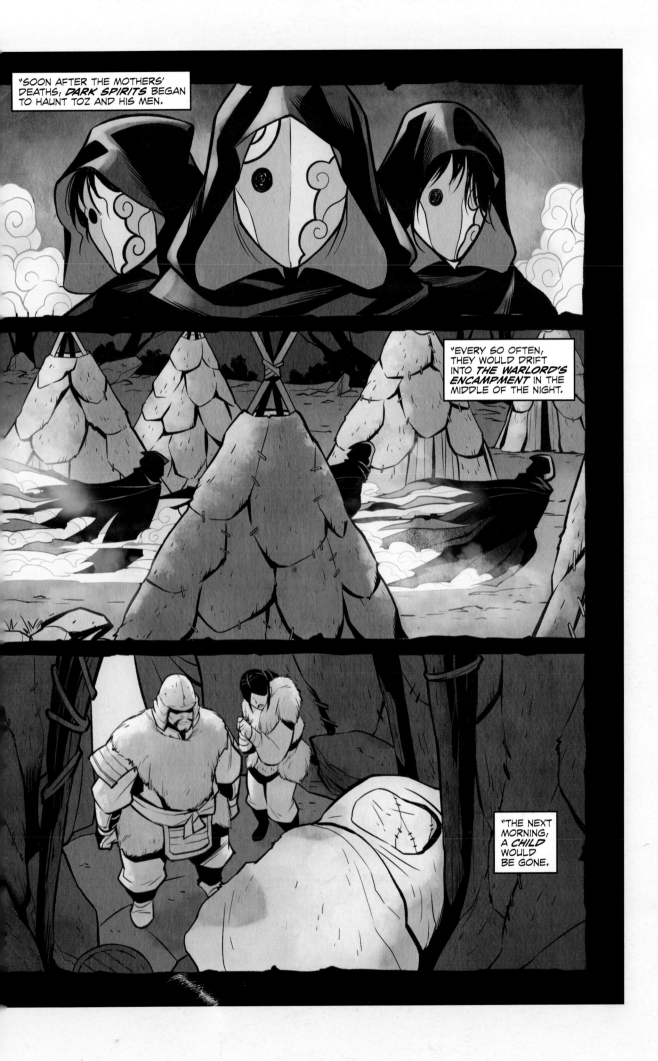

"SOON AFTER THE MOTHERS' DEATHS, *DARK SPIRITS* BEGAN TO HAUNT TOZ AND HIS MEN.

"EVERY SO OFTEN, THEY WOULD DRIFT INTO *THE WARLORD'S ENCAMPMENT* IN THE MIDDLE OF THE NIGHT.

"THE NEXT MORNING, A *CHILD* WOULD BE GONE.

GLY: *I just love the way Gurihiru did the bottom of this page. It slows down the action perfectly.*

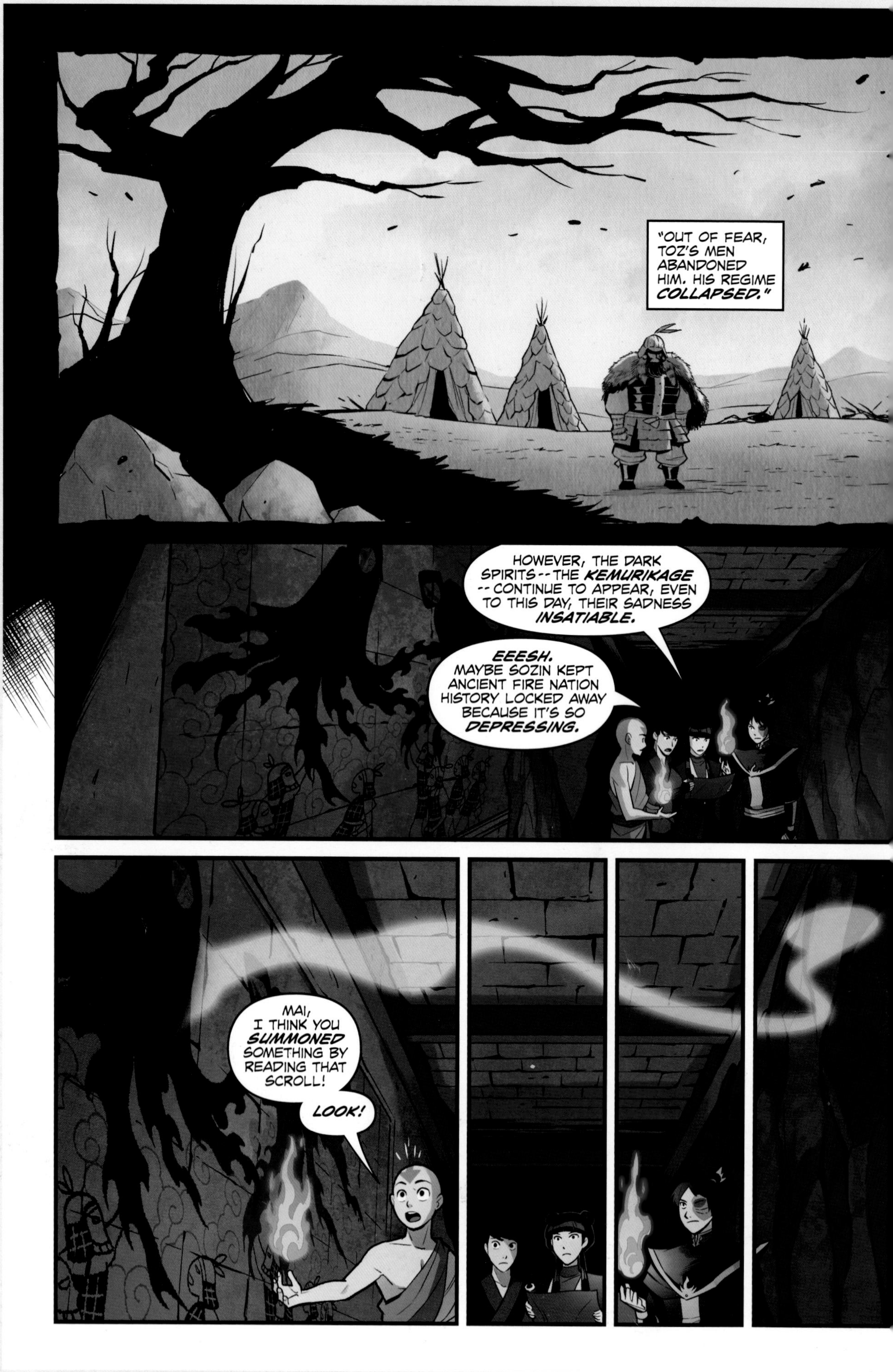
"OUT OF FEAR, TOZ'S MEN ABANDONED HIM. HIS REGIME COLLAPSED."
HOWEVER, THE DARK SPIRITS--THE KEMURIKAGE--CONTINUE TO APPEAR, EVEN TO THIS DAY, THEIR SADNESS INSATIABLE.
EEESH. MAYBE SOZIN KEPT ANCIENT FIRE NATION HISTORY LOCKED AWAY BECAUSE IT'S SO DEPRESSING.
MAI, I THINK YOU SUMMONED SOMETHING BY READING THAT SCROLL!
LOOK!

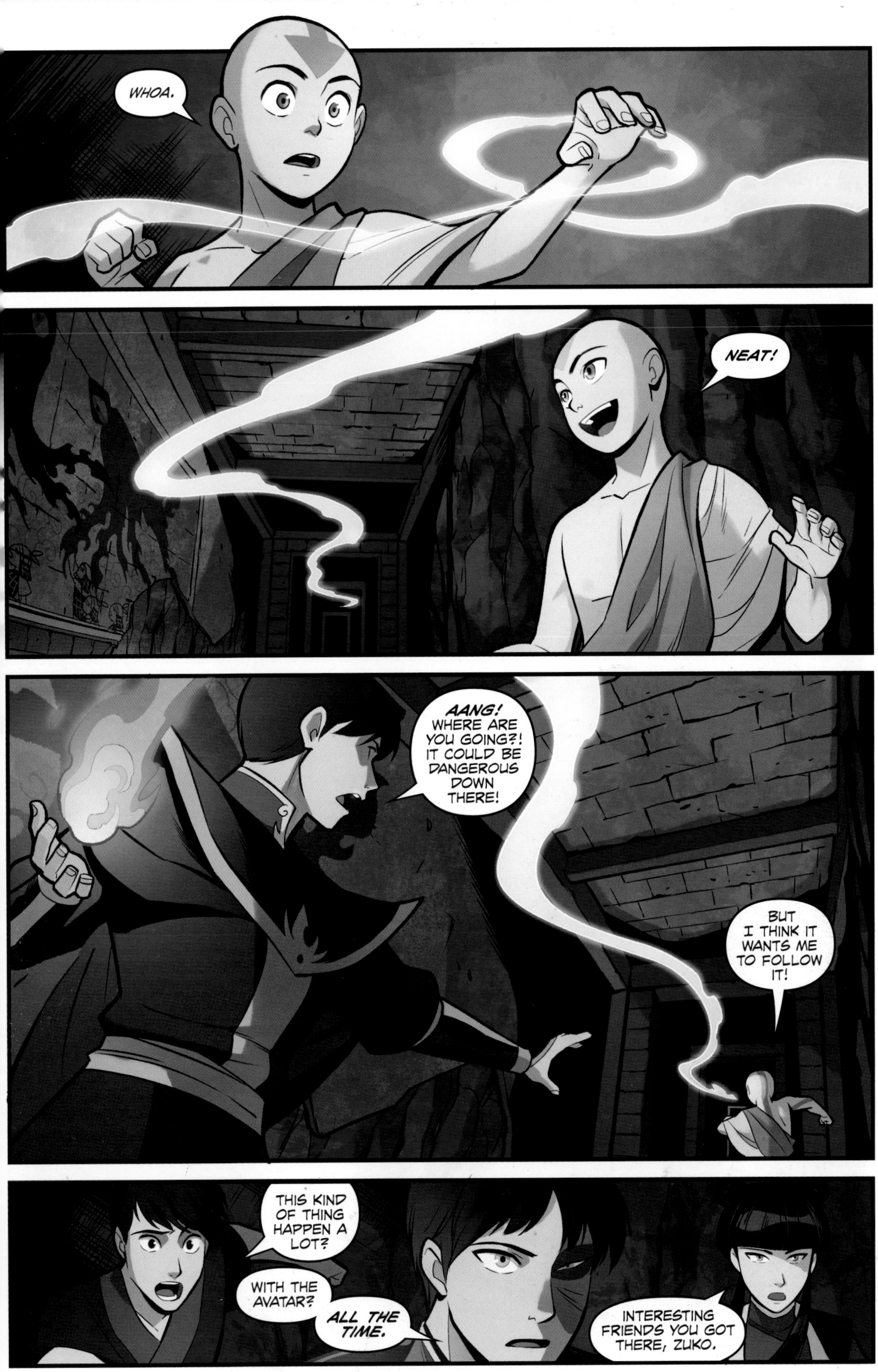
WHOA.
NEAT!
AANG! WHERE ARE YOU GOING?! IT COULD BE DANGEROUS DOWN THERE!
BUT I THINK IT WANTS ME TO FOLLOW IT!
THIS KIND OF THING HAPPEN A LOT?
WITH THE AVATAR?
ALL THE TIME.
INTERESTING FRIENDS YOU GOT THERE, ZUKO.

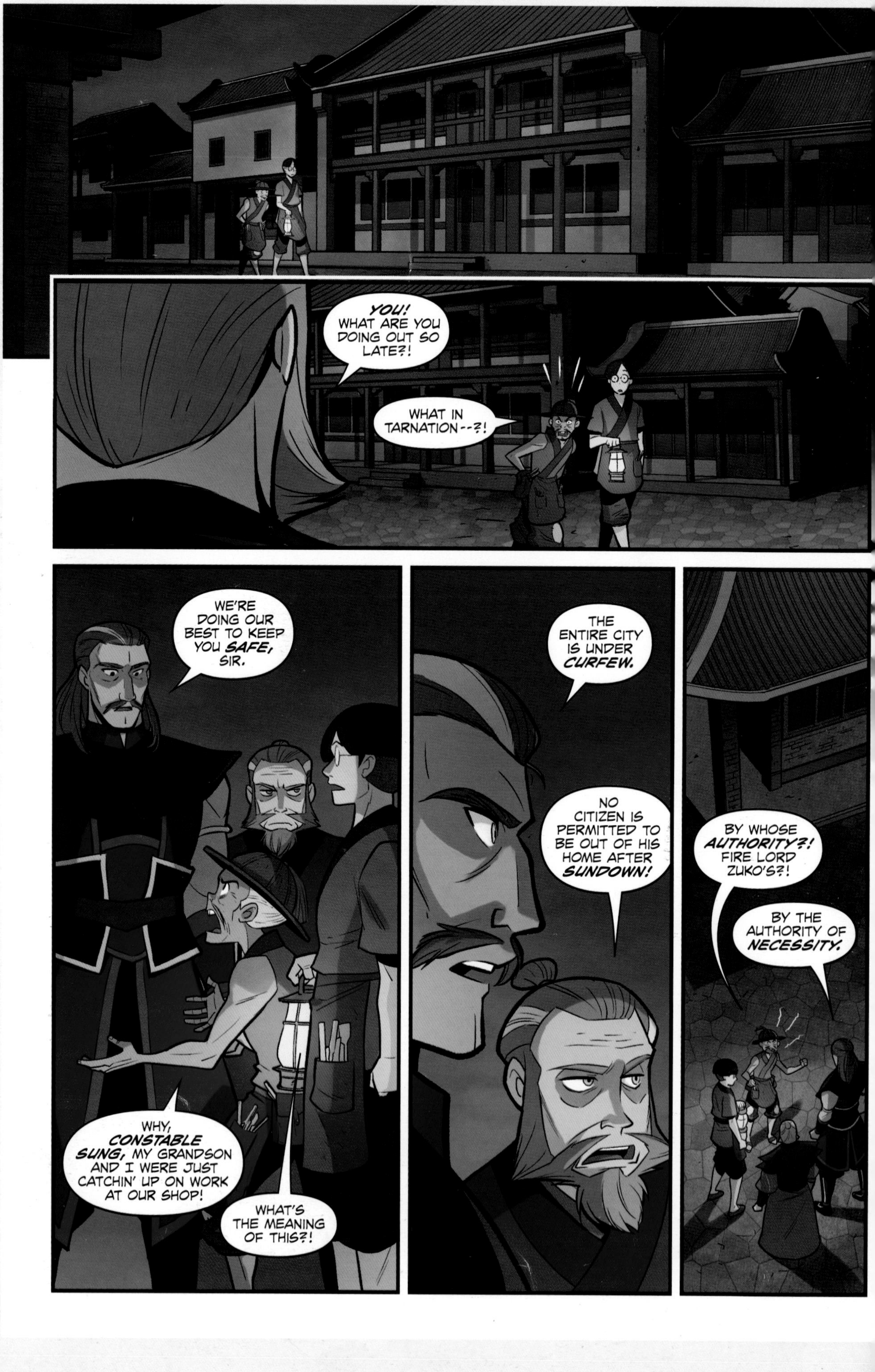
YOU! WHAT ARE YOU DOING OUT SO LATE?!
WHAT IN TARNATION--?!
WE'RE DOING OUR BEST TO KEEP YOU SAFE, SIR.
WHY, CONSTABLE SUNG, MY GRANDSON AND I WERE JUST CATCHIN' UP ON WORK AT OUR SHOP!
WHAT'S THE MEANING OF THIS?!
THE ENTIRE CITY IS UNDER CURFEW.
NO CITIZEN IS PERMITTED TO BE OUT OF HIS HOME AFTER SUNDOWN!
BY WHOSE AUTHORITY?! FIRE LORD ZUKO'S?!
BY THE AUTHORITY OF NECESSITY.

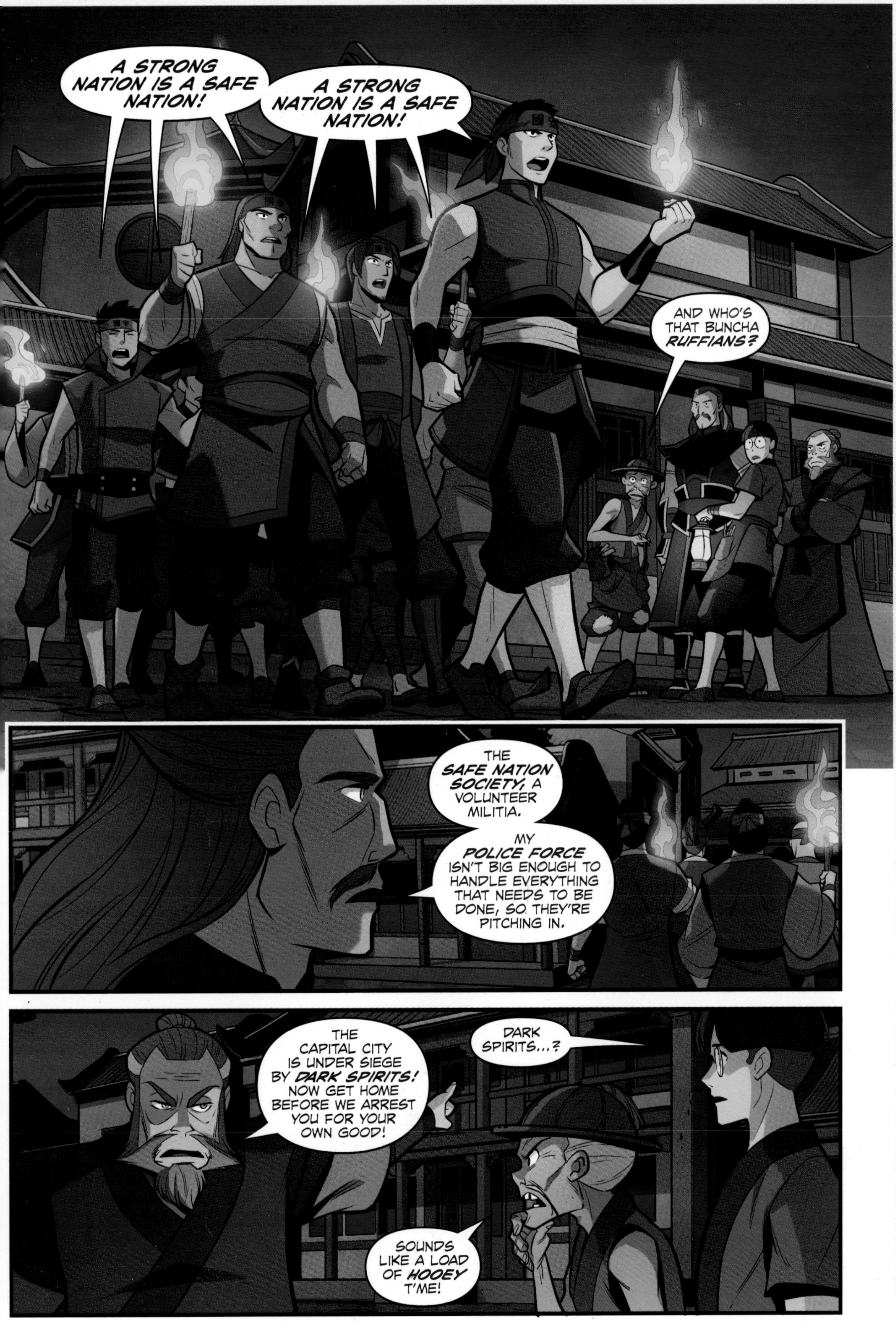
A STRONG NATION IS A SAFE NATION!
A STRONG NATION IS A SAFE NATION!
AND WHO'S THAT BUNCHA RUFFIANS?
THE SAFE NATION SOCIETY, A VOLUNTEER MILITIA.
MY POLICE FORCE ISN'T BIG ENOUGH TO HANDLE EVERYTHING THAT NEEDS TO BE DONE, SO THEY'RE PITCHING IN.
THE CAPITAL CITY IS UNDER SIEGE BY DARK SPIRITS! NOW GET HOME BEFORE WE ARREST YOU FOR YOUR OWN GOOD!
DARK SPIRITS...?
SOUNDS LIKE A LOAD OF HOOEY T'ME!

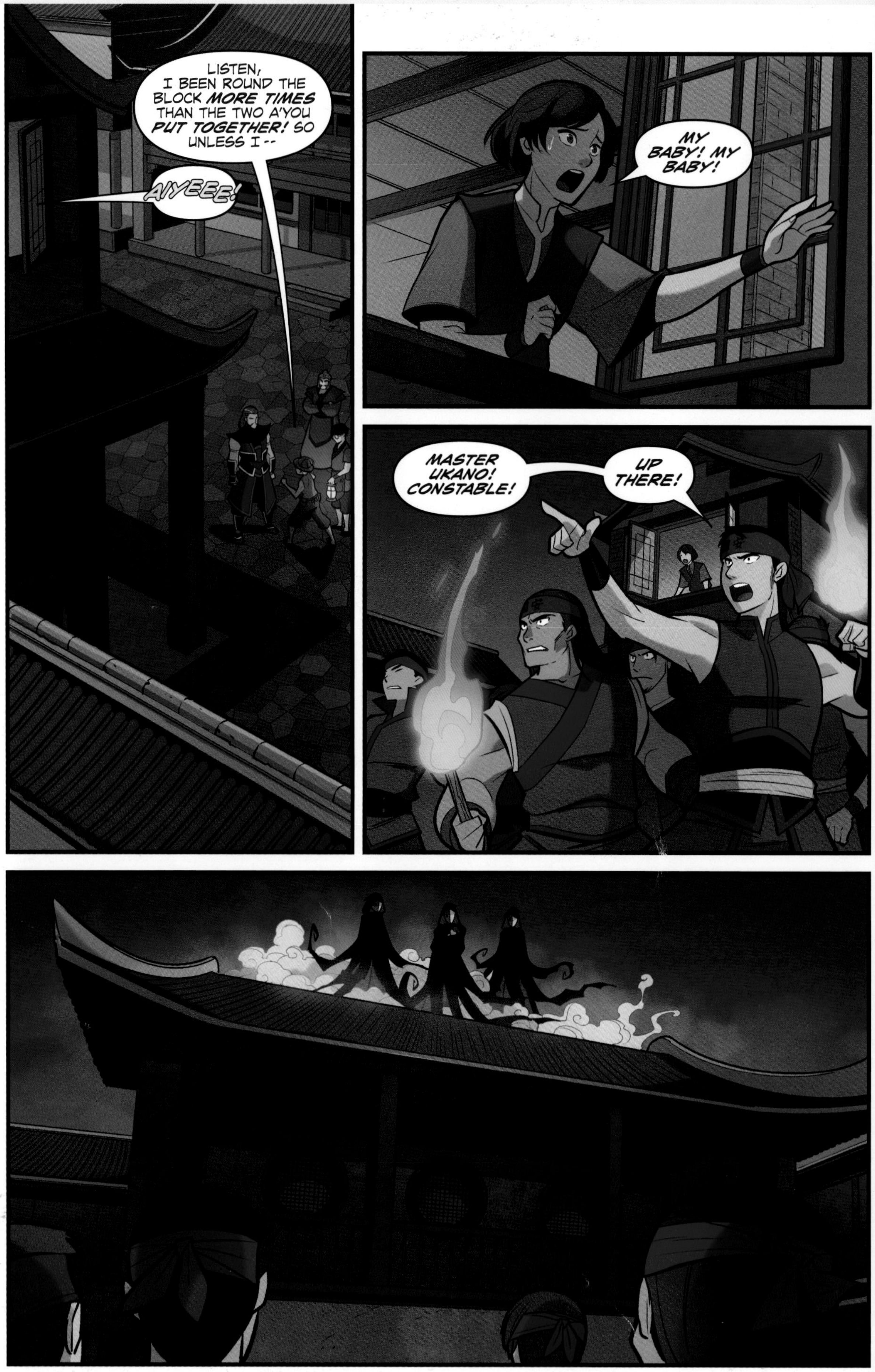
LISTEN, I BEEN ROUND THE BLOCK MORE TIMES THAN THE TWO A'YOU PUT TOGETHER! SO UNLESS I --
AIYEEE!
MY BABY! MY BABY!
MASTER UKANO! CONSTABLE!
UP THERE!

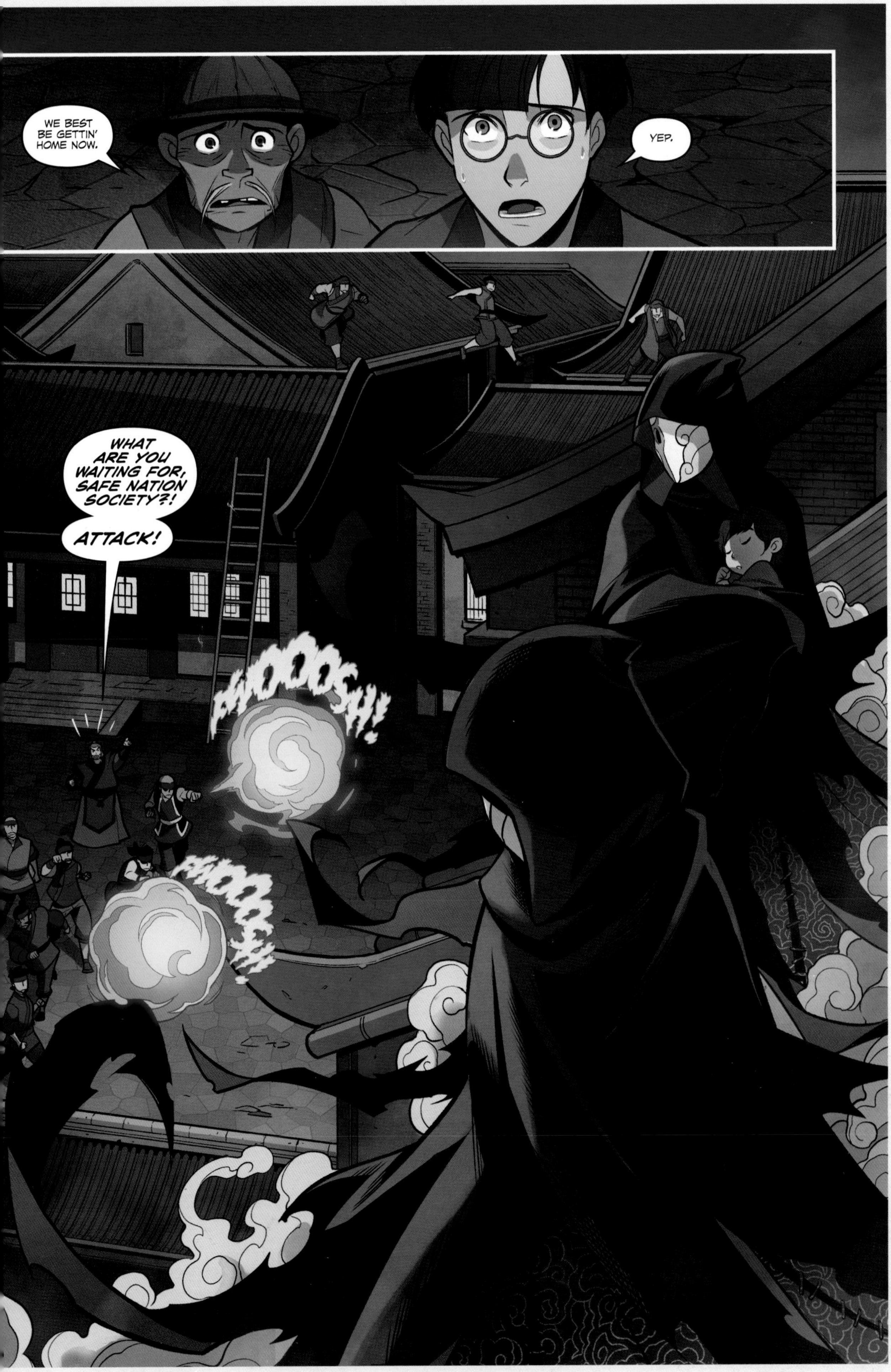
WE BEST BE GETTIN' HOME NOW.
YEP.
WHAT ARE YOU WAITING FOR, SAFE NATION SOCIETY?!
ATTACK!
FWOOOSH!
FWOOOSH!

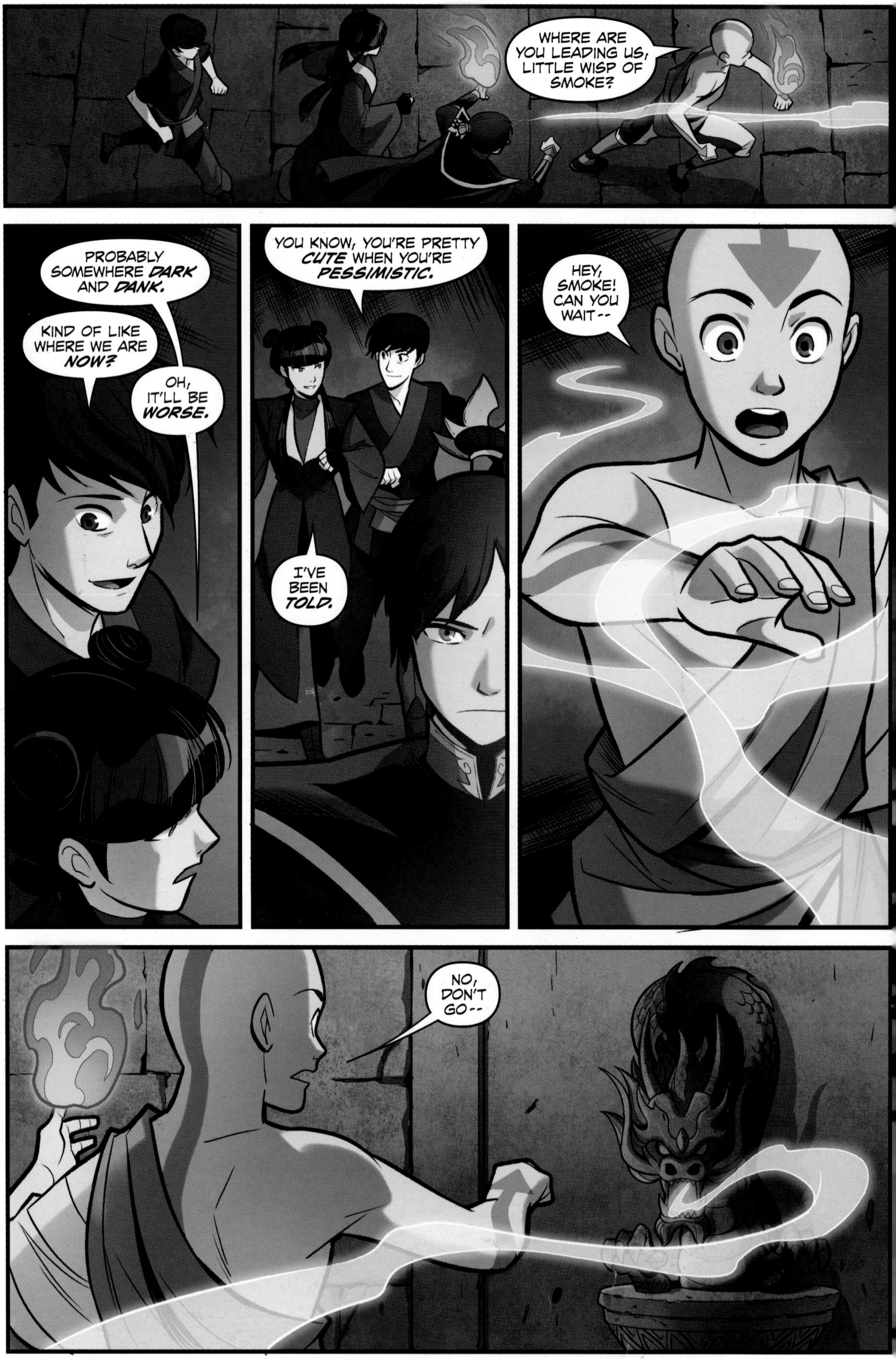
WHERE ARE YOU LEADING US, LITTLE WISP OF SMOKE?
PROBABLY SOMEWHERE DARK AND DANK.
KIND OF LIKE WHERE WE ARE NOW?
OH, IT'LL BE WORSE.
YOU KNOW, YOU'RE PRETTY CUTE WHEN YOU'RE PESSIMISTIC.
I'VE BEEN TOLD.
HEY, SMOKE! CAN YOU WAIT--
NO, DON'T GO--

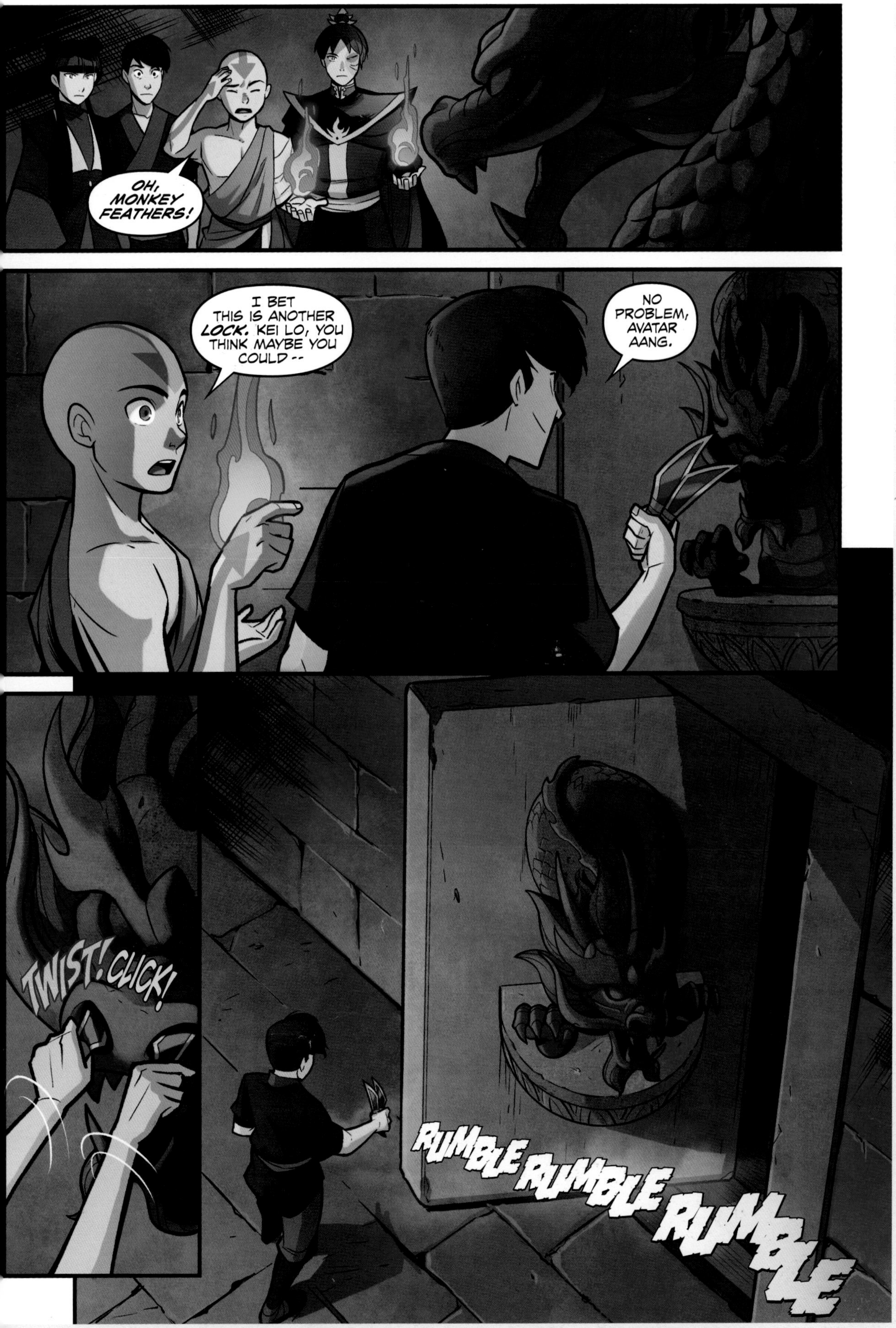
OH, MONKEY FEATHERS!
I BET THIS IS ANOTHER LOCK. KEI LO, YOU THINK MAYBE YOU COULD --
NO PROBLEM, AVATAR AANG.
TWIST! CLICK!
RUMBLE RUMBLE RUMBLE

GLY: *"Monkey feathers" is such a great phrase. I try to have Aang use it whenever I can.*

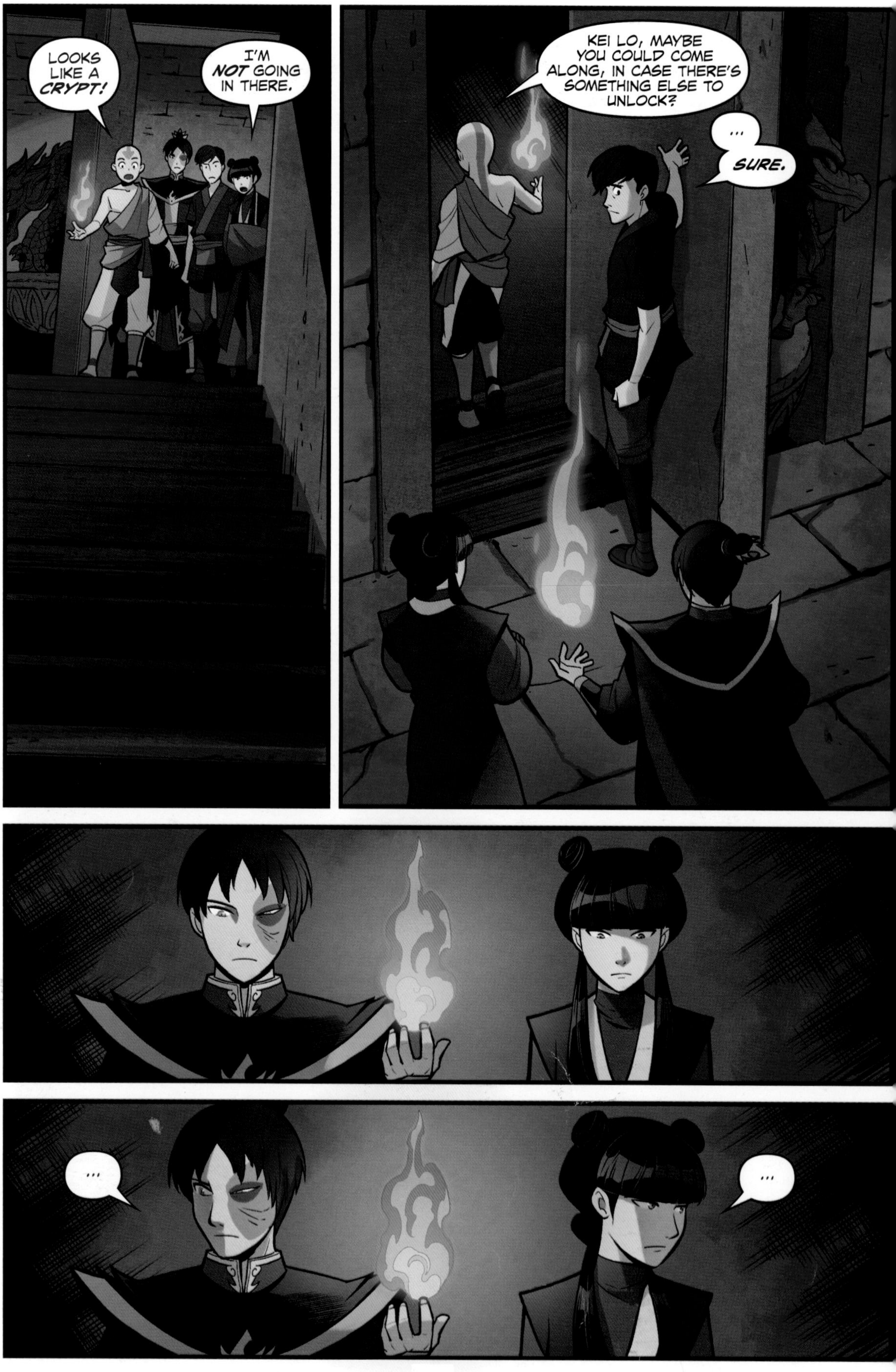
LOOKS LIKE A CRYPT!
I'M NOT GOING IN THERE.
KEI LO, MAYBE YOU COULD COME ALONG, IN CASE THERE'S SOMETHING ELSE TO UNLOCK?
... SURE.
...
...

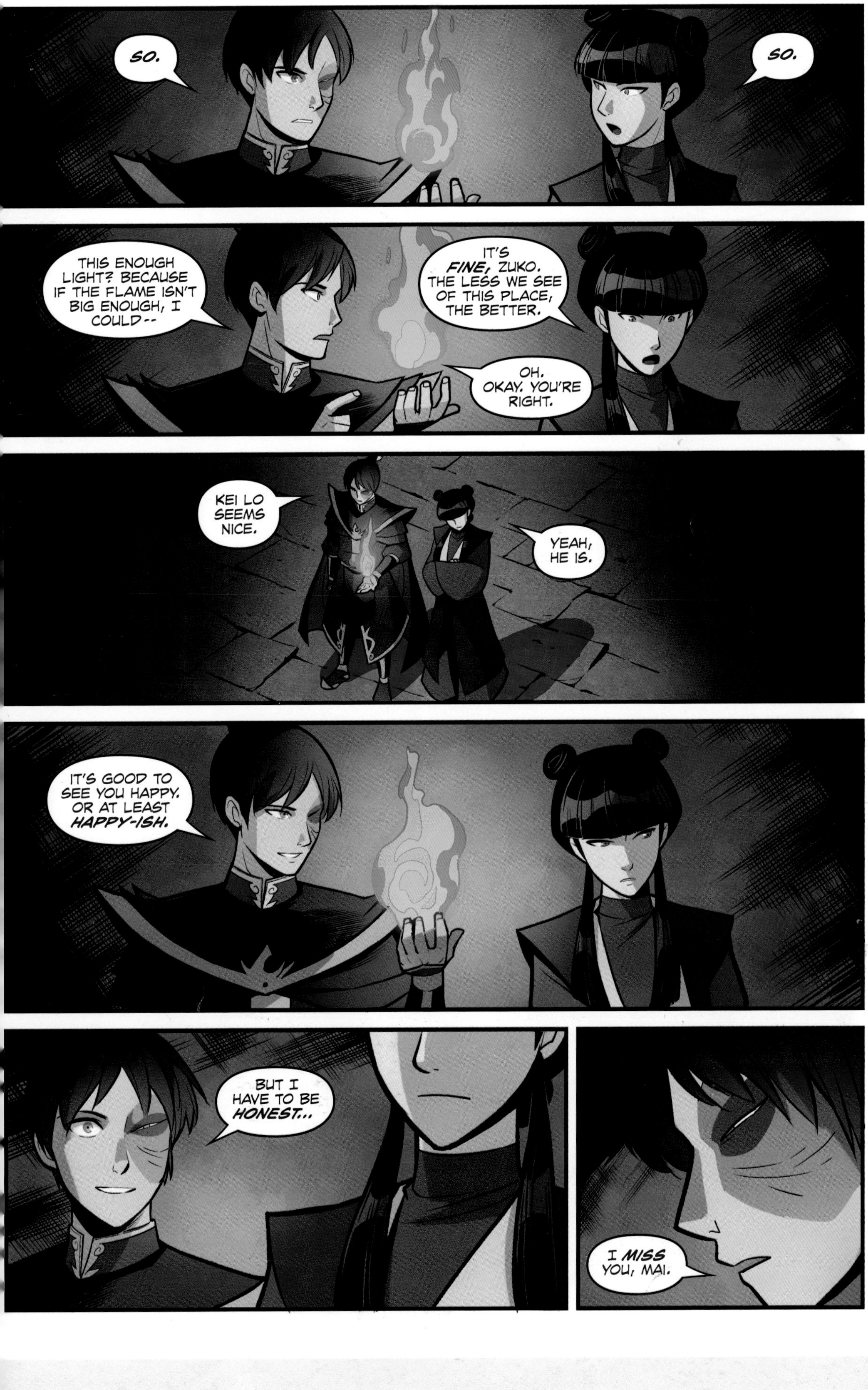
SO.
SO.
THIS ENOUGH LIGHT? BECAUSE IF THE FLAME ISN'T BIG ENOUGH, I COULD--
IT'S FINE, ZUKO. THE LESS WE SEE OF THIS PLACE, THE BETTER.
OH. OKAY. YOU'RE RIGHT.
KEI LO SEEMS NICE.
YEAH, HE IS.
IT'S GOOD TO SEE YOU HAPPY. OR AT LEAST HAPPY-ISH.
BUT I HAVE TO BE HONEST...
I MISS YOU, MAI.

GLY: *I've only had a couple of girlfriends in my life, so I haven't experienced all that many breakups. But the ones I did have to go through were pretty rough. I drew on some of that emotion to write this scene.*

G: *We liked Mai's changes of expression here and the way we drew them. We hope we were able to show her inner strength.*

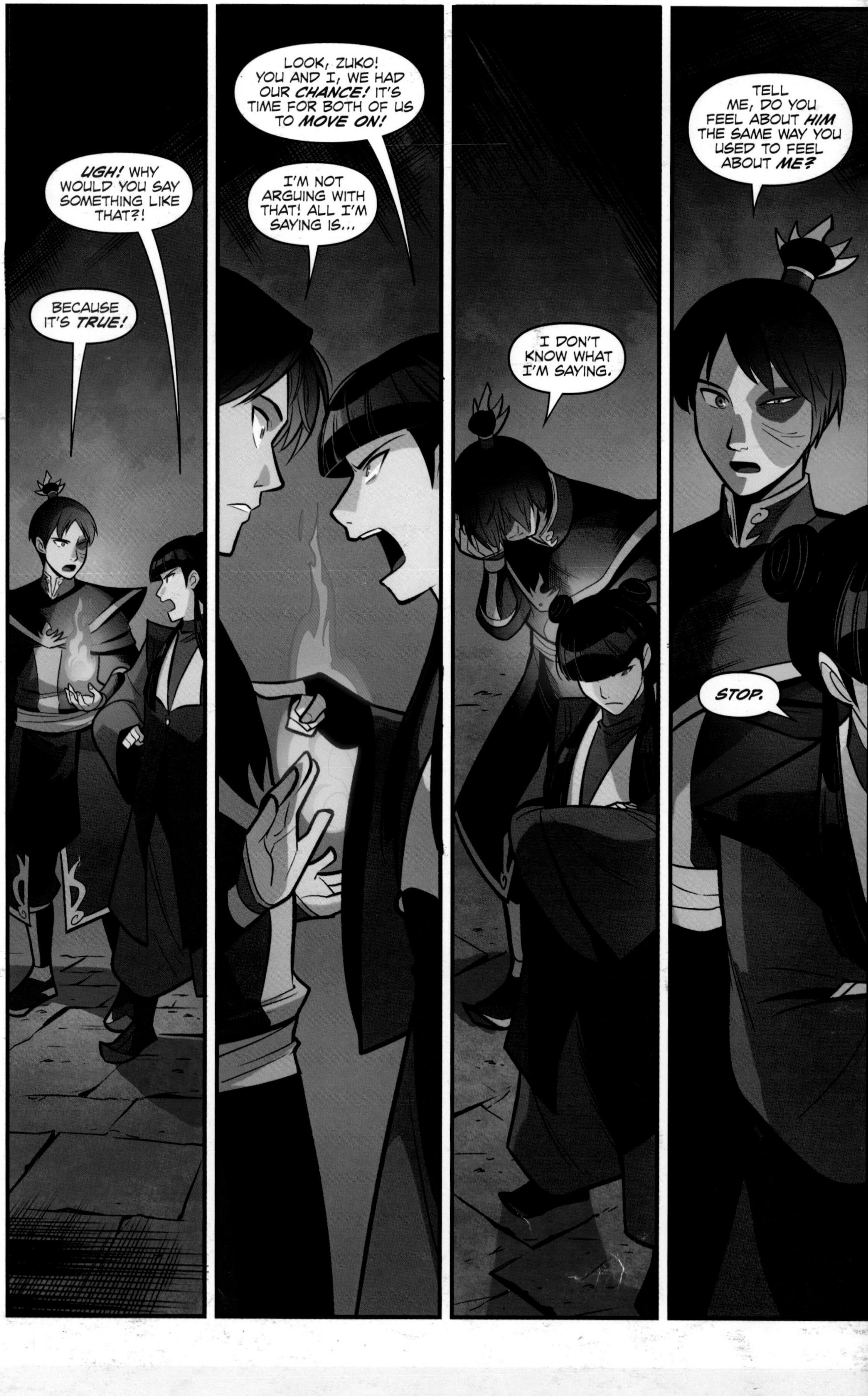
UGH! WHY WOULD YOU SAY SOMETHING LIKE THAT?!
BECAUSE IT'S TRUE!
LOOK, ZUKO! YOU AND I, WE HAD OUR CHANCE! IT'S TIME FOR BOTH OF US TO MOVE ON!
I'M NOT ARGUING WITH THAT! ALL I'M SAYING IS...
I DON'T KNOW WHAT I'M SAYING.
TELL ME, DO YOU FEEL ABOUT HIM THE SAME WAY YOU USED TO FEEL ABOUT ME?
STOP.

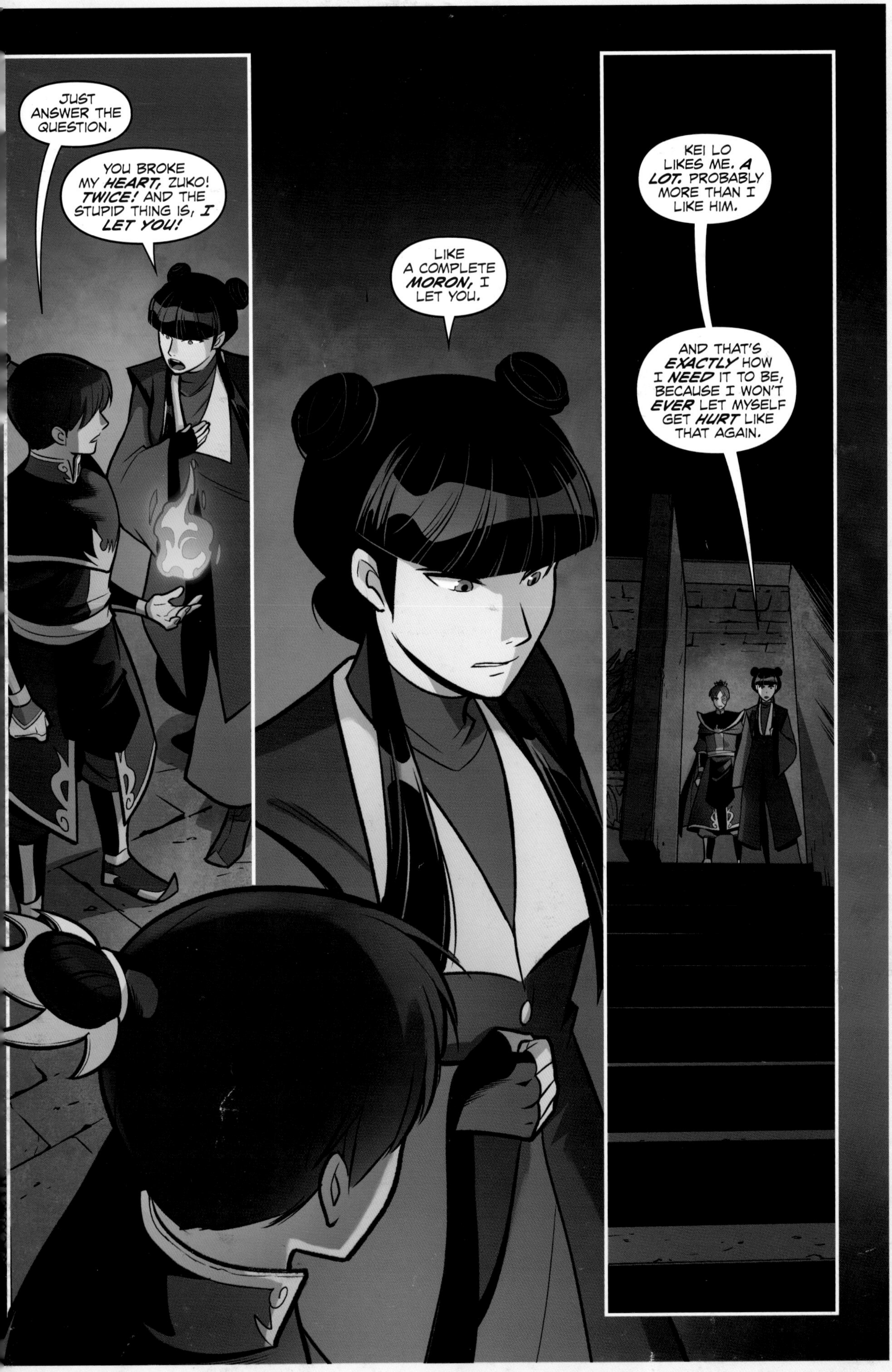
JUST ANSWER THE QUESTION.
YOU BROKE MY HEART, ZUKO! TWICE! AND THE STUPID THING IS, I LET YOU!
LIKE A COMPLETE MORON, I LET YOU.
KEI LO LIKES ME. A LOT. PROBABLY MORE THAN I LIKE HIM.
AND THAT'S EXACTLY HOW I NEED IT TO BE, BECAUSE I WON'T EVER LET MYSELF GET HURT LIKE THAT AGAIN.

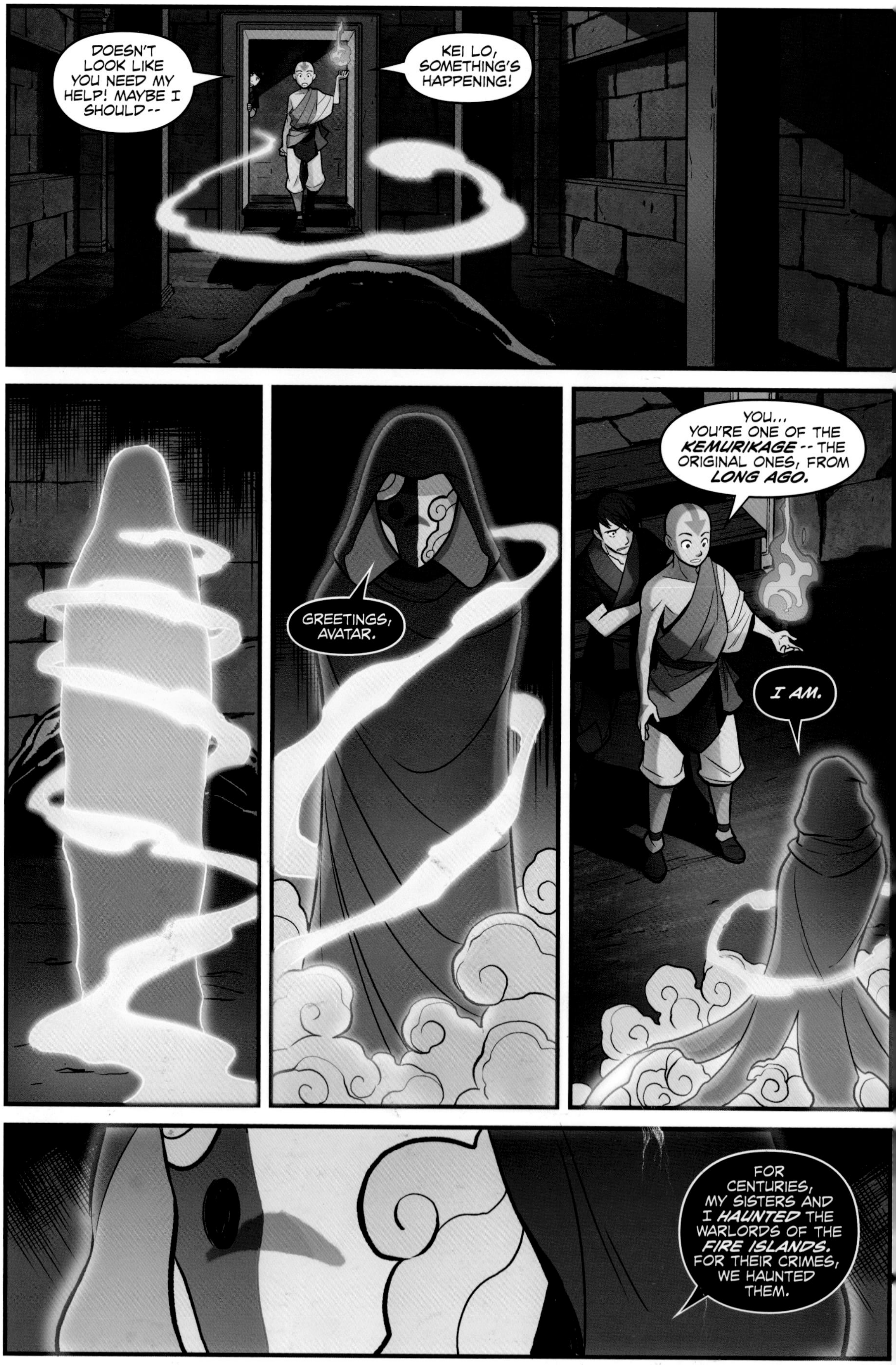
DOESN'T LOOK LIKE YOU NEED MY HELP! MAYBE I SHOULD--
KEI LO, SOMETHING'S HAPPENING!
GREETINGS, AVATAR.
YOU... YOU'RE ONE OF THE KEMURIKAGE -- THE ORIGINAL ONES, FROM LONG AGO.
I AM.
FOR CENTURIES, MY SISTERS AND I HAUNTED THE WARLORDS OF THE FIRE ISLANDS. FOR THEIR CRIMES, WE HAUNTED THEM.

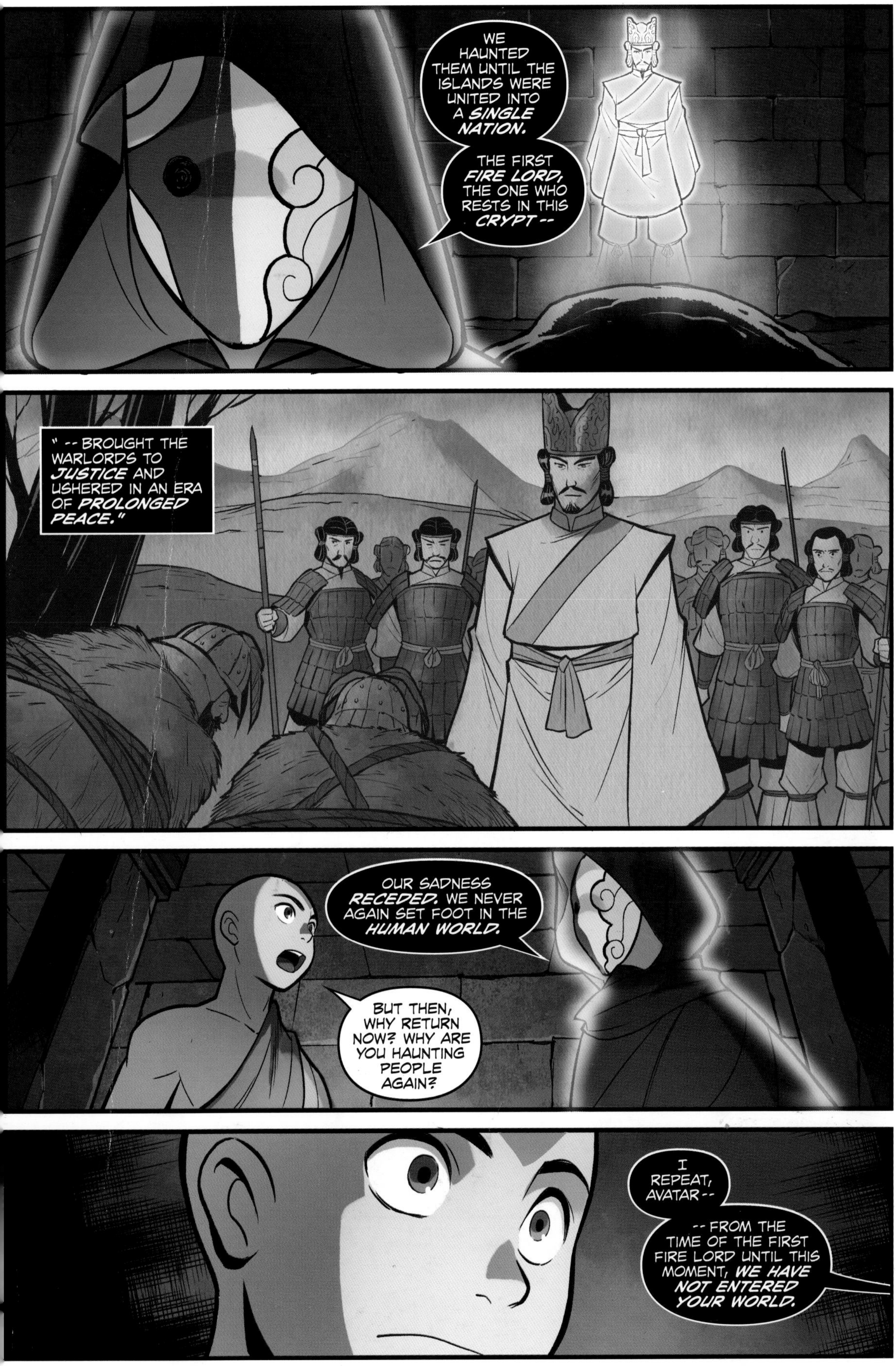
WE HAUNTED THEM UNTIL THE ISLANDS WERE UNITED INTO A *SINGLE NATION.*
THE FIRST *FIRE LORD,* THE ONE WHO RESTS IN THIS *CRYPT --*
" -- BROUGHT THE WARLORDS TO *JUSTICE* AND USHERED IN AN ERA OF *PROLONGED PEACE.*"
OUR SADNESS *RECEDED.* WE NEVER AGAIN SET FOOT IN THE *HUMAN WORLD.*
BUT THEN, WHY RETURN NOW? WHY ARE YOU HAUNTING PEOPLE AGAIN?
I REPEAT, AVATAR --
-- FROM THE TIME OF THE FIRST FIRE LORD UNTIL THIS MOMENT, *WE HAVE NOT ENTERED YOUR WORLD.*

GLY: *Here, we wanted to show that the position of the Fire Lord is rooted in good. Not every Fire Lord is like Ozai, Azulon, and Sozin.*

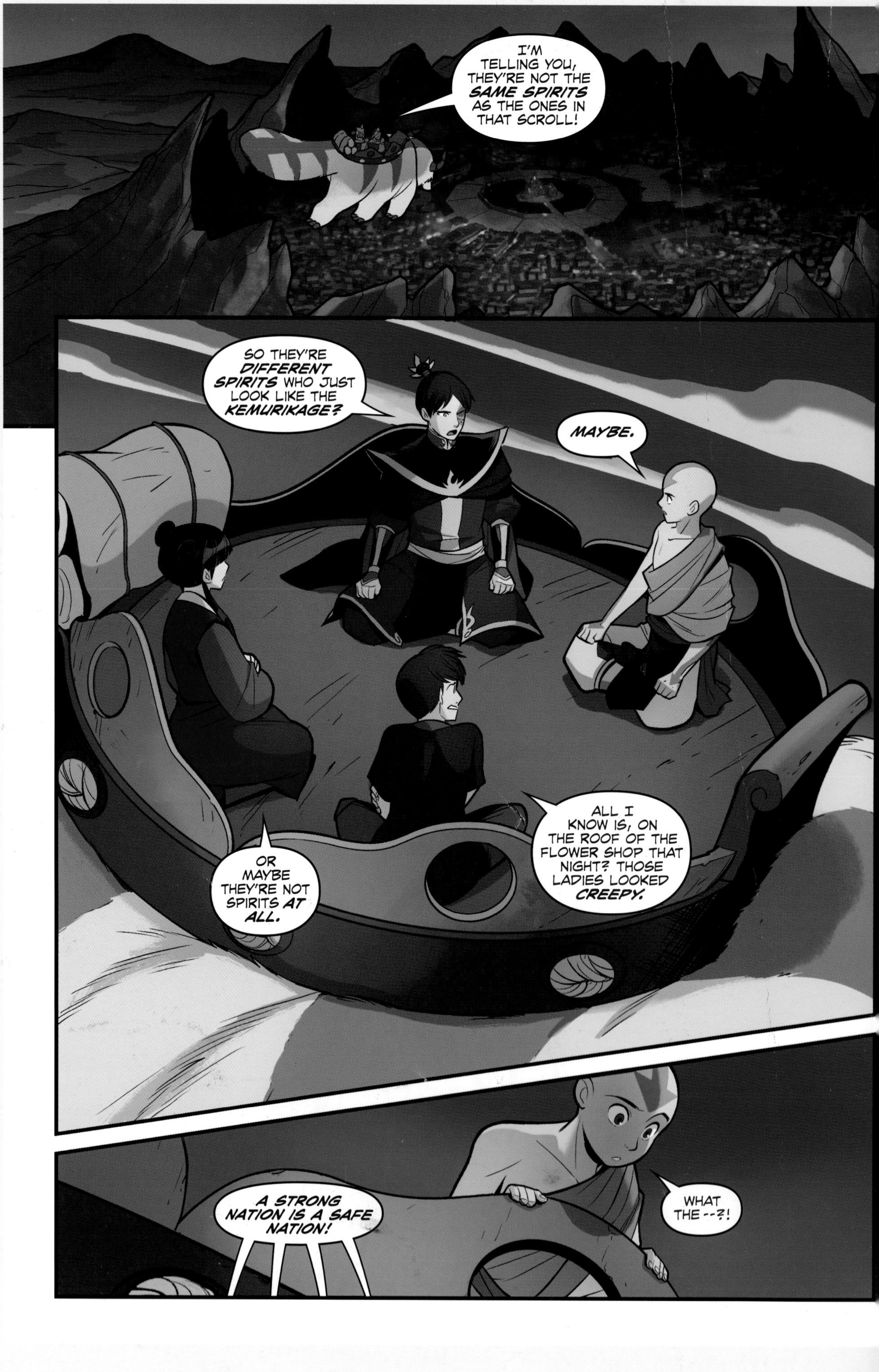
I'M TELLING YOU, THEY'RE NOT THE SAME SPIRITS AS THE ONES IN THAT SCROLL!
SO THEY'RE DIFFERENT SPIRITS WHO JUST LOOK LIKE THE KEMURIKAGE?
MAYBE.
OR MAYBE THEY'RE NOT SPIRITS AT ALL.
ALL I KNOW IS, ON THE ROOF OF THE FLOWER SHOP THAT NIGHT? THOSE LADIES LOOKED CREEPY.
A STRONG NATION IS A SAFE NATION!
WHAT THE--?!

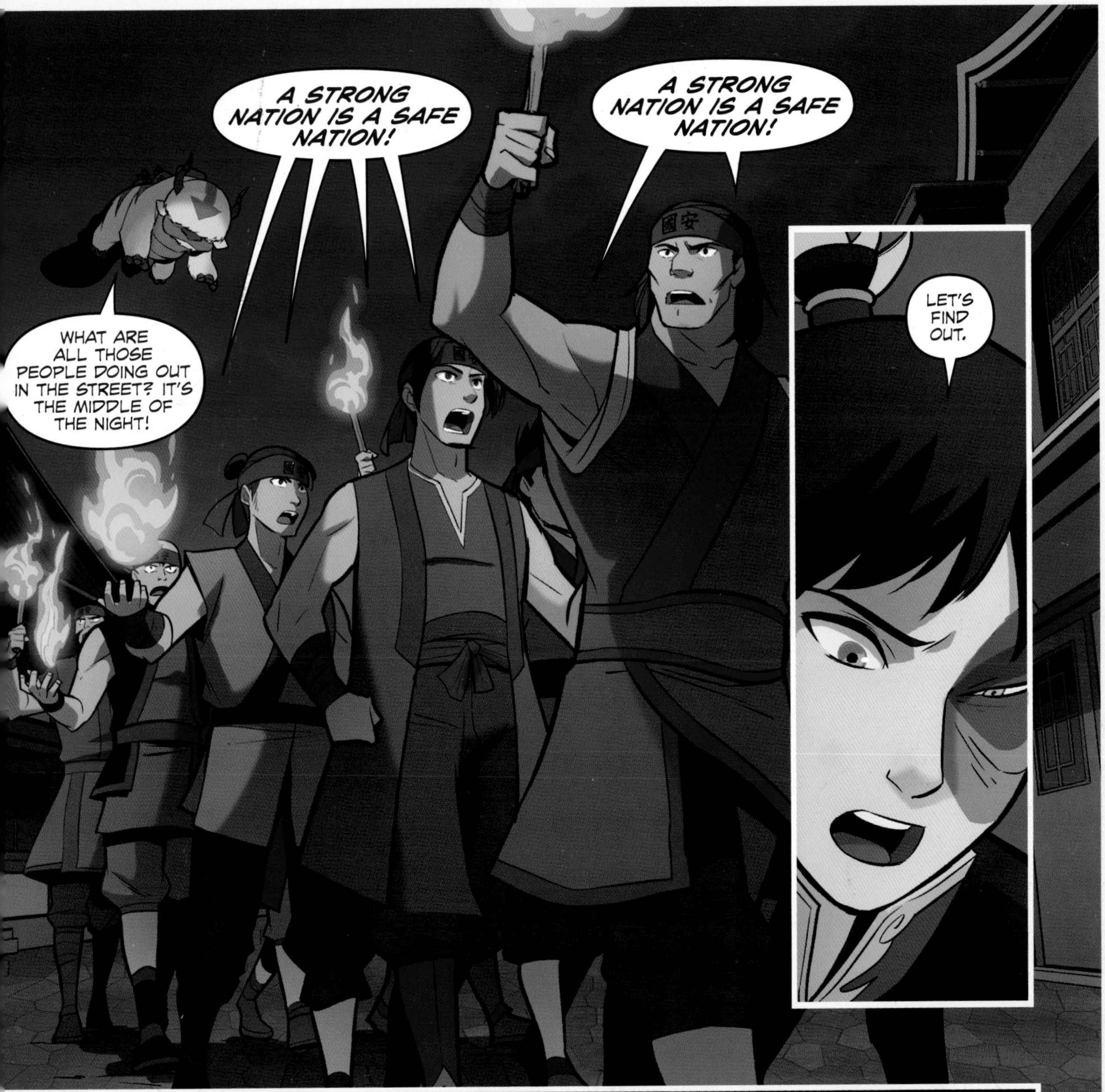
WHAT ARE ALL THOSE PEOPLE DOING OUT IN THE STREET? IT'S THE MIDDLE OF THE NIGHT!
A STRONG NATION IS A SAFE NATION!
A STRONG NATION IS A SAFE NATION!
LET'S FIND OUT.

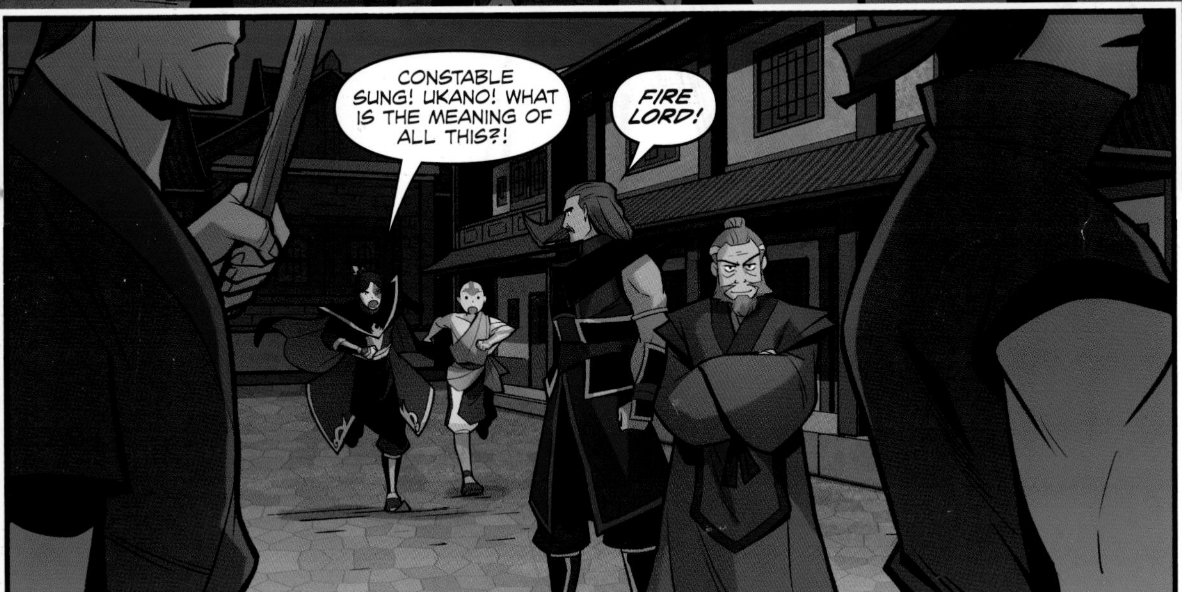
CONSTABLE SUNG! UKANO! WHAT IS THE MEANING OF ALL THIS?!
FIRE LORD!

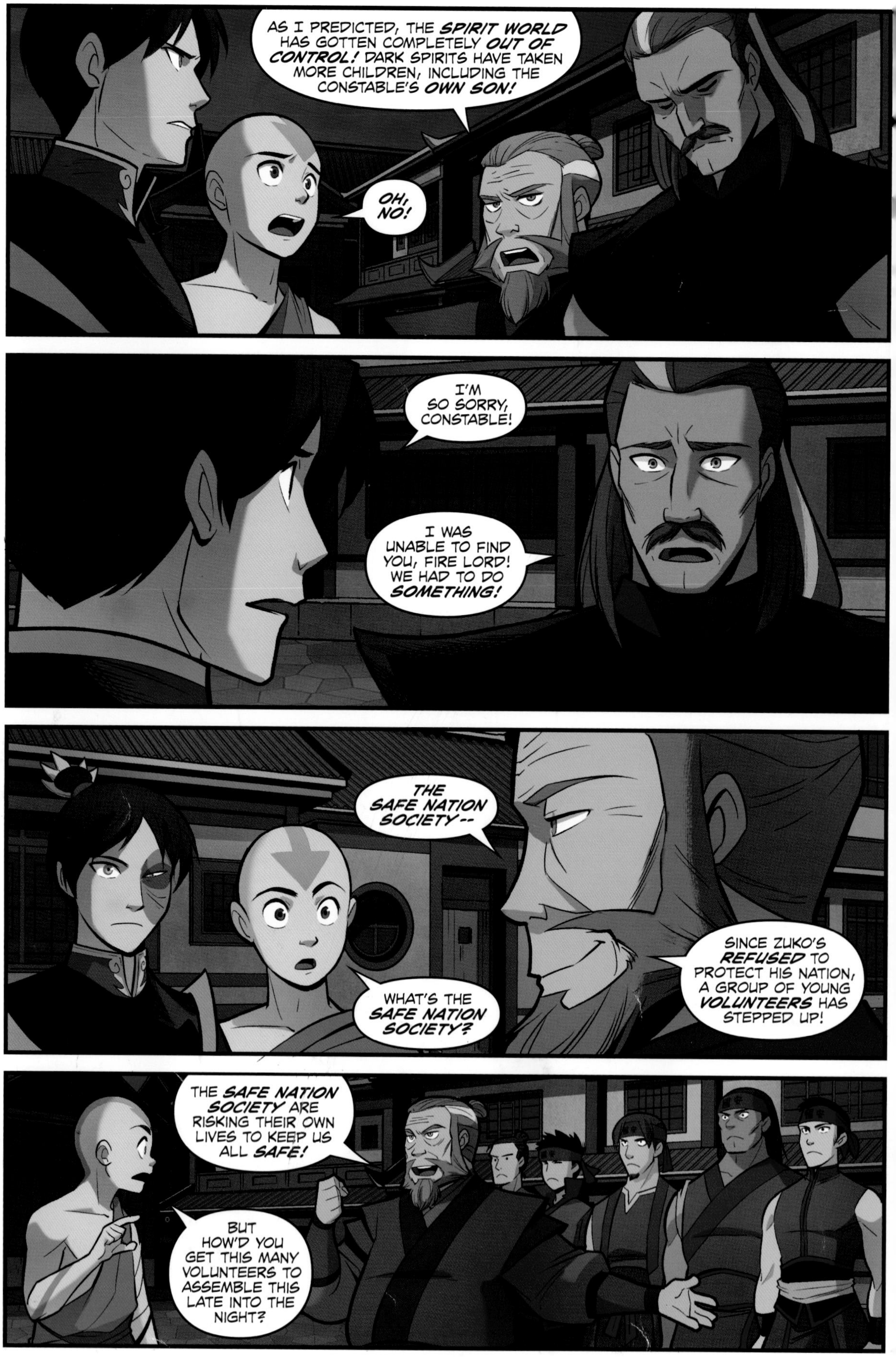
AS I PREDICTED, THE SPIRIT WORLD HAS GOTTEN COMPLETELY OUT OF CONTROL! DARK SPIRITS HAVE TAKEN MORE CHILDREN, INCLUDING THE CONSTABLE'S OWN SON!
OH, NO!
I'M SO SORRY, CONSTABLE!
I WAS UNABLE TO FIND YOU, FIRE LORD! WE HAD TO DO SOMETHING!
THE SAFE NATION SOCIETY --
WHAT'S THE SAFE NATION SOCIETY?
SINCE ZUKO'S REFUSED TO PROTECT HIS NATION, A GROUP OF YOUNG VOLUNTEERS HAS STEPPED UP!
THE SAFE NATION SOCIETY ARE RISKING THEIR OWN LIVES TO KEEP US ALL SAFE!
BUT HOW'D YOU GET THIS MANY VOLUNTEERS TO ASSEMBLE THIS LATE INTO THE NIGHT?

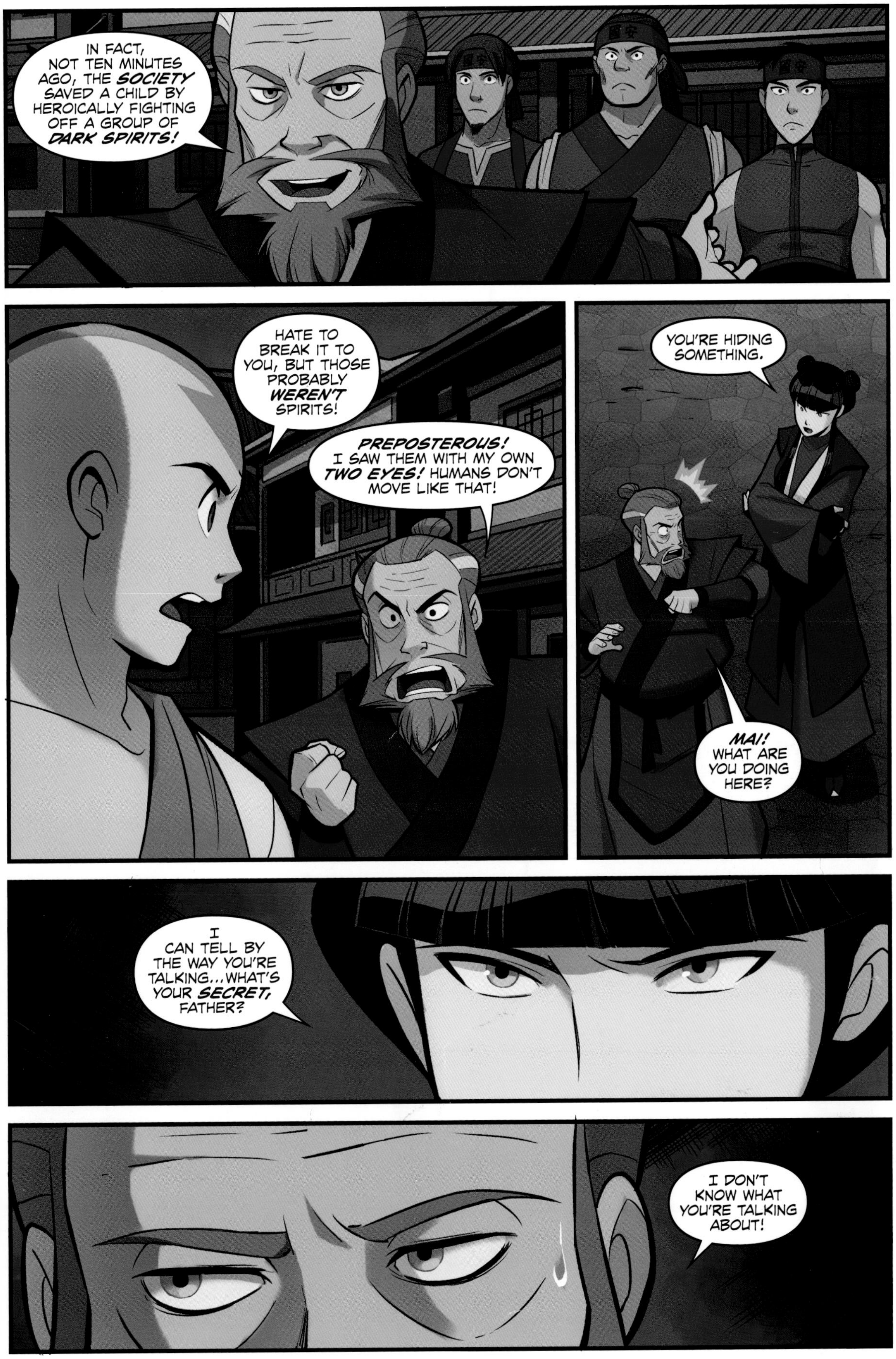
IN FACT, NOT TEN MINUTES AGO, THE SOCIETY SAVED A CHILD BY HEROICALLY FIGHTING OFF A GROUP OF DARK SPIRITS!
HATE TO BREAK IT TO YOU, BUT THOSE PROBABLY WEREN'T SPIRITS!
PREPOSTEROUS! I SAW THEM WITH MY OWN TWO EYES! HUMANS DON'T MOVE LIKE THAT!
YOU'RE HIDING SOMETHING.
MAI! WHAT ARE YOU DOING HERE?
I CAN TELL BY THE WAY YOU'RE TALKING... WHAT'S YOUR SECRET, FATHER?
I DON'T KNOW WHAT YOU'RE TALKING ABOUT!

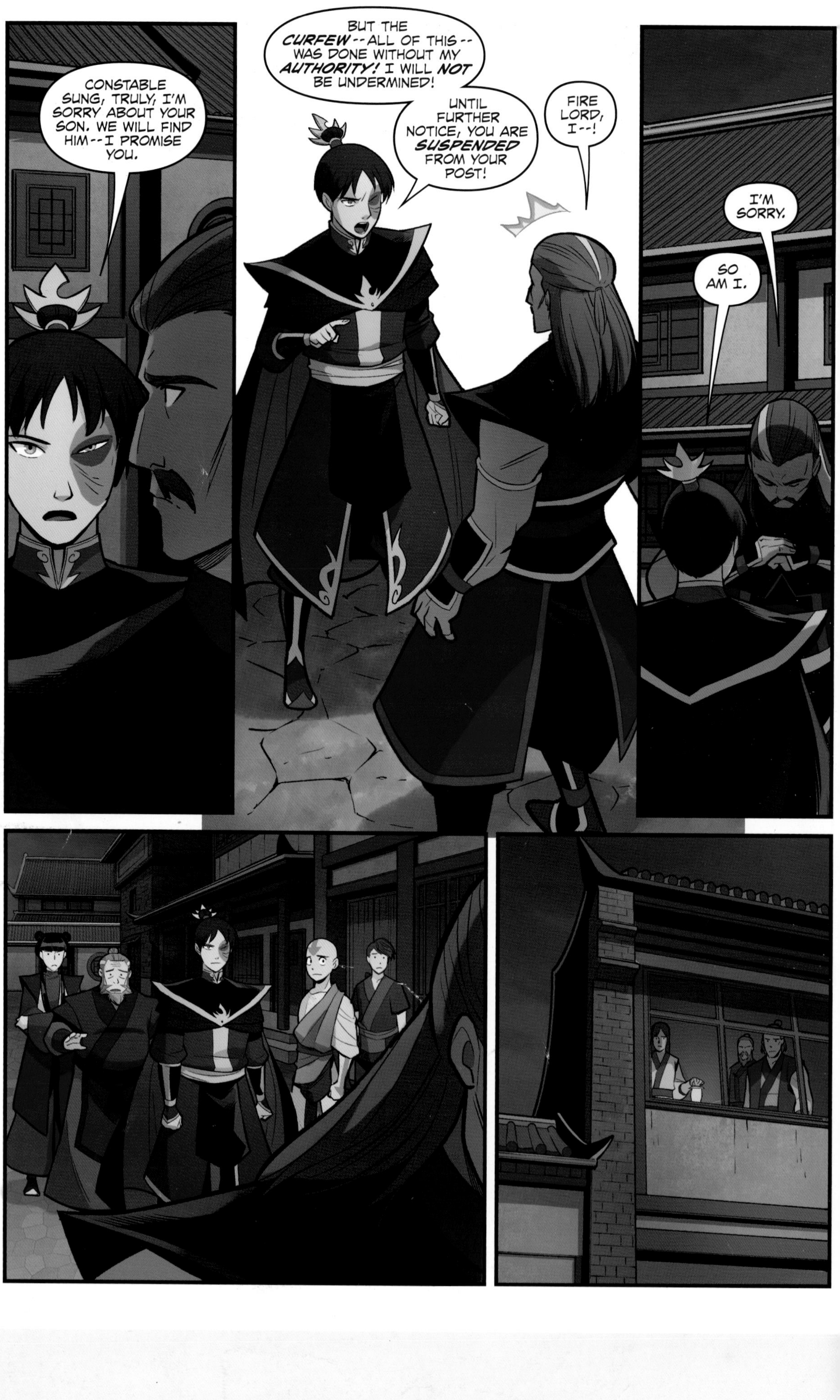
CONSTABLE SUNG, TRULY, I'M SORRY ABOUT YOUR SON. WE WILL FIND HIM--I PROMISE YOU.
BUT THE CURFEW--ALL OF THIS--WAS DONE WITHOUT MY AUTHORITY! I WILL NOT BE UNDERMINED!
UNTIL FURTHER NOTICE, YOU ARE SUSPENDED FROM YOUR POST!
FIRE LORD, I--!
I'M SORRY.
SO AM I.

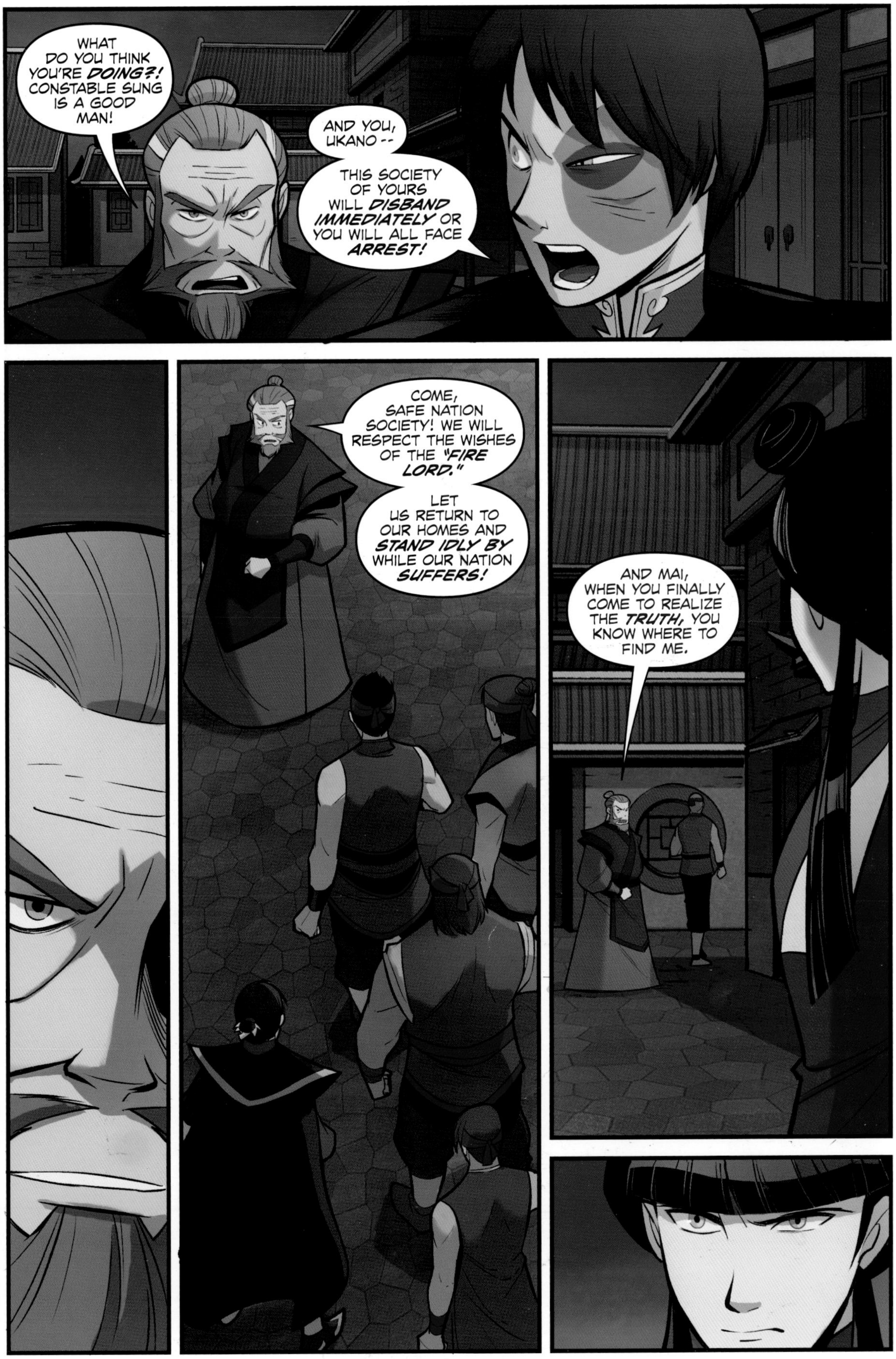
WHAT DO YOU THINK YOU'RE DOING?! CONSTABLE SUNG IS A GOOD MAN!
AND YOU, UKANO --
THIS SOCIETY OF YOURS WILL DISBAND IMMEDIATELY OR YOU WILL ALL FACE ARREST!
COME, SAFE NATION SOCIETY! WE WILL RESPECT THE WISHES OF THE "FIRE LORD."
LET US RETURN TO OUR HOMES AND STAND IDLY BY WHILE OUR NATION SUFFERS!
AND MAI, WHEN YOU FINALLY COME TO REALIZE THE TRUTH, YOU KNOW WHERE TO FIND ME.

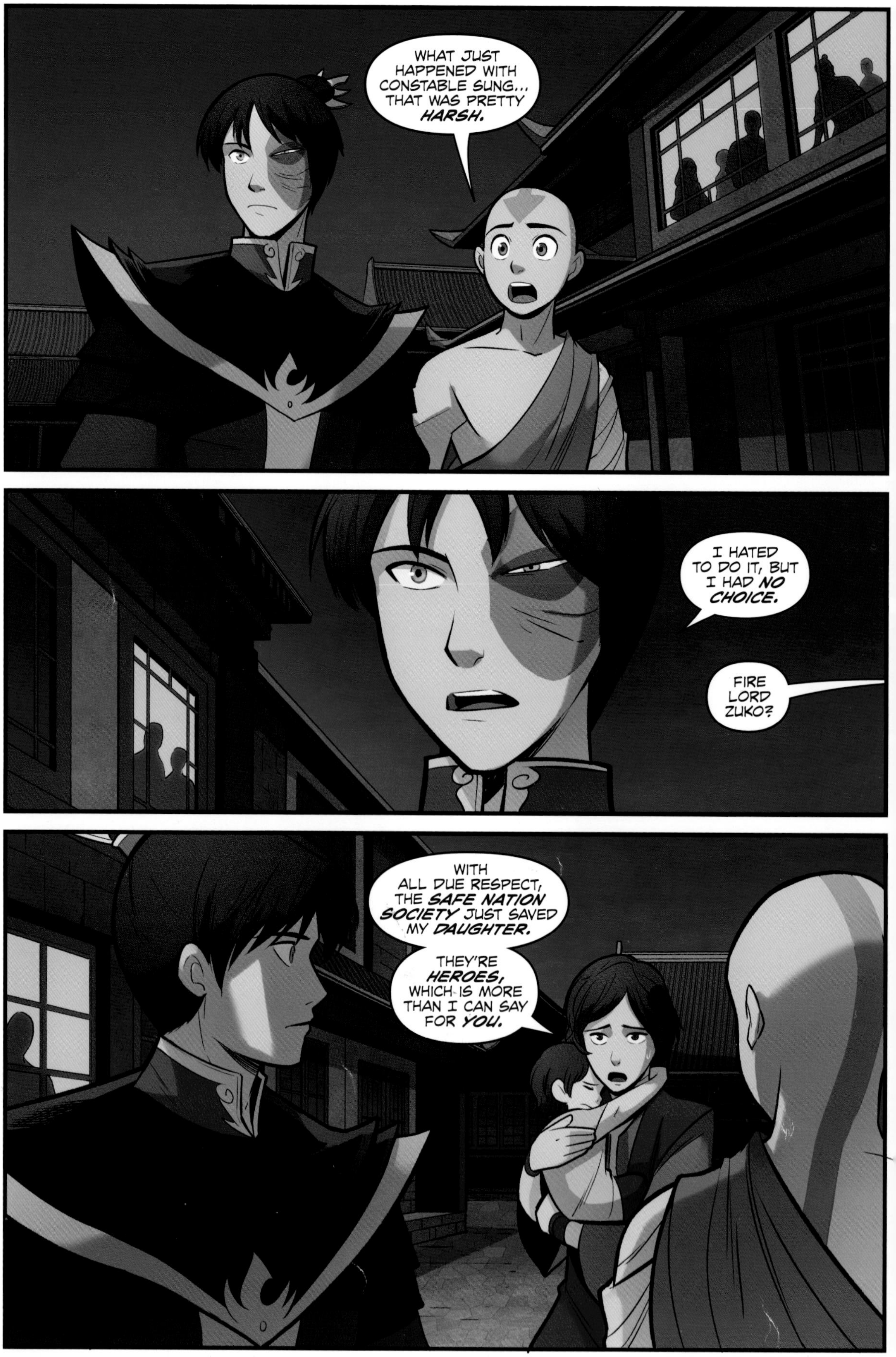
WHAT JUST HAPPENED WITH CONSTABLE SUNG... THAT WAS PRETTY HARSH.
I HATED TO DO IT, BUT I HAD NO CHOICE.
FIRE LORD ZUKO?
WITH ALL DUE RESPECT, THE SAFE NATION SOCIETY JUST SAVED MY DAUGHTER.
THEY'RE HEROES, WHICH IS MORE THAN I CAN SAY FOR YOU.

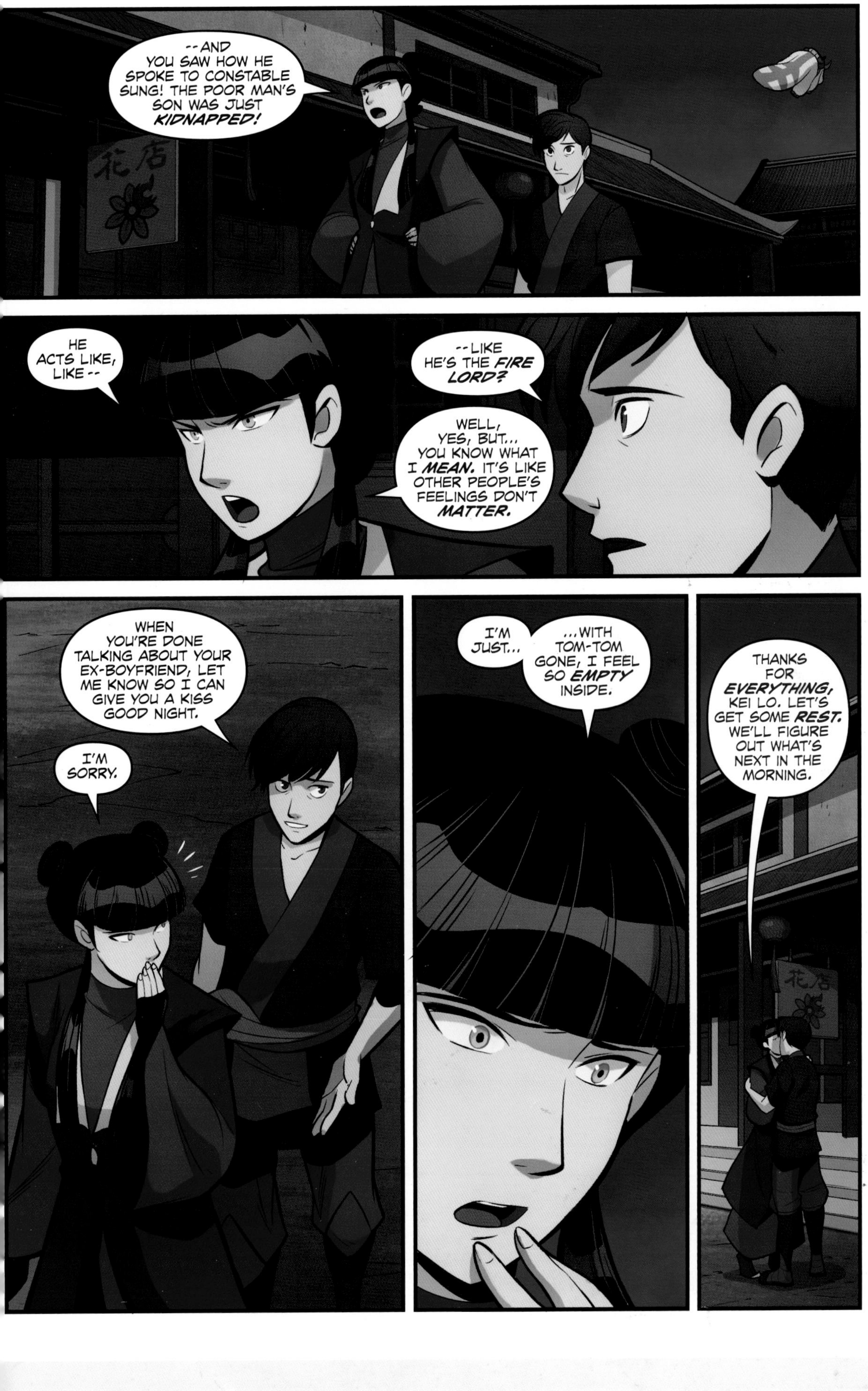
--AND YOU SAW HOW HE SPOKE TO CONSTABLE SUNG! THE POOR MAN'S SON WAS JUST KIDNAPPED!
HE ACTS LIKE, LIKE --
--LIKE HE'S THE FIRE LORD?
WELL, YES, BUT... YOU KNOW WHAT I MEAN. IT'S LIKE OTHER PEOPLE'S FEELINGS DON'T MATTER.
WHEN YOU'RE DONE TALKING ABOUT YOUR EX-BOYFRIEND, LET ME KNOW SO I CAN GIVE YOU A KISS GOOD NIGHT.
I'M SORRY.
I'M JUST...
...WITH TOM-TOM GONE, I FEEL SO EMPTY INSIDE.
THANKS FOR EVERYTHING, KEI LO. LET'S GET SOME REST. WE'LL FIGURE OUT WHAT'S NEXT IN THE MORNING.

GLY: *When Mai, Tom-Tom, and their parents first appeared in "Return to Omashu," Mai wasn't all that warm toward her little brother. In fact, she was willing to go along with Azula's plan to give him up to Team Avatar.*

As the series progressed, however, we saw Mai opening up. She made a place in her heart for Zuko. She gathered her courage and stood up to Azula. These changes allowed her to warm up to her brother, too.

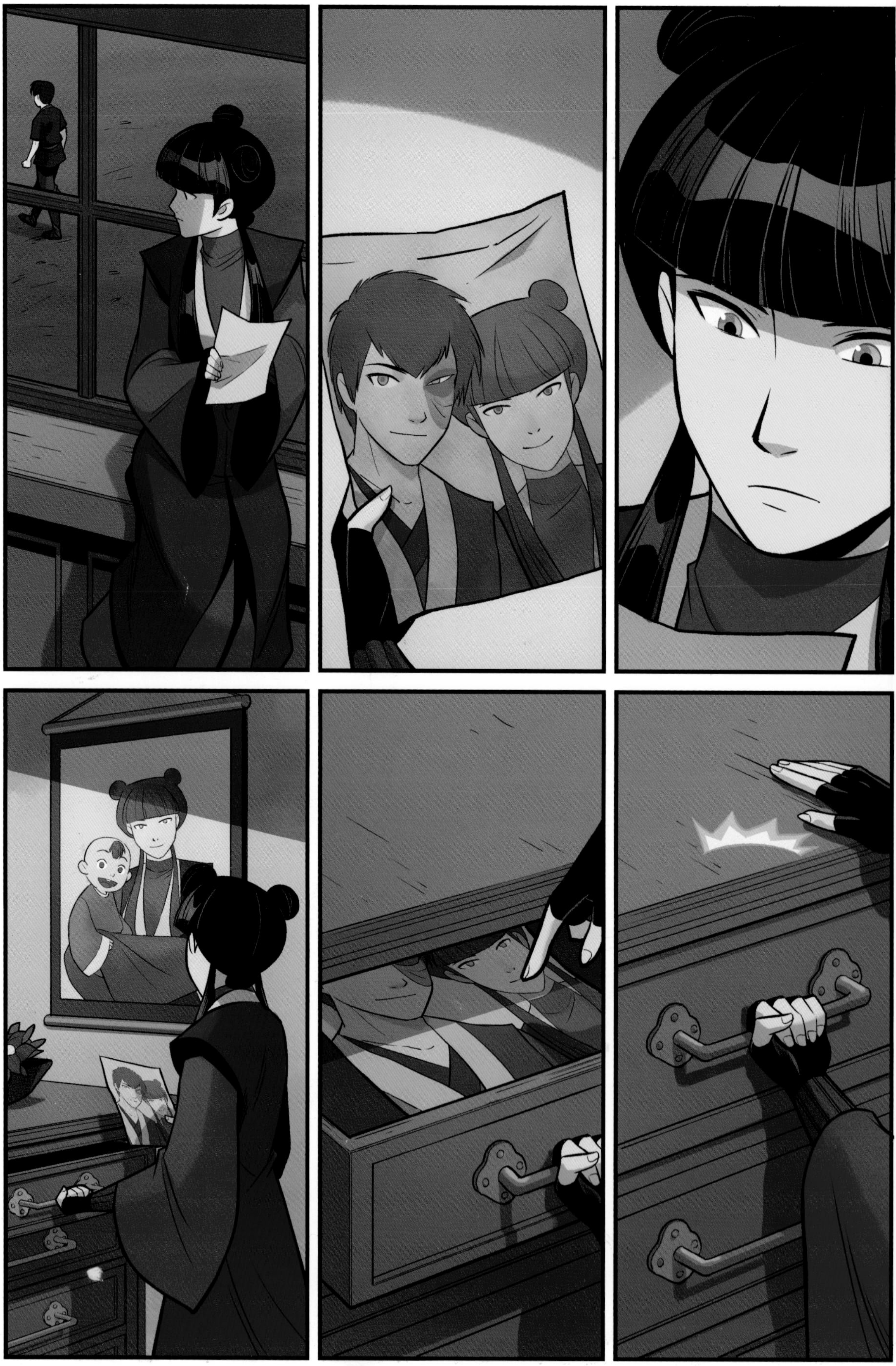

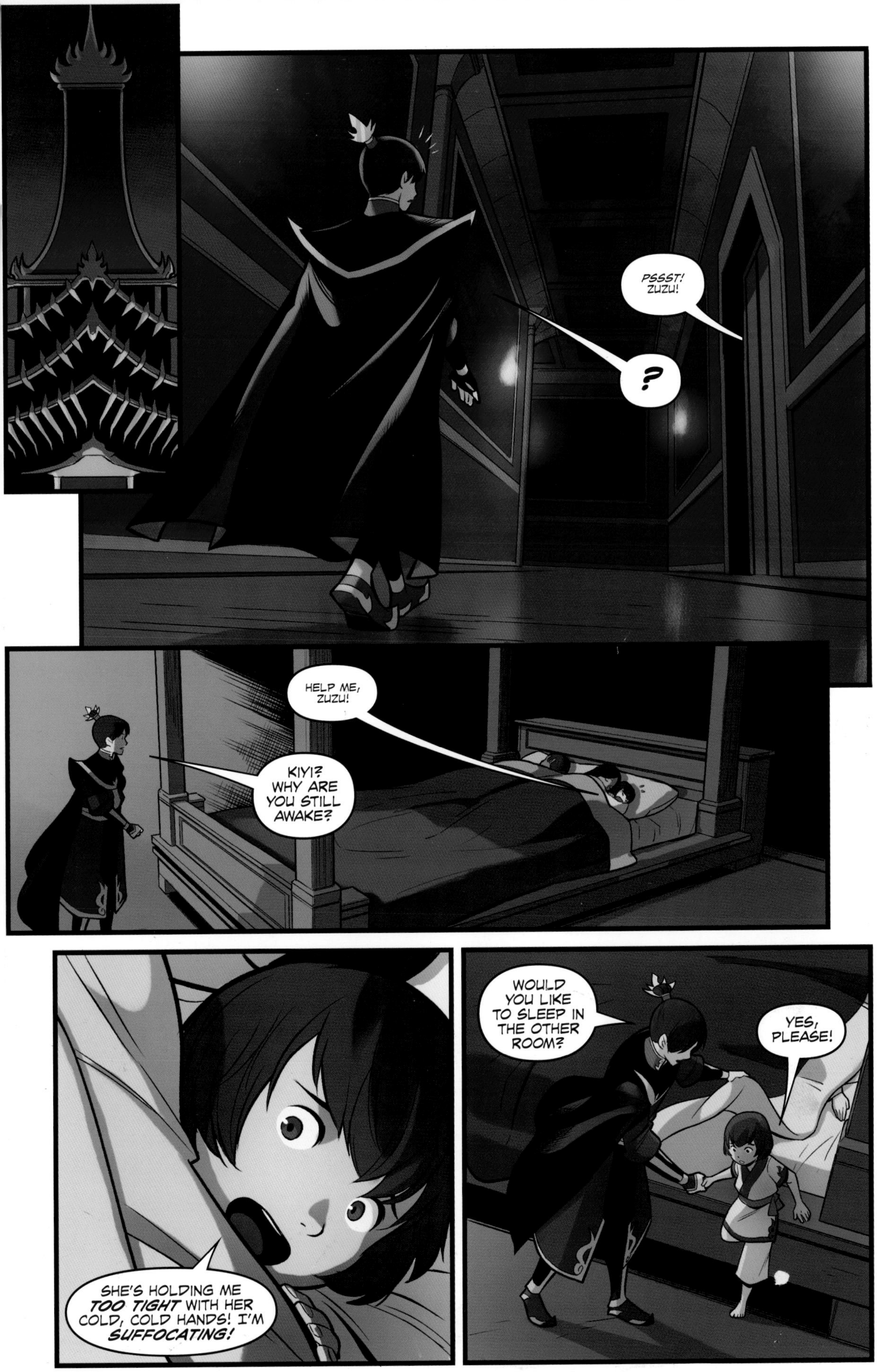
PSSST! ZUZU!
?
HELP ME, ZUZU!
KIYI? WHY ARE YOU STILL AWAKE?
SHE'S HOLDING ME *TOO TIGHT* WITH HER COLD, COLD HANDS! I'M *SUFFOCATING!*
WOULD YOU LIKE TO SLEEP IN THE OTHER ROOM?
YES, PLEASE!

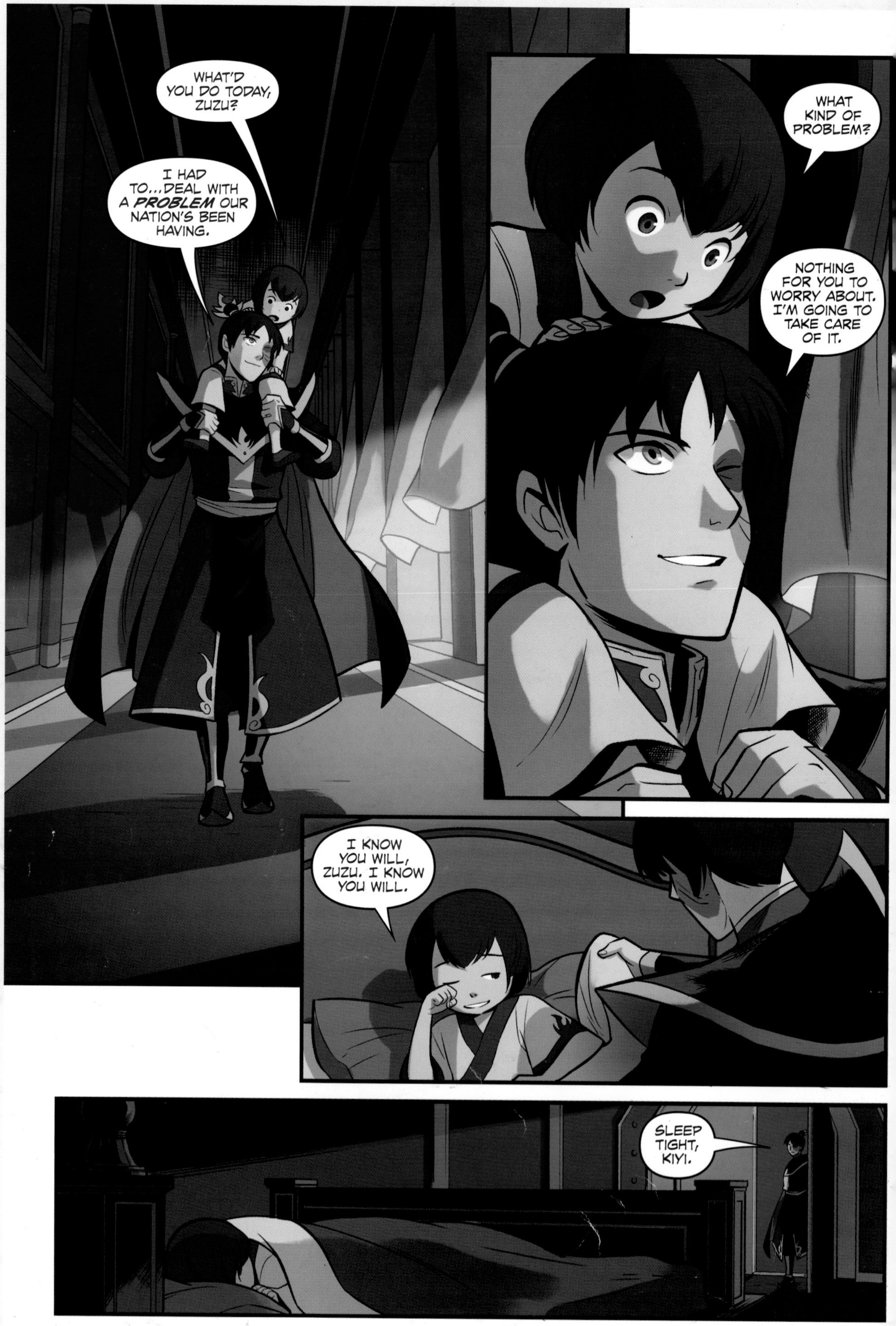
WHAT'D YOU DO TODAY, ZUZU?
I HAD TO...DEAL WITH A PROBLEM OUR NATION'S BEEN HAVING.
WHAT KIND OF PROBLEM?
NOTHING FOR YOU TO WORRY ABOUT. I'M GOING TO TAKE CARE OF IT.
I KNOW YOU WILL, ZUZU. I KNOW YOU WILL.
SLEEP TIGHT, KIYI.

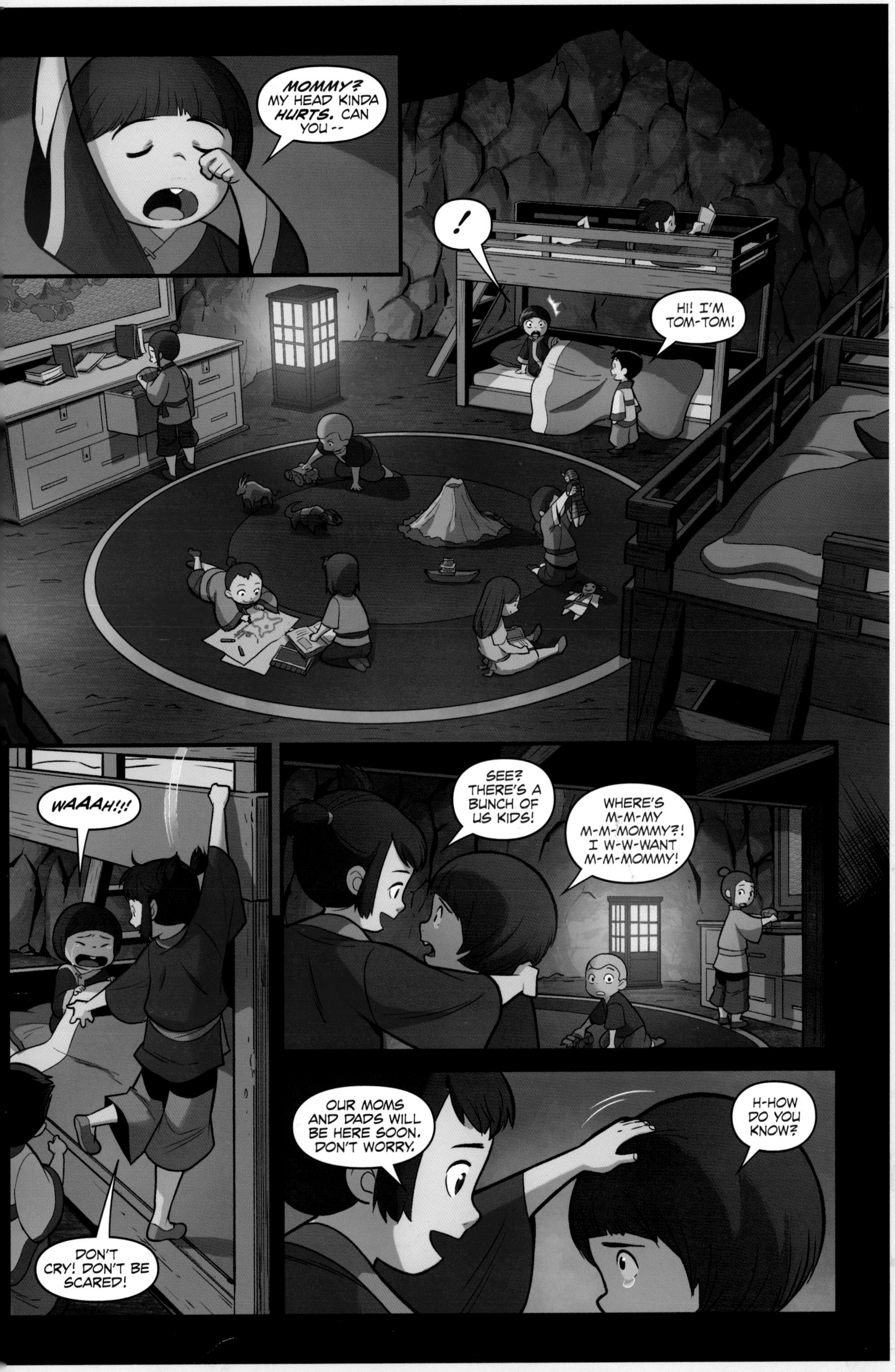
MOMMY? MY HEAD KINDA HURTS. CAN YOU --
!
HI! I'M TOM-TOM!
WAAAH!!!
DON'T CRY! DON'T BE SCARED!
SEE? THERE'S A BUNCH OF US KIDS!
WHERE'S M-M-MY M-M-MOMMY?! I W-W-WANT M-M-MOMMY!
OUR MOMS AND DADS WILL BE HERE SOON. DON'T WORRY.
H-HOW DO YOU KNOW?

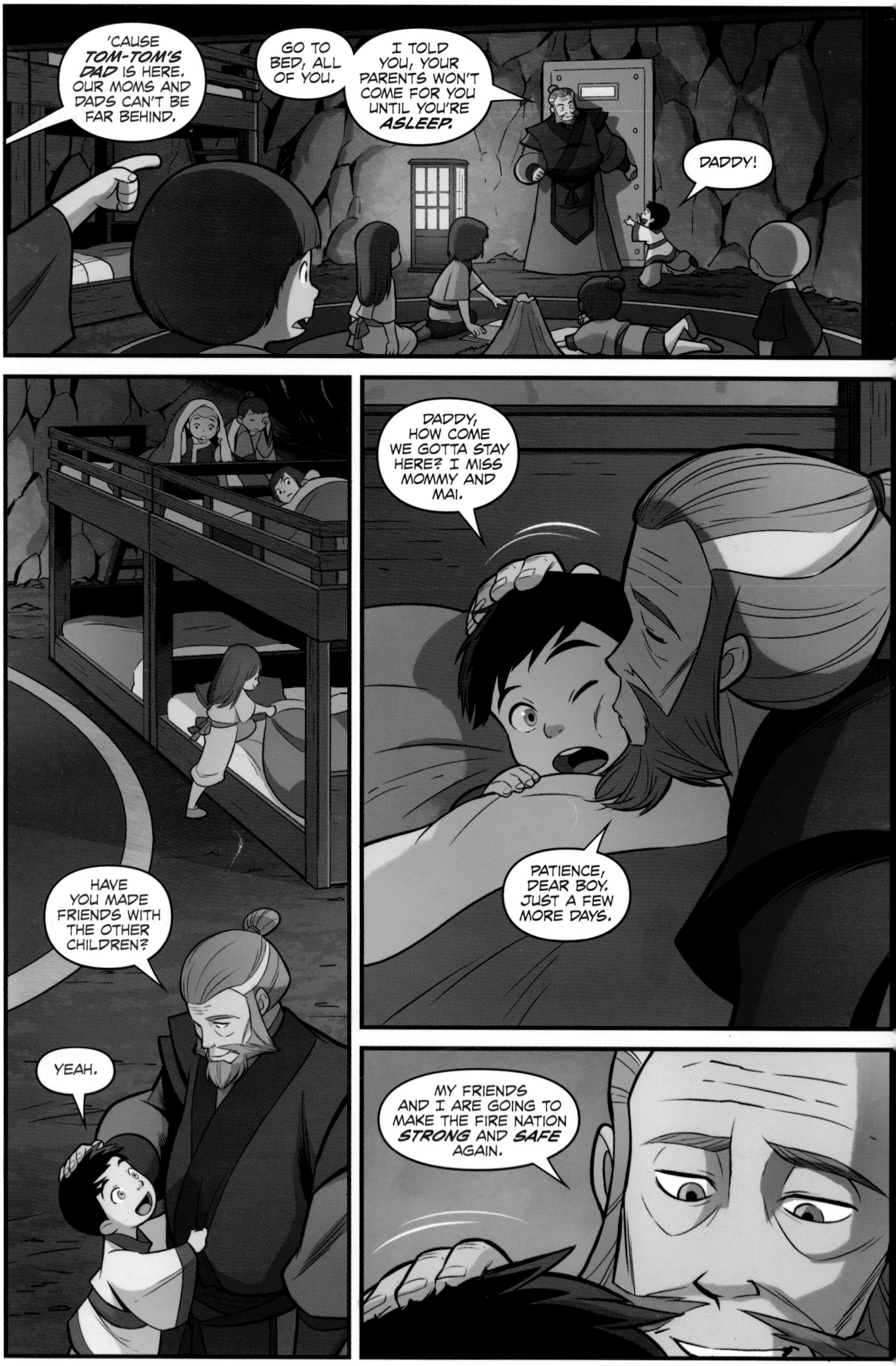
'CAUSE *TOM-TOM'S DAD* IS HERE. OUR MOMS AND DADS CAN'T BE FAR BEHIND.
GO TO BED, ALL OF YOU.
I TOLD YOU, YOUR PARENTS WON'T COME FOR YOU UNTIL YOU'RE *ASLEEP.*
DADDY!
HAVE YOU MADE FRIENDS WITH THE OTHER CHILDREN?
YEAH.
DADDY, HOW COME WE GOTTA STAY HERE? I MISS MOMMY AND MAI.
PATIENCE, DEAR BOY. JUST A FEW MORE DAYS.
MY FRIENDS AND I ARE GOING TO MAKE THE FIRE NATION *STRONG* AND *SAFE* AGAIN.

GLY: *Gurihiru needed to make the children's chamber creepy, but not too creepy. I think they did a great job.*

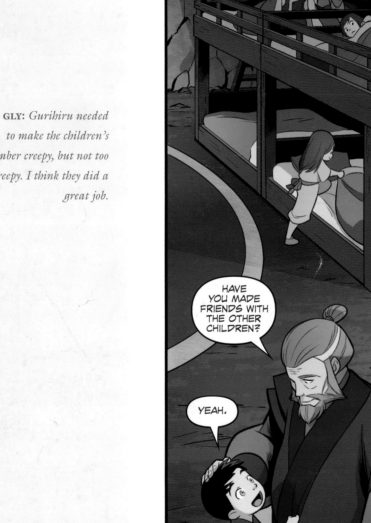

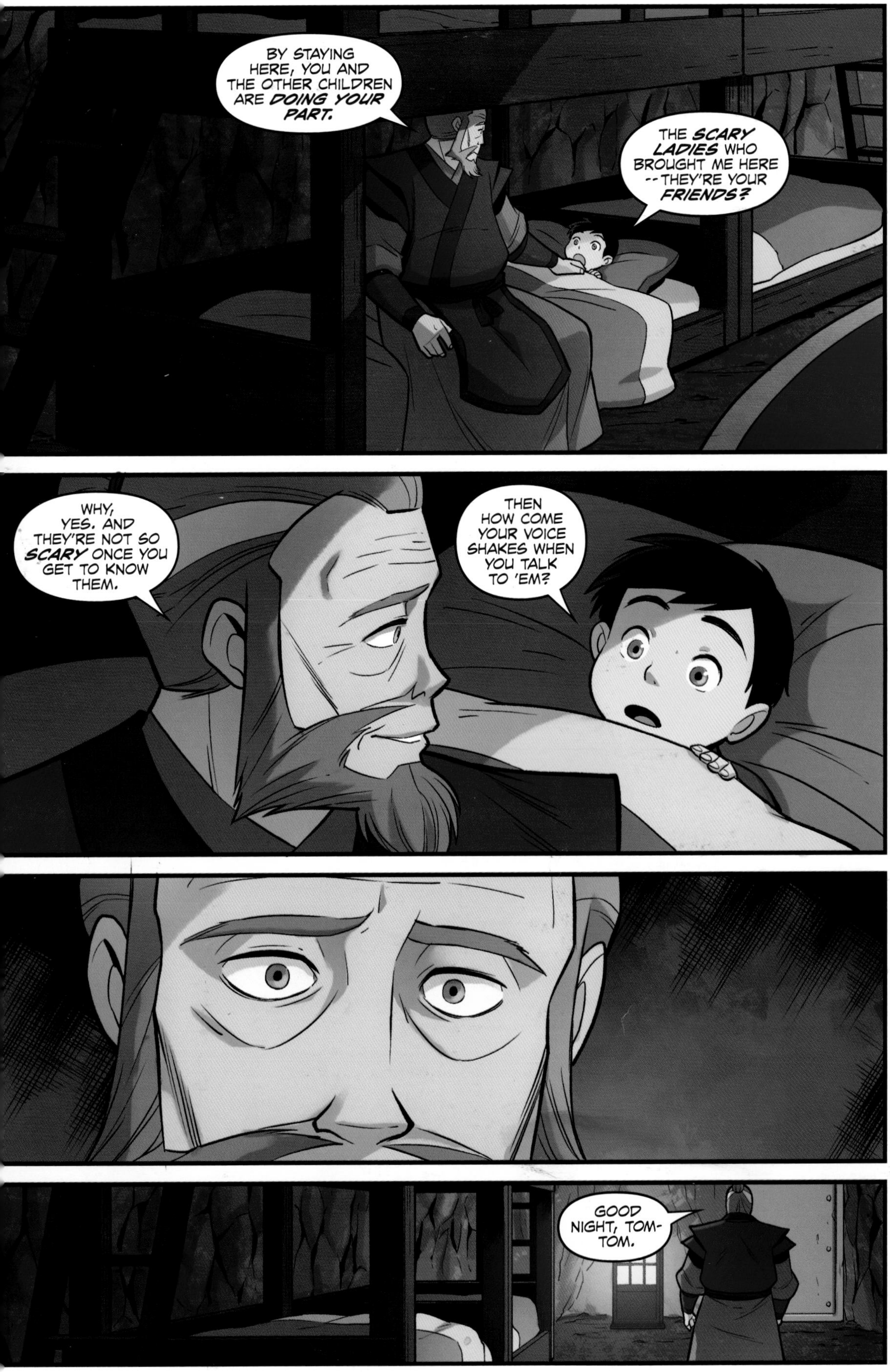
BY STAYING HERE, YOU AND THE OTHER CHILDREN ARE DOING YOUR PART.
THE SCARY LADIES WHO BROUGHT ME HERE --THEY'RE YOUR FRIENDS?
WHY, YES. AND THEY'RE NOT SO SCARY ONCE YOU GET TO KNOW THEM.
THEN HOW COME YOUR VOICE SHAKES WHEN YOU TALK TO 'EM?
GOOD NIGHT, TOM-TOM.

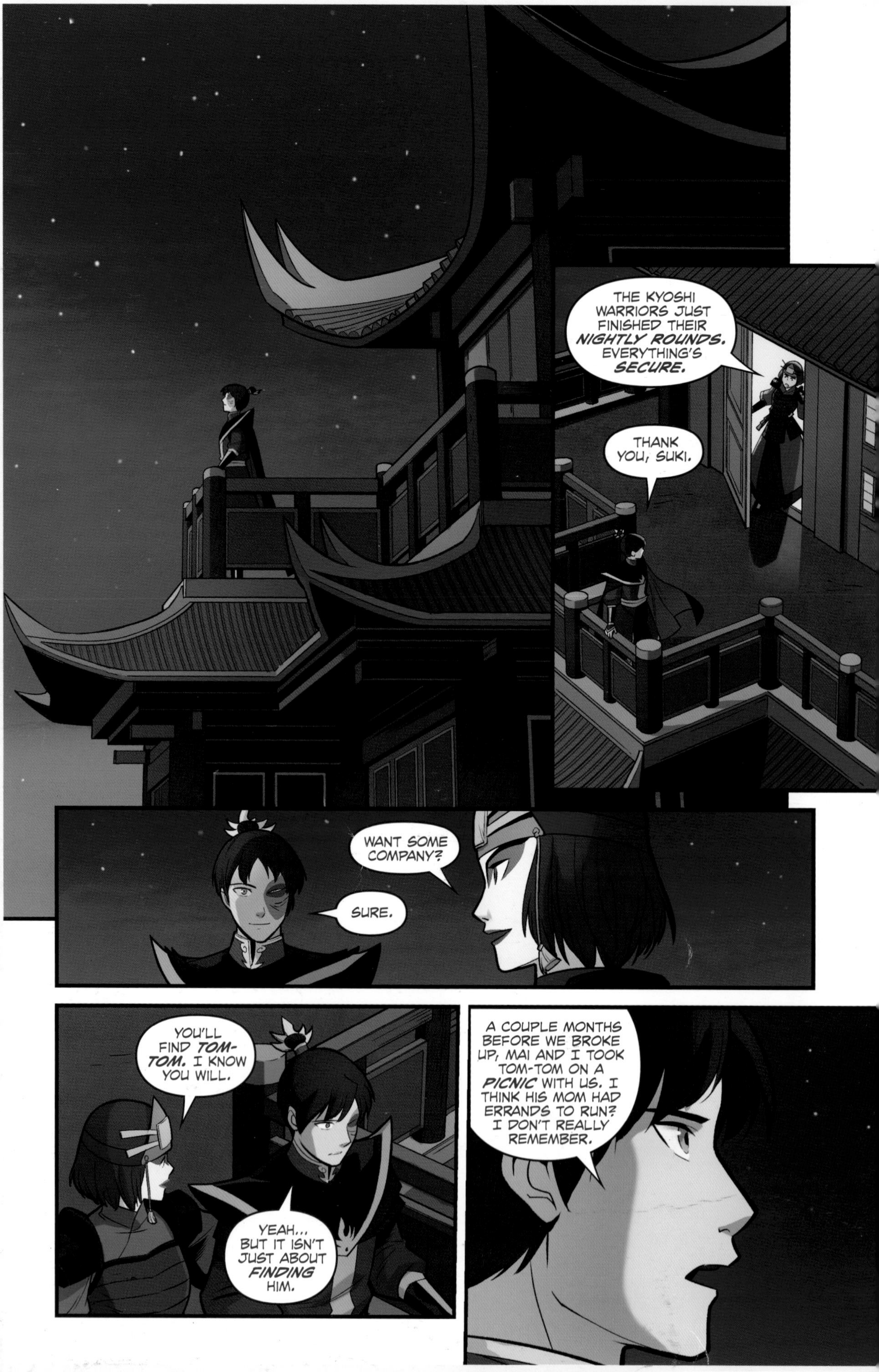
THE KYOSHI WARRIORS JUST FINISHED THEIR NIGHTLY ROUNDS. EVERYTHING'S SECURE.
THANK YOU, SUKI.
WANT SOME COMPANY?
SURE.
YOU'LL FIND TOM-TOM. I KNOW YOU WILL.
YEAH... BUT IT ISN'T JUST ABOUT FINDING HIM.
A COUPLE MONTHS BEFORE WE BROKE UP, MAI AND I TOOK TOM-TOM ON A PICNIC WITH US. I THINK HIS MOM HAD ERRANDS TO RUN? I DON'T REALLY REMEMBER.

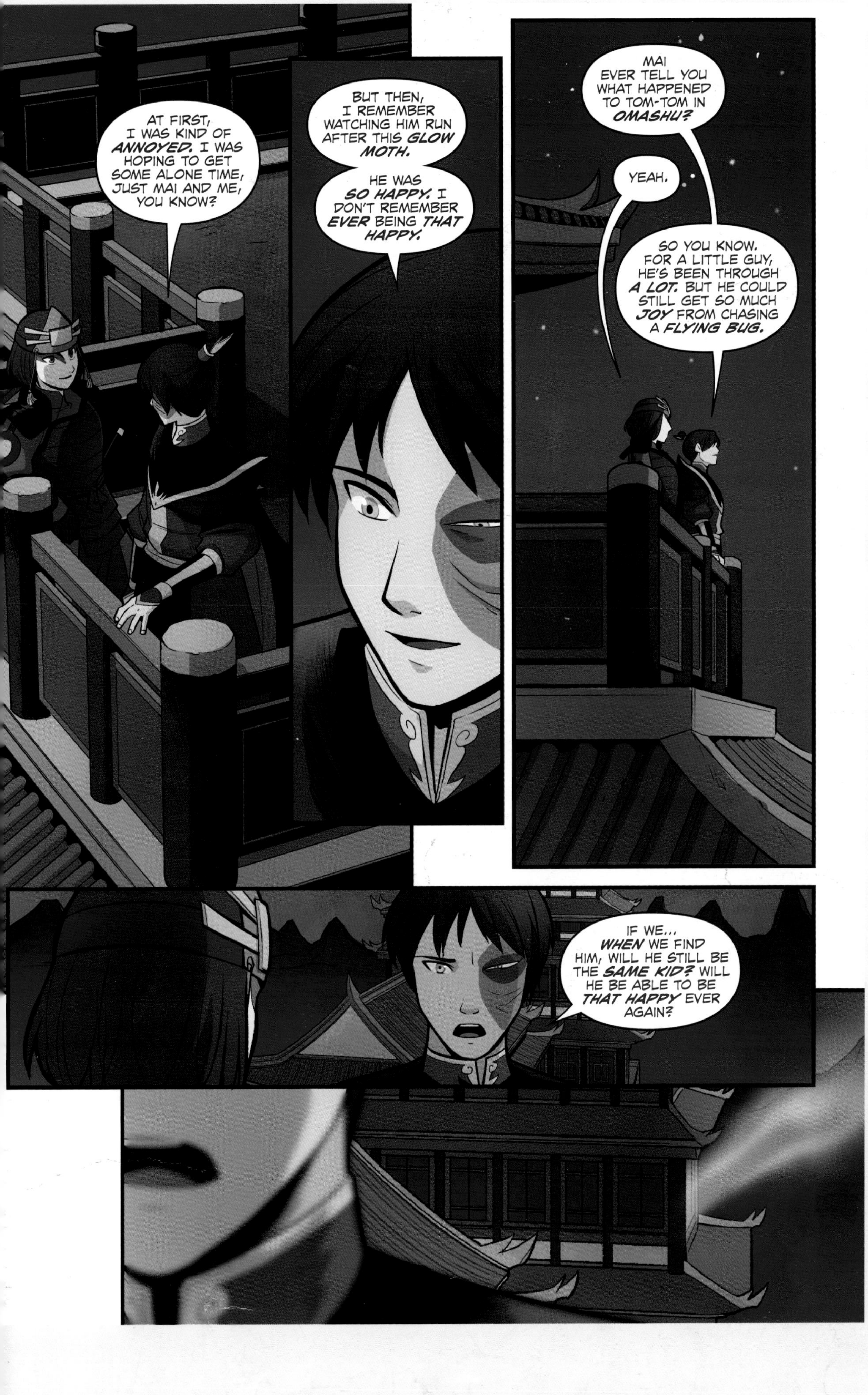
AT FIRST, I WAS KIND OF ANNOYED. I WAS HOPING TO GET SOME ALONE TIME, JUST MAI AND ME, YOU KNOW?
BUT THEN, I REMEMBER WATCHING HIM RUN AFTER THIS GLOW MOTH.
HE WAS SO HAPPY. I DON'T REMEMBER EVER BEING THAT HAPPY.
MAI EVER TELL YOU WHAT HAPPENED TO TOM-TOM IN OMASHU?
YEAH.
SO YOU KNOW. FOR A LITTLE GUY, HE'S BEEN THROUGH A LOT. BUT HE COULD STILL GET SO MUCH JOY FROM CHASING A FLYING BUG.
IF WE... WHEN WE FIND HIM, WILL HE STILL BE THE SAME KID? WILL HE BE ABLE TO BE THAT HAPPY EVER AGAIN?

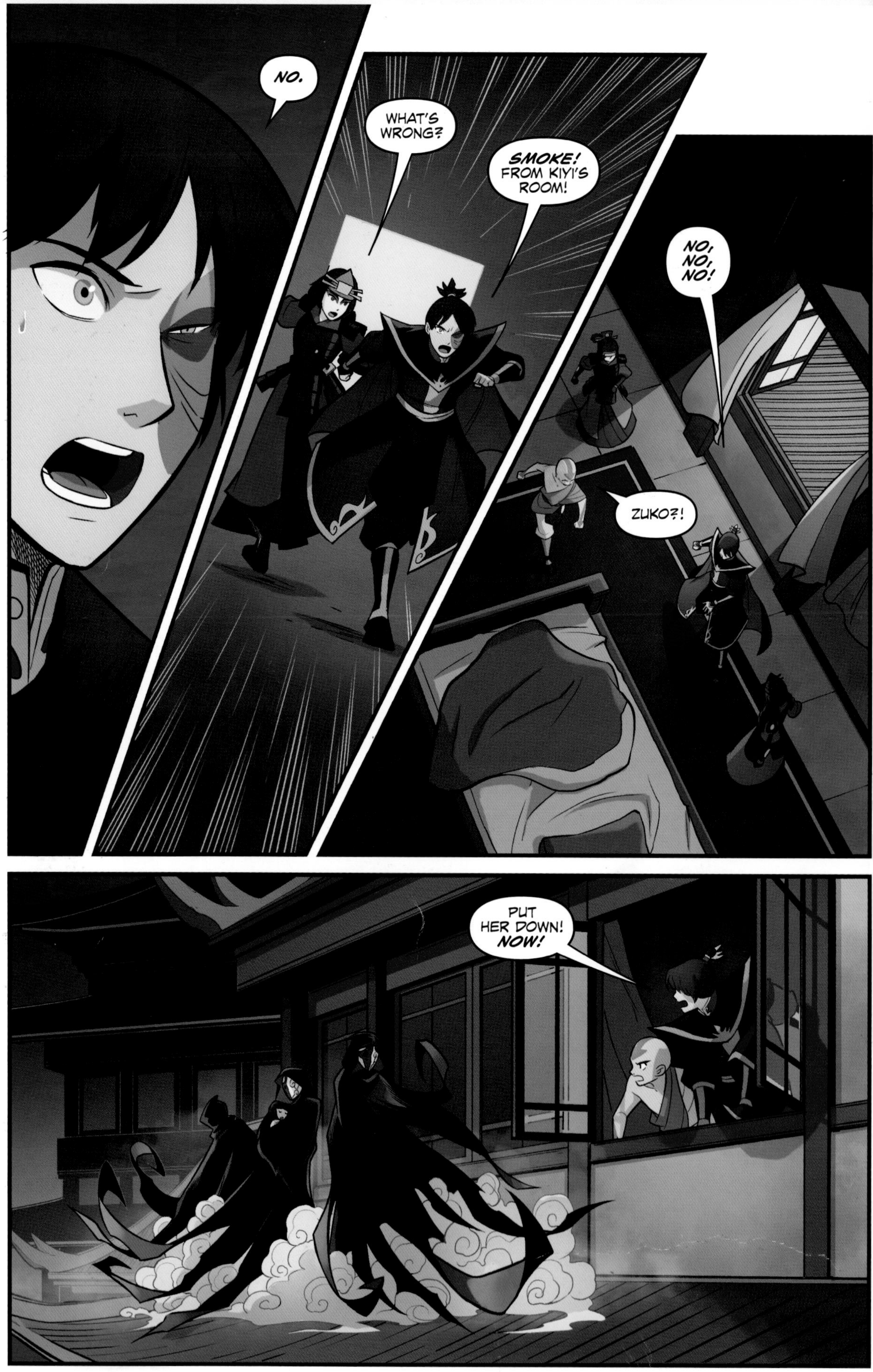
NO.
WHAT'S WRONG?
SMOKE! FROM KIYI'S ROOM!
NO, NO, NO!
ZUKO?!
PUT HER DOWN! NOW!

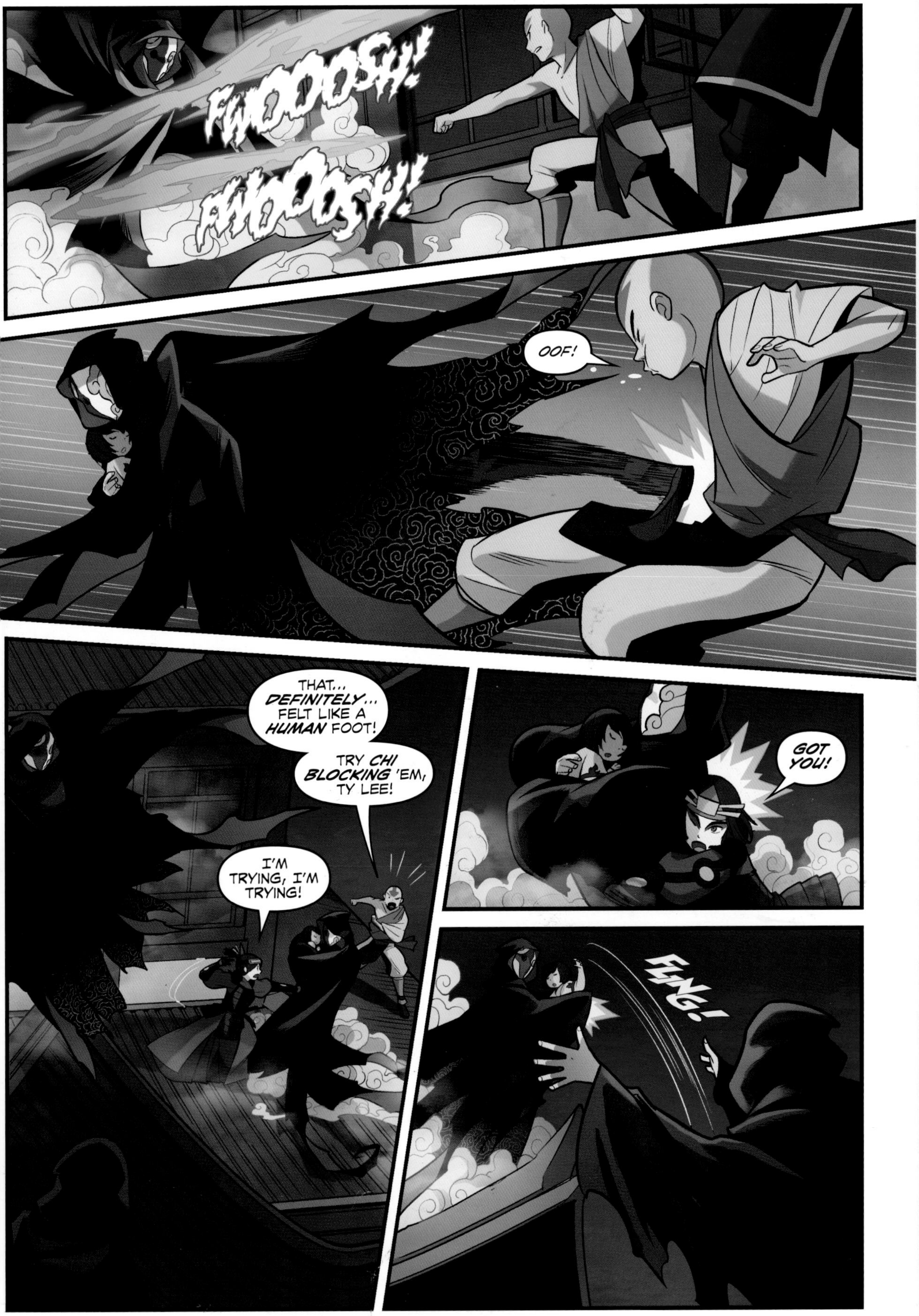
FWOOOSH!
FWOOOSH!
OOF!
THAT... DEFINITELY... FELT LIKE A HUMAN FOOT!
TRY CHI BLOCKING 'EM, TY LEE!
I'M TRYING, I'M TRYING!
GOT YOU!
FLING!

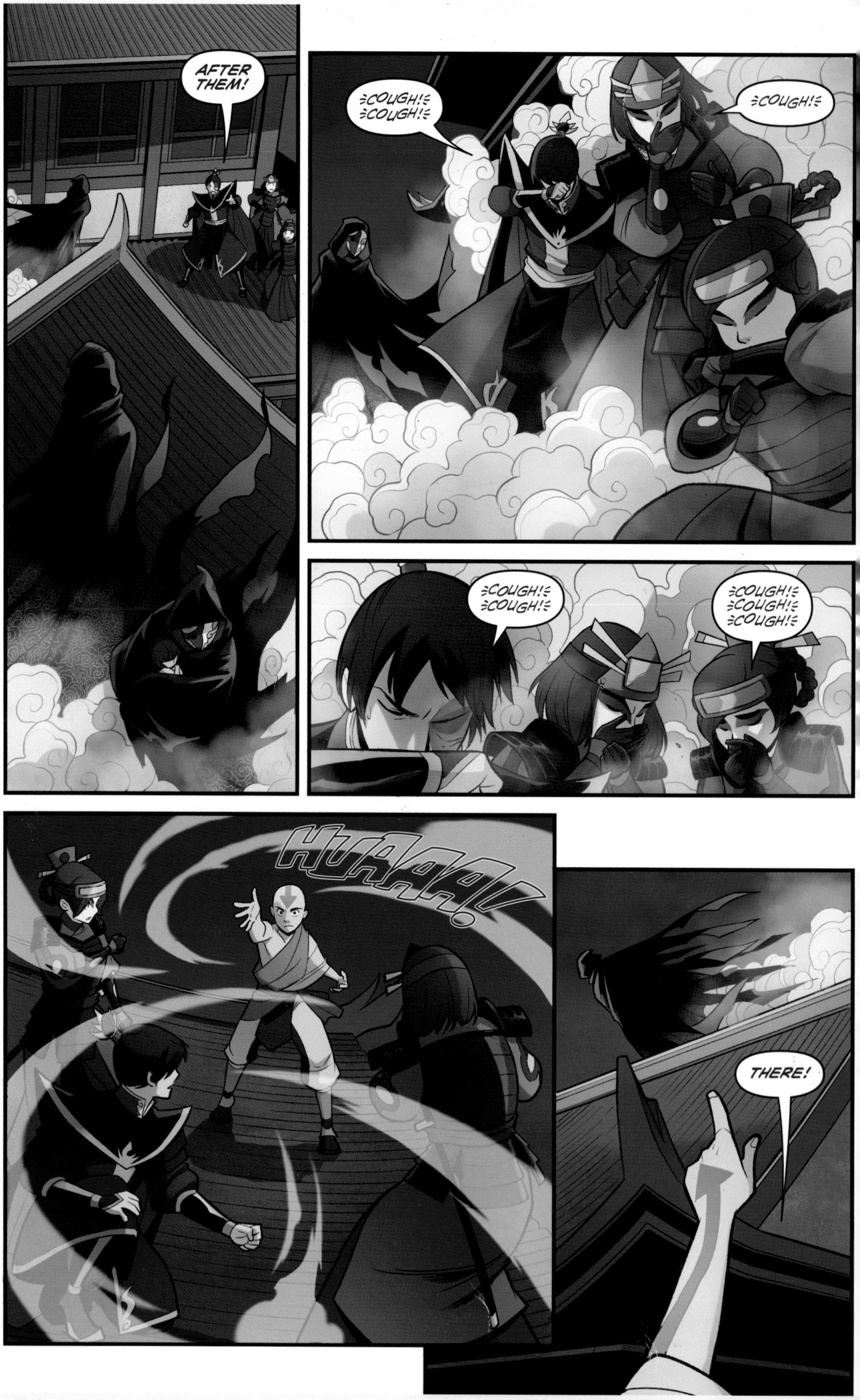
AFTER THEM!
COUGH! COUGH!
COUGH!
COUGH! COUGH!
COUGH! COUGH! COUGH!
HUAAAA!
THERE!

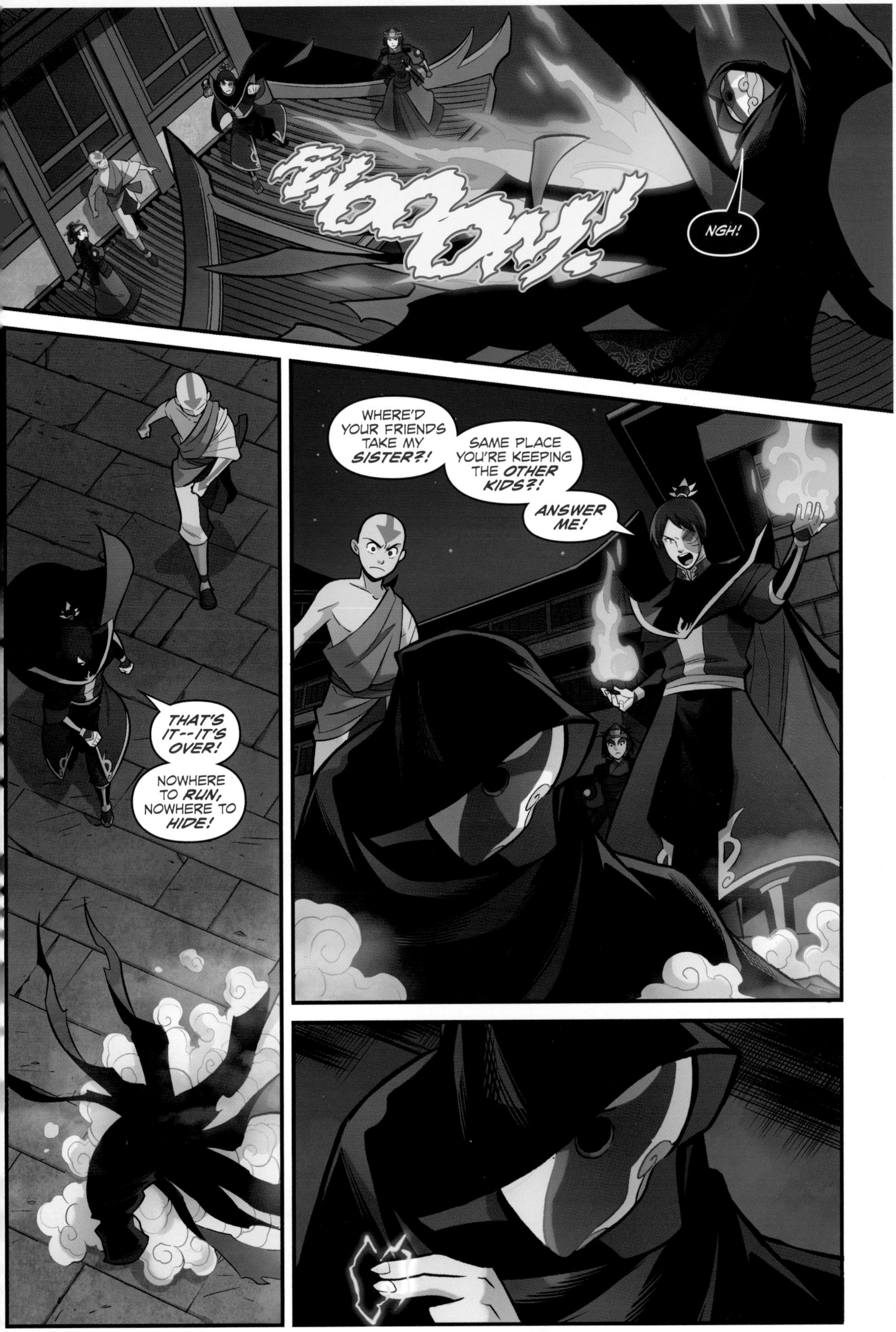
FWOOOM!
NGH!
THAT'S IT--IT'S OVER!
NOWHERE TO RUN, NOWHERE TO HIDE!
WHERE'D YOUR FRIENDS TAKE MY SISTER?!
SAME PLACE YOU'RE KEEPING THE OTHER KIDS?!
ANSWER ME!

GLY: Were you surprised by Azula's appearance? I hope so. The Kemurikage are the embodiment of fear. Since Azula's most potent weapon is fear, it seemed fitting to make her the leader.

As she said herself in the series finale, "Trust is for fools! Fear is the only reliable way."

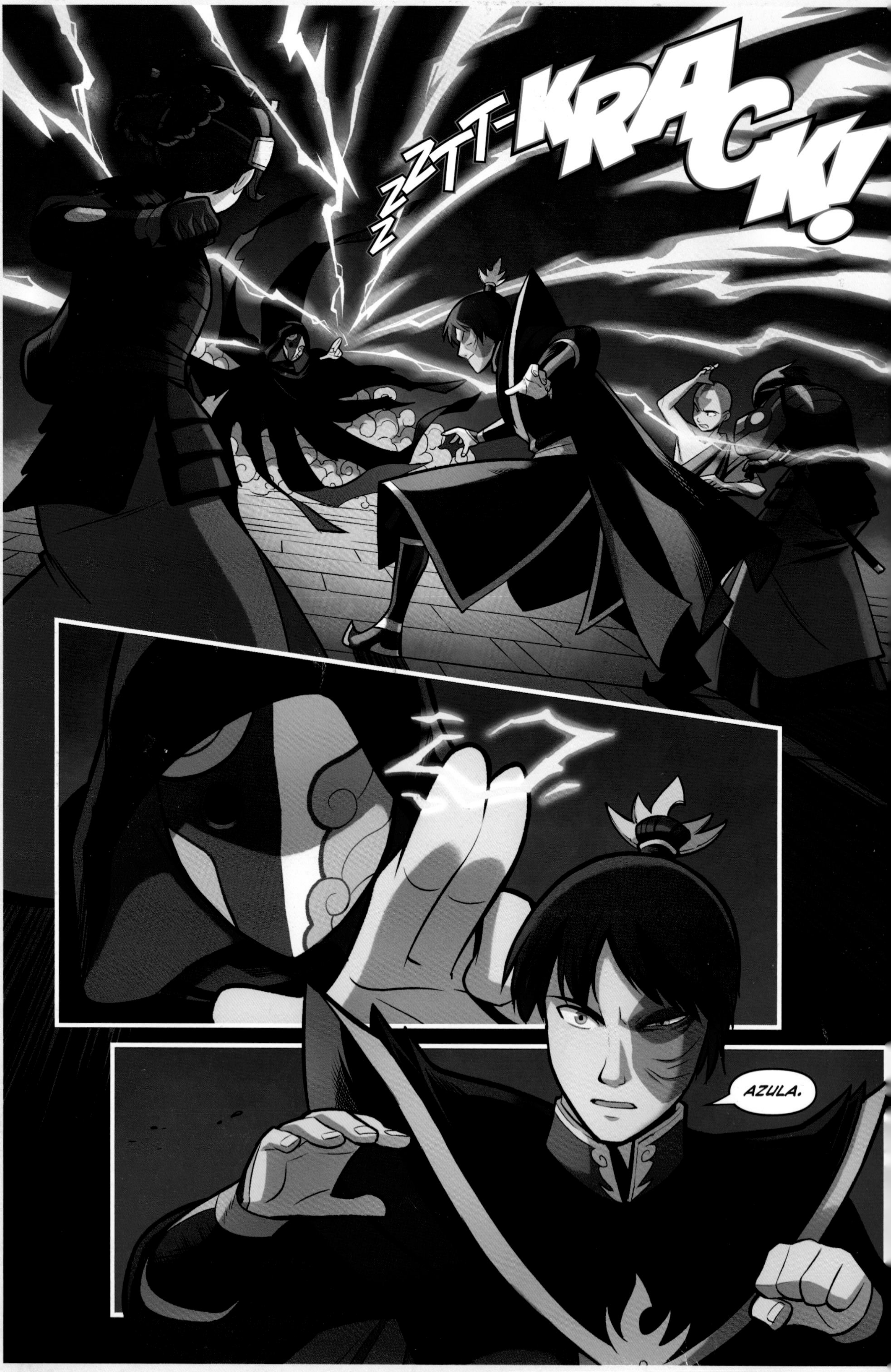
ZZZTT-KRACK!
AZULA.

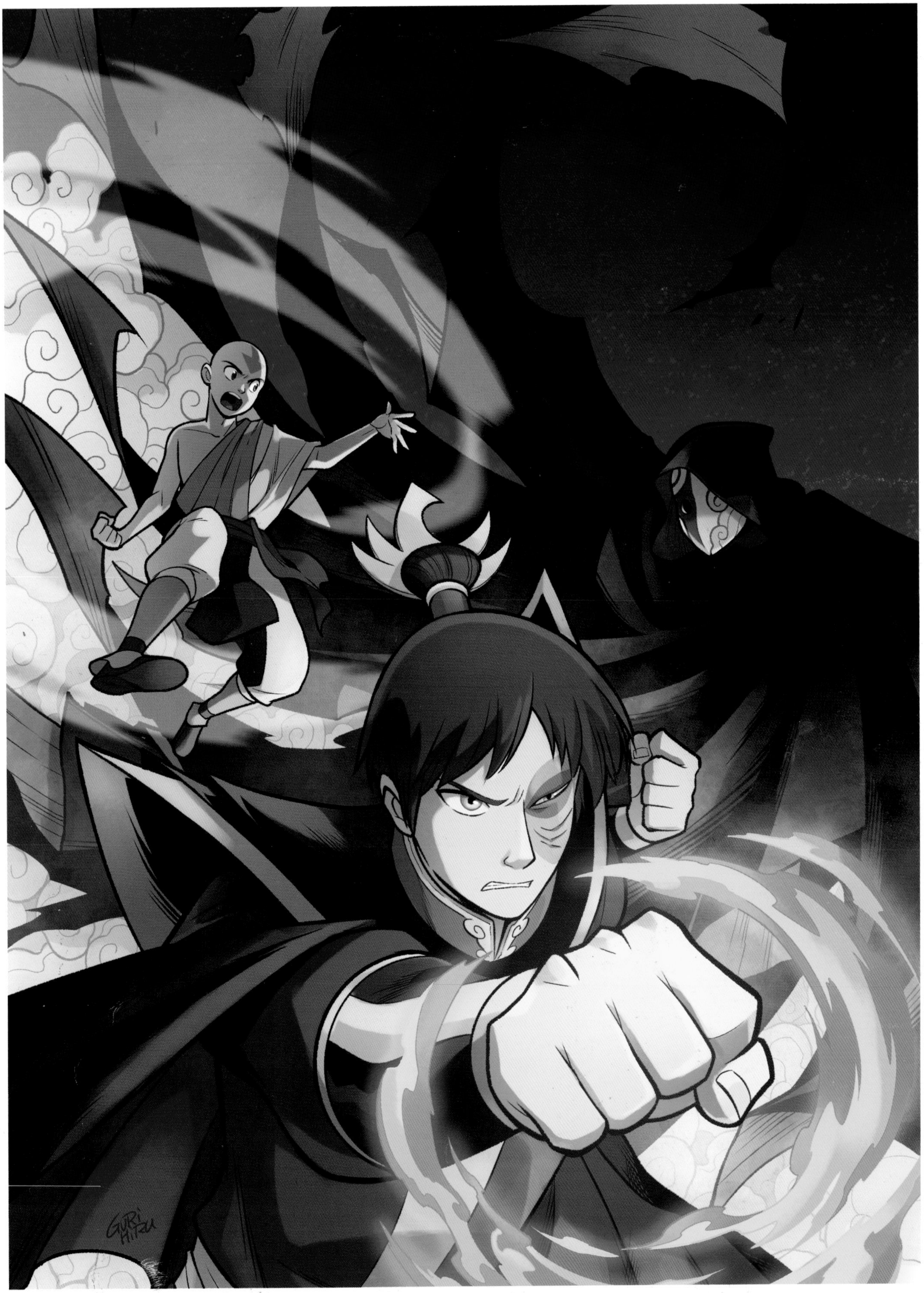
GURI HIRU

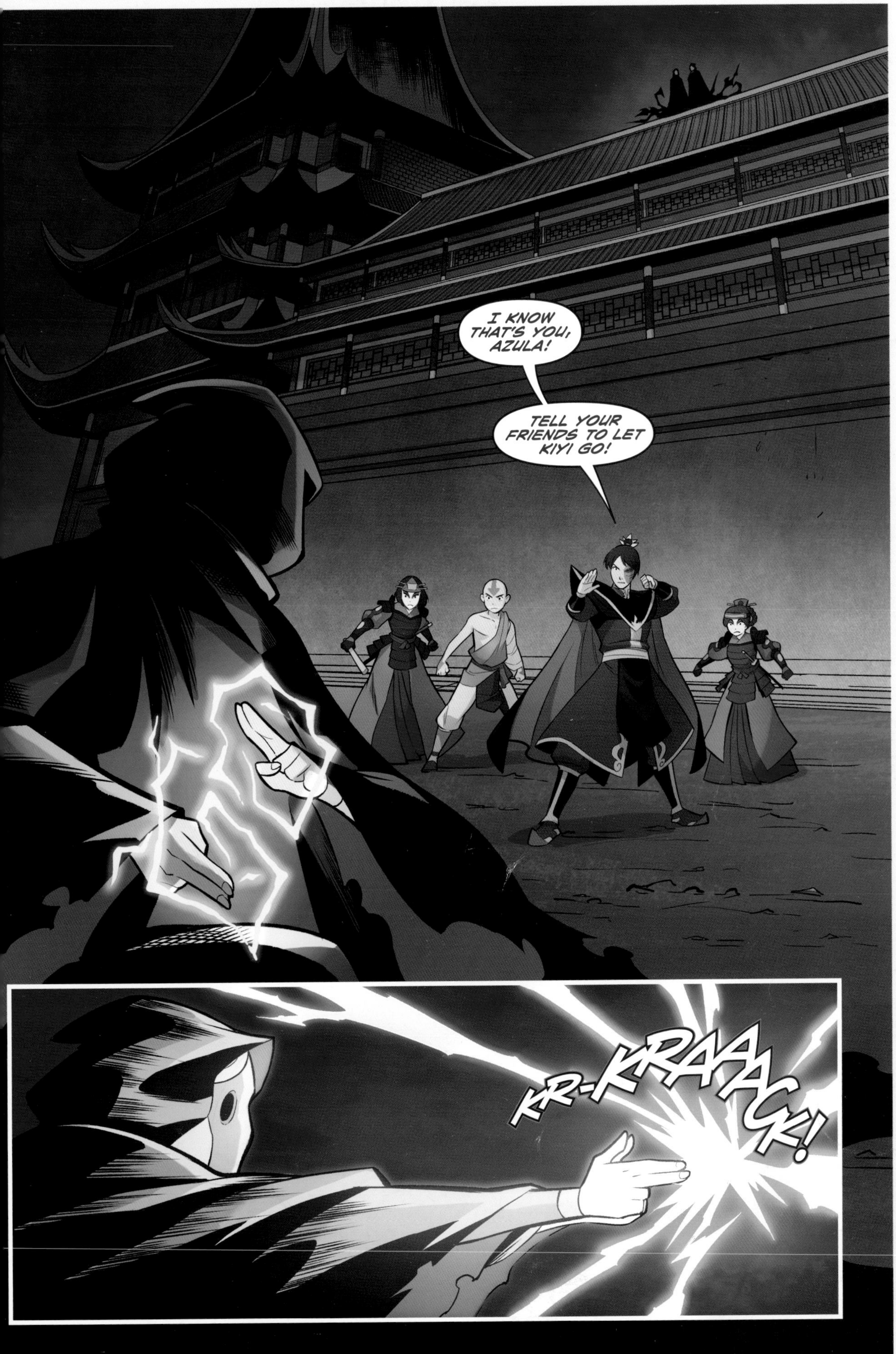
I KNOW THAT'S YOU, AZULA!
TELL YOUR FRIENDS TO LET KIYI GO!
KR-KRAAAACK!

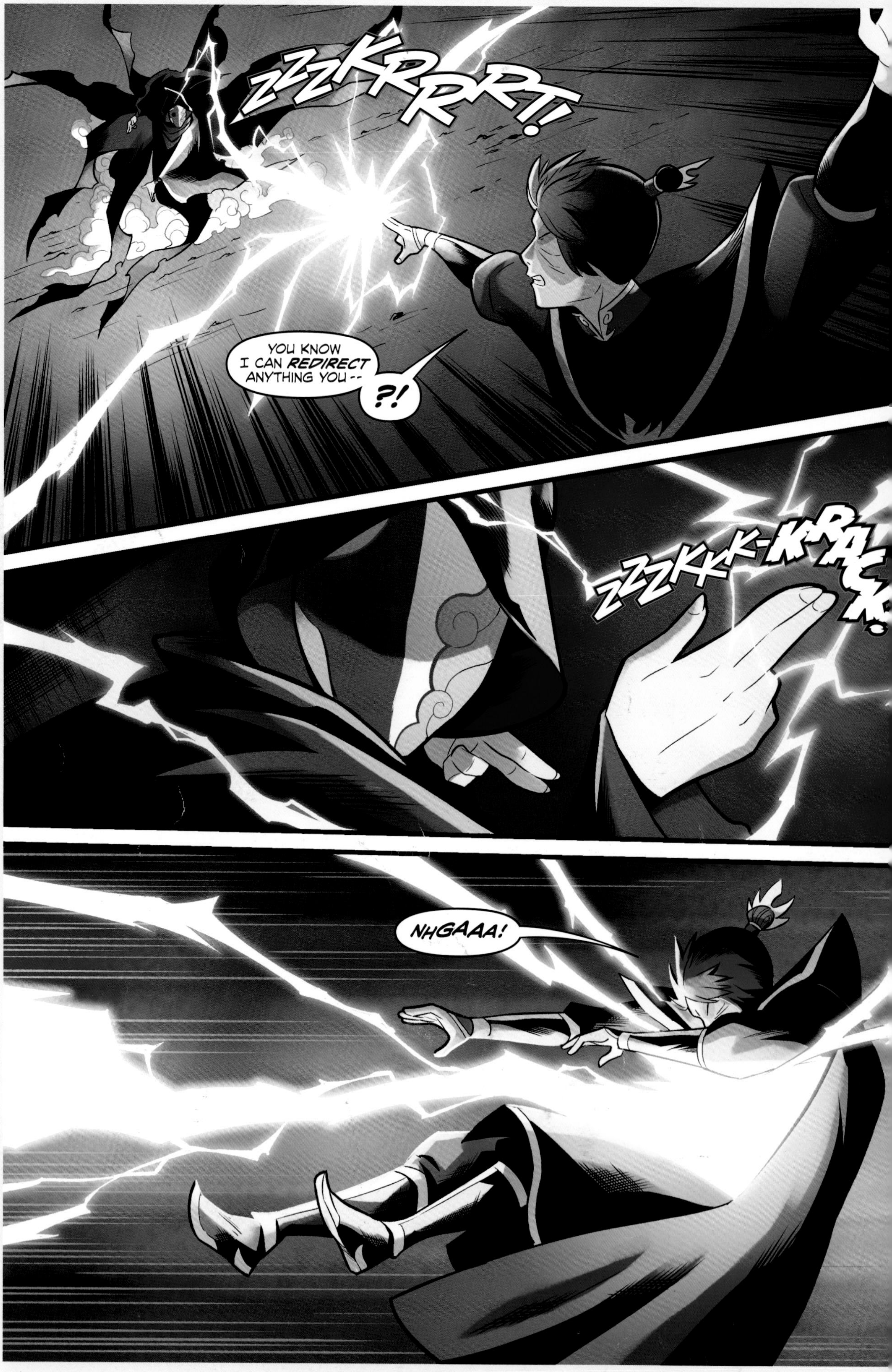
ZZZKRRRT!
YOU KNOW I CAN *REDIRECT* ANYTHING YOU--
?!
ZZZKKK-KRACK!
NHGAAA!

GLY: *Uncle Iroh trained Zuko to redirect lightning in "Bitter Work." He later used his new skill against both Ozai and Azula. In both the animated series and the comics, lightning redirection was used to show Zuko's power, his mastery of firebending.*

In this scene, we're using it in the same way, only for Azula.

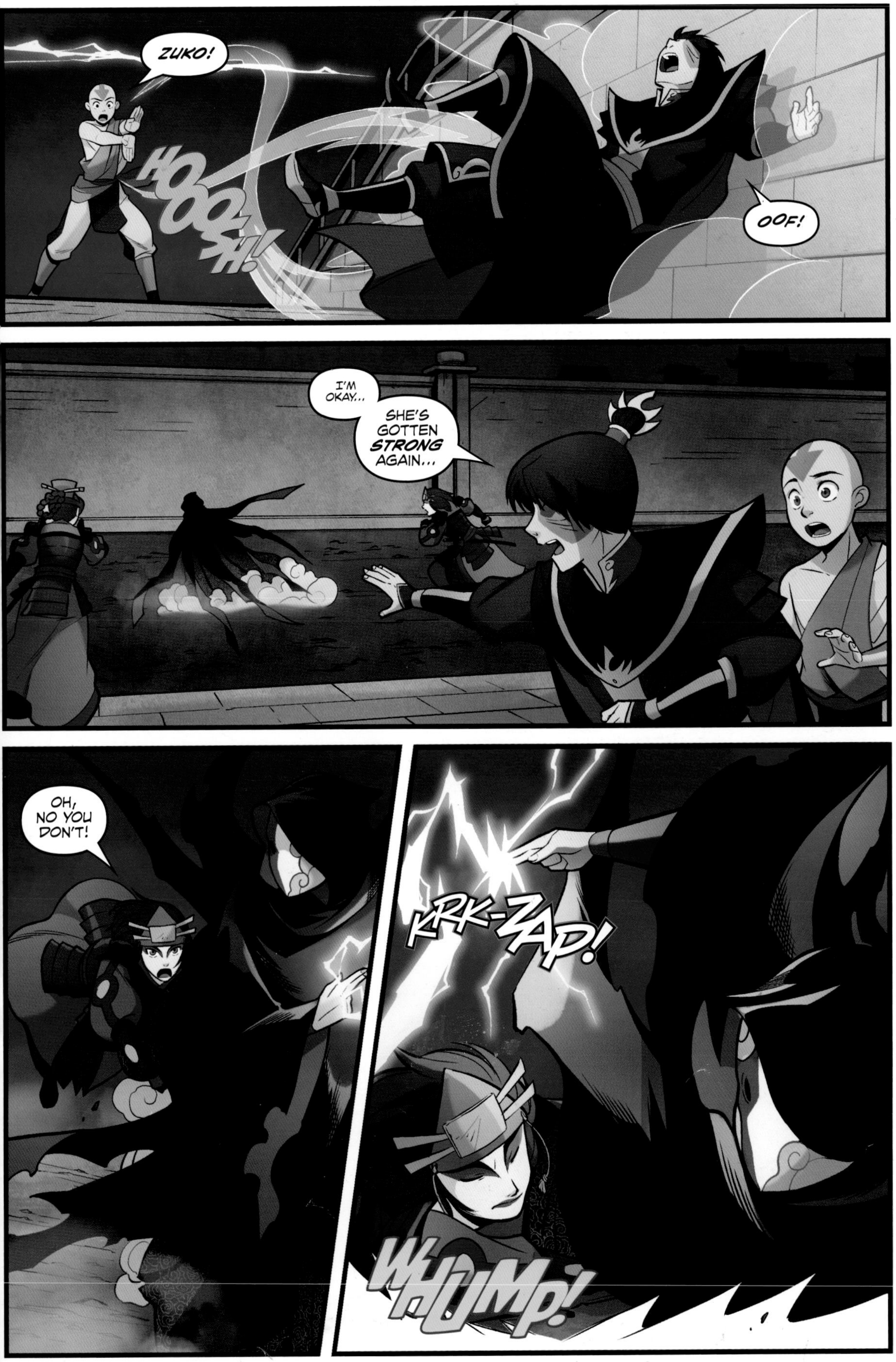
ZUKO!
HOOOSH!
OOF!
I'M OKAY...
SHE'S GOTTEN STRONG AGAIN...
OH, NO YOU DON'T!
KRK-ZAP!
WHUMP!

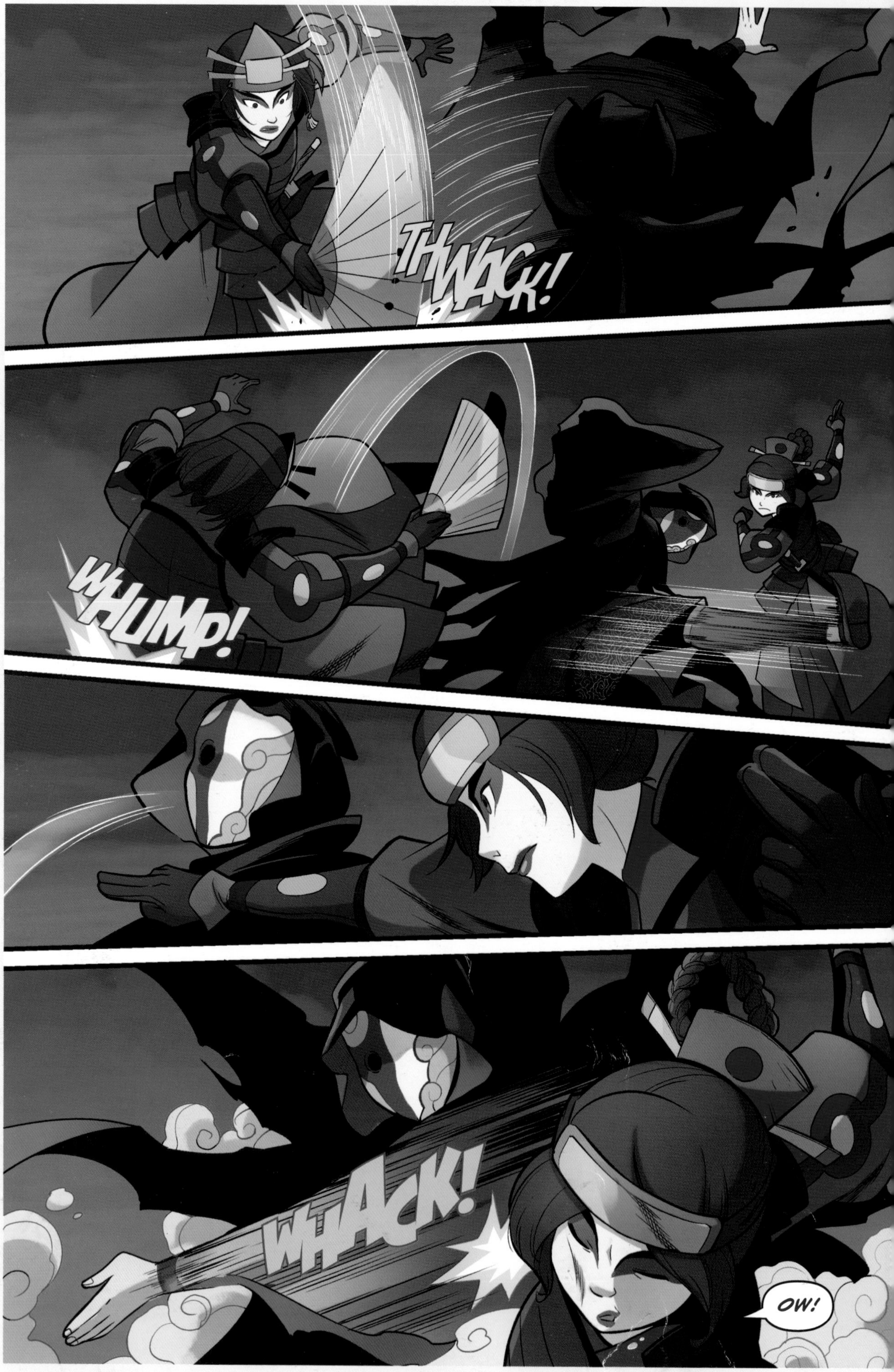
THWACK!
WHUMP!
WHACK!
OW!

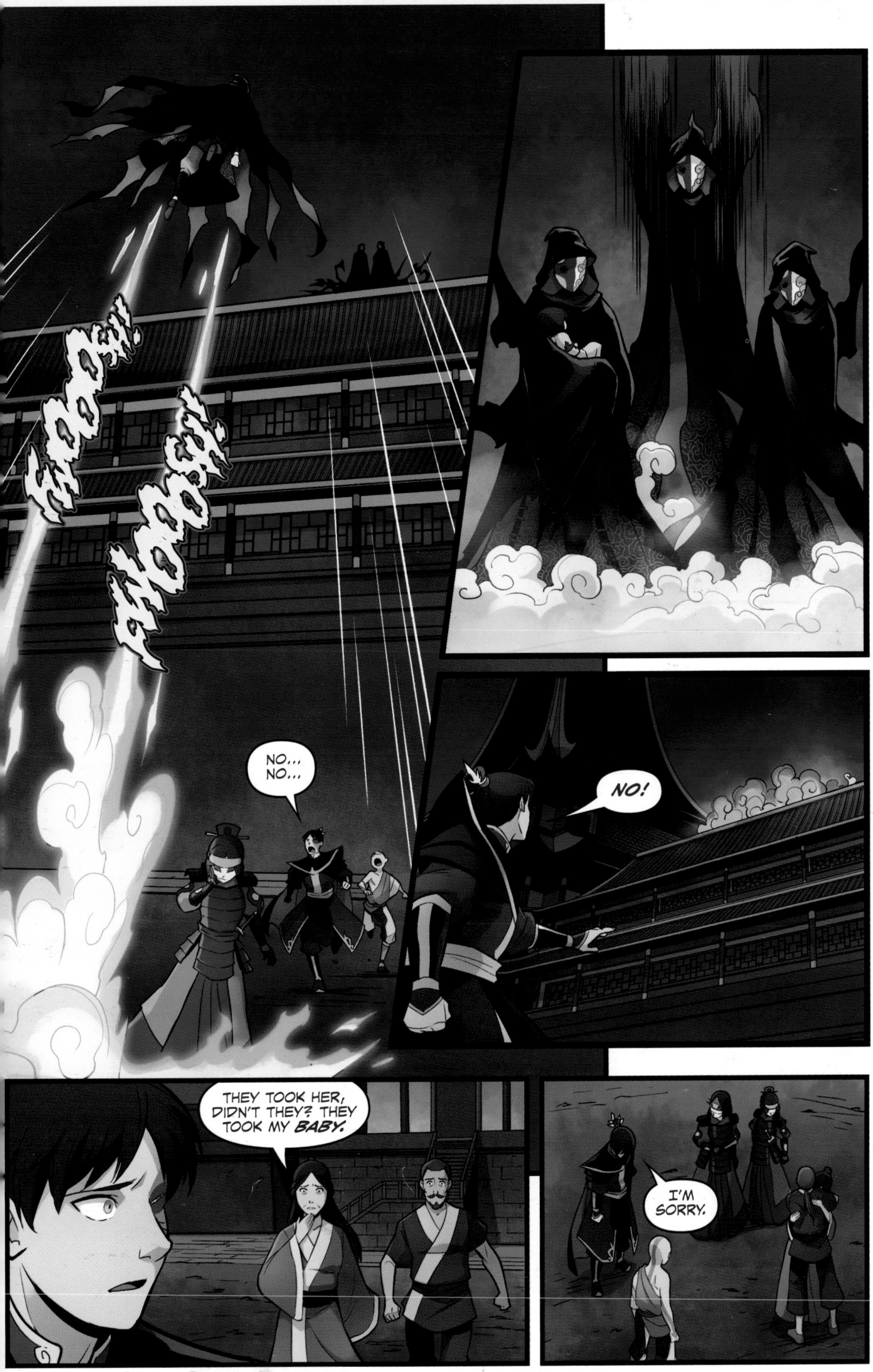
FOOSH!!
WHOOSH!!
NO... NO...
NO!
THEY TOOK HER, DIDN'T THEY? THEY TOOK MY BABY.
I'M SORRY.

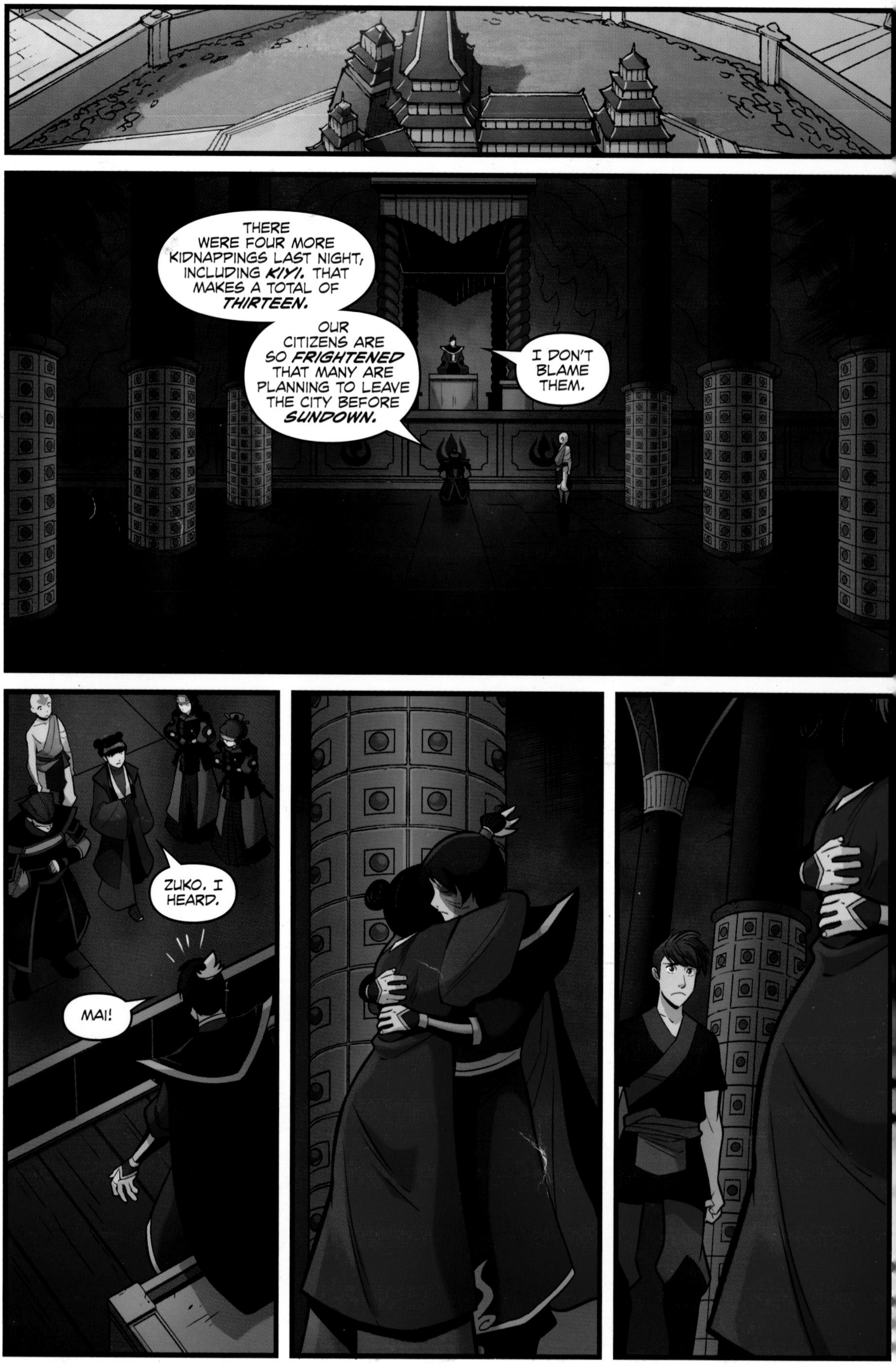
THERE WERE FOUR MORE KIDNAPPINGS LAST NIGHT, INCLUDING KIYI. THAT MAKES A TOTAL OF THIRTEEN.
OUR CITIZENS ARE SO FRIGHTENED THAT MANY ARE PLANNING TO LEAVE THE CITY BEFORE SUNDOWN.
I DON'T BLAME THEM.
ZUKO. I HEARD.
MAI!

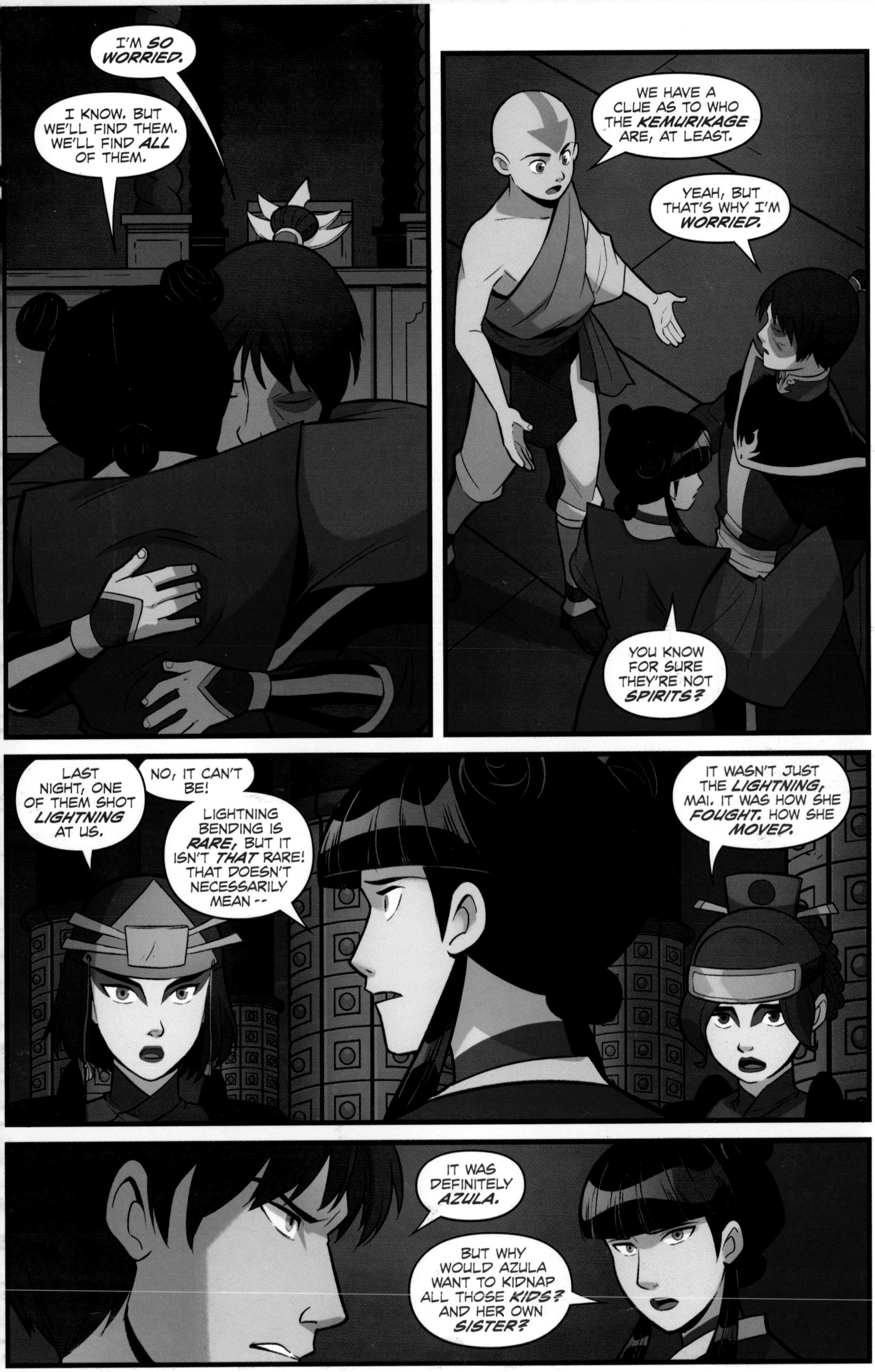
I'M SO WORRIED.
I KNOW. BUT WE'LL FIND THEM. WE'LL FIND ALL OF THEM.
WE HAVE A CLUE AS TO WHO THE KEMURIKAGE ARE, AT LEAST.
YEAH, BUT THAT'S WHY I'M WORRIED.
YOU KNOW FOR SURE THEY'RE NOT SPIRITS?
LAST NIGHT, ONE OF THEM SHOT LIGHTNING AT US.
NO, IT CAN'T BE!
LIGHTNING BENDING IS RARE, BUT IT ISN'T THAT RARE! THAT DOESN'T NECESSARILY MEAN --
IT WASN'T JUST THE LIGHTNING, MAI. IT WAS HOW SHE FOUGHT. HOW SHE MOVED.
IT WAS DEFINITELY AZULA.
BUT WHY WOULD AZULA WANT TO KIDNAP ALL THOSE KIDS? AND HER OWN SISTER?

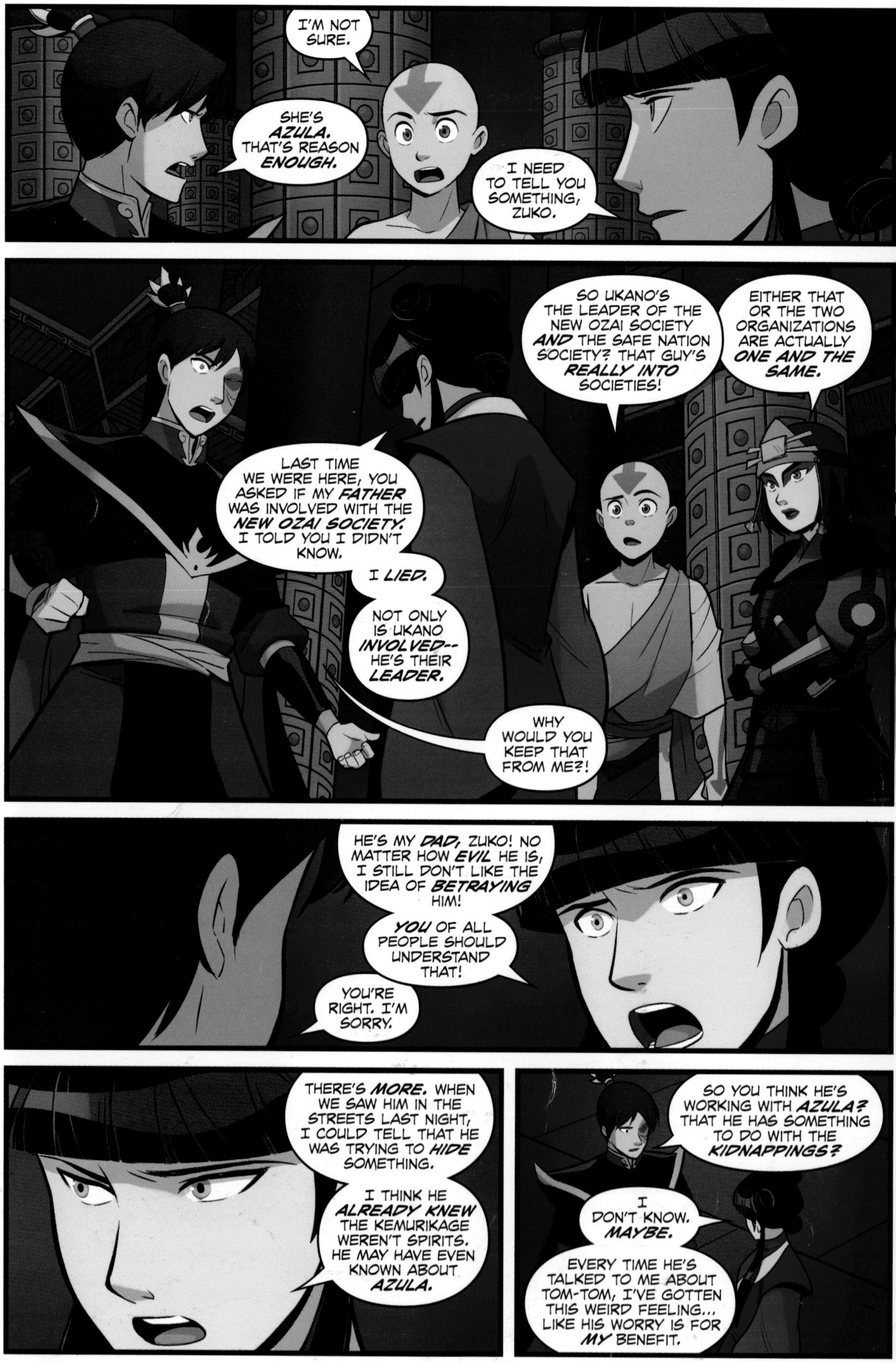
I'M NOT SURE.
SHE'S AZULA. THAT'S REASON ENOUGH.
I NEED TO TELL YOU SOMETHING, ZUKO.
SO UKANO'S THE LEADER OF THE NEW OZAI SOCIETY AND THE SAFE NATION SOCIETY? THAT GUY'S REALLY INTO SOCIETIES!
EITHER THAT OR THE TWO ORGANIZATIONS ARE ACTUALLY ONE AND THE SAME.
LAST TIME WE WERE HERE, YOU ASKED IF MY FATHER WAS INVOLVED WITH THE NEW OZAI SOCIETY. I TOLD YOU I DIDN'T KNOW.
I LIED.
NOT ONLY IS UKANO INVOLVED-- HE'S THEIR LEADER.
WHY WOULD YOU KEEP THAT FROM ME?!
HE'S MY DAD, ZUKO! NO MATTER HOW EVIL HE IS, I STILL DON'T LIKE THE IDEA OF BETRAYING HIM!
YOU OF ALL PEOPLE SHOULD UNDERSTAND THAT!
YOU'RE RIGHT. I'M SORRY.
THERE'S MORE. WHEN WE SAW HIM IN THE STREETS LAST NIGHT, I COULD TELL THAT HE WAS TRYING TO HIDE SOMETHING.
I THINK HE ALREADY KNEW THE KEMURIKAGE WEREN'T SPIRITS. HE MAY HAVE EVEN KNOWN ABOUT AZULA.
SO YOU THINK HE'S WORKING WITH AZULA? THAT HE HAS SOMETHING TO DO WITH THE KIDNAPPINGS?
I DON'T KNOW. MAYBE.
EVERY TIME HE'S TALKED TO ME ABOUT TOM-TOM, I'VE GOTTEN THIS WEIRD FEELING... LIKE HIS WORRY IS FOR MY BENEFIT.

GLY: *Ukano's affinity for secret societies mirrors China's in the early 1900s.*

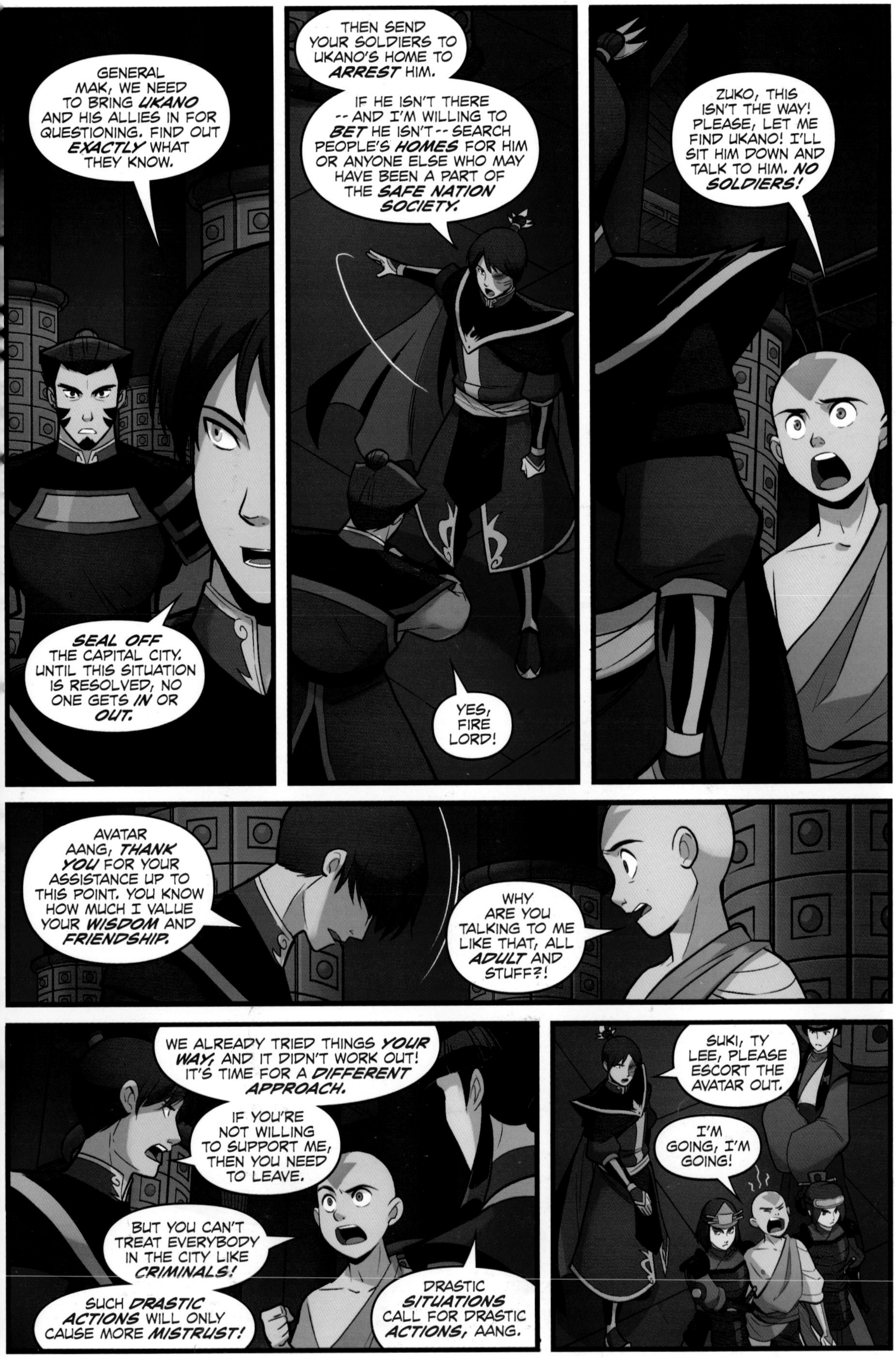
GENERAL MAK, WE NEED TO BRING UKANO AND HIS ALLIES IN FOR QUESTIONING. FIND OUT EXACTLY WHAT THEY KNOW.
SEAL OFF THE CAPITAL CITY. UNTIL THIS SITUATION IS RESOLVED, NO ONE GETS IN OR OUT.
THEN SEND YOUR SOLDIERS TO UKANO'S HOME TO ARREST HIM.
IF HE ISN'T THERE -- AND I'M WILLING TO BET HE ISN'T -- SEARCH PEOPLE'S HOMES FOR HIM OR ANYONE ELSE WHO MAY HAVE BEEN A PART OF THE SAFE NATION SOCIETY.
YES, FIRE LORD!
ZUKO, THIS ISN'T THE WAY! PLEASE, LET ME FIND UKANO! I'LL SIT HIM DOWN AND TALK TO HIM. NO SOLDIERS!
AVATAR AANG, THANK YOU FOR YOUR ASSISTANCE UP TO THIS POINT. YOU KNOW HOW MUCH I VALUE YOUR WISDOM AND FRIENDSHIP.
WHY ARE YOU TALKING TO ME LIKE THAT, ALL ADULT AND STUFF?!
WE ALREADY TRIED THINGS YOUR WAY, AND IT DIDN'T WORK OUT! IT'S TIME FOR A DIFFERENT APPROACH.
IF YOU'RE NOT WILLING TO SUPPORT ME, THEN YOU NEED TO LEAVE.
BUT YOU CAN'T TREAT EVERYBODY IN THE CITY LIKE CRIMINALS!
SUCH DRASTIC ACTIONS WILL ONLY CAUSE MORE MISTRUST!
DRASTIC SITUATIONS CALL FOR DRASTIC ACTIONS, AANG.
SUKI, TY LEE, PLEASE ESCORT THE AVATAR OUT.
I'M GOING, I'M GOING!

GLY: *General Mak first showed up in* The Promise.

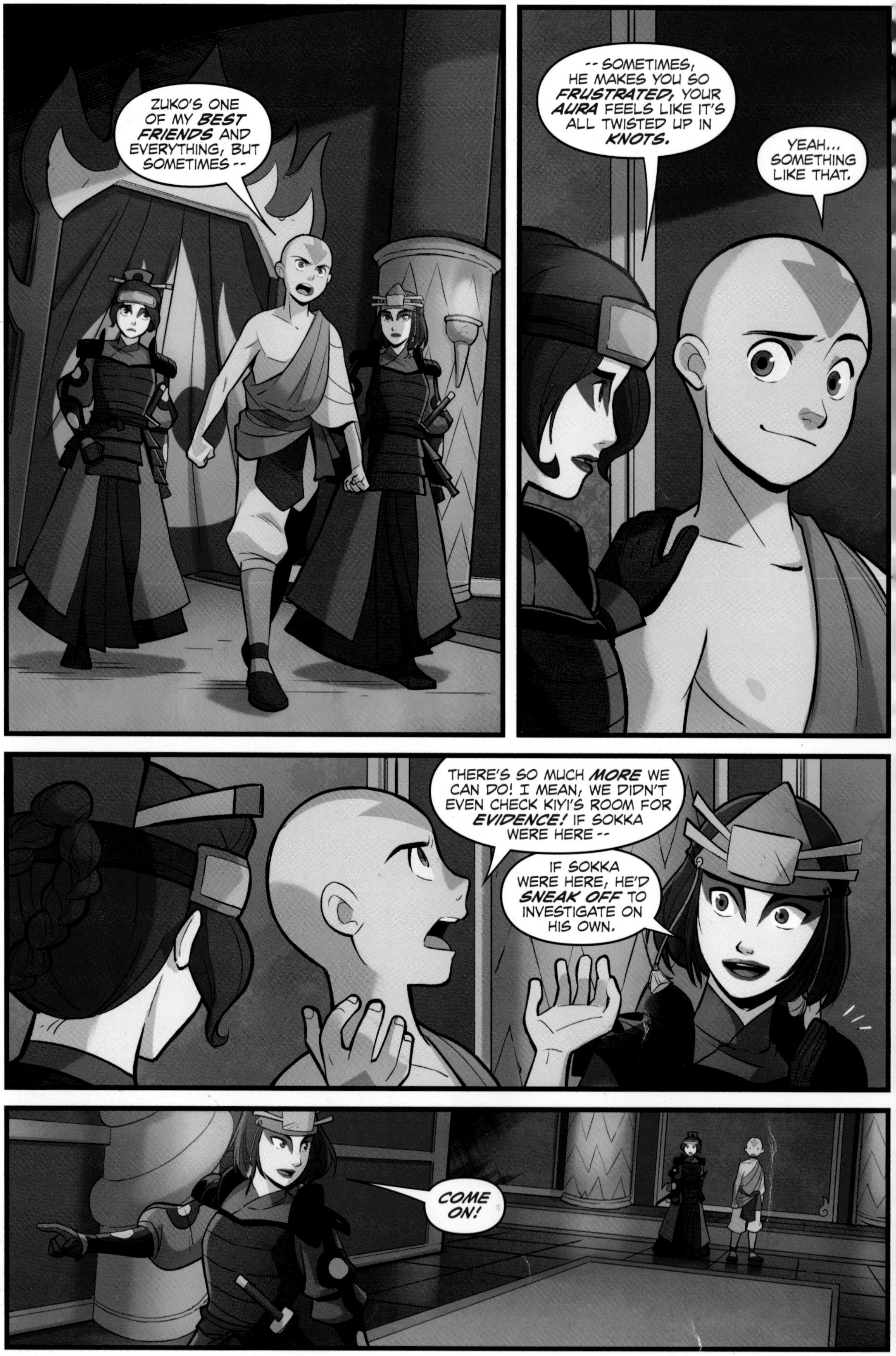
ZUKO'S ONE OF MY BEST FRIENDS AND EVERYTHING, BUT SOMETIMES --
-- SOMETIMES, HE MAKES YOU SO FRUSTRATED, YOUR AURA FEELS LIKE IT'S ALL TWISTED UP IN KNOTS.
YEAH... SOMETHING LIKE THAT.
THERE'S SO MUCH MORE WE CAN DO! I MEAN, WE DIDN'T EVEN CHECK KIYI'S ROOM FOR EVIDENCE! IF SOKKA WERE HERE --
IF SOKKA WERE HERE, HE'D SNEAK OFF TO INVESTIGATE ON HIS OWN.
COME ON!

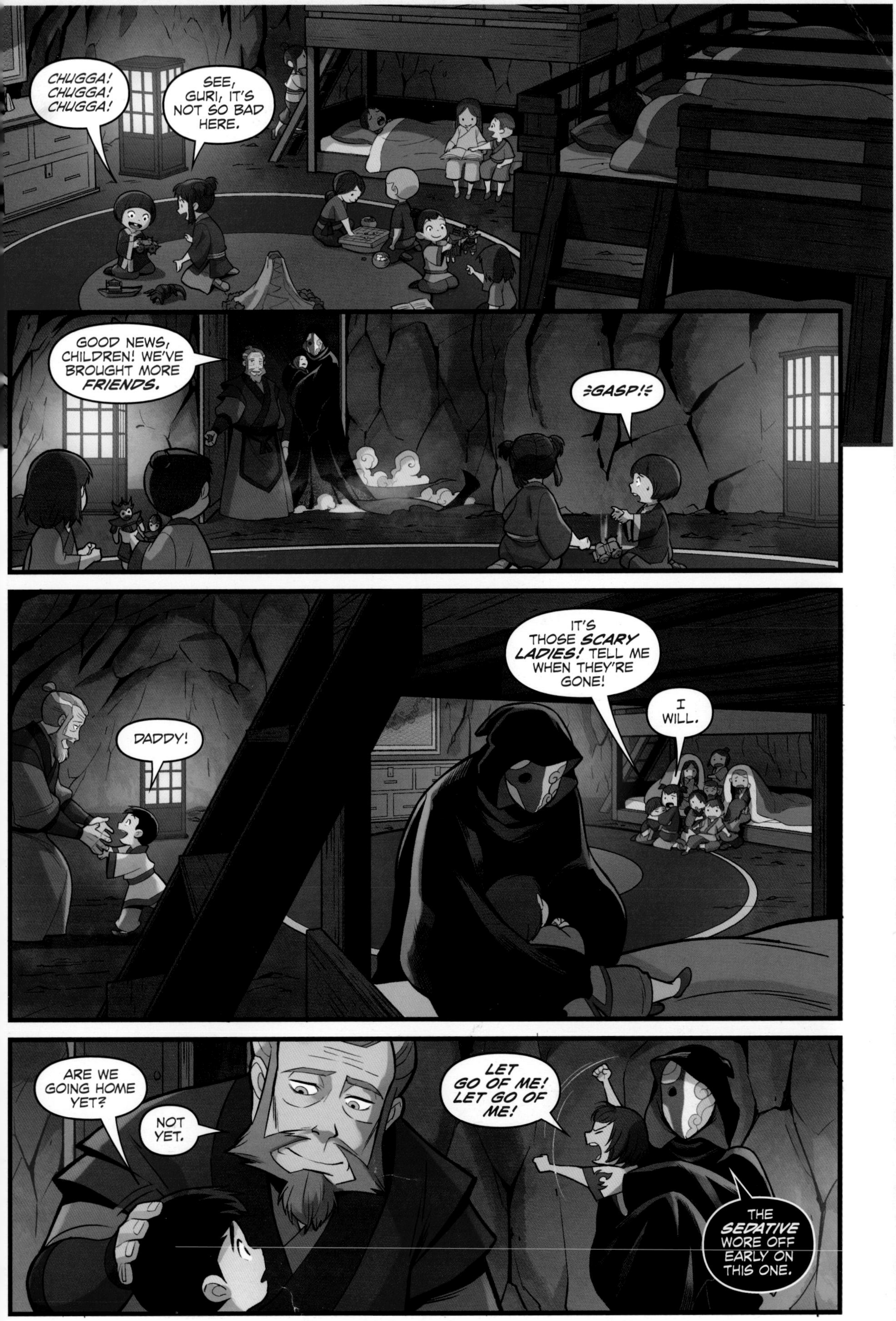
CHUGGA! CHUGGA! CHUGGA!
SEE, GURI, IT'S NOT SO BAD HERE.
GOOD NEWS, CHILDREN! WE'VE BROUGHT MORE FRIENDS.
GASP!
DADDY!
IT'S THOSE SCARY LADIES! TELL ME WHEN THEY'RE GONE!
I WILL.
ARE WE GOING HOME YET?
NOT YET.
LET GO OF ME! LET GO OF ME!
THE SEDATIVE WORE OFF EARLY ON THIS ONE.

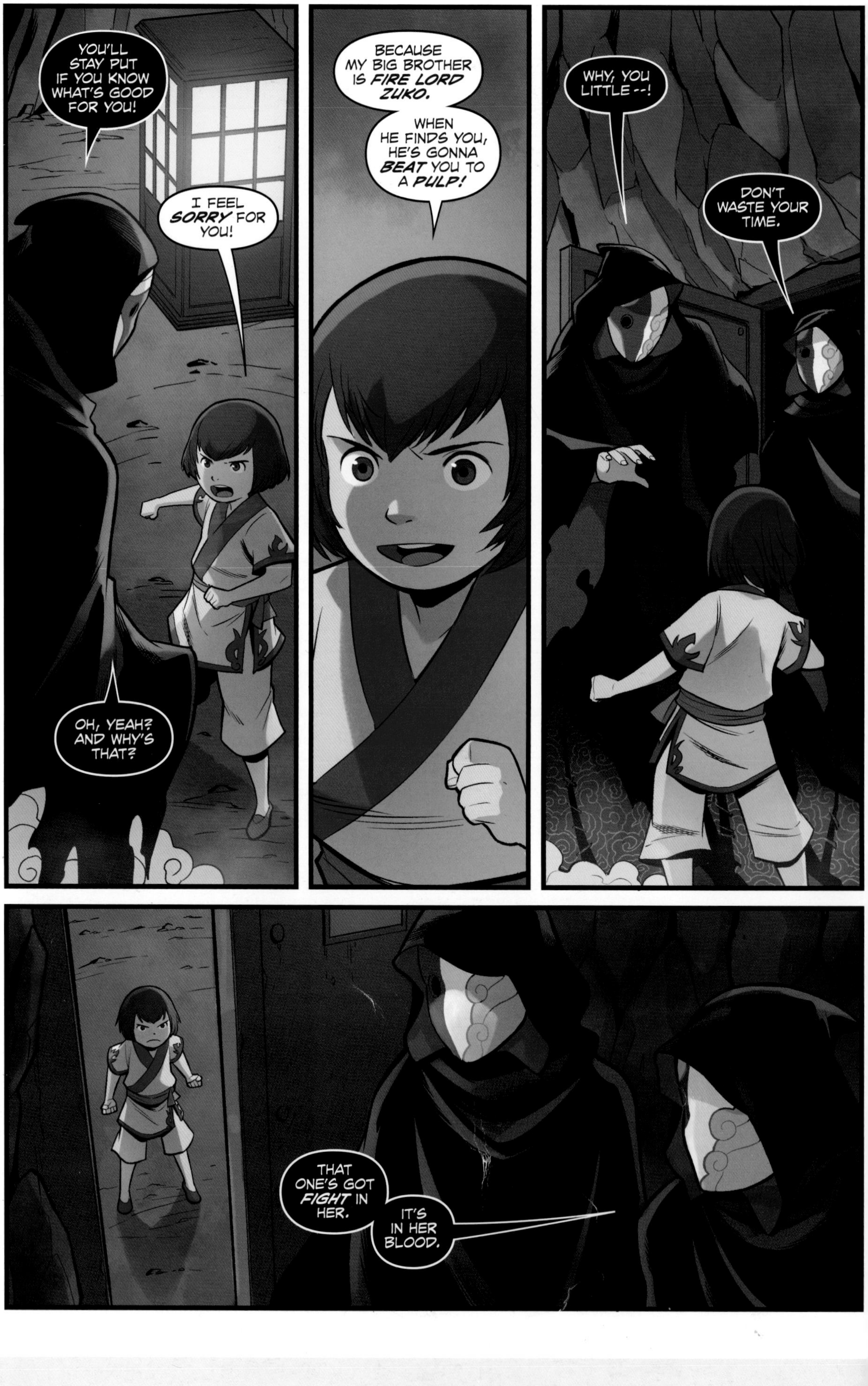
YOU'LL STAY PUT IF YOU KNOW WHAT'S GOOD FOR YOU!
OH, YEAH? AND WHY'S THAT?
I FEEL SORRY FOR YOU!
BECAUSE MY BIG BROTHER IS FIRE LORD ZUKO.
WHEN HE FINDS YOU, HE'S GONNA BEAT YOU TO A PULP!
WHY, YOU LITTLE--!
DON'T WASTE YOUR TIME.
THAT ONE'S GOT FIGHT IN HER.
IT'S IN HER BLOOD.

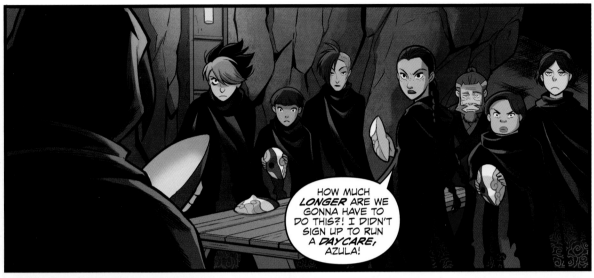

HOW MUCH *LONGER* ARE WE GONNA HAVE TO DO THIS?! I DIDN'T SIGN UP TO RUN A *DAYCARE*, AZULA!

PATIENCE, ZIRIN.

I BROKE YOU OUT OF THAT *HORRIBLE INSTITUTION*, REMEMBER? WATCHING OVER A FEW BRATS IS THE *LEAST* YOU COULD DO FOR *ME*.

GLY: *Azula met most of these ladies during her time in the mental institution.*

G: *We were happy to have Azula back. She seems to be much more calm and not like the irrational person she used to be.*

LADIES, CAN YOU GIVE ME A MOMENT WITH UKANO? HE AND I NEED TO DISCUSS *NEXT STEPS*.

AZULA, ZIRIN IS *RIGHT*. WE CAN'T SUSTAIN THIS FOR MUCH LONGER!

HOW MUCH DO YOU LOVE THE *FIRE NATION*, UKANO?

YOU KNOW MY *COMMITMENT!* I EMPTIED MY BANK ACCOUNT TO BUILD THIS *HEADQUARTERS* FOR YOU!

I SUBJECTED MY FAMILY TO *HORRORS BEYOND IMAGINING!*

I'M WILLING TO DO *ANYTHING* FOR THE SAKE OF MY NATION!

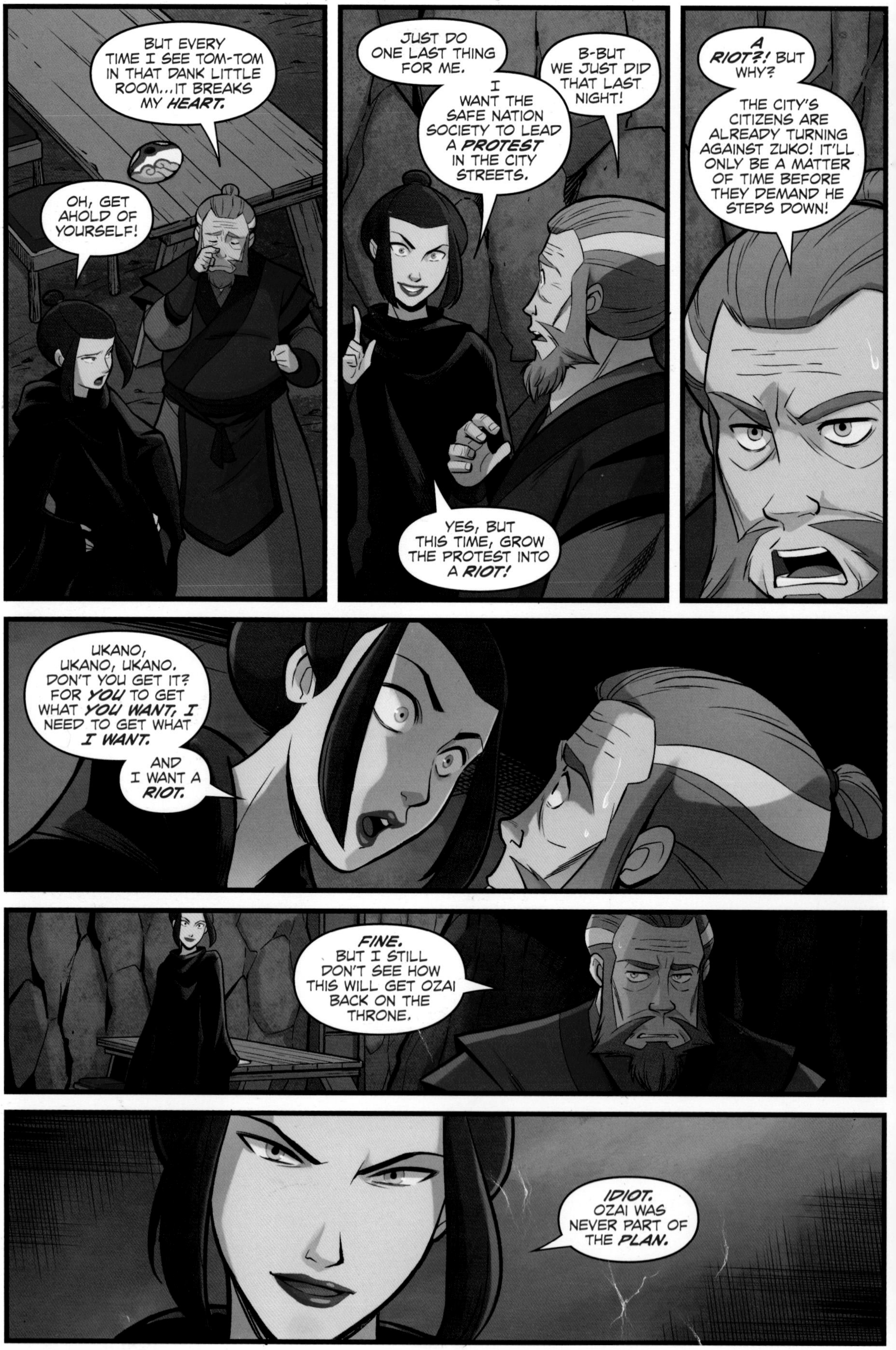
BUT EVERY TIME I SEE TOM-TOM IN THAT DANK LITTLE ROOM...IT BREAKS MY HEART.
OH, GET AHOLD OF YOURSELF!
JUST DO ONE LAST THING FOR ME.
I WANT THE SAFE NATION SOCIETY TO LEAD A PROTEST IN THE CITY STREETS.
B-BUT WE JUST DID THAT LAST NIGHT!
YES, BUT THIS TIME, GROW THE PROTEST INTO A RIOT!
A RIOT?! BUT WHY?
THE CITY'S CITIZENS ARE ALREADY TURNING AGAINST ZUKO! IT'LL ONLY BE A MATTER OF TIME BEFORE THEY DEMAND HE STEPS DOWN!
UKANO, UKANO, UKANO. DON'T YOU GET IT? FOR YOU TO GET WHAT YOU WANT, I NEED TO GET WHAT I WANT.
AND I WANT A RIOT.
FINE. BUT I STILL DON'T SEE HOW THIS WILL GET OZAI BACK ON THE THRONE.
IDIOT. OZAI WAS NEVER PART OF THE PLAN.

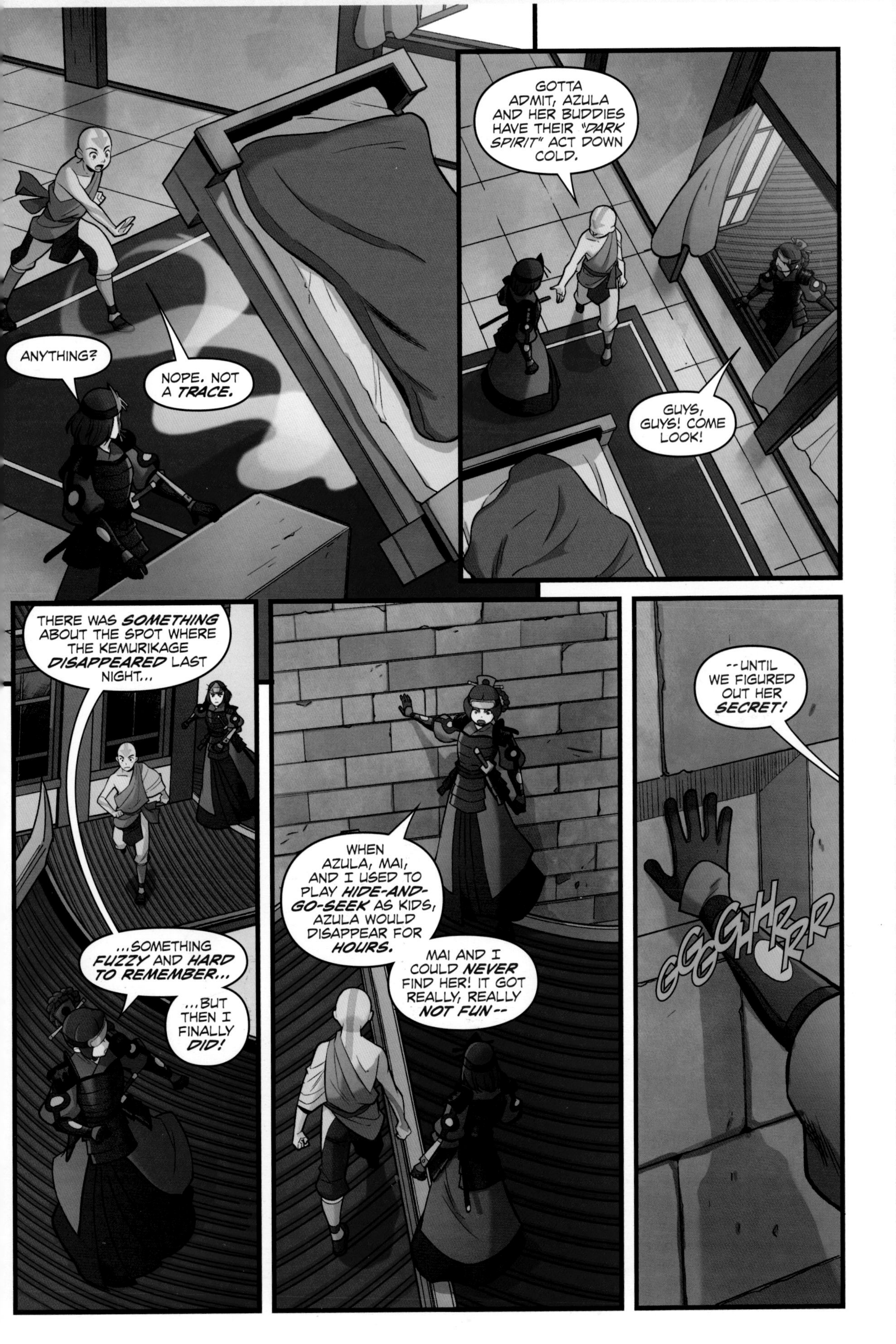
ANYTHING?
NOPE. NOT A TRACE.
GOTTA ADMIT, AZULA AND HER BUDDIES HAVE THEIR "DARK SPIRIT" ACT DOWN COLD.
GUYS, GUYS! COME LOOK!
THERE WAS SOMETHING ABOUT THE SPOT WHERE THE KEMURIKAGE DISAPPEARED LAST NIGHT...
...SOMETHING FUZZY AND HARD TO REMEMBER...
...BUT THEN I FINALLY DID!
WHEN AZULA, MAI, AND I USED TO PLAY HIDE-AND-GO-SEEK AS KIDS, AZULA WOULD DISAPPEAR FOR HOURS.
MAI AND I COULD NEVER FIND HER! IT GOT REALLY, REALLY NOT FUN--
--UNTIL WE FIGURED OUT HER SECRET!
GGGGHRRR

GLY: *We also showed secret passageways in the Fire Nation Royal Palace in* The Search.

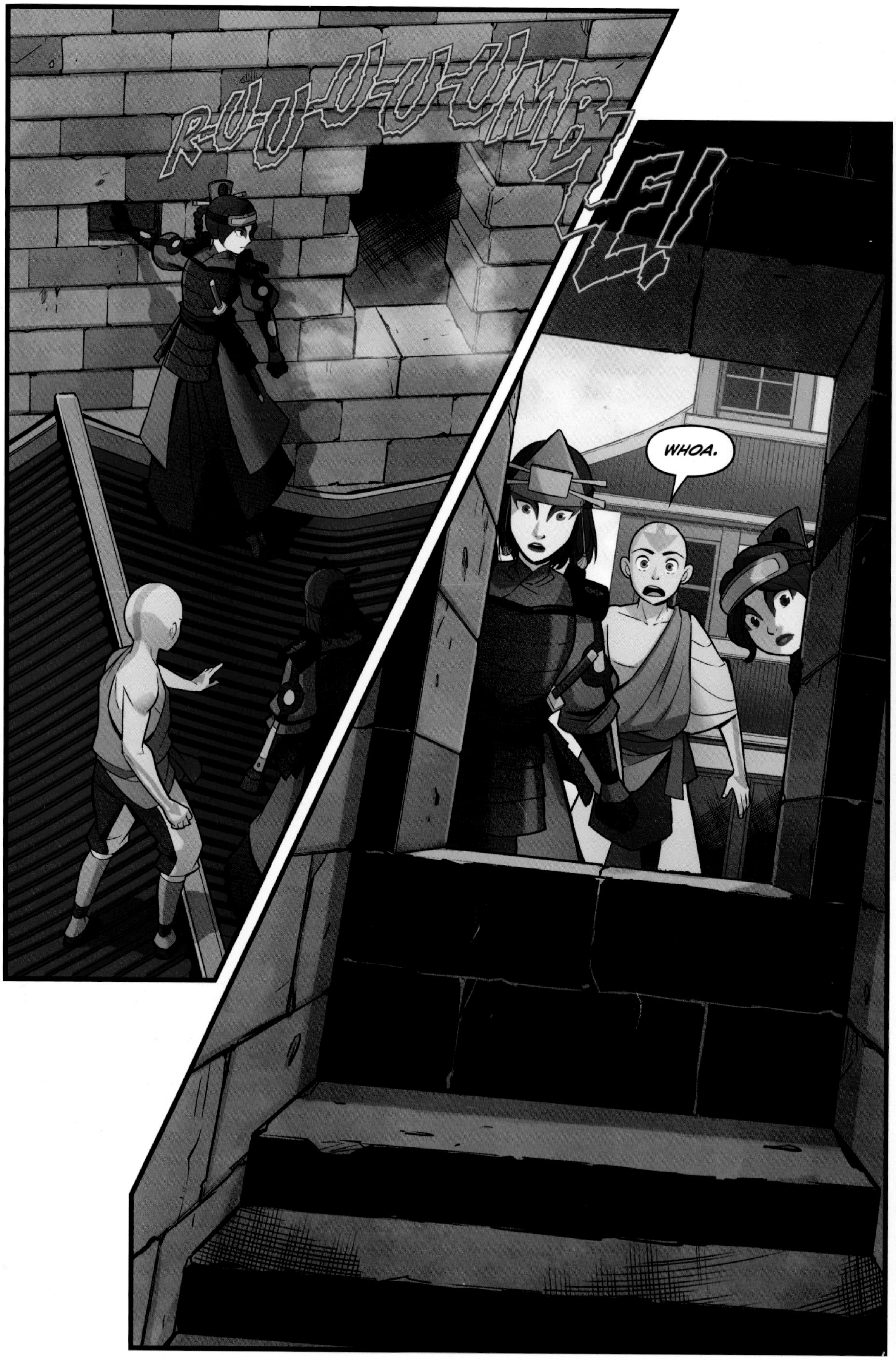
RUUUUUMBLE!
WHOA.

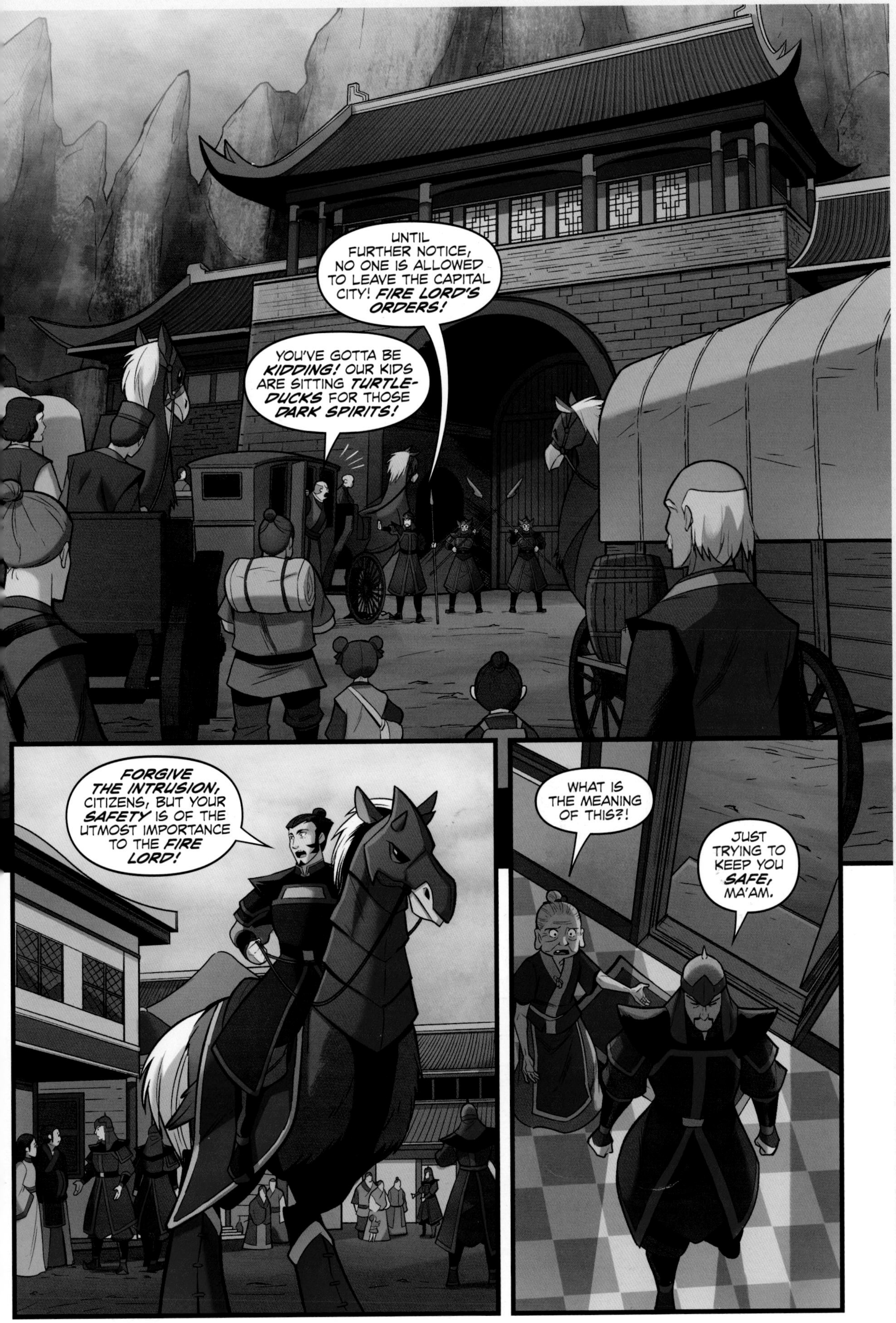
UNTIL FURTHER NOTICE, NO ONE IS ALLOWED TO LEAVE THE CAPITAL CITY! FIRE LORD'S ORDERS!
YOU'VE GOTTA BE KIDDING! OUR KIDS ARE SITTING TURTLE-DUCKS FOR THOSE DARK SPIRITS!
FORGIVE THE INTRUSION, CITIZENS, BUT YOUR SAFETY IS OF THE UTMOST IMPORTANCE TO THE FIRE LORD!
WHAT IS THE MEANING OF THIS?!
JUST TRYING TO KEEP YOU SAFE, MA'AM.

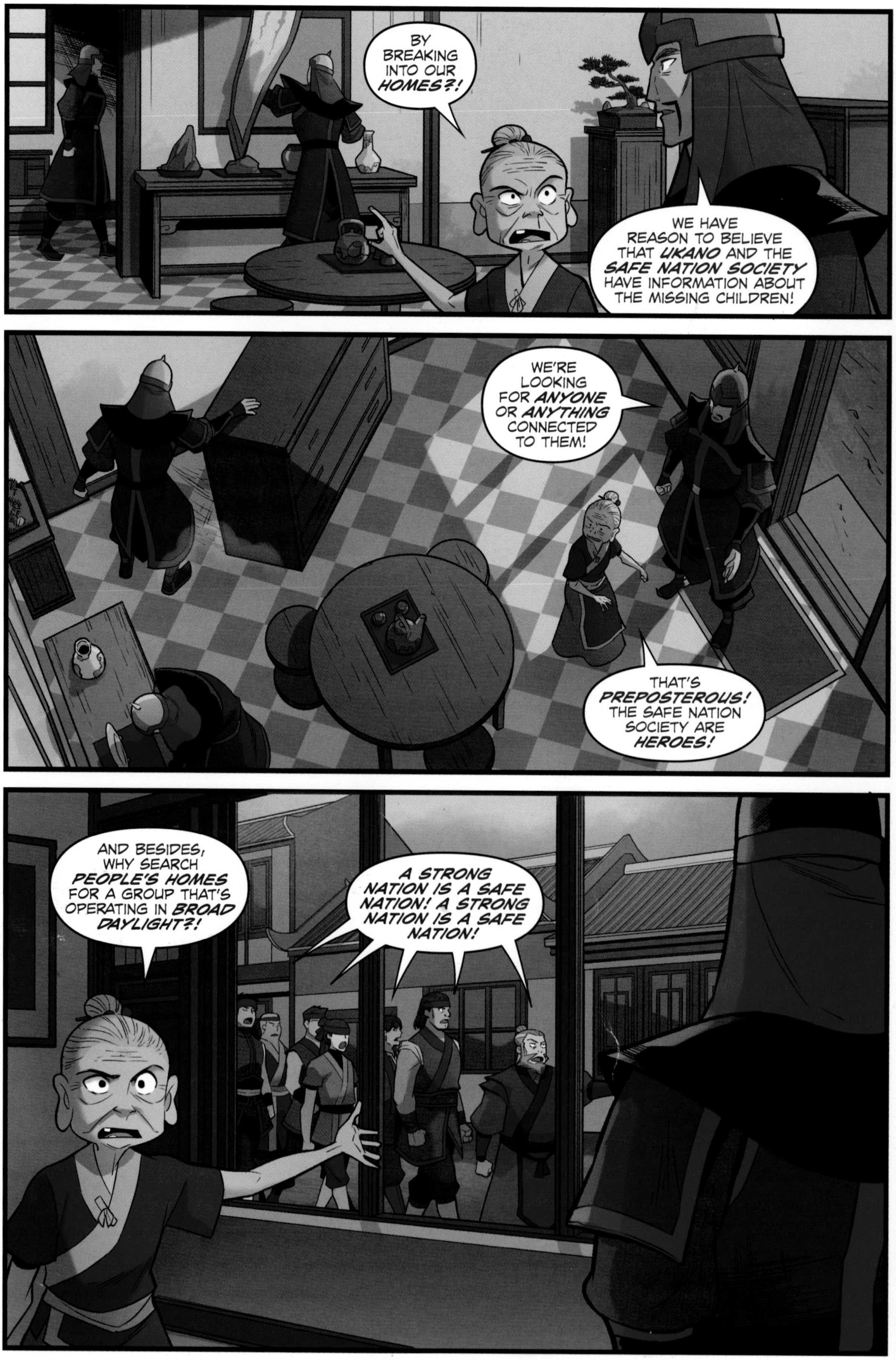
BY BREAKING INTO OUR HOMES?!
WE HAVE REASON TO BELIEVE THAT UKANO AND THE SAFE NATION SOCIETY HAVE INFORMATION ABOUT THE MISSING CHILDREN!
WE'RE LOOKING FOR ANYONE OR ANYTHING CONNECTED TO THEM!
THAT'S PREPOSTEROUS! THE SAFE NATION SOCIETY ARE HEROES!
AND BESIDES, WHY SEARCH PEOPLE'S HOMES FOR A GROUP THAT'S OPERATING IN BROAD DAYLIGHT?!
A STRONG NATION IS A SAFE NATION! A STRONG NATION IS A SAFE NATION!

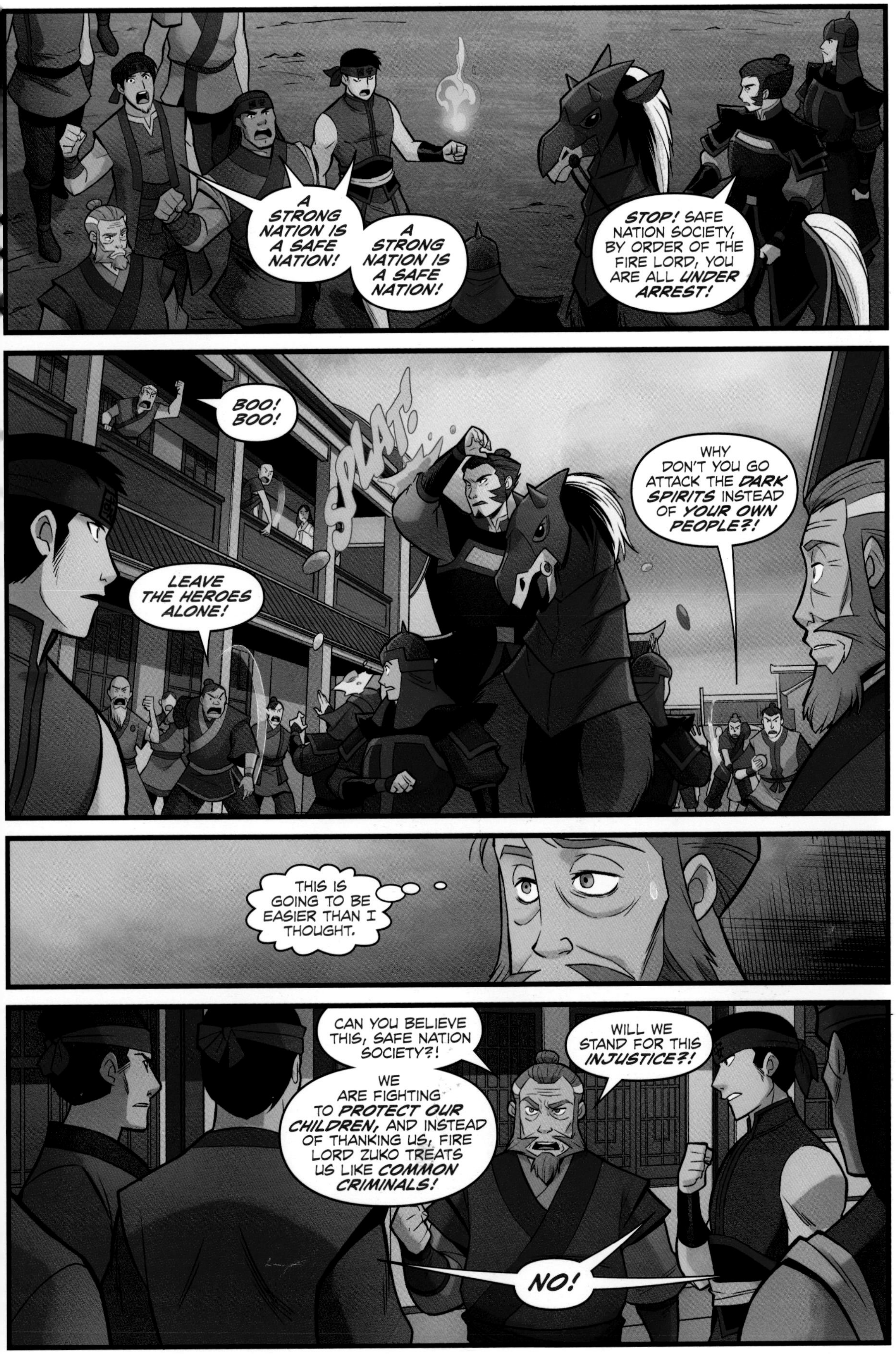
A STRONG NATION IS A SAFE NATION!
A STRONG NATION IS A SAFE NATION!
STOP! SAFE NATION SOCIETY, BY ORDER OF THE FIRE LORD, YOU ARE ALL UNDER ARREST!
BOO! BOO!
SPLAT!
LEAVE THE HEROES ALONE!
WHY DON'T YOU GO ATTACK THE DARK SPIRITS INSTEAD OF YOUR OWN PEOPLE?!
THIS IS GOING TO BE EASIER THAN I THOUGHT.
CAN YOU BELIEVE THIS, SAFE NATION SOCIETY?!
WE ARE FIGHTING TO PROTECT OUR CHILDREN, AND INSTEAD OF THANKING US, FIRE LORD ZUKO TREATS US LIKE COMMON CRIMINALS!
WILL WE STAND FOR THIS INJUSTICE?!
NO!

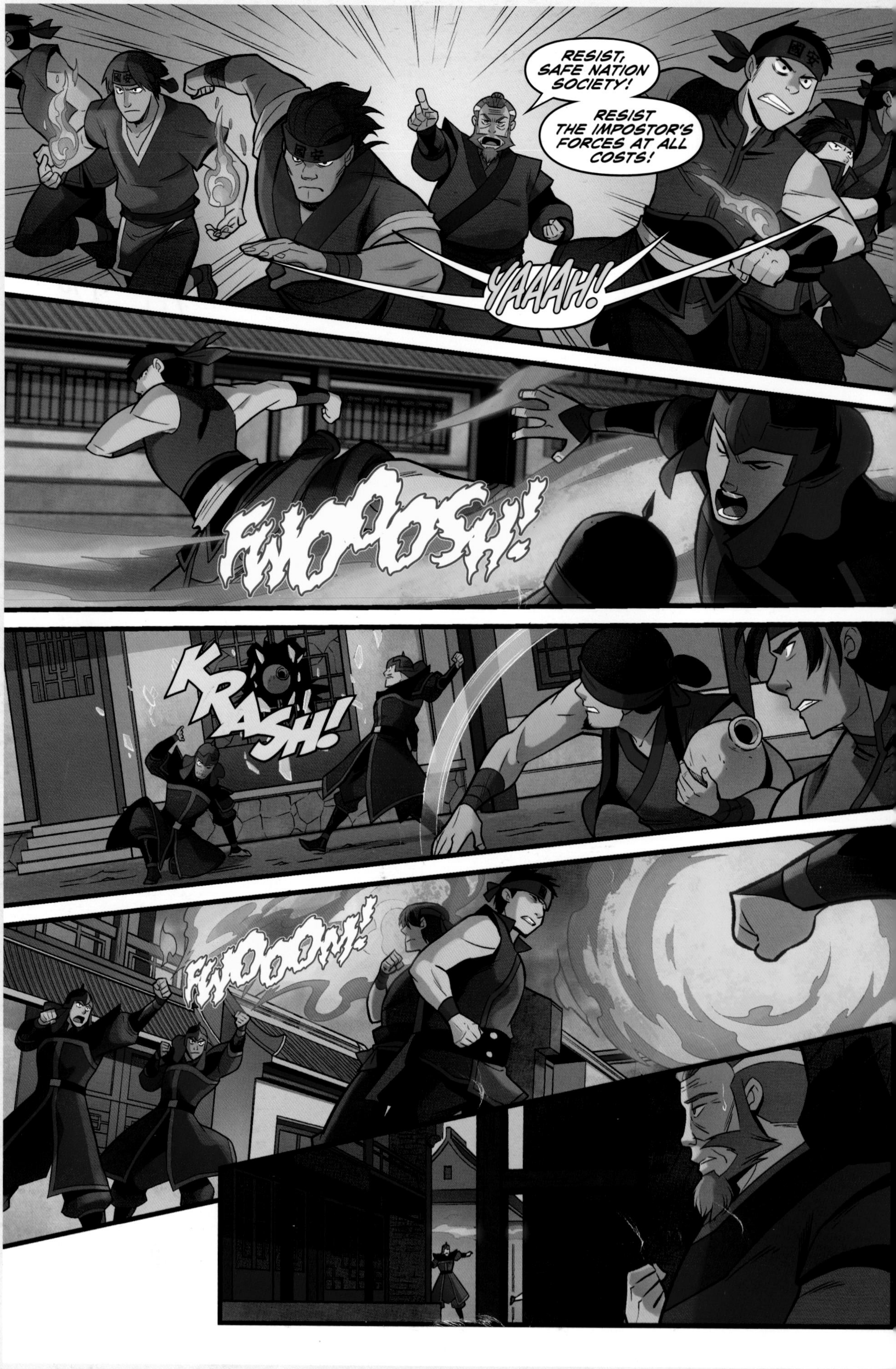
RESIST, SAFE NATION SOCIETY!
RESIST THE IMPOSTOR'S FORCES AT ALL COSTS!
YAAAH!
FWOOOSH!
KRASH!
FWOOOM!

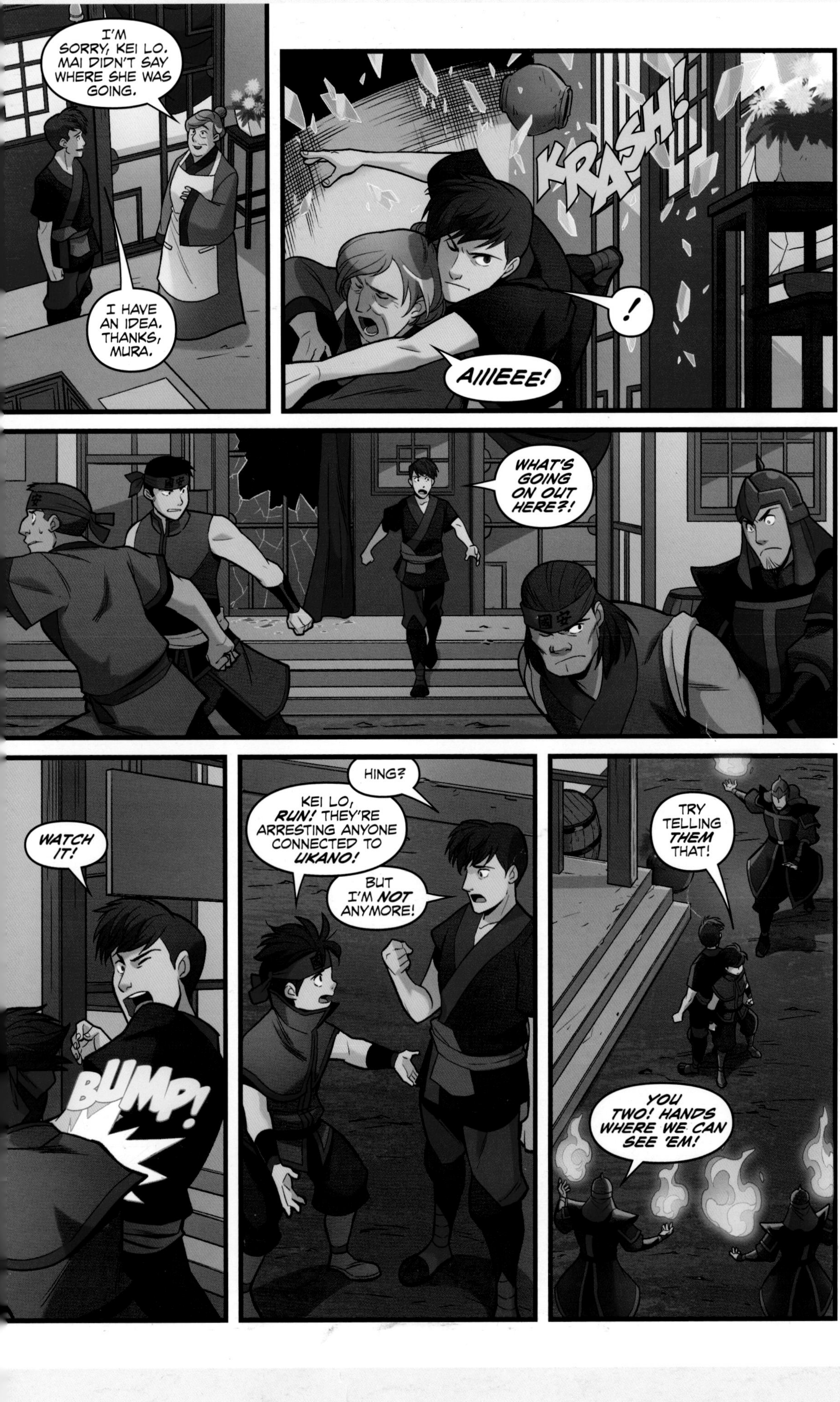
I'M SORRY, KEI LO. MAI DIDN'T SAY WHERE SHE WAS GOING.
I HAVE AN IDEA. THANKS, MURA.
KRASH!!
!
AIIIEEE!
WHAT'S GOING ON OUT HERE?!
WATCH IT!
BUMP!
HING?
KEI LO, RUN! THEY'RE ARRESTING ANYONE CONNECTED TO UKANO!
BUT I'M NOT ANYMORE!
TRY TELLING THEM THAT!
YOU TWO! HANDS WHERE WE CAN SEE 'EM!

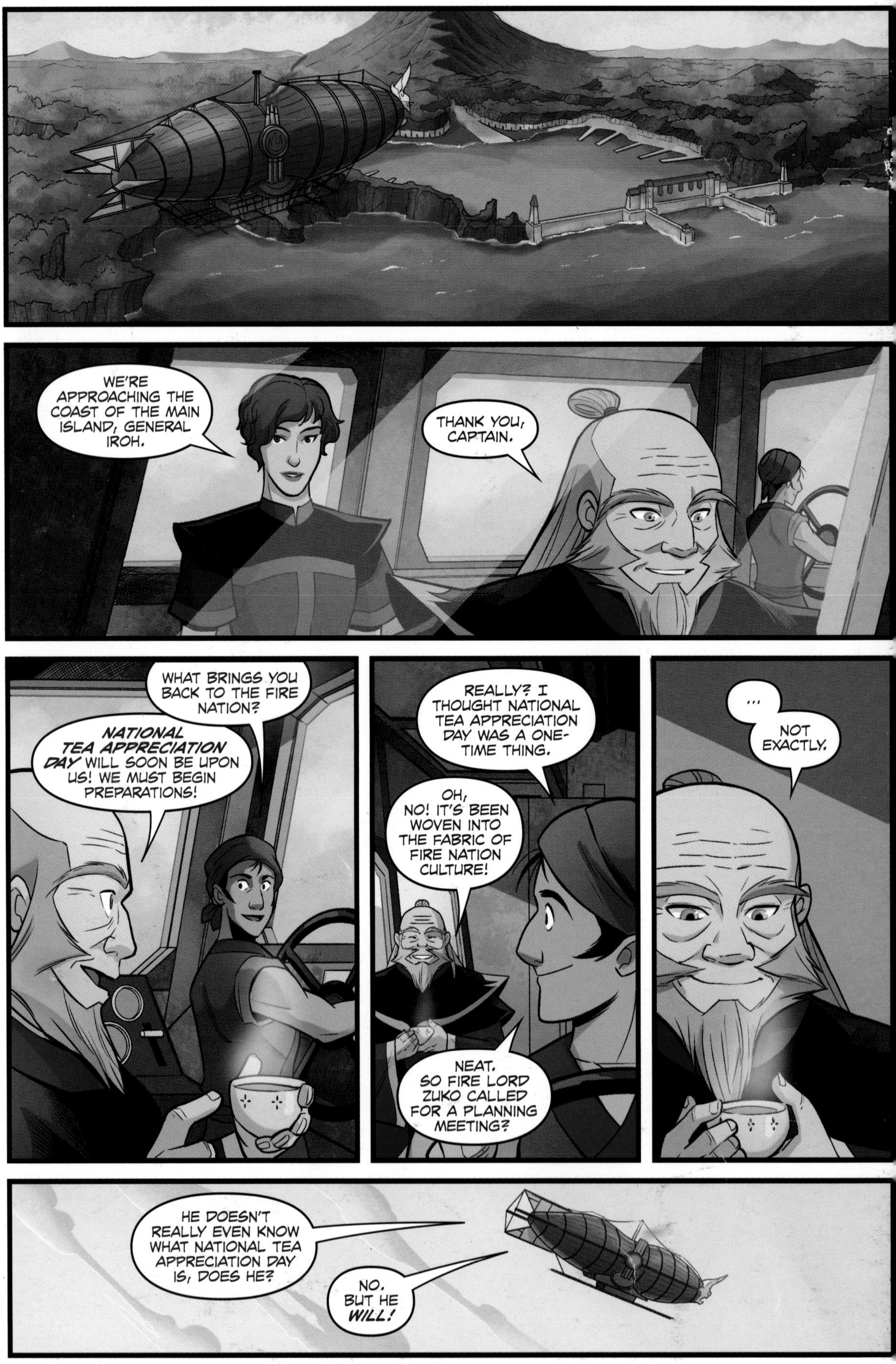
WE'RE APPROACHING THE COAST OF THE MAIN ISLAND, GENERAL IROH.
THANK YOU, CAPTAIN.
WHAT BRINGS YOU BACK TO THE FIRE NATION?
NATIONAL TEA APPRECIATION DAY WILL SOON BE UPON US! WE MUST BEGIN PREPARATIONS!
REALLY? I THOUGHT NATIONAL TEA APPRECIATION DAY WAS A ONE-TIME THING.
OH, NO! IT'S BEEN WOVEN INTO THE FABRIC OF FIRE NATION CULTURE!
NEAT. SO FIRE LORD ZUKO CALLED FOR A PLANNING MEETING?
... NOT EXACTLY.
HE DOESN'T REALLY EVEN KNOW WHAT NATIONAL TEA APPRECIATION DAY IS, DOES HE?
NO. BUT HE ***WILL!***

GLY: *Uncle Iroh instituted the first National Tea Appreciation Day while he was interim Fire Lord.*

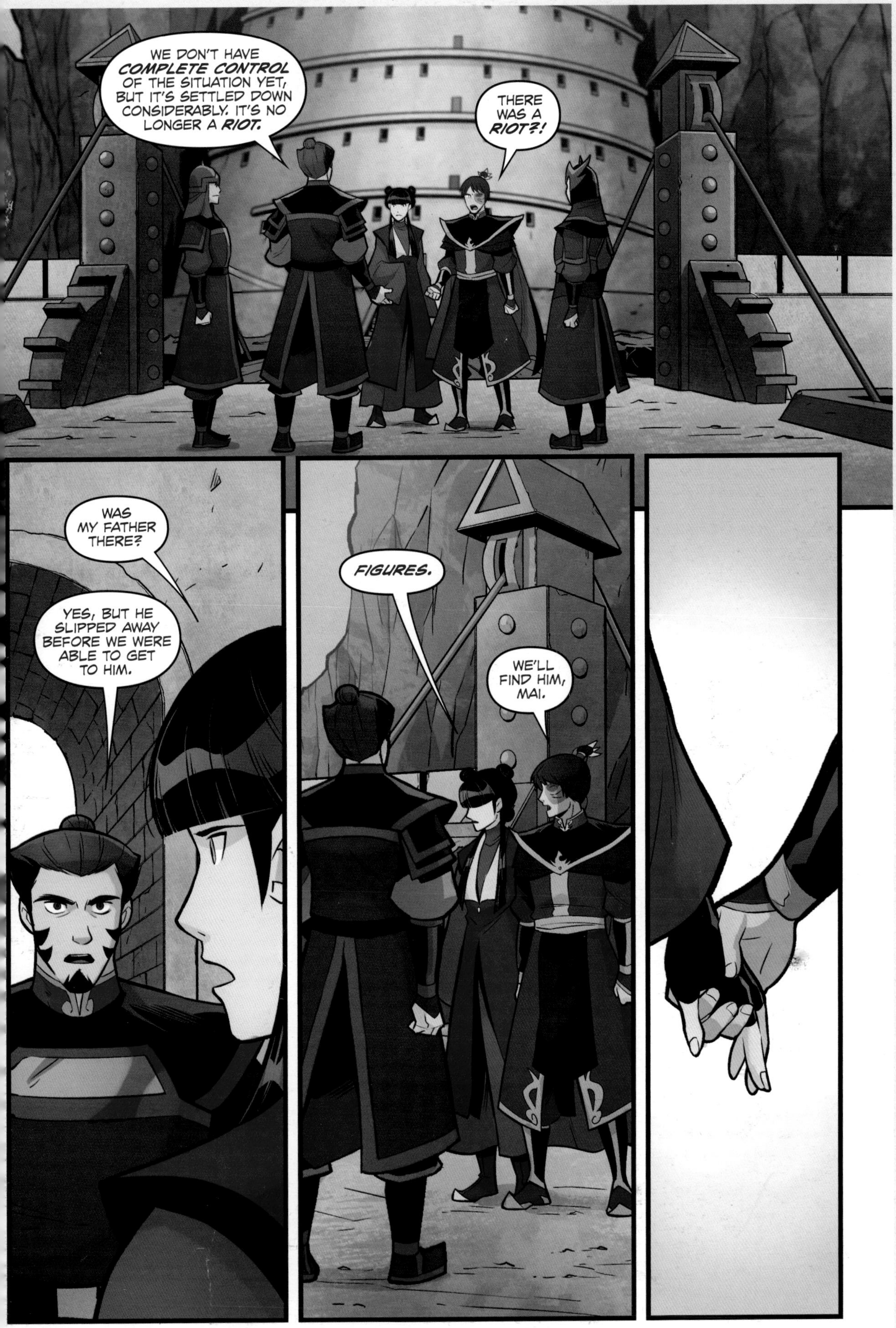
WE DON'T HAVE COMPLETE CONTROL OF THE SITUATION YET, BUT IT'S SETTLED DOWN CONSIDERABLY. IT'S NO LONGER A RIOT.
THERE WAS A RIOT?!
WAS MY FATHER THERE?
YES, BUT HE SLIPPED AWAY BEFORE WE WERE ABLE TO GET TO HIM.
FIGURES.
WE'LL FIND HIM, MAI.

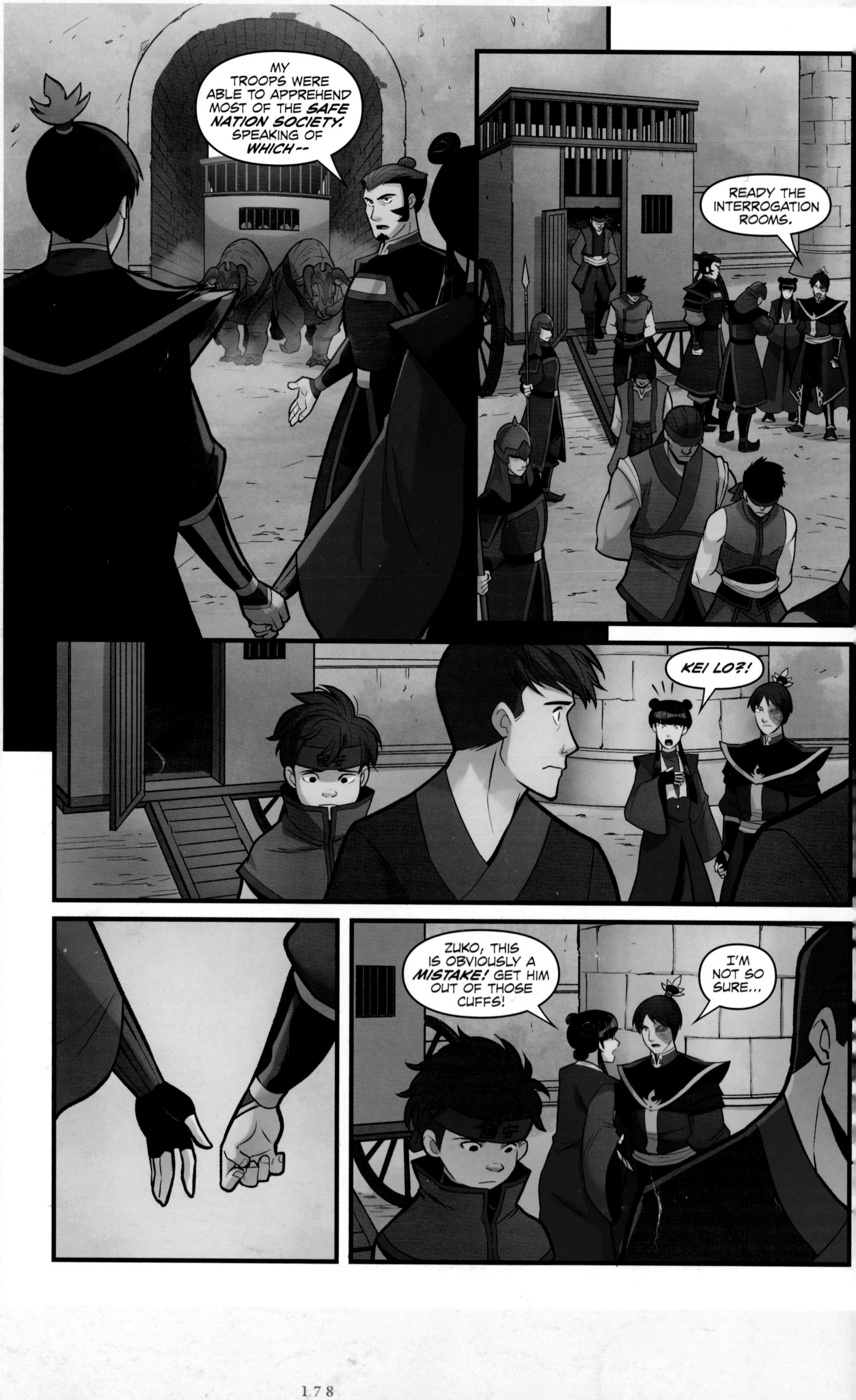
MY TROOPS WERE ABLE TO APPREHEND MOST OF THE SAFE NATION SOCIETY. SPEAKING OF WHICH--
READY THE INTERROGATION ROOMS.
KEI LO?!
ZUKO, THIS IS OBVIOUSLY A MISTAKE! GET HIM OUT OF THOSE CUFFS!
I'M NOT SO SURE...

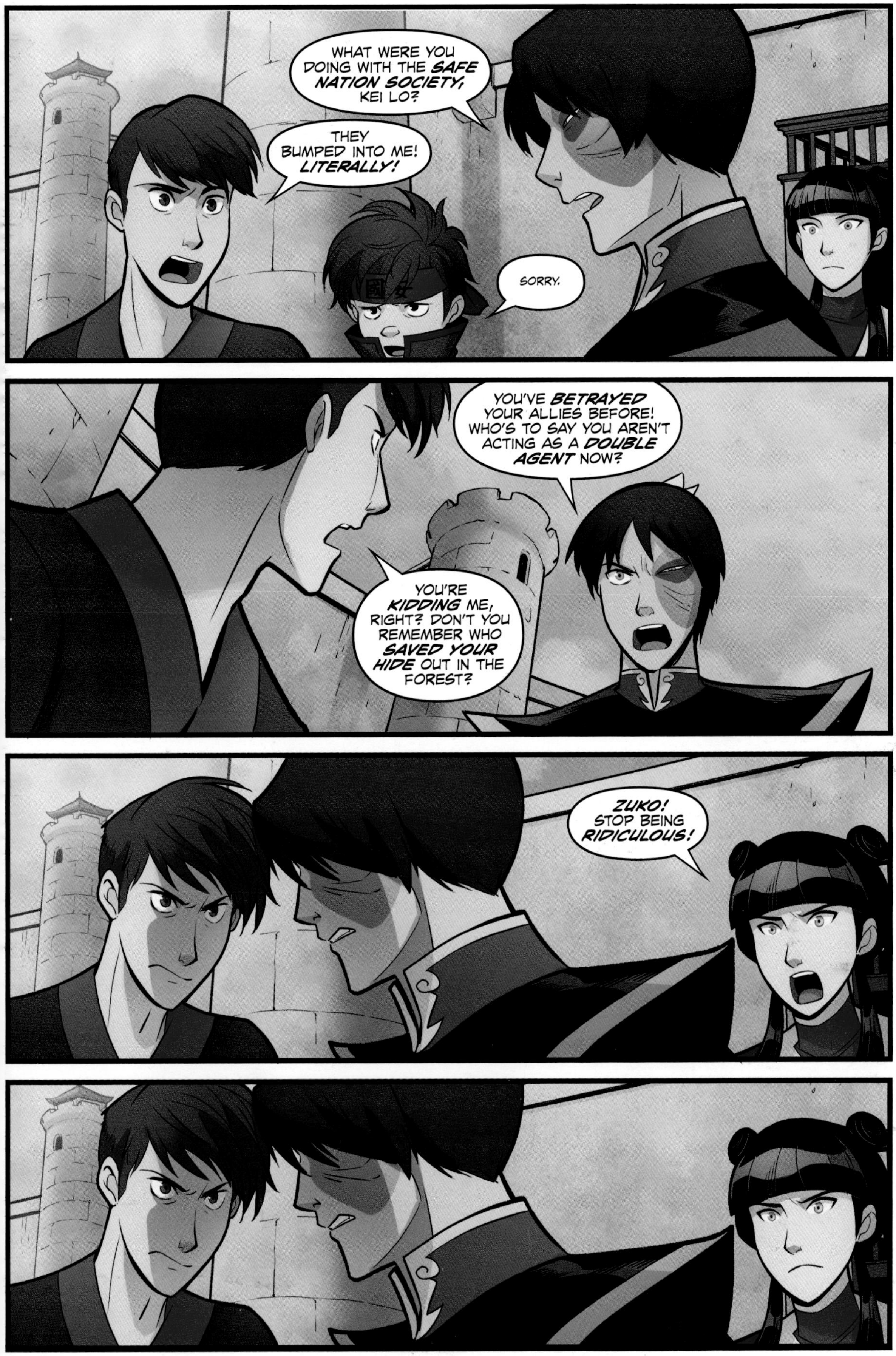
WHAT WERE YOU DOING WITH THE SAFE NATION SOCIETY, KEI LO?
THEY BUMPED INTO ME! LITERALLY!
SORRY.
YOU'VE BETRAYED YOUR ALLIES BEFORE! WHO'S TO SAY YOU AREN'T ACTING AS A DOUBLE AGENT NOW?
YOU'RE KIDDING ME, RIGHT? DON'T YOU REMEMBER WHO SAVED YOUR HIDE OUT IN THE FOREST?
ZUKO! STOP BEING RIDICULOUS!

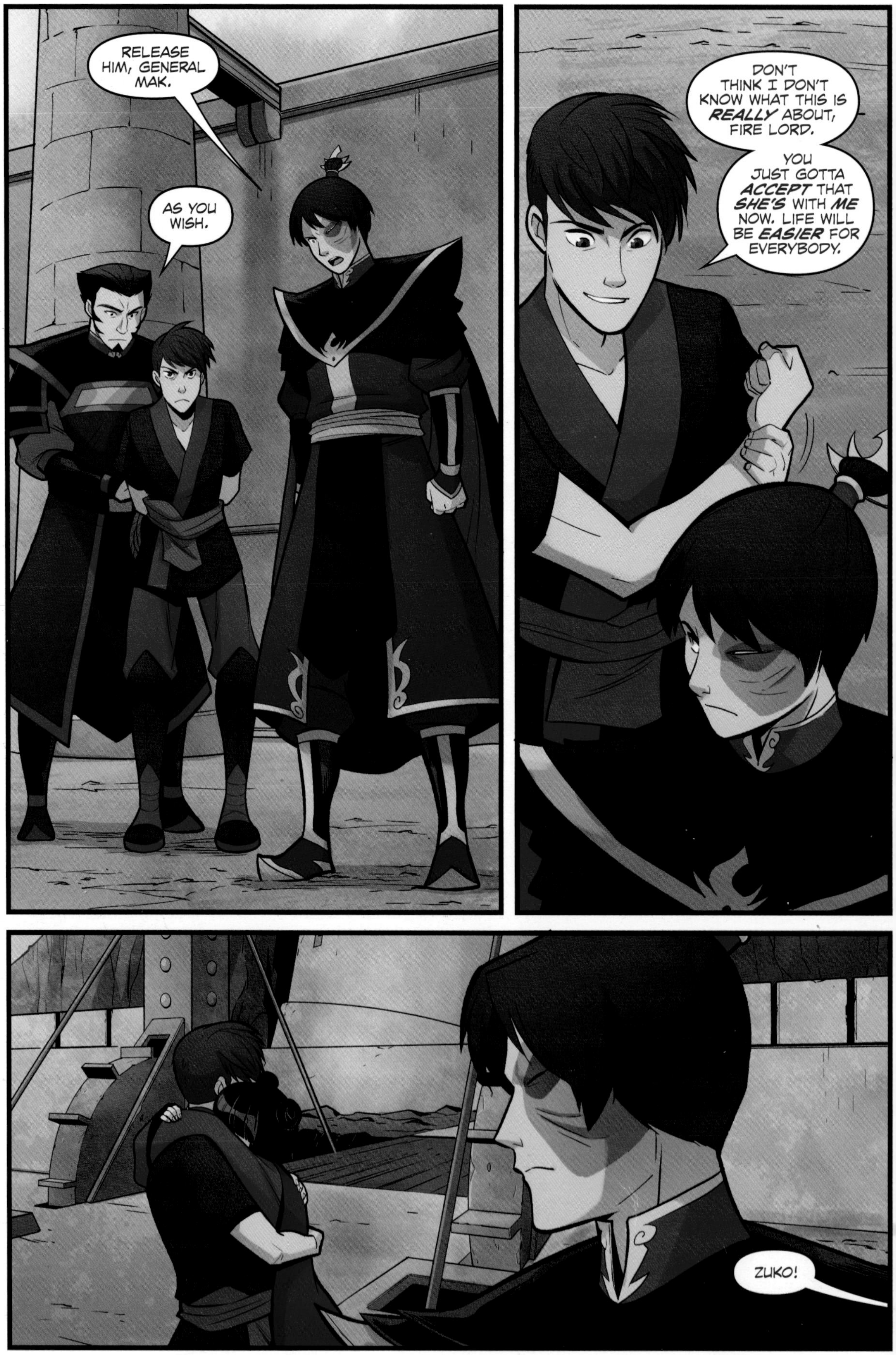
RELEASE HIM, GENERAL MAK.
AS YOU WISH.
DON'T THINK I DON'T KNOW WHAT THIS IS REALLY ABOUT, FIRE LORD.
YOU JUST GOTTA ACCEPT THAT SHE'S WITH ME NOW. LIFE WILL BE EASIER FOR EVERYBODY.
ZUKO!

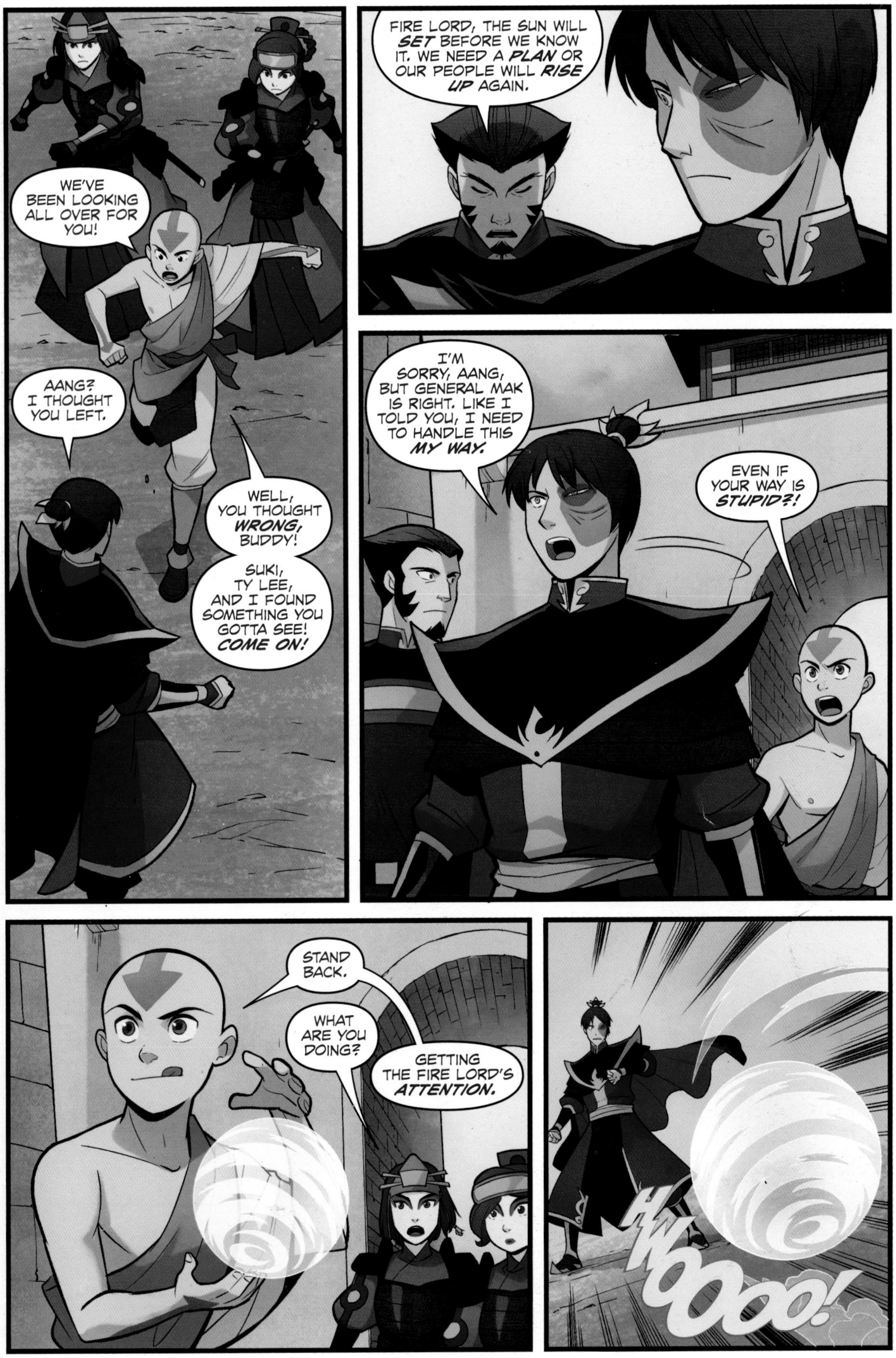
WE'VE BEEN LOOKING ALL OVER FOR YOU!
AANG? I THOUGHT YOU LEFT.
WELL, YOU THOUGHT WRONG, BUDDY!
SUKI, TY LEE, AND I FOUND SOMETHING YOU GOTTA SEE! COME ON!
FIRE LORD, THE SUN WILL SET BEFORE WE KNOW IT. WE NEED A PLAN OR OUR PEOPLE WILL RISE UP AGAIN.
I'M SORRY, AANG, BUT GENERAL MAK IS RIGHT. LIKE I TOLD YOU, I NEED TO HANDLE THIS MY WAY.
EVEN IF YOUR WAY IS STUPID?!
STAND BACK.
WHAT ARE YOU DOING?
GETTING THE FIRE LORD'S ATTENTION.
HWOOOOO!

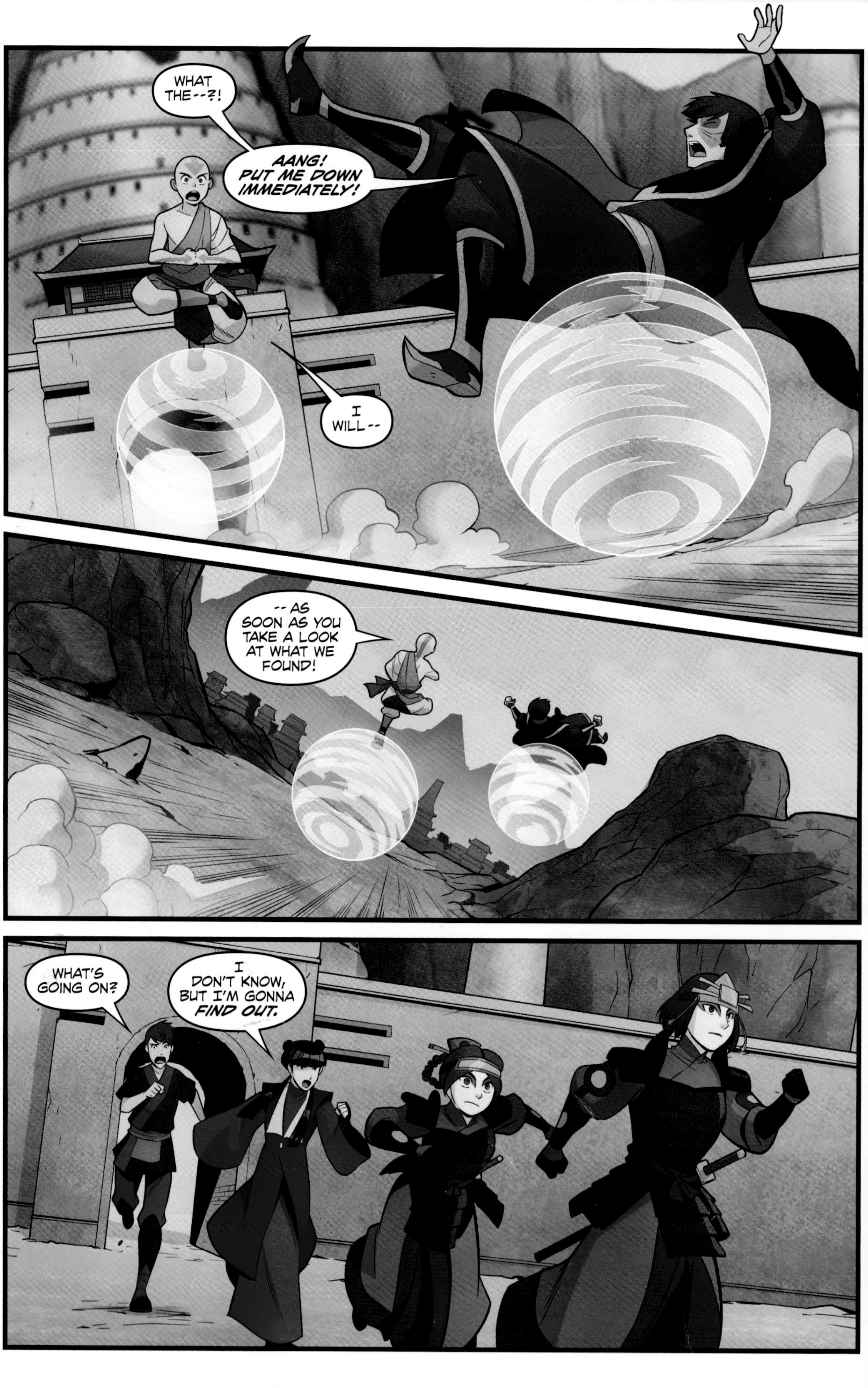
WHAT THE--?!
AANG! PUT ME DOWN IMMEDIATELY!
I WILL--
--AS SOON AS YOU TAKE A LOOK AT WHAT WE FOUND!
WHAT'S GOING ON?
I DON'T KNOW, BUT I'M GONNA FIND OUT.

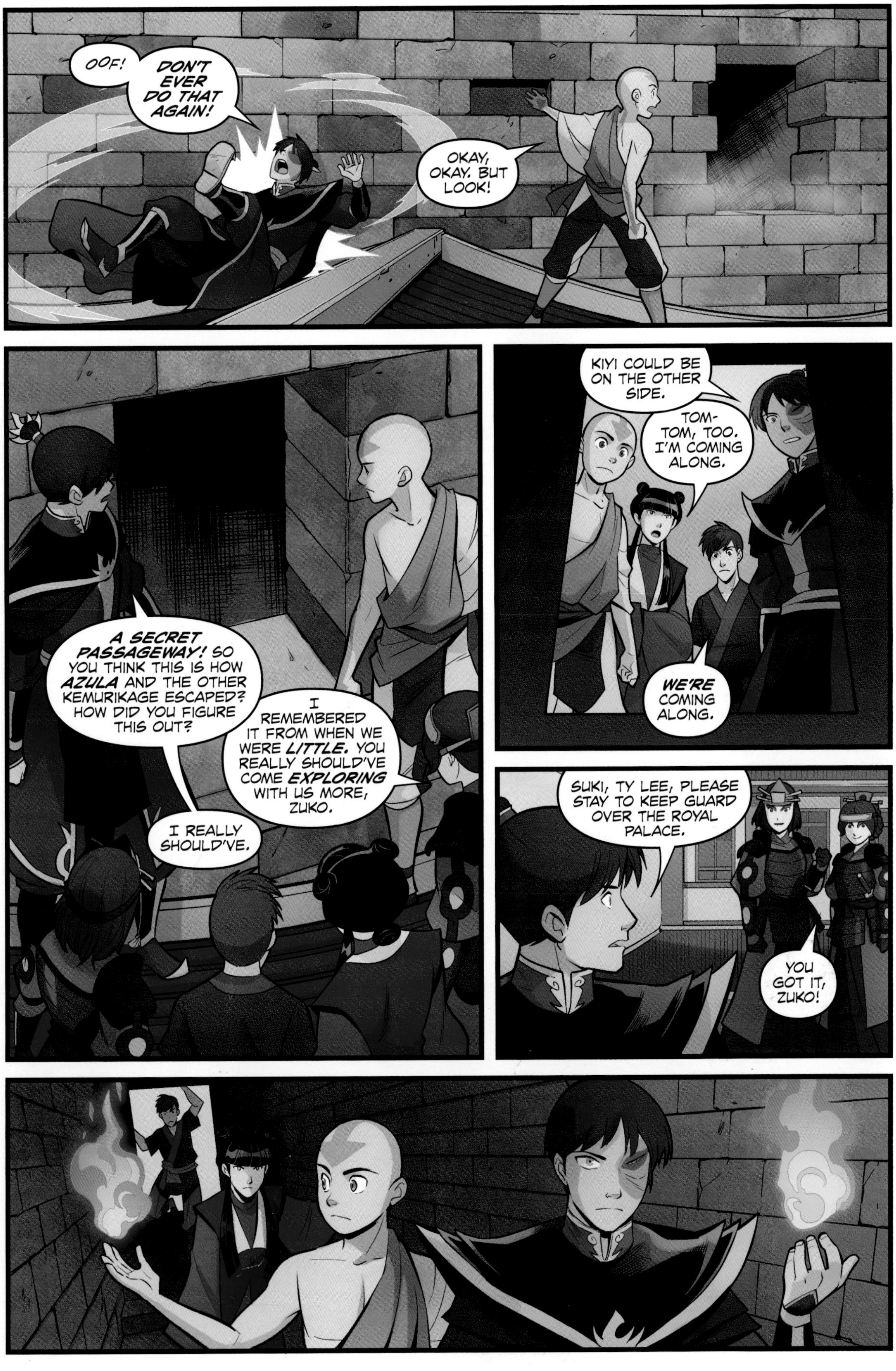
OOF!
DON'T EVER DO THAT AGAIN!
OKAY, OKAY. BUT LOOK!
A SECRET PASSAGEWAY! SO YOU THINK THIS IS HOW AZULA AND THE OTHER KEMURIKAGE ESCAPED? HOW DID YOU FIGURE THIS OUT?
I REMEMBERED IT FROM WHEN WE WERE LITTLE. YOU REALLY SHOULD'VE COME EXPLORING WITH US MORE, ZUKO.
I REALLY SHOULD'VE.
KIYI COULD BE ON THE OTHER SIDE.
TOM-TOM, TOO. I'M COMING ALONG.
WE'RE COMING ALONG.
SUKI, TY LEE, PLEASE STAY TO KEEP GUARD OVER THE ROYAL PALACE.
YOU GOT IT, ZUKO!

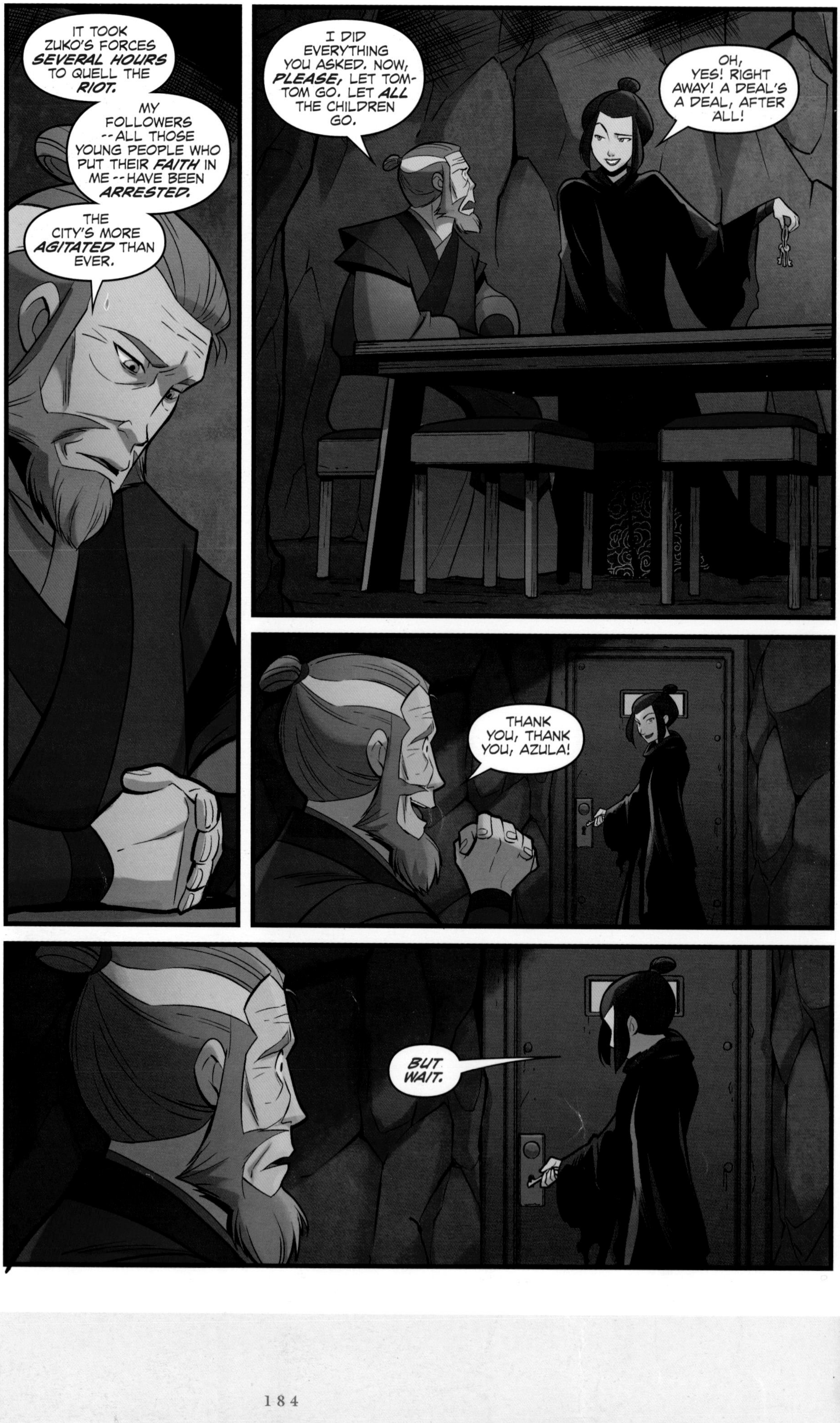
IT TOOK ZUKO'S FORCES SEVERAL HOURS TO QUELL THE RIOT.
MY FOLLOWERS --ALL THOSE YOUNG PEOPLE WHO PUT THEIR FAITH IN ME --HAVE BEEN ARRESTED.
THE CITY'S MORE AGITATED THAN EVER.
I DID EVERYTHING YOU ASKED. NOW, PLEASE, LET TOM-TOM GO. LET ALL THE CHILDREN GO.
OH, YES! RIGHT AWAY! A DEAL'S A DEAL, AFTER ALL!
THANK YOU, THANK YOU, AZULA!
BUT WAIT.

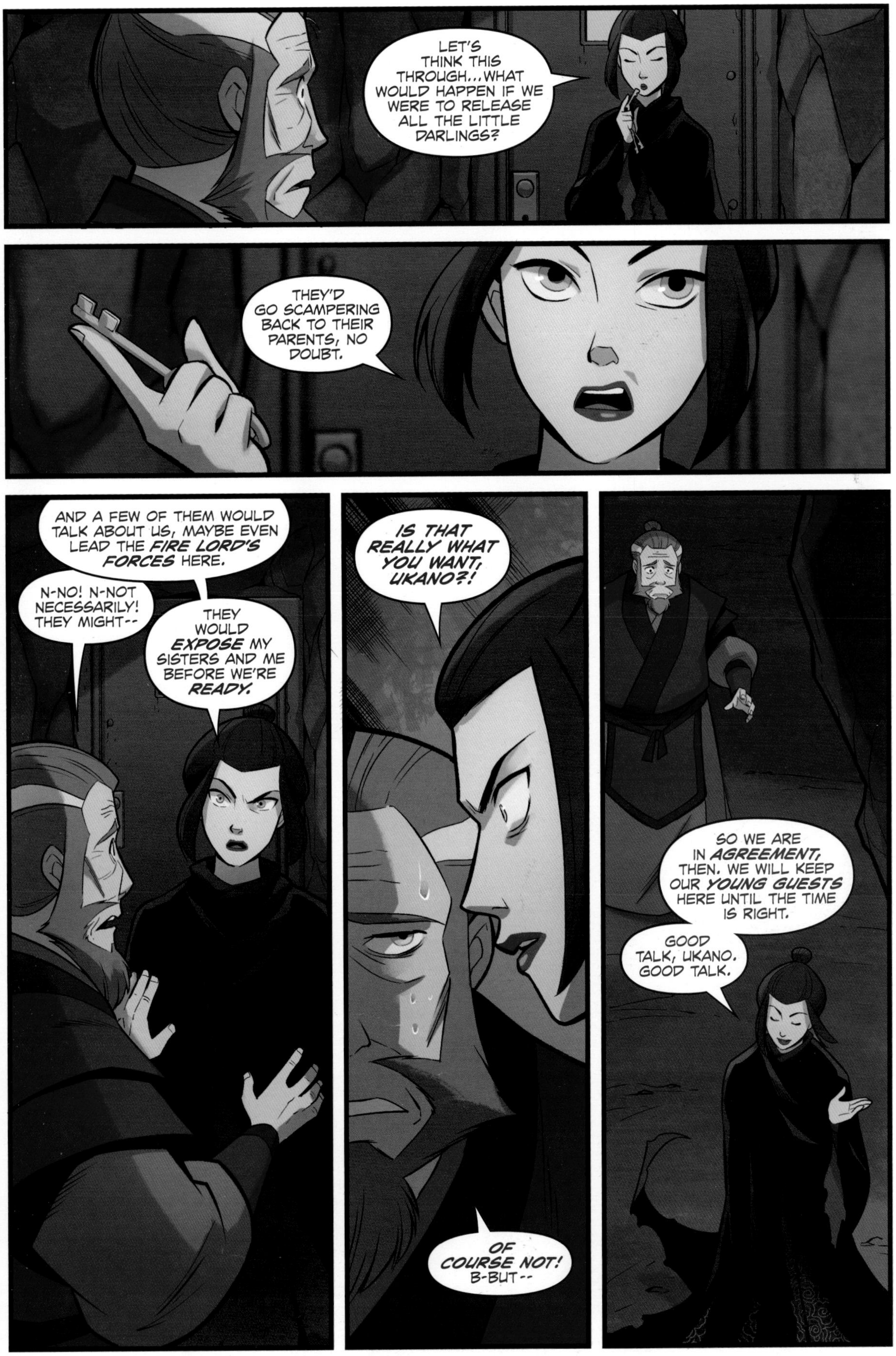
LET'S THINK THIS THROUGH...WHAT WOULD HAPPEN IF WE WERE TO RELEASE ALL THE LITTLE DARLINGS?
THEY'D GO SCAMPERING BACK TO THEIR PARENTS, NO DOUBT.
AND A FEW OF THEM WOULD TALK ABOUT US, MAYBE EVEN LEAD THE FIRE LORD'S FORCES HERE.
N-NO! N-NOT NECESSARILY! THEY MIGHT--
THEY WOULD EXPOSE MY SISTERS AND ME BEFORE WE'RE READY.
IS THAT REALLY WHAT YOU WANT, UKANO?!
OF COURSE NOT! B-BUT--
SO WE ARE IN AGREEMENT, THEN. WE WILL KEEP OUR YOUNG GUESTS HERE UNTIL THE TIME IS RIGHT.
GOOD TALK, UKANO. GOOD TALK.

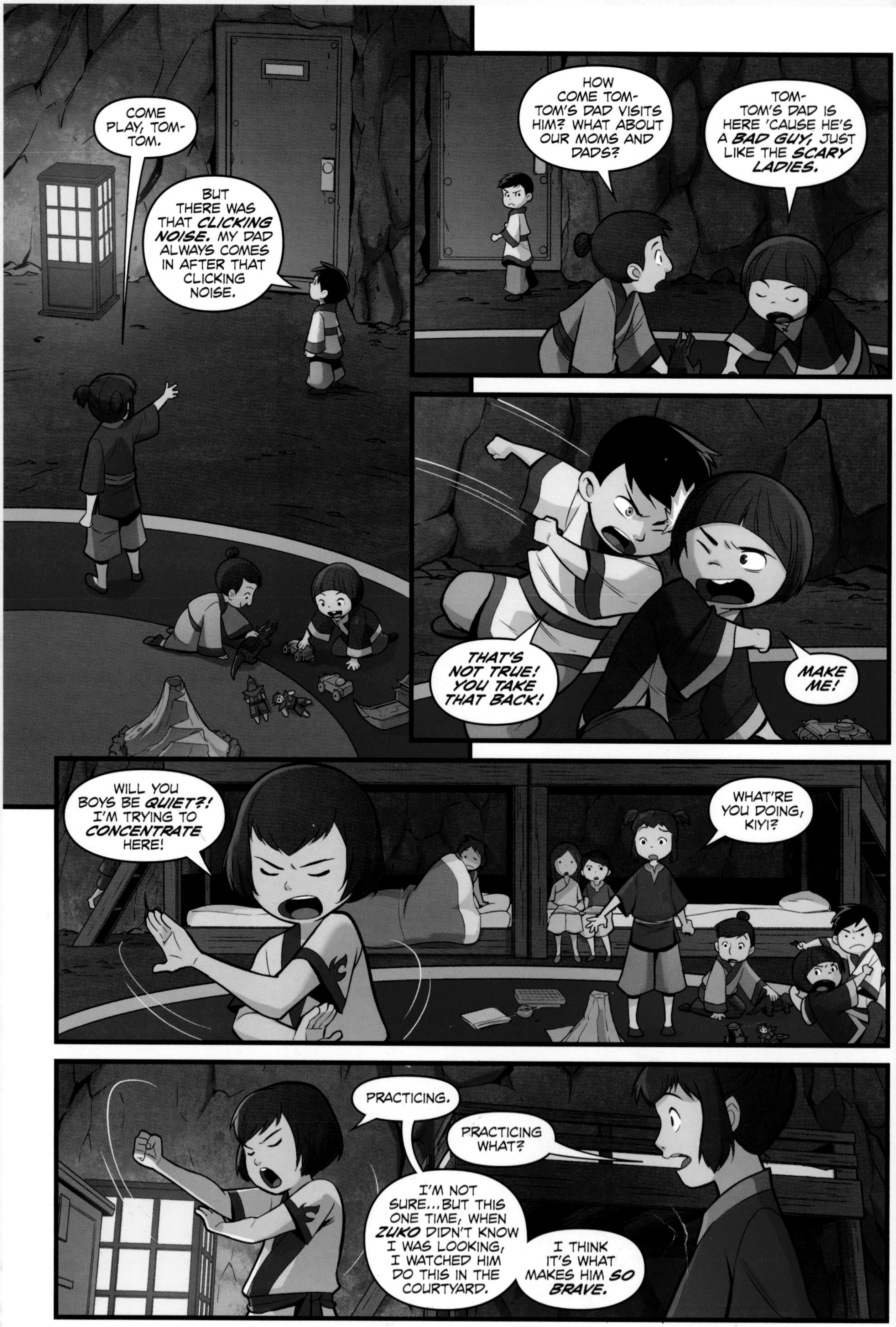
COME PLAY, TOM-TOM.
BUT THERE WAS THAT CLICKING NOISE. MY DAD ALWAYS COMES IN AFTER THAT CLICKING NOISE.
HOW COME TOM-TOM'S DAD VISITS HIM? WHAT ABOUT OUR MOMS AND DADS?
TOM-TOM'S DAD IS HERE 'CAUSE HE'S A BAD GUY, JUST LIKE THE SCARY LADIES.
THAT'S NOT TRUE! YOU TAKE THAT BACK!
MAKE ME!
WILL YOU BOYS BE QUIET?! I'M TRYING TO CONCENTRATE HERE!
WHAT'RE YOU DOING, KIYI?
PRACTICING.
PRACTICING WHAT?
I'M NOT SURE...BUT THIS ONE TIME, WHEN ZUKO DIDN'T KNOW I WAS LOOKING, I WATCHED HIM DO THIS IN THE COURTYARD.
I THINK IT'S WHAT MAKES HIM SO BRAVE.

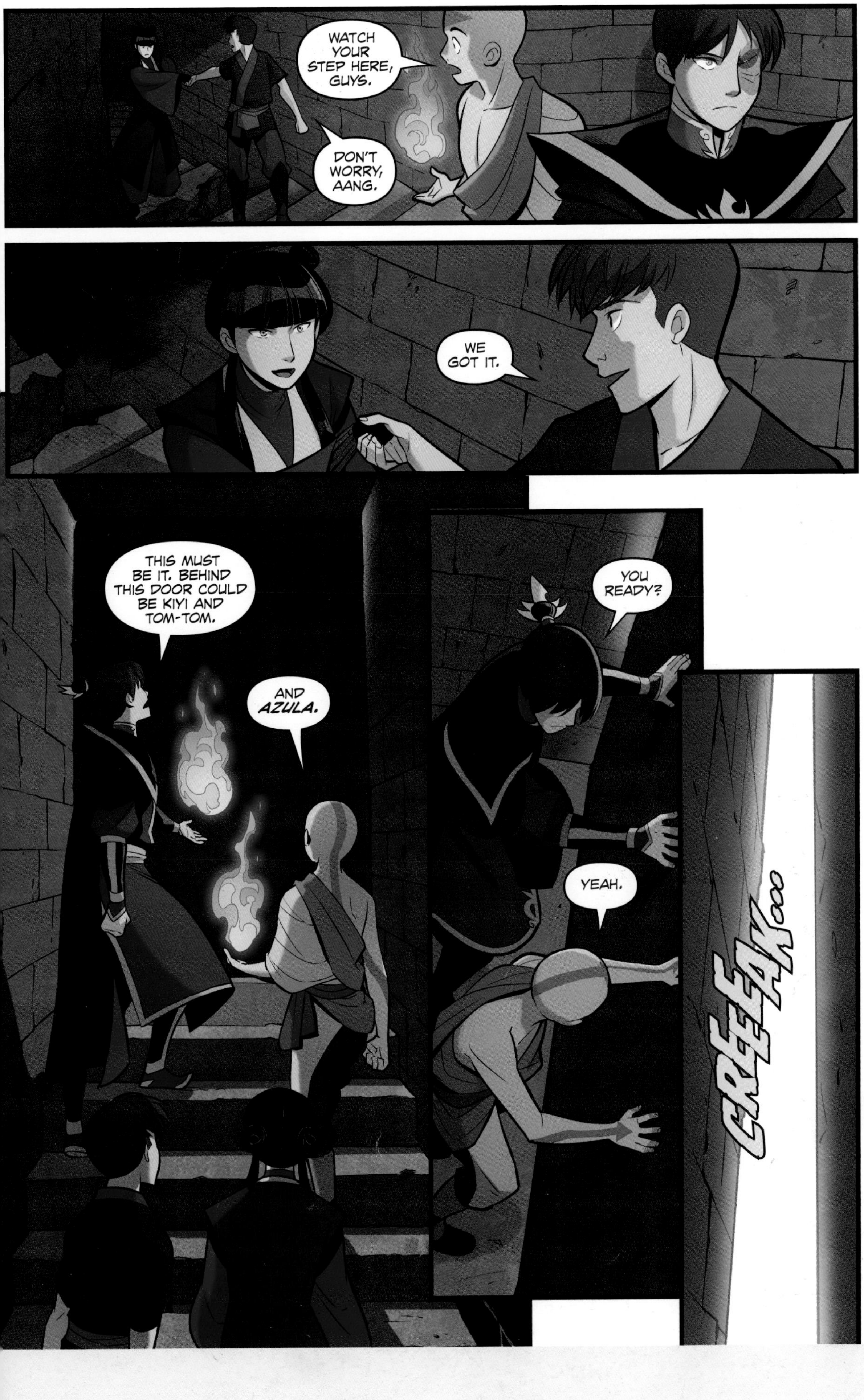
WATCH YOUR STEP HERE, GUYS.
DON'T WORRY, AANG.
WE GOT IT.
THIS MUST BE IT. BEHIND THIS DOOR COULD BE KIYI AND TOM-TOM.
AND *AZULA.*
YOU READY?
YEAH.
CREEEAK...

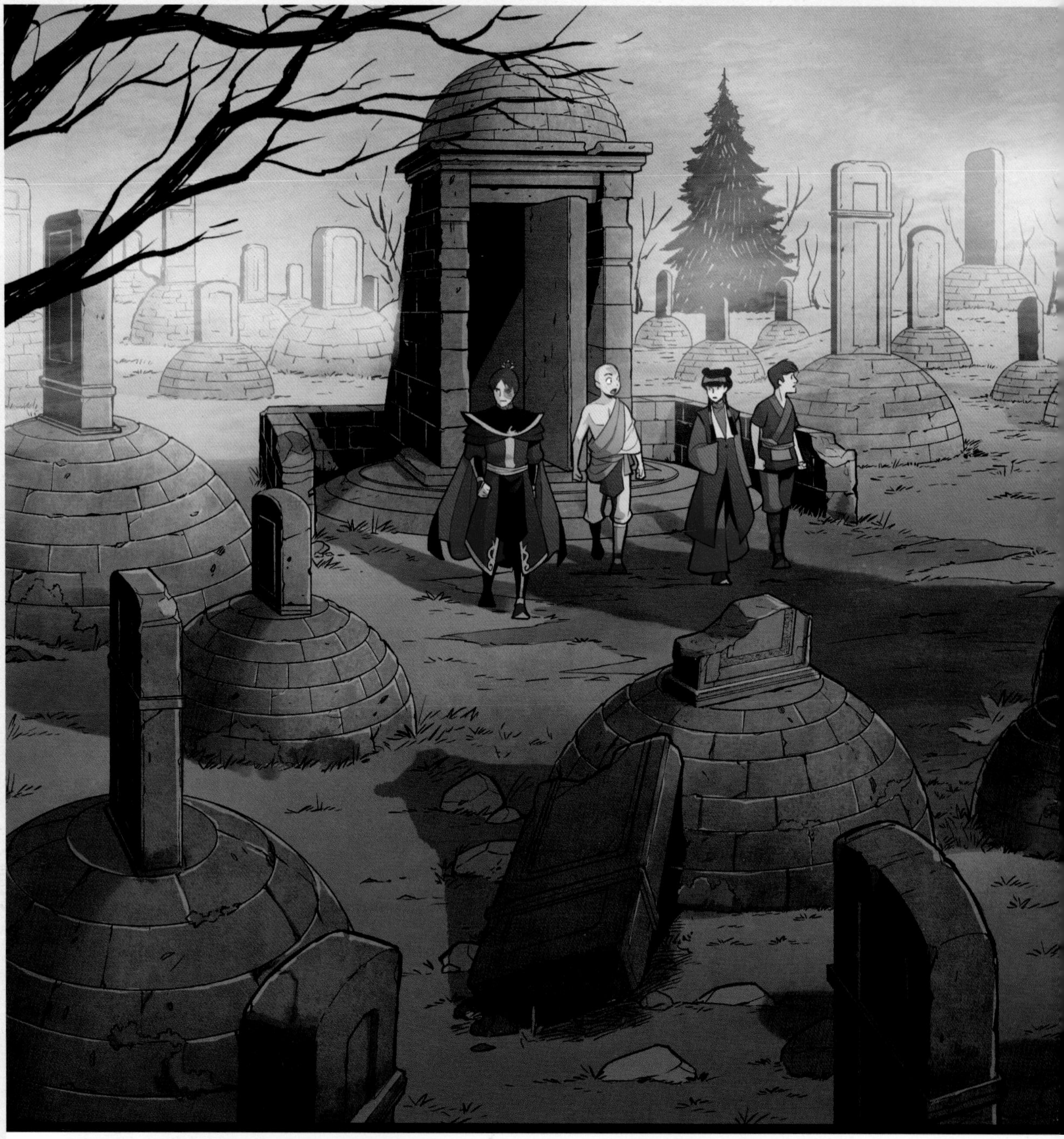

GLY: *The dome-shaped tombs in this graveyard were inspired by ancient Asian graveyards. In China's Fujian Province and in Japan's Ryukyu Islands, tombs were sometimes made to look like tortoiseshells. People smarter than me speculate that this was done to put the deceased under the care of the Black Tortoise, one of the Four Celestial Beings in Asian folklore.*

Incidentally, I used the Four Celestial Beings in The Shadow Hero, *a graphic novel I did with my friend Sonny Liew.*

G: *We used the tomb we saw on our trip to China as reference.*

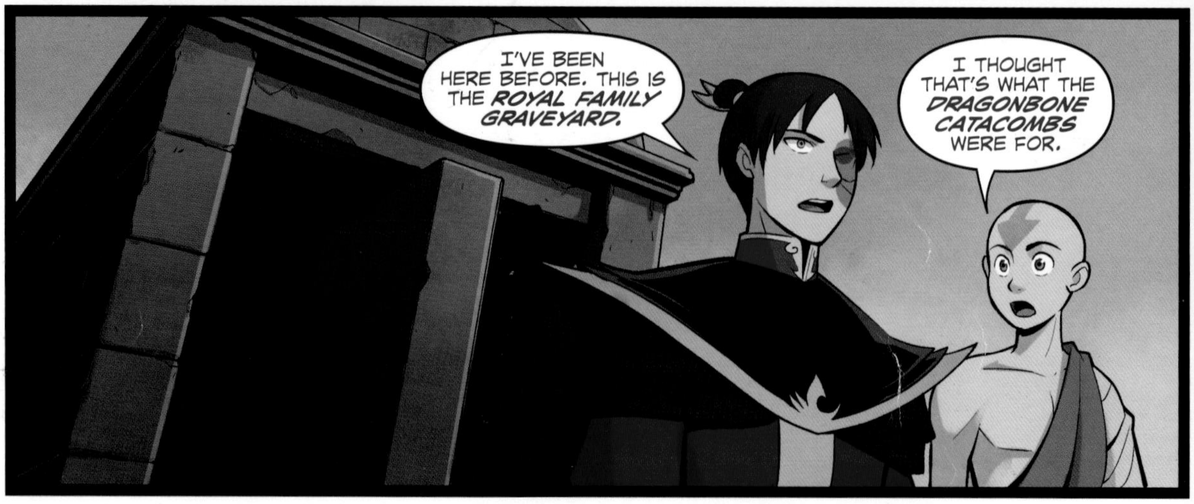
I'VE BEEN HERE BEFORE. THIS IS THE ROYAL FAMILY GRAVEYARD.
I THOUGHT THAT'S WHAT THE DRAGONBONE CATACOMBS WERE FOR.

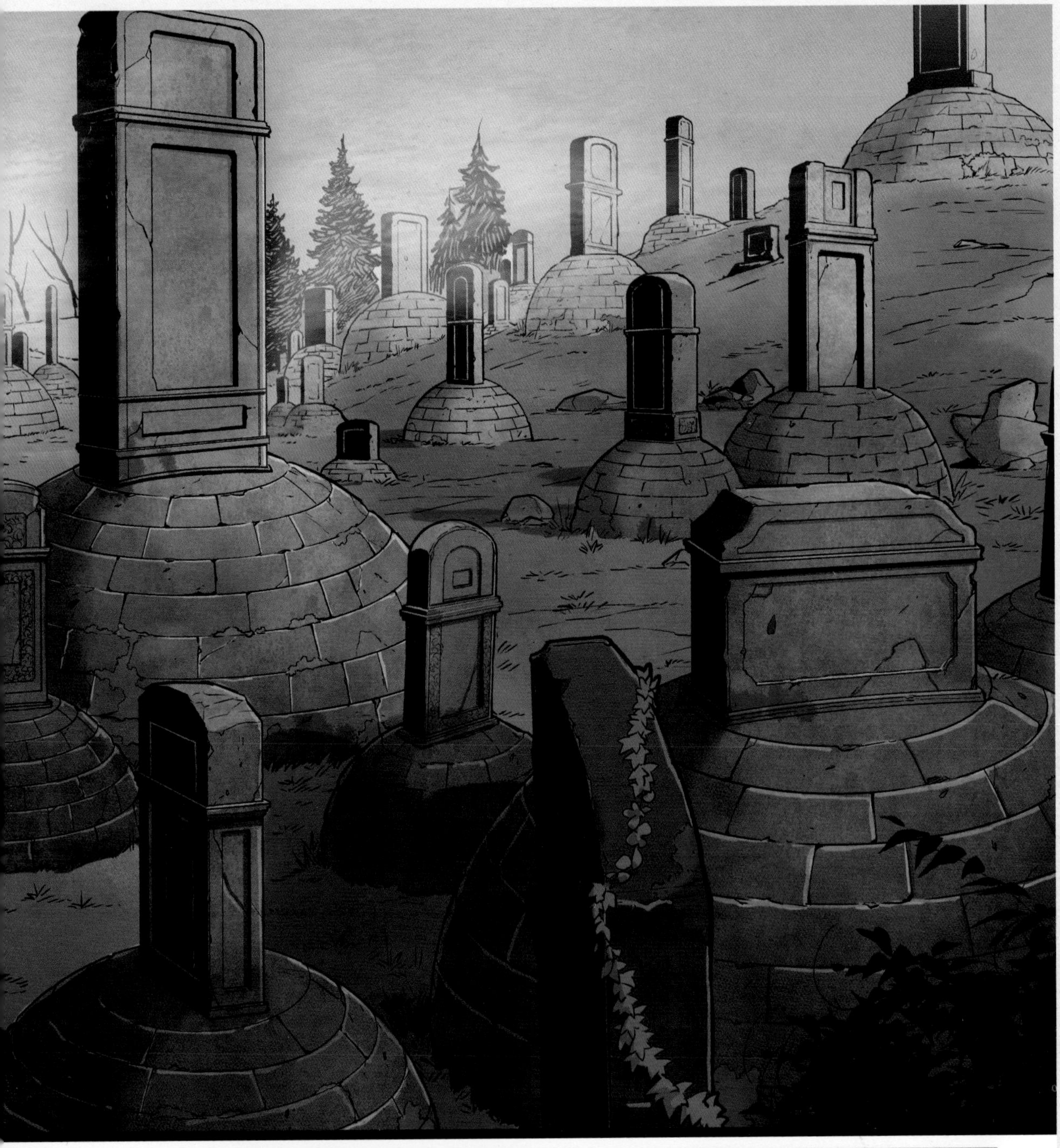

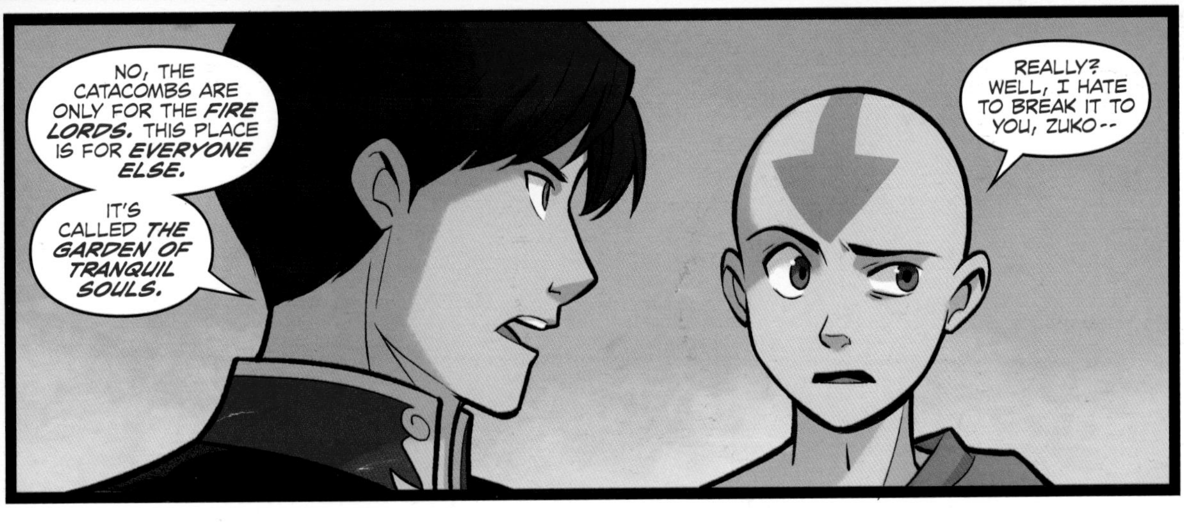
NO, THE CATACOMBS ARE ONLY FOR THE *FIRE LORDS.* THIS PLACE IS FOR *EVERYONE ELSE.*
IT'S CALLED *THE GARDEN OF TRANQUIL SOULS.*
REALLY? WELL, I HATE TO BREAK IT TO YOU, ZUKO--

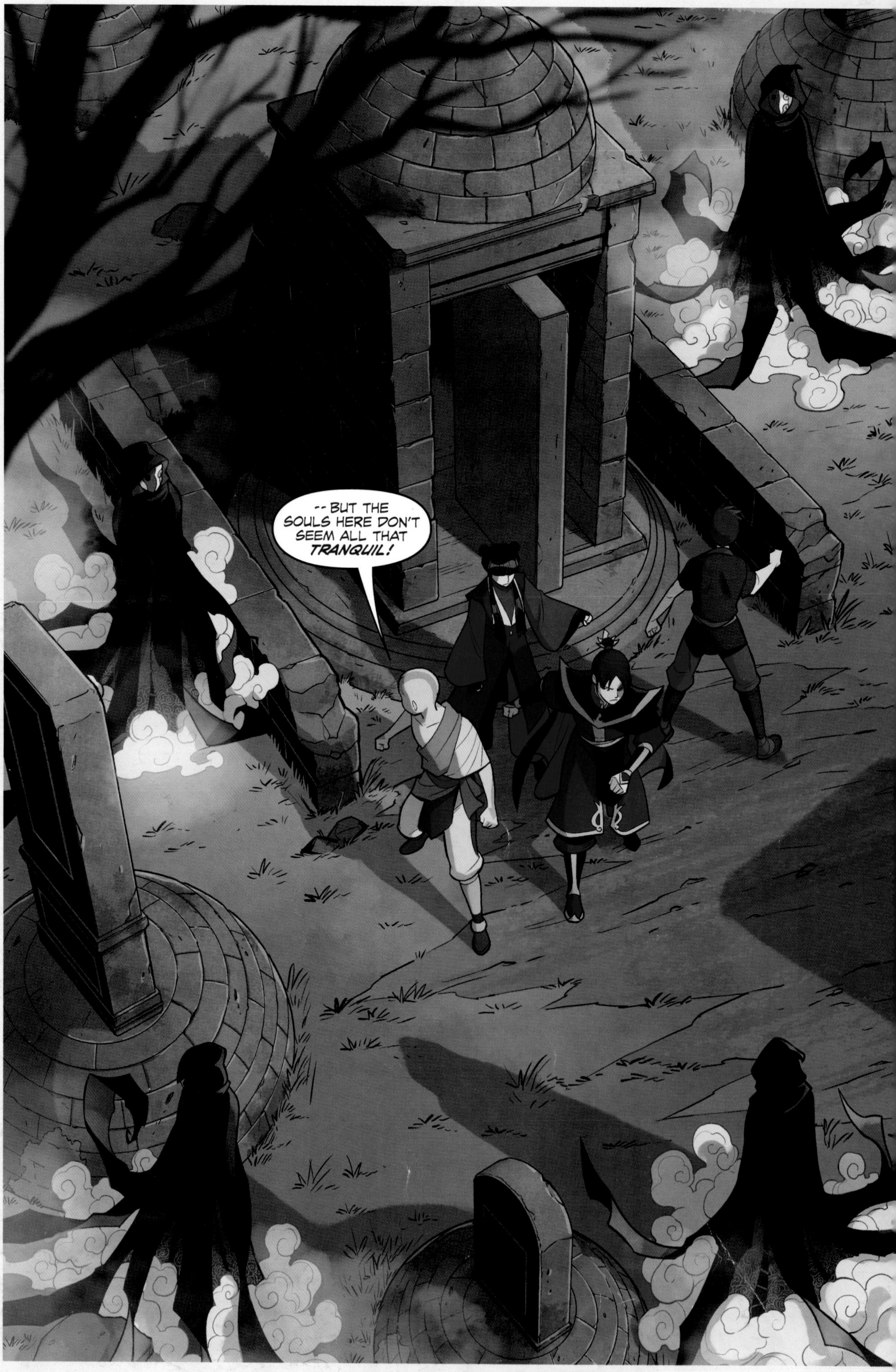
-- BUT THE SOULS HERE DON'T SEEM ALL THAT *TRANQUIL!*

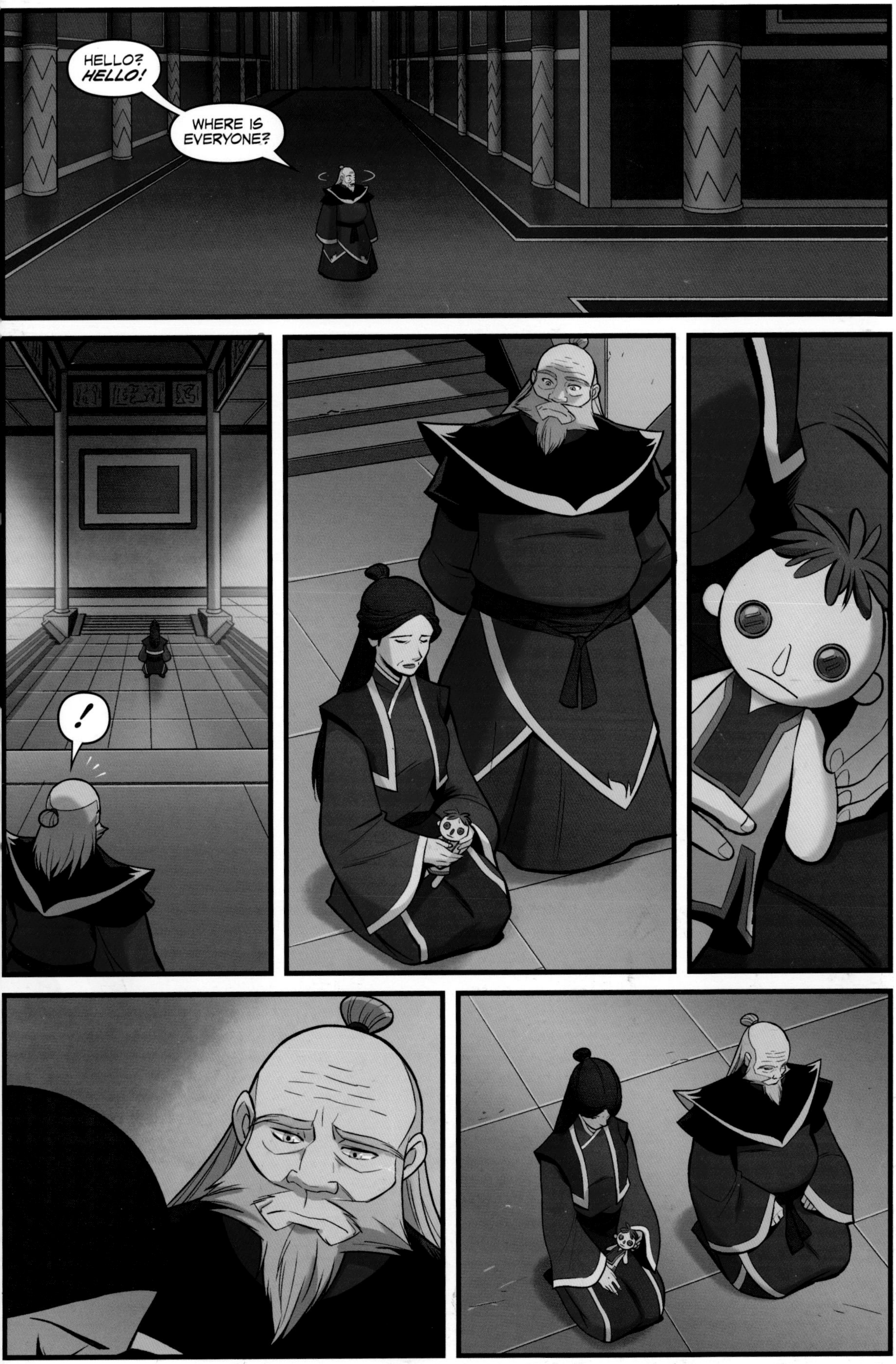
HELLO? HELLO!
WHERE IS EVERYONE?
!

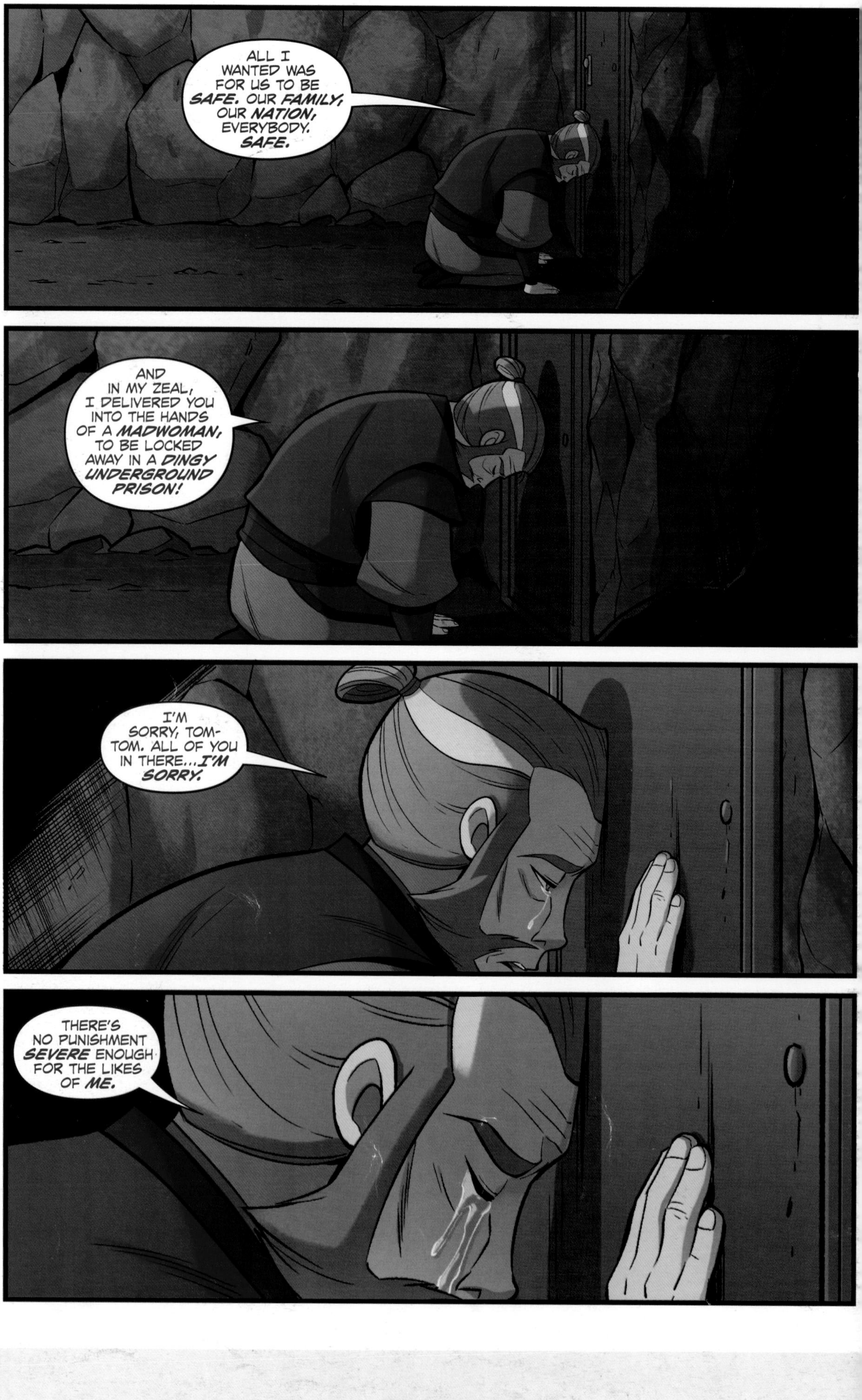
ALL I WANTED WAS FOR US TO BE SAFE. OUR FAMILY, OUR NATION, EVERYBODY. SAFE.
AND IN MY ZEAL, I DELIVERED YOU INTO THE HANDS OF A MADWOMAN, TO BE LOCKED AWAY IN A DINGY UNDERGROUND PRISON!
I'M SORRY, TOM-TOM. ALL OF YOU IN THERE... I'M SORRY.
THERE'S NO PUNISHMENT SEVERE ENOUGH FOR THE LIKES OF ME.

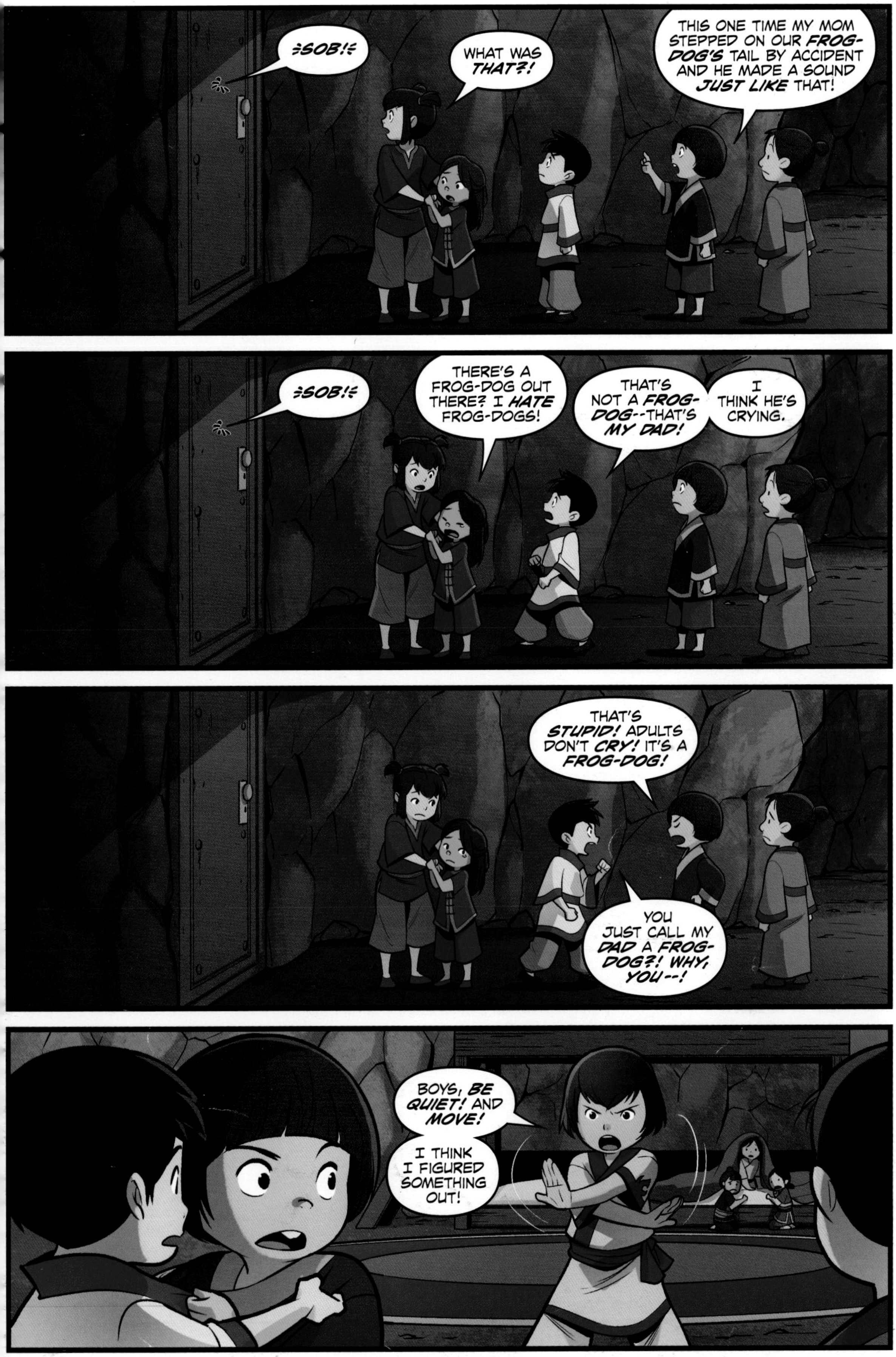
SOB!
WHAT WAS THAT?!
THIS ONE TIME MY MOM STEPPED ON OUR FROG-DOG'S TAIL BY ACCIDENT AND HE MADE A SOUND JUST LIKE THAT!
SOB!
THERE'S A FROG-DOG OUT THERE? I HATE FROG-DOGS!
THAT'S NOT A FROG-DOG--THAT'S MY DAD!
I THINK HE'S CRYING.
THAT'S STUPID! ADULTS DON'T CRY! IT'S A FROG-DOG!
YOU JUST CALL MY DAD A FROG-DOG?! WHY, YOU--!
BOYS, BE QUIET! AND MOVE!
I THINK I FIGURED SOMETHING OUT!

G: *We actually laughed at the children's reactions when we drew this. Sorry, Ukano! You are looking so sad.*

GLY: *We discussed whether or not Kiyi should be a Firebender. You can see our conclusion on this page.*

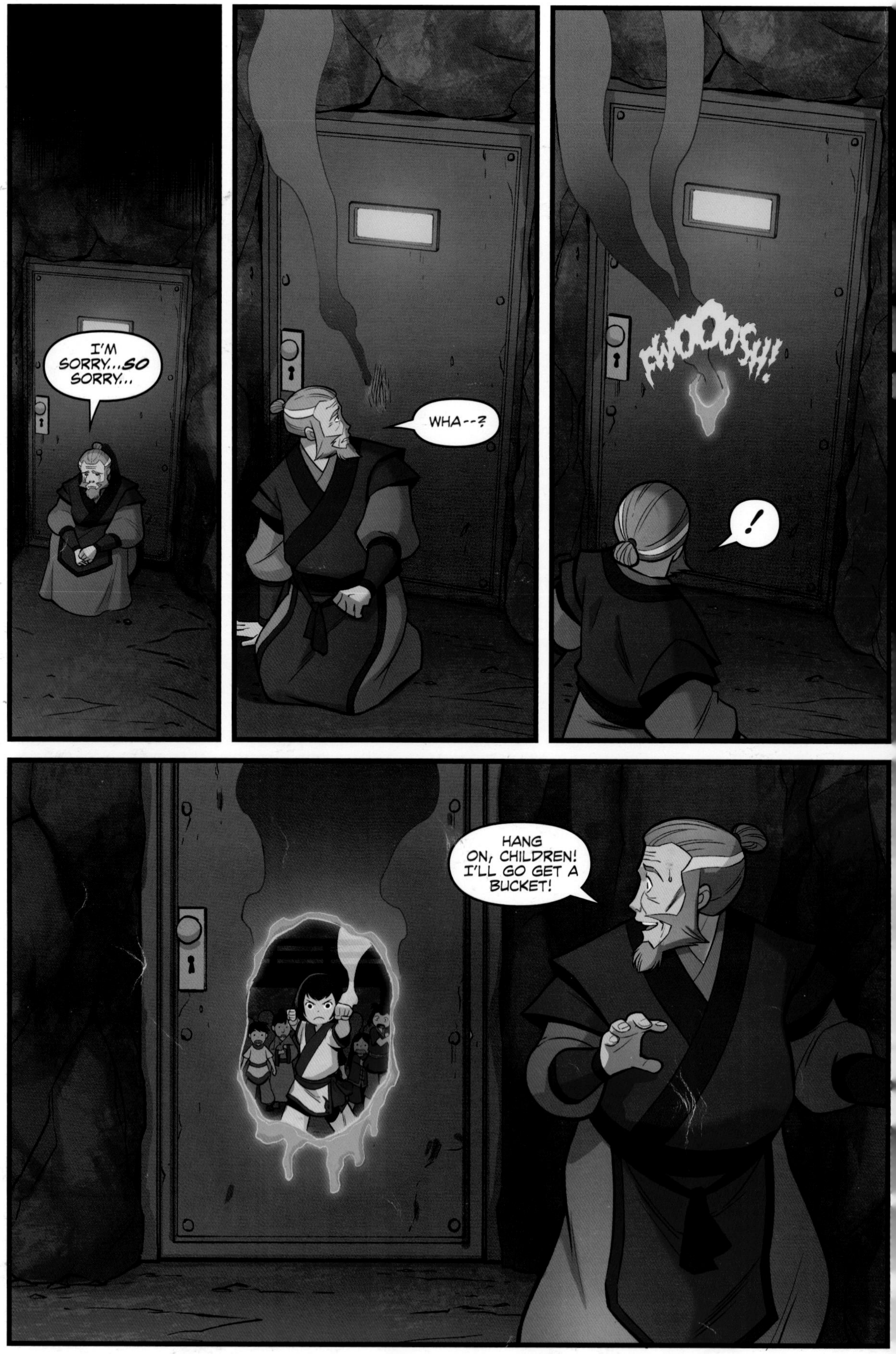
I'M SORRY...SO SORRY...
WHA--?
FWOOOSH!
!
HANG ON, CHILDREN! I'LL GO GET A BUCKET!

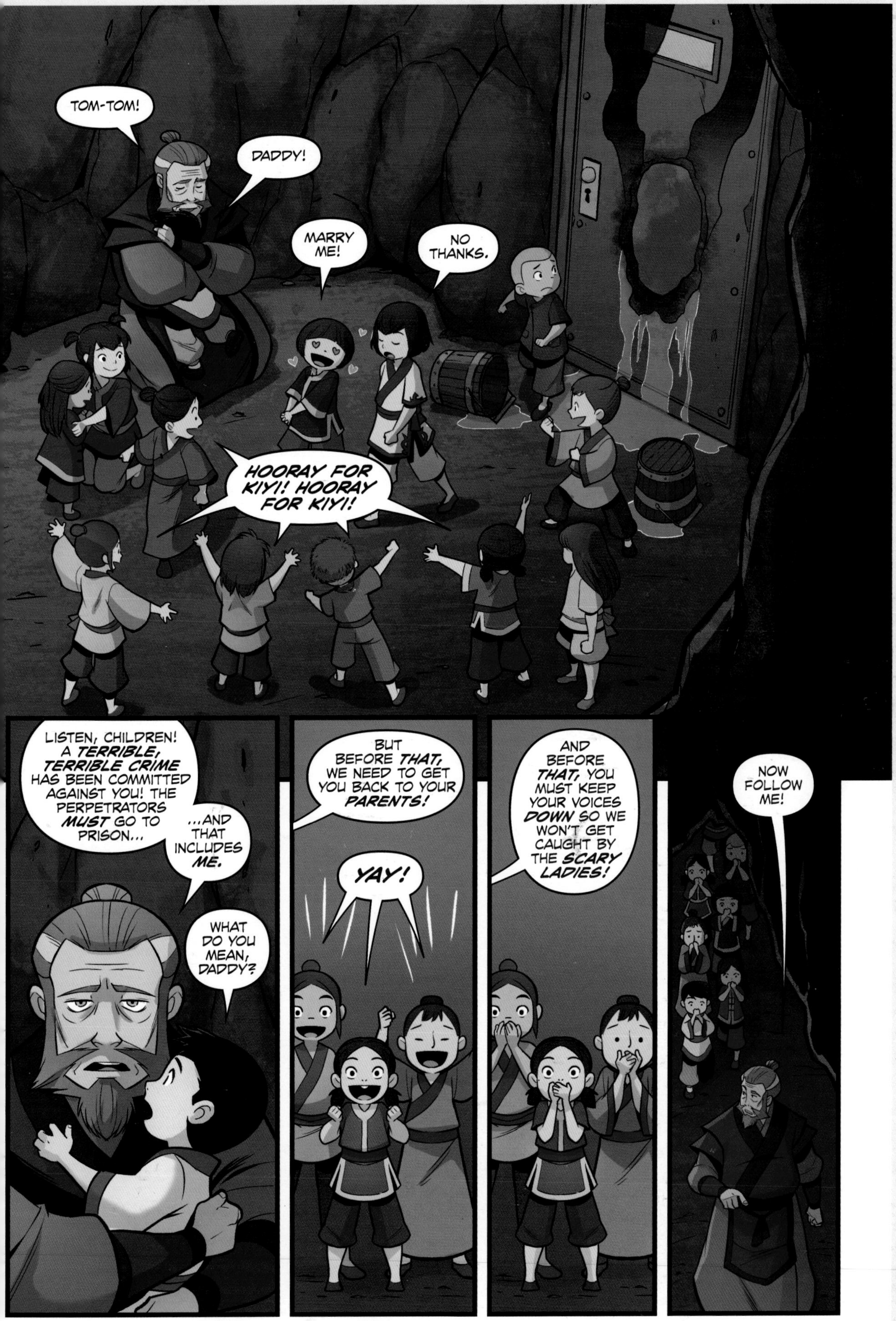
TOM-TOM!
DADDY!
MARRY ME!
NO THANKS.
HOORAY FOR KIYI! HOORAY FOR KIYI!
LISTEN, CHILDREN! A TERRIBLE, TERRIBLE CRIME HAS BEEN COMMITTED AGAINST YOU! THE PERPETRATORS MUST GO TO PRISON...
...AND THAT INCLUDES ME.
WHAT DO YOU MEAN, DADDY?
BUT BEFORE THAT, WE NEED TO GET YOU BACK TO YOUR PARENTS!
YAY!
AND BEFORE THAT, YOU MUST KEEP YOUR VOICES DOWN SO WE WON'T GET CAUGHT BY THE SCARY LADIES!
NOW FOLLOW ME!

GLY: *In panels 3 and 4 on this page, Gurihiru perfectly capture the goofy expressions children make.*

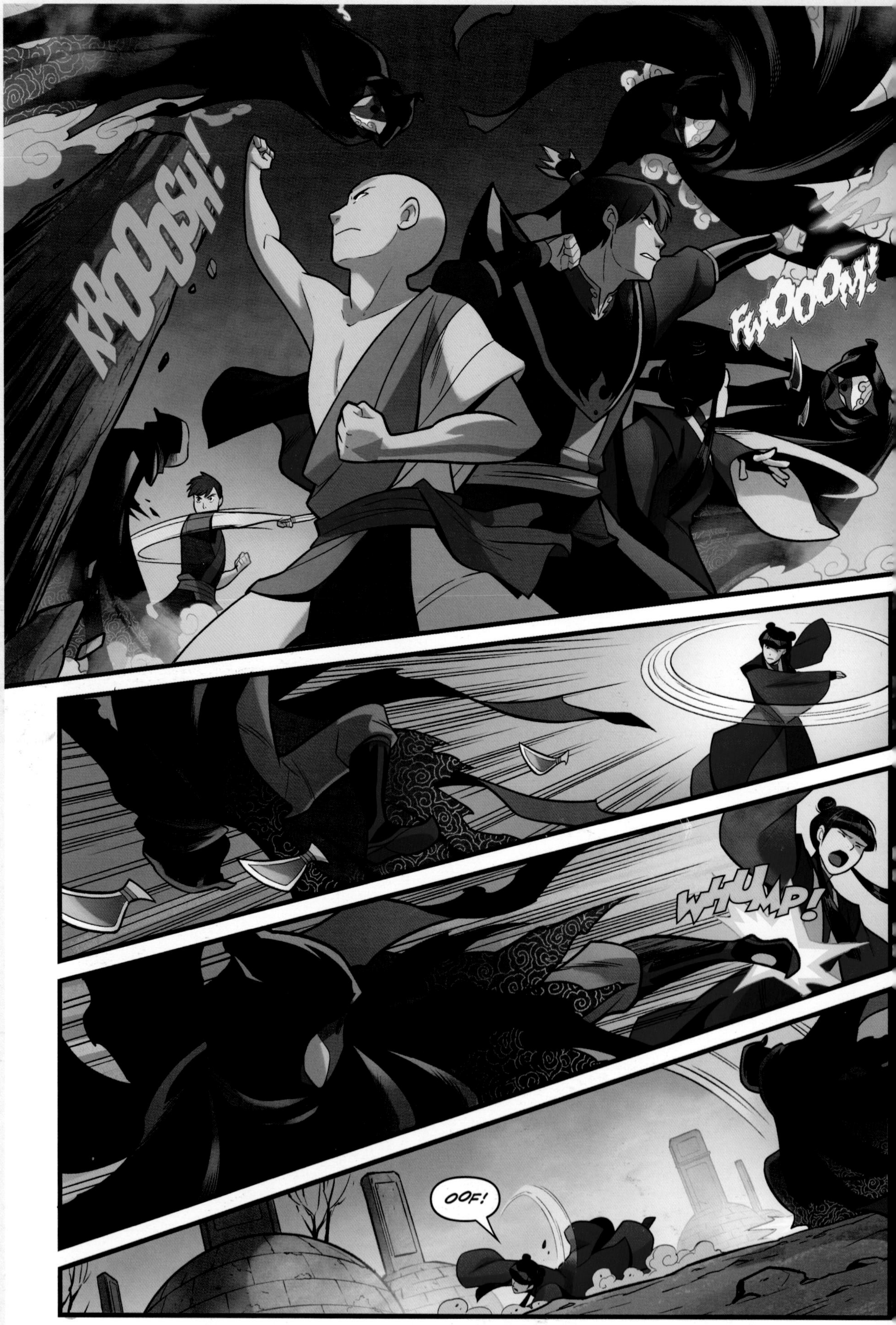
KROOOSH!
FWOOOM!
WHUMP!
OOF!

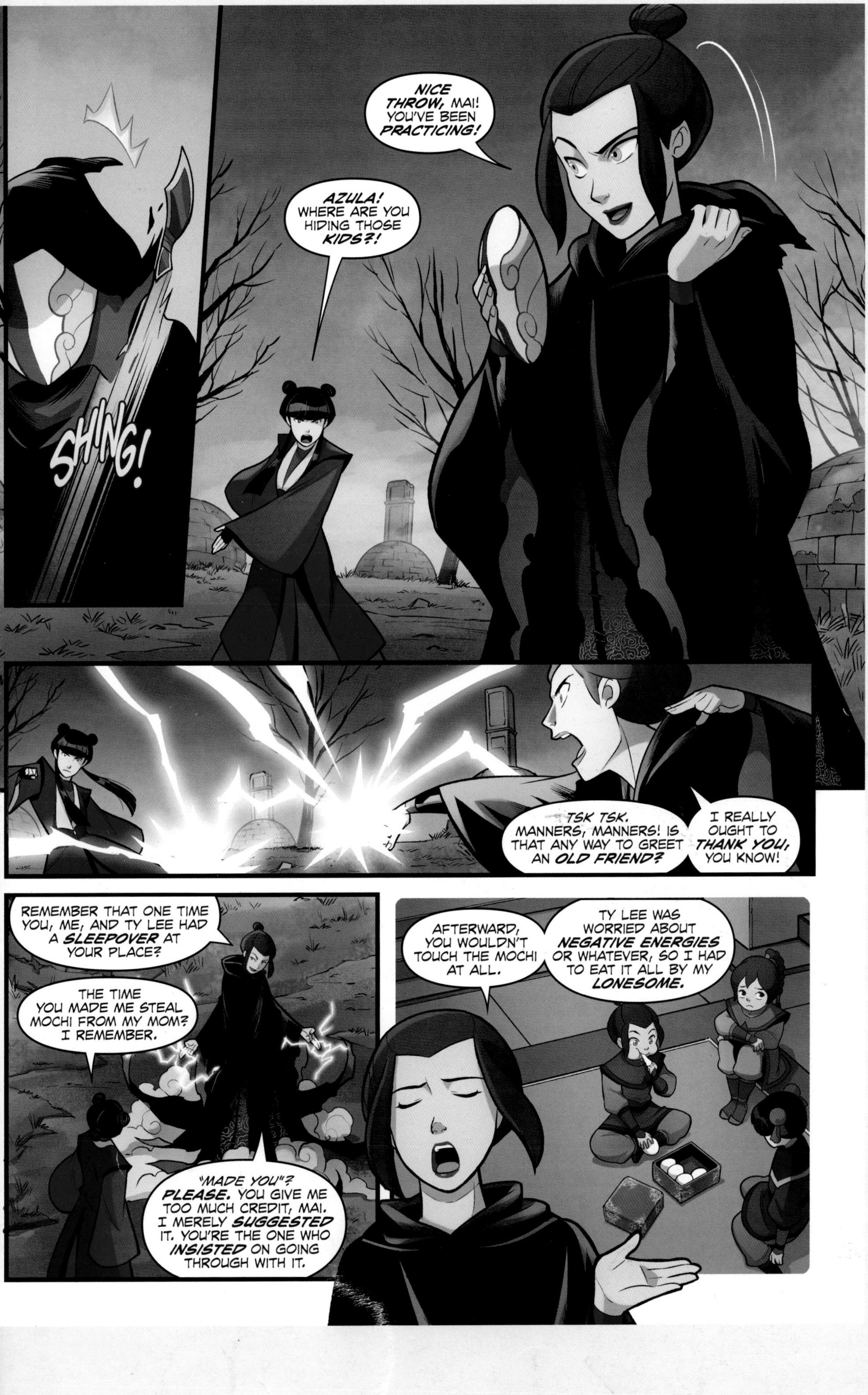
SHING!
AZULA! WHERE ARE YOU HIDING THOSE KIDS?!
NICE THROW, MAI! YOU'VE BEEN PRACTICING!
TSK TSK. MANNERS, MANNERS! IS THAT ANY WAY TO GREET AN OLD FRIEND?
I REALLY OUGHT TO THANK YOU, YOU KNOW!
REMEMBER THAT ONE TIME YOU, ME, AND TY LEE HAD A SLEEPOVER AT YOUR PLACE?
THE TIME YOU MADE ME STEAL MOCHI FROM MY MOM? I REMEMBER.
"MADE YOU"? PLEASE. YOU GIVE ME TOO MUCH CREDIT, MAI. I MERELY SUGGESTED IT. YOU'RE THE ONE WHO INSISTED ON GOING THROUGH WITH IT.
AFTERWARD, YOU WOULDN'T TOUCH THE MOCHI AT ALL.
TY LEE WAS WORRIED ABOUT NEGATIVE ENERGIES OR WHATEVER, SO I HAD TO EAT IT ALL BY MY LONESOME.

GLY: *The flashback here is inspired by a story my parents used to tell me when I was a kid. Whenever I misbehaved, they would threaten to call an old witch who lived in the hills. Sometimes, for extra drama, they would even pick up the phone and begin to dial. Supposedly, the witch would come down and drag disobedient children back up to her hovel by their earlobes. My parents told me you could tell which children were bad by how long their earlobes were.*

Don't worry. I'm all better now.

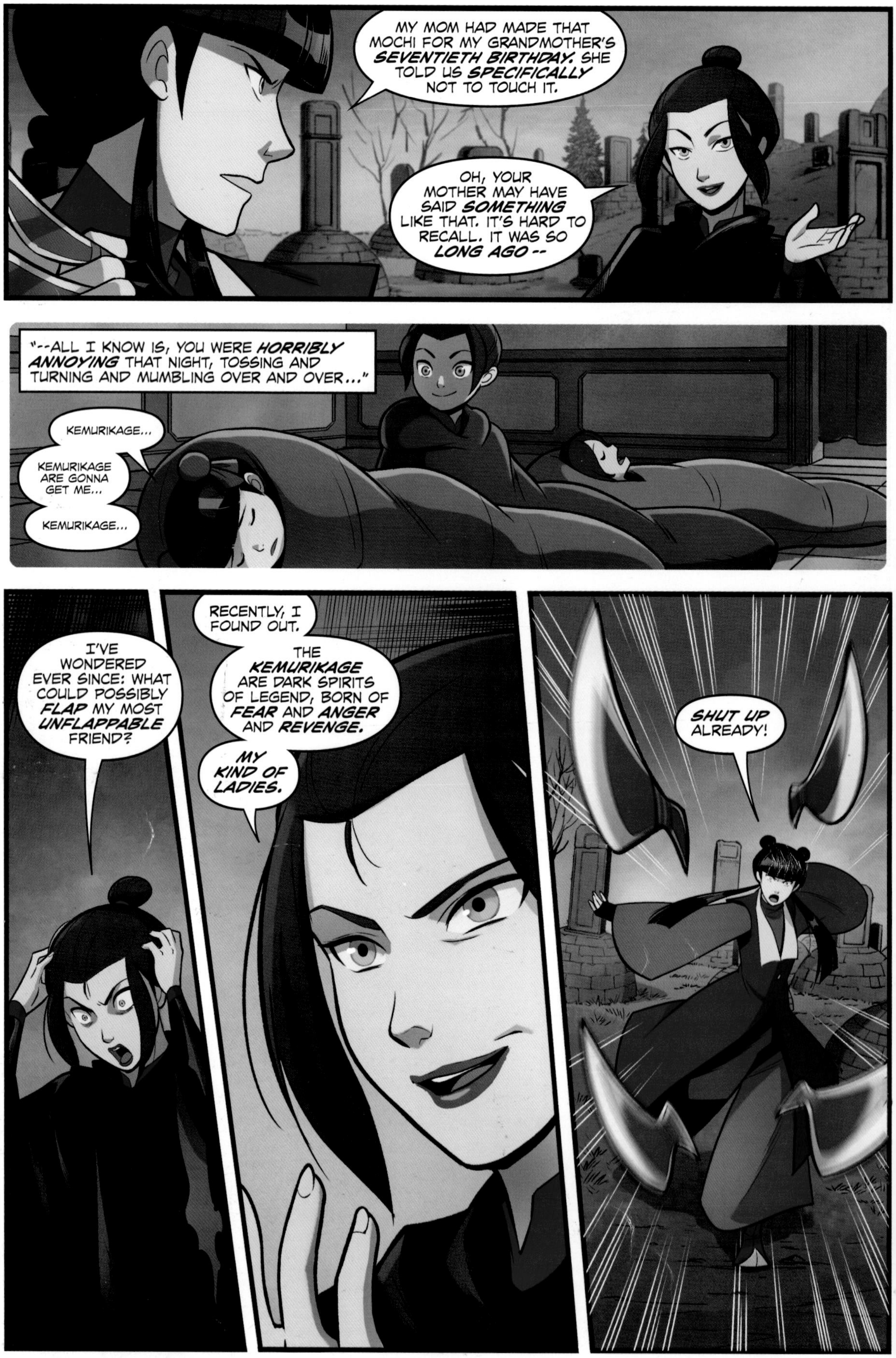
MY MOM HAD MADE THAT MOCHI FOR MY GRANDMOTHER'S SEVENTIETH BIRTHDAY. SHE TOLD US SPECIFICALLY NOT TO TOUCH IT.
OH, YOUR MOTHER MAY HAVE SAID SOMETHING LIKE THAT. IT'S HARD TO RECALL. IT WAS SO LONG AGO --
"--ALL I KNOW IS, YOU WERE HORRIBLY ANNOYING THAT NIGHT, TOSSING AND TURNING AND MUMBLING OVER AND OVER..."
KEMURIKAGE...
KEMURIKAGE ARE GONNA GET ME...
KEMURIKAGE...
I'VE WONDERED EVER SINCE: WHAT COULD POSSIBLY FLAP MY MOST UNFLAPPABLE FRIEND?
RECENTLY, I FOUND OUT.
THE KEMURIKAGE ARE DARK SPIRITS OF LEGEND, BORN OF FEAR AND ANGER AND REVENGE.
MY KIND OF LADIES.
SHUT UP ALREADY!

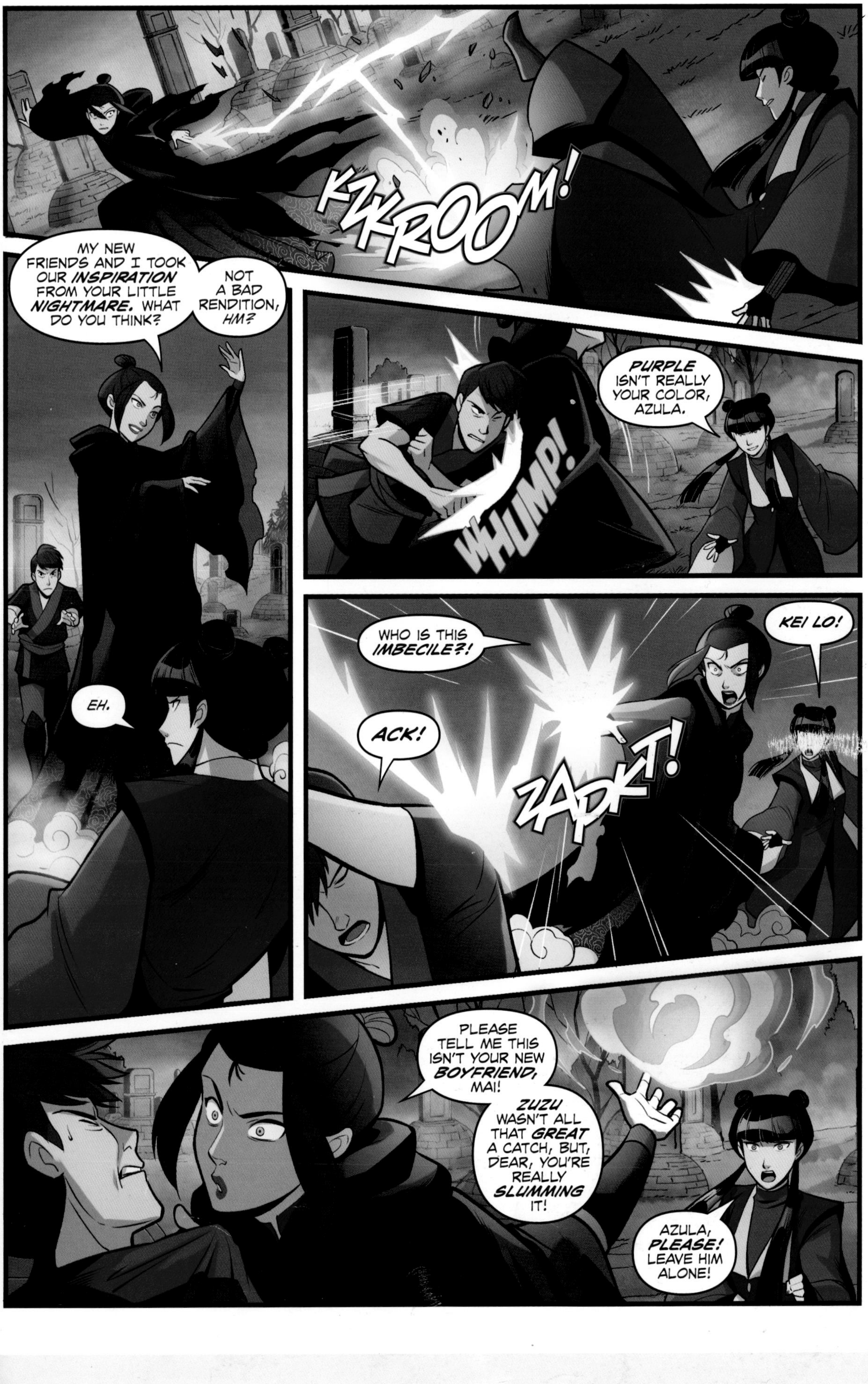
KZZKROOOM!
MY NEW FRIENDS AND I TOOK OUR INSPIRATION FROM YOUR LITTLE NIGHTMARE. WHAT DO YOU THINK?
NOT A BAD RENDITION, HM?
EH.
PURPLE ISN'T REALLY YOUR COLOR, AZULA.
WHUMP!
WHO IS THIS IMBECILE?!
KEI LO!
ACK!
ZAPKT!
PLEASE TELL ME THIS ISN'T YOUR NEW BOYFRIEND, MAI!
ZUZU WASN'T ALL THAT GREAT A CATCH, BUT, DEAR, YOU'RE REALLY SLUMMING IT!
AZULA, PLEASE! LEAVE HIM ALONE!

GLY: *I disagree with Mai. I think Azula looks great in purple.*

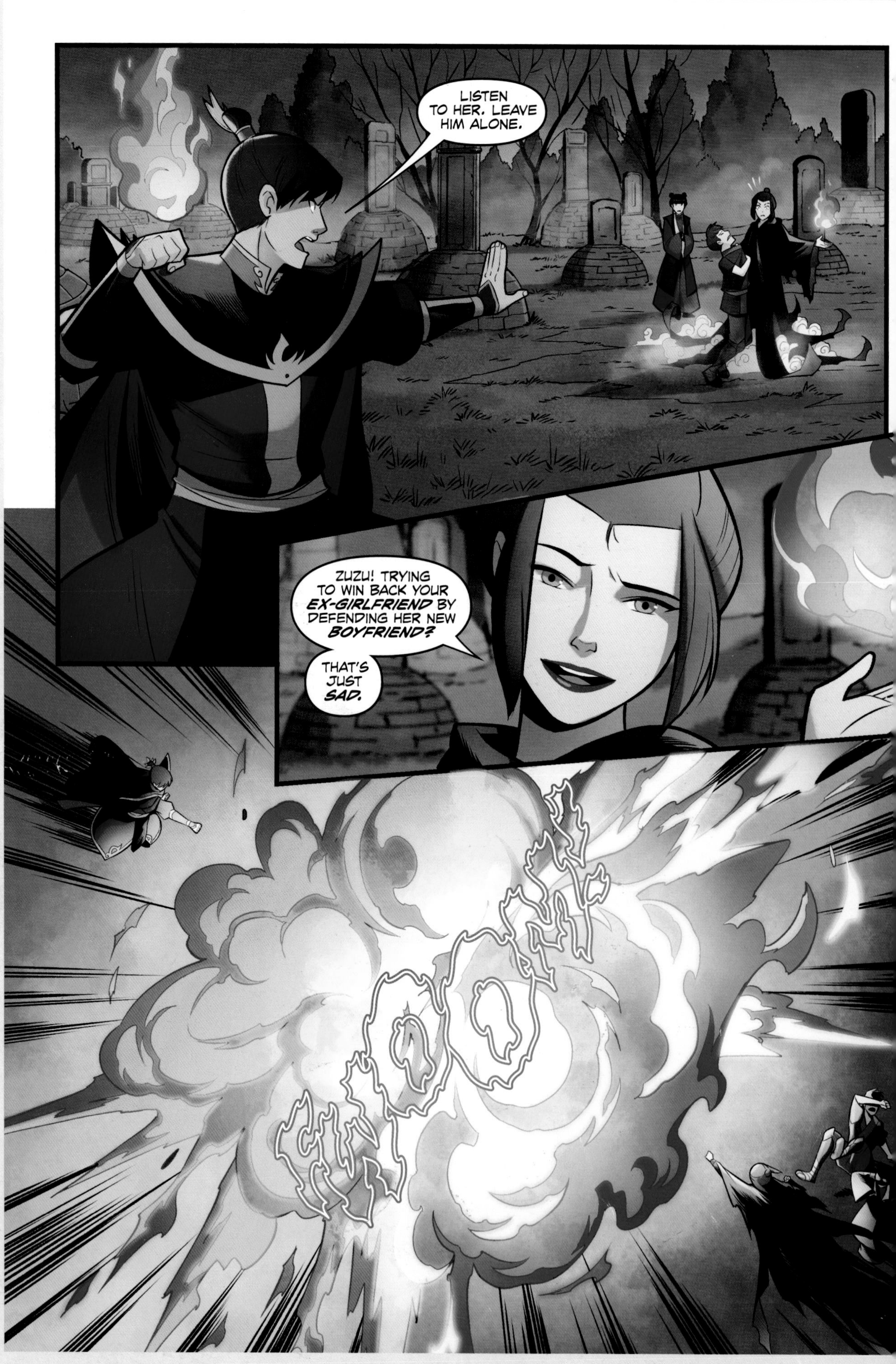
LISTEN TO HER. LEAVE HIM ALONE.
ZUZU! TRYING TO WIN BACK YOUR EX-GIRLFRIEND BY DEFENDING HER NEW BOYFRIEND?
THAT'S JUST SAD.

GLY: *This is a nod to Zuko and Azula's final confrontation in the series finale, one of the most beautifully rendered martial arts fights ever, in my opinion.*

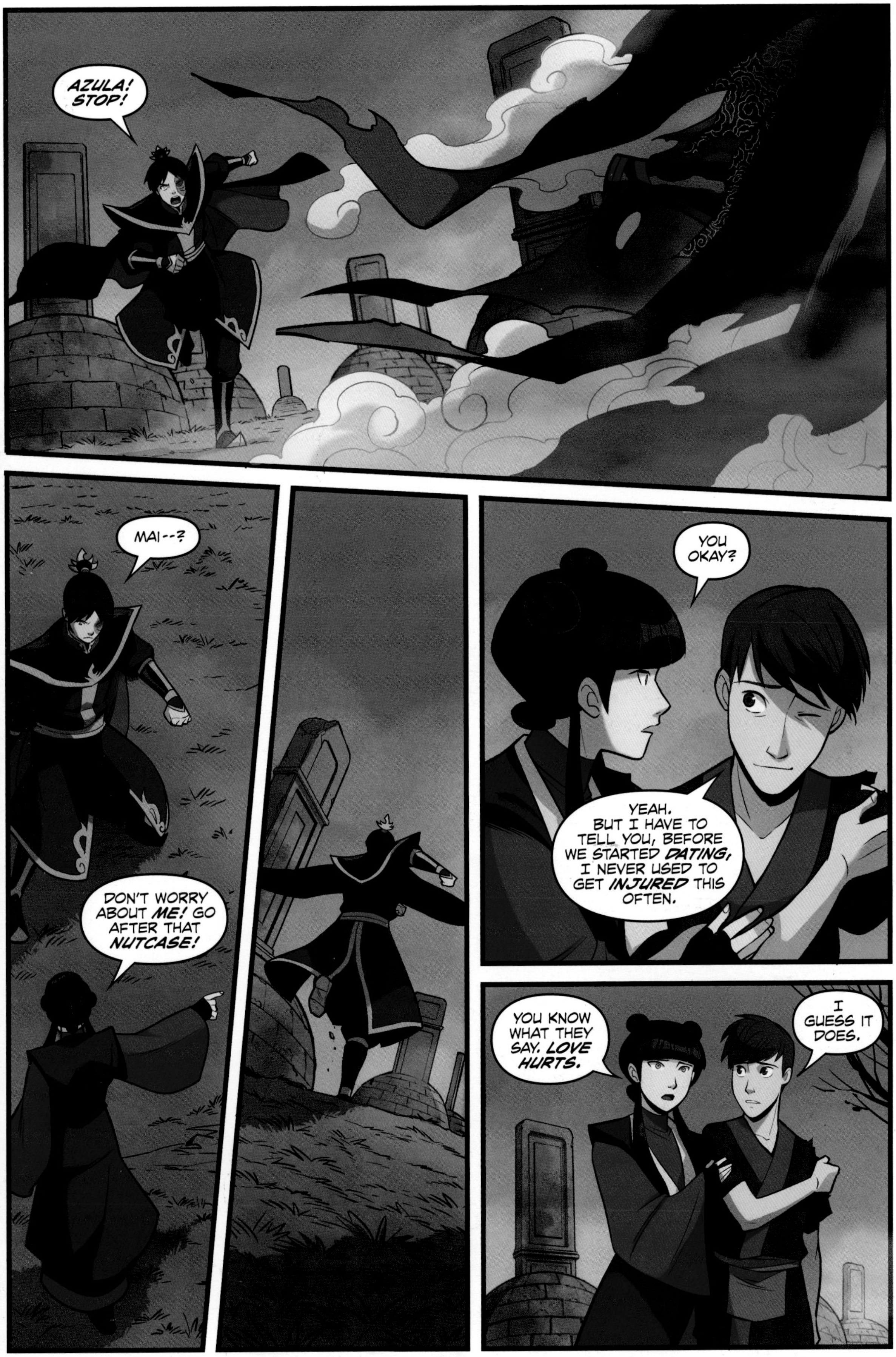
AZULA! STOP!
MAI--?
DON'T WORRY ABOUT *ME!* GO AFTER THAT *NUTCASE!*
YOU OKAY?
YEAH. BUT I HAVE TO TELL YOU, BEFORE WE STARTED *DATING,* I NEVER USED TO GET *INJURED* THIS OFTEN.
YOU KNOW WHAT THEY SAY. *LOVE HURTS.*
I GUESS IT DOES.

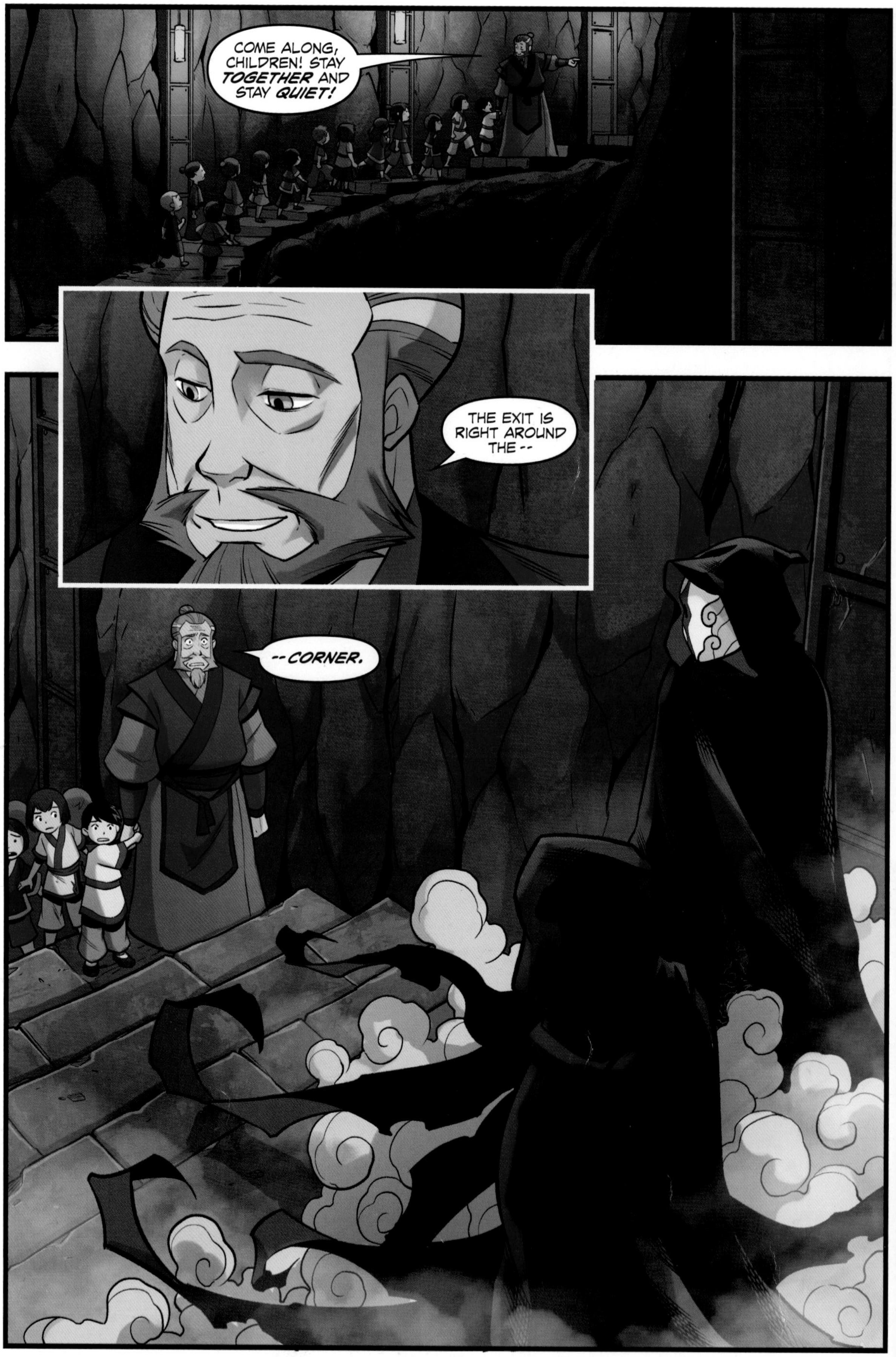
COME ALONG, CHILDREN! STAY TOGETHER AND STAY QUIET!
THE EXIT IS RIGHT AROUND THE --
--CORNER.

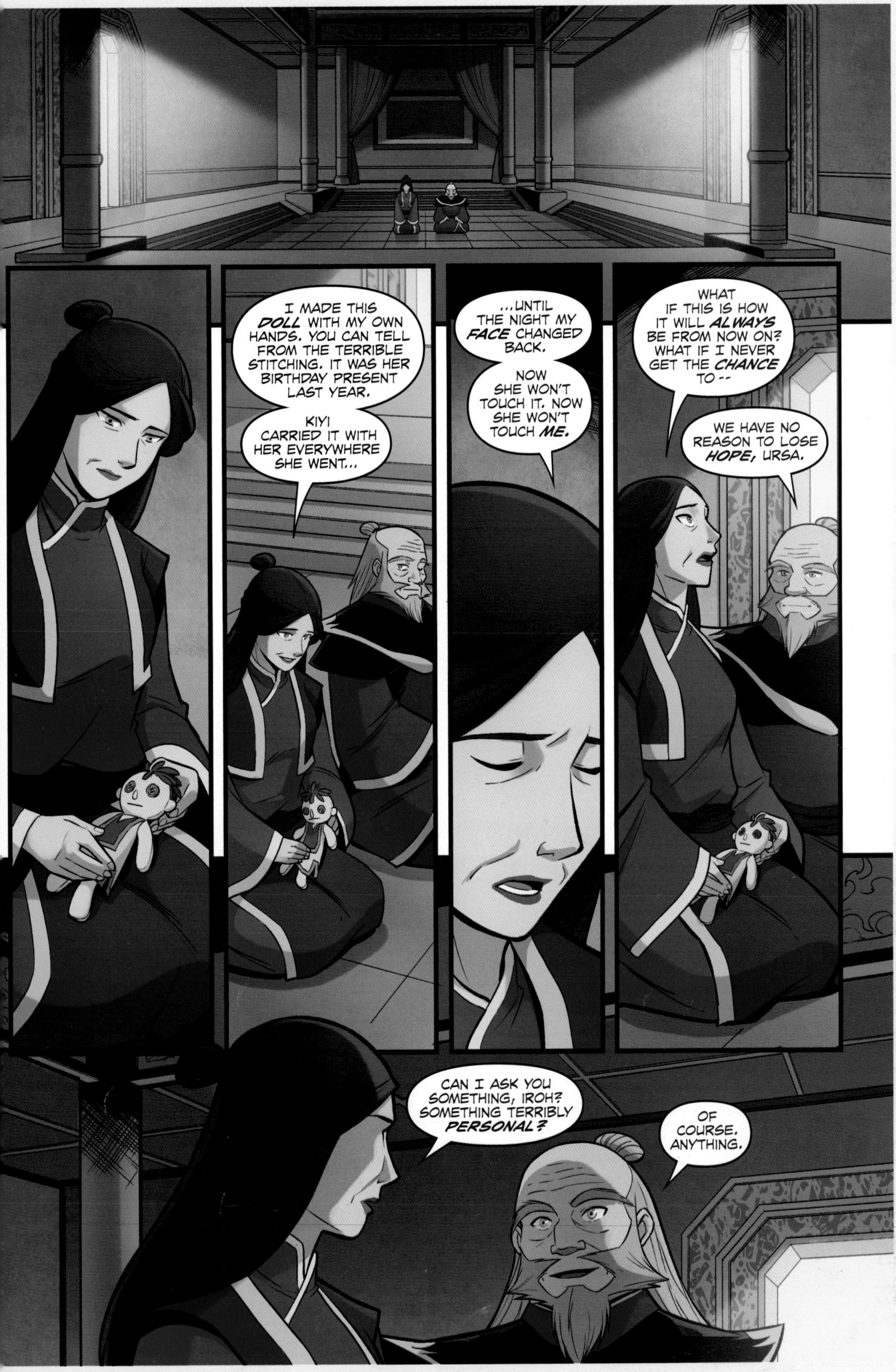
I MADE THIS DOLL WITH MY OWN HANDS. YOU CAN TELL FROM THE TERRIBLE STITCHING. IT WAS HER BIRTHDAY PRESENT LAST YEAR.
KIYI CARRIED IT WITH HER EVERYWHERE SHE WENT...
...UNTIL THE NIGHT MY FACE CHANGED BACK.
NOW SHE WON'T TOUCH IT. NOW SHE WON'T TOUCH ME.
WHAT IF THIS IS HOW IT WILL ALWAYS BE FROM NOW ON? WHAT IF I NEVER GET THE CHANCE TO --
WE HAVE NO REASON TO LOSE HOPE, URSA.
CAN I ASK YOU SOMETHING, IROH? SOMETHING TERRIBLY PERSONAL?
OF COURSE. ANYTHING.

GLY: *Iroh's words here echo a parental pep talk a friend gave me.*

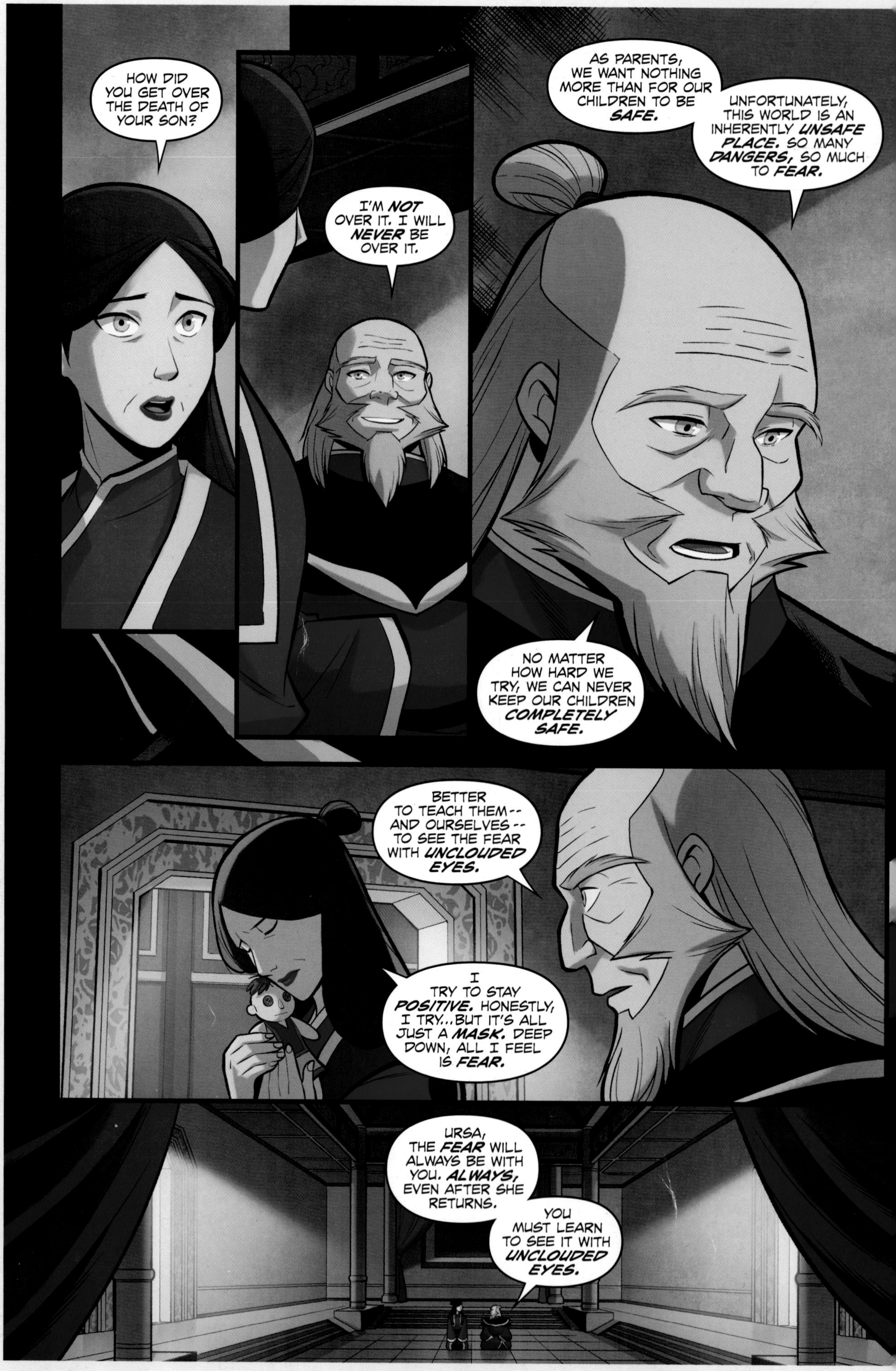
HOW DID YOU GET OVER THE DEATH OF YOUR SON?
I'M NOT OVER IT. I WILL NEVER BE OVER IT.
AS PARENTS, WE WANT NOTHING MORE THAN FOR OUR CHILDREN TO BE SAFE.
UNFORTUNATELY, THIS WORLD IS AN INHERENTLY UNSAFE PLACE. SO MANY DANGERS, SO MUCH TO FEAR.
NO MATTER HOW HARD WE TRY, WE CAN NEVER KEEP OUR CHILDREN COMPLETELY SAFE.
BETTER TO TEACH THEM-- AND OURSELVES-- TO SEE THE FEAR WITH UNCLOUDED EYES.
I TRY TO STAY POSITIVE. HONESTLY, I TRY...BUT IT'S ALL JUST A MASK. DEEP DOWN, ALL I FEEL IS FEAR.
URSA, THE FEAR WILL ALWAYS BE WITH YOU. ALWAYS, EVEN AFTER SHE RETURNS.
YOU MUST LEARN TO SEE IT WITH UNCLOUDED EYES.

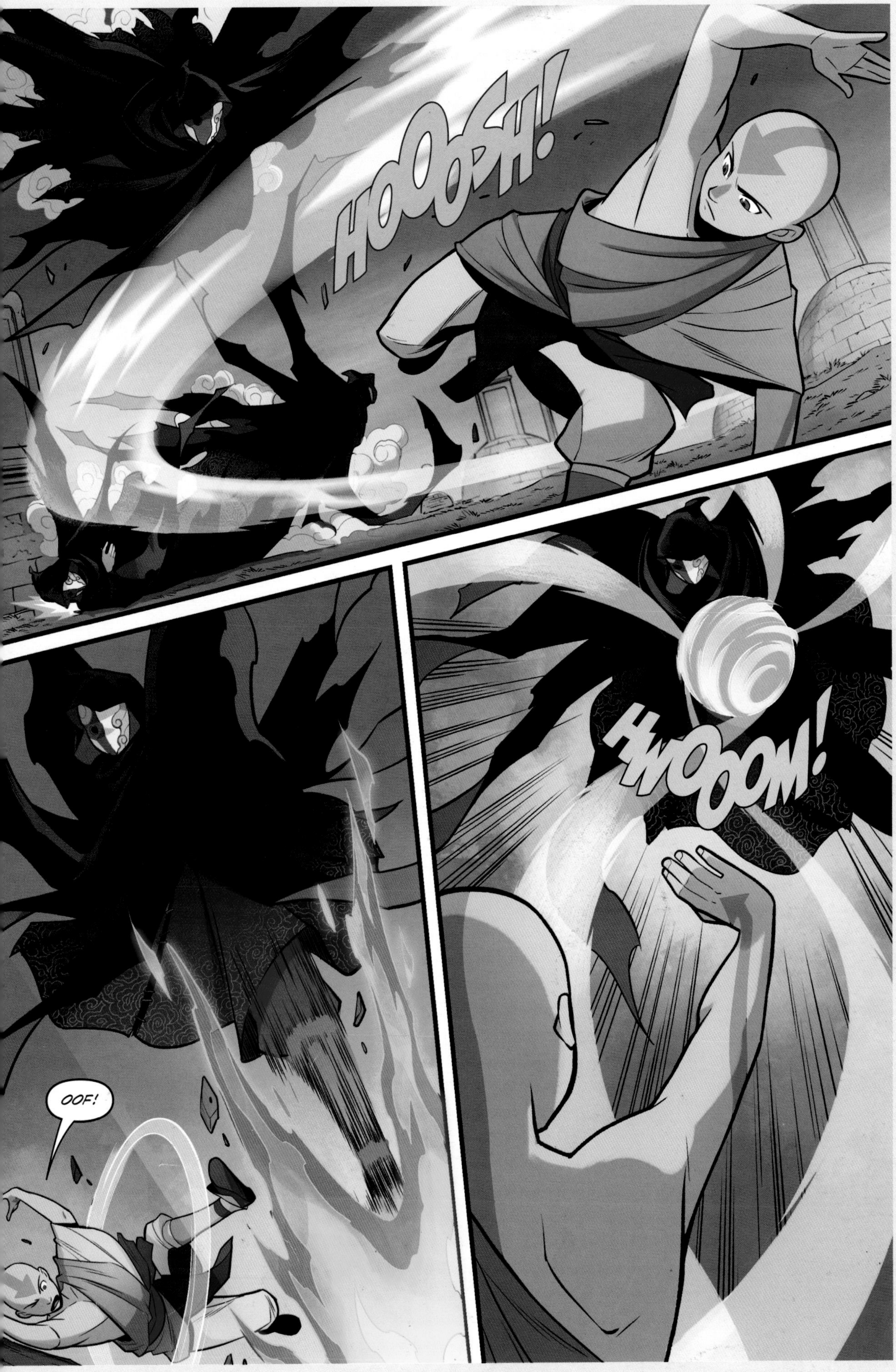
HOOOOSH!
HWOOOM!
OOF!

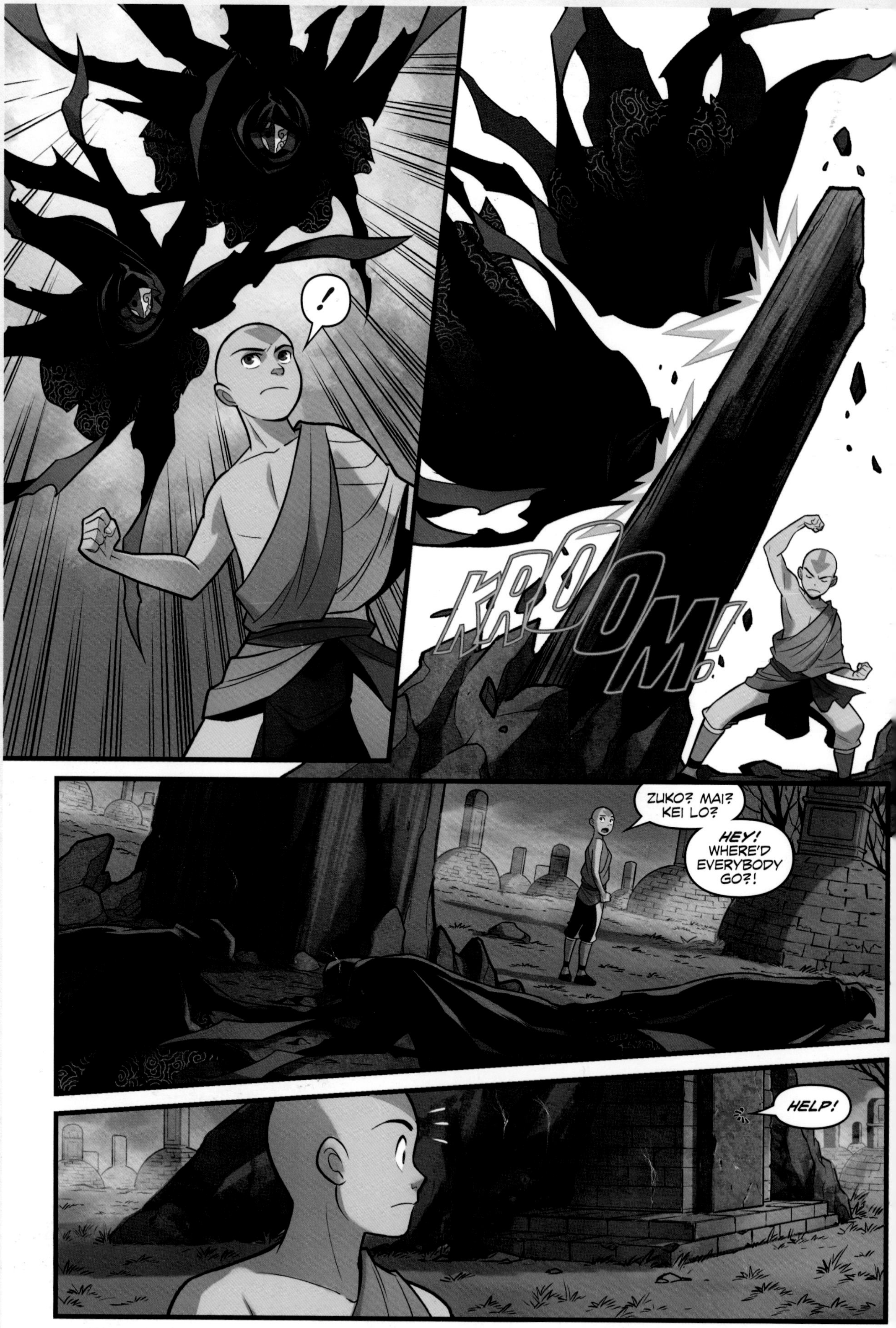
!
KROOOM!
ZUKO? MAI? KEI LO?
HEY! WHERE'D EVERYBODY GO?!
HELP!

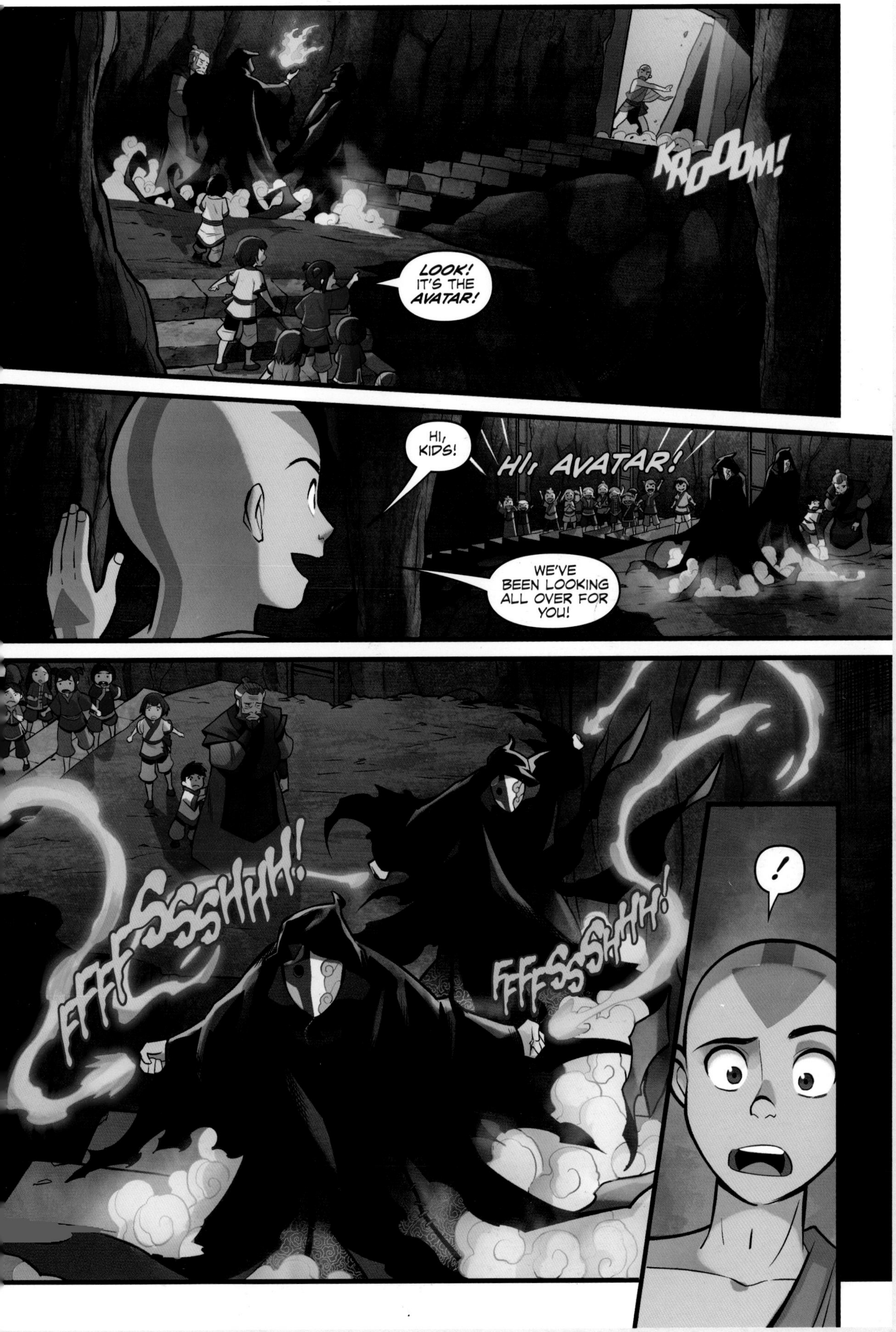
KROOOM!
LOOK! IT'S THE AVATAR!
HI, KIDS!
HI, AVATAR!
WE'VE BEEN LOOKING ALL OVER FOR YOU!
FFFFSSSHHH!
FFFFSSSHHH!
!

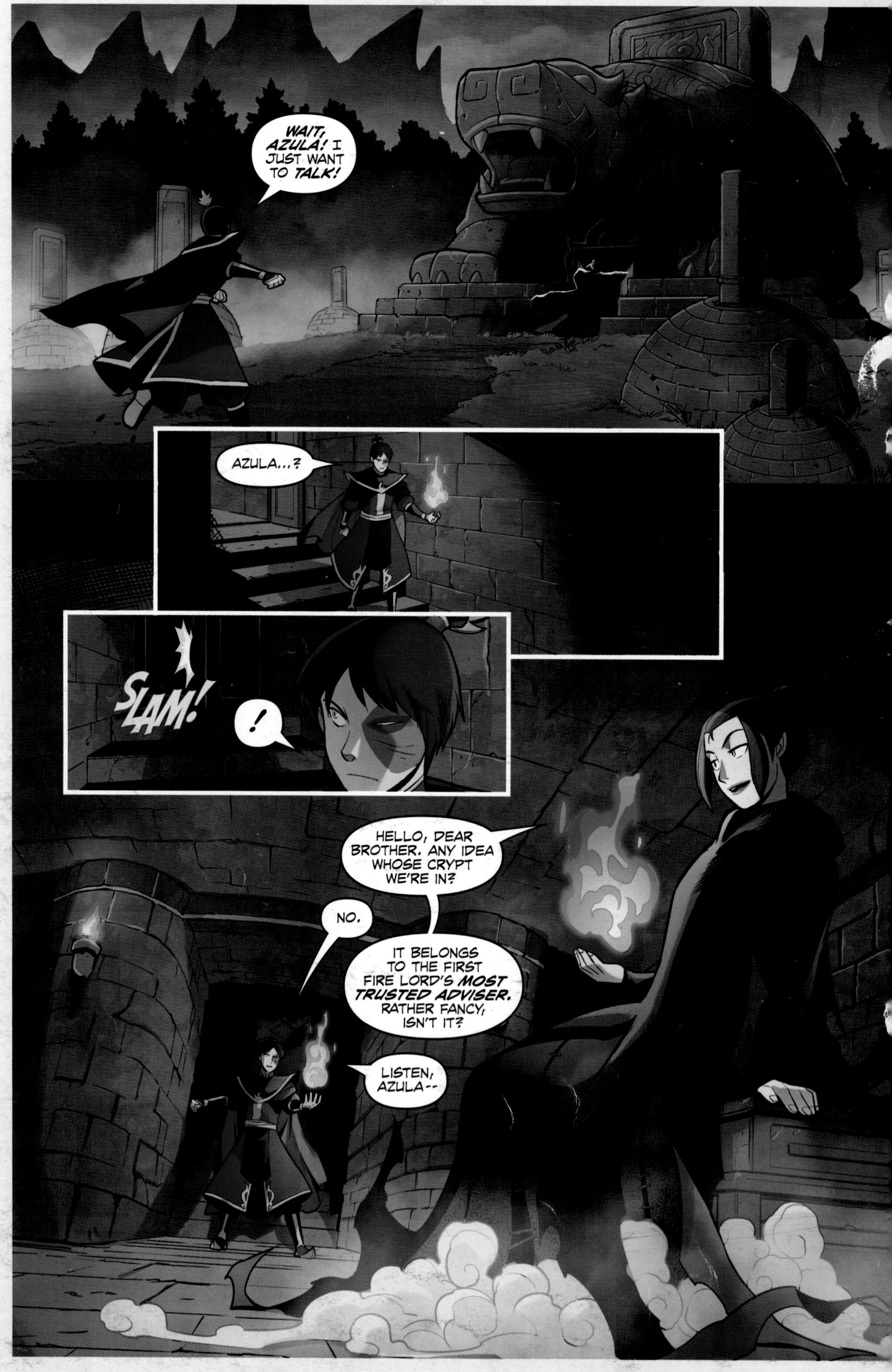
WAIT, AZULA! I JUST WANT TO TALK!
AZULA...?
SLAM!
!
HELLO, DEAR BROTHER. ANY IDEA WHOSE CRYPT WE'RE IN?
NO.
IT BELONGS TO THE FIRST FIRE LORD'S MOST TRUSTED ADVISER. RATHER FANCY, ISN'T IT?
LISTEN, AZULA--

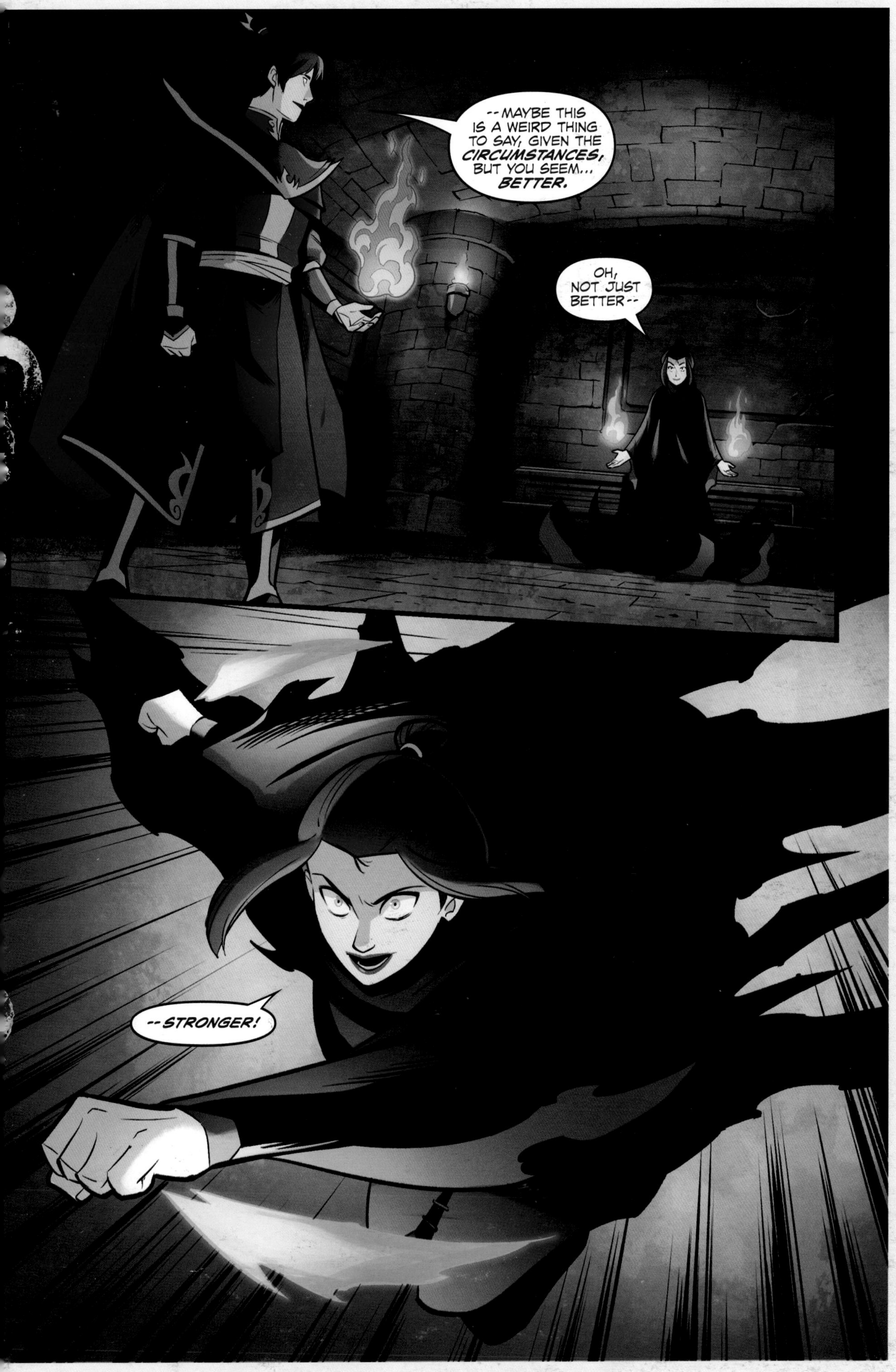
--MAYBE THIS IS A WEIRD THING TO SAY, GIVEN THE *CIRCUMSTANCES*, BUT YOU SEEM... *BETTER*.
OH, NOT JUST BETTER--
--*STRONGER!*

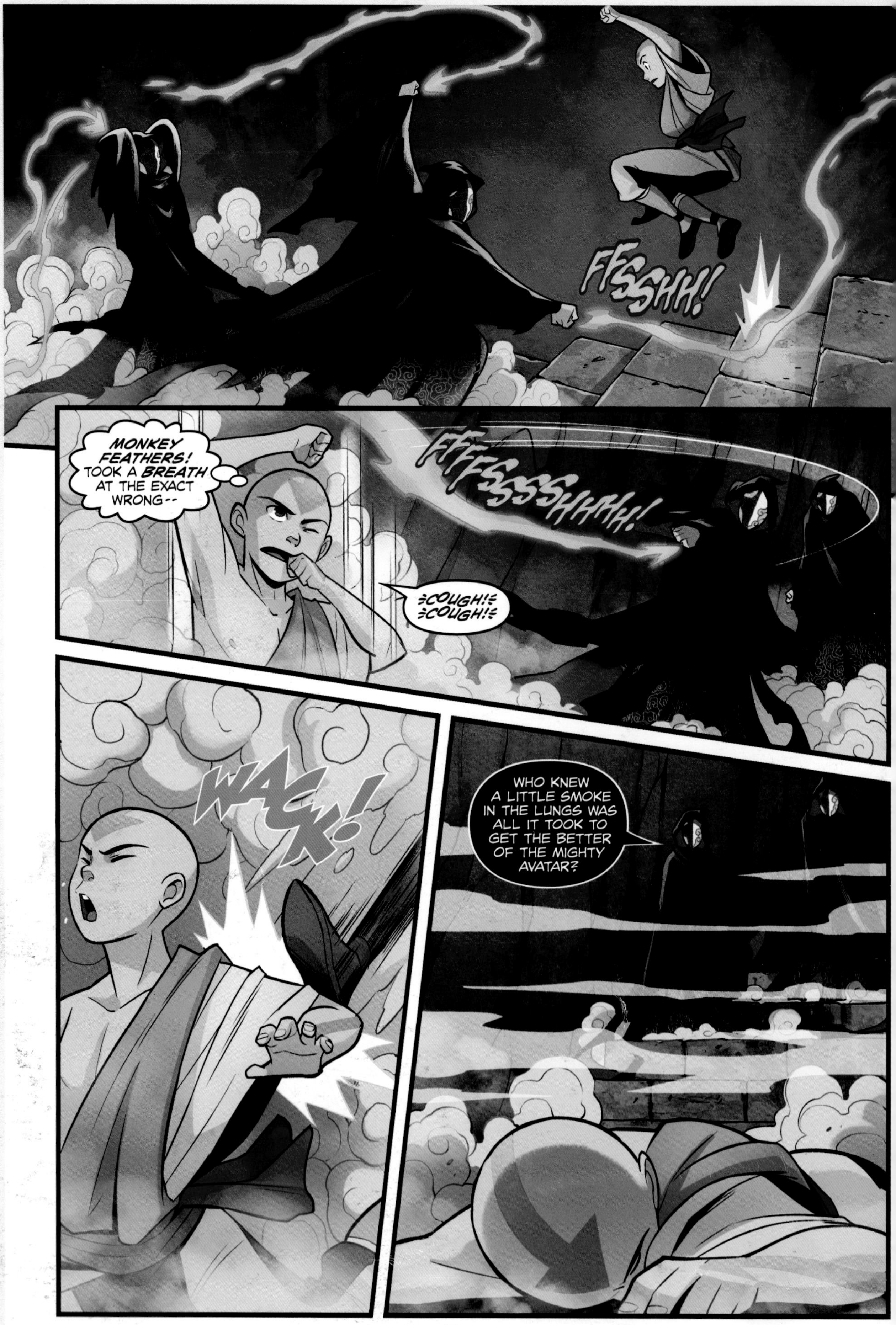
FFSSHH!
MONKEY FEATHERS! TOOK A BREATH AT THE EXACT WRONG--
FFFFSSSSHHHH!
COUGH! COUGH!
WACK!
WHO KNEW A LITTLE SMOKE IN THE LUNGS WAS ALL IT TOOK TO GET THE BETTER OF THE MIGHTY AVATAR?

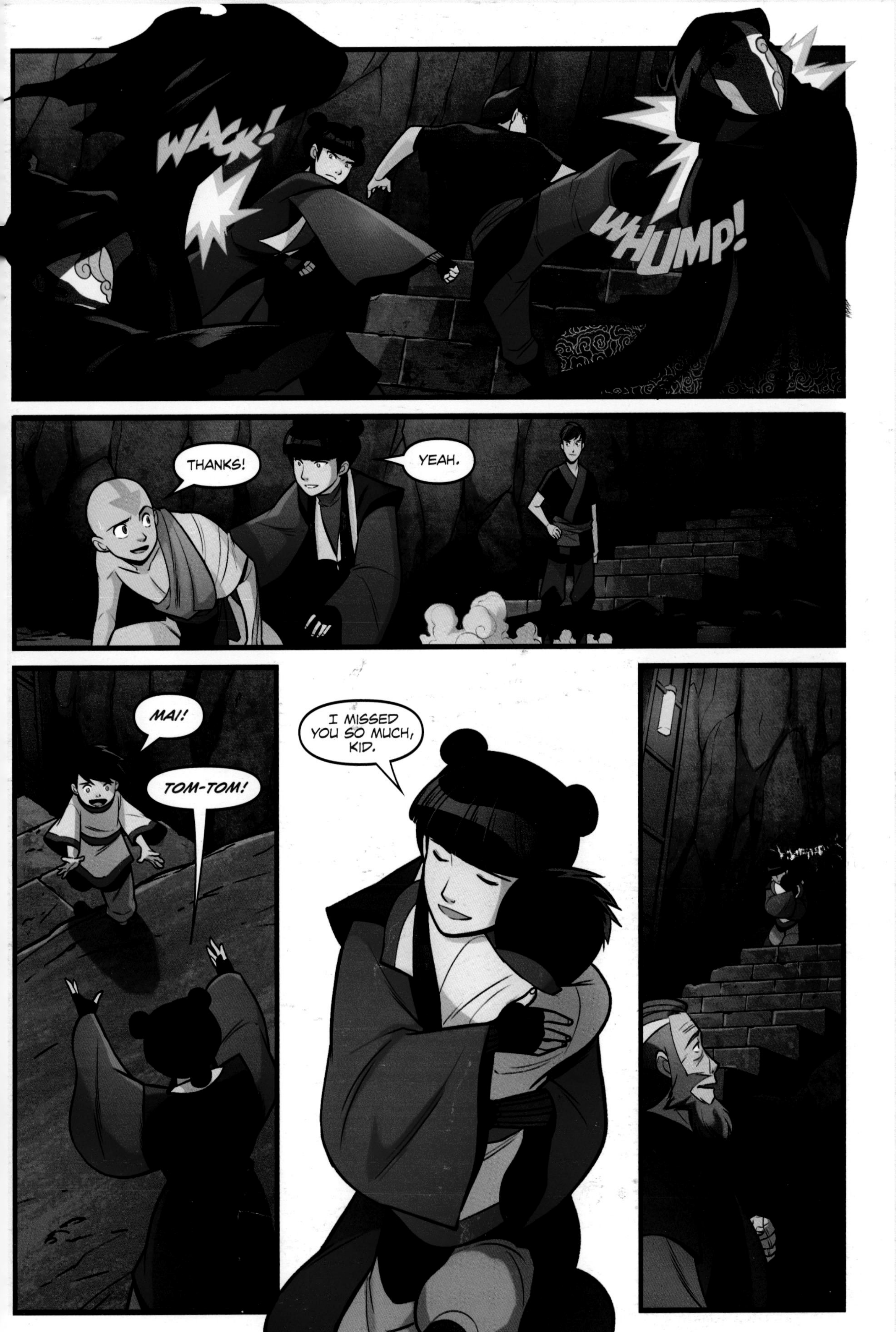
WACK!
WHUMP!
THANKS!
YEAH.
MAI!
TOM-TOM!
I MISSED YOU SO MUCH, KID.

GLY: *We wanted Zuko and Azula's fight to feel grittier than any of their previous fights. Hence, fire daggers.*

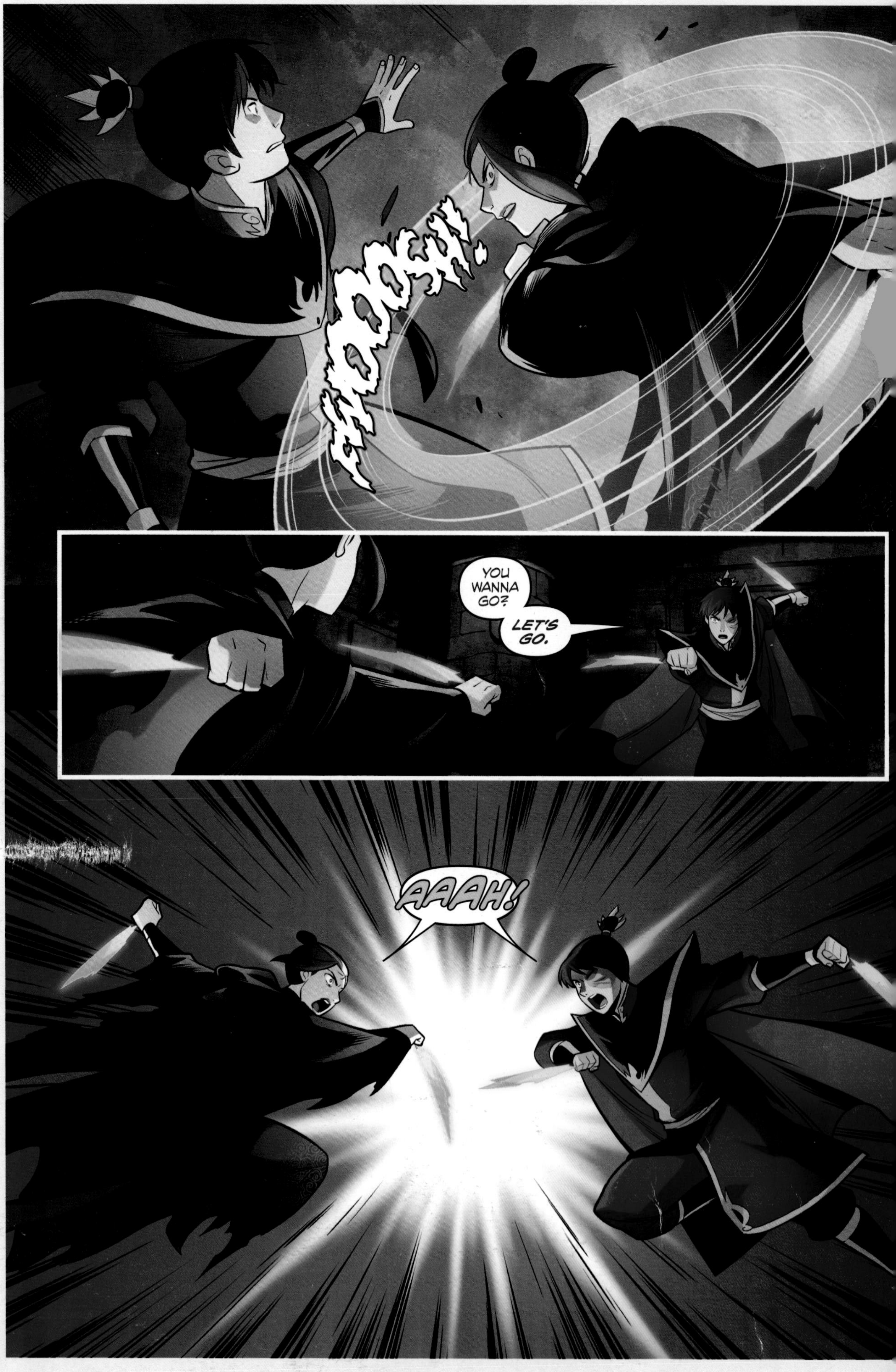
FWOOSH!!
YOU WANNA GO?
LET'S GO.
AAAH!

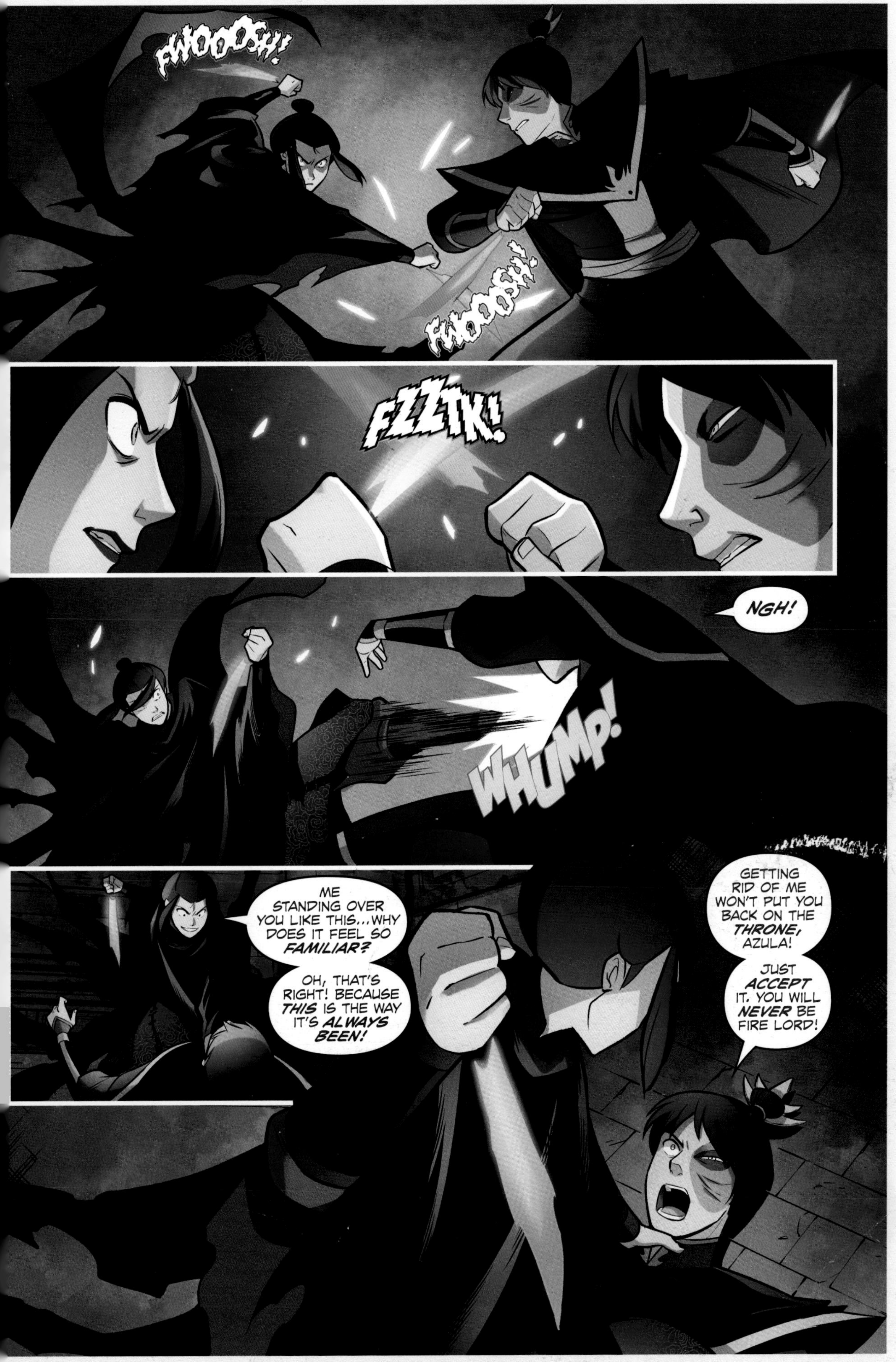
FWOOOSH!
FWOOOSH!
FZZZTK!
NGH!
WHUMP!
ME STANDING OVER YOU LIKE THIS... WHY DOES IT FEEL SO FAMILIAR?
OH, THAT'S RIGHT! BECAUSE THIS IS THE WAY IT'S ALWAYS BEEN!
GETTING RID OF ME WON'T PUT YOU BACK ON THE THRONE, AZULA!
JUST ACCEPT IT. YOU WILL NEVER BE FIRE LORD!

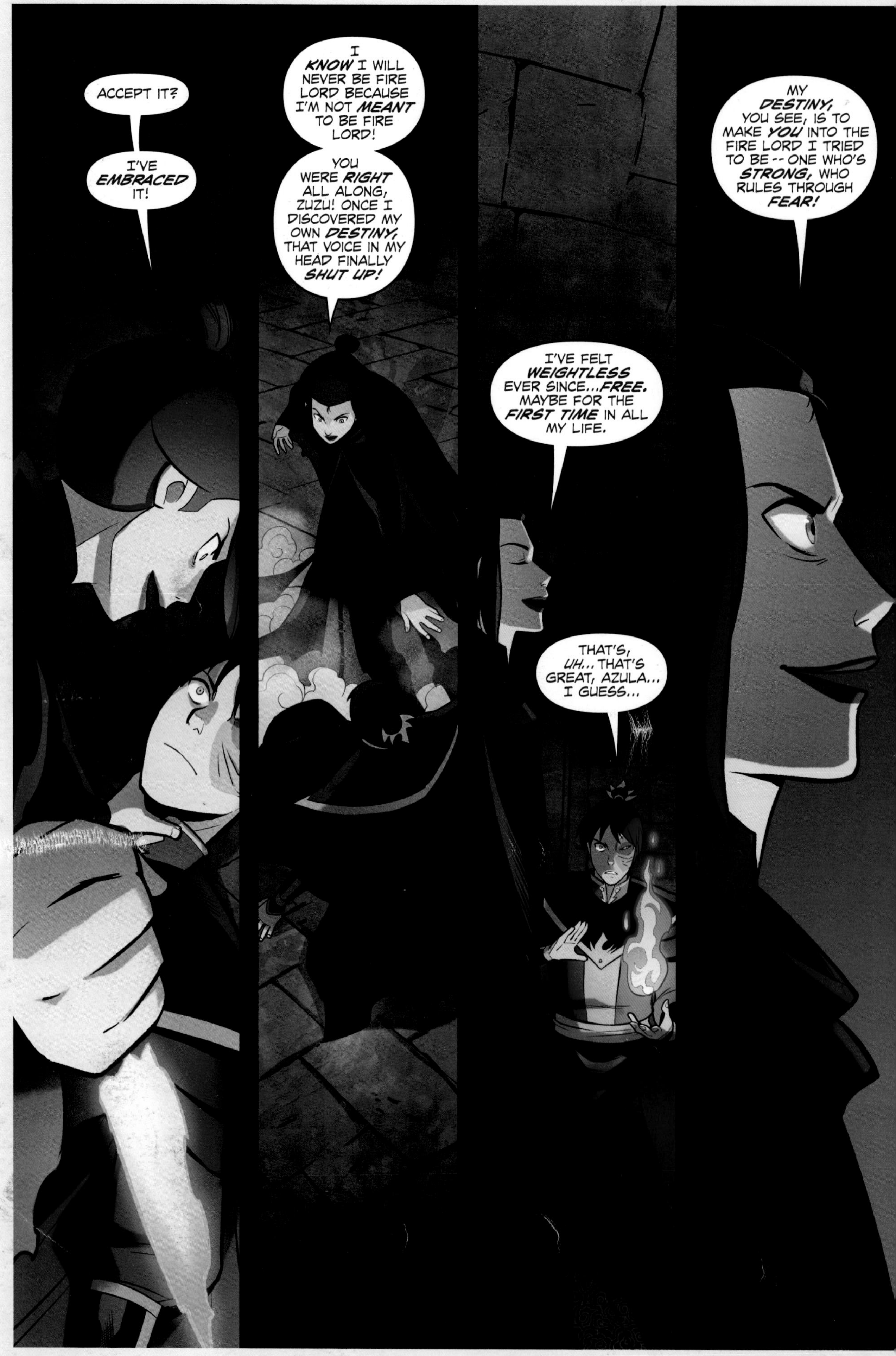
ACCEPT IT?
I'VE EMBRACED IT!
I KNOW I WILL NEVER BE FIRE LORD BECAUSE I'M NOT MEANT TO BE FIRE LORD!
YOU WERE RIGHT ALL ALONG, ZUZU! ONCE I DISCOVERED MY OWN DESTINY, THAT VOICE IN MY HEAD FINALLY SHUT UP!
I'VE FELT WEIGHTLESS EVER SINCE...FREE. MAYBE FOR THE FIRST TIME IN ALL MY LIFE.
THAT'S, UH... THAT'S GREAT, AZULA... I GUESS...
MY DESTINY, YOU SEE, IS TO MAKE YOU INTO THE FIRE LORD I TRIED TO BE -- ONE WHO'S STRONG, WHO RULES THROUGH FEAR!

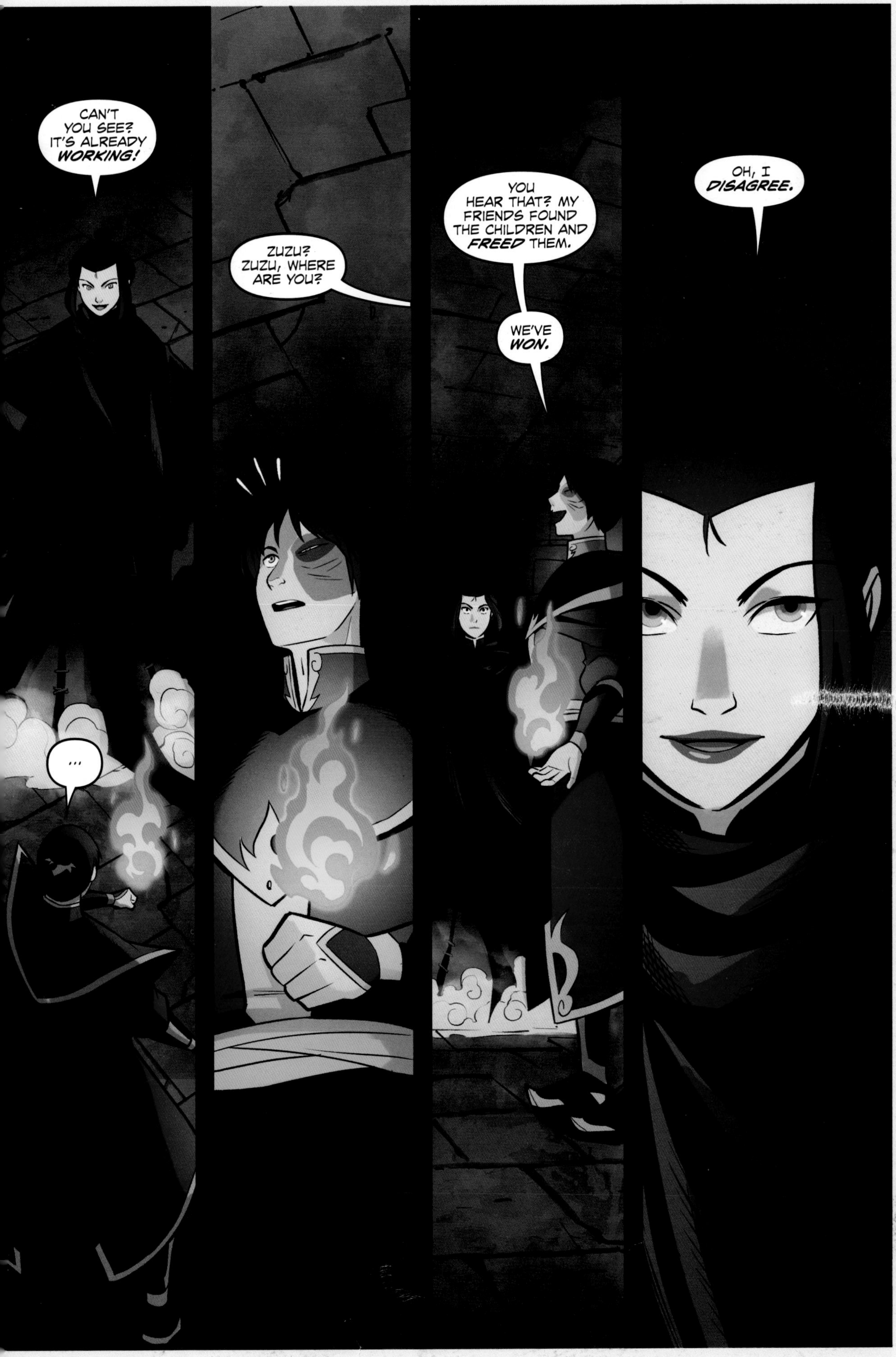
CAN'T YOU SEE? IT'S ALREADY WORKING!
...
ZUZU? ZUZU, WHERE ARE YOU?
YOU HEAR THAT? MY FRIENDS FOUND THE CHILDREN AND FREED THEM.
WE'VE WON.
OH, I DISAGREE.

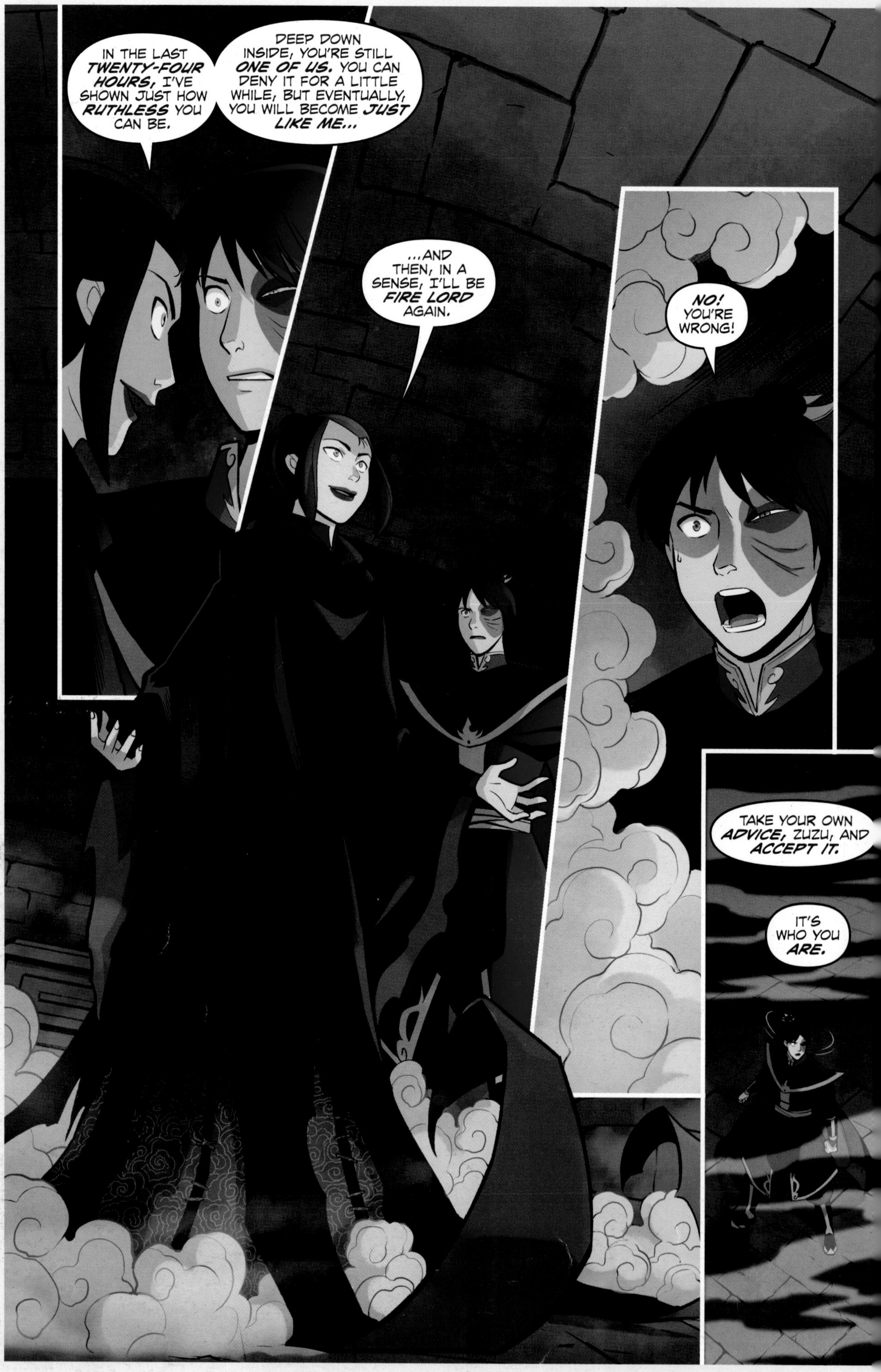
IN THE LAST TWENTY-FOUR HOURS, I'VE SHOWN JUST HOW RUTHLESS YOU CAN BE.
DEEP DOWN INSIDE, YOU'RE STILL ONE OF US. YOU CAN DENY IT FOR A LITTLE WHILE, BUT EVENTUALLY, YOU WILL BECOME JUST LIKE ME...
...AND THEN, IN A SENSE, I'LL BE FIRE LORD AGAIN.
NO! YOU'RE WRONG!
TAKE YOUR OWN ADVICE, ZUZU, AND ACCEPT IT.
IT'S WHO YOU ARE.

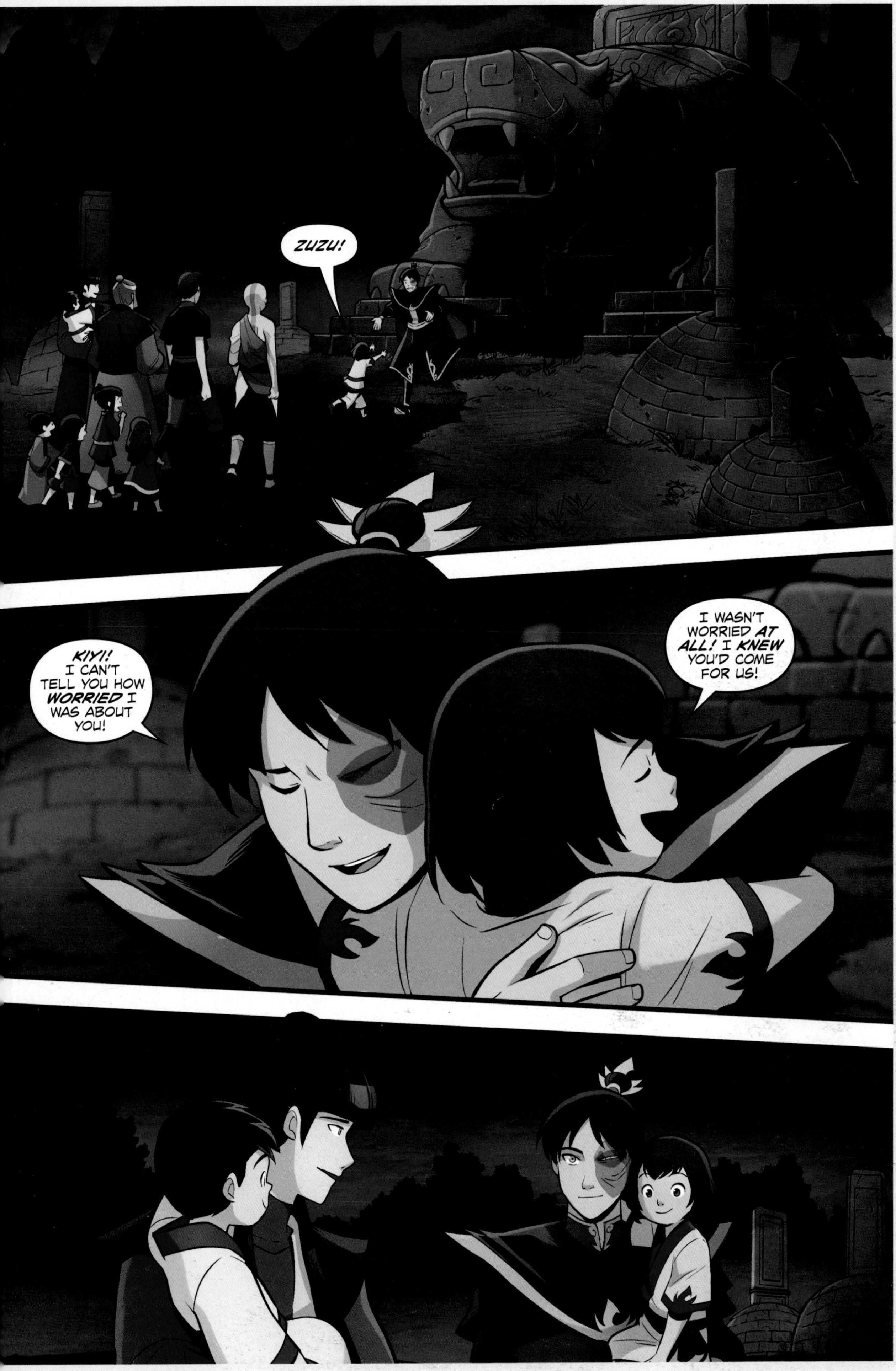
ZUZU!
KIYI! I CAN'T TELL YOU HOW WORRIED I WAS ABOUT YOU!
I WASN'T WORRIED AT ALL! I KNEW YOU'D COME FOR US!

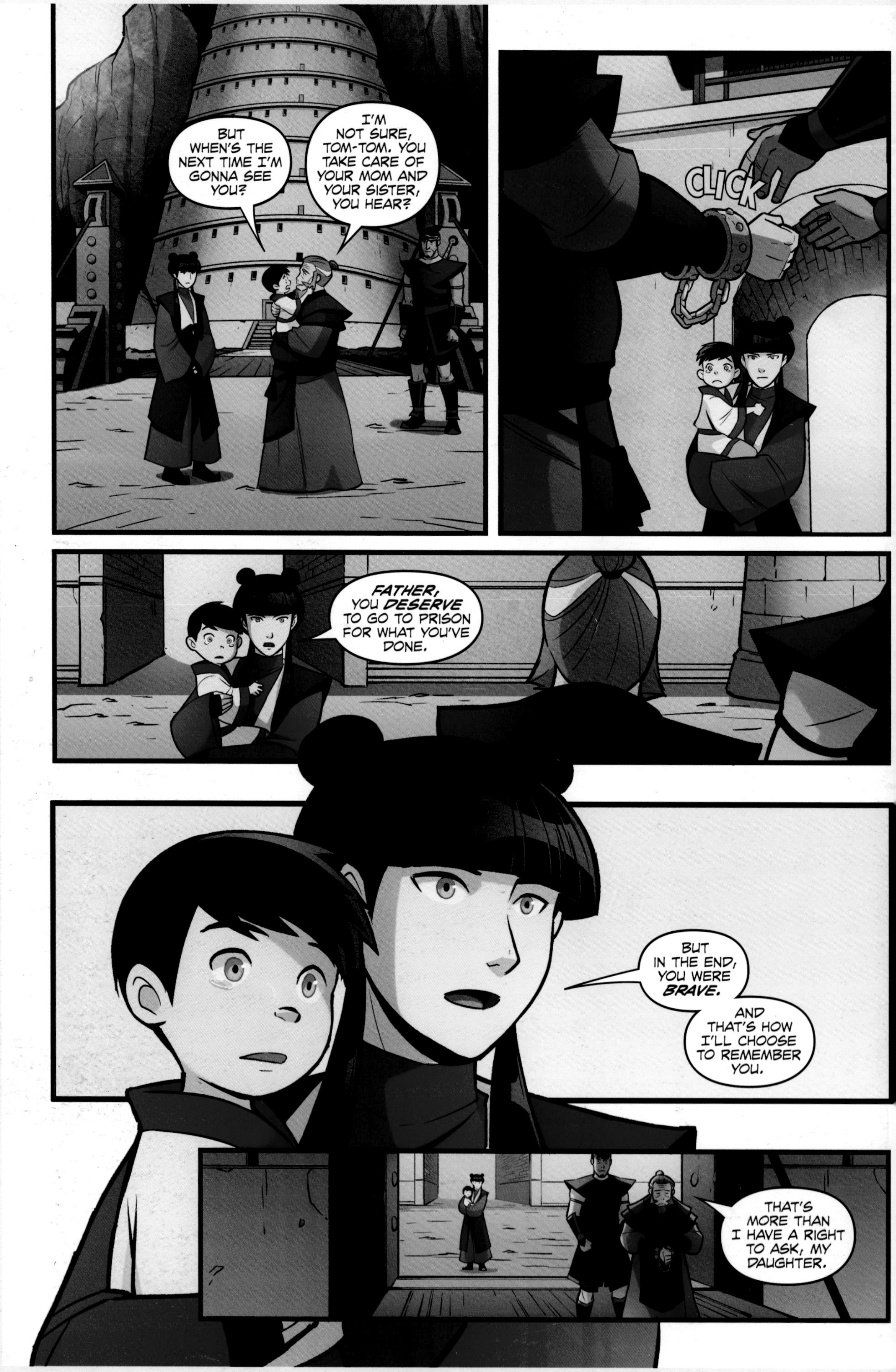
BUT WHEN'S THE NEXT TIME I'M GONNA SEE YOU?
I'M NOT SURE, TOM-TOM. YOU TAKE CARE OF YOUR MOM AND YOUR SISTER, YOU HEAR?
CLICK
FATHER, YOU DESERVE TO GO TO PRISON FOR WHAT YOU'VE DONE.
BUT IN THE END, YOU WERE BRAVE.
AND THAT'S HOW I'LL CHOOSE TO REMEMBER YOU.
THAT'S MORE THAN I HAVE A RIGHT TO ASK, MY DAUGHTER.

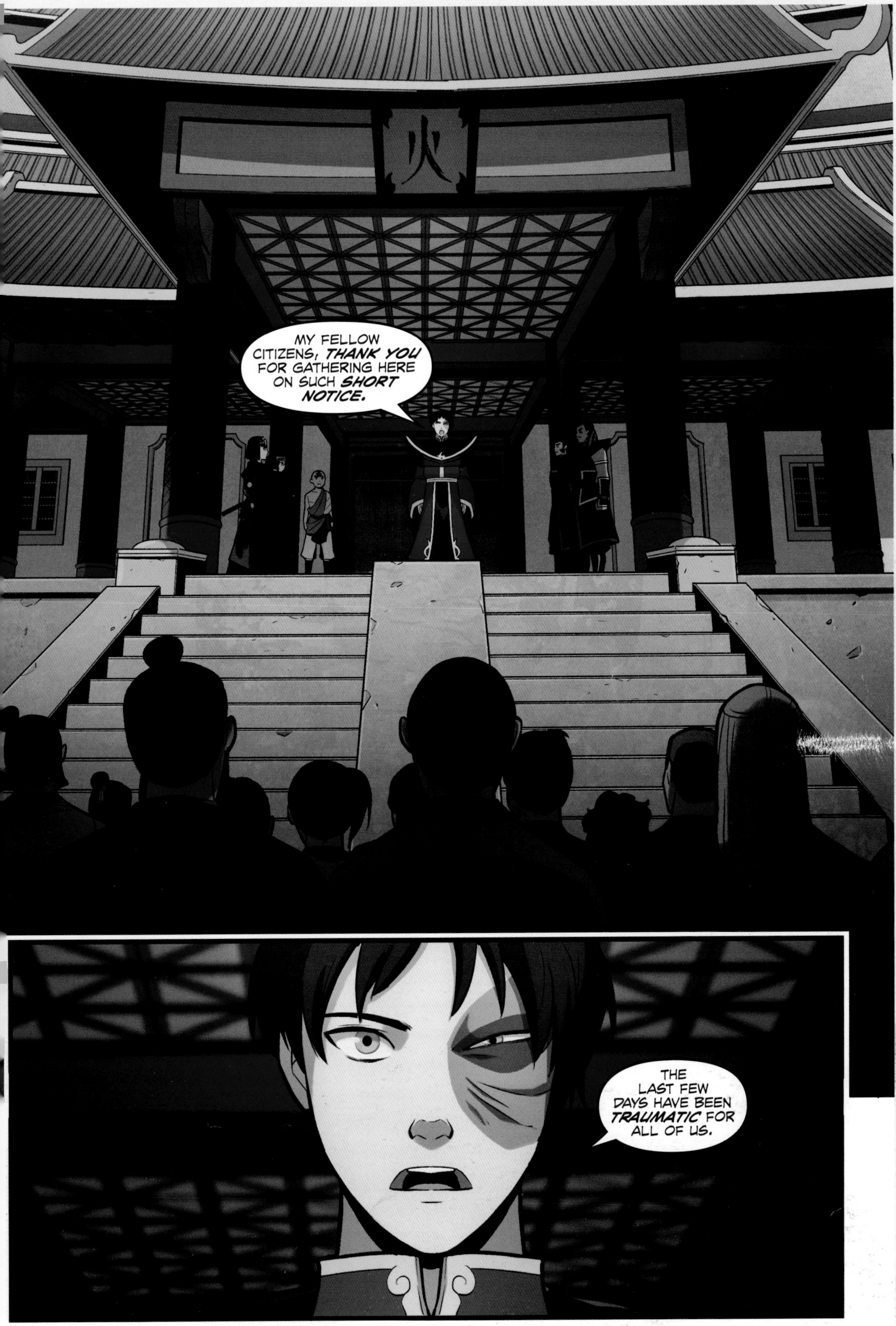
MY FELLOW CITIZENS, THANK YOU FOR GATHERING HERE ON SUCH SHORT NOTICE.
THE LAST FEW DAYS HAVE BEEN TRAUMATIC FOR ALL OF US.

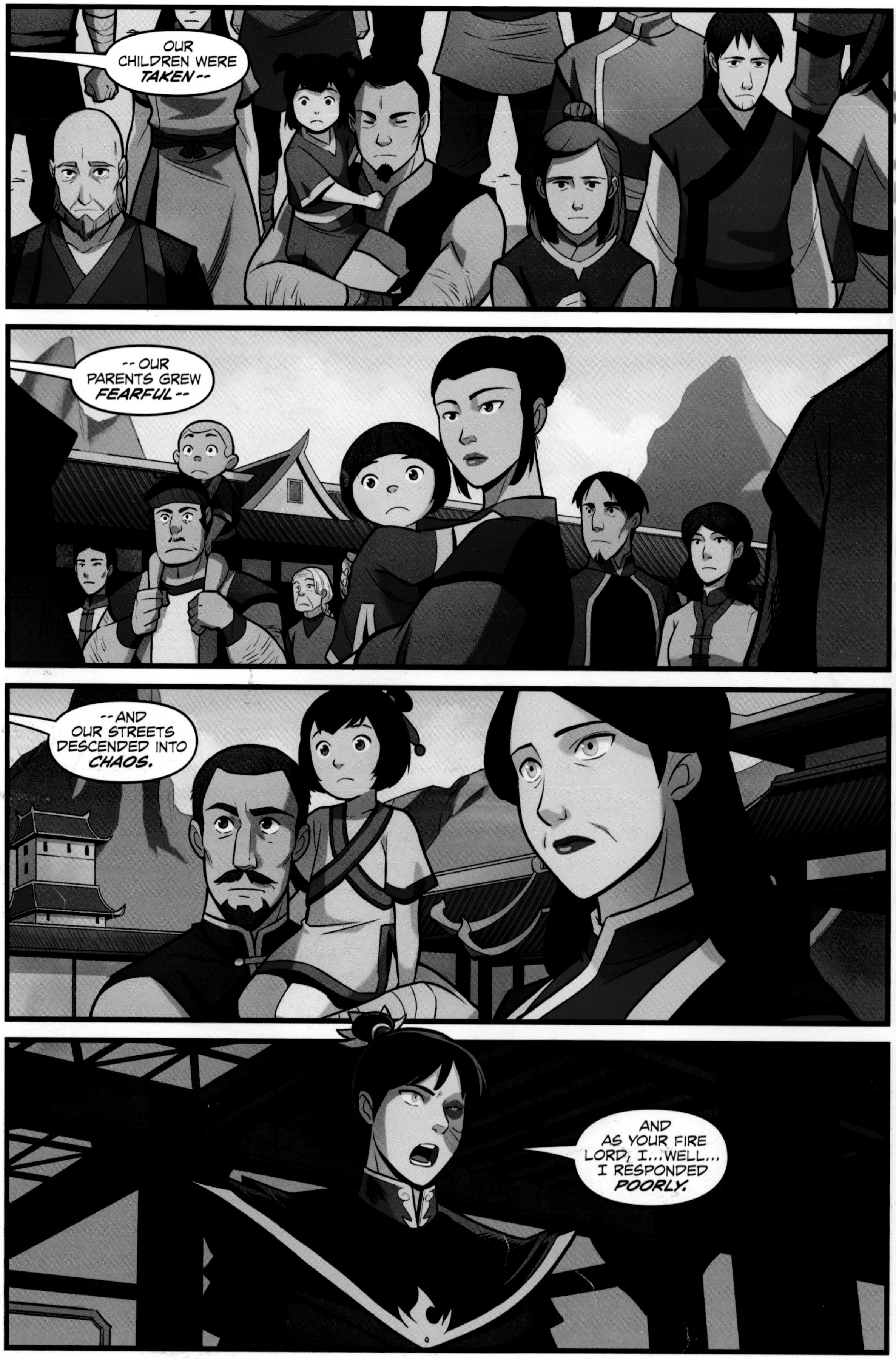
OUR CHILDREN WERE TAKEN--
--OUR PARENTS GREW FEARFUL--
--AND OUR STREETS DESCENDED INTO CHAOS.
AND AS YOUR FIRE LORD, I...WELL... I RESPONDED POORLY.

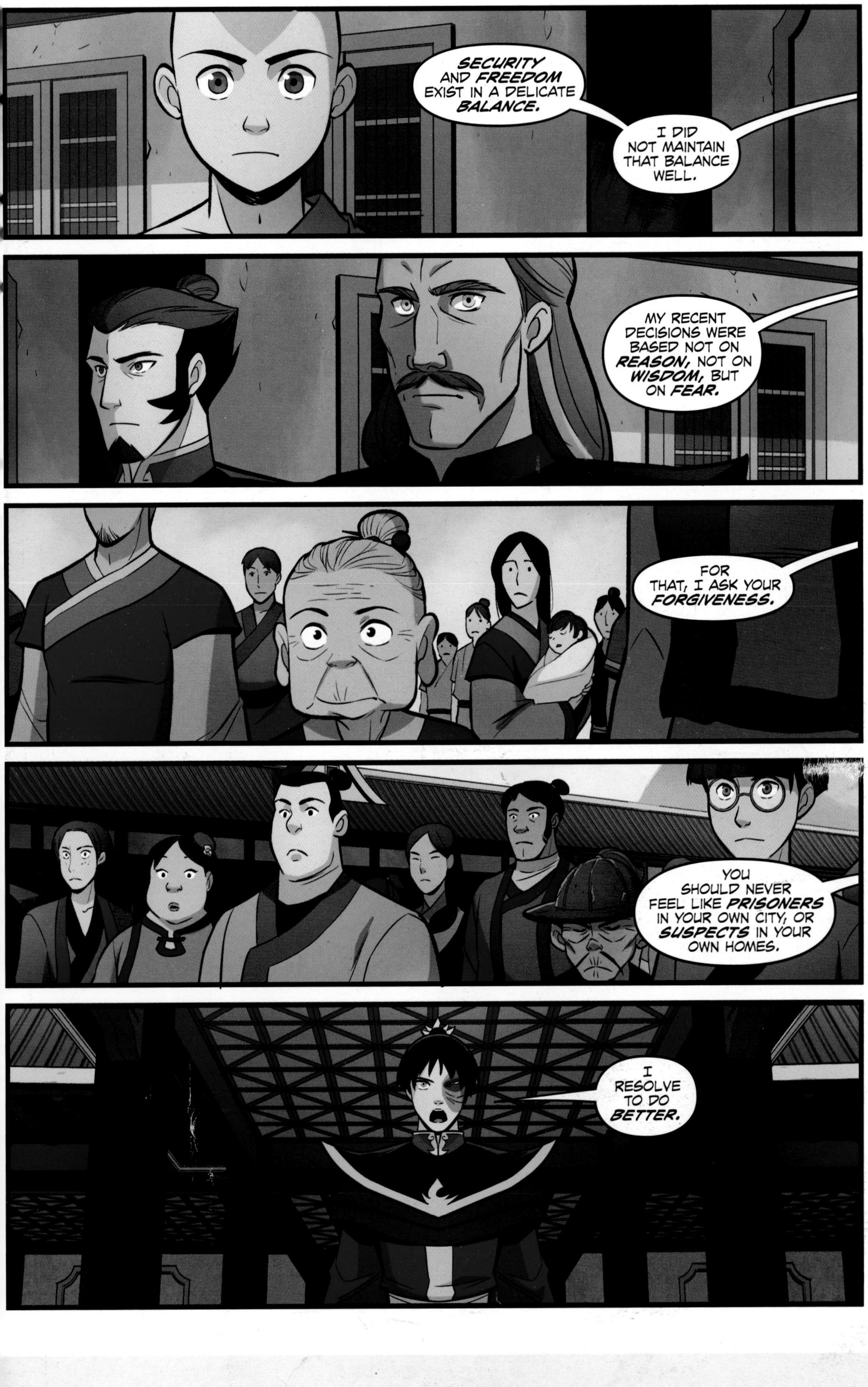
SECURITY AND FREEDOM EXIST IN A DELICATE BALANCE.
I DID NOT MAINTAIN THAT BALANCE WELL.
MY RECENT DECISIONS WERE BASED NOT ON REASON, NOT ON WISDOM, BUT ON FEAR.
FOR THAT, I ASK YOUR FORGIVENESS.
YOU SHOULD NEVER FEEL LIKE PRISONERS IN YOUR OWN CITY, OR SUSPECTS IN YOUR OWN HOMES.
I RESOLVE TO DO BETTER.

GLY: *So many of our political disagreements these days can be boiled down to a tension between security and freedom, don't you think?*

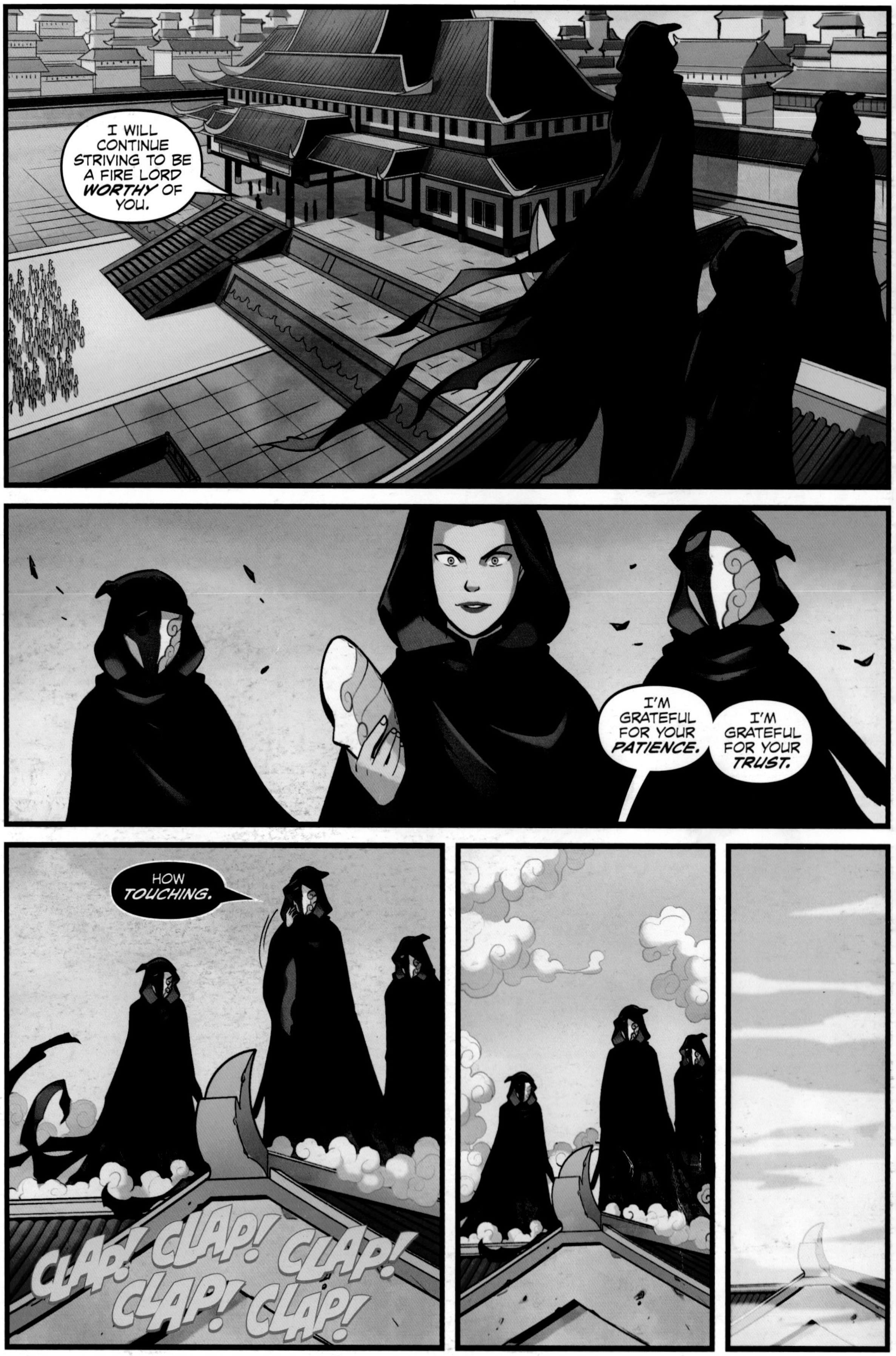
I WILL CONTINUE STRIVING TO BE A FIRE LORD WORTHY OF YOU.
I'M GRATEFUL FOR YOUR PATIENCE.
I'M GRATEFUL FOR YOUR TRUST.
HOW TOUCHING.
CLAP! CLAP! CLAP! CLAP! CLAP!

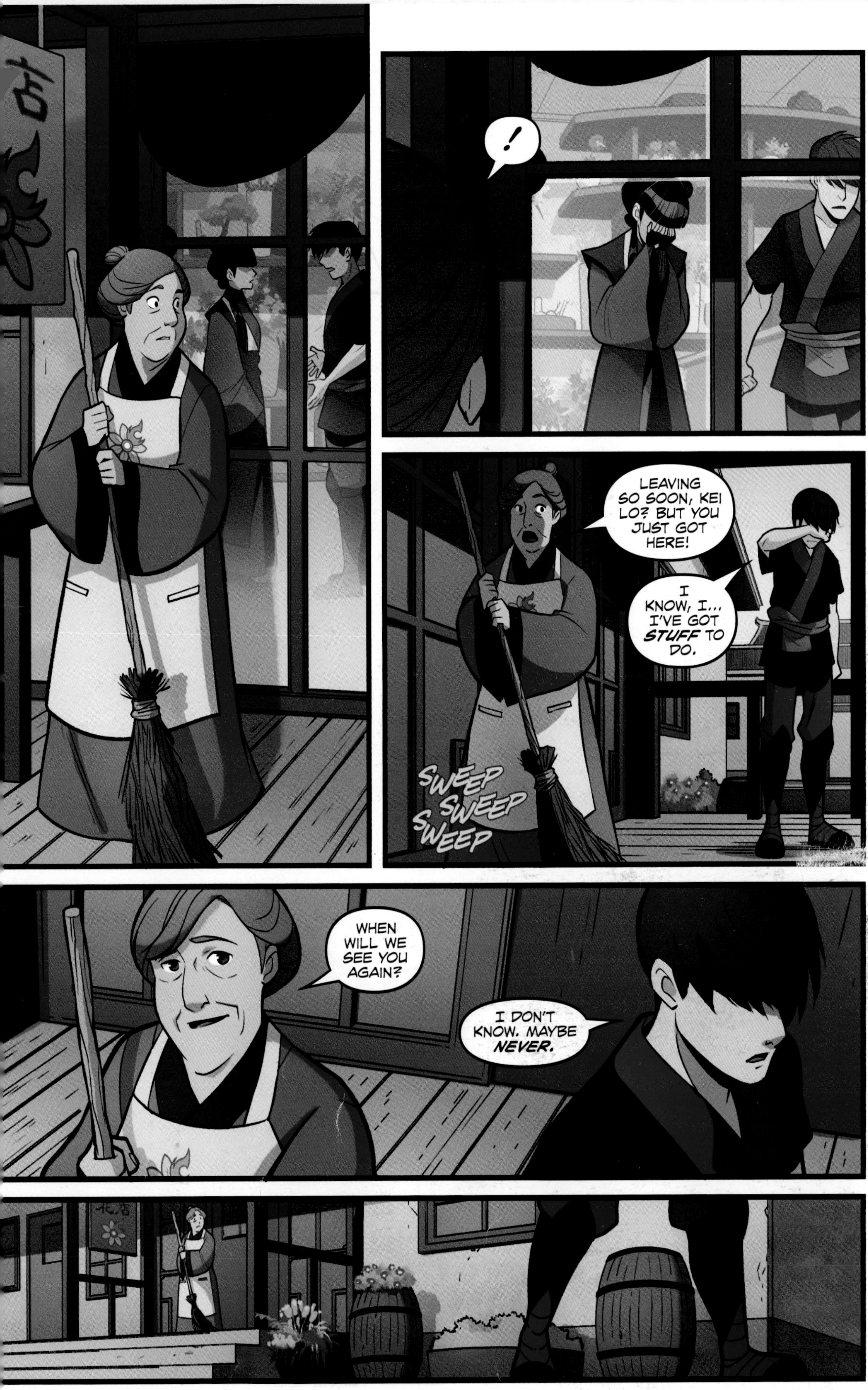
!
LEAVING SO SOON, KEI LO? BUT YOU JUST GOT HERE!
I KNOW, I... I'VE GOT *STUFF* TO DO.
SWEEP SWEEP SWEEP
WHEN WILL WE SEE YOU AGAIN?
I DON'T KNOW. MAYBE *NEVER.*

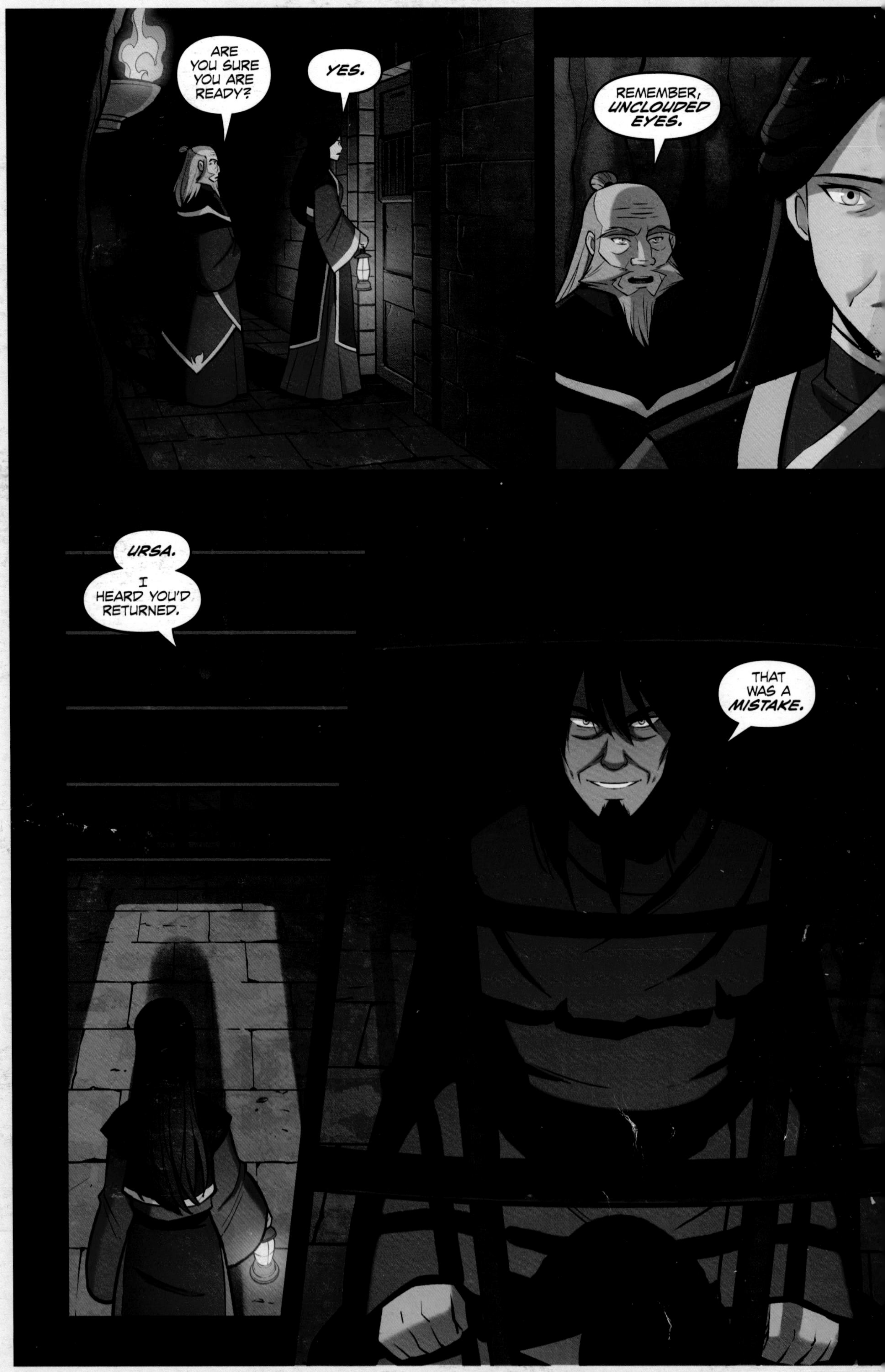
ARE YOU SURE YOU ARE READY?
YES.
REMEMBER, UNCLOUDED EYES.
URSA.
I HEARD YOU'D RETURNED.
THAT WAS A MISTAKE.

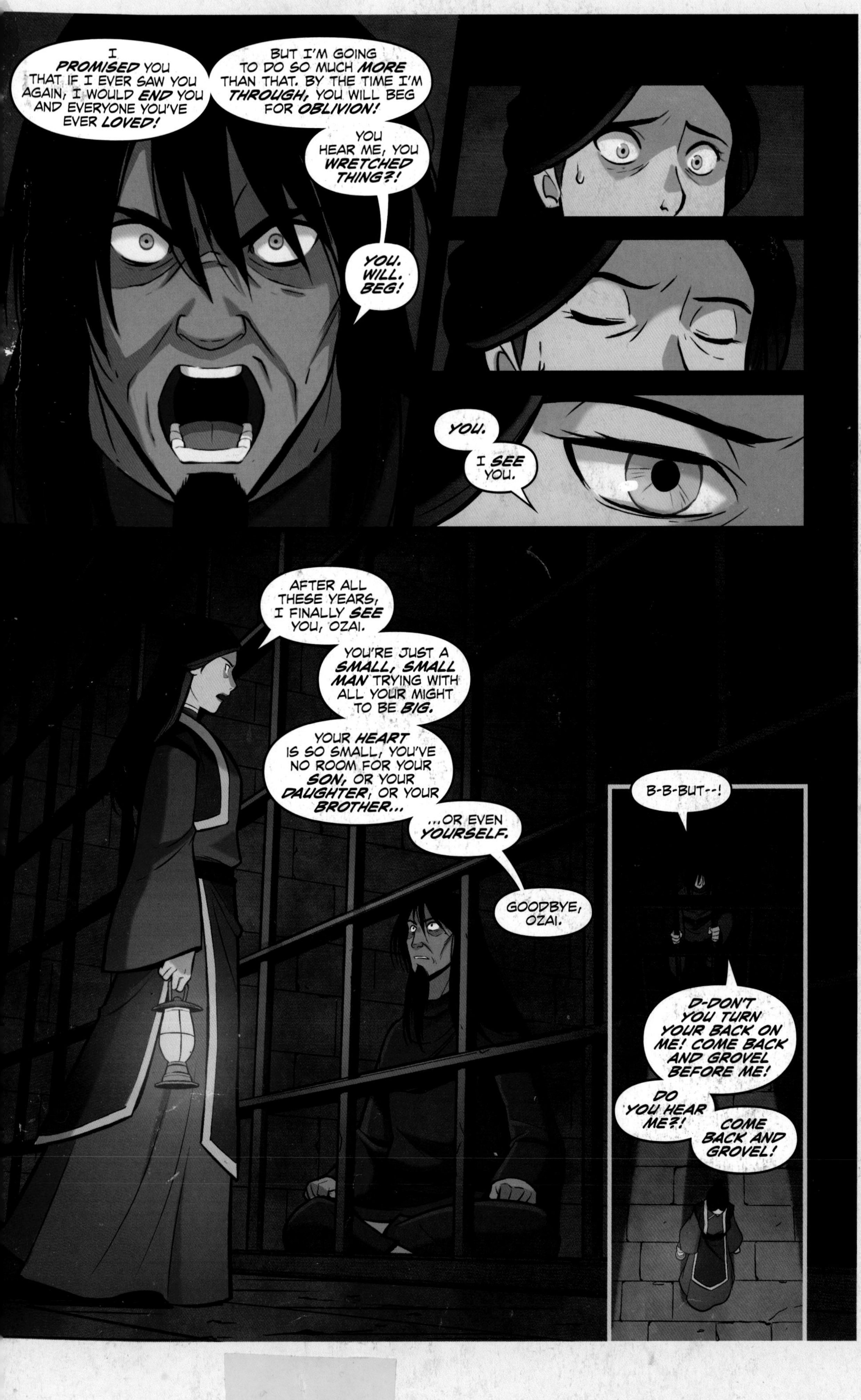
I PROMISED YOU THAT IF I EVER SAW YOU AGAIN, I WOULD END YOU AND EVERYONE YOU'VE EVER LOVED!
BUT I'M GOING TO DO SO MUCH MORE THAN THAT. BY THE TIME I'M THROUGH, YOU WILL BEG FOR OBLIVION!
YOU HEAR ME, YOU WRETCHED THING?!
YOU. WILL. BEG!
YOU.
I SEE YOU.
AFTER ALL THESE YEARS, I FINALLY SEE YOU, OZAI.
YOU'RE JUST A SMALL, SMALL MAN TRYING WITH ALL YOUR MIGHT TO BE BIG.
YOUR HEART IS SO SMALL, YOU'VE NO ROOM FOR YOUR SON, OR YOUR DAUGHTER, OR YOUR BROTHER...
...OR EVEN YOURSELF.
GOODBYE, OZAI.
B-B-BUT--!
D-DON'T YOU TURN YOUR BACK ON ME! COME BACK AND GROVEL BEFORE ME!
DO YOU HEAR ME?!
COME BACK AND GROVEL!

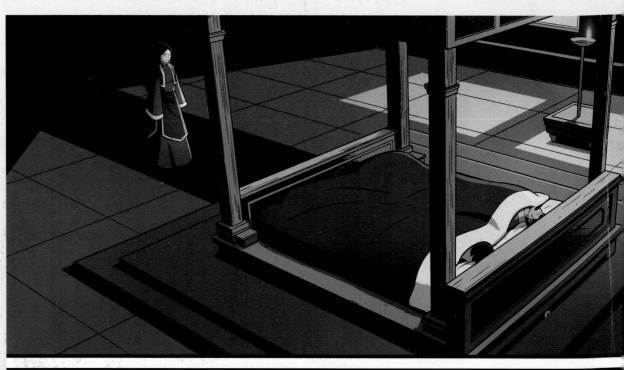

GLY: *It took us a long time, both in the script and in the art, to get the second-to-last panel right.*

MOMMY... YOU'RE BACK.

I'M BACK.

Artwork and captions by Gurihiru

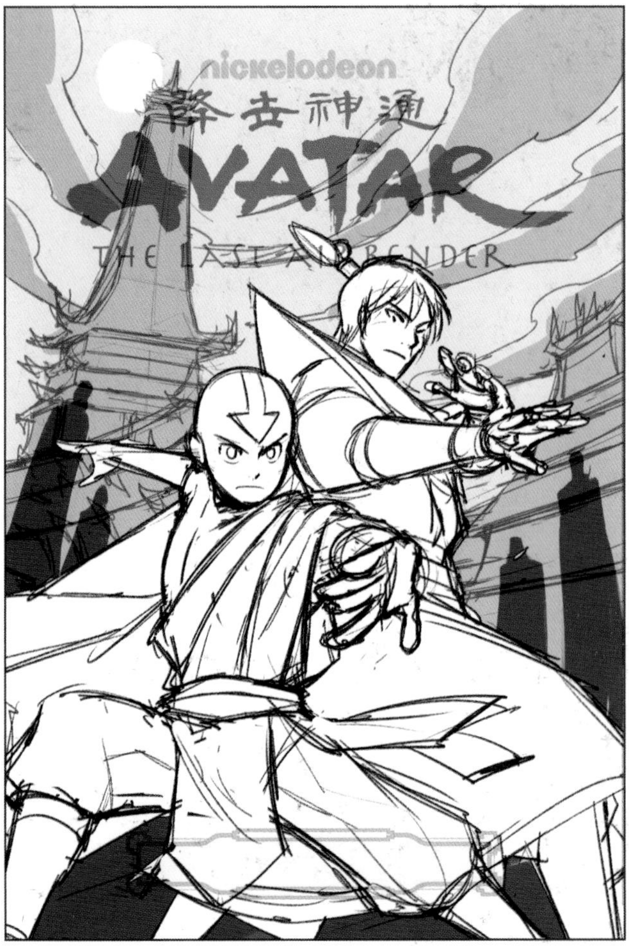
nickelodeon
降去神通
AVATAR
THE LAST AIRBENDER

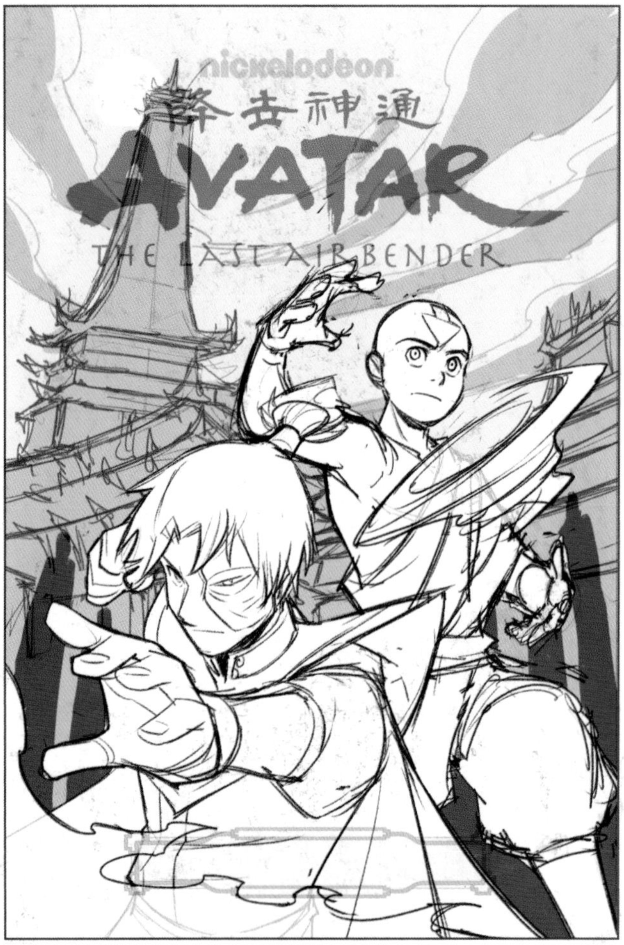
nickelodeon
降去神通
AVATAR
THE LAST AIRBENDER

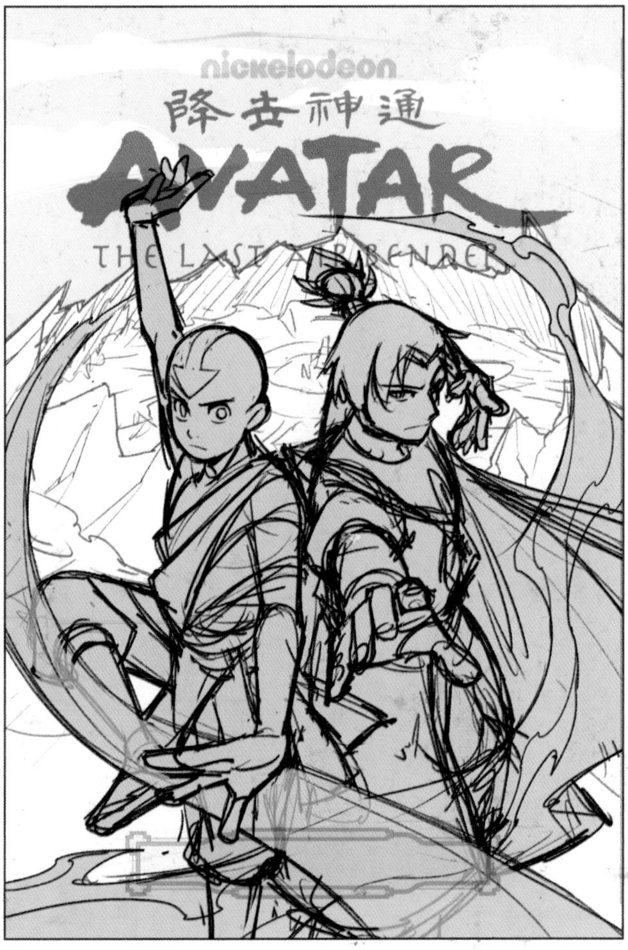
nickelodeon
降去神通
AVATAR
THE LAST AIRBENDER

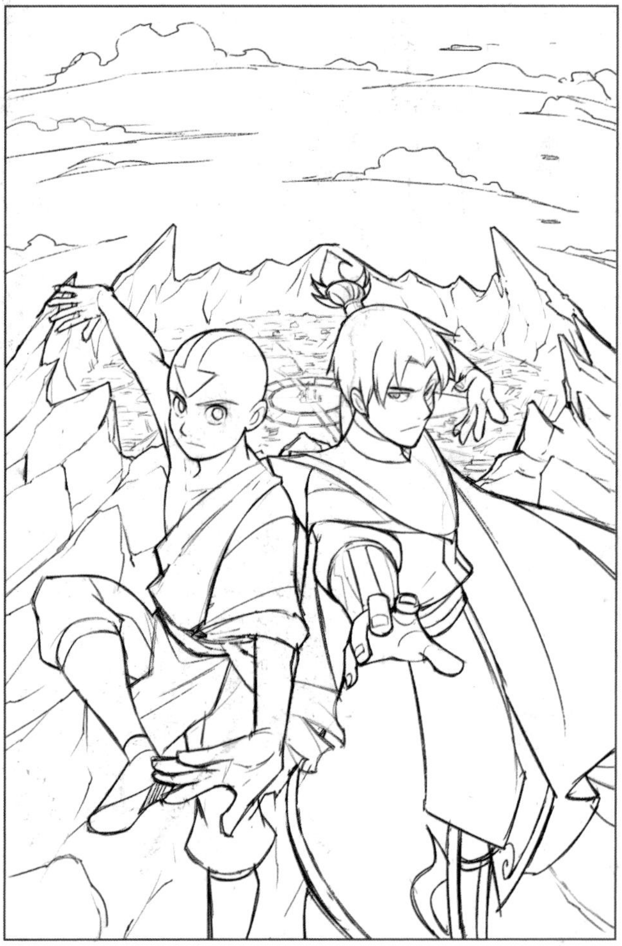

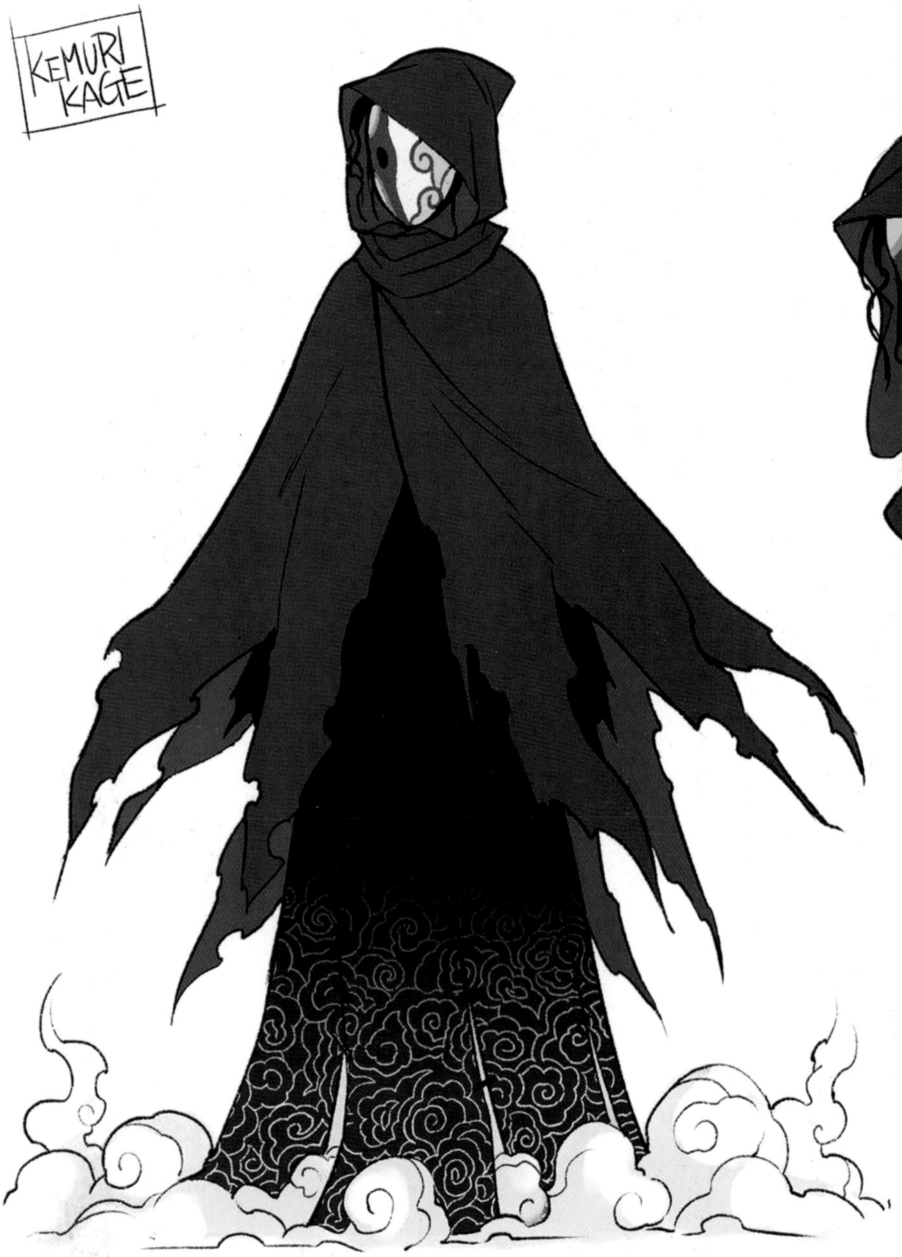
KEMURI
KAGE

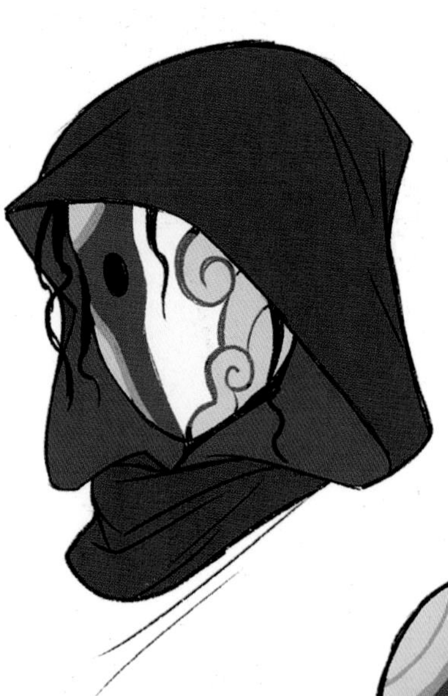

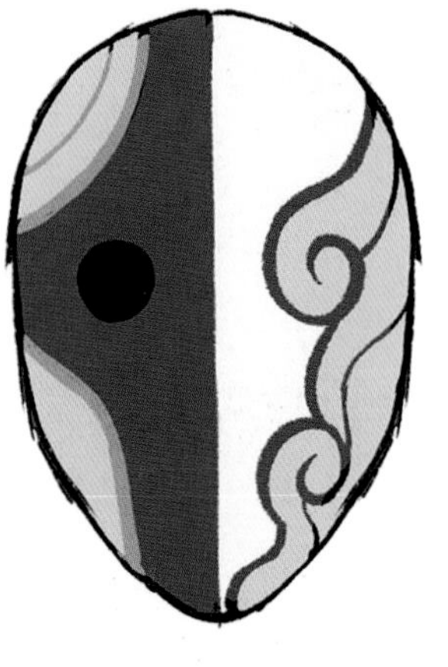

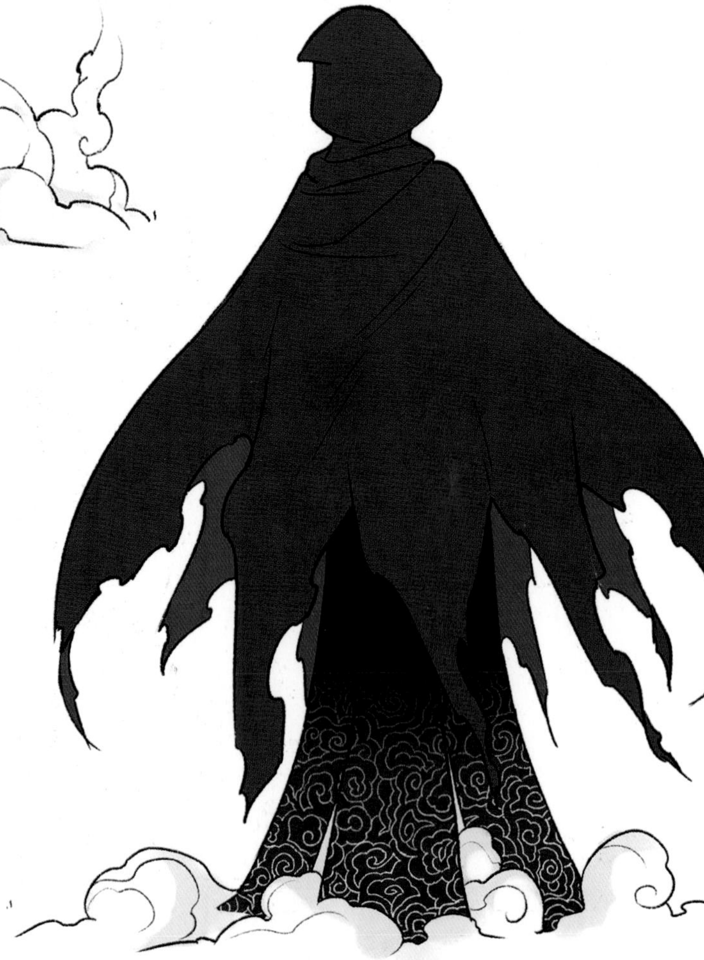

KEMURIKAGE

In Japanese, kemuri *means "smoke," and* kage *means "shadow," so we designed the Kemurikage with dark cloaks and spooky, expressionless masks. The mask is asymmetrical, which evokes a sense of unease, and to make them look like spirits, smoke comes out from the bottom of the cloak.*

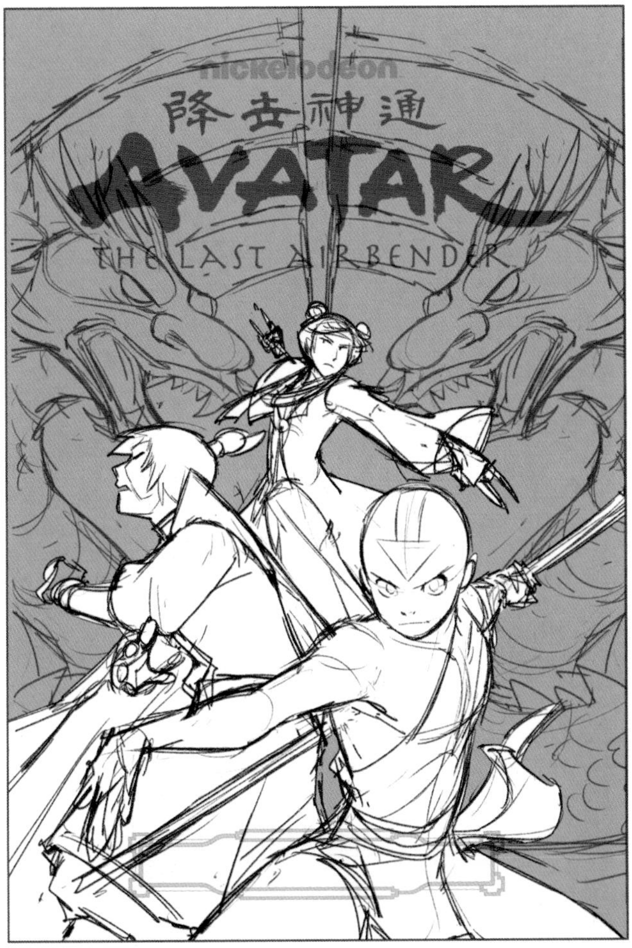
nickelodeon
AVATAR
THE LAST AIRBENDER

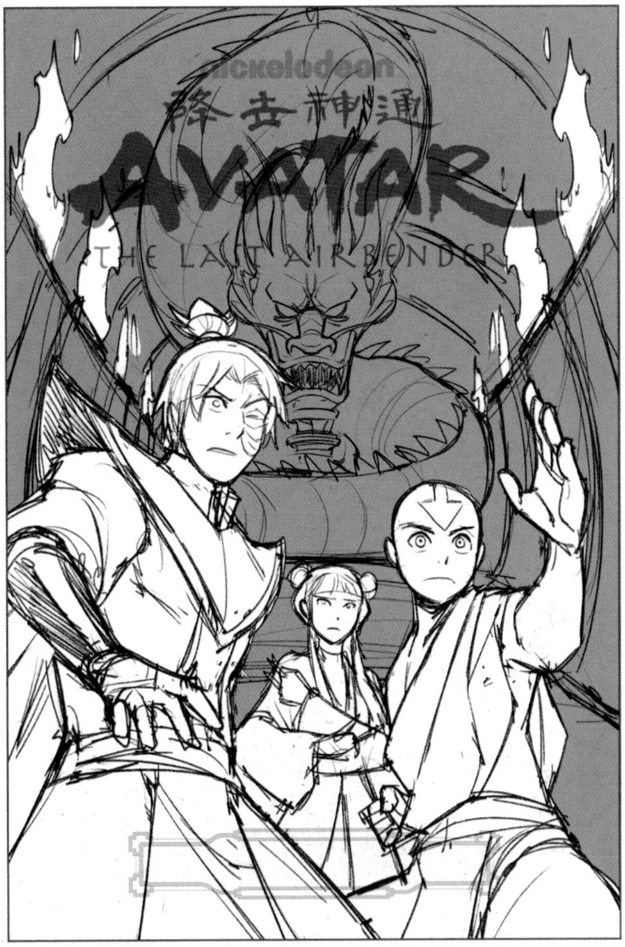
nickelodeon
AVATAR
THE LAST AIRBENDER

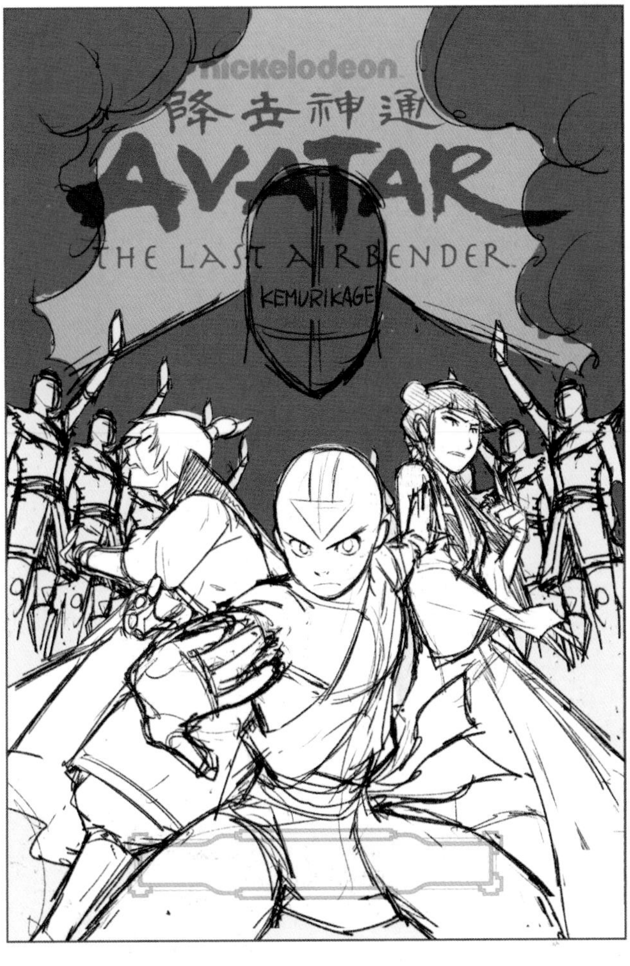
nickelodeon
AVATAR
THE LAST AIRBENDER
KEMURIKAGE

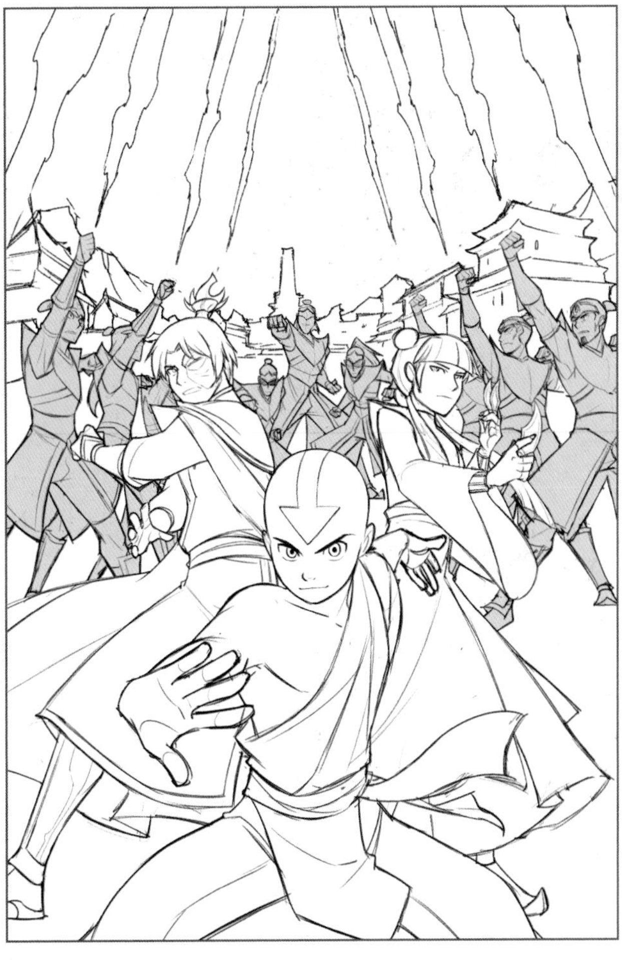

NEW OZAI SOCIETY

The members of the New Ozai Society wear Ozai's headband, but in order to hide their identity, we designed it to cover half of their face. Since they work in the dark, we chose dark colors for their costumes.

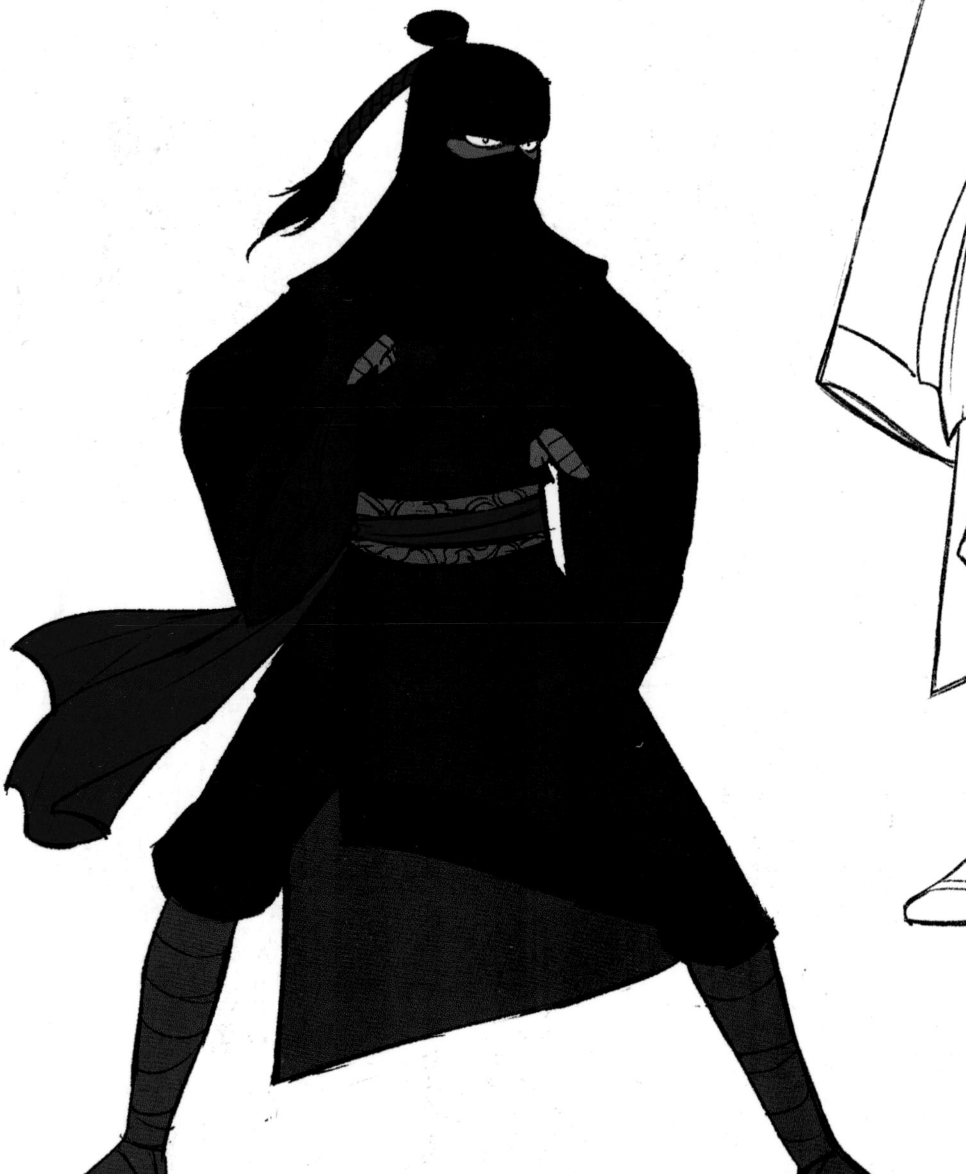

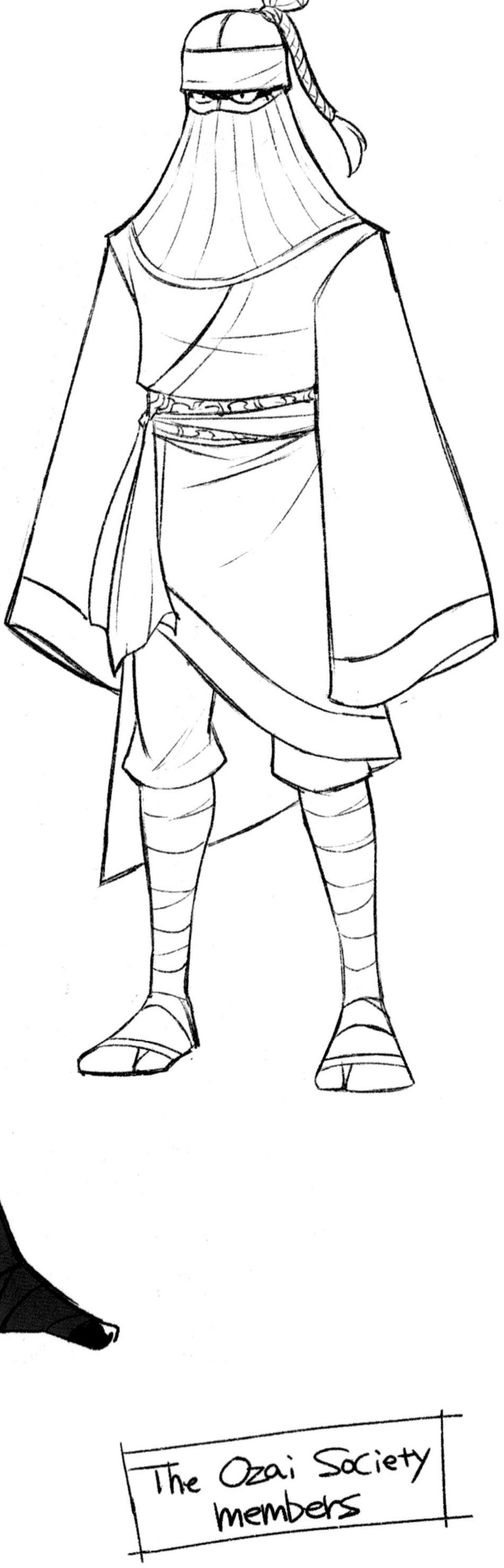
The Ozai Society members

降世神通
AVATAR
THE LAST AIRBENDER

nickelodeon
降世神通
AVATAR
THE LAST AIRBENDER

nickelodeon
降世神通
AVATAR
THE LAST AIRBENDER

降世神通
AVATAR
THE LAST AIRBENDER

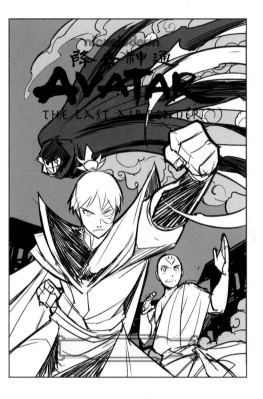

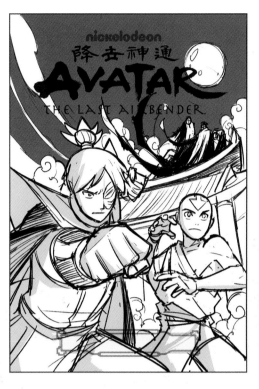

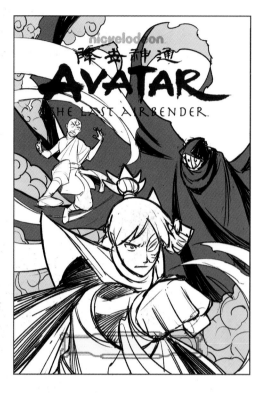

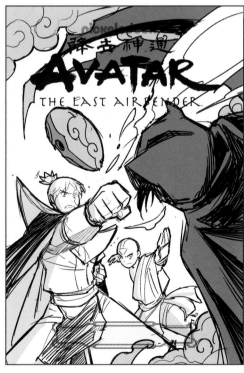

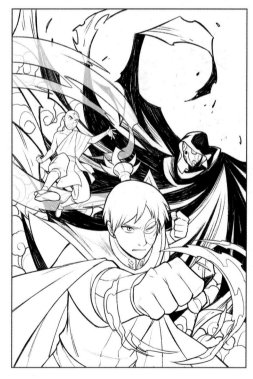

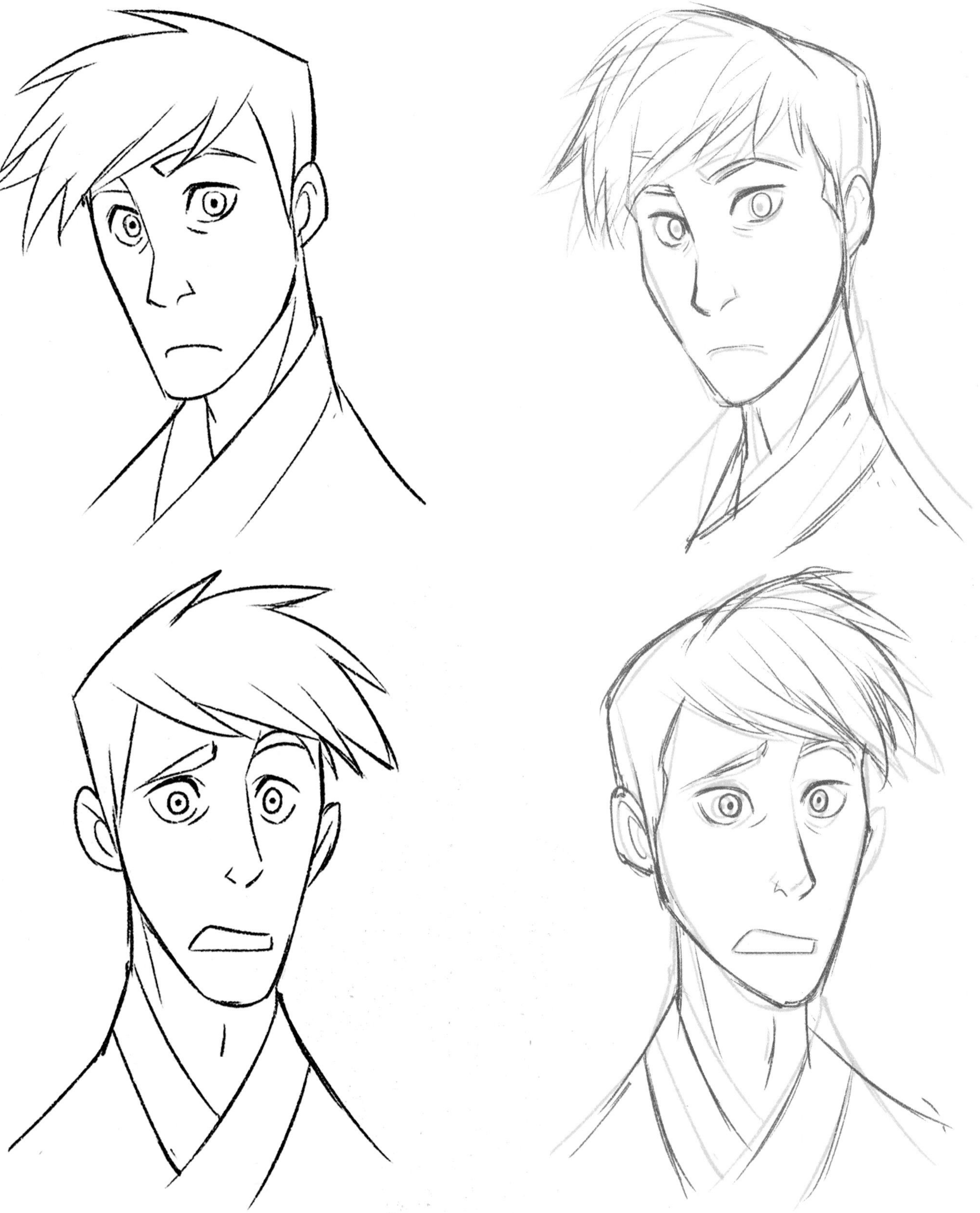

KEI LO

Kei Lo first appeared in the Free Comic Book Day short story "Rebound." The design here is basically the same, but we made him a more strong-willed young man by changing his eyes a little bit.

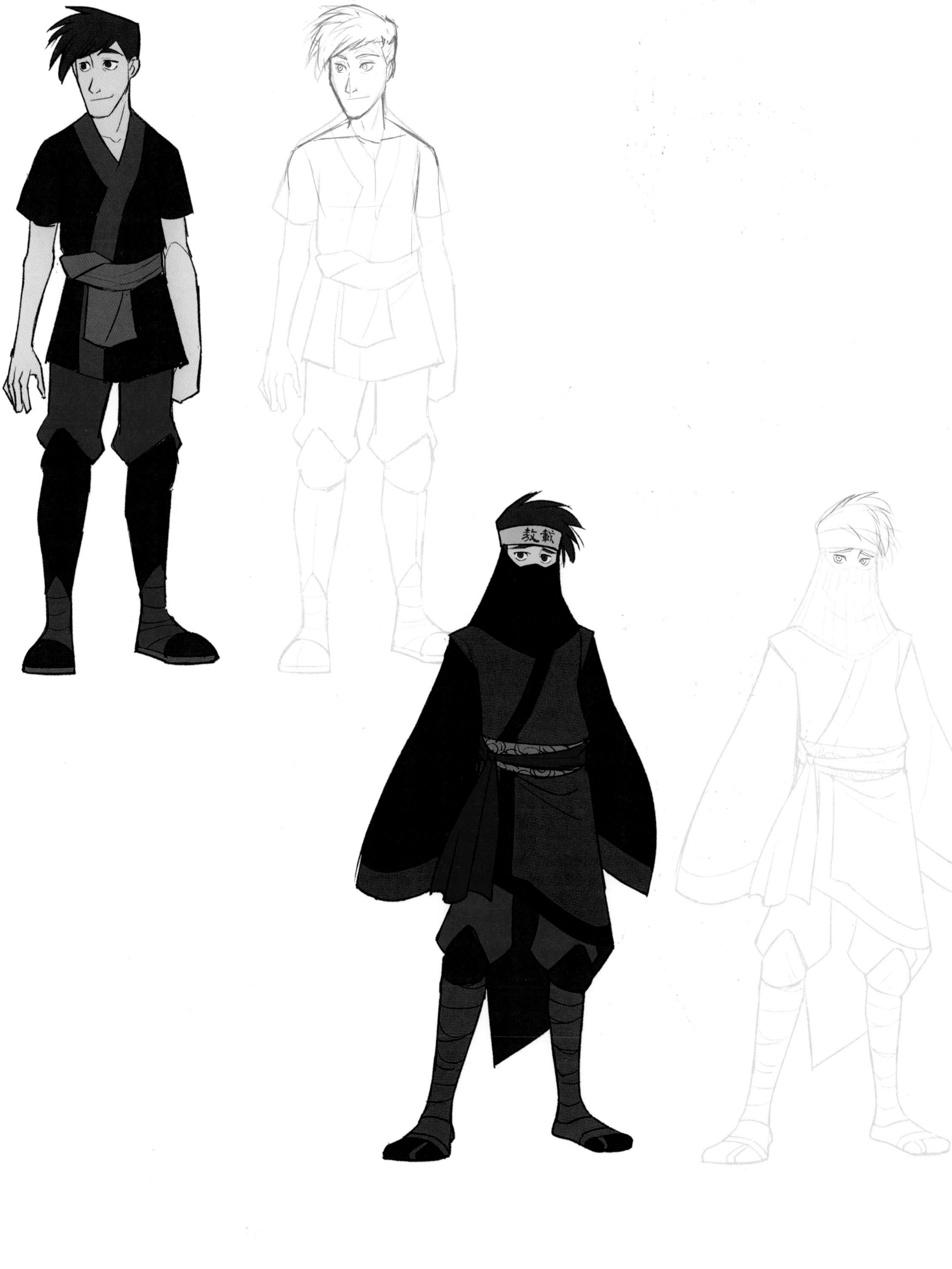

1

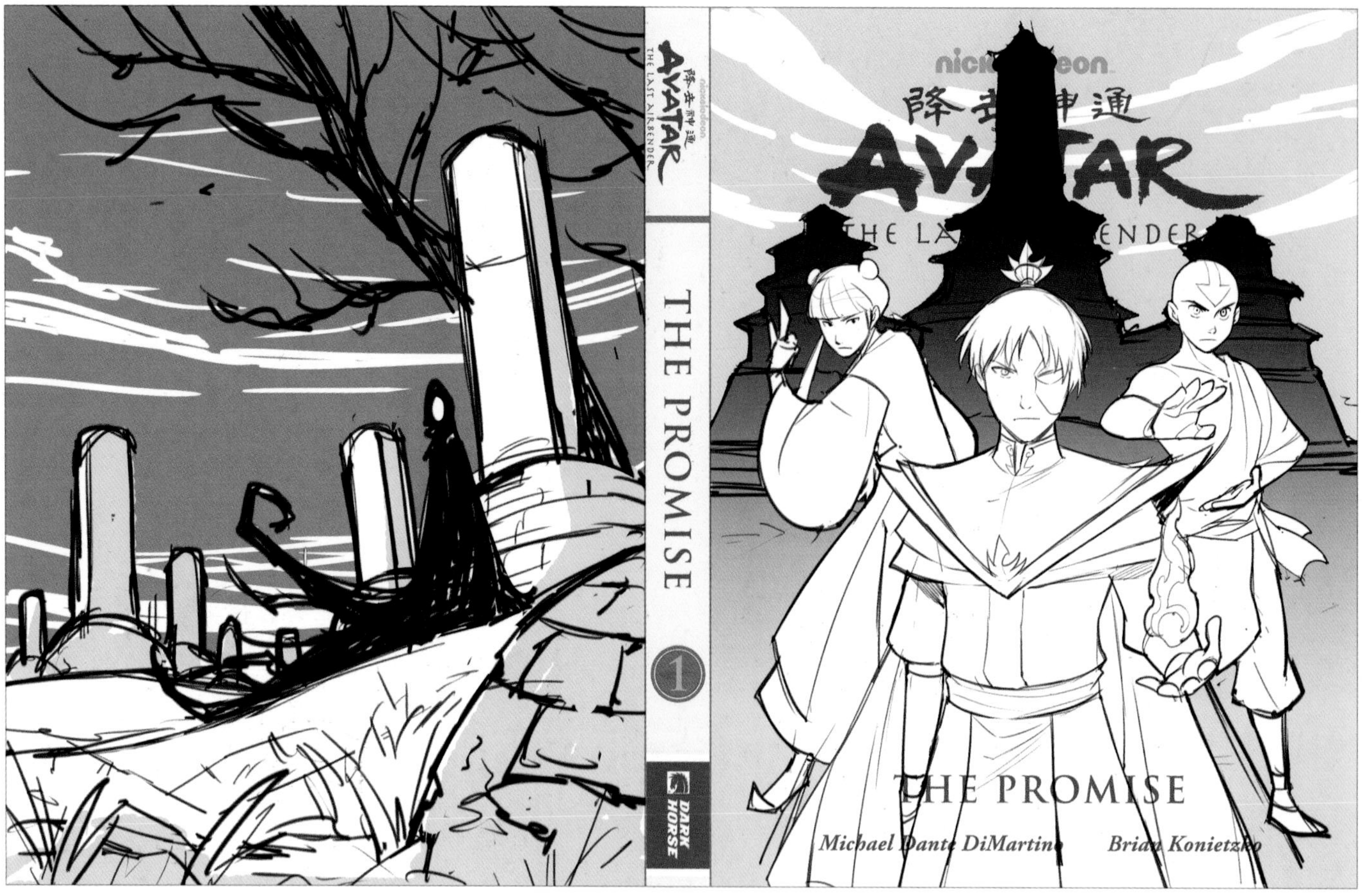
降世神通
AVATAR
THE LAST AIRBENDER
THE PROMISE
1
DARK HORSE
降世神通
AVATAR
THE PROMISE
Michael Dante DiMartino
Brian Konietzko

2

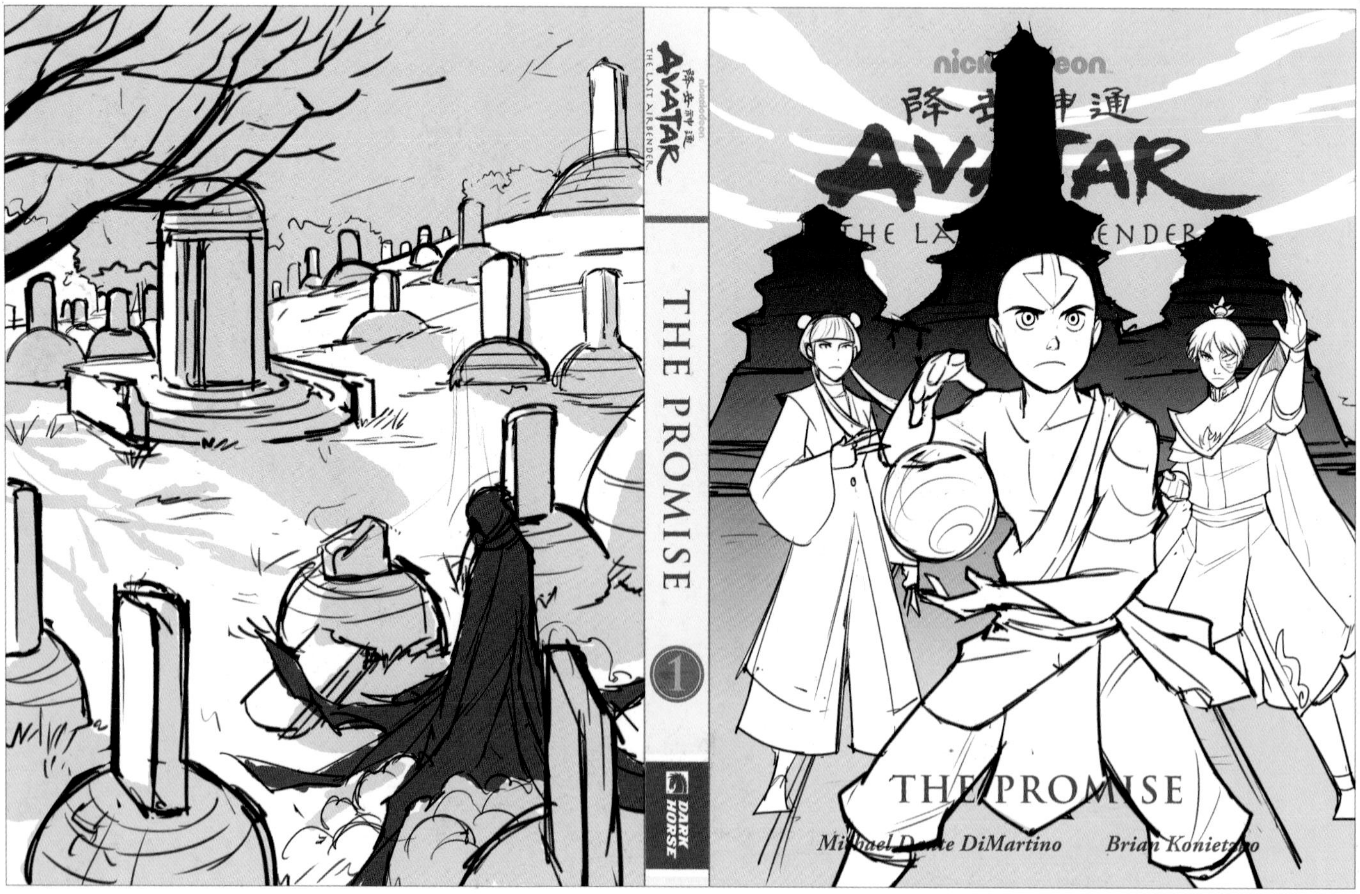
降世神通
AVATAR
THE LAST AIRBENDER
THE PROMISE
1
DARK HORSE
降世神通
AVATAR
THE PROMISE
Michael Dante DiMartino
Brian Konietzko

3

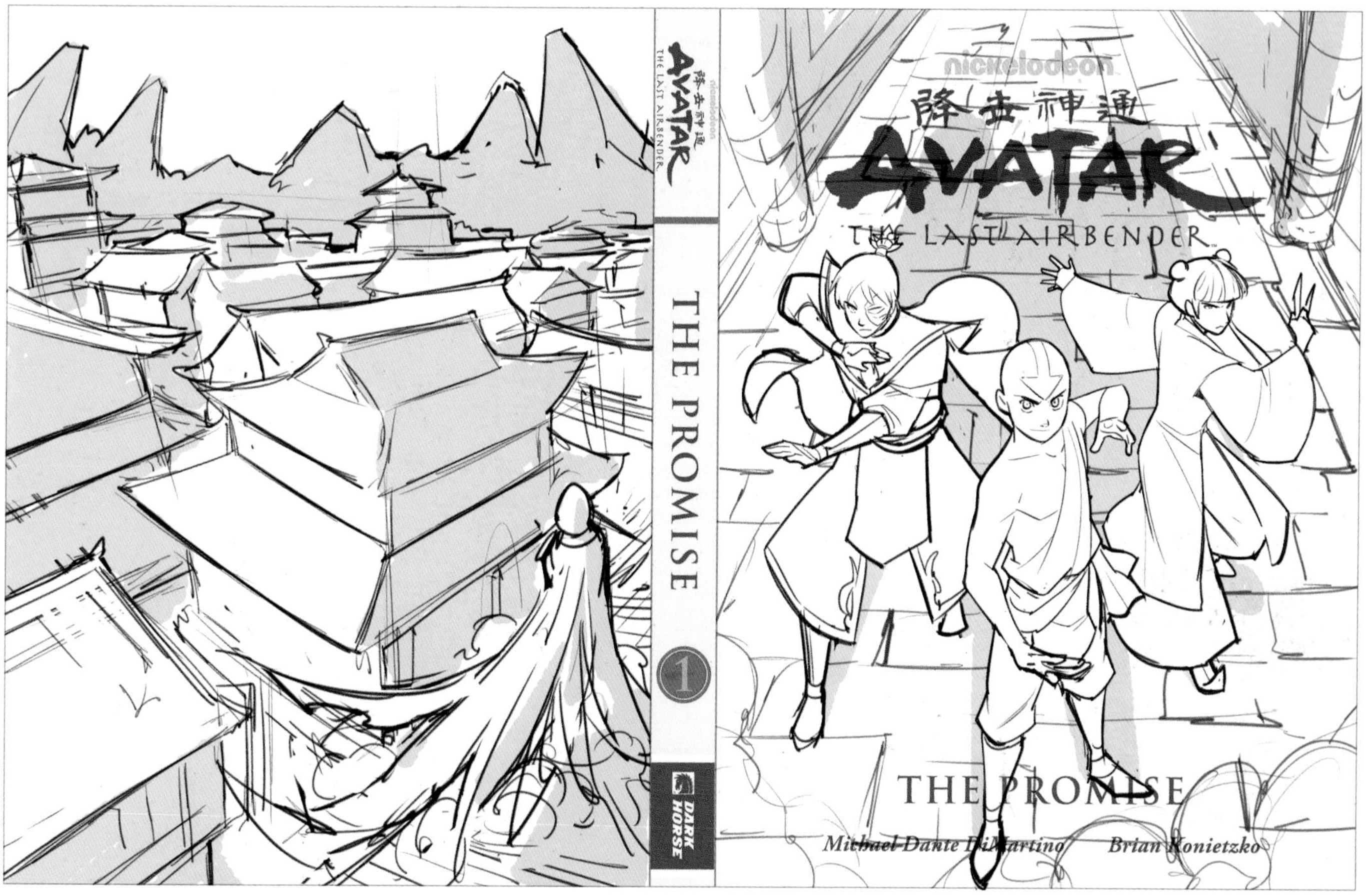
AVATAR
THE LAST AIRBENDER
THE PROMISE
1
DARK HORSE
nickelodeon
降世神通
AVATAR
THE LAST AIRBENDER
THE PROMISE
Michael Dante DiMartino
Brian Konietzko

4

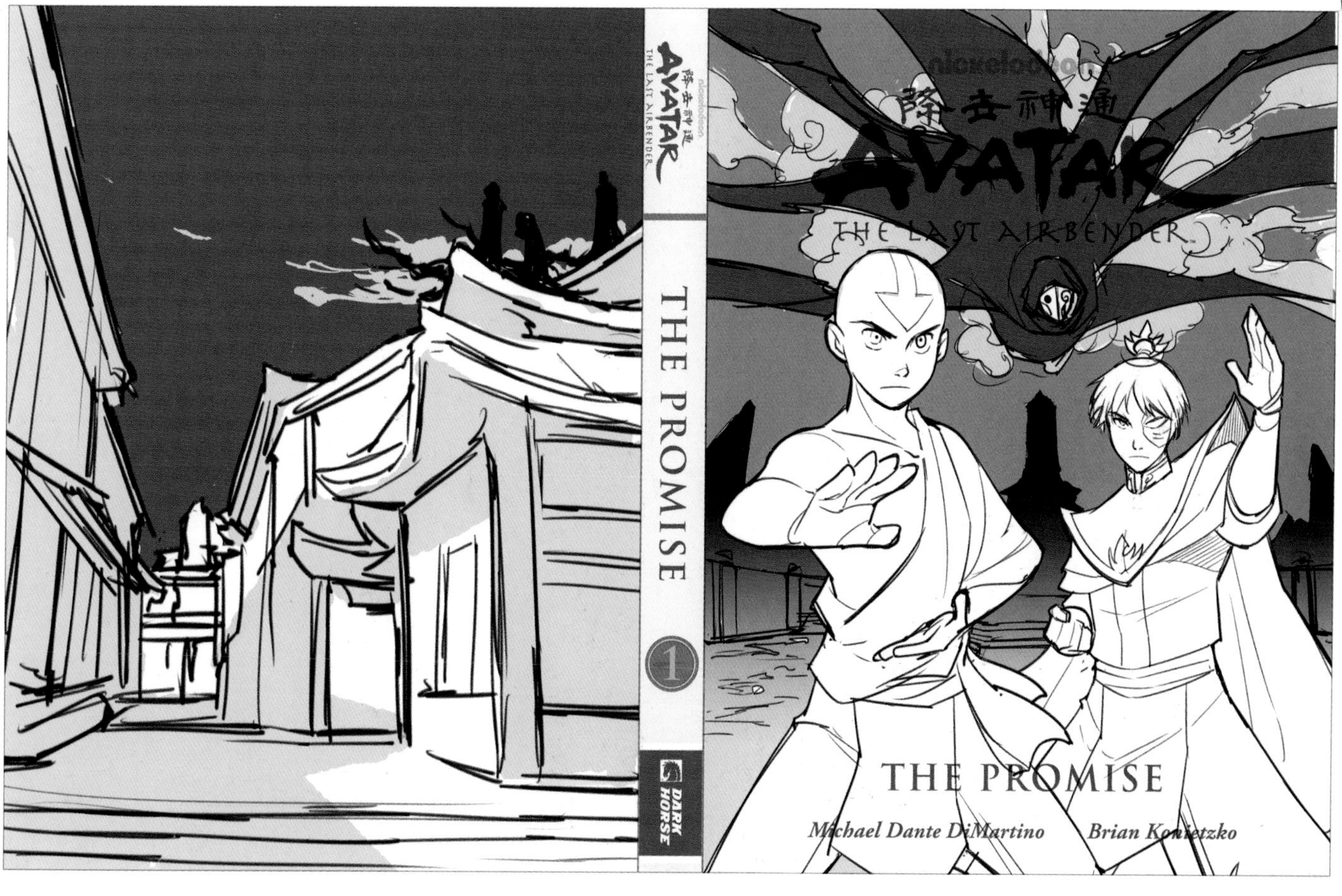
nickelodeon
降世神通
AVATAR
THE LAST AIRBENDER
THE PROMISE
1
DARK HORSE
nickelodeon
降世神通
AVATAR
THE LAST AIRBENDER
THE PROMISE
Michael Dante DiMartino
Brian Konietzko

UKANO

nickelodeon

降去神通

AVATAR

THE LAST AIRBENDER

BE PART OF THE INCREDIBLE JOURNEY!

Check out the best-selling graphic novels by acclaimed writer Gene Luen Yang.

nickelodeon
AVATAR
THE LAST AIRBENDER
NORTH AND SOUTH · PART ONE

Avatar: The Last Airbender—North and South Part 1
978-1-50670-022-9 $10.99

nickelodeon
降去神通
AVATAR
THE LAST AIRBENDER
SMOKE AND SHADOW

AVATAR
THE LAST AIRBENDER
SMOKE AND SHADOW · PART THREE

Avatar: The Last Airbender—Smoke and Shadow Library Edition
978-1-50670-013-7 $39.99

Avatar: The Last Airbender—Smoke and Shadow Part 1
978-1-61655-761-4 $10.99

Avatar: The Last Airbender—Smoke and Shadow Part 2
978-1-61655-790-4 $10.99

Avatar: The Last Airbender—Smoke and Shadow Part 3
978-1-61655-838-3 $10.99

nickelodeon
AVATAR
THE RIFT · PART THREE

nickelodeon
降去神通
AVATAR
THE LAST AIRBENDER
THE RIFT

Avatar: The Last Airbender—The Rift Library Edition
978-1-61655-550-4 $39.99

Avatar: The Last Airbender—The Rift Part 1
978-1-61655-295-4 $10.99

Avatar: The Last Airbender—The Rift Part 2
978-1-61655-296-1 $10.99

Avatar: The Last Airbender—The Rift Part 3
978-1-61655-297-8 $10.99

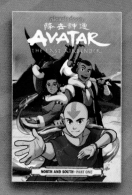

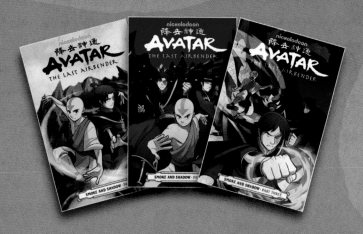

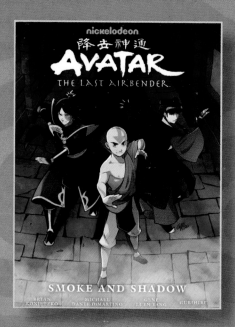

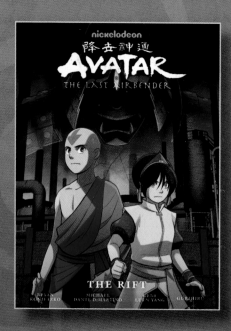

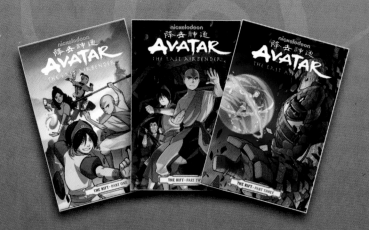

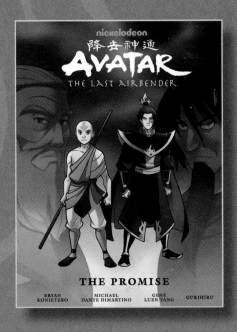

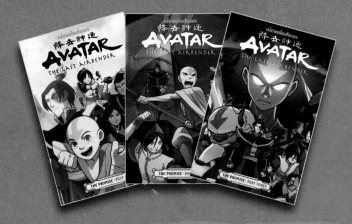

nickelodeon
降世神通
AVATAR
THE LAST AIRBENDER
THE PROMISE
BRYAN KONIETZKO
MICHAEL DANTE DiMARTINO
GENE LUEN YANG
GURIHIRU

AVATAR
THE LAST AIRBENDER
THE PROMISE · PART THREE

Avatar: The Last Airbender—The Promise Library Edition
978-1-61655-074-5 $39.99

Avatar: The Last Airbender—The Promise Part 1
978-1-59582-811-8 $10.99

Avatar: The Last Airbender—The Promise Part 2
978-1-59582-875-0 $10.99

Avatar: The Last Airbender—The Promise Part 3
978-1-59582-941-2 $10.99

nickelodeon
降世神通
AVATAR
THE LAST AIRBENDER
THE SEARCH
BRYAN KONIETZKO
MICHAEL DANTE DiMARTINO
GENE LUEN YANG
GURIHIRU

AVATAR
THE SEARCH · PART ONE
THE SEARCH · PART THREE

Avatar: The Last Airbender—The Search Library Edition
978-1-61655-226-8 $39.99

Avatar: The Last Airbender—The Search Part 1
978-1-61655-054-7 $10.99

Avatar: The Last Airbender—The Search Part 2
978-1-61655-190-2 $10.99

Avatar: The Last Airbender—The Search Part 3
978-1-61655-184-1 $10.99

nickelodeon
降世神通
AVATAR
THE LAST AIRBENDER
THE LOST ADVENTURES

Avatar: The Last Airbender—The Art of the Animated Series
978-1-59582-504-9 $34.99

Avatar: The Last Airbender—The Lost Adventures
978-1-59582-748-7 $14.99

AVAILABLE AT YOUR LOCAL COMICS SHOP OR BOOKSTORE.
To find a comics shop in your area, call 1-888-266-4226
For more information or to order direct, visit DarkHorse.com or call 1-800-862-0052

DARK HORSE BOOKS

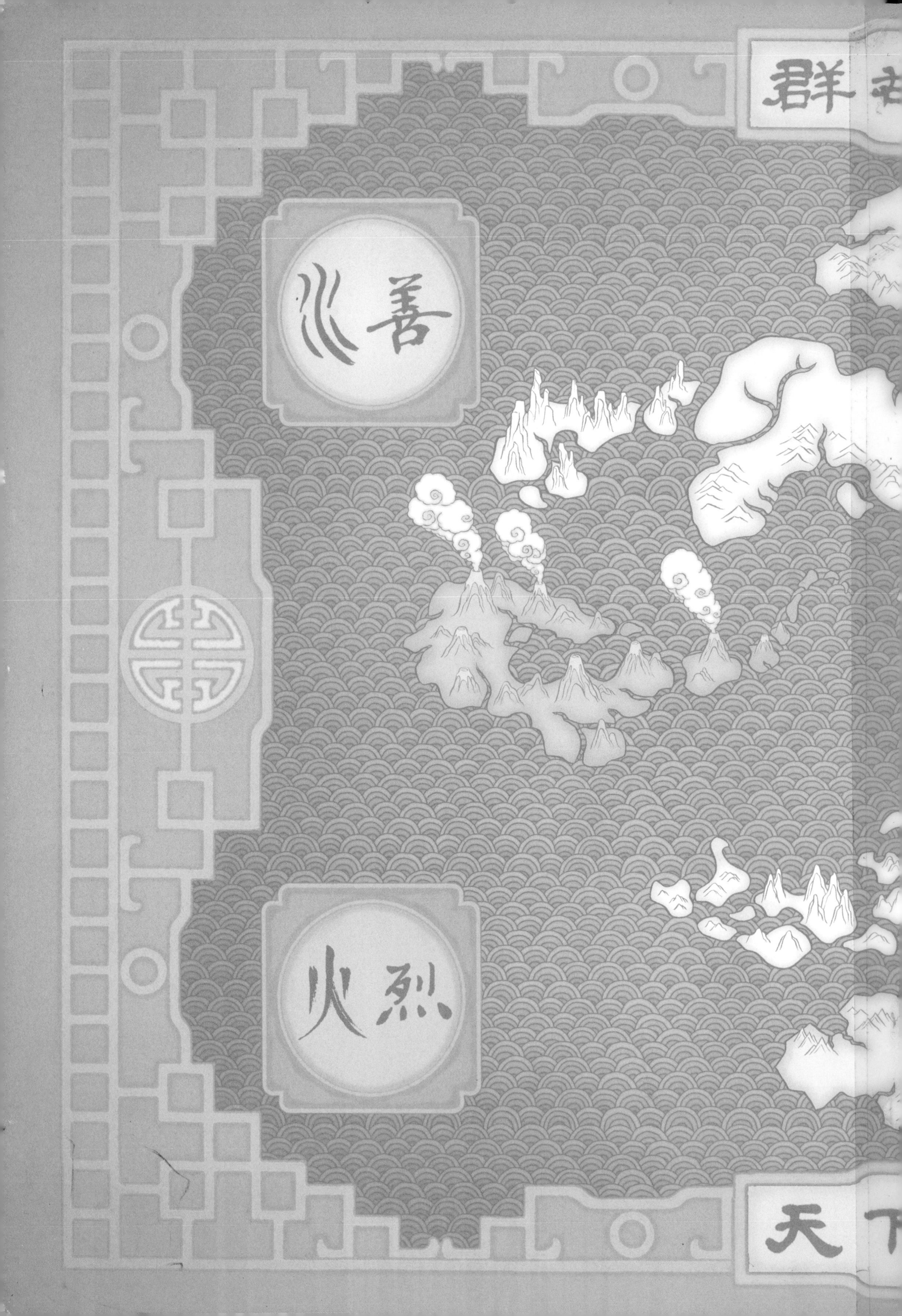

群
善
火 烈
天